CRISPIAN VILLENEUVE was born in England in 1950 and met anthroposophy in London in 1973. He has worked for many years in centres of the Camphill Movement, caring for people with special needs. He is the author of the two-volume work *Rudolf Steiner in Britain*.

Francis Bacon in Paris in 1578, in his eighteenth year (miniature by Nicholas Hilliard)

RUDOLF STEINER: THE BRITISH CONNECTION

ELEMENTS FROM HIS EARLY LIFE AND CULTURAL DEVELOPMENT

CRISPIAN VILLENEUVE

TEMPLE LODGE

Temple Lodge Publishing
Hillside House, The Square
Forest Row, RH18 5ES

www.templelodge.com

Published by Temple Lodge 2011

A catalogue record for this book is available from the British Library

ISBN 978 1 906999 29 2

Cover by Andrew Morgan Design
Typeset by DP Photosetting, Neath, West Glamorgan
Printed and bound in Great Britain by 4edge Ltd, Hockley.

CONTENTS

To
EKKEHARD MEFFERT
(1940–2010)

My dear Meffert,

Although never having met you or made any contact with you during your earthly life, I nonetheless consider it especially appropriate to dedicate to you the present book. My reason for so doing lies in the great admiration which I have always harboured for your slim but elegant and highly perceptive biography of Carl Gustav Carus. In course of that work you finely sketched out the relations of your subject to well-known Middle European figures of his time, and it was this which led me to wonder whether the present study might not broaden that same picture by also examining his relationship to another notable contemporary, who came however from a Western European background.

That in your now discarnate state you may follow the thoughts of such earthly readers as peruse these present pages is the hope of,

My dear Meffert,

Your affectionate friend,

C. Villeneuve

PREFACE

The present book grew out of my work *Rudolf Steiner in Britain*, published in 2004,[1] which documented the series of Steiner's ten visits to England and Wales in the first quarter of the twentieth century.

As observed by Marie Steiner in her foreword to the 1924 Torquay course, the Initiate's tenth and last visit to Britain in August of that year already formed part of the climactic finale of his earthly incarnation, ending with his death in Switzerland in March 1925. It did not therefore seem to me appropriate simply to end my text at the point in August 1924 where Steiner left Britain for the last time, so I continued the account for another year in order to cover his death and its immediate aftermath—all from a British perspective—as far as August 1925.

Once that decision had been made, however, the question began to arise about the chronologically polar subject of Steiner's relationship to Britain *before* any of his visits to that country had taken place at all. Extending the whole work backwards in order to explore this further topic was of course a much larger proposition, since it would mean adding a preliminary period of over 40 years. Nonetheless at a certain point during the lengthy composition of the book I decided also to undertake this additional task, prompted especially by the fact that much of the relevant literary material lay buried in such volumes of Steiner's *Gesamtausagabe* as otherwise seemed extremely unlikely ever as a whole to be translated into English.

After some time it became evident that the task when fully carried out would extend what was already growing into a very large work beyond all feasible limits. Moreover, much of the subject-matter in this additional text began as if by itself to take on a different character of a kind not readily compatible with the themes unfolding in the main part of my account. Eventually in the year 2003, therefore, I abandoned altogether the notion of including this preliminary period.

By that stage, however, the additional part of my text exploring this extra topic had already progressed so far, and become in its own way so interesting, that after finally completing the earlier work it seemed only right then to return to this abandoned portion, develop the content further in such manner as seemed appropriate, and bring it to completion in its own right as a quite separate publicational project.

⋆

As with the previous work, it is important to stress that this present book is not intended to be a general account of Steiner's early life of a kind already available, but rather a specialist study examining, sometimes in depth, certain selected portions quite deliberately extracted from their overall context. Even so, to have strictly confined myself to Steiner's connection with British culture during his early years would of course have resulted in an absurdly misshapen book. That connection however serves especially to open up the larger topic of his relation to natural science as a whole, highlighting the polarity and tension—ultimately for Steiner a creative one—between on the one hand the Goethean view of science arising from Middle Europe and on the other those different scientific attitudes emanating from Western Europe which may generally be described as Baconian.

In this regard an important stimulus was given by Steiner's first literary work, namely his edition of Goethe's scientific writings. After his death in 1925 his editorial introductions were reprinted as a separate book—now also available in English—from which passages have often been quoted by anthroposophical authors. But although the five-volume edition has been reprinted as well, its Gothic typography has proved rather a barrier even to many readers who are fluent in German. And yet besides Steiner's editorial introductions it also contains a multitude of his sometimes quite extensive and often revealing footnotes. Here one may follow so to speak at first hand the interweaving of his own thought with the relevant Goethean texts even more closely and continuously than in his more discursively argued introductions. Although including brief extracts from the latter, I have therefore given much more space to reproducing passages from Goethe's original texts and Steiner's footnotes. In taking this action it was difficult to know where to stop, and sometimes painful to have to do so. But I hope to have rescued at any rate some of these footnotes from the relative obscurity in which they have long been left to languish.

The major criterion for deciding which texts to include was a statement made by Goethe himself on 10 January 1825 to a visiting Englishman at Weimar named Mr Hutton, as later recorded by Eckermann:

> I have been studying the English language and English literature for the last fifty years, so that I know your writers and your national way of life and institutions very well. If I were to come over to England I should be no stranger.

★

All researchers into the early part of Steiner's life must first come to terms with his unfinished autobiography,[2] *Mein Lebensgang*, and no apology is given for including at many points in the present book relevant passages from this incomparable work, to which those who concern themselves with its author will find themselves again and again returning. As before, translations from both this and other writings by Steiner are my own. Further autobiographical statements or letters by Steiner are also woven into the account, along with some biographical material about his teacher Karl Julius Schröer.

Regarding the Baconian tradition, a prominent place has been accorded to the early- and mid-nineteenth-century figure of William Whewell, fleetingly mentioned in the *Lebensgang* but hitherto unexamined in anthroposophical literature. The reason for the present prominence lies in the fascinating paradox that although Whewell may be regarded as perhaps the greatest admirer of Francis Bacon in recorded history his life as a whole is also noticeably coloured by what were for an Englishman of his time unusually strong connections to Middle Europe.

The most appropriate way of interweaving these contrasting Baconian and Goethean traditions into a reasonably balanced account seemed to be to provide primary texts from both of them, and fill out the resultant assemblage with related material of more general interest either by or about Steiner during the nineteenth century, especially of such kind as was otherwise scarcely or not at all accessible to an English readership.

This account of Rudolf Steiner's relation to British culture in the early part of his life is now offered to any interested readers, and above all to those who have enjoyed my previous work.

Crispian Villeneuve
2011

1
THE CONTINENTAL SITUATION

As a Small Child

Towards the end of February 1861 the 26-year-old wife of a 31-year-old Austrian railway telegraphist stationed at the village of Kraljevec in Croatia gave birth to her first child, a son.

Although Kraljevec had its own church, at the time this was only a subsidiary of the main parish church in Drascovec, another village some three miles to the south-east. So the newborn child was taken by his parents on the first of the countless journeys which he was to make in the following 64 years of his earthly life, over to Drascovec to be baptized in the Catholic church. The service was held in the age-old cultic Latin. And it was also in that language that the baby's names, or at any rate his three forenames, were entered into the parish baptismal register as 'Adolphus Josephus Laurentius'.

The locally spoken language was Serbo-Croat. Not that the baby's Austrian parents, who had only arrived in the district shortly before his birth, would have been able to speak much, if indeed anything at all, of that particular language. To them it probably sounded just as foreign as their own native German tongue must certainly have been felt by their neighbours in that region.

Decades later, in a lecture at Dornach on 28 April 1920, the grown-up man himself reported:

> As a small child I used to give terrible screams and was always carried around the house, because I would scream so much that it disturbed the neighbours.

Those tranquil Kraljevec neighbours simply had to accustom themselves to the disturbance, for that family of Austrian newcomers stayed on in their village for another year and a half.

★

In late 1862 the Austrian family with that disturbing baby—maybe to the relief of their Kraljevec neighbours—finally packed their bags and moved back to their own country. The telegraphist had been reposted to Mödling, just south of Vienna.

Here the family stayed for some six months. Probably during this time the baby first began to speak. And since the language spoken both by his parents and by all the travellers passing through the station was German, the baby naturally picked up the German language too.

During all the remaining years of his life, this particular language may be said to have constituted a defining element of his earthly personality.

⋆

Around the time of his second birthday in early 1863 the parents of little Rudl, as they called their toddler, moved with him again, southwards to another railway station—the only kind of home he knew—at Pottschach in Lower Austria. And there he remained for the rest of his early childhood.

Having reached the age of three, Rudl was joined in the family by a sister, who in contrast to himself was given an elegant polysyllabic name: Leopoldine. Since that must have been rather a mouthful for her brother to pronounce, it is perhaps understandable that she came to be known as Poldi.

After another couple of years Rudl and Poldi were further joined by a younger brother, Gustav, deaf and dumb but very friendly.

⋆

On reaching the age of six Rudl was first sent to school, but soon withdrawn when his father fell out with the old Pottschach schoolmaster. The father then taught his son at home—i.e. in the station—reading and counting.

Writing gave the little boy more difficulty.

An Artistic Element

Rudolf—the correct vernacular form of his first forename—Steiner described the early part of his life in various contexts, each time a little differently. In examining his biography it is sometimes necessary to collate the details of his separate accounts.

In Berlin on 4 February 1913, a set of complex circumstances in the Theosophical Society induced Steiner to give an autobiographical lecture. Referring to himself largely in the third person, he related his family's move to Neudörfl:

> When the boy in question was eight to nine years old, his father was transferred to another railway station, lying at the boundary between—as one says in Austria—Cisleithania and Transleithania, the Austrian and Hungarian lands, though the station was really situated towards Hungary . . .

In his autobiography he stated that the move took place 'when I was in the eighth year of my life', i.e. at the age of seven. The generally accepted date is 1869, the mean of these differing indications.

Somewhat later in the lecture, Steiner continued:

> After the father had been transferred, as previously mentioned, to the place situated between Austria and Hungary, but still in Hungary, the boy in that place came into the village school. It was a peasant school of the old type still existing at the time, where boys and girls were together as a matter of course. What could be learnt in this school, which of course was not a particularly great deal, never had a fully intensive effect on the boy in question for the simple reason that the excellent teacher there—excellent in his way within the limits of possibility—had a special predilection for drawing . . .

Heinrich Gangl, assistant teacher at Neudörfl School, was according to his pupil's account more interested in drawing than in the subject-matter of his own teaching. And the young child naturally picked up this interest. For Steiner went on:

> . . . Since the boy showed quite early an aptitude for drawing, that teacher simply took him out of the schoolroom during the time when other pupils were being shown how to learn reading and writing, and led him into his little study, where the boy always had to draw. So relatively soon he managed to draw quite nicely—as individual people said—one of the most significant political persons in Hungary, namely Count Sczéchenyi.

Count Széchenyi was a Hungarian statesman of the early nineteenth century, whose portrait adorned the walls in many Hungarian schools.

Steiner stated that in the teacher's library he found a geometry book, which he proceeded to study. In his autobiography he discussed for no less than two and a half pages the significance to him of this book. He located in it the first seed of what was to become his 'view', meaning of course his view of the world.

These pages were rounded off as follows:

> By means of his geometry book the assistant teacher at Neudörfl provided me with a justification of the spiritual world which at that time I needed.
>
> I also owe him many other things. He brought me an artistic element. He played the violin and the piano. And he did a lot of drawing. Both these things strongly attracted me to him. I was with him as much as possible. He particularly loved to draw. Already in my ninth year he made me draw with charcoal. In this way I had to copy pictures under his guidance . . .

So Gangl had two artistic interests. 'Both of these things'—music and drawing—'strongly attracted' the young boy to the teacher.

It is however clear which of the two arts Gangl preferred, and which of them he encouraged Steiner to take up—drawing. The statement in the

Berlin lecture that 'the boy showed quite early an aptitude for drawing' indicated latent creative capacities in this art, no doubt also affected by the forms in the geometry book. His teacher fostered these capacities, and the boy's talents developed. Indeed when in the late twentieth century the copied portrait of Count Széchenyi eventually turned up, folded inside one of the boy's school exercise books preserved in the Dornach archives, it was found to show a good sense of proportion and detail, and care in technical execution.

Now Steiner composed his autobiography over the years 1923–5, under circumstances set out in its opening paragraphs, as a serial narrative intended for general reading. But about three years earlier, some time in 1920 or early 1921, he had already begun to set down an account of his own life, if perhaps only for private circulation. At any rate there has survived in his handwriting a six-page autobiographical fragment, shown to at least one friend during this time. It describes the beginning of Steiner's life from his birth at Kraljevec down to his early Neudörfl years.

Like the autobiographical lecture and the autobiography, this fragment too refers both to the geometry book found in the teacher's library and to the teacher's drawing instruction. It also refers to the teacher's musical instruction, but in a sentence which provides a further detail:

> I always took part as a listener in the piano lessons given in my teacher's room.

The school piano must then have been located in Gangl's little study where Steiner 'always had to draw'.

It is interesting to reflect that, depending on when exactly in 1869 the move to Neudörfl may have taken place, Steiner was a pupil in the school of that village for three or perhaps even three-and-a-half years. So during this whole period of time when he 'always had to draw', he was in addition 'always' listening to piano lessons being given to other pupils in the school.

Of the two instruments which Gangl played, Steiner mentioned firstly the violin, but did not record his teacher giving any violin lessons. However, in a lecture at Stuttgart on 8 March 1923 he stated:

> Any pipe or fiddle is something which musically comes down from the higher world. But a piano is like a philistine who no longer contains in himself a higher man. It is the philistine instrument. We are lucky that it exists, for otherwise philistines would have no music at all. But it has arisen from a materialistic experience of music. The piano is then . . . the instrument which must in fact be musically overcome. A human being who wishes to experience what is actually musical must be freed from the impression of the piano.

The continual 'impression of the piano' which Steiner was over some three years receiving at very close quarters in the music lessons at Neudörfl had then a materialistic character in comparison to the freer and more directly spirit-related sound of a violin. And although Gangl's playing of musical instruments 'strongly attracted' the child to this teacher, Steiner remained to the end of his days only a musical listener, never taking steps towards becoming a practitioner. He did not learn to play either the piano or the violin, or indeed any other musical instrument either.

It seems therefore reasonable to deduce that this boy who 'showed quite early an aptitude for drawing' did not by contrast demonstrate any particular aptitude for playing musical instruments.

French and Hungarian

Another passage in Rudolf Steiner's autobiography relating to his Neudörfl years reads:

> On the foothills of the Alps could be seen the mansions of both Pitten and Frohsdorf. The latter was inhabited at the time by Count Chambord, who at the start of the seventies wanted to become King of France as Henry the Fifth. I received deep impressions from the part of life related to Frohsdorf Mansion . . .

The 'part of life related to Frohsdorf Mansion' is recorded in various other sources, such as a section on the Count of Chambord contributed by Joanni d'Arsac to the 1892 volume of a series of *Biographies du XIX Siècle*.

D'Arsac stated that at Frohsdorf

> . . . on n'entendit parler que le français, tous les services étaient uniquement remplis par les français; l'esprit et le coeur y étaient essentiellement français.

The 'deep impressions' received by Steiner of the aristocratic culture still being fostered at Frohsdorf must then have included some impressions of the French language, which however he was not himself able to speak.

★

Steiner's autobiography continued:

> In connection with Frohsdorf a part of social life was also revealed to me. The assistant teacher at Neudörfl, whom I was often allowed to watch as he worked in his little room, prepared innumerable begging-appeals to Count Chambord for the poorer inhabitants of the village and neighbourhood. In response to every such appeal would come a subsidy of one guilder, out of which, for his trouble, the teacher was always allowed to keep six kreutzer.

> He needed this income. For his post brought him every year—fifty-eight guilders. In addition he had his morning coffee and midday meal with the 'schoolmaster'. He then also gave 'extra lessons' to some ten children, including myself. For this he was paid every month one guilder.

Elaborating on the magnanimity of Count Chambord, d'Arsac reported the sentiments of the lucky beneficiaries:

> A Frohsdorf, Henri V fit le bien à profusion, avec passion, comme autrefois Saint Louis ou Charles V. Il ne pouvait pas voir une misère, entendre parler d'un malheur, sans éprouver le besoin de l'adoucir par le bienfait.
>
> Cette grande vertu royale de la charité, Henri V l'avait eue dès l'aurore de son adolescence. 'Je n'ai jamais vu,' disait une vieille femme de Frohsdorf à un journaliste français, 'de plus grand chrétien que notre seigneur le roi Henri V; il est le père de tous les malheureux, de tous les pauvres gens; il est tous les jours la Providence de ceux qui sont dans le besoin, et ce sera tant pis pour les pauvres le jour où il ira régner en France.'

In the event the successive attempts made at that time by the French royalist party to have the Bourbon dynasty returned to the throne were unsuccessful. So the wealthy and generous Count Chambord went on living at Frohsdorf right up to his death in 1883—to the continued economic benefit of poorer Austrians in the neighbourhood and of their literary intermediary Heinrich Gangl.

★

The account in Steiner's autobiography went on:

> Next to the assistant teacher, the person whom I loved among those involved in running the school was the parish priest...

Franz Maráz had been Catholic priest at Neudörfl since 1860, some nine years before the Steiner family arrived in the village.

> ...He came regularly twice a week to give the religion lesson, and often at other times as well to inspect the school. The picture of this man became deeply engraved in my soul, and throughout my whole life he would repeatedly arise in my memory. He was by far the most significant person I came to know up to my tenth or eleventh year. He was an energetic Hungarian patriot, and took vigorous part in the Magyarizing of Hungarian territory then taking place. Out of this attitude he wrote articles in the Hungarian language; I came to know these articles because the assistant teacher had to make fair copies of them, and in spite of my youth he always discussed their content with me...

If Gangl could discuss the content of the articles, he too, like Maráz, must have been bilingual. And for the discussion to have had much purpose, the boy too must already have gained at least some understanding of Hungarian.[3]

In order to appreciate Steiner's relationship to foreign languages it is important to examine such details. Although at that time the village of Neudörfl was officially situated in Hungary, in practice it had for centuries been largely peopled by German-speaking Austrians. Hungarian history was taught at the school, for Steiner mentioned that the boys sitting in his row in the classroom had to copy out the story of King Arpad, a famous Hungarian figure of the late ninth and early tenth centuries. But the teaching itself was all done in German. As far as is known, other languages were not officially introduced. Steiner must have heard Gangl and Maráz speaking together in Hungarian, but what the boy picked up of this language at school was quite incidental to the curriculum.

Indeed it may be observed that although Gangl was a musician, singing is not recorded as having been taught at the school either, not even in German—let alone in French or Hungarian, or any other modern language.

It is therefore quite understandable that this boy who 'showed quite early an aptitude for drawing' was able to absorb Hungarian in a way natural to children, but otherwise did not show any particular aptitude for foreign languages.

★

The significant impulse received from Maráz was of a scientific character, as described by Steiner in his autobiography:

> Through *one* strong impression in particular I also owe this parish priest a very great deal for my later spiritual orientation. He once entered the school, gathered around him the 'more mature' pupils, among whom he included me, unrolled a drawing he had made, and with its help explained to us the Copernican system of the universe. He spoke very vividly about the movement of the Earth around the Sun, about the axial rotation, the tilted position of the earthly axis, about summer and winter, and about the terrestrial zones. I was completely absorbed by the matter, spending days copying the drawing; I had another special lesson from the parish priest about solar and lunar eclipses, and from then onwards all my desire for knowledge was directed onto this subject.
>
> At the time I was about ten years old, and still unable to write correctly in regard to either spelling or grammar.

According to the autobiographical fragment he was introduced to the Copernican system of the universe 'in the ninth year of my life', i.e. when aged only eight. But whether in fact he was eight, nine or ten years old does not much matter. What he emphasized in his autobiography by juxtaposing two paragraphs of such dissimilar length was the contrast between his total absorption in an eye-opening scientific subject—astronomy—and on the other hand his relatively slow progress in mastering the formal written features of his own mother-tongue.

The Latin Language

In course of his autobiographical lecture, Rudolf Steiner went on:

> The place where all this happened was a very peculiar place, because important political and cultural relationships once again as it were peered in. It was the very time when Hungary began to Magyarize and especially in such borderlands much was happening as a result of the connection between different peoples, in particular the Magyar and German peoples. One came to know an extraordinary amount of cultural relationships—without everything being then categorized—so here too the boy became acquainted with the most modern conditions.
>
> Now what has been misunderstood is that the boy, like other schoolboys in that place—this only happened for quite a short time—had to be a server in the village church. It was simply stated: 'Today this and that boy are to ring the bells and put on their vestments and do the serving.' This had not been going on for a very long time when the boy's father—for most remarkable reasons—insisted that the serving should not get too prolonged. Owing to certain circumstances, the boy was from time to time unable to avoid coming too late . . .

Although Steiner stated that his serving 'only happened for quite a short time', the context of the statement was a lecture provoked by an accusation that he had been educated by Jesuits. To counter this accusation he took pains to stress the small influence exercised by the religious element within his upbringing as a whole.

In the different context of his autobiography he gave a full account:

> The proximity of the church and its surrounding graveyard was of deep importance in my life as a boy. Everything happening at the village school was connected with it. This was due not only to social and administrative conditions then prevailing, but above all to the parish priest being a significant person. The assistant teacher was at the same time church organist, as well as custodian of vestments and other church objects; he gave the parish priest every assistance in looking after the cult. We schoolboys acted as servers and choristers at masses, memorial services and funerals. The ceremonial of the Latin language and cult was an element in which my

> boyish soul was fond of living. Since up to my tenth year I took an intense part in this church serving I was often in the company of the parish priest whom I regarded so highly.

At an earlier point Steiner stated that he moved to Neudörfl 'in the eighth year of my life', so it seems to be implied that he was a church server for about two years. In relation to a total of some ten years spent in the village, this could still be justifiably described as 'quite a short time'.

Further reference is made in his account to an occasion when Maráz preached a sermon aimed partly at a member of the village's Masonic lodge. Since however the 'Humanitas' Lodge at Neudörfl was only founded on 9 March 1871, when Steiner had already entered his eleventh year, his time as church server must have continued for longer in his childhood than he later estimated.

★

In order to picture the impressions received by the eight-, nine- or ten-year-old child who after ringing the bells in the little parish church of Saint Nicholas at Neudörfl was then vested as server or chorister for a sacramental or other cultic service celebrated by Franz Maráz and accompanied on the organ by Heinrich Gangl, a few observations may be made about the services concerned. For in the autobiographical fragment Steiner stated that

> As 'churchboy' I served at the sacrifice of the Mass, at afternoon service, at funerals and at Corpus Christi festivals.

The Mass is the principal sacrament of Catholicism, celebrated especially on Sundays and at festivals. At this time the only part spoken in the vernacular was the sermon. All cultic and liturgical texts were still in Latin—apart from the 'Kyrie' in Greek. Most were assigned to the priest, but responses were made by servers. Normally the texts were spoken, but at major festivals, even in a small country parish, there may well have been a sung Mass with parts rendered in a Gregorian mode by the celebrant on one hand and the congregation or a representative choir on the other.

Of particular interest is the allusion to 'afternoon service'. Except on Good Friday, there is no Catholic service pertaining specifically to the afternoon. But it may be supposed that Steiner was referring to the short service called Benediction, chiefly celebrated in the late afternoon or evening. In this service a consecrated host was brought out from the tabernacle and exhibited on the altar inside a monstrance—as sometimes discussed in Stener's lectures, often with blackboard illustrations. The monstrance was then incensed, to the accompaniment of various readings, prayers and hymns.

'Funerals', amplified in the autobiography to 'funerals and memorial services', were occasions when the young boy—who already at Pottschach had met the discarnate entity of his deceased maternal aunt—now also experienced within a sombre cultic atmosphere the physical reality of human death. The solemnity of the Catholic 'Requiem Mass', spoken or sung, reached the apogee of its liturgical expression in Thomas of Celano's famous sequence *Dies Irae*.

Corpus Christi festivals fall on Thursday after Trinity Sunday, the date of which is determined by Easter. Whether these festivals included that on 27 May 1869 depends on when during that year the Steiners first arrived at Neudörfl, but certainly the young boy served at this festival on 16 June 1870, and possibly still on 8 June 1871. The reason for singling out these particular festivals must have been the associated procession, wherein a priest accompanied by servers would carry around his parish a monstrance displaying a consecrated host, thus blessing the surrounding land.

In origin, Corpus Christi was a medieval festival dating from the year 1264. Its liturgy was commissioned from Thomas Aquinas, who both chose appropriate scriptural texts and also composed for it the magnificent sequence *Lauda Sion* in a metre of rhyming octo- and heptasyllabic lines. This begins:

> Lauda Sion Salvatorem,
> Lauda ducem et pastorem
> In hymnis et canticis.
>
> Quantum potes, tantum aude
> Quia major omni laude
> Nec laudare sufficis . . .

Since the festival only comes round once a year, a remark may be adduced from another context in the autobiographical lecture, stating that the boy

> . . . did not have much sense for the connection of words with things, if the words were seldom expressed. But he had a remarkable sense for the sound of words, for what can be discerned through the sound of words.

⋆

Steiner concluded his autobiographical fragment as follows:

> This church serving came one day to an abrupt end. In the morning several 'churchboys', myself included, had arrived too late to be able to serve. All of them were now to be caned in the school. I had a quite irresistible aversion to this, and knew how to get out of it. I always made my escape in such a

way as never to have been caned. But my father was so enraged at the thought that 'his son' should have been caned that he said: 'Church serving is now out. You're never going there again.'

Not Naturally Accessible

A passage in Christoph Lindenberg's two-volume biography of Rudolf Steiner reads:

> Attendance at the *Realschule* in Wiener-Neustadt began in autumn 1872. During his first two years at this school Rudolf Steiner's interest in lessons was not yet awakened. He had real trouble keeping up. He was often bored and would hide somewhere in the back rows, trying to read fairy stories in the textbook, until one day he was found out and then 'questioned' every day. Moreover in certain subjects the teaching was pretty awful. 'We had two Carmelites, one of whom was supposed to teach us French, the other English. The one for English in particular could... hardly speak an English word at all—well, anyway not a sentence. For natural history we had a man who really understood absolutely nothing about either God or the world.' In religion lessons the book—admittedly an excellent one—was simply learnt by heart. But to Rudolf Steiner languages were not naturally accessible. He himself relates: 'He had difficulty in everything linguistic, even in German. Up to his fourteenth or fifteenth year this boy'—he himself is meant—'made in his homework the most foolish mistakes in German language.'

The scholastic years 1872–4, when the boy was aged 11 to 13, must therefore have been educationally rather unfulfilling, and in a general account of Steiner's life such as presented in Lindenberg's biography there was no reason to dwell unduly upon them. One may however consider what development did or did not take place in the subjects mentioned—fairy stories, religion, natural history, languages—during the further course of the boy's school career.

The anecdote of the 11-year-old Steiner at the *Realschule* surreptitiously reading fairy stories during a German lesson until caught by the one-eyed teacher Franz Schubert was recorded by a fellow pupil named Albert Pliwa—later a coinage official and eventually Director of the Mint in Vienna. Pliwa further stated that during his early years at the school Steiner while sitting in the train from Neudörfl to Wiener-Neustadt would be reading children's stories. So outside school hours the boy continued to find nourishment for his imaginative life.

Religion was a subject to which Steiner had a somewhat ambivalent relation. According to the autobiographical lecture he only attended religion lessons at the *Realschule* during the first four years, out of duty, and when released by the school timetable attended them no more. But right up to the age of 15 he was receiving religious instruction. In his autobiography he mentioned that the school had excellent textbooks in this very subject, adding:

> I lived very strongly in these teachings. But my relation to them was determined by the spiritual world being for me a content of human perception. These teachings penetrated my soul so deeply because I felt in them that the human spirit can find a way through knowledge into the supersensible . . .

Nothing further seems recorded about Steiner's studies in natural history, nor indeed about his teacher in this particular subject. But Laurenz Jelinek, who in 1874 began to teach him mathematics and physics, and remained his class-teacher for all his subsequent years at the *Realschule*, had no interest in biology. So although the boy had an excellent teacher in geometry—the club-footed and square-headed Georg Kosak—and later also in chemistry—the taciturn but sharply-gazing Hugo von Gilm—and therefore made good progress in the field of inorganic sciences, he evidently came short in the field of the life sciences.

The subject of languages was complex. On the one hand, Steiner's initially imperfect relation to the literary forms of his own mother-tongue stabilized when he reached the age of puberty. A significant stimulus was given by the friendly doctor in Wiener-Neustadt, the 64-year-old Carl Hickel, who introduced the teenager to classical German writings by Lessing, Goethe and Schiller. Steiner's exceptionally deep connection to the German *Sprachgenius* must have been largely formed under this influence during his later teenage years.

Poorly taught foreign languages, on the other hand, made little impression upon him. Whether those of Western Europe formed part of the curriculum already presented during his first year at the *Realschule*, as implied by Lindenberg, or were only added at a later stage—for instance in 1876 when religion lessons fell out—does not seem recorded. But comparison may certainly be drawn with the youth's attitude towards the closest Eastern European language, as coloured by the awkward position of his father described in the autobiography:

> . . . My father did not approve of Hungary at all. He was indeed living at the Hungarian border-spot Neudörfl during the Magyarizing time. The sword of Damocles always hung over his head that he might be unable to be stationmaster at Neudörfl because he could not speak Magyar. This was actually quite unnecessary in that archetypally German region. But the Hungarian government was endeavouring to man Hungarian railway lines,

> even privately owned ones, with Magyar-speaking employees. My father wanted to keep his position at Neudörfl until I had finished school in Wiener-Neustadt. All this gave him very little sympathy towards Hungary . . .

Steiner here characterized his home region as 'archetypally German'. But this was not the whole story. In the autobiographical lecture he had previously admitted that

> It was the very time when Hungary was beginning to Magyarize and especially in such borderlands much happened as a result of the connection between different peoples, especially the Magyar and German peoples. One came to know an extraordinary amount of cultural relationships . . .

Among things happening as a result of the connection between the Magyar and German peoples was a political policy recorded by Pliwa in an interesting anecdote, which shows how the youth came to know one cultural relationship—that between the German and Hungarian languages—in what may be called a very striking way:

> Hungary decided in these years to erase German station names and put up on station buildings Hungarian ones instead. Neudörfl was now called Laitha-Szent-Miklós and Sauerbrunn Savanyûkût. Once when Rudolf Steiner got out at Sauerbrunn, he proudly refused to give the porter his ticket because the German name Sauerbrunn was not on the station building and he did not understand the 'Hunnish' Savanyûkût. The stationmaster came up, a furious Magyar, and swung out on him with an enormous clip over the ears, whereupon Rudolf Steiner taunted him as a 'Hun' and got out of range from this readily striking person.

The anecdote is remarkable. Sauerbrunn, the neighbouring village to which the youth, as described in his autobiography, made a daily walk during his holidays in order to fill a pitcher with delicious bubbling spring water, was also a place where he 'could often listen to the deeply impressive music of the Hungarian Gypsies'.

But Gypsy music was one thing, toponymy quite another. Music did not affect this boy nearly as much as did his own native tongue. The shock of finding a familiar German place name replaced at the station by a foreign, 'Hunnish', one proved too great to surmount.

My Unbounded Interest

Life in a railway station sometimes provided Rudolf Steiner with a useful opening. His autobiography recorded:

> It happened that one of the officials who relieved my father on duty knew how to bind books. From him I learned bookbinding, and in the holidays between the fourth and fifth classes of the *Realschule* was able to bind my school books for myself...

This official was named Balus, and he came from Sauerbrunn. So he must have known the railway employees of the previously recorded anecdote: the porter at the station exit, and the Magyar stationmaster who clouted Steiner over the ear. Maybe when Balus during the summer of 1876 instructed the teenager about the art of bookbinding he also gave him sensible advice about tolerance and courtesy towards speakers or supporters of foreign languages...

⋆

In the autumn of that year Steiner moved up to the fifth class, to which was assigned as German teacher the 'particularly strict' Joseph Mayer. The autobiography records:

> His lessons gave me a lot to do. In the fifth class they included Greek and Latin poetry, of which samples were brought forward in German translation. Only now did I sometimes feel sad that my father had not sent me to the *Gymnasium* but to the *Realschule*. For I felt how little I was affected by the peculiarity of Greek and Latin art. So I bought myself Greek and Latin textbooks and alongside the *Realschule* education quietly pursued a private *Gymnasium* education. This took up much time...

The reason why it took up much time must have been that Steiner found it quite difficult. He would still have remembered the sound of Latin—and to a tiny extent that of Greek—from his period as a 'church-boy' five or six years previously. But mastering the vocabulary, grammatical forms and syntactic patterns from the classical periods of these two languages was not an activity for which he had any natural aptitude.

The sequence of events in his autobiography is occasionally given out of order. He reported his first explorations of the classical languages only *after* describing the following event, which however took place at a later point:

> One day I passed a bookshop. In the display window I saw a copy of Kant's *Kritik der reinen Vernunft* in Reclam's edition. I did everything I could to buy this book as fast as possible.

Although in the 1909 foreword to the *Geheimwissenschaft* he claimed to have begun studying Kant in his sixteenth year, and in the autobiographical lecture of 1913 that it was between his fourteenth and fifteenth year, Lindenberg pointed out that the Reclam edition of the *Kritik der reinen Vernunft* was only published in May 1877, after Steiner had a few months previously reached the age of 16, being in other words in his seventeenth year.

The account continues:

> When Kant at this time entered my sphere of thought, I did not yet have the slightest knowledge of the position he occupied in mankind's spiritual history. Whatever anyone had thought about him, whether in agreement or dissent, was completely unknown to me. My unbounded interest in the critique of pure reason was aroused by my quite personal soul-life. In my boyish way I was striving to understand what human reason is capable of achieving by way of real insight into the essence of things.
>
> My reading of Kant met various hindrances in external facts of life. Because of the long distance to be covered between home and school, I lost at least three hours every day, not reaching home before six o'clock. There was then an endless amount of homework to be done. And on Sundays I devoted myself almost exclusively to descriptive geometry. My ideal was to attain the greatest exactness in geometrical constructions and immaculate neatness in handling of shaded drawings and application of colour.

Sundays would still have begun with the sound of bells at the adjacent village church. But campanology and church services belonged to the past. Even Franz Maráz had left Neudörfl four years previously, transferred elsewhere.

The Lord's Day was now devoted to homework set by the 41-year-old Georg Kosak, whom the teenage Steiner loved dearly, as narrated in the karma lecture given at Breslau on 11 June 1924, but who never once in all the time he taught this pupil geometry—six years, as implied in the autobiography, or seven, as stated in the lecture—gave him opportunity to speak even a single private word with him!

The autobiography goes on:

> So just then there was hardly any time left to read the *Kritik der reinen Vernunft*. I found the following solution. History was being taught in such a way that the teacher seemed to be lecturing, but was really reading from a book. What was presented to us in this way we then had to learn from one lesson to the next from our book. I thought I could read what was in the book at home. From the teacher's 'lecture' I got nothing. I did not take in the least thing by listening to what he was reading.

The history teacher in the fifth class was a Tyrolean named Franz Kofler.

In the autobiographical lecture Steiner described how he found the solution to his lack of time:

> ... The only remaining time which could be usefully applied was the lesson when the history teacher lectured so boringly. The youth now pondered how this time might be used. He was acquainted with bookbinding ...

So he put to good effect what he had learned from Balus in the previous summer holidays, recounting in the autobiography:

> I separated the sections of Kant's little book and fastened them into the history book lying in front of me during the history lesson, and now read Kant while from the rostrum history was being 'taught'. Of course this was a great offence against school discipline; but it disturbed no one and detracted so little from what was required of me that at this very time I was marked as 'excellent' in history.

The surreptitious reading of fairy stories some four years earlier thus found its continuation—or metamorphosis—in the teenager's even more surreptitious perusal of the most influential work in the field of modern philosophy.

> During the holidays my reading of Kant was eagerly continued. I must have read many pages more than twenty times over . . .

⋆

Now ever since its second edition of 1787, the *Kritik der reinen Vernunft* by Immanuel Kant carried straight after the title page the following epigraph:

BACO DE VERULAMIO
INSTAURATIO MAGNA. PRAEFATIO

> De nobis ipsis silemus. De re autem quae agitur, petimus: ut homines eam non Opinionem, sed Opus esse cogitent; ac pro certo habeant, non Sectae nos alicuius, aut Placiti, sed utilitatis et amplitudinis humanae fundamenta moliri. Deinde ut suis commodis aequi . . . in commune consulant . . . et ipsi in partem veniant. Praeterea ut bene sperent, neque Instaurationem nostram ut quiddam infinitum et ultra mortale fingent, et animo concipiant; quuum revera sit infiniti erroris finis et terminus legitimus.

This motto was taken from the preface to Francis Bacon's projected *Instauratio Magna*, of which the *Novum Organum* was designed as second part. Since the first part was represented only by a later, separately published work, the preface originally appeared in 1620, and is still usually given, as introductory to the *Novum Organum*.

Some five years later, in May 1625, the ailing 64-year-old Bacon began to draw up his last will. It was completed in December, only a few months before his death on the following Easter Sunday, 9 April 1626.[4]

Among legacies set out in the will was this:

> For my name and memory, I leave it to men's charitable speeches, and to foreign nations, and the next ages.

Prominent among 'foreign nations' in 'the next ages' who by literary counterparts of 'charitable speeches' may be said to have laid claim to that particular legacy were the German-speaking nation-states of Middle Europe in the eighteenth century.

★

The young Steiner, who by the time he first read the Baconian epigraph heading the *Kritik der reinen Vernunft* had been studying Latin for about a year previously, should not have had much difficulty in working out the meaning. In English translation the epigraph may be rendered:

> About our own selves we are silent. But as to the matter concerned, we ask that men think of it not as an opinion, but as a work; and hold it for certain that we are laying the foundations not of any sect or pleasing doctrine, but of human usefulness and empowerment. And then that being well disposed to their own interests . . . they take common counsel . . . and themselves undertake their share. Moreover, that they be of good hope, nor imagine and conceive in soul of our *Instauration* as something infinite and superhuman, when in true fact it is the end of infinite error, and a legitimate goal.

One can hardly help wondering whether the epigraphic page at the front of the *Kritik der reinen Vernunft* reproducing this passage in its original Latin form may not have been one of the very ones which Steiner read 20 times over.

By the time the youth reached the end of Kant's substantial work he must also have noted how its very last paragraph echoed the Baconian phrase 'et ipsi in partem veniant':

> As regards those who wish to pursue a *scientific* method, they have here the choice of proceeding either *dogmatically* or *sceptically*, but in either case they have the obligation of proceeding *systematically*. If I here name with regard to the former the famous Wolff, and with regard to the latter David Hume, then for my present purposes I can leave the others unnamed. The *critical* path alone is still open. If the reader has had pleasure and patience in travelling along in my company, then he can now judge, if it pleases him to contribute his part to making this footpath into a highway, whether or not what many centuries have failed to accomplish might not be attained even before the close of the present one: namely, to bring reason to full satisfaction in regard to what has always, but until now vainly, occupied her powers and engaged her desire for knowledge.

The eighteenth century referred to had closed long since, and Steiner was reading these words in 1877, almost a hundred years after their first publication in 1781.

Something Inward

After a few more paragraphs in his autobiography, Rudolf Steiner recounted a further literary discovery:

> One day around this time, in a second-hand bookshop in Wiener-Neustadt, I discovered Rotteck's history of the world...

The *Allgemeine Weltgeschichte* of Karl von Rotteck originally appeared in nine volumes published over the years 1812–27. It was reissued in 1846 in a different format reordering the work into four volumes and adding a fifth which brought the author's historical account up to the year 1840.

Steiner continued:

> Although I was receiving the highest marks at school, history had previously been for me something external...

This was hardly surprising if his Tyrolean teacher Franz Kofler had merely been reading from a textbook.

> ...It now became something inward. I was delighted by the warmth with which Rotteck grasped and described historical events. I did not yet notice his one-sidedness in presentation...

In order that readers may appreciate Rotteck's warmth of description and thus share in Steiner's delight, a few characteristic passages will be brought forward which however also reveal the one-sidedness in presentation. References are to the numeration of the volumes in the revised edition of 1846.

★

After covering in his first volume the history of the ancient world, Rotteck moved in his second volume into the medieval period. Here are some paragraphs from a chapter on the Wars of the Roses in the fifteenth century:

> Encouraged by the weakness of Henry VI and the nation's discontent, this Richard of York now set up his ambiguous pretensions, and so plunged his country for thirty years into an abyss of evils. A contest began between the Red Rose (Lancaster) and the White Rose (York). In no people's annals is recorded a more terrible civil war. Unexampled was the fury of battles, horrible the work of the executioner, murder and assassination the tale of every day. No less than eighty members of the royal house died by violence. For this they could accuse themselves alone. The contest was their own. What they suffered, most of them had themselves inflicted or designed to inflict upon their relatives. With and beside them, for and by them, hun-

dreds of thousands of people died as well. The noblest families vanished in a deplorable way, the flower of the nation was destroyed by arms and by the miseries of war, the country wore the saddest aspect of desolation, and human character was degraded to brutal ferocity by the incessant spectacle of crime and the perpetual fermenting of passion, and by intolerable suffering and misery.

All this was done in order to decide whether the posterity of the daughter of King Edward's second son or the descendants of his third son should sit upon the English throne. The nation *itself* was not asked by whom it wanted to be governed. Only to keep up a *semblance* of justice and give legal authority to the work of weapons did the victors always solicit the acknowledgement of Parliament, and this was never refused. What a national destiny!

★

During his autobiographical lecture Steiner recorded that

> The youth really immersed himself at depth in the history of the Thirty Years' War, being able to obtain Rotteck's *Weltgeschichte*. It made a great impression through the warmth with which the first volumes of this world-history were written.

In course of Rotteck's third volume, where his account moved into the modern age, he included a chapter on 'The Times of the Thirty Years' War'. A reader may indeed 'immerse himself at depth', for the chapter comprised no less than 37 sections, giving detailed coverage to the history of this period both on the Continent and also in Britain.

The penultimate section, 'Characteristics of the Revolution', described the contemporaneous English Civil War:

> Henceforth the torrent of revolution swelled visibly and formidably. A horrid rising of the Irish against English Protestants was artfully employed by Parliament to increase hatred against the monarch, represented as the author of these bloody scenes, which he himself deplored and abhorred. Parliament presented to him a list of grievances as a remonstration of state (1642), drawn up with much bitterness, and containing a long series of complaints about injustice old and new, real and pretended, proceeding from the throne, and spread it among the people to increase the fire.

The fire of Rotteck's words burned through another paragraph recounting the Royalist defeats at the battles of Marston Moor and Naseby, and then blazed up against the Scots:

> In this extremity, Charles resolved to throw himself into the arms of the Scottish army—a resolution of which he soon repented. For when after a

dangerous flight he arrived at the Scottish camp he was immediately treated as a prisoner, and in a short space of time delivered up to his mortal enemy, the English Parliament. The Scots infamously sold their hereditary prince for the sum of £400,000, staining their history with an indelible blot.

A further paragraph describing background politics led onto the next section, 'Oliver Cromwell. Charles Executed'. Preparing readers for the worst, Rotteck reached out for a string of adjectives wherewith to preface Cromwell's very name:

> Since dissolution of the state's legal form and the raging civil war had given free rein to wild power, the more violent had according to the nature of things gained victory over the moderate. The 'Independents' in Parliament and in the army who, animated by a partisan spirit, rejected all positive authority both in religious and political matters, soon became the dominant party. They had at their head the knavish and fanatically pious, equally cunning and valiant Oliver Cromwell...

The account went on to describe Cromwell's rule and Charles's detainment. On reaching the year 1649, the whole chapter was brought to a dramatic finale:

> Amidst many personal outrages Charles was dragged before this iniquitous tribunal. On the 17th of January, the villains pronounced sentence of death upon the king, regarding neither the most sacred rights nor the intercession of many ambassadors and powers. On the 30th of January, Charles suffered death at the executioner's hand, in public before his palace of Whitehall, with firmness and dignity. The nation was plunged into grief and horror. Europe shuddered at the unheard-of deed.

The Deepest Impression

After describing in his autobiography the effect made on him by Rotteck's history of the world, Rudolf Steiner continued:

> ...Through him I was led towards two other historians whose style and historical view of life made the deepest impression upon me: Johannes von Müller and Tacitus. Under such impressions I found it quite difficult to find my way into the lessons on history and literature. But I tried to enliven these lessons by everything acquired outside them. This was how I spent my time in the three upper classes of the seven in the *Realschule*.

To picture the way in which this youth was enlivening his history and literature lessons, a reader must again sample certain works by the named historians.

★

Johannes von Müller lived at the end of the eighteenth and beginning of the nineteenth century, a little earlier than Rotteck. Among his writings was a work entitled *Vier und zwanzig Bücher Allgemeiner Geschichten bes. der Europäischen Menschheit*, published posthumously in 1810. The last volume of this work included a whole chapter about Great Britain. Here are its final paragraphs:

> The system of excise, a tax on consumption, is a Dutch invention. It was adopted by the Long Parliament which dethroned Charles I, and was confirmed under the reign of Charles II. Since then this imposition has been many times extended to other articles; its amount has been increased, and the system for collecting it improved. The uniform object of the ministry has been to render this tax as productive and as little disagreeable as possible; and to collect it with utmost attention to accuracy and equity. The increase of price caused by this tax is usually confounded with the price of the goods; and on that account it is in appearance by far the least burdensome imposition. In the year 1772 it produced £3,800,000.
>
> In the reign of William III, a tax of 3s. 4d. was imposed on every bushel of salt. Under Anne, this imposition was transferred to the excise; and since the time of George II it has been rendered perpetual. Stamp duties are imposed on contracts, records, playing cards, newspapers, advertisements and almanacs; and vary according to the value of the instrument, from 6d. to £10.
>
> The customs, which owing to the prodigious increase in manufacture and commerce take the place of old and new subsidies, already amounted to £2,500,000 (A.D. 1754). Bounties granted on the export of some articles, and drawbacks on others, are deducted from the above sum; and Swift's witty remark that in custom-house language twice two does not always make four is not without foundation. In fact, exports are increased both by vanity and speculation; and the high rate of the customs is a real bounty on smuggling.
>
> Little can be said respecting the produce of the Crown lands, as William III rewarded his adherents with very long leases on these domains. This prince had a civil list of £700,000; arising from the customs, the excise, the courts, the Post Office, a tax upon fermented liquors, and a contribution from the commons. Queen Anne was content with a similar sum; and George I contrived to save out of this amount £23,000, which he bestowed on his natural daughter, Malusina von Schulenburg. Under the reign of George II the sources supplying the civil list were so productive that it often amounted to £1,000,000; and this king, despite expenses occasioned by his love of magnificence, his numerous journeys and children and the Countess of Yarmouth, left at his death a property amounting to £1,700,000. George III gave up the funds of the civil list; in lieu of which Parliament allotted him

a fixed income of £800,000. He also enjoyed revenue arising from Wales and Cornwall and had at his own disposal income from West-Indian property as well. Within twenty years Parliament twice discharged debts of the civil list amounting to upwards of £1,000,000.

In the glorious period of the Seven Years' War, Great Britain maintained an army of 337,000 men in its pay; and possessed 61 ships of the line and 353 smaller vessels of war. After the conclusion of the peace of 1763, land forces were limited to 40,000 men. Resources of military talents have never been more successfully applied by any modern people than by the Britons during that contest. So much care was taken to provide for all the wants of the soldiery that normal mortality among the wounded was not more than 1 in 20; and out of 14,000 men employed in the year 1760 in cruising through the Bay of Biscay, scarcely 20 were attacked by disease. Inventions, even of foreigners, were nobly rewarded by the British Parliament.

The spirit of the nation produced such exertions that after 3 unsuccessful or fruitless campaigns its perseverance was rewarded with 12 victories, by which it gained the distant province of Canada, 25 islands, 9 fortified towns, 40 forts, 100 vessels of war, and a booty to the value of £10,000,000.

The same spirit which since the restoration of their ancient freedom had animated the Britons afforded the astonishing spectacle of a nation reduced to the brink of ruin, amidst the desertion of its colonies, the commotions of Ireland and the tumults of faction, groaning under the burden of an enormous taxation, destitute of allies and without any assistance, which yet withstood the united power of the House of Bourbon and its ancient confederate Holland.

What a lofty eminence this nation would attain if, among the treasures of plundered Hindustan and the corruptions of avarice, the spirit of its laws could remain powerful enough to render moderation and equity the foundations of its political system!

★

Turning back to Publius Cornelius Tacitus, the Roman historian of the late first and early second century, a reader may consider another description of British scenery and habits.

In the *Agricola*, written during the years 97–8, Tacitus celebrated the career of his father-in-law Gnaeus Julius Agricola, praetorian legate in Britain from 78 to 84. The narrative includes the first detailed account of the island:

> Although the geographical position and the inhabitants of Britain have been described by many authors, I shall describe them once again, not to match my industry and ability against theirs, but because the conquest was only completed in this period. Where my predecessors relied on graces of style to

make their guesswork sound attractive, I shall offer ascertained fact. Britain, the largest of the islands known to us Romans, is of such a size and so situated as to run parallel to the coast of Germany on the east and of Spain on the west, while to the south it actually lies within sight of Gaul. Its northern shores, with no land facing them, are beaten by a wild and open sea. The general shape of Britain has been compared by Livy and by Fabius Rusticus—the finest of ancient and modern writers respectively—to an elongated diamond or a double-headed axe. Such indeed is its shape south of Caledonia, and so the same shape has been attributed to the whole. But when you go farther north you find a huge and shapeless tract of country, jutting out to form what is actually the most distant coastline and finally tapering into a kind of wedge. These remotest shores were now circumnavigated, for the first time, by a Roman fleet, which thus established the fact that Britain is an island . . . I will add just one observation. Nowhere does the sea hold wider sway; it carries to and fro in its motion a mass of tidal currents, and in its ebb and flow does not stop at the coast, but penetrates deep inland and winds about, pushing its way even among highlands and mountains, as if in its own domain.

Who the first inhabitants of Britain were, whether natives or immigrants, is open to question. One must remember we are dealing with barbarians. But their physical characteristics vary, and the variation is suggestive. The reddish hair and large limbs of the Caledonians proclaim a German origin; the swarthy faces of the Silures, the tendency of their hair to curl, and the fact that Spain lies opposite, all lead one to believe that Spaniards crossed in ancient times and occupied that part of the country. The peoples nearest to the Gauls likewise resemble them. It may be that they still show the effect of a common origin; or perhaps it is climatic conditions which have produced this physical type in lands converging so closely from north and south. On the whole, however, it seems likely that Gauls settled in the island lying so close to their shores. In both countries you find the same ritual and religious beliefs. There is no great difference in language, and there is the same hardihood in challenging danger, the same cowardice in shirking it when it comes close. But the Britons show more spirit: they have not yet been enervated by protracted peace . . .

Their strength is in their infantry. Some tribes also fight from chariots. The nobleman drives, and dependants fight in his defence. Once they showed obedience to kings; now they are distracted between warring factions of rival chiefs. Indeed, nothing has helped us more in fighting against their very powerful nations than their inability to cooperate. It is only seldom that two or three states unite to repel a common danger; so, fighting in separate groups, all are conquered. The climate is wretched, with frequent rains and mists, but no extreme cold. Their day is longer than in our part of the world. The nights are light, and in the extreme north so short

> that evening and morning twilight are scarcely distinguishable . . . The soil will produce good crops, apart from olives, vines and other plants which usually grow in warmer lands. They are slow to ripen, though they shoot up quickly—both facts being due to the same cause, the extreme moistness of the soil and atmosphere. Britain yields gold, silver and other metals, to make it worth conquering. Its seas, too, produce pearls, but of a dark, bluish-grey colour. Some think the natives unskilful in gathering them; for whereas in the Indian Ocean oysters are torn alive and breathing from the rocks, in Britain they are collected as the sea throws them up. I find it easier to believe that the pearls are of inferior quality than that people miss a chance of making a larger profit.

The History of Modern Times

In a further passage of his autobiography, Rudolf Steiner reported:

> Only in the final class at the *Realschule* did I have a teacher who also gripped me by his teaching of history. He taught history and geography . . .

This was Albert Löger.

> . . . The new teacher strongly affected his pupils through his teaching of history. To us he was a personality in the fullest sense. He was a party man, totally enthused by the progressive ideas directing what was then Austrian Liberalism. At the school nothing of this was noticed. He brought nothing of his party views into it. But his involvement in life made his history teaching come strongly alive. With the results of reading Rotteck in my mind I listened to this teacher's historical expositions. They made a fine blend. I consider it important that I was able to absorb in this way precisely the history of modern times.

If Löger's historical expositions on modern times made a fine blend with the results of reading Rotteck, one can imagine what they must have been like by turning to the later volumes of the latter's *Weltgeschichte.*

⋆

The fourth volume, for instance, contains a chapter with a section on 'England', subtitled 'Conquests in the East Indies'. Most of it recounted the British conquest of India and other neighbouring islands at the end of the eighteenth and beginning of the nineteenth centuries.

In the final paragraph, however, Rotteck, although supposedly writing about the past, simply switched his narrative into the present tense and gave a graphic description of the contemporary and still continuing effects:

> It is not precisely the dominion of these countries, but the resultant security and extension of commerce with the richest lands of the Earth that makes the possession of them precious to England. By the East Indies, as well as by many other possessions and colonies, in all seas and in the most important ports of the commercial world, the mother-country becomes mistress of the treasures of the nations. Her industry makes incessantly new progress; machines alone double in their effect the productive mass of the population. About 30,000 vessels serve for foreign commerce, and 1000 vessels of war maintain the dominion of the seas. Every day there arise upon English soil precious new foundations and new monuments of Britain's grandeur. She supports without much difficulty the immense expenses of her government and the annual payment of more than £40,000,000 for the interest of her enormous debt, according to some of about £1,000,000,000, and according to others far more, and if circumstances require it pays with her gold most of the armies of Europe . . .

The fifth and last volume contained a further chapter with a section on 'Great Britain', giving an overview of this country's relationship to the rest of Europe:

> At the fall of Napoleon, Great Britain, above all other powers, celebrated a brilliant triumph. She had annihilated the long-feared enemy, set a king over France, procured command of the European army of occupation for her general, Wellington, exercised a predominant influence in the new regulation of the European system, and at once made the precious acquisition of the Ionian islands and in place of the regained Hanover several finely situated German provinces. The continental countries, closed to her commerce under Napoleon, were now opened to it again, and she practised anew her well-learned art of keeping these countries permanently tributary to her industry and closing her own market to their productions. In other parts of the world she also augmented either her commercial preponderance or—especially in the East Indies—her political and military power. Yet the kingdom's internal condition did not correspond to such a brilliant exterior. The weight of the enormous public debt, the boundlessly disproportionate distribution of property, the stagnation or decay of many branches of industry as a result of the peace, the precarious condition of the manufacturers, the arrogance of the rich and eminent, the annually increasing fermentation in the poorer classes, the justified exasperation of the oppressed Catholics in Ireland which led to desperate civil war, and many other sufferings or symptoms of disease presented the sea-ruling state to the eyes of the observer under an aspect far from exciting envy, and filled the mind of the thinking Briton himself with great apprehension.
>
> But the worst result of the revolutionary struggle was the reaction produced and maintained by it against the ideas of the age. The government's

power became more absolute in proportion as the standing troops increased; the aristocracy, revolted by the democratic character of the French Revolution, redoubled their arrogance and severity, and the people themselves, seduced by national rivalry, did not generally see, or saw without repugnance, that their government's policy, instead of preceding other powers as formerly, now remained far behind the spirit of the age, and trifled away its claim to the love and confidence of the nations. National vanity was flattered that the Bourbons, as protégés of Britain, had ascended the throne of France, and passionate zeal overlooked that the principle of legitimacy to which on this occasion English ministers rendered homage was sapping the foundations of the House of Hanover's rights to the throne of England.

Although from considerations relative to the form of her government England had refused to accede to the Holy Alliance she nonetheless followed its tendency, and thus lost a great part of her political importance. Had she hitherto played the part of a protector of the weaker against the strong (particularly in recent times of a protector of national laws against Napoleon's world dominion) and thereby obtained respect and powerful influence, she now sank from a leading position down to a subordinate one. After the restoration of the Bourbons and the fall of Naploeon, British aid was but little needed for maintaining the principle of legitimacy in Europe. At the head of the new system stood the great continental powers, and compared with them England almost retreated into political insignificance. Congresses of monarchs and ministers which ordered dictatorially the affairs of the European continent took place partly without England and partly with only her subordinate participation, and among the intelligent of all nations the voice of hatred and contempt was raised against the government of aristocrats and the people of traders on the Thames.

The Result Hearafter Described

In his autobiography Rudolf Steiner recounted one notable aspect of his time in the upper classes at the *Realschule*: his tense relationship to the German teacher, Joseph Mayer. Having discovered the latter to be an adherent of Herbart's philosophy, the youth bought a couple of Herbartian textbooks and began to play a kind of hidden game with this teacher by spicing his German essays with Herbartian ideas.

The matter was also recalled by Albert Pliwa, who described the consequences of Steiner's philosophical reading:

> On being asked how he had come to have an inclination for this study, he replied that the splendid lecture about Herbart's philosophy by Dr Joseph Mayer (our teacher for German literature) had appealed to him. But once in Class VII Prof. Mayer, while returning exercise books relating to home-

work where Rudolf Steiner had used very many philosophical expressions and in Mayer's view had been applying them badly, said: 'You seem to possess at home a philosophical literature! I advise you not to read it, since you are unable at present to understand it!' There then followed a long explanation about 'psychological freedom' which, as Mayer said, Rudolf Steiner in his German essay 'had just been throwing around', allegedly without grasping it in the least. Our ironic remarks made no impression on Rudolf Steiner; on the contrary, he immersed himself ever more in his favourite study (Kant).

Steiner gave an additional reason for Mayer's displeasure with him, recounting in the autobiographical lecture that

> ... the teacher for German literature, who was otherwise a splendid man and made great contributions to the school, could not abide the youth Rudolf Steiner reading things which led him to write such dreadfully long essays, sometimes even filling a whole exercise book.

★

For the school-leaving examination in the summer of 1879 Mayer set his pupils to write a German essay on the theme 'The patriotism of citizens is the firmest support to the state (illustrated by historical examples)'.

Steiner with his extensive reading in the historical works of Rotteck, Johannes von Müller and Tacitus would have been able to bring forward plenty of examples on this theme, and no doubt the essay he wrote was again a lengthy one.

In his autobiography he recorded:

> ... The teacher took a long time to read my essays. At the leavers' festival after the final exam, when for the first time he was 'pleasantly' together with us pupils, he told me how my lengthy essays had annoyed him.

The autobiographical lecture reported Mayer's very words:

> ... After the school-leaving exam, when it was usual for pupils to be once more with the teachers before leaving the school, he said to the youth: 'Yes, you were my strongest phraser; I was always frightened when your exercise book arrived.'

★

Pliwa too remembered the day of the leavers' festival. He described the headmaster's speech:

> At the leaving festival (Valet), given by leavers on the 5th of July 1879 to teachers and fellow pupils of the upper class at the *Realschule* and the *Maschinenbauschule* (connected to the *Realschule*), the headmaster Andreas

Rudolf Steiner at Wiener Neustadt in 1879, aged 18

Pöschko said: 'Of all the pupils who entered our establishment in the year 1872,' (about 140) 'there remained after the IVth Class' (1876) 'only 23 who proceeded into the Upper School. Most of these dropped out because of their poor study,' (the Wiener-Neustadt *Realschule* was said at the time to be among the 'hardest' in the whole of Austria), 'while some went for two or three years into other schools. So only three are left of those who arrived in 1872 and thus went through all seven classes in the establishment, and these three have passed the exam with distinction: Steiner, Deutsch, Pliwa!'

There seems a strange kind of appropriateness, almost symbolism, in the fact that Steiner had been studying the German language for no less than seven years alongside a fellow pupil with the name of 'Deutsch'.

Sigmund Deutsch, of Jewish extraction, was stated by Pliwa to have had 'a glorious manner of expression in German essays'—evidently quite different from Steiner's pompous philosophical jargon. Maybe in the school-leaving exam Mayer gave Deutsch a good mark for German.

⋆

On the day of this leavers' festival, certificates were drawn up and handed out to all the leavers.

The first page of one certificate read:

School-leaving Certificate

Rudolf Steiner from Kraljevec in Hungary began studies *in the school year 1872/3 at the Landesoberrealschule in Wiener-Neustadt and until 1879 in all classes at the same* completed them, in moral qualities attained the mark *exemplary*, and took the school-leaving examination set by the undersigned examination board with the result hereafter described:

Languages:

German Language:	*Satisfactory*
French Language:	*Praiseworthy*
English Language:	*Praiseworthy*

A second page listed other school subjects, which on Steiner's certificate were mostly marked as 'excellent'.

On the third page, dated 5 July 1879, were the signatures of the school inspectorate, the headmaster and each of the teachers, including

... Pet. Lambertz for Fr. Language ... W. Schmeisser for English ... Dr J. Mayer for German ...

It is amusing to find that Dr Mayer, adversely affected by the irritation he had received from his pupil's Herbartian terminology and the exhaustion to which he was driven by the length of the same pupil's essays, characterized the level of Steiner's German as merely 'satisfactory', whereas both the Carmelite teachers, Father Lambertz and Father Schmeisser, awarded the same pupil laudatory epithets for his performance in French and English! The resultant impression given by the certificate was that its holder had more ability in foreign languages than in his own mother-tongue. This may well be regarded as the biggest joke in Steiner's whole earthly life.

Talking of jokes, one can also hardly avoid commenting on the surname of his English teacher, Father Schmeisser. *Schmeisser* is a noun meaning 'chucker, slinger', being derived from the colloquial verb *schmeissen* used in such German expressions as *mit Fremdwörtern um sich schmeissen*—'to bandy foreign words about'.

The Second-hand Bookseller

In his autobiographical lecture Rudolf Steiner described the ensuing summer holidays:

Now when his schooltime was over, there arose in the youth a whole series of philosophical questions. The school-leaving exam was finished, and the

> father had himself transferred to a station near Vienna so that the youth could attend the Technical College. In the holiday-time following the school-leaving exam a deep longing really arose to solve philosophical questions. There was only one way by which this longing could be quenched. A number of schoolbooks accumulated down the years were taken to the second-hand bookseller and a nice little sum acquired, which was at once exchanged for books on philosophy. The youth now read what he had not yet read by Kant, for instance his treatise from the year 1763 about the *Versuch, den Begriff der negativen Grössen in die Weltweisheit einzuführen* or Kant's *Träume eines Geistersehers, erläutert durch Träume der Metaphysik* where a connection is made to Swedenborg. Not just Kant, but the whole of literature could be followed through representative books by Hegel, Schelling, Fichte and their pupils—for instance Karl Leonhard Reinhold—Darwin etc . . .

It is revealing to find here the name of Charles Darwin casually tacked on, almost like an afterthought, to this list of long-dead German philosophers. The famous English scientist was then the only contemporary author whose writings were purchased by the 18-year-old youth in that second-hand bookshop during his first visit to Vienna at the very dawn of the Michael Age.

Charles Darwin on the veranda at Down House, c. 1879

The reason for Steiner's interest in Darwin may easily be deduced. At the *Realschule* in Wiener-Neustadt he had been taught natural history by 'a man who really understood nothing at all about either God or the world'. With regard to the subject in question this suggests someone teaching a kind of crude creationism. Although on his school-leaving certificate Steiner was marked as 'excellent' in the subject, and was entered at the Technical College to study *inter alia* botany and zoology, he must have become aware that in relation to natural history there also existed in modern times a new theory or set of theories quite different to those he had been taught.

★

At the dawn of the Michael Age Charles Darwin, just like Rudolf Steiner, was on holiday. But their holidays were completely different.

The 18-year-old youth, having spent his 'nice little sum' on books, stayed at home in the Viennese suburbs, studying the spiritual landscape of German philosophy as well as its more recent and radically variant Darwinian counterpart.

The wealthy septuagenarian scientist, by contrast, spent what must have been a nice big sum in taking his family far from their Kentish home on an extended tour through the physical landscape of a beautiful part of north-west England.

In the second volume, *The Power of Place*, of her authoritative biography *Charles Darwin*, Janet Browne relates:

> Eager for a diversion, the remaining family set out in August 1879 for a month's holiday in the Lake District, travelling by train with Henrietta, Francis, and two-year-old Bernard in a private railway carriage hired for the occasion. Darwin complained about the extravagance but Emma said 'we should have been quite killed but for the saloon carriage'. Admitting defeat, he jettisoned all pretence at invalidism and enjoyed the journey with 'the freshness of a boy', greatly savouring the vista of Morecambe Bay as the train snaked around the edge, one of the most dramatic combinations of railway engineering and coastal scenery in the United Kingdom. They stayed in a hotel in Coniston owned by Victor Marshall, cousin of their architect at Down House, with views over the lake and gardens. Everyone remembered this holiday with pleasure. Darwin was more relaxed than the family had known him for a long time. On a day's excursion to Grasmere, Henrietta said, 'I shall never forget my father's enthusiastic delight, jumping up from his seat in the carriage to see better at every striking moment.' Darwin recognized the unusual situation himself. 'The scenery gave me more pleasure than I thought my soul, or whatever remains of it, was capable of feeling,' he told Romanes afterwards. Jovially, he wrote to Marshall to

> express his thanks, and volunteered to send him a young oak tree from Down House grown from an unusual specimen in his father's garden at Shrewsbury. He agreed to return to the Lake District to Ullswater for another visit in 1881.
>
> On that first trip, Darwin made the acquaintance of John Ruskin, the critic and author, who lived in seclusion at Brantwood on the shore of Lake Coniston. The two had much to talk about, not least the friends they held in common. Richard Litchfield knew Ruskin well from their time as teachers together at the Working Men's College . . .

Litchfield was Darwin's son-in-law, married to his second (surviving) daughter Henrietta.

> Darwin listened sympathetically while Ruskin confided that his mind was becoming 'clouded'. A few days later Darwin paid a return call during which Ruskin took him into a back room to show him his collection of J.M. Turner's watercolours. Politely, Darwin murmured some appreciative words. Afterwards, he confessed he could make out 'absolutely nothing of what Mr. Ruskin saw in them'. Victor Marshall reported that Ruskin subsequently spoke about this meeting in high good humour, mentioning Darwin's 'deep & tender interest about the brightly coloured hinder half of certain monkeys'.

A Most Extensive Programme

In October 1879 Rudolf Steiner matriculated at the *Technische Hochschule* (Technical Highschool, or Technical College) in Vienna.

Christoph Lindenberg observes:

> It is clear from his study-book that Rudolf Steiner undertook a very extensive programme of studies. Besides mathematics, physics and chemistry he attended courses on botany, zoology, mineralogy and geology, as well as law. Since he received every year a scholarship of 300 guilders (600 gold marks), he was obliged to give regular evidence of his success in these studies.

The regular evidence was in the form of examination results.

★

Among the courses Steiner attended during his first year at the college were those on 'Geology' and 'Mineralogy with Exercises'. The latter comprised three hours of lectures every week, and two of exercises.

Both courses were given by Ferdinand Hochstetter, a widely travelled man whose life merits perhaps a paragraph.[5] Born in Esslingen in 1829, he first studied theology in Tübingen. There however his interests turned towards natural science, and he wrote a doctoral dissertation on limestone spars. From 1853 to 1856 he undertook geological explorations in Bohemia, as a result of which he was invited to join a scientific expedition circumnavigating the world under the sponsorship of the Austrian government. Engaged as the expedition's geologist, he prepared himself thoroughly for the enterprise by travelling to Berlin in order to consult the scientist and geographer Alexander von Humboldt, by then well into his eighties, and also to England. Over the years 1857–9 this expedition sailed in the frigate *Novara* right around the world, giving Hochstetter opportunity to carry out geological research in Gibraltar, Brazil, South Africa and Ceylon, as well as on smaller islands in both the Indian and Pacific Oceans. On reaching the antipodes, he was commissioned by the government of New Zealand to make a geological survey of their whole country. This took some nine months, and resulted in his drawing up the first geological map of New Zealand. Returning to Austria, he was appointed in 1860 to the chair of Geology and Mineralogy at the Vienna Polytechnic—later renamed Technical College—where he modernized the teaching of these subjects. In 1869 he was engaged on geological work in Turkey preparatory to some railway construction, and in 1872 on similar work in the Urals for the Trans-Siberian railway. During the next academic year he was among the science teachers of the ill-fated Crown Prince Rudolf. In 1875 he published *Die Erde*, and on appointment in 1876 as Director of the Natural History Museum in Vienna also his *Leitfaden der Geologie und Mineralogie*, which soon established itself as a standard textbook, going into further editions.

Now in his autobiography Steiner recorded that at the *Realschule* in Wiener-Neustadt he was 'all eyes and ears' when Franz Kofler, during whose history lessons he had been surreptitiously reading Kant, set out on the blackboard the geological and geographical relations of the Alps. At the Technical College in Vienna he must have further developed his knowledge of geology, for when examined in this subject on 13 March 1880 by Andreas Kornhuber he was marked as 'excellent'. Four months later, on 5 July, he was examined by Hochstetter himself on mineralogy, and again marked 'excellent'.

★

Kornhuber, who took the geology exam, was Professor of Botany and Zoology. A qualified medical doctor and also veterinary surgeon, he specialized in palaeobiology. His own courses that year included 'Botany with Exercises'—a weekly three hours of lectures and two of exercises—and 'Systematic Overview of the Lower Animals'—two hours per week.

In his autobiography Steiner recalled that

> Wherever I came across the sciences of organic nature, they were permeated by Darwinian ideas. The highest ideas of Darwinism seemed to me at the time a scientific impossibility. I had gradually come to build up for myself a picture of man's inner being. This was of a spiritual kind, thought of as a member of a spiritual world. It was pictured as being submerged from the spiritual world into natural existence, and inserted into a natural organism in order thereby to perceive and act in the world of the senses.
>
> This picture I could not even disavow through having a certain respect for the thought processes in the teachings of organic evolution. The idea of higher organisms proceeding out of lower ones seemed to me fruitful. But to combine this idea with what I knew as the spirit-world was immeasurably difficult.

The implication is that 'the highest ideas of Darwinism' were concerned with the human being. The reference to 'higher organisms proceeding out of lower ones' may lead a reader to wonder whether during his 'Systematic Overview of the Lower Animals' Professor Kornhuber might not have expounded this part of the Darwinian theory and in the process alluded to the human being as a higher kind of animal.

Although Steiner claimed that for him it was 'immeasurably' hard to combine the Darwinian theory with what he knew as the spirit-world, his difficulty does in a sense seem to have been academically measured by his performance in the exams. For in none of the biological subjects did he gain any superlatives. Kornhuber—also acting that year as Rector of the College—must have been absent, for the exams were taken by Alexander Bauer, Professor of Chemistry. In the botany exam on 10 July Bauer only marked Steiner as 'good', and a week later, in the zoology exam on the 17th, once again as simply 'good'.

To judge therefore by his examination results, Steiner was making better progress in the inorganic than in the organic sciences.

A Most Charming and Attractive Man

In his account of Rudolf Steiner's years at the Technical College, Christoph Lindenberg makes the following remark:

> It is striking that Steiner in his autobiography and also elsewhere is largely silent about his official studies.

This observation may be extended to cover also Steiner's official teachers. Since he mentioned Hochstetter only once in a Dornach lecture and nowhere for instance Kornhuber or Bauer, it must be supposed that for all their scientific expertise these academics were not in respect to the art of teaching particularly inspiring. The autobiographical lecture records that Steiner was

> ... little inclined to listen with quite pedantic regularity to lectures at the Technical College, though he took part in everything...

On the whole he was more interested in attending courses about quite different subjects such as philosophy or aesthetics being given at Vienna University, of which however he was not himself actually a member.

The teacher at the Technical College from whom Steiner did gain inspiration and to whom he always made reference was Karl Julius Schröer, Professor of German Literature, whose courses he attended from the very start of his Viennese years in 1879 and whose influence was to remain of paramount importance for the rest of his life. And yet it is precisely by switching the focus away from Schröer and onto the latter's various academic colleagues like Hochstetter, Kornhuber or Bauer that one may come to appreciate Lindenberg's remarks about the anomaly of Schröer's position:

> It is certainly correct that Schröer was teaching at the Technical College and that Steiner met him there. But the fact that Schröer taught at the Technical

Karl Julius Schröer

> College was actually an 'objective misunderstanding'. Schröer did not represent acknowledged science, and was not regarded by the philological gang as one of their company. In 1875 Schröer's work *Die Dichtung des 19 Jahrhunderts in ihren bedeutenden Erscheinungen* had been torn to shreds in a review by Hebbel's biographer Emil Kuh, as a 'history of literature shaken from the cuff'. Erich Schmidt [from 1880 Professor of German at Vienna University and later Director of the Goethe Archives at Weimar] considered Schröer to be an utter dimwit, and for the technicians and scientists at the Technical College Schröer must have been an exotic phenomenon.

The reason why in that given context Schröer must have been an exotic phenomenon was elaborated by Walter Johannes Stein in an article entitled 'A Contribution to the History of Rudolf Steiner's Life', contributed in 1934 to the *Korrespondenz der anthroposophischen Arbeitsgemeinschaft*. This article, which reported a talk with Steiner during a conference at the Hague in April 1922, began as follows:

> On becoming a student at the Technical College in Vienna, Rudolf Steiner was led by destiny to a person of outstanding significance. Karl Julius Schröer, then Professor of the History of German Literature at the Technical College in Vienna, was a solitary person weaving thoughts of universal import and comprehensiveness. His meeting with the young Rudolf Steiner was a spiritual event.
>
> The significance of Schröer can be gauged if one takes the trouble to make a serious study of his individual sentences and aphoristic remarks. In his history of German literature, for instance, sentences are found shedding wide light on the evolutionary course of peoples throughout the centuries. I indicated some of this in my introduction to Schröer's important edition of *Faust*. Unfortunately Rudolf Steiner could no longer bring out this new edition. Had this still happened, we would have been able to recognize in his additions to Schröer's commentary how his mind provided a complement to the spiritual manner of Schröer.
>
> In a conversation I was able to have with him during a conference in Holland, Rudolf Steiner told me something about his meeting with Schröer which can also be of value to others, so perhaps it may here be related.
>
> Rudolf Steiner found Schröer involved in preparing collected writings by Goethe for Kürschner's comprehensive work of German literature, *Kürschners deutsche Nationalliteratur*. Schröer felt himself capable, and indeed was in the comprehensive sense of the word, of editing Goethe's literary and dramatic work. But he drew back from commenting on Goethe's *scientific* work. The path of Schröer's own destiny had made him into a teacher of German at a *Technical* College, but he could not form the resolve to overcome his feeling of being a layman in the domain of physics, mineralogy and biology.

An account has been given of the personnel at the Technical College who had expertise in mineralogy and biology, subjects which Steiner was studying during his first year.

Physics, by contrast, only entered Steiner's curriculum at the College from his second year onwards, i.e. from the autumn of 1880. Over the academic year of 1880–1 he attended courses given by several teachers on general and technical physics, the theory of heat, optics, mathematical physics, the mechanical theory of heat, and the history of physics.

In his autobiography he stated:

> Physics studies were completely permeated by the mechanical theory of heat and the wave theory of the phenomena of light and colour.
>
> The study of the mechanical theory of heat had a personally coloured appeal for me because I heard lectures about this physical domain from a personality whom I quite exceptionally revered. It was Edmund Reitlinger, author of the fine book *Freie Blicke*.
>
> He was a most charming and attractive man. When I became his pupil he was already suffering from an advanced disease of the lungs. For two whole years I attended lectures by him on the mechanical theory of heat, physics for chemists, and the history of physics. I worked under him in the physics laboratory in many fields, especially that of spectral analysis . . .

Edmund Reitlinger

Born in 1830 in Pest, Reitlinger came—just like Schröer—from what was politically a Hungarian background. He had been Professor of Physics at the Technical College since 1866—the very same year in which Schröer, some five years his senior, was appointed Professor of German Literature.

2
THE FINE BOOK *FREIE BLICKE*

The Poetry of Reality

If when describing Edmund Reitlinger in his autobiography the very first thing that Rudolf Steiner mentioned about this person whom he 'quite exceptionally revered' was his authorship of a 'fine book', an interested reader will naturally turn to the book in question in order to discover what was so fine about it.

A detailed look will therefore be taken at Reitlinger's *Freie Blicke.* Although to begin with this diversion naturally leads the present narrative somewhat away from the course of Steiner's life, its ultimate relevance will gradually become apparent.

★

Freie Blicke was published in Berlin in 1874—six years before Steiner made his first acquaintance with its author at the Technical College in Vienna.

The noun *Blick* means 'look, sight', so the title might be translated into English as 'Free Sights'. There was also a subtitle, 'Popular Scientific Articles', and a dedication to Heinrich Wilhelm Dove.

After this came a foreword, here reproduced in full:

> Foreword
>
> The more do I believe myself to have attained in the following book that objectivity beyond which an author may be forgotten, the more do I feel a need to say some words in advance so as to communicate with the reader in person.
>
> From earliest youth onwards, indeed I might say from the time to which my first memories go back, I was always filled with a most vivid longing for knowledge. If at first this urge merely presented itself as the novel desire of an awakened child, in youth and manhood it later became a need to know which was directed towards everything cognizable and much that was not. In spite of any danger I too would have lifted the veil from the image at Saïs, and as soon as I felt capable, I hurried from one philosophical system to another. But what happened to me was like what happens to those tuberculous persons who try, one after another, the infallible miracle cures being extolled, without success . . .

This must have been a veiled autobiographical reference, showing that

Reitlinger's lung-disease, described by Steiner as (six years later) 'advanced', was a chronic condition from which he had long been suffering, and for which he could find no remedy.

> ...In the end I confessed myself to no particular philosophy—out of philosophy. I was not however dissatisfied. It was at least elevating to consort in mind with profound thinkers who had attempted to fathom the world by speculative means, and at the same time I had come to know through mathematical, historical, linguistic and scientific studies manifold splendid details. The experiential sciences (or if the name of the most important part be transferred to the whole, natural sciences) offered a possibility, through observation, transmission and calculation, but above all through experiment—that powerful mediator between subject and object—of penetrating ever more deeply into the world's correlation according to law, and of attaining a knowledge which, if not limitless, was yet every day expanding...

The phrase 'mediator between subject and object' implicitly alluded to Goethe's essay of 1793 'Experiment as Mediator between Subject and Object'.

> ...I therefore decided to act according to Dante's call:
>
> Verwendet jetzt, um neues zu erfahren
> Weil Seele noch und Leib zusammenhält
> Den kurzen Rest von eurem Erdenleben!
>
> Not long before the need arose for me to choose a profession, physics had risen to an achievement of most general importance, the law of the conservation of energy. This rules the interaction of all natural forces, and on contemplating the mathematical formula any person might believe they saw before them the sign of the macrocosm, and could call out with Faust:
>
> Wie Alles sich zum Ganzen webt,
> Eins in dem andern wirkt und lebt!
>
> And yet the so-called imponderables—light, heat, electricity and magnetism—were by the law of the conservation of energy still subjected only in general to the mechanical order of the world. Neither was their essential nature yet fully unravelled, nor the wealth of their manifestations completely investigated. It had merely become undeniable that studying them was highly significant for the goal of all knowledge, for cognizing the whole order of the world. One might then hope not to have lived in vain by acting according to Goethe's saying: 'Join yourself to a whole as a serving member.' Consequently I chose experimental physics as my profession in life and my area of work.

In this book the reader will not however encounter the results of my experimental researches in electricity and spectral analysis, published elsewhere. The book arose rather from a spiritual need which was as it were contrasted to a physicist's special professional activity. At a meeting of scientists in Innsbruck, Helmholtz aptly said of experimental researchers: 'We cannot deny that the more an individual is obliged to limit the field of his work, the more he must feel a spiritual need not to lose connection with the whole.' No one through his own individual work wants to lose from sight the historical development of science, or through his own perhaps lost position the battlefield itself, where mastery over Nature beckons as the prize of victory. To me this sensation necessarily became so much more vivid, since I had devoted myself for years on end to philosophical and historical studies.

Unveilings of monuments and centennial festivals first offered opportunity and occasion to express publicly this feeling of general progress. By presenting not only the discoveries and inventions of the great immortals being celebrated, but also the most remarkable events from their life, it was easier for me to take both scientific and aesthetic viewpoints into account. This possibility seemed equally present in all cases where science was unveiling the past of the Earth or of our race beyond the bounds of historical records, where earthly and heavenly distances were vanishing away through telegraph and spectral apparatus, or where even the opaquely mysterious top of the skull could not prevent insight into the relation between brain and sensory instruments—in a word where the discoveries and inventions of science were so increasing our knowledge and mastery of Nature that we might say like Schiller: reality itself is becoming a poem. This reality which science makes manifest, hovering in a double infinity of space and time, with its interaction and metamorphosis of appearances, under the twofold law of the conservation of matter and of energy, presents such a splendid drama, filled with elevation and harmony, that on recalling Hegel's saying 'Everything real is reasonable' we may venture on the expression 'Everything real is beautiful'. We are of course speaking here only of that higher reality known through science, not of the mundane one of our own struggles and sufferings.

What science was proclaiming about the origin, size and constitution of the world, about time and eternity, far surpassed everything which religious myth or folk-saga had thought up. If it was granted to me to express in words the poetry of reality as it stood before my mind, I also believed that I might perhaps reckon on interest in wider circles. Led by this endeavour, I composed the articles which I am now presenting in collected form to friends of German literature. In accord with their exoteric tendency, I welcomed the fact that the greater number, individually as I wrote them, were published by Austria's widest-read papers, the earlier ones by the

Presse, the later ones by the *Neue Freie Presse*. Two appeared in *Auerbachs Volkskalender*, one in the popular astronomical journal *Sirius*. In the following collection they are not printed in chronological sequence, but ordered to present as it were a panorama of the world surrounding us, from heavenly space to the human brain, from macrocosm to microcosm. I may be allowed gratefully to add that on showing some of the oldest articles, before publication, to the well-known writer Dr Alfred Königsberg, I was able to take up his various suggestions. Berthold Auerbach referred me to the title of the final article.

'If a natural scientist,' says Goethe, 'wants to claim his own right to free inspection and observation, he must make it a duty to secure the rights of Nature. Only where she is free will he be free. Where she is bound by human rules, he will be fettered too.' The nature of freedom implies that the freedom of Nature which Goethe demands can only flourish where all other claims to freedom by modern civilization—like freedom of thought or belief—are secured and guaranteed. Thus arises that inseparable interaction between freedom and natural science which is indicated from the start of the book to the finish, and indeed runs as a red thread throughout.

The articles collected here arose individually and by occasion, each of them forming originally a completed whole. These 'free sights' therefore look out as through separate little windows, or individual facets of an insect's eye. One and the same real world surrounding us is nonetheless the object of observation in all. Truth is mirrored and painted by them, and is what they are both looking at and aiming towards. They all arise from one same world-conception, which regards materialism and idealism, science and philosophy as evolutionary steps of one Nature and one Spirit with a comprehensive and illuminating knowledge of the world. I have called these 'sights' free since they have tried to be free from the half-timbered construct of an artificial division of knowledge created by ourselves, free from the exclusivity of a scholarly language of signs and formulae, and free from the narrowness of national and religious prejudices. They also rest entirely on the free standpoints of that pure humanity which numbers among its representatives the greatest heroes of German poetry and science, Goethe and Schiller, Kant and Humboldt, and which doubtless will also emerge victorious from the present cultural battle.

Mediating between scholarship and popular education is among a writer's most difficult tasks. For such a case even an Alexander von Humboldt found it necessary to invoke the reader's forbearance. In my regard I may be allowed to recall the following words by Humboldt from the third edition of his *Ansichten der Natur*: 'The union of literary and purely scientific purpose—wishing to occupy fantasy and at the same time enrich life with ideas through the acquisition of knowledge—brings separate parts into disorder, and makes the required unity of composition hard to achieve.'

Vienna, on the 1st of July 1874.

Dr Edmund Reitlinger,
Professor of Physics at the Technical College in Vienna.

Freedom and Scientific Research

The foreword to Edmund Reitlinger's *Freie Blicke* was followed by a list of contents, giving titles and page numbers of 30 individual articles: 'The Solar Worship of a Natural Scientist', 'How is the Sun Heated?', 'The Solar Eclipse on the 6th of March 1867', 'A Look into the Universe', 'Our Ancestors from the Stone Age', 'From the Egyptian *Book of the Dead*', 'The Egyptian Monuments in Miramar', 'Of the Antipodes', 'Of the World Market', 'Zoo Studies', 'From the Green Room', 'A Prize of 50,000 Francs', 'From the History of Telegraphy', 'Science and the Lightning Flash', 'The Globe in Flight', 'Nicolas Copernicus', 'Kepler's *Dream of the Moon*', 'Galileo Galilei', 'Franz Arago', 'A Hundred Years after the Birth of Alexander v. Humboldt', 'For the Centenary of Alexander v. Humboldt', 'Joseph Ressel, Inventor of the Propeller-driven Steamer', 'Carl Rokitansky', 'Alteration of Sound and Colour through Movement', 'The Piano in the Ear', 'Disputational Art', 'Doctor Faust and Natural Science', 'Computation of Time', 'Man of the Future', 'Into the Interior of Nature'.

This list of titles shows sufficiently the variety of subject-matter, and in the present work it is of course not possible to examine the content of all these articles. Whoever takes the trouble to peruse them will however admire the skill with which Reitlinger presented for the readership of his day a popular but nonetheless reliable exposition of this or that topic from widely separate areas in which science interacted with general culture.

It may be added that the author's style of writing sometimes gave rise to quite trenchant statements. Witness for instance the final sentences of the article 'A Look into the Universe':

> There are today only two classes of nations at all, those sunk in the night of despotism, receiving sluggishly and dreamily the benefits of science, and those walking in the daylight of freedom, contemplating the harmony of the universe and tirelessly striving by their own power and activity to wrest from Nature new treasures and new secrets. Only those nations who unite freedom and scientific research can thus today rightfully say that they are heading for the peak of civilization.

★

A closer look may be taken at the article on 'Galileo Galilei', written for the tercentenary of the great scientist's birth on 18 February 1864. It began as follows:

> In this year natural science and poetry celebrate the third centenary of their heroes: Galilei and Shakespeare. It was Galilei who, having received fleeting news about the invention of a telescope in Holland, put one together in a single night in 1609. The first among all mortals, he directed it towards the sky and thus founded a new epoch in astronomy. On the Moon he perceived mountains and valleys; to the then known fixed stars he added a new class; in the Milky Way he saw a girdle beset with countless stars; in Orion alone he found over 500 new stars; he resolved patches of mist into a host of little stars, and discovered the four moons of Jupiter, the ring of Saturn and the phases of Venus. These discoveries, which frequently contradicted traditional views, were mostly set down in his *Sidereus Nuncius* (The starry messenger). But blind supporters of Aristotle ventured to explain the discoveries as an optical deception. Indeed at Padua, where he held the chair of mathematics, they were even contested by his professional colleagues. In vain did he challenge them, as he complains in a letter to our Kepler, to look through the telescope towards the sky and gain conviction with their own eyes. They did not even wish to see the telescope itself.
>
> It was especially the moons of Jupiter and the phases of Venus which decided the great controversy of the time between the Ptolemaic and Copernican systems of the universe . . .

Over several further pages Reitlinger recounted the dramatic story of how Galilei's pioneering scientific ideas brought him into conflict with the Italian ecclesiastical establishment of his time. He included observations like this:

> Perhaps the remembrance that he owed some of his finest discoveries to a church contributed to Galilei's vivid desire to reconcile the Church with research in natural science. A swinging lamp in the cathedral of his home city of Pisa had led him to pendular motion as a measure of time, from which derived the pendular clock. With an eye of genius he used the leaning tower of Pisa for his famous experiments with falling objects.

The author went on to describe Galilei's trial in 1633, his forced recantation, and the verdict of confinement in old age to his villa in Arcetri.

> He once more plucked up courage and composed the *Dialogue on Movement*, where he layed down the immortal foundations of rational mechanics. The treatment in this work of the trajectory was particularly important for the science of war. Already as a professor in Padua he held the view that military science was nothing else than applied natural science. Respected foreigners

> from all countries crowded into his lessons on fortress construction, the art of laying sieges, and the application of geometry and mechanics to military purposes. Gustavus Adolphus of Sweden is supposed to have been his pupil, and his statue can still be seen on the Prato Navale of the old university town. He was therefore the Carnot of his time and had a no less famous applier of his theory than the modern man has in Napoleon. He paved the way for all progress. Even Newton's doctrine of gravitation can be said to have arisen from the union of Galilei's mechanics with the laws of Kepler.
>
> A new misfortune now befell the much-tested old man: the light of his eyes began to dim. Already completely blind in one eye, he made one last great telescopic discovery, that of the oscillation (libration) of the Moon. In 1638 his second eye went blind as well, and he himself writes: 'I have become wholly and incurably blind. This sky, this Earth, this universe, which through wonderful observations I have extended a thousandfold beyond the boundaries believed in by past times, are now shrivelled up to the narrow space occupied by my body.'
>
> Despite the ban of the Inquisition, he was visited at that time by the young Milton, fated to be like him in a destiny of fame and blindness...

The allusion was to the exordium to Book III of *Paradise Lost* where the blind English poet, recounting his wanderings in thought to the Castalian spring (on Mount Parnassus) and his nightly spiritual journeys to Mount Sion and its brooks (Kidron and Siloa, associated with the Pool of Siloam where the blind man recovered sight) compared his own fate to that of similar figures from Greek antiquity: the legendary Thamyris who challenged the Muses to a contest in which he failed and lost his eyes, and the epic poet Homer, referred to by his surname of Maeonides:

> ...Yet not the more
> Cease I to wander where the Muses haunt
> Clear Spring, or shady Grove, or Sunny Hill,
> Smit with the love of sacred Song; but chief
> Thee *Sion* and the flow'ry Brooks beneath
> That wash thy hallow'd feet, and warbling flow,
> Nightly I visit: nor sometimes forget
> Those other two equall'd with me in fate,
> So were I equall'd with them in renown,
> Blind *Thamyris* and blind *Maeonides*...

Reitlinger then brought his article to an end:

> During his last four years Galilei was looked after by his second daughter, Arcangela, and his enthusiastic disciple Viviani. In 1638 he still writes: 'Even in my darkness I am brooding now over this, now over that object of Nature, and cannot bring my restless head to peace.' On the 4th of January

1642, the same year in which Newton was born, death brought the 78-year-old man to a longed-for repose. Despite difficulties created by the Inquisition, whose prisoner he still was, Galilei was according to his wish buried alongside his ancestors in the church of Santa Croce. But for almost a century he had to remain without a memorial. He gained one under the will of his disciple Viviani.

For centuries the Sphinx of Nature had set man a great riddle, on whose solution mastery over her kingdom should depend. How does what is resting come into motion, and what is mobile come to rest? Galilei found the riddle's solution. What is mobile remains forever in continuous motion, without external influence, and what is resting eternally at rest. This is a property of matter, and motion and rest are only relative. Like Oedipus, Galilei too was led to ruin by research pressing restlessly onwards, and the eyes of both were finally closed by blindness. To the two old men, in Colonos and in Arcetri, there only then remains the tender care of their daughter: a movingly tragic drama! Galilei's epitaph reads therefore rightly: *Naturae Oedipo*.

And the mechanics created by Galilei grew on and on: it has altered the Earth with machines, and as celestial mechanics has fathomed the movements of the planets. It finally also succeded in acquiring what Archimedes so much longed for—that free point independent from the Earth. A suitably hung pendulum gains its level of oscillation just as if it were fixed to a point outside the Earth. Thereby the walls of an experimenting hall can be perceived to rotate during the Earth's daily movement in 24 hours around a vertical drawn from the pendulum's point of suspension to the Earth's central point, and this movement can thus be followed so to speak with the eyes. This glorious experiment was made a few years ago by Foucault, who also first grasped the idea put into effect by Kirchhoff of a chemistry of the Sun and stars through spectral analysis. Germans saw Foucault's pendulum experiment in Cologne Cathedral, and even in Rome it is supposed to have been seen by the present Pope. But the pendulum of Foucault writes with an invisible spirit-hand onto the walls '*e pur si muove*'—a serious warning to any Power desiring within one realm to decree away motion forever.

The Basis for All Cognition

Certain parts of Edmund Reitlinger's article in *Freie Blicke* on 'Doctor Faust and Natural Science' also deserve to be set out.

This article, written in 1866, was concerned with the German 'folk-book' about Faust published in the late sixteenth century. For several pages Reitlinger discussed the content of the work and its historical background—mentioning also the contemporary English play on the same figure by Christopher Marlowe.

The article then continued:

It is known that a play by Grabbe placed Don Juan and Faust opposite each other. But already Hebbel observed this to be false: every Faust would turn into a Don Juan and every Don Juan into a Faust. Don Juan, however, is of all people the one who forms a least correct opposite to the counterfeiter of natural science, the Faust of saga and folk-book. The opposite is formed by those true, genuine and great scientists enthused by the divinity of Nature: Kepler, Galilei, Newton, Humboldt.

This comes before us with particular clarity in the noble figure of Kepler. Our readers will know that by inferring from experience the true orbits of the planets Kepler became the creator of modern astronomy. But he also found the actual seat of sight in the human eye, and was the first to explain in a correct manner the working of the telescope. He put forward instances of induction crowned with the highest success, where Bacon later set down rules erroneously exemplified. Precisely for observers and experimenters does the saying 'exempla trahunt' seem invented. There is thus no doubt whatsoever that it is Kepler, not Bacon, who stands before us as the founder of modern science. He lived only a few decades after the origin of the Faust saga, and his discoveries coincided with the time when the folk-book was travelling around the world. Without denying the devout spirit of his time, Kepler placed the Bible of Nature alongside the written one. In the latter, God's thoughts are read; but in the former, they are seen. Knowledge of natural laws is to him a thinking of the thoughts by which God created the universe. So he finds God in Nature. He believes that a human being is called upon and empowered to penetrate her, by the very 'gifts which have thus been graciously bestowed on him and communicated from *above*'. This is just what Faust had despaired of. In every respect, therefore, Kepler travels an opposite path from the Faust of saga. He too, with Faust, takes 'eagle's wings', but they carry him up to the Sun of truth.

Kepler thus turns to God in order to investigate the divine laws. What Faust hopes from the devil Kepler seeks in God. Both of them are filled by an innermost thirst to fathom Nature. With Faust it is a 'dark urge', and with Kepler a light-filled endeavour. They are connected like prophecy and fulfilment.

After a couple more pages about Kepler, Faust and Goethe, the article ended with these sentences:

Even if the word 'homeopathy' were to disappear from medicine entirely, the saying 'healing of like by like' will always be the only correct one as regards the urge for knowledge. A person gripped by the desire to know can only healthily bathe in the dew of truth. However, it is never granted us to know the total and complete truth. But if a Lessing went as far as to put striving after truth before truth itself, so we too may feel some satisfaction, more at least than in pleasure, by always broadening our knowledge and pushing its limits further back. This indeed is what is happening. Ever more do Egyptologists unveil for us the veiled image of Saïs, the land of priestly hieroglyphs. Sanskrit experts show us in the holy books of ancient Indians the purest and most original form of metaphysical problems. Through comparison of tongues, linguists draw nearer to the very essence of speech and the riddle of its origin. Physicists demonstrate to us terrestrial matter in the Sun and fixed stars, and by the law of the conservation of energy melt together time and eternity. Chemists ban the chimera of life force through artificial union of organic substances. Physiologists supplement Kant's critique of pure reason, i.e. *of the cognizing capacity*, by researching the *organ of cognition*, by investigating sensory perceptions and the activity of brain and nerves. Palaeontologists and Darwinists explain to us the origin of species by the transformation of one into another. Are not all these researches and discoveries which belong to our time directly related to the aims and purposes of the highest philosophical cognition? Since they all rest on 'experience', as though proving the applicability of scientific method, if we put them together under the word 'science' in the widest and most general sense, this must consequently form the basis for all cognition. Our striving after truth then finds satisfaction in a progress which is every day reactivated. When Plato wished briefly to describe the essence of poetic art, which illuminates what is low by humour and what is high by enthusiasm, he stated that the best tragic poet would also be the best writer of comedies. Shakespeare was not so far removed from this ideal, since in him Aeschylus and Plautus were united. We however may be allowed to imitate Plato by stating our conviction of a necessary union between science and philosophy in this sentence: the desire for knowledge—and the Faust-saga—will only reach a satisfactory conclusion when the best physicist and the best metaphysician, Kepler and Kant, are united in one person.

'Into the Interior of Nature'

With regard to the present work the most arresting article in Edmund Reitlinger's *Freie Blicke* was the very last one, 'Into the Interior of Nature'. It was a lengthy article—the longest in the whole collection—and had only just been written in 1874, the year the book came out. As previously seen, in his foreword the author stated that the title was referred to him by Berthold Auerbach.

The article began:

> Nichts ist drinnen, nichts ist draussen,
> Denn was innen, das ist aussen.
>
> Goethe

> Goethe's finest creations were, as is known, self-liberations of his spirit, by which he mastered the morbid moods of his person or time. In this way arose the sufferings of Werther, and while more than one enthusiast laid hands on themselves in an overexcited manner Goethe himself recovered and could say in Shakespeare's words: 'Der gesunde hüpft und lacht...'

Literally this means 'The healthy man hops and laughs'. The present writer is unable to say where this supposed Shakespearean quotation comes from.

> ... It is interesting that when the Bishop of Bristol wanted to attribute to him the suicides caused by his youthful work, the grey-haired Goethe replied by referring to the hundreds of thousands who kill each other at the command of princes and encourage each other to murder, robbery and plunder. 'After such horrors you give thanks to God,' he exclaimed, 'and thereupon sing a Te Deum!...'

The person concerned was not the Bishop of Bristol, but rather Lord Bristol, Bishop of Derry in Ireland, one of the great English eccentrics of his day. He often travelled on the Continent and met Goethe in Jena in 1797—as the latter recounted to Soret in 1830.

Reitlinger continued to discuss Goethe:

> ... When he withdrew from conditions threatening his whole existence by a sudden journey to Italy, like a flight, it was through the immortal creation of his *Tasso* that according to certain statements he shook off 'that painful annoyance still clinging to him from Weimar impressions and memories'. He therefore agreed when J.J. Ampère, son of the famous physicist, called *Tasso* an 'intensified *Werther*'.
>
> Something similar is true of *Faust*, and Goethe himself stated that not only the unbounded and dissatisfied striving of the main character but also the scorn and cruel irony of Mephistopheles presented and incorporated parts of his own being. In *Werther* and *Tasso* the poet is supposed to have lent thoughts and words from his own course of development without completely identifying with them, indeed through these very works to have freed himself from the one-sidednesses there presented. But with *Faust* it appears taken for granted that statements may be read of the most personal Goethean convictions. We acknowledge this in regard to the place where the dying Faust says:
>
> Das ist der Weisheit letzter Schluss;
> Nur der verdient sich Freiheit wie das Leben,
> Der täglich sie erobern muss.
>
> This however is not nearly the case with countless statements—coming at very different times—about Nature, art and science contained in that most thoughtful of all poetic works. We particularly object to the notion that

Goethe himself despaired of Nature's explorability and held that striving after knowledge of her was idle trouble, like Faust in the tragedy's first scene. Ever since the first part of *Faust* came out, winged words from this scene are quoted by both open and concealed opponents of science for the same purpose as was formerly a well-known statement by Haller. In *Dichtung und Wahrheit* Goethe says about the interest aroused in him by the puppet-play fable of Faust that he too had been beating about all knowledge and early enough had its vanity pointed out to him. But later he wholly recognized the importance of investigating Nature, which he regarded as a most successful and appropriate method of activating our desire for knowledge. Indeed he saw in poetry and science the most essential and mutually complementary tasks of his own personality, and went so far as to consider his scientific studies and discoveries equally valuable, if not even superior to his poetic creations and achievements. By acknowledging that after Shakespeare and Spinoza the greatest influence on him was from Linnaeus, he indicates that he sought to re-establish in his own person the ancient trinity of poet, philosopher and scientist, and evidently believed that he had not been unsuccesful. His studies of Nature led him to the conviction that very often pathways to what is held unresearchable suddenly open up, and what seemed inaccessible might be approached from a previously undreamt-of side. He therefore found himself in a vividly felt contradiction to a famous saying by Haller. Albrecht von Haller too represented that spiritual trinity of philosophy, science and poetry, and the higher Haller stood in science the more did Goethe see that he needed to defend his claims against the 'Swiss poems'. So there is found in those writings on morphology a 'Friendly Call' where he expresses a 'joy repeatedly pressing on him'. He feels happy agreement with earnest, active researchers near and far. Together with them he asserts that the unresearchable be presupposed and admitted but a boundary then also drawn up for the researcher himself. How widely and deeply the human mind manages to penetrate into its own secrets and those of the world is never determined or finalized. A subsequent amusing piece of rhyme may be taken in that sense. Here follow the verses marked in his collection of poems 'However', where he dryly mocks Haller's statement:

> Ins Innere der Natur
> Dringt kein erschaffner Geist,
> Glückselig, wem sie nur
> Die äussere Schale weist!

and says:

> Das hör' ich sechzig Jahre wiederholen,
> Und fluche drauf, aber verstohlen.

> Since that time the same saying has been quoted for a further fifty years. But a few Faustian passages have been joined to it, e.g.:
>
> Geheimnisvoll am lichten Tag,
> Lässt sich Natur des Schleiers nicht berauben.
>
> In these and similar words we meet, as in *Werther* and *Tasso*, fleeting impressions of the poet's, who just by presenting them frees himself from them. In no case are they concerned with final opinions belonging to Goethe, who devoted such a great part of his life to scientific studies. At a later place in the tragedy even Faust himself is found contradicting them, when he thanks the Spirit of the World for having allowed him into Nature's
>
> Tiefe Brust
> Wie in den Busen eines Freunds zu schauen.
>
> This emerges even more clearly from the above-quoted poem of protest against Haller; from the passage used as motto and numerous others of the same tendency; from the tireless persistence and perseverance with which Goethe for many years sought to investigate Nature's physical and physiological laws; from all his many writings dedicated to science, which he composed into ripe old age, until a few days before his death, and from which shines out the happy belief of penetrating into the interior of Nature!
>
> All this was merely the opening of the article.

It is evident that the kind of reader Reitlinger was seeking to engage was one of mainly literary interests. He not only referred to several of Goethe's literary works, but also included brief poetic quotations. To English readers such quotes may mean little or nothing at all, but to the ear and mind of a German-speaking person they form recognizable touchstones from a significant area of feeling and consciousness.

Elevating Sensation

No reader up to this point of Edmund Reitlinger's article 'Into the Interior of Nature' would yet have been able to guess what became apparent in the next paragraph—that it was in fact a review-article.

> Goethe's scientific correspondence may now remind a later-born generation of his passionate love for science, his reverence for its world-compelling power and his confidence in its boundless future . . .

A footnote gave details:

> *Goethes Naturwissenschaftliche Correspondenz (1812–1832)*, edited on behalf of

the von Goethe family by F.Th. Bratranek, two volumes, Leipzig, F.U. Brockhaus, 1874.

The main text went on:

. . . In the year 1818 Goethe wrote to Carus: 'Old age can sense no loftier happiness than to feel itself having grown into youth, and to be growing further with it. The years of my life which I had to spend in solitary devotion to science, because I found the present moment objectionable, now come highly to my benefit. At a stage in life when one would otherwise only be praising a time gone by, I feel myself in agreement with the present.' This concordance of Goethe with his contemporaries increased year after year, right up to his death. In Germany the 'new union', to use his own words, gained ever more supporters and fellow workers, while in France a way was paved for Goethe's botanical views by a translation of his *Metamorphosis of Plants*. During the last years of Goethe's life his greatest scientific thought, the unity in the plan of the animal world, found an enthusiastic defender in Geoffroy de St Hilaire. Thus arose the well-known misunderstanding of Soret when visiting Goethe on the 2nd of August 1830, after news had arrived of the July revolution. Goethe called out: 'Now what do you think of this great event? The volcano has erupted!' When Soret replied that the expulsion of the royal family was to be expected, it transpired that Goethe did not mean the political event, but the famous battle in the Académie des Sciences between Geoffroy St Hilaire and Cuvier. Soret's naive confession that when Goethe explained this he felt in his thoughts 'a complete standstill' shows how far ahead of his contemporaries Goethe was. Even at present many will be astonished, though Goethe's great thought championed by Geoffroy has now become master of the day, if in essentially altered form, as Darwinism. It claims the participation of the really educated in higher measure than does the drama of intrigue of those three dynasties combatting each other in France. The convergence between Goethe's method of perceiving and that of other men has anyway since his death continued. Publication of his scientific correspondence encounters today a prepared generation, where no longer a few select minds but the majority of educated people can both grasp and share Goethe's method of scientific perception.

That great fruitful thought of a typical unity in all living beings brings Goethe the highest fame of having enriched knowledge, and forms a most important issue in this method of perception. Apart from the name *Morphology*, Goethe gave his botanical and osteological writings a second title, *Formation and Reformation of Organic Natures*, and further set before them a profound motto from Job, 'See, he passes over me before I am aware, and changes before I notice.' This at once rouses a present-day reader to suppose that what he had in mind here was the cardinal question of the origin and development of species, including the human being. So indeed it was. Already in 1784 Goethe directed conscious endeavour towards this question by seeking and finding in man the intermaxillary bone. At the time, it was believed that the intermaxillary substantiated the difference between man and ape. However, in the human skull too Goethe discovered faint traces of that suture joining the upper jaw and the intermaxillary in animals. His explanation is that man too originally possessed an intermaxillary, which later vanished by fusion with the upper jaw. In animals the latter contains the molar and canine teeth, the former the incisors. Fusion of both bones eliminates the animal snout, and effects the noble formation of a human face. From this subsequent fusion of bones originally also separate in man, Goethe concludes that the difference between a human being and an animal cannot be found in anything particular. Already in 1784, forwarding his work on the intermaxillary, Goethe wrote this to Knebel: 'Every creature is only a tone, a shade in a great harmony which must be studied as a whole, otherwise every individual part is a dead letter. This little work is written from that viewpoint. Here really lies the interest hidden within it.' In sketches for an introduction into comparative anatomy put onto paper in 1795 and 1796, he teaches that all differences in the formation of animal species are brought forth from a basic type through fusion, division, transformation, reduction or total elimination of individual parts. The possibility that a man might change into a bird or wild animal—which had risen before the power of poetic imagination—was after final observation of these parts by ingenious scientists also put forward by them to the understanding. Coincidence of structure was indeed followed even further by Camper into the kingdom of the fishes. Effects of climate, mountain altitude, warmth and cold, moisture and dryness, methods of nutrition and life become visible to us in the structural difference of species. The same parts are, in man and ape, arms with hands; in horses and ruminants, forefeet with hooves; in cats, paws with claws; in fishes, fins; in birds, wings. To Goethe's credit, it is not in any way necessary to identify this teaching with that of Darwin, which is in fact essentially different. The general thought of a typical and genetic unity in the animal world is already so elevated and momentous that it justifies to the full Goethe's enthusiastic words:

> Freue dich, höchstes Geschöpf der Natur, du fühlest dich fähig,
> Ihr den höchsten Gedanken, zu dem sie schaffend sich aufschwang,
> Nachzudenken . . .

It is interesting to compare these words of Goethe, which express his delight over the unity recognized in the world of animals, with those produced in Kepler from discovering the law-bound harmony of our planetary system. 'Father of the world, what moved you so to elevate a poor earthly creature that it now stands there like a king ruling wide spaces, almost a god—reflecting to you your thoughts!' One and the same elevating sensation, the same thankful joy, merely in the garb of different centuries!

The Poet of Natural Science

Within the present context there is no need to reproduce the whole of Edmund Retlinger's review-article 'Into the Interior of Nature', which as already stated was rather lengthy. Suffice to say that the article went on for some pages discussing other scientific work undertaken by Goethe in both the organic and inorganic realms. Then came these paragraphs:

> On the same tree where a person is plucking figs today he will want to pluck them again tomorrow, and if sloes had grown on it overnight his face would be very morose; but whoever is a friend to sloes will turn towards the thorns. According to these words of Goethe's, people had become too used to the precious fruits of his poetry to seek in him the thorn-surrounded one of science. As a result his scientific writings, when they appeared, found only little interest and even less approval. 'Nowhere,' he says, 'would people admit that science and poetry were compatible. That science had developed out of poetry was forgotten. People did not consider that after a change of times both of them might quite well meet again as friends on a higher level, to mutual advantage.'
>
> The prejudices combatted here by Goethe are still present today, and it must partly be attributable to them that his scientific writings are only little known to a contemporary readership. Partly this is also because they are written in a language admittedly beautiful, but nonetheless specialist. Even of his poetical works Goethe had said: 'My productions cannot become popular. Anyone who thinks this and strives towards it is in error. They are not written for the crowds, but only for individual persons who desire and seek something of the kind and are proceeding in similar directions.' He underestimated the assiduous educability of Germans, through which a great deal originally intended for exquisite, indeed courtly circles has since become the nation's common property. That he composed his scientific writings led by this view, without aiming for a popular method of presentation, is all the more explicable since at the time no such method existed for scientific subjects. Humboldt first led the German people, who had already long since entered the temple of Art, to enter that of Nature as well. By their inclusion in his collected works, Goethe's writings on science are certainly now possessed by everyone. So far, however, this has only given occasion for the curious fact that people could refer to them with the jocular riddle: 'What writings are as widely disseminated as they are little read?'
>
> One cannot concern oneself with Goethe's scientific correspondence without turning one's gaze onto his literary and research activity in different

areas of science, and asking what place the poet occupies as scientist, and how the scientist is at work in poetic creativity. Professor Bratranek, editor of Goethe's scientific correspondence, speaks about this in an introduction he entitles 'Goethe's Scientific Importance'. Outlining and assessing Goethe's scientific achievements, he basically in his own words follows an excellent lecture by Virchow from the year 1861, 'Goethe as a Natural Scientist and in Particular Relation to Schiller'. By contrast, he answers the question of what influence Goethe's science exercised on his poetry in a splendid piece of research into the aesthetic author himself. He links onto the 'anthropomorphism' of the Goethean conception of Nature. This word, he says, expresses a unity of natural knowledge and poetry living in Goethe. The humanizing or raising of a natural phenomenon into the mental domain of law, never progressing to abstraction, but just recognizing it as something observed, as a primal phenomenon or primal type, is when applied in another area the highest natural truth of Goethe's poetry. In treating natural phenomena Goethe unites incomparable fidelity with complete humanization, and thus attains a beauty and vividness of depiction as no poet before him. Using the example of cloud formation, Bratranek tries to bring forward evidence that Goethe in depicting this surpassed the two greatest poets of previous times, Homer and Shakespeare. Observing Nature enables Goethe to give his presentation that exactitude by which fantasy can experience the enjoyable power of a reproduction mirroring reality—a poet's highest triumph. Bratranek concludes that since he united the sharply heard consonants of Nature with the strongest vowels of a human breast no one let sound in such full tones as he did the eighteenth century's call: 'Retournons à la nature.'

Goethe himself boasts of owing to his observation of Nature new pictures and comparisons, and in this regard brings forward the passage:

> Wie traurig steigt die unvollkommne Scheide
> Des späten Monds mit seuchter Glut heran.

Glorious poems like 'Bei Betrachtung von Schiller's Schädel' repose on his study of Nature like golden fruits on a silver dish. Without it, he would never have been able to describe 'the veil of poetry from the hand of truth' as the gift imparted to him.

Goethe's science has therefore done unforgettable service to German poetry, just through its effect on his poetic creativity. German history, however, as already stressed by Virchow, has another special reason for valuing Goethe's immersion in Nature. This initially gave rise to that memorable union between Goethe and Schiller, which Palleske called the first shy outline of a new national formation. The stormy works of Schiller's youth filled Goethe, on his return from Italy, not with any admiration of their power but only with displeasure at their formlessness. He saw ideals of

> beauty which he had scarcely attained placed once more into question. Even after Schiller found a place of refuge and permanent home in Jena, no convergence took place. As Goethe expressly testifies, it was only thanks to plant metamorphosis that there developed a relation to Schiller surpassing all his wishes and hopes. In 1794 Goethe and Schiller are known to have met in the scientific society at Jena. On the occasion of a lecture, Schiller remarked to Goethe that there was no way in which the usual dismembered manner of treating Nature could attract any layman who might want to be involved. Goethe countered by referring to his own method of not taking Nature as separate and isolated, but presenting it as active and living, striving from the whole towards the parts. Having in the meantime entered Schiller's house, he vividly put forward the metamorphosis of plants. Schiller listened with great involvement, and although their subsequent conversation did not lead to total agreement a first step had nonetheless been taken. A relation arose which Goethe states was for him a new spring, when everything happily germinated together, emerging from seeds and upshooting twigs. Goethe, however, described his relation to Schiller in the words: 'He preached the *gospel of freedom*, while I wanted to secure the *rights of Nature*.' Schiller and Goethe therefore complemented each other like freedom and science. In the mouth of the people, the creator of *Tell* has long been called 'poet of freedom', and in 1859 was celebrated as such. Even with Goethe, however, it was not the case of a mere personal union between poetry and knowledge of Nature. Rather as Aristotle, the philosopher of experience, stands beside Plato, the philosopher of ideas, so does Goethe, the poet of science, stand beside Schiller, the poet of freedom. Who would deny this, on learning how Goethe describes man's highest purpose as being the revelation to him of 'God—Nature'? Or on reading the glorious words of the 'eternal weaver's masterpiece', where Nature's sway and activity are already depicted, under restless transformation yet continual inertia of her forces, just as though Goethe had seen before him the law of the conservation of energy? What J.R. Mayer and Helmholtz recognized Goethe already divined . . .

A Genuine Human Education

Over the next few pages of his article 'Into the Interior of Nature', Edmund Reitlinger examined various further details of the book under review and other issues relating to Goethe's researches in anatomy and botany. He then went on:

> His teaching on colour, too, remained not wholly fruitless for science. Although unable either to repress or supplant the optics of the physical 'guild', it nonetheless sowed the seed of important discoveries in the field of

sensory physiology. Especially Purkinje and Johannes Müller took up this Goethean legacy. In the collection letters are found from both of them which shed closer light on this relationship. Through the doctrine of colours Purkinje was led to his important investigations on sight in a subjective regard, and in the relevant letter (Nr. 196) Johannes Müller also recognizes himself as belonging to the 'new union'. Goethe's scientific researches, he writes, have stimulated him to penetrate the secrets of organic Nature. The great services shown by Goethe in regard to a doctrine of the sense of sight arouse in him a vivid regret that Goethe did not concern himself with the sense of hearing too. He believes that the processes through which we draw near to the essence of one sense must lead towards the physiology of all the others. It cannot be denied that such statements on the part of the immortal discoverer of specific sense-energies, who numbers among his pupils Helmholtz, Dubois-Reymond, Brücke and Ludwig, possess the highest significance.

In general, we learn from numerous letters about seeds whose resultant growths have since come to light, and whose ripened fruits we greet as long since known and admired. In this connection we may just mention the letter from Poggendorff on the 10th of August 1824 (Nr. 290). Poggendorff here forwards to Goethe the first issue of those *Annalen für Physik und Chemie* whose fifty-year existence gave occasion a few months ago for a worthy celebration in Berlin. Doyen Poggendorff had the rare fortune of experiencing this jubilee of his excellent journal. The unforgettable upswing of German physical science in the last fifty years is indivisibly united to this journal's brilliant effect.

After a couple of pages further discussing Goethe's letters and some results of his scientific works, Reitlinger brought his article—and thereby the whole book *Freie Blicke*—to a conclusion in these two paragraphs:

We have however not the slightest doubt that in the great cultural battle of the present Goethe would regard science as the best and most powerful confederate of progress. Its first modern success, the discovery of the Copernican world-system, already led to hefty conflict with Ultramontanism. Chiefly on account of science, the latter finds modern civilization incompatible. So too science offers the most effective enlightenment for superstition, and the best support in educating people to unite freedom with respect for law. Goethe stated in words we may here apply: 'Mankind needs to transmit what is positive from one generation to another, and it would be good for the positive to be at the same time what is both right and true. In this regard I would be delighted for us to come clean and persevere in what was right in science, and not go again transcendent, after everything feasible has been done.'

That science is increasingly 'coming clean', however, he would certainly

> not deny. Indeed, already then (1827) he stated: 'Progress is now being made such as I could not foresee, and on ways introduced by myself. I feel like a person heading towards the dawn, who when the Sun shines forth is astonished at its brilliance.' In the half-century which has since passed by, the Sun has no doubt risen considerably, greeted at the same time by the lark of freedom with her morning song. Though till now only gilding the peaks of education, she must yet, the higher she rises, send her rays into ever deeper valleys. By filling with equally bright light the German palace and the German hut, may she soon perfect, at least as far as the German tongue extends, what Schiller and Goethe were striving after: a genuine human education, founded on love of freedom and on knowledge of Nature.

Reitlinger wrote this article in 1874. It was concerned with Goethe's scientific impulse, but the opening paragraphs were aimed especially at a literary reader, and the foreword to *Freie Blicke* presented the book in which it was included 'to friends of German literature'.

Anyone perusing this article today can scarcely help thinking about a certain literary-minded Goetheanist in the author's immediate vicinity, namely his academic colleague at the Technical College, that exotic phenomenon the Professor of German Literature.

The life of this figure is finely set out in the biography *Karl Julius Schröer*

Goethe in 1828

by Walter Beck. Schröer was born in 1825. Already from a young age he wrote poetry of his own, and the evidence of unpublished poems from the period 1850–5 suggests that in his late twenties he was having supersensible nocturnal meetings with the entelechy of the discarnate Goethe (who in 1836 had previously—though Beck does not mention this—appeared in a dream to Eckermann). Apart from composing poetry, however, such meetings led on the earthly plane to no further result. And only a few years later, in another poem published in 1856, when he was aged 31, Schröer even stated that he saw a wide path ahead but was unable to go forward along it.

Instead, the path along which he may be said to have subsequently gone—with great energy and enthusiasm—was an essentially narrower one which kept him within the humanistic confines of linguistic, literary and folk studies, but at a distance from the evolving science of his day. From Beck's biography one may compare what Schröer was doing in 1874 at the very time when his academic colleague the Professor of Physics was publishing *Freie Blicke*:

> The Schröer family spent the summer holidays in July at Baden near Vienna, and in August, at Warmbad Villach.
>
> During the entire year 1874, however, Schröer concentrated on writing his book which appeared at the beginning of the following year, *Die Deutsche Dichtung des 19. Jahrhunderts*. After nine years of lecturing at the Polytechnic and Technical College, this book came out as his most extensive but also most controverted publication. He wished to present therein the poetry of the nineteenth century, not with scientific comprehensiveness, but as 'Popular Lectures'...

How striking that the book by the 44-year-old Reitlinger, published in late 1874, was subtitled 'Popular Scientific Articles', and that by the 50-year-old Schröer, appearing in early 1875, 'Popular Lectures'! Both academic authors were striving after popularity, but in completely different fields—one in science and the other in literature.

It was precisely the arbitrary, unscientific character of *Die Deutsche Dichtung des 19. Jahrhunderts* which led to strong disapproval of this book by professional literary scholars of the day. On 8 March 1875 Erich Schmidt wrote to Wilhelm Scherer in Berlin:

> Have you read Schröer's wretched book about German poetry in the 19th century? Yet why do I say 'read'? I've seldom seen anything so bad, and in such poor taste. Starting with the feature articles on Goethe and Fräulein Ziegler! The unknown dialectal poet Misson! Herman Grimm together with the summerhouse poetess E. Marlitt and Werner!...

Four years later, in 1879, Schröer was still lecturing on precisely such themes, as recorded in the first autobiographical account which Rudolf Steiner committed to paper, the so-called 'documents de Barr' written down for Edouard Schuré at the Alsatian town of Barr in September 1907. These state:

> In my first year at the Technical College in Vienna I became acquainted with Karl Julius Schröer. To start with I heard his lectures on the history of German poetry from the first emergence of Goethe, on Goethe and Schiller, on the history of German poetry in the 19th century . . . Schröer himself kept his distance from science.
>
> But I was then working from the beginning of 1880 onwards at Goethe's scientific studies.

At what point Steiner went on to examine Goethe's scientific correspondence is not exactly known. But when later that year, in October 1880, he became acquainted also with Reitlinger and probably soon afterwards read his book *Freie Blicke*, he would have found in its final article 'Into the Interior of Nature' an appreciative approach to Goethean science in the general direction of his own incipient studies within this very same field.

3
THE CANTABRIGIAN CORRELATION

You'll Do

In his autobiography Rudolf Steiner continued his description of Edmund Reitlinger as follows:

> Of special importance for me were Reitlinger's lectures on the history of physics. One felt him speaking in such a way that because of his illness every word was difficult. And yet his lectures were in the best sense inspiring. He was a person with a strictly inductive way of research; for everything physically methodical he was fond of quoting Whewell's book on inductive sciences. Newton represented for him the high point of research in physics. His course on the history of physics was divided into two parts: firstly from ancient times to Newton, and secondly from Newton to recent times. He was a universal thinker . . .

To readers in the English-speaking world this passage is given especial interest by the statement that Reitlinger 'was fond of quoting Whewell's book on inductive sciences'. The reference is to a work by one of the leading figures in British academic and scientific circles of the mid-nineteenth century.

In order to set the work in question within a suitable context, the present part will be devoted to a general account of its author's life and writings, drawn from various kinds of documentary sources. It may be stated at the outset that in the very nature of the case this account also involves some interrelated discussion of other associated figures connected to his remarkable destiny.

★

William Whewell came originally from the north of England. He was born on 27 May 1794 in Brock Street, Lancaster. His father was by profession a master carpenter in that town. His mother sometimes contributed poems to the town's local paper, the *Lancaster Gazette*. Altogether the parents had seven children, but two died in infancy and a third in childhood. The four surviving ones consisted of William—the eldest—and three sisters.

★

In 1804, when William was ten years old, another person who was to play an important role on the scientific scene of nineteenth-century Britain was also born in Brock Street, Lancaster, at the end where it led into Dalton Square: the future anatomist and physiologist Richard Owen.

Owen's reminiscences form the main source of information about Whewell's Lancastrian years, and they centre on a particular event which took place in about 1808, when Whewell was 14 years old. Although Owen at that time was aged no more than four, his account may nonetheless be considered trustworthy because of his position as a close neighbour in the street.

Owen lost his father at an early age, and was brought up by his widowed mother with the support of his godfather, who lived next door. This was a young curate named Joseph Rowley, Headmaster of the town's Grammar School.

Owen recorded:

> In a court lower down Brock Street, Whewell the carpenter dwelt and had his workshop. I remember both the father and grandfather of Dr. Whewell. The grandfather was a most venerable-looking old man, who used to be brought out to sit in the sun in the square. He could tell of the passage through the town of the 'Scotch rebels' in 1745. The gardens of Mr. Rowley and my mother 'marched', as the Scotch say; and it happened that Whewell, the father, was employed in some repairs of the dividing rail fence. Between noon and two p.m. we left school for dinner...

At the time Owen himself was not yet at the school, which he first entered at the age of six, but in this account he was using his later knowledge of the school timetable.

> ...and Mr. Rowley found Whewell's son in the garden, his father having gone to dinner. He entered into conversation with the boy, who then was at the 'Blue School', and about to be apprenticed to his father, and was struck with his replies to questions as to what he had learnt, and especially in regard to his arithmetic. The father returning, Mr. Rowley expressing his opinion of the superior abilities of the youth, proposed that he should go to the Grammar School. The carpenter was a man of sound sense and much esteemed, and stated obvious objections: 'He knows more about parts of my business now than I do, and has a special turn for it.' However, out of deference to the clergyman and Headmaster, he asked for a week to think it over. Mr. Rowley said he would find him books, and there would be no expense for the teaching. So Whewell went.

Whewell's mother had died in the previous year, 1807. Was she maybe looking down from another world and lending support to her teenage son?

⋆

Newly entered at Lancaster Grammar School, the teenager made remarkable progress in his studies, so much so that only a year later Rowley arranged for him to meet the mathematician John Hudson, another northener who was now Fellow of Trinity College in the University of Cambridge. For during university vacations Hudson often returned from the south-east of England to stay at his own family home near Kendal.

The 15-year-old Whewell walked over to meet Hudson at the Bridge Inn, between Kendal and Lancaster. After some conversation in which he assessed the lad's attainments, the Cambridge don observed: 'You'll do. You'll be among the first six wranglers.' A 'wrangler' is a leading candidate in the Cambridge mathematical tripos.

Hudson recommended that Whewell be transferred to his own old school at Heversham, just over the Westmoreland border. The reason was that Heversham Grammar School had an exhibition to Trinity College.

★

So in the following year, 1810, the 16-year-old Whewell changed school yet again, moving from Lancaster several miles further north to Heversham. Probably he boarded at the school. And already in 1811 his scholastic career was crowned with success when indeed he duly won the exhibition to Trinity College in Cambridge. At the time, however, he was still too young to attend university, so he had to spend another year at Heversham Grammar School.

Towards the end of 1811 it happened that the headmaster of the school died. During the ensuing months when the trustees were searching for a successor they requested the 17-year-old Whewell to become acting headmaster and take charge of the whole school!

Arrangements were also made—probably by Hudson—for the youth to have private tuition from John Gough, the famous blind mathematician and scientist who lived in nearby Kendal. The subjects which Gough taught this teenage headmaster were algebra, trigonometry, conic sections, fluxions and mechanics.

And finally in the autumn of 1812 the 18-year-old Whewell set out from his native Lancashire on what was then a three-day journey right down to Cambridge. On eventually arriving there he duly matriculated in Trinity College.

Through Strange Seas of Thought

Trinity College Cambridge is especially famous as the college of Isaac Newton, who in the late seventeenth century spent there a large part of his life. Newton studied in this college from 1661 to 1665, and a couple of years later in 1667 became a Fellow. In 1669 he was appointed Professor of Mathematics at Cambridge, a chair which he held for 32 years, right down to 1701 when he abandoned his academic career and left Cambridge altogether, taking up the post of Master of the Mint in London, where he eventually died in 1727.

⋆

Already during his lifetime Newton attained international fame, and after his death his fame grew even more. So in 1755 his posthumous presence was sculpted onto the material plane in the form of a statue erected in a room immediately adjacent to the most sacred part of Trinity College: the antechapel which leads into the chapel.

The college chapel lies on the north side of the great court. Entrance is gained by ascending a couple of steps and passing through a closed porch giving further access to a door. On opening this door a visitor finds himself entering the antechapel, a large rectangular hall of considerable height. Stone walls extend around on all four sides, with light falling down from windows high above on north and south. The larger part of the room stretches away to the east, towards a wall upholding a large organ under which a pair of double doors leads into the chapel.

But it is the smaller part of the antechapel, extending a little to the west, which engages the attention. One's eyes are drawn towards a work of art which stands in a dominating place on a pedestal set in the very centre of the west end: the marble statue of Newton sculpted by Louis François Roubiliac.

From an artistic point of view, this is indeed a magnificent piece. A visitor may just stand for some moments gazing at it from the side. If he then desires a closer look, and begins to move towards it, he starts to diminish in relation. For since the pedestal on which the statue is placed rises some three feet off the floor, by coming right in front of the statue one finds oneself standing so to speak at Newton's feet. In that position one may also savour to the full the simple but all the more telling inscription at the statue's base:

NEWTON
Qui genus humanum ingenio superavit.

This statue is especially celebrated in lines written by the poet William Wordsworth, who as an undergraduate from 1787 to 1791 at the neighbouring college of St John's was living in rooms just across the lane which divides the buildings of the two colleges,

Statue of Newton by Louis-François Roubiliac

. . . And from my pillow, looking forth by light
Of moon or favouring stars, I could behold
The antechapel where the statue stood
Of Newton with his prism and silent face,
The marble index of a mind for ever
Voyaging through strange seas of Thought, alone . . .

After absorbing the impression made by this statue, a visitor may turn round in the other direction, and make his way eastwards across the antechapel towards the doors leading into the chapel. When the chapel itself has been entered, and the doors behind closed, one is in quite another space, of similar dimensions but with the atmosphere of a standardly designed church. Wooden stalls are set on either side, and the attention is naturally directed to the altar at the eastern end.

It is not difficult to imagine a member of Trinity College sitting in this chapel after the close of a service, immersed still in the solemnity of thought, intensification of feelings or resolutions of will to which such a service might lead. Rising at last to his feet and stepping out of the wooden stalls onto the chequered marble floor, he would then turn westwards towards the exit and move up to the double doors. As soon as the doors opened to let him through, they would reveal again the statue of Isaac Newton at the far end of the antechapel, perfectly framed in the chapel doorway.

Passing through that doorway and re-entering the antechapel, one would then pace towards that statue—as if towards the presence of an incarnate god, far exalted above other mortals, yet visible here in a kind of temple—before then turning southwards to the exit, and crossing back over the threshold to emerge again into the great court, the open air, and normal daytime consciousness.

In the course of the nineteenth century William Whewell would have been regularly going through this very experience down all the long years that he was to spend in Trinity College.

Man Seeks Acquaintance

Making his home inside the congenial Cambridge ambience, the 18-year-old William Whewell entered into quite new circles of people. He formed connections to various slightly older contemporaries who had already started on careers of distinction, such as the budding economist Richard Jones or, in the neighbouring college of St John's, the brilliant John Herschel—son of the famous astronomer Sir William. He also made several friends of his own age at Trinity, including Connop Thirlwall, Thomas Worsley, and in particular the remarkable Julius Charles Hare. Within the context of the present work the significance of this latter friendship lies in the fact that as an eight-year-old child Hare had lived for several months in 1804 in Weimar, where he had met both Schiller—during the last year of his life—and Goethe. He remained ever after passionately devoted to German culture, acquiring a knowledge of German literature and scholarship to an extent then quite unusual in England.

⋆

As an undergraduate at the university Whewell studied mathematics under John Hudson as well as other scientific and classical subjects, at all of which he worked assiduously. He performed well in the regular college exams, and with an essay on Brutus and Caesar won in 1813 a 'declamation prize'.

Perhaps still influenced by his deceased mother, he also started to write poetry. Here for instance is the opening of an untitled poem from July 1813:

> O thou who bid'st th' adventurous spirit roam
> Beyond the narrow boundaries of home;
> Who view'st the distant shores with piercing eye

That hid by half the world's big convex lie;
Who mak'st the East and West join hands to pour
Their mingled produce on each other's shore;
Thou that can'st tread the sea and ride the gale,
O heaven-born GENIUS OF DISCOVERY, hail!
Inspired by thee, since first the world began
Man seeks acquaintance with his brother man;
Phoenicia's early sons, inspired by thee,
Ranged every shore that bounds their inland sea;
And while fond self-complacent Athens own'd
Alcides's pillars Earth's remotest bound,
Thy favoured Carthage sought on Albion's shore
Her precious mineral and her sparkling ore:
And though when clouds of Gothic gloom opprest
The setting glories of the darkened West,
Though then amid the night of science chain'd
Barbarian fetters long thy flight restrain'd,
Yet the first breath of Europe's balmy morn
Shook off thy bonds; beneath thy influence born
Pleased Commerce bask'd on thy Venetian isles,
And wealthy Genoa felt thy cheering smiles;
Beneath thy sheltering wing did Vasco brave
The storm-clad spirit of the Indian wave;
But chief thy soul-expanding power possest
Its spacious temple in Columbus's breast...

★

A little later, Whewell composed in the same metre—rhyming decasyllabic couplets—another poem of 340 lines on a well-known figure from early British history, which in 1814 won the Chancellor's English medal and was immediately published as a little pamphlet: *Boadicea.*

Richard Owen recorded how the news was received back in Lancaster:

> One day after the noontide meal my godfather came in, as usual when he had any topic to impart to his neighbour (and he had a great respect for my mother's judgement). 'I've sad news for you, Mrs. Owen, today. I've just had a letter from Cambridge. That boy Whewell has ruined himself, he'll never get his wranglership now!' 'Why, good gracious, Mr. Rowley, what has Whewell been doing?' 'Why, he has gone and got the Chancellor's gold medal for some trumpery poem, "Boadicea" or something of the kind, when he ought to have been sticking to his mathematics. I give him up now. Taking after his poor mother, I suppose.' The relief to my mother's mind was immense, for we all had the greatest interest in the career of our neighbour-

prodigy, and she pacified the worthy curate by urging that young men must have some amusement, and this seemed a very innocent one.

I remember the intense interest with which *Boadicea* was read in the family circle when copies found their way to Dalton Square.

★

In 1815 Whewell came to be taught by another rising star among Cambridge mathematicians, George Peacock. And in January 1816 his student years at Cambridge culminated with distinction when he graduated not only—as foretold by Hudson seven years previously—among the top six wranglers, but indeed among the top two, narrowly missing first place through not being able to write fast enough during the exam.

The widowed carpenter in far-distant Lancaster learnt of his son's success, which gave him joy during the last months of his life. He died in July of that year.

Adventurous Spirit

For a person of the interests and ability of William Whewell, an academic career was what naturally now opened out. Although after graduation he at first occupied himself as a private tutor, he remained closely involved with the university and was indeed elected President of the Cambridge Union Society, where he took part in vigorous political debates.

This was however a time when a widespread fear of radicalism and revolution was sweeping through Britain, and the government of the day suspended habeas corpus. The same fear took hold of the minds of administrators at Cambridge, and in March 1817 the Vice-Chancellor, escorted by beadles and proctors, arrived at the Union and demanded that the members disperse and meet no more. Although Whewell stood his ground and achieved a private audience with the Vice-Chancellor, it was to no purpose. The Union had to abandon its meetings, which were not reconvened for the next four years.

With the Union disbanded, the only permissible social activity left was communal reading. Under the direction of Julius Hare, Whewell and his circle therefore spent the long evenings together immersed in the study of the German language.

★

In October 1817 Whewell was elected a Fellow of Trinity College, and in 1818 he gained further appointments as college tutor and as Lecturer in Mathematics.

Many years later, a pupil from this time, Kenelm Digby, set down in a letter some reminiscences:

> You will understand that though my acquaintance with Dr. Whewell began very early at Cambridge, it is chiefly of his genial and generous disposition as a friend and companion that I can speak. This anyone could observe who knew him as intimately as I did. Though on my first coming up to college he consented to have me as a pupil, I can only venture to say of him, as a tutor, that he was always encouraging and indulgent, possessing a singular facility for reconciling those whom he instructed to subjects of study for which they would otherwise have felt no inclination.
>
> Having formed one of a party of Trinity men who spent a long vacation with him in North Wales for the sake of study, at the expiration of the time he refused to take any remuneration from me, saying that he would not be justified in doing so as I had not paid any attention to his lectures. In fact, I liked him better on horseback than in the professorial chair, and he was always, during the intervals of study, scouring the hills with some of us . . .

★

Various subjects of study on which Whewell lectured to such pupils would have been scientific. In 1819 he published *An Elementary Treatise on Mechanics*, described by a contemporary as

> . . . a work of great value, and very far in advance of any then existing textbook, for the clearness and correctness of its treatment of bodies in contact, and in the precision with which the assumptions involved in the laws of motion and the composition of forces are stated and illustrated.

It was among the earliest books written in English to make use of calculus in solving dynamical problems. Several revised editions were to appear during later years.

★

In the summer vacation of 1819, rather in accord with the theme of his earlier poem, the 'adventurous spirit' of the young Cambridge don decided to 'roam / beyond the narrow boundaries of home' by making a journey to the Continent. But although he set out with high hopes, he never arrived at all, because the ferry from Brighton to Dieppe on which he was endeavouring to cross the Channel collided at night with another vessel, and went down.

In a letter to his sister, Whewell recounted the story:

> It was a fine starlit night, and we had a fair breeze, so that we were likely to make a remarkably short passage, and expected to breakfast in France next morning. We had been out between one and two hours. I did not like the

cabin, and had laid myself down on deck between dozing and sleeping, when I was roused by a furious shock and crash caused by our ship striking against another. By the time I could look about me, I found the two ships alongside of each other, and people getting out of ours into the other as fast as they could. I understood afterwards that orders had been given to do this, though at the time I did not see the necessity, for I did not perceive that our vessel was damaged. However, I was in the other ship immediately. Everybody was easily got on board, though some French ladies who were with us were exceedingly frightened, and I thought would have fainted. We came in such a hurry that we left our hats, and the ladies their shoes, on board the packet, so of course we brought no luggage with us. Soon after, the ships began to roll and work very violently, and after some time the mast of the packet we had left came thundering down. Shortly after, they got the ships clear of each other, and we sailed away from our unfortunate vessel, the *Nancy*, leaving her a complete wreck. It was still however expected that our goods would be got out of her, and as soon as they could they got out a boat, and sent it to examine her. As it was dark we soon left her out of sight, but the boat returned with intelligence that she was sinking fast, and already so deep in the water that there was no chance of saving anything. Our captain, who went in the boat, just contrived to save his own portmanteau. I suppose that in half an hour after, all would be gone to the bottom . . .

What I most grieved for were the two £5 notes which were in my trunk, and might just as well have been in my pocket!

The ship on board which we got was the brig *Henry*, going to the Mediterranean. However, they sailed about all night, and landed us next morning at Brighton.

So the would-be European traveller found himself back where he started, without hat, luggage or money. With no further funds to hand, there was nothing else to do but return again to Cambridge.

Adapting once more the phraseology of Whewell's earlier poem, one might say that if the 'soul-expanding power' of the 'Genius of Discovery' which could 'tread the sea and ride the gale' really 'possest / its spacious temple' in the breast not only of the long-dead Columbus but also in that of the living poet who had written those words, he would have to show still greater determination in order to reach 'the distant shores' beyond the English Channel and make 'acquaintance with his brother man' on the continental part of Europe.

The Men of Science

The personal physique and constitution of William Whewell are succinctly described in *The Dictionary of National Biography*:

> ... Tall and massively built, Whewell enjoyed good health throughout his life ...

Together with scholars like George Peacock and Adam Sedgwick he formed part of a group at Cambridge known as 'The Northern Lights', since its members all originated from the north of England. In 1819 this group in association with others like John Stevens Henslow founded the Cambridge Philosophical Society.

At the time the adjective 'philosophical' was used in Britain to cover a range of subjects which nowadays would be termed 'scientific', and the first paper contributed by Whewell to the Society's *Transactions* had an astronomical theme: 'On the Position of the Apsides in Orbits of Great Eccentricity'.

Owing to the promise shown by a steady stream of such papers as well as by his book on mechanics, Whewell was in the spring of 1820 elected—at the remarkably early age of 26—a Fellow of the Royal Society.

★

When summer of that year came round, Whewell, accompanied now by Richard Jones, set out again over the Channel—this time taking the shorter crossing from Dover. Having arrived safely at Calais the friends travelled down to Paris, and stayed a whole fortnight in the French capital. Afterwards they went on south-east through Melun and Auxerre to Chalon-sur-Saône, where they took a boat down the river as far as Lyons. There they disembarked and headed towards Mont Blanc. Crossing into Switzerland, they spent some weeks climbing around in the Bernese Alps. The return journey went through Geneva, north via Basel, and down the Rhine, again partly by boat, as far as Cologne. They then turned west, passed through Aachen towards Brussels, made a short detour to Waterloo—site of the great battle of five years previously—and on through Lille to the coast, where they regained a ferry to England.

This was Whewell's first journey of orientation over a fair part of the European continent and landscape.

★

In 1820 John Herschel, the computer pioneer Charles Babbage and others founded the Astronomical Society (later Royal Astronomical Society). In 1821 Whewell too was elected a member.

During the following year, 1822, Whewell made another trip to Paris, reporting in a letter:

> ... The men of science and the lectures, which were what I principally wished to visit, I found easy access to.

Georges Cuvier

These men of science included the famous Georges Cuvier, who was building up in the French capital the finest zoological and palaeontological collection in Europe, and also Alexander von Humboldt, then mainly resident in Paris and publishing the reports of his travels in the Americas.

Early in 1823 Whewell made a third journey to France. He spent two days in Amiens absorbed by the vast Gothic cathedral, and went on again to Paris, where this time he visited the Observatory.

Back in England, he brought out a sequel to his previous work on mechanics, entitled *A Treatise on Dynamics*. With such publications he was moving into the forefront of British science of his day.

The Entire Devotion of his Powers

During the summer of 1823, William Whewell crossed again over the Channel, accompanied now by his former pupil Kenelm Digby, to make an architectural tour of churches in Picardy and Normandy. Their main route went from Calais south towards Abbeville, west to Dieppe, down to Rouen, west again through Lisieux, on to Caen and over to Mont Saint Michel.

In reminiscences of Whewell, Digby reported that

> As a travelling companion he was unrivalled, being always ready to rough it and to take everything in a good-humoured way, and I shall not easily forget his riding with me on the post-horses to visit St. Michel 'au péril de la mer'.

At the time, Whewell himself described the famous pilgrimage site in a letter to his sisters:

> ... The farthest point of our travels was St. Michael's Mount, a most remarkable insulated rock, surrounded on all sides, for a great distance, by the sands of the sea, and covered with very lofty and picturesque buildings, which formerly composed a monastery. It was considered a place of extraordinary sanctity, and an immense number of persons have at various times come in pilgrimage hither. They give you the names of kings and queens of France and England, princes and statesmen, bishops and warriors without end who have visited the shrine of 'St. Michel au péril de la mer'. Even yet the reputation of its holiness is not quite gone. Many persons still come in a spirit of devotion, and I bought there a little book which related a great number of miracles performed by the assistance of St. Michael, and which the good priest who narrates them maintains to be quite as certain as those of Scripture ...

★

Among articles published by Whewell in the *Transactions* of both the Cambridge Philosophical Society and of the Royal Society were some on the subject of crystallography, demonstrating the nature of crystal twinning and introducing a new notation of crystal planes. In the summer of 1825, seeking to gain further instruction in this science, Whewell decided to consult the foremost crystallographer of the day, Friedrich Mohs, successor at Freiberg to the famous Abraham Werner.

Crossing the Channel this time by ferry to Hamburg, Whewell travelled down through Germany towards the Harz—where he climbed up the Brocken—and then south-east through Leipzig. On eventually arriving at Freiberg, however, he found that Professor Mohs was just setting out on his own summer holidays, which were going to be spent in Vienna.

Mohs invited the Englishman to accompany him on this trip, and so the two of them travelled on together. They made for Dresden, took the road south towards Prague and onwards for five whole days until—as related by Whewell in a letter—looking out through the window of their stagecoach, they saw one day in the distance 'the lofty Gothic spire' of St Stephen's Cathedral, and soon after arrived at long last in Vienna. Whewell then spent a whole month studying under Mohs's guidance the mineralogical collections of the very city where some 55 years later the young Rudolf

William Whewell in 1825, aged 30

Steiner would be listening to Edmund Reitlinger quoting his work on inductive science!

For the return journey through Germany Whewell took a more northerly route, going by way of Berlin. But when he attempted in Potsdam to call on Alexander von Humboldt the latter missed him, subsequently explaining in a letter what had happened:

> C'est votre admirable connoissance de la langue allemande qui m'a porté malheur. J'avois ordonné de laisser entrer tout gentleman *anglais* qui se présenteroit. Vous avez parlé allemand comme un habitant du pays!!

⋆

Always a person of strong religious conviction, Whewell completed the theological training then still customary for fellows of Cambridge colleges, and on Trinity Sunday 1826, at the age of 32, was ordained to the Anglican priesthood.

A later account commented:

> He accepted no college living, however, or special care of souls—not from any want of appreciation of the importance of the ministerial office, or doubt of his own aptitude for its exercise, but from a conscientious per-

suasion that his true sphere of utility would be found in the entire devotion of his powers to the furtherance of the objects of the University as a place of education, and to the improvement of its system of instruction in those great branches of mental culture in which it was beginning to be felt at that epoch that such improvement was not only possible, but largely needed.

★

In this year Whewell contributed to the *Encyclopaedia Metropolitana* part of a treatise on 'Electricity', and an article on 'Archimedes—Greek Mathematics' which was later also reprinted in another collection.

Helped by his assistant tutor George Biddell Airy, he undertook experiments with a pendulum down a Cornish mine with a view to determining the density of the Earth. At a depth of 1200 feet below ground he wrote a lengthy letter—well over two pages in the printed edition—to John Herschel describing both their progress and their difficulties. After returning to the surface, he composed in due course a proper record, *Account of Experiments made at Dolcoath Mine.*

During the summer Whewell made another journey to France, reporting that

> ... I spent my time pleasantly enough whilst in Paris, seeing almost all the remarkable men of science who are to be found there.

Towards the end of the year he made a further trip to Paris along with Adam Sedgwick, staying in the French capital over Christmas and the Holy Nights.

★

In 1827 Whewell was elected a Fellow of the Geological Society. And in March 1828 he was appointed Professor of Mineralogy at Cambridge—succeeding John Henslow who had resigned from that chair on being made Professor of Botany.

Now during that same year there matriculated at Christ's College Cambridge an 18-year-old undergraduate by the name of Charles Darwin.

The City of our Solemnities

On 17 December 1828, the annual Commemoration Day of Trinity College, William Whewell preached a sermon in the college chapel.

It is perhaps appropriate to imagine the scene. Probably the service included suitable hymns, sung to organ accompaniment. At the end of one of them, as the sound of the organ died away, the congregation would have sat down.

William Whewell in 1828

When they had settled into their stalls, and quiet was restored, they would have directed their attention towards the only person remaining on his feet: the University's recently appointed Professor of Mineralogy, robed in a white surplice covered over the shoulders with a colourful academic hood. This preacher for his part would have turned his gaze towards the congregation and, after a suitable pause, begun his sermon.

The subsequently printed text opens as follows:

> 'Look upon Zion, the city of our solemnities; thine eyes shall see Jerusalem a quiet habitation, a tabernacle that shall not be taken down.' Isaiah XXXIII, 20.

We are now met here to celebrate the return of a day, on which our ordinances call upon us annually to revive the feelings arising from our relation to the institution within whose walls we live. We come to disentangle from the tumult of daily thoughts and passions, the sentiments suggested by a calm consideration of the character of this establishment, whose children we are; to animate thus our emotions of admiration, of gratitude, of hope; to excite and confirm no less our self-watchfulness, our humility, our good resolutions. We come to a yearly office of household piety: to trim the lamp of our domestic hearth with odorous deeds, and words of kindly and solemn affection; that thus its light may fall with no waning or wavering ray on our path, as we travel rapidly to the close of another departing year.

This is, I repeat, an office of mingled joy and fear, of triumph and solicitude: it demands alike our thanksgivings and our prayers. For if indeed it be that we can look upon this our allotted place with no unfounded pleasure; if we find to have issued from its courts a portion of that family of great names, that inheritance of great thoughts and actions, to which the eyes of all ages turn with admiration; if its precincts have, even to this hour, been full of beneficial influences, motives, and aids: we may well rejoice at these our blessings. But, standing as we here do in the presence of our God and Judge, we may not forget that to man on Earth no blessing can be given without corresponding duties; no eminence without its appropriate responsibility; that no exultation can be blameless which assumes the form of pride, no satisfaction in the past which makes us secure of the future. In the mid draught of our joy, in the very source of our self-gratulation, is mixed a sobering infusion of danger and trial; a remembrance that we have to act and to abstain, as well as to exult and hope; that the glory is to them that fight the good fight even to the end; and that the splendour of our arms and the brightness of our weapons, this wanting, are idle and unprofitable objects of our gaze.

With this monitory reflection attending our thoughts and hallowing their employment, we may throw open our minds to that which offers itself as worthy matter for thankfulness and admiration, in the recollections to which this day is dedicated. We may turn to the past—to the names bright with the learning of lustre and genius, of wisdom and piety, which adorn the various periods of our records. We may cheer and elevate our own souls by this spectacle of the excellence that man may reach. We may drink in strength and hope and firm resolve and lofty thought, from the contemplation of their characters and destinies. We may consider with pleasure all that is good and fair in the habits of the institution under which they lived here, and under which we live; that this *our* nursing mother and *theirs* loves to minister food and encouragement alike to the reason and to the imagination; that for the cup which she presses to our lips, she mingles the most costly ingredients of ancient and of modern times—all the treasured stores of antique genius and taste, all the teeming fruits of modern intellect and discovery; that she engages those who sit at her feet in a daily intercourse and communion where various ranks and stations and ages, persons with various pursuits and views and destinations, meeting, we trust, in no harsh or narrow spirit, no suspicious and unkindly temper, stimulate and restrain each other; that this our common body feels, and has felt, within its frame, the influences of a principle which teaches its members to reverence and cling to the institutions of the past; to consider them as a most precious inheritance transmitted to us from other times; as supplying, whether in matters of intellectual speculation or of practical life, the best correctives to the hasty impulses of human caprice and restlessness and passion; and yet that not the less, it cherishes a sensibility to the free and active working of those vital principles in the mind and in the progress of man, by which traditionary ordinances require, from time to time, to be in their details regulated and enlarged, interpreted and revivified.

With all these grateful recollections, these golden bands, to connect us with the past history of our college, we may well feel that we are not aliens to those departed worthies whose memories we reverence and admire. Though we may be far removed from the splendour of their intellectual rank, we are yet their poor kindred in virtue of our common connexion with this our parent institution. We claim with them an incorporeal blood. They are our ancestry. And we point to the long lines of their pictures and statues as the images that testify of our family; the badges of our high descent; the evidences that the spiritual world is open to our highest

> ambition; that in the aristocracy of thought and virtue there is no station to which we are precluded from aspiring.
>
> Any enumeration of our great names would be now but superfluous. The glittering procession is of too lengthened an extent; and even *our* reverence and admiration might be vulnerable to weariness and distraction. Yet grateful and profitable it must be to fix our thoughts for a moment on some object of those better feelings. And it can seldom happen, but that with each returning season, some portion of our history shall have a more especial claim on our remembrance and attention. At our last anniversary the great name of NEWTON was pressed upon our minds with a more peculiar prominency, by the thought that with that year one century had passed since his removal from this mortal life; that it was, as it were, the birth-year of his immortality. The present year is similarly marked in that with it two hundred years have rolled away since the birth of another of our most illustrious elders: he too, like that other, a founder and leader in the science which he cultivated; one whose works and example have directed the course of later times; and to whom, even in the present day, men look as one of the great original authors and promoters of those studies of Nature which formed the joy and business of his life . . .

The reference was to John Ray, mathematician and naturalist, born in 1628. For a couple of further pages in the printed text, the preacher extolled in splendid rhetorical manner Ray's virtues and accomplishments.

After briefly mentioning other well-known fellows in the college history—such as Newton's teacher Isaac Barrow—he then continued:

> It was here that they pondered and discovered, that they went on from page to page and from thought to thought. Our walls have been conscious of their soliloquies. Their walks are the paths where we still roam. Their books are in our hands. Our hearths have been consecrated by their presence. We tread on ground hallowed by their thoughtful steps, amid the same reverend forms of tower and grove which met their contemplative eyes. And if the moonbeams or the night-breezes as they touch our battlements can still minister to us a calmness of repose, and refresh our spirits from the intensity of thought or the turmoil of daily life, can we refrain from imagining that they also must have felt these soothing and kindly influences mingle with their high thoughts, and that the workings of their great minds may have been tinged and pervaded by the unseen spirit of the place which still lingers around us?
>
> It were a pleasing and grateful task to call up the recollection of those who have thus given a sacredness to this our home by making it the scene of their enduring works as well as of their disciplinal studies; who have lingered in no ignoble rest by the side of that fountain from which they drank their earlier draughts of knowledge . . .

The preacher went on discoursing in this magniloquent style about other long-deceased fellows, such as the poets Abraham Cowley and George Herbert.

This part of his sermon covers three whole pages in the printed text.

The Lofty Call

The congregation seated in the chapel of Trinity College Cambridge on 17 December 1828 was still listening to the sermon being preached by Professor William Whewell.

After what must have been several more minutes, the preacher brought to a conclusion his eulogy of the departed fellows. Perhaps he then briefly paused for breath, before resuming his discourse:

> But it needs not that we should longer dwell on such examples. Let it be allowed us to turn for an instant to one other reflection. It is not from the instances of those only who have spent within her walls a contemplative and studious life that we may thus draw nutriment to the feelings of reverence which we bear to 'our Zion, the city of our solemnities'. It is no less grateful to notice that those whose higher fortune has, often with a doubtful kindness, transferred them after a short sojourn here into the world of active and social life, have not seldom carried with them a cordial and duteous feeling which made them, when good achieved in speculation or action had earned them fame, glad and ready to wreath *their* glory with that of this their nursing mother.
>
> There is a name upon our rolls which is by men esteemed scarcely second even to that of Newton. There is a book of which the first words thus declare: 'FRANCIS OF VERULAM thus thought and reasoned; and deemed that, for his thoughts to be known to the living and to future generations, was of concern to them.' And of which book, nevertheless, men have ever agreed to confess that he spake not too proudly. For this man was, as it were, invested by Nature with the privilege of declaring *her* laws, as by his sovereign he was invested with the dignity of declaring the laws of his kingdom. And this book contains a legislation delivered almost in the spirit of prophecy, for that kingdom of science which Newton afterwards conquered. And let it be permitted us on this day to bring forth from our records the words which he addressed to this community, when, unfolding that view of the nature of knowledge which was thereafter to govern all men's minds, he made of his work an offering of kindness and duty, not unworthy to be placed among the most valued of our treasures.
>
> 'All things owe that which they are, and their advancement, unto their origins. Since therefore I drank from your fountains the beginning of

sciences, it hath seemed right to me to return to you the augmentations of the same. And I trust that these our studies will grow up the more prosperously among you, as it were in that which hath been their native soil. Wherefore I exhort you, that retaining the modesty of your minds, and the reverence which is due to antiquity, you be not wanting also to the advancement of knowledge; but rather that, next to the sacred volume of God's word and scripture, you do in the second place perpetually and diligently peruse that great volume of God's works and creatures, whereunto all other books are but as commentaries. Fare you well.'

This was the dignified strain of filial regard, the lofty call to share his high career, which that eloquent voice, as well became it, uttered. And these are sentences which, in no unsubstantial aspiration, we might inscribe upon our gates and within our halls, to remind ourselves and all of the high aims which should ever here guide and animate our course. Nor need we fear to remember that such an appeal was made to those whose successors we are, when we recollect how worthy a response to this high-toned summons was, in no protracted course of years, echoed from among these walls; that of those who did, as he exhorted, unroll and read the great volume of Nature, they who have been already spoken of, Newton and Ray, were both the foremost and the greatest; and that each of them, with regard to the page which he more peculiarly studied, has been the master from whom others, in later days, have derived the best elements of their lessons. We may, too, not unwillingly recollect that Herbert, already the theme of our remembrances, was the friend and valued counsellor of that great lawgiver; and that none more deeply understood or spoke more worthily of that mighty intellectual code, than the philosophic Cowley. If therefore it is our boast that *that* book of THE PRINCIPLES OF THE PHILOSOPHY OF THE UNIVERSE which must ever stand single and unparalleled among the works of men, is entirely ours; had here its conception and birth and growth; it is also true that *that* NEW ORGAN OF PHILOSOPHIZING, a volume no less of peculiar and unrivalled dignity, pertains to us by no slight or doubtful claim. It had within the circuit of our walls its first germ and origin; and, though born under another roof, it returned, as it were, to this its ancestral home; found in our schools those who recognized its language; who exulted in its excellencies; who promoted with the zealous affection of kindred and lovers the yet obscure beginnings of its majestic fortunes.

It is, therefore, with no vain and overweening fondness that we consider the fame and character of such immortal names as those now mentioned, to belong to the institution of which we are members. This their intellectual parent has a portion of their glory, as she awoke their speculations and invigorated their powers. *Hither, as to their fountain,* those bright *stars repairing, drew in their golden urns* that *light* which they have since been pouring among the generations of men . . .

The printed text of the sermon continues with this magnificent Ciceronian oratory for several further pages.

★

As Whewell pointed out in his sermon, Francis Bacon was indeed a former member of the College. Under the different educational circumstances obtaining in the sixteenth century, Bacon spent three years of his early adolescence, between the ages of 12 and 15, studying at Trinity College, from 1573 to 1576.

In the earliest account of Bacon's life, appended in 1657—31 years after his death—to an edition of his writings brought out under the title *Resuscitatio*, his chaplain and literary executor William Rawley stated:

> Whilst he was commorant in the University (As his Lordship hath been pleased to impart unto my Self) he first fell into the Dislike of the Philosophy of Aristotle; Not for the Worthlessnesse of the Authour, to whom he would ever ascribe all High Attributes, But for the Unfruitfullnesse of the way; Being a Philosophy (as His Lordship used to say) onely strong for Disputations and Contentions, But Barren of the Production of Works for the Benefit of the Life of Man. In which Mind he continued to his Dying Day.

Every New Prospect

Regarding the year 1828 in the biography of William Whewell's academic colleague Adam Sedgwick, the authors record this anecdote:

> Christmas was spent, in company with Whewell, at Viscount Milton's house near Peterborough. At that time many of the Fellows of Trinity used to find their way to that hospitable mansion, and Whewell spent his Christmas there for many years in succession. On one of these occasions—possibly in 1828—he was asked if he would like to go out hunting. Of course he said 'Yes'. Mounted on a first-rate horse, well up to his weight, he inquired how he could see most of the run. 'Keep close to Sebright' (the huntsman) was the reply. Whewell did as he was bid, and followed that splendid rider over everything. They had an unusually good run, over a difficult country, in course of which Sebright took an especially stout and high fence. Looking round to see what had become of the stranger, he found him at his side, safe and sound. 'That was a rasper, Sir,' he exclaimed, in admiration at his pluck. 'I did not observe that it was anything more than ordinary,' answered Whewell.

★

In 1828 Whewell published an *Essay on Mineralogical Classification*, followed in the next year by a companion volume in a different field, *Essay on Chemical Elements and Nomenclature.*

During the summer of 1829 he made an extensive continental tour, travelling through Holland and France into Germany and Switzerland. His main purpose was to study medieval ecclesiastical architecture. But he also used the occasion to visit the source of the Danube, go on towards the Bodensee—'a most glorious prospect'—and then to the Rhinefall at Schaffhausen, the mightiest waterfall in Europe, where the great river plunges over a 75-foot drop. Whewell described it in a letter:

> It is grand in all aspects, but standing in the gallery, all the surrounding objects confused by the blinding spray and a sort of eternity of waters hurrying past and filling the eye, one can scarce believe that the solid universe is not drifting away with immeasurable violence...

After this he walked for 20 or 30 miles a day in some of the highest parts of the Alps, especially to view the glaciers, and then journeyed down into Italy as far as Milan. Recrossing the Alps back into Germany, he finished by attending a scientific congress at Heidelberg, where he was elected to the Gesellschaft für Naturwissenschaft und Heilkunde.

In 1830 the results of this tour were published as *Architectural Notes on German Churches, with Remarks on the Origin of Gothic Architecture.* The final chapter of this work ends with a 'List of Churches' naming all those the author had visited. They numbered 97 in Germany, as well as four in Switzerland. Cologne was clearly his favourite place, since even apart from the cathedral the list includes 13 other churches in that city. The remainder of the list names other cathedrals or churches in and around Bonn, Koblenz, Mainz, the Rheingau, Frankfurt, Worms, Speyer, Strasbourg, Freiburg, Regensburg, Nuremberg, Bamberg and Würzburg, as well as four Swiss churches in Schaffhausen, Zurich, Lucerne and Berne.

The author's identity was not revealed, for this book came out anonymously.

⋆

The experience of Whewell's continental travels was also incorporated into his work in a more general way, as in 1831 when his review of John Herschel's *Preliminary Discourse on the Study of Natural Philosophy* included the following analogy:

> It is ever thus in the progress of inductive philosophy as in the wanderings of the Alpine traveller. The hill which at starting seemed the only barrier between him and his journey's end serves but as a point from which he descries higher mountains to climb, and wider fields to traverse. But still

every step is an ascent, every new prospect is a gain. And the august forms which surround him, and the pure atmosphere into which he rises, make his toil a sport and his perseverance a delight.

The Language of Electricity

In the course of a lecture given at Dornach on 18 December 1916, Rudolf Steiner had occasion to refer to Michael Faraday as 'a great mind, one of the greatest minds of all times'. In the light of this description, it seems of interest here to examine one particular aspect of Faraday's epoch-making electrical discoveries,[6] especially that of electromagnetic induction in 1831.

In his biography *Faraday—The Life* (2002), James Hamilton writes:

> The new impetus that Faraday's discoveries had given to the world of science, and to the wider world, demanded a new language to ease their flow out of the laboratory and into everyday speech. This need became particularly pronounced as Faraday and others continued to describe and demonstrate electricity in lectures: a phrase such as 'electrical fluid', even though it 'flowed' and had 'current', could no longer carry the burden of

Michael Faraday

meaning that Faraday's discoveries were placing upon it, and was obsolete. In one of the first recorded instances of a backlash against technical jargon of the type that was to bedevil the late twentieth century, Faraday wrote to Revd. William Whewell at Trinity College, Cambridge in February 1831, raising just that problem—the need for words for these new things. Whewell was an open, helpful scholar, generous with his time and ideas, the ideal confidant for Faraday. Maria Edgeworth described him to perfection: 'Fair, handsome, most agreeable, quick conversation, shining playfully with science and literature—and free from all testiness and susceptibility of some of the scientific grandees—vide Babbage par excellence.'

The question that Faraday had for him would challenge Whewell's powers of free-thinking, and indeed the playfulness of his language:

'I cannot help thinking it a most unfortunate thing that men who as experimentalists & philosophers are the most fitted to advance the general cause of science & knowledge should by the promulgation of their own theoretical views under the form of nomenclature, notation or scale actually retard its progress—It would not be of so much consequence if it was only theory & hypothesis which they thus treated, but they put facts or the current coin of science into the same limited circulation when they describe them in such a way that the initiated only can read them.'

Faraday well knew the passage in the Bible—*Genesis* 2: 19–20—in which Adam named the animals, thus putting dangers into context and fear of the unknown into perspective. To give names to the various functions, tenses, participles, conjunctions and other parts of speech of electricity was the essential next step, releasing the power of this natural force from latter-day alchemists, or whatever other silent priestly caste might arise, before they got their hands on it. With their truly public duty in the forefront of their minds, the non-conformist Christian and the deeply-established Anglican churchman forged a language for electricity that caught on rapidly and is with us today, now too deep-rooted to be superseded.

Faraday first came to Whewell with some words that he had invented but which he remained dubious about—'exode', 'zetode', 'zetexode', and even 'eastode' and 'westode', for the terminals of a battery. Whewell in his reply suggested 'anode' and 'cathode'; and these names happily remain. In creating a new terminology for the newly harnessed natural power, Faraday and Whewell were going back to the crucible of Western language, ancient Greek. 'I may mention . . . that *anodos* and *cathodos* are good genuine Greek words,' Whewell assured Faraday, 'and not compounds coined for the purpose . . . Upon the whole I think anode and cathode much the best.' Nevertheless Faraday was at first sceptical about 'anode' and 'cathode', and used 'dexiode' and 'skaiode'—from the Greek for right and left—in the first published edition of his seventh series of *Experimental Researches in Electricity* (1834), telling Whewell, 'I like Anode & Cathode better as to sound, but all

> to whom I have shewn them have supposed at first that by *Anode* I meant *No way*.'
>
> Faraday was given some wonderfully clear instruction in Greek from Whewell, and relished the correspondence, which was in its own way as creative as the discovery of the laws of electricity themselves. An animal is merely a beast without its name. Whewell was an essential expert witness for Faraday:
>
> 'As to the objection to *anode* I do not think it is worth hesitating about. *Anodos* and *cathodos* do really mean in Greek a way up and a way down; and *anodos* does not mean, and cannot mean according to the analogy of the Greek language, *no way*. It is true that the prefix *an* put before adjectives beginning with a vowel gives a negative signification, but not to substantives, except through the medium of adjectives. *Anarchos* means without government, and hence *anarchia*, *anarchy*, means the absence of government: but *anodos* does not and cannot mean the absence of way ...'
>
> This gave Faraday the support he needed in his linguistic arguments at the Royal Institution. He wrote to Whewell:
>
> 'I had some hot objections made to [your nomenclature] here and found myself very much in the condition of the man with his son and ass who tried to please everybody; but when I held up the shield of your authority it was wonderful to observe how the tone of objection melted away.'
>
> With Whewell's help, the language of electricity kept pace with the steady progress of Faraday's researches. When Faraday had a problem of expression of a new idea, Whewell would generally reply by return of post with a suggestion. Thus, 'ion' and 'dielectric' came to Faraday's aid, and, much later in their correspondence, 'diamagnetic' and 'paramagnetic', and words with English roots such as 'inducteity' ...

The extent of the correspondence is shown by the number of letters from Whewell to Faraday preserved today in the archives of Trinity College Cambridge: no less than 156.

Hamilton continues:

> To Faraday a good name had not only to look right in print, but also to sound right; he indeed would be at the front line of its usage, the first to spin the word before the public. He tolerated the coinage of the word 'scientist' to describe his profession—this had first come into use at the meeting of the embryonic British Association for the Advancement of Science in York in 1831—but wanted Whewell to suggest an alternative to the French word '*physicien*'. Faraday disliked 'physicist' on aural grounds: '... "Physicist" is both to my mouth & ears so awkward that I think I shall never be able to use it. The equivalent of three separate sounds in *s* in one word is too much.' In this case Whewell does not appear to have come up with an alternative, but he was aware of the importance of the task he was engaged on with Faraday:

'Such a coinage (of words) has always taken place at the great epochs of discovery; like the medals that are struck at the beginning of a new reign—or rather like the change of currency produced by the accession of a new sovereign; for their value and influence consists in their coming into common circulation.'

The importance of clarity of meaning for Faraday, his understanding of the power of the right word, was a quality that had its roots and expression not only in the Bible, but further in his love of poetry. We have seen how Byron's *Childe Harold* entranced him, as did Thomas Moore's *Lalla Rookh*, and Gray's 'Elegy', and he was also engaged by Laurence Sterne's wordplay. His own facility as a letter writer and diarist is further expression of his literary side, as is his enjoyment of his duties as a teacher and showman. In *Childe Harold* there is a verse which Faraday must have known, and which might have touched his heart both in its relevance to his own feelings and as a poetic expression of the most powerful force in Nature:

> Could I embody and unbosom now
> That which is most within me,—could I wreak
> My thoughts upon expression, and thus throw
> Soul, heart, mind, passions, feelings strong or weak,
> All that I would have sought, and all I seek,
> Bear, know, feel, and yet breathe—into *one* word,
> And that one word were lightning, I would speak;
> But as it is, I live and die unheard,
> With a most voiceless thought, sheathing it as a sword.

The Establishment of General Laws

In course of his *Autobiography*, Charles Darwin recorded the significant connection he formed as a Cambridge undergraduate to the Professor of Botany:

> I have not yet mentioned a circumstance which influenced my whole career more than any other. This was my friendship with Professor Henslow. Before coming up to Cambridge, I had heard of him from my brother as a man who knew every branch of science, and I was accordingly prepared to reverence him. He kept open house once every week when all undergraduates and some older members of the University who were attached to science used to meet in the evening. I soon got, through Fox, an invitation, and went there regularly. Before long I became well acquainted with Henslow, and during the latter half of my time at Cambridge took long walks with him on most days, so that I was called by some of the dons 'the man who walks with Henslow'; and in the evening I was very often asked to

John Stevens Henslow

join his family dinner. His knowledge was great in botany, entomology, chemistry, mineralogy and geology. His strongest taste was to draw conclusions from long-continued minute observations. His judgement was excellent, and his whole mind well-balanced...

Dr. Whewell was one of the older and distinguished men who sometimes visited Henslow, and on several occasions I walked home with him at night. Next to Sir J. Mackintosh he was the best discourser on grave subjects to whom I ever listened...

Now in August 1831 the Cambridge mathematician George Peacock paid a visit in London to Francis Beaufort, Hydrographer of the Admiralty. Straight after this visit, Peacock wrote to John Henslow in Cambridge, stating:

Captain Fitzroy is going out to survey the southern coast of Tierra del Fuego and afterwards to visit many of the South Sea islands and return by the Indian archipelago. The vessel is fitted out expressly for scientific purposes combined with the survey. It will furnish therefore a rare opportunity for a naturalist, and it will be a great misfortune that it should be lost. An offer has been made to me to recommend the proper person to go out as naturalist with this expedition. He will be treated with every consideration... Is there any person who you can strongly recommend? He must be such a person as would do credit to our recommendation.

In reply, Henslow put forward the name of his recently graduated 22-year-old pupil Charles Darwin.

Some months earlier Robert Fitzroy, captain of the proposed expedition, had met the geologist Charles Lyell (also then corresponding about geological nomenclature with Whewell, who suggested suitable terms for various periods: 'Eocene', 'Miocene', 'Pliocene', 'Pleistocene'). Lyell asked for observations to be made in South America on his behalf. And shortly before leaving England, Fitzroy presented Darwin with the recently published first volume of Lyell's *Principles of Geology*. In the course of the journey further volumes were forwarded to Darwin by Henslow.

Departing from Plymouth on the south Devon coast, the *Beagle* set sail in November 1831 on its voyage around the world. The ship did not return to Britain for another five years.

⋆

At this point it may be noted that during the very next year, 1832—while Darwin was engaged in exploring various parts of South America—the deaths occurred in Europe of two major scientific figures. One came from Middle Europe and the other from Western Europe, and they represented radically different tendencies from one another: Johann Wolfgang von Goethe, and Georges Cuvier.

⋆

Although William Whewell was prevented by college business from being present at the founding of the British Association for the Advancement of Science, he came to play straight afterwards an active part in this body, making friends especially with its Scottish co-founder James David Forbes. The first meeting Whewell attended was that at Oxford in June 1832, where John Dalton (also tutored in Kendal by the blind John Gough) and Michael Faraday were given honorary degrees. During this year Whewell himself was elected an honorary member of the Royal Geological Society of Cornwall, the Yorkshire Philosophical Society, and the Naval and Military Library and Institution, as well as a Fellow of the Society of Antiquaries.

While still retaining his fellowship at Trinity College, he now however resigned from his Cantabrigian chair. He presented to the university his mineralogical collection of about a thousand specimens, along with a substantial sum towards the provision of a suitable museum.

For he had come to find that his interests could not be limited to any single discipline. He travelled over to France on a further architectural tour of Normandy, visiting no fewer than 130 different churches. He was also bringing out books on other subjects: in 1832 the first volume, *On the Free Motion of Points*, of an expanded edition of his *Treatise on Dynamics*, as well as two new works, *The First Principles of Mechanics* and an *Introduction to Dynamics*. And as a pioneer in the new field of tidology he published in 1833 an *Essay towards a First Approximation to a Map of Co-Tidal Lines*.

★

Another work brought out by Whewell in 1833 was entitled *Astronomy and General Physics considered with Reference to Natural Theology*. This was one of the so-called Bridgewater Treatises, sponsored under the will of Francis, Earl of Bridgewater, who had left a large sum for the Royal Society to 'appoint persons to write, print and publish one thousand copies of a work on the power, wisdom and goodness of God as manifested in the creation; illustrating such work by all reasonable arguments'.

Whewell's book opened with a dedicatory letter:

TO THE
RIGHT HONOURABLE AND RIGHT REVEREND
CHARLES JAMES,
LORD BISHOP OF LONDON.

My Lord,

I owe it you that I was selected for the task attempted in the following pages, a distinction which I feel to be honourable; and on this account alone I should have a peculiar pleasure in dedicating the work to your Lordship. I do so with additional gratification on another account: the Treatise has been written within the walls of the College of which your Lordship was formerly a resident member, and its merits, if it have any, are mainly due to the spirit and habits of the place. The society is always pleased and proud to recollect that a person of the eminent talents and high character of your Lordship is one of its members; and I am persuaded that any effort in the cause of letters and religion coming from that quarter will have for you an interest beyond what it would otherwise possess.

The subject proposed to me was limited. My prescribed object is to lead the friends of religion to look with confidence and pleasure on the progress of the physical sciences, by showing how admirably every advance in our knowledge of the universe harmonizes with the belief of a most wise and good God. To do this effectually may be, I trust, a useful labour. Yet I feel most deeply, what I would take this occasion to express, that this and all that the speculator concerning Natural Theology can do is utterly insufficient for the great ends of Religion; namely, for the purpose of reforming men's lives, of purifying and elevating their characters, of preparing them for a more exalted state of being. It is the need of something fitted to do this which gives to Religion its vast and incomparable importance; and this can, I well know, be achieved only by that Revealed Religion of which we are ministers, but on which the plan of the present work did not allow me to dwell.

That Divine Providence may prosper the labours of your Lordship and of all who are joined with you in the task of maintaining and promoting *this* Religion, is, my Lord, the earnest wish and prayer of

Your very faithful

and much obliged Servant,

William Whewell.

Trinity College, Cambridge,
Feb. 25, 1833.

After an introduction, the work was divided into three 'books', of which the first two were on 'Terrestrial Adaptations' and 'Cosmical Arrangements'.

The third 'book' was entitled 'Religious Views'. It contained nine chapters, of which the penultimate one was headed 'On the Physical Agency of the Deity'. This chapter began:

William Whewell in 1834, aged 40

> We are not to expect that physical investigation can enable us to conceive the manner in which God acts upon the members of the universe. The question 'Canst thou by searching find out God?' must silence the boastings of science as well as the repinings of adversity. Indeed science shows us, far more clearly than the conceptions of everyday reason, at what an immeasurable distance we are from any faculty of conceiving how the universe, material and moral, is the work of the Deity. But with regard to the material world, we can at least go as far as this—we can perceive that events are brought about, not by insulated interpositions of Divine power exerted in each particular case, but by the establishment of general laws. This, which is the view of the universe proper to science, whose office it is to search out these laws, is also the view which throughout this work we have endeavoured to keep present to the mind of the reader. We have attempted to show that it combines itself most readily and harmoniously with the doctrines of Natural Theology; that the arguments for those doctrines are strengthened, the difficulties which affect them removed, by keeping it steadily before us. We conceive, therefore, that the religious philosopher will do well to bear this conception in his mind. God is the author and governor of the universe through the laws which he has given to its parts, the properties which he has impressed upon its constituent elements. These laws and properties are, as we have already said, the instruments with which he works: the institution of such laws, the selection of the quantities which they involve, their combination and application, are the modes in which he exerts and manifests his power, his wisdom, his goodness. Through these attributes, thus exercised, the Creator of all shapes, moves, sustains and guides the visible creation.

A Good Discussion

At the meeting of the British Association held in 1833 at Cambridge, presided over by Adam Sedgwick, William Whewell gave an address expounding his principles of scientific enquiry. He described astronomy as 'not only the queen of the sciences, but in a stricter sense of the term the only perfect science'.

This meeting was attended by the 60-year-old poet and writer Samuel Taylor Coleridge, who later noted his impressions of another speaker:

> I was exceedingly pleased with Faraday, he seemed to me to have the true temperament of genius—that carrying on of the spring and freshness of youthful, nay boyish feelings, into the mature strength of manhood.

In 1834 Whewell went on to visit Coleridge at Highgate, stating in a letter:

> ... I had the pleasure of seeing Coleridge a few weeks before his death, and, what was also a great pleasure, took Worsley to him, who had never seen him before. He talked wonderfully well ...

★

Turning next to the field of meteorology, Whewell climbed up Skiddaw in 1834 together with George Biddell Airy—now Professor of Astronomy—to conduct experiments with hygrometers. Whewell went on to design a device of his own to measure the time and velocity of the wind: a self-regulating anemometer. It had a set of vanes like a miniature windmill driving a series of reduction screws to produce a slow vertical movement on a rotating drum. The device was later improved by other inventors working in this field.

During this year Whewell published the second volume, *On the Motion of Points Constrained*, of the expanded edition of his *Treatise on Dynamics*. In the course of internal controversies at Trinity College aroused by his historian friend Connop Thirlwall he also composed a couple of pamphlets, *Remarks on Mr. Thirlwall's Letter* and *Additional Remarks to Mr. Thirlwall's Two Letters*.

William Whewell in 1836, aged 42

★

There would be little point in detailing Whewell's continuous travels around Britain throughout all the years of his life (or his visit to St Kilda, right out in the Atlantic), but his involvement in different British localities found expression in honorary membership of various provincial societies of the kind springing up at that time: the Bristol Institute for the Advancement of Science, the Shropshire and North Wales Natural History Society, the Literary and Philosophical Society of Manchester, the Historic Society of Lancashire and Cheshire, and the Royal Society of Edinburgh. On a journey made through Ireland—partly to study the famous round towers—he was given honorary membership of the Royal Irish Academy. Later he was elected to that of the Institute of British Architects and of the Institution of Civil Engineers.

In 1835 he brought out under his own name a second edition of *Architectural Notes on German Churches*, enlarged with matter relating to his tours in Picardy and Normandy, and a pamphlet entitled *Thoughts on the Study of Mathematics* which brought him into controversy with the Scottish philosopher Sir William Hamilton. Further works in 1836 were *Newton and Flamsteed* and an edition of *The Progress of Ethical Philosophy* by the now deceased James Mackintosh—the very figure whom Darwin put higher than Whewell as a 'discourser on grave subjects'.

★

After spending almost four years in the waters of South America, the *Beagle* finally crossed over the Pacific, passed some time in various parts of Australasia, and then sailed over the Indian Ocean.

At the end of May 1836 it docked in South Africa about 20 miles from Cape Town. Robert Fitzroy took chronometrical readings at the British observatory and conferred with (the now knighted) Sir John Herschel, who was resident there for four years charting the stars of the southern hemisphere.

In his *Autobiography*, Charles Darwin recorded:

> I felt a high reverence for Sir J. Herschel, and was delighted to dine with him at his charming house at the Cape of Good Hope ... He never talked much, but every word which he uttered was worth listening to ...

Such talk as there was may have been about Charles Lyell, whom Herschel knew personally, and from whom he had recently received a new edition of the *Principles of Geology*. For soon after leaving South Africa, Darwin wrote from the *Beagle* to Henslow asking if Adam Sedgwick would propose him as a member of the Geological Society.

On 2 October, the *Beagle* reached again the south Devon coast, and docked in Falmouth. After an absence of almost five years, Darwin had returned to Britain.

⋆

At the end of the month, Darwin had his first meeting in London with Lyell, then President of the Geological Society, and also with Richard Owen, who (having acted as host to Cuvier during the Frenchman's visit to England in 1830, and himself gone on to visit him in Paris in 1831) was now Professor of Comparative Anatomy at the Royal College of Surgeons. Owen undertook to examine the fossil specimens Darwin had brought back from his world tour.

The presidency of the Geological Society is a post tenable for two years, and in February 1837 Lyell's term of office came to an end. He was succeeded in the post by Whewell. Towards the end of that month, Darwin wrote from Cambridge to his sister Caroline stating:

> I have just been reading a short paper to the Philosoph. Socy. of this place, and exhibiting some specimens & giving a verbal account of them. It went off very prosperously & we had a good discussion in which Whewell & Sedgwick took an active part.

Richard Owen

A week later, Whewell as the new President asked Darwin to become Secretary of the Geological Society. Darwin at first declined.

★

It has been seen that several years previously Whewell had begun work—with assistance from the Admiralty, the East India Company, and even various foreign governments—on studying the movements of the tides. Under his guidance a vast mass of data on the subject was systematically accumulated, far exceeding both in bulk and in accuracy anything previously available. Whewell summarized the information in a series of papers to the Royal Society, and constructed a map showing the march of the tide-wave round the Earth, as well as a more detailed diurnal co-tidal chart for the British Isles. These labours effectively constituted the foundation of modern tidology, and in 1837 gained him a Royal Medal, as well as election to the Royal Geographical Society and to honorary membership of the Société Française de Statistique Universelle.

In the summer of 1837 he made another continental tour, going down to Paris, south-west to Chartres to visit the cathedral, back through Paris and north-east to Rheims, across into Germany at Trier, along the Mosel to Koblenz and down the Rhine to his favourite Cologne, over again to Aachen, and then north to The Hague—viewing the picture galleries—and Amsterdam, returning by ferry from Rotterdam.

★

Whewell's Bridgewater treatise *Astronomy and General Physics* was now brought out in a German translation, published at Stuttgart under the title *Die Sternenwelt.* At Cambridge, meanwhile, its author completed new works on different subjects which also came out in this year: firstly a textbook on mechanics and hydrostatics, *The Mechanical Euclid*, later reappearing in improved editions, and secondly a book *On the Principles of English University Education*—*inter alia* incorporating his previous *Thoughts on the Study of Mathematics*, with a suitable reply to the criticisms of Sir William Hamilton.

Whisper the Fortunate Word

The third and most important publication brought out by William Whewell in 1837 was an enormous work he had been engaged on for a number of years, which attempted to present a full-scale historical account of the entire scientific field: *The History of the Inductive Sciences.* It comprised three octavo volumes running altogether to over 1600 pages.

The work opened with a dedicatory letter:

TO
SIR JOHN FREDERICK WILLIAM HERSCHEL,
K.G.H.

My dear Herschel,

It is with no common pleasure that I take up my pen to dedicate these volumes to you. They are the result of trains of thought which have often been the subject of our conversation, and of which the origin goes back to the period of our early companionship at the University. And if I had ever wavered in my purpose of combining such reflections and researches into a whole, I should have derived a renewed impulse and increased animation from your delightful *Discourse* on a kindred subject. For I could not have read it without finding this portion of philosophy invested with a fresh charm; and though I might be well aware that I could not aspire to that large share of popularity which your work so justly gained, I should still have reflected that something was due to the subject itself, and should have hoped that my own aim was so far similar to yours that the present work might have a chance of exciting an interest in some of your readers. That it will interest you, I do not at all hesitate to believe.

Sir John Herschel

If you were now in England I should stop here. But when a friend is removed for years to a far distant land, we seem to acquire a right to speak openly of his good qualities. I cannot, therefore, prevail upon myself to lay down my pen without alluding to the affectionate admiration of your moral and social, as well as intellectual excellencies, which springs up in the hearts of your friends whenever you are thought of. They are much delighted to look upon the halo of deserved fame which plays round your head; but still more to recollect, as one of them said, that your head is far from being the best part about you.

May your sojourn in the southern hemisphere be as happy and successful as its object is noble and worthy of you; and may your return home be speedy and prosperous, as soon as your purpose is attained.

Ever, my dear Herschel, yours,

W. Whewell
22nd March, 1837.

There seems a curious appropriateness in Whewell having signed this dedicatory letter prefacing *The History of the Inductive Sciences* on the fifth anniversary of the death of Johann Wolfgang von Goethe. For indeed the range of the work had something Goethean about it. The three volumes were divided into a number of 'books', and a general idea of their content can be gained from listing the titles.

Those in the first volume were 'The History of Greek School Philosophy with reference to Physical Science', 'The History of Physical Sciences in Ancient Greece', 'The History of Greek Astronomy', 'The History of Physical Science in the Middle Ages' and 'The History of Formal Astronomy after the Stationary Period'.

Those in the second volume were 'The History of Mechanics, including Fluid Mechanics', 'The History of Physical Astronomy', 'The History of Acoustics', 'The History of Optics, Formal and Physical', and 'The History of Thermotics and Atmology'.

Those in the third volume were 'The History of Electricity', 'The History of Magnetism', 'The History of Galvanism, or Voltaic Electricity', 'The History of Chemistry', 'The History of Mineralogy', 'The History of Systematic Botany and Zoology', 'The History of Physiology and Comparative Anatomy', and 'The History of Geology'.

★

Naturally it is not possible here to enter into detail about the author's treatment of all these different subjects, but attention may perhaps be drawn to the 'book' in the third volume about the 'History of Physiology and Comparative Anatomy'.

This 'book' contained several chapters, of which the sixth, 'Introduction of the Principle of Developed and Metamorphosed Symmetry', opened with a section on 'Vegetable Morphology' which began as follows:

> Before we proceed to consider the progress of principles which belong to animal and human life, such as have just been pointed at, we must look round for doctrines, if any such there be, as apply alike to all organized beings, conscious or unconscious, fixed or locomotive—to laws which regulate vegetable as well as animal forms and functions. Though we are very far from being able to present a clear and connected code of such laws, we may refer to one law at least which appears to be of genuine authority and validity, and is worthy our attention as an example of a properly organical or physiological principle, distinct from all mechanical, chemical or other physical forces, and such as cannot even be conceived to be resolvable into those. I speak of the tendency which produces such results as have been brought together in recent speculations upon *Morphology*.
>
> It may perhaps be regarded as indicating how peculiar are the principles of organic life, and how far removed from any mere mechanical action, that the leading idea in these speculations was first strongly and effectively apprehended, not by a laborious experimenter and reasoner, but by a man of singularly brilliant and creative fancy; not by a mathematician or chemist, but by a poet. And we may add further that this poet had already shown himself incapable of rightly apprehending the relation of physical facts to their principles; and had, in trying his powers on such subjects, exhibited a signal instance of the ineffectual and perverse operation of the method of philosophizing to which the constitution of his mind led him. The person of whom we speak is John Wolfgang Göthe, who is held, by the unanimous voice of Europe, to have been one of the greatest poets of our own, or of any time, and whose *Doctrine of Colours* we have already had to describe, in the History of Optics, as an entire failure. Yet his views on the laws which connect forms of plants into one simple system have been generally accepted and followed up. We might almost be led to think that this writer's poetical endowments contributed to this scientific discovery—the love of beauty of form, by fixing attention upon the symmetry of plants; and the creative habit of thought, by making constant development of a familiar process.

Whewell's devastatingly critical remarks about Goethe's theory of colours and indeed mental constitution were certainly sharply worded. All the more revealing is it then to follow his contrasting appreciation of Goethe's botanical ideas. For at this point a large footnote taking up almost half the page reproduced a passage from Goethe's hexametric poem 'The Metamorphosis of Plants', to which Whewell added an English translation of his own in the same metre.

> We may quote some of the poet's own verses as an illustration of his feelings on this subject. They are addressed to a lady.

Dich verwirret, geliebte, die tausendfältige mischung
Dieses blumengewühls über dem garten umher;
Viele namen hörest du an, und immer verdränget,
Mit barbarischem klang, einer den andern im ohr.
Alle gestalten sich ähnlich und keine gleichet der andern;
Und so deutet das chor auf ein geheimes gesetz,
Auf ein heiliges räthsel. O! könnte ich dich, liebliche freundinn,
Ueberliefern so gleich glücklich das lösende wort.

Thou, my love, art perplext with the endless seeming confusion
Of the luxuriant wealth which in the garden is spread;
Name upon name thou hearest, and in thy dissatisfied hearing,
With a barbarian noise one drives another along.
All the forms resemble, yet none is the same as another;
Thus the whole of the throng points at a deep hidden law,
Points at a sacred riddle. Oh! Could I to thee, my beloved friend,
Whisper the fortunate word by which the riddle is read!

The translation of these Goethean verses into English hexameters was to receive special commendation from the dedicatee Sir John Herschel in a review of the work.

After this footnote, Whewell's main text resumed:

> But though we cannot but remark the peculiarity of our being indebted to a poet for the discovery of a scientific principle, we must not forget that he himself held that in making this step he had been guided not by his invention but by observation. He repelled with extreme repugnance the notion that he had submitted fancy for fact, or imposed ideal laws on actual things. While he was earnestly pursuing his morphological speculations, he attempted to impress them upon Schiller. 'I expounded to him, in as lively a manner as possible, the metamorphosis of plants, drawing on paper, with many characteristic strokes, a symbolic plant before his eyes. He heard me,' Göthe says (*Zur Morphologie*, p. 24) 'with much interest and distinct comprehension; but when I had done, he shook his head and said "That is not Experience; that is an Idea." I stopt with some degree of irritation; for the point which separated us was marked most luminously by this expression.' And in the same work he relates his botanical studies and his habit of observation, from which it is easily seen that no common amount of knowledge and notice of details were involved in the course of thought which led him to the principle of the Metamorphosis of Plants.

Whewell set out this principle in some detail over a couple of pages, giving as example a metamorphic form of the common snapdragon (*Linaria vulgaris*) as discussed in the *Principles of Botany* by his colleague John Henslow—the teacher of Charles Darwin.

The Philosophy of Life

After a further paragraph discussing the history of the idea of plant metamorphosis prior to Goethe, the account by William Whewell continued:

> Göthe was led to his system on this subject by general views of Nature. He saw, he says (*Zur Morph.* i. 30), that a whole life of talent and labour was requisite to enable anyone to arrange the infinitely copious organic forms of a single kingdom of Nature. 'Yet I felt,' he adds, 'that for me there must be another way, analogous to the rest of my habits. The appearance of the changes, round and round, of organic creatures had taken strong hold on my mind. Imagination and Nature appeared to me to vie with each other which could go on most boldly yet most consistently.' His observation of Nature, directed by such a thought, led him to the doctrine of metamorphosis.
>
> In a later republication of his work (*Zur Morphologie*, 1817) he gives a very agreeable account of the various circumstances which affected the reception and progress of his doctrine. Wildenow (Zur *Morph.* i. 121) quoted him thus: 'The life of plants is, as Mr. Göthe very prettily says, an expansion and contraction, and these alternations make the various periods of life.' 'This "*prettily*",' says Göthe, 'I can be well content with, but the "*egregie*" of Usteri is much more pretty and obliging.' Usteri had used this term respecting Göthe in an edition of Jussieu.
>
> The application of the notion of metamorphosis to the explanation of double and monstrous flowers had been made previously by Jussieu. Göthe's merit was to have referred to it the *regular* formation of the flower. And as Sprengel justly says (*Gesch. Botan* ii. 304), his view had so profound a meaning, made so strong an appeal by its simplicity, and was so fruitful in the most valuable consequences that it was not to be wondered at if it occasioned further examination of the subject; although many persons pretend to slight it. The task of confirming and verifying the doctrine by a general application of it to all cases—a labour so important and necessary after the promulgation of any great principle—Göthe himself did not execute. At first he collected specimens and made drawings with some such view (*Zur Morph.* i. 129), but was interrupted and diverted to other matters. 'And now,' says he in his later publication, 'when I look back on this undertaking, it is easy to see that the object I had before my eyes was for me, in my position, with my habits and mode of thinking, unattainable. For it was no less than this: that I was to take that which I had stated in general and presented to the conception, to the mental intuition, in words; and that I should, in a particularly visible, orderly, and gradual manner, present it to the eye; so as to show to the outward sense that out of the germ of this idea might grow a tree of physiology fit to overshadow the world.'
>
> Voigt, professor at Jena, was one of the first who adopted Göthe's view

into an elementary work, which he did in 1808. Other botanists laboured in the direction which had thus been pointed out...

Whewell went on to review subsequent scholarly progress in this field.

The next section, headed 'Application of Vegetable Morphology', showed how the doctrine of metamorphosis was used to solve various botanical problems. It ended as follows:

We find, therefore, that a principle we may call the *Principle of Developed and Metamorphosed Symmetry* is firmly established and recognized, and familiarly and successfully applied by botanists. And it will be apparent, on reflection, that though *symmetry* is a notion which applies to inorganic as well as to organic things, and is in fact a conception of certain relations of space and position, such *development* and *metamorphosis* as are here spoken of are ideas entirely different from any of those to which the physical sciences have led us in our previous survey; and are, in short, genuine *organical* or *physiological* ideas—real elements of the philosophy of *life*.

We must, however imperfectly, endeavour to trace the application of this idea in the other great department of the world of life; we must folllow the history of Animal Morphology.

A further chapter, 'Progress of Animal Morphology', opened with a section headed 'Rise of Comparative Anatomy', which gave first a brief history of this subject in the sixteenth, seventeenth and early eighteenth centuries.

The text then continued:

Such is Cuvier's outline of the earlier history of comparative anatomy. We shall not go into detail upon this subject; but may observe that such studies had fixed in the minds of naturalists the conviction of the possibility and propriety of considering large divisions of the animal kingdom as modifications of one common *type*. Belon, as early as 1555, had placed the skeleton of a man and a bird side by side, and shown the correspondence of parts. So far as the case of vertebrated animals extends, this correspondence is generally allowed; although it required some ingenuity to detect its details in some cases; for instance, to see the analogy of parts between the head of a man and of a fish.

In tracing these less obvious correspondencies, some curious steps have been made in recent times. And here we must, I conceive, again ascribe no small merit to the same remarkable man who, as we have already had to point out, gave so great an impulse to vegetable morphology. Göthe, whose talent and disposition for speculating on all parts of Nature were truly admirable, was excited to the study of anatomy by his propinquity to the Duke of Weimar's cabinet of natural history. In 1786 he published a little essay, the object of which was to show that in man, as well as in beasts, the

> upper jaw contains an intermaxillary bone, although the sutures are obliterated. After 1790 (*Zur Morphologie*, i. 234), animated and impelled by the same passion for natural observation and for general views which had produced his Metamorphosis of Plants, he pursued his speculations on these subjects eagerly and successfully. And in 1795 he published a *Sketch of a Universal Introduction into Comparative Anatomy, beginning with Osteology*; in which he attempts to establish an 'osteological type', to which skeletons of all animals may be referred. I do not pretend that Göthe's anatomical works have had any influence on the progress of the science comparable with that exercised by the labours of professional anatomists; but the ingenuity and value of the views they contained was acknowledged by the best authorities; and the clearer introduction and application of the principle of developed and metamorphosed symmetry may be dated from about this time. Göthe declares that at an early period of these speculations he was convinced (ib. 250) that the bony head of beasts is to be derived from six vertebrae . . .

When reading all this today it is easy to point out that Goethe himself did not regard symmetry as a law of Nature, and in that sense the *context* of Whewell's discussion—in a 'book' on 'The History of Anatomy and Physiology', with reference to the 'principle of developed and metamorphosed symmetry'—may be regarded as quite contrary to the whole Goethean approach. But nonetheless Whewell's brief account of Goethe's ideas on organic morphology is sufficiently appreciative in tone to place its author within his own chosen manner among the earliest exponents in the English-speaking world of this particular area of Goethean science.

We Stand Here by the Well

In November 1837 Willam Whewell preached a series of four sermons before the University of Cambridge, the assembled texts of which then appeared as his fourth publication of that same year, entitled *On the Foundations of Morals*.

This work too opened with a dedicatory letter:

> TO THE
> REV. JULIUS CHARLES HARE,
> RECTOR OF HERSTMONCEAUX, SUSSEX
>
> ———
>
> My dear Hare,
>
> If in writing a multitude of books there is much weariness, there is at least this satisfaction—that the writer may sweeten each portion of his toil by making it the memorial of some valued friendship. I look upon the fol-

Julius Charles Hare

lowing pages with much greater pleasure because I have prefixed your name to them; and I turn the speculations which they contain with a more cheerful and kindly spirit because they carry me back to the days when you still resided in our much-loved Trinity College; when I had the delight of constant intercourse with you, and such themes were not unfamiliar to our conversation. In the main purpose of my sermons, I know that I shall have you for my favourer, for I had you for my forerunner.

You are now removed from us, to my great sorrow and that of many more; and are transferred to a situation where your daily walk is among the practical duties and household feelings, which you cultivate so earnestly and well, and which, if I am not mistaken, you deem the fit employment and true business of man. Nor am I disposed to doubt that such a life is, for most men, more truly wise and happy than one in which our tasks lie chiefly in the world of speculation; and in which the principal events consist in our own solitary intellectual struggles. Yet to you I may say, without any doubt of receiving your assent, that this employment of guessing at truth is both in itself praiseworthy and, if carried on with a humble trust in the Divine Giver of all Truth, is full of deep and wide sources of practical blessing. I therefore dedicate these discourses to you, in the full confidence of receiving from you not only the kind wishes of a friend and the interest of a lover of speculative truth, but the approbation of a good man.

I am always, my dear Hare,

Affectionately yours,

W. Whewell

Trinity College Cambridge
Dec. 16, 1837

The text of the first sermon began:

'For the invisible things of Him from the creation of the world are clearly seen, being understood by the things that are made; even His eternal power and Godhead; so that they are without excuse.' (Romans 1:20.)

The constant object of the Christian preacher should be to lead men to love and glorify their heavenly Master, and to live suitably to their Christian profession. 'Hallowed be thy name . . . Thy will be done on earth' might be his standing texts, and his perpetual theme. But this unity in his end may include a vast variety in the means which he employs. It may often be best that he should take his place by the side of the living waters, and call aloud: 'Ho, every one that thirsteth!' But it may sometimes be no less proper for him to stand by the *fountain-heads* of truth; to watch over the well from which distant streams are derived; to repair its crumbling wall; to complete its broken rim; above all, to remove carefully all pollution and impurity, all poisonous or unwholesome taint, which mistake or negligence may have shed into it. Instead of practically appealing to the great rules of duty, and the affections and motives which may urge men to obedience and love, it may at times be profitable to examine how these rules of duty are to be discovered and known by man; on what grounds they rest; how they are consistent with themselves, and with human nature. For man—a creature born to think as well as to feel, impelled to speculate no less than to act, whose business it is to render, not a blind but a 'reasonable service'—cannot restrain himself from demanding such consistency; cannot refrain from thus enquiring after the ground of that which is enjoined him. It is the irresistible impulse of his nature, which receives a warrant in the injunction to 'scrutinize all things, and hold fast that which is right.' (1 Thess. 5:21.)

Nor are such employments of man's understanding without influence on his life and conduct: far otherwise. Although enquiries concerning truths of doctrine may be actively prosecuted by a few only, they exert a mighty power in a thousand ways upon the daily thoughts and practice of the bulk of mankind. The prevalent opinions concerning the first principles of religion and morality tinge, through innumerable channels, the remotest streams of religious and moral teaching; and thus affect the spiritual welfare of millions of our fellow-Christians. Those who employ themselves in the examination of such original principles and sources of truth may therefore feel themselves entitled to utter the prayer of the faithful servant of old, 'O Lord God, I pray thee send me good speed this day, and shew kindness unto my master Abraham—Behold, I stand here by the well.' (Gen. 24:12.)

We stand here by the well. We here teach those who are to teach others; we here communicate those governing principles which in a great degree guide and shape the course of intellectual activity in after-life. What is here imparted to those who repair to our fountains is transmitted to the whole of our nation by the various lines of communication which belong to our civil and spiritual condition—by the channels of our domestic and social life, of our literature, and of our ecclesiastical polity. Who among us can doubt that in this way we exercise a vast power, for good or for evil? Men may sometimes scoff at such influences; but what serious man can fail to see that the doctrines to which we give our sanction here *must* sway and *have* swayed the general bent of men's reasonings and convictions upon the most important points of moral and religious truth?

It cannot then be deemed improper if, in this and the following discourses, we endeavour to ascertain what view of the nature of moral and Christian duty is most conformable to the true constitution and condition of man . . .

Thoughts of Grace and Beauty

Charles Darwin finally accepted the Secretaryship of the Geological Society, and remained in that post for the next three years. On 21 January 1838, he wrote to John Henslow in Cambridge stating:

> I have accepted the Secret. of G. Soc.; as Whewell asked me again in a very pleasant manner, & as the duties are lessened, I could not refuse with fairness, although it is an office which I do not relish.—
>
> I have sent a copy of my journal, as far as complete, to Mr. Whewell, for him to review the Geolog. part in his anniversary speech.

This speech was given on 16 February, with William Whewell as the Society's President announcing the award for that year of the prestigious Wollaston Medal

> . . . to Mr. Richard Owen for his services to fossil zoology in general, and in particular for the part already published of his description of the fossil remains collected by Mr. Darwin in the voyage of H.M.S. *Beagle.*

A year later, in his outgoing speech as President, Whewell announced the award of this medal to Christian Ehrenberg, Professor of Medicine in the University of Berlin (who *inter alia* had accompanied Alexander von

Humboldt on the great Asiatic journey of 1829 taking them right across Siberia to the very borders of China).

★

During 1838 Whewell made frequent visits to London, partly in order to officiate every fortnight as President of the Geological Society and partly to consult a specialist about injuries sustained in a fall from his horse. For as a rider he was rather carefree, and throughout his life experienced many falls. Indeed he used to joke that he had personally measured the depth of every ditch in the Cambridge neighbourhood by tumbling into them all!

In June of that year he was appointed to another Cantabrigian chair: the Professorship of Moral Philosophy. But for several months he did not take up this new appointment, being still too engaged in other business. He brought out a further mathematical textbook, *The Doctrine of Limits, with its Applications*, and also a volume of eclogues in rhyming couplets about the Bartlow Hills in Essex, with the Latin title *Nugae Bartlovianae.*

★

It seems to have been in the summer of 1838 that William Whewell first met Cordelia Marshall.

Cordelia, like William, came from the north but, unlike him, belonged to a wealthy family. Her father, John Marshall, had made a fortune as a cotton and flax manufacturer in Leeds, and also owned a house in London and a large estate on the edge of Ullswater in the Lake District. In this capacity he was a close friend of the poet William Wordsworth—whom he had accompanied on a tour of Ireland in 1829.

Whewell was introduced to the Marshall family through the poet's younger brother Christopher Wordsworth, at the time Master of Trinity College.

★

During this summer vacation Whewell travelled once again to the Continent. Although his letters only show that he visited Germany, another piece of evidence composed during that year might suggest that his tour was more extensive. It is a poem of 124 lines in blank verse (iambic pentameter).

The opening describes the poet journeying in Italy, along the Mediterranean coastline, and viewing a temple with Greek associations. May one then deduce that Whewell not only crossed over the Alps but even travelled down the Italian peninsula as far south as Paestum? This poem at any rate vividly conjures up the atmosphere of the Paestum temples.

I wander'd long amid Ausonian plains,
And on the bright shore of the Tideless Sea;
Bright shores—for there on high Apollo drives
Nearer his golden car; but glorified
Far more by jewels which Apollo's child,
Art, heav'n-taught Art, has fixt upon the verge
Of the blue sea, or on the cliff abrupt,
Or deep in groves, and by the torrent's war.

O! wondrous Art, I cried, how, touch'd by thee,
The inert rock smooth hewn, and passive shaft
That bears up ponderous stone, can fill the mind
With thoughts of grace and beauty! Lo, I see
Before my soothèd eye the temple's form,
See side by side the shapely pillars rise,
All fair proportioned, like a stately row
Of graceful virgins or of youths, that stand
Serene and mild at even distances,
While o'er their heads the long entablature,
Parted through all its length in slighter forms,
Smooth beam, and sculptured frieze, and jutting crown
Connects, but crushes not. From end to end
Part answers part with thoughtful symmetry.
Through the dark shade that parts the marble stems
Dimly I see the simple inner wall,
But nought that troubles or that loads the mind,
Well-pleased to step from graceful shaft to shaft,
As on the soft feet of some numerous verse,
Proportion'd, simple, and symmetrical—
Such should Art ever be.

I turned me back
And clomb the barrier of bright Italy,
And travelled pensive to my native North,
Bearing within me, rich possession! still
The treasured memories of Ancient Art—
The pillar'd temple in its leafy grove,
The giant columns on the sounding shore . . .

A Fierce and Destructive Sword

In the first volume of her biography of Charles Darwin, *Voyaging* (1995), Janet Browne describes this crucial point in her subject's life, in the chapter entitled 'A Theory by Which to Work':

All through August and September, Darwin ploughed through a wide range of philosophical and metaphysical texts, following up references, checking review journals, finding out what the best European minds had made of some of the questions he was attempting to answer. His pocket notebooks proved too small for exploring all the thoughts he wanted to record; and he started composing longer and longer essays . . .

If ever an individual was primed to make the most of another man's views at that time, it was Darwin. One book invariably led to another, as he searched for the next piece of his puzzle. David Brewster's review of Comte's *Cours de Philosophie Positive*, for instance, which Darwin read in the *Edinburgh Review* in September 1838, inspired him to hunt for papers by the Belgian statistician Adolphe Quetelet, whom Brewster mentioned in passing. Quetelet was famous for codifying the idea of an 'average' man in 1835, and interesting to Darwin for 'facts there mentioned about proportion of sexes at birth & causes' . . .

So it is not too surprising that on 28 September 1838, Darwin began reading Thomas Robert Malthus's *Essay on the Principle of Population*—for amusement, he claimed, but clearly following up lines of enquiry relating to individual variation, averages and chance, as well as seeking information on human population statistics.

Other reasons for reading Malthus were not far behind. A good case can be made for at least some of his initial interest lying in the fact that Malthus dealt with the question of the 'fruitfulness of marriages', an issue running high in his notebooks. Practical statements relating to human fecundity were just the kind of details he sought at that moment . . .

Nor were Malthus's doctrines entirely unknown to Darwin personally. They were as pervasive in biology as they were in general nineteenth-century culture, intimately related to continuing debates within natural theology and social reform in the wider political sphere. Darwin came across them in the books by Paley which were a fixed part of the Cambridge degree course; and William Whewell discussed them in a paper delivered in 1829 at the Cambridge Philosophical Society. Lyell frequently described the Malthusian struggle to survive in his *Principles*, citing Augustin de Candolle's writings on the subject, as well as giving his own stirring descriptions of human endeavour and colonial warfare where the best fighter always won. More generally still, long reviews of Malthus's works, or of newly-issued anti-Malthusian works, constantly appeared in the literary journals Darwin was methodically reading. It would have been hard for him to avoid hearing about the principle of population while controversy raged over the new Poor Laws and when food riots, inflammatory addresses and unprecedented economic depression flared in distant parts of the country. Every publication in the land discussed the Chartist question during that summer and autumn: every member of the 'exasperated populace' knew his or her distress was aggravated by large numbers of people to feed and the high price of corn.

The full impact of Malthus's *Essay on Population* became plain after Darwin finished reading it on 3 October. Excitedly, he set about rethinking his transmutation work.

First and foremost, he recognized that differential death rates gave him a mechanism for explaining the preservation of adaptations, until then a mysterious unknown quantity. Every individual death, bit by bit, contributed to a larger piecemeal shift in animal or plant form, with the result that each species became better adapted to external conditions...

★

Just over a month later, 11 November, Darwin proposed marriage to his cousin Emma Wedgwood.

Janet Browne continues:

Over the next few weeks, Darwin and Emma tried to say in letters the important things they had both left unsaid during their brief meetings...

Emma was devout in a quiet, steadfast way. She had been brought up as a traditional Anglican, with few of the Unitarian leanings of her Wedgwood grandparents. Her father, like his brothers and countless other sons of the dissenting manufacturing elite, willingly embraced the conventional outlook of the Church of England as he turned himself into one of the landed gentry...

She had a special request of Darwin. 'It is perhaps foolish of me to say this much but my own dear Charlie we now do belong to each other & I cannot help being open with you. Will you do me a favour? yes I am sure you will, it is to read our Saviours farewell discourse to his disciples which begins at the end of the 13th chap of St. John. It is so full of love to them & devotion & every beautiful feeling. It is the part of the New Testament I love best.'

Emma surely saw Darwin as one of the doubters who could, if they only stopped questioning, find themselves able to believe...

Unerringly, she also recognized something of the dichotomy characterizing Darwin's mental life. His sense of duty to his fellows, his innate conservatism, his inbuilt appreciation of the values of gentlemanly society and unthinking acceptance of the advantages of Britain's hierarchies of power lay uneasily together with the radical thrust of his philosophical views. He had yet to find a way to keep his life and work running smoothly together. Mostly, the problem was a consequence of the structure of English society—religion was as much a question of class and behaviour as doctrine, and a formal subscription to Church of England principles went hand in hand with his own position in society...

Darwin was still struggling to come to terms with this dichotomy when he proposed to Emma. No one knew better than he how far his changing views about species were leading him along the path of disbelief. No one knew better than he how far he was wedded to an entirely natural origin of man. Every time he opened one of his notebooks he felt the seductive call of a godless Universe. Even his dreams warned him about wandering too far off the straight and narrow. Yet he also felt himself an integral part of the upper echelons of British society; and he was fully accepted as such by his scientific colleagues. For the moment, he could call on some residual belief in an external deity. But he still felt it was important to tell Emma his generalized uncertainty about a range of Church axioms: how he rejected the Bible's status as an infallible text in relation to the history of the Earth; and that he was no longer sure about miracles and revelation.

To a large degree, Emma accepted these confessions calmly. She was not so strait-laced that she could not admit a preference for avoiding one of 'Allen's temperance sermons'. She was not shocked by Lyell's tearing apart Genesis and geology . . .

However, she was much more religious than Darwin, and genuinely believed in the Anglican faith she was brought up in. She was relieved when Darwin complied with her request to read parts of the Bible and told her he felt 'earnest on the subject'. Luckily, he reassured her, 'there were no doubts as to how one ought to act'.

He was far more acerbic with himself in his notebooks. The only doubts he allowed during those weeks at the end of 1838 were whether his arguments for transmutation were fully effective. A hard edge suddenly flashed: an incisiveness about the full scope of a naturalistic view of the world which cut through the thicket of compromise and self-illusion he had carefully built up over the years. Fresh from thinking about Emma's religious beliefs, he confronted the raw bones of his theory. Did he really mean to threaten the status of the human mind, and mankind's hopes for a moral meaning to life outside of life itself? Was the whole system of morality to go? The answer, he bravely concluded, was yes. Religious belief was merely a natural property of humanity. 'Belief allied to instinct,' he wrote on a slip of paper. Even better, he daringly ventured, the 'love of the deity' was a mere 'effect of organization'. Emotions of terror and sublimity inevitably prompted a feeling that there was some external cause, one that primitive mankind could not help personifying and turning into a deity. 'How completely men must have personified the deity.'

Malthus had given him a fierce and destructive sword:

'When two races of men meet they act precisely like two species of animals—they fight, eat each other, bring diseases to each other &c., but then comes the more deadly struggle, namely which have the best fitted organizations, or instincts (i.e. intellect in man) to gain the day ... Man acts on & is acted on by the organic and inorganic agents of this earth like every other animal.'

There was little space left for divinity or moral redemption in this bleak view of life.

The Canter of the Verses

On 29 January 1839, the 30-year-old Charles Darwin, Secretary of the Geological Society, was after a short engagement married at the village of Maer in Staffordshire to his cousin Emma Wedgwood.

⋆

A few months later, William Whewell printed privately a small book entitled *Herman and Dorothea, translated from the hexameters of Göthe.*[7]

Whether this work was inspired by the translator's growing friendship with Cordelia Marshall is not known. But at any rate one person to whom he sent a copy was the newly married Charles Darwin:

Trin. Col.
Ap. 11. 1839

My dear Darwin,

I want to be allowed to present the accompanying little book as a marriage gift to you and Mrs. Darwin. It is a very humble gift, to be sure, but it may serve to remind you of my good wishes, which are very cordially yours. Moreover, if you can accommodate yourself to the canter of the verses, you will find in it a very pretty love story.

Believe me always

Very truly yours,

W. Whewell

'The canter of the verses' was a horseman's reference to the poem's hexametric form, also reproduced in this English rendering. Indeed, the equestrian translator even prefaced Goethe's poem with a hexametric introduction of his own, where the verses already canter nicely along. The form is quite different from the iambic pentameters in his poem from the previous year, but sounds very appropriate to its content.

Ancient Rhine! On thee are blessings breathed by the German
When, by thy bounties cheer'd, his heart expands in his bosom.
Beautiful Rhine! The traveller too oft wafts thee a blessing
Bearing away in his thought full many a cherisht remembrance.
For who, once that has roved on the beauteous banks of the Rhine-stream,

Joys not still to recal those castled rocks with their vine-clad
Slopes, and the winding stream, broad-dimpled, rushing between them;
Godesberg gay, and the Dragon's Rock, and the Corner of Roland,
Fair Saint Goar, and the Switzer Dale, and the voice of the Lurley
Heard in the silence of eve, sweet answering over the water;
Cölln with its lofty vaults, where sacred harmonies float, while
Sound and stony shaft seem both aspiring to heavèn;
Towns with their nightly pomp, when, seen from the balconied window
Lamps and serener stars reflected beam in the river,
And the tumult of day-life, softening, sinks to its slumber!
Wanderer, lov'st thou the Rhine? Then list to a tale of its borders
Flung from its Master's lyre; by me, as a labour of love, thus
Tuned, but ah, I fear me in vain! for the ear of the Briton;
And yet never in vain, if it once to the sad or the weary
Bring those visions again in the soothing pow'r of their beauty
Linking the fair with the fair; that so the forms of the poet
Ever may float in his mind with scenes of memory blended.

In contrast to this translator who had made himself quite familiar with the Rhineland, the world-travelled Darwin had only once ventured onto the European Continent, on a brief visit to France which took him no further than Paris,[8] so he had no 'scenes of memory' relating to 'the beauteous banks of the Rhine-stream' at all. Nor indeed did he ever travel to the Continent again in the remaining 43 years of his life.

Nonetheless he was sufficiently pleased by the gift to send an appreciative reply:

12 Upper Gower St.
April 16th—

My dear Whewell,

I have been much flattered by your 'marriage gift' and kind note. I assure you very few have given me more pleasure.—Mrs. Darwin desires me to give you her best thanks for it.—I hope sometime when you are in town and happen to be disengaged, we may see you in this house.—I have hardly done more than dip into Herman & D. but I intend beginning it immediately.

A short time since I finished, having only skimmed parts before, another & quite different production of yours—the Hist. of Inductive Sciences—& I will run the risk of appearing exceedingly presumptuous by telling you how much I enjoyed it—to see so clearly the steps by which all the great scientific discoveries have been come to is a capital lesson to everyone, even to the humblest follower of science & I hope I have profited by it.—When I closed your third volume I wished much to say my thanks to you, and now, however presumptuous it may have been, I have satisfied myself by saying them.

Believe me

Most truly yours

Chas. Darwin

Such Useful and Even Necessary Value

On 22 April 1839 William Whewell finally delivered his inaugural lecture as Professor of Moral Philosophy in Cambridge University. The last paragraph of the subsequently printed text reads:

> In the meantime, I must not terminate my first lecture without again begging the indulgence of the university for the very imperfect manner in which at the present time I am able to execute the office of delivering such lectures as the Professorship requires. The proper study of Moral Philosophy requires no ordinary amount of reading and of thought. I trust that hereafter I shall be able to bring before my hearers the results of a longer course of labour employed on this study, and in a maturer form. But I was desirous that after so long an interruption of the activity of an office which may be so useful in this university, not a single year should elapse without something being done by me to mark its revival; and I conceived that by taking a limited field, the history of Moral Philosophy in England, and especially in this university, and by tracing only the more prominent features of this history, I might be able to offer some views not uninstructive, even with so short a time of preparation and among other employments. In future years I may attempt perhaps a wider range of research, although I would beg to be excused at present from laying down any definite plan or fixed period. My power of giving a full attention to the subject may for some time be limited by the prosecution of other speculations which I would not willingly resign. Moreover, these wider speculations to which I refer, although at first they may appear to have no direct bearing upon the special study which belongs to this Professorship, will, I can venture to say, be found in the end to be subservient in a very important manner to the clearness and soundness of our ethical reasonings. Inquiries into the nature of truth, the means and methods of its discovery, and the philosophy of science, even though they set out from the study of physical science, if they are at all successful cannot fail to exercise a strong and favourable influence upon our studies with regard to moral truth, moral science, and the true philosophy of human life.

★

One of the 'other employments' with which Whewell had not ceased to be concerned was the subject-matter of his previous chair—mineralogy. In

1840 he negotiated the gift to Cambridge of the foremost British mineral collection of the day, left by the recently deceased Sir Abraham Hume. At the same time a rare mineral, calcium oxalate hydrate ($CaC_2O_4H_2O$), was even named in his own honour: Whewellite.

★

Since Whewell's fame had begun to spread outside his own country, academic honours from other lands also came his way. In America he was made an Honorary Member of the Boston Society of Natural History, and in France a Vice-President of the Institut d'Afrique.

A different kind of compliment was paid to him in German-speaking lands. For during the same year 1840—in which Whewell also went on a further tour through Holland and Germany—the first two volumes of his *History of the Inductive Sciences* came out in Stuttgart in a German version: *Die Geschichte der induktiven Wissenschaften*. The translation was undertaken by Joseph Johann von Littrow, a mathematical and astronomical writer widely read in Middle Europe. Littrow had indeed a peculiar relation to the science of astronomy, having been born at Bischofteinitz during the very night, 13 March 1781, when in the garden of 19 King Street in Bath the 42-year-old organist William Herschel, gazing through a telescope towards the constellation of the Twins, first set eyes on the planet Uranus. It was therefore singularly appropriate for him to translate into German a work dedicated to the discoverer's son.

From 1819 onwards Littrow was Professor of Astronomy at the University of Vienna and Director of the Imperial Observatory. Since in 1823 Whewell had visited the Observatory in Paris, one may wonder whether Littrow and Whewell might have met during the latter's stay in Vienna in 1825—at the time when the Viennese Observatory was being rebuilt.

In 1832 Littrow published a work *Über den gefürchteten Kometen des gegenwärtigen Jahres*, referred to by Rudolf Steiner in a lecture on 20 September 1924 during the priests' Apocalypse course at Dornach as written by

> ... a significant astronomer, Littrow, and it was very interesting. Even today I can only advise you to concern yourselves with it. It was highly interesting, with fine calculations agreeing exactly. This matter was examined by an illuminated man ...

The illuminated man had already reviewed Whewell's Bridgewater Treatise *Die Sternenwelt* in the 1838 number of the Viennese *Jahrbuch der Literatur*. And he now prefaced the first volume of *Die Geschichte der Induktiven Wissenschaften* with the following translator's note:

> The present history of natural sciences (*History of the Inductive Sciences from the earliest to the present times*. By the Rev. William Whewell, M.A., Fellow and

Tutor of Trinity College, Cambridge, President of the Geological Society of London. III vols., London, J.W. Parker) which I received from the author himself shortly after its completion, seemed to me such an excellent one, and also of such useful and even necessary value to my countrymen, that I believe myself to be meeting their general desire by presenting it to them here in German garb. It would please me very much to have assessed this desire in a suitable way, and also to have met it to the satisfaction of my readers.

Littrow supplemented the original text of Whewell's work with extensive footnotes of his own giving a German-language readership further relevant information of scientific, biographical and bibliographical character.

★

On reading Thomas Carlyle's *Chartism*, also published in 1840, Whewell printed privately as 'a kind of adaptation of some passages of that remarkable book' a poem of 190 hexameters, the *Isle of the Sirens*.

The poem sets these passages into an imaginary Homeric adventure undertaken by Telemachus. Here is the opening, inspired by the well-known episode in Book XII of the *Odyssey*, and showing a similar vigour:

Over the broad-spread sea the thoughtful son of Ulysses
Steered his well-built bark. Full long he had sought for his father,
Till Hope, lingering, fled; for the face of the water is trackless.
Then rose strong in his mind the thought of his home and his island;
And he desired to return; to behold his Ithacan people,
Listen their just complaints, restrain the fierce and the lawless.
Strong prest the wind on the bellying sail, and fleetly the bark flew,
Flew o'er the dark blue wave, till near to the Isle of the Sirens
Glided its onward course. Then suddenly pausèd the breezes,
And in the air was a calm, and the waves were still'd into slumber.
Rose from their seats his companions bold, and haulèd the sail down,
Lifted the mast from its step, and laid it along in the bottom,
Sat on the thwarts, and stoutly they rowed till near was the island,
Where—but they knew it not—the deep-soul'd Ithacan sovereign
Past before, and alone of his crew heard the song of the Sirens:
For he had stopped their ears, wise, kneading wax with his fingers,
He there bound to the mast, by his own wise counsel protected.
Yet so sweet was the song, he beckoned his friends to release him,
Making signs with his brows; but they more lustily rowed on;
And from his seat then rose Eurylochus, rose Perimedes,
And they bound him with cords still more, close pinching his members . . .

A Philosophy of Science

In the previously quoted passage from his inaugural lecture in the chair of Moral Philosophy at Cambridge, William Whewell indicated that he was still engaged on another scientific work. This too appeared in 1840 under the title *The Philosophy of the Inductive Sciences Founded upon their History*, in two octavo volumes running altogether to over 1200 pages.

It opened with a dedicatory letter:

TO THE
REV. ADAM SEDGWICK, M.A.,
SENIOR FELLOW OF TRINITY COLLEGE,
WOODWARDIAN PROFESSOR OF GEOLOGY IN THE
UNIVERSITY OF CAMBRIDGE, AND PREBENDARY
OF NORWICH.

———

My dear Sedgwick,

When I showed you the last sheet of my *History of the Inductive Sciences* in its transit through the press, you told me that I ought to add a paragraph or two at the end, by way of moral to the story; and I replied that the moral

Adam Sedgwick

would be as long as the story itself. The present work, the *moral* which you then desired, I have, with some effort, reduced within a somewhat smaller compass than I then spoke of; and I cannot dedicate it to anyone with so much pleasure as to you.

It has always been my wish that, as far and as long as men might know anything of me by my writings, they should hear of me along with the friends with whom I have lived, whom I have loved, and by whose conversation I have been animated to hope that I too might add something to the literature of our country. There is no-one whose name has, on such grounds, a better claim than yours to stand in the front of a work which has been the subject of my labours for no small portion of our long period of friendship. But there is another reason which gives a peculiar propriety to this dedication of my *Philosophy* to you. I have little doubt that if your life had not been absorbed in struggling with many of the most difficult problems of a difficult science, you would have been my fellow-labourer or master in the work which I have here undertaken. The same spirit which dictated your vigorous protest against some of the errors which I also attempt to expose would have led you, if your thoughts had been more free, to take a leading share in that reform of philosophy which all who are alive to such errors must see to be now indispensable. To you I may most justly inscribe a work which contains a criticism of the fallacies of the ultra-Lockean school.

I will mention one other reason with which I place your name at the head of my *Philosophy*. By doing so, I may consider myself as dedicating it to the College to which we both belong, to which we both owe so much of all that we are, and in which we have lived together so long and so happily; and *that*, be it remembered, the College of Bacon and of Newton. That College, I know, holds a strong place in your affections, as in mine; and among many reasons, not least on this account—we believe that sound and enduring philosophy ever finds there a congenial soil and a fostering shelter. If the doctrines which the present work contains be really true and valuable, my unhesitating trust is that they will spread gradually from these precincts to every part of the land.

That this office of being the fosterer and diffuser of truth may ever belong to our common nursing mother, and that you, my dear Sedgwick, may long witness and contribute to these beneficial influences is the hearty wish of

Yours affectionately,

W. Whewell

Trinity College, May 1, 1840.

There then followed a preface, which began:

The work now before the reader is intended as an application of the plan of Bacon's *Novum Organum* to the present condition of physical science. The progress of such science during the last three centuries has given us the means of inquiring, with advantages which former generations did not possess, what that *organ*, or intellectual method is, by which solid truth is to be extracted from the observation of Nature; and though the attempt to discover this cannot but be an arduous undertaking, it is so plainly required of the present generation that anyone engaging in it with sobriety and industry may claim to have his labours soberly and tolerantly estimated. I shall therefore make no apology for what might otherwise appear the presumption of such a design. My scheme is however narrower than Bacon's in this respect, that I have in the present work confined myself to those branches of human knowledge which have external Nature for their object, and are often exclusively termed *sciences*. The reason given for this limitation in the following pages (namely that it seemed proper to collect our philosophy of knowledge from the most certain and distinct portions of knowledge alone) will, I trust, be considered as an adequate justification of the course pursued.

Many writers, both before and since Bacon, have employed themselves upon the subjects with which we are here concerned—the philosophy of knowledge, and the methods of arriving at science; and I have availed myself of their conclusions, where they appeared to be real additions to sound philosophy. I must add that I have not scrupled to subject their speculations to a critical examination, and to reject all that was thus found to be erroneous or worthless. A system which professes to give a view of the nature of knowledge supplies canons of criticism by which all other philosophical doctrines must be tried, in order to determine their import and reality. It is an office essentially connected with the exposition of such a system, to pronounce on the value of previous essays of the same kind. Hence I have not hesitated on some occasions to dissent from the great masters of the philosophy of science, from Bacon, from Cuvier, and even from Newton himself; believing that they, upon maturer consideration, would have been led to those doctrines and precepts which I have preferred to theirs. In like manner, although I have adopted Kant's reasoning respecting the nature of space and time, it will be found by anyone acquainted with the system of that acute metaphysician that my views differ widely from his. I have also ventured to condemn some of the opinions respecting physical philosophy published by another eminent German writer (Schelling) to whose works I have in other subjects great obligations.

The present work was announced in the outset of a *History of the Inductive Sciences* published three years ago. That history was indeed the result of labours undertaken with a view to the formation of a philosophy of science, and was intended from the first as an introduction to a work on that subject. I may therefore take the liberty of saying that I have as yet seen no reason to wish to make any material change in the *History*, as it is now before the world. I will not omit this opportunity of expressing my obligations to the German translator of the *History* . . .

A footnote here stated:

The History of the Inductive Sciences has been translated into German by M. von Littrow, Director of the Imperial Observatory at Vienna, and author of many well-known mathematical works.

The main text continued:

. . . It is a testimony which may well give an author some confidence in the value of his work that one of the most eminent men of science in Europe should spontaneously postpone other tasks in order to give it, with the most flattering expressions, to the public of his own country . . .

After some further discussion of other matters, Whewell ended his preface with these remarks:

Bacon's purpose and promise was that his New Organ should produce material as well as intellectual profit—works, as well as knowledge. That the study of the order of Nature does add to man's power, the history of the sciences since Bacon has abundantly shown. But though this hope of derivative advantages may stimulate our exertions, it cannot govern our methods of seeking knowledge without leading us away from the most general and genuine forms of knowledge. The nature of knowledge must be studied in itself and for its own sake before we attempt to learn what external rewards it will bring us. I have therefore not aimed at imitating Bacon in those parts of his work in which he contemplates the increase of man's dominion over Nature as the main object of natural philosophy; being fully persuaded that if Bacon himself had had unfolded before him the great theories which have been established since his time, he would have acquiesced in the contemplation of them; and would have readily proclaimed the real reason for aiming at the knowledge of such truths to be that they are *true*. Thus I have ventured to separate his first aphorism ('Homo naturae minister et interpres tantum facit et intelligit quantum de naturae ordine re vel mente observaverit; nec amplius scit aut potest') into two; to consider the *interpretation* as our primary object, not the *ministration*; the *knowing*, not the *doing*; the *intelligence*, not the *power*.

The mode of delivering the philosophy of science in aphorisms which Bacon has adopted would not well suffice for the treatment of the subject at present, since many questions must be discussed, many perplexities explained. No writer upon such subjects can expect to be either understood or assented to, beyond the limits of a narrow school, who is not prepared with good arguments, as well as magisterial decisions, upon the many obscure and controverted points which the subject brings before him. But though an aphoristic philosophy, unsupported by reasoning, is thus unsuited to the time, it may be satisfactory to many readers to see the philosophy to which in the present work we are led presented in aphoristic form. I have therefore expressed in aphorisms a large part of the doctrines resulting from the discussions which occupy the following pages. These aphorisms are given at the end of this preface.

Along with these, I shall add some other aphorisms on the subject of the language of science; a subject in which it appears to be time to collect, from the usage of the most judicious writers, some rules which may tend to preserve the purity and analogies of scientific language from wanton and needless violation. As this subject is not discussed in the work itself, I have given, along with these aphorisms, such examples as may tend to confirm and illustrate them, and have applied them to some cases at present unsettled.

Of Ideas in General

Exactly as stated, the preface to William Whewell's *Philosophy of the Inductive Sciences* was immediately followed, not by any opening chapter, but rather by a section headed 'Aphorisms Concerning Ideas'.

These began:

I.

Man is the Interpreter of Nature, Science the right interpretation.

II.

The *Senses* place before us the *Characters* of the Book of Nature; but these convey no knowledge to us, till we have discovered the Alphabet by which they are to be read.

III.

The *Alphabet*, by means of which we interpret Phenomena, consists of the *Ideas* existing in our own minds; for these give to the phenomena that coherence and significance which is not an object of sense.

IV.

The antithesis of *Sense* and *Ideas* is the foundation of the Philosophy of Science. No knowledge can exist without the union, no philosophy without the separation of these two elements.

Already from the opening aphorism it is apparent that not only had Whewell, as stated in his preface, divided the first of Bacon's aphorisms into two, but in his own aphorisms he then simply discarded the concepts contained in the second part of Bacon's.

The sequence of Whewell's aphorisms continued in similar fashion for no less than CXIII. Most of them, like those quoted above, consisted of just one or two sentences, but some were expanded into a whole paragraph.

There then came a further section headed 'Aphorisms Concerning Science', of which there were another LVI.

These were followed by 'Aphorisms Concerning the Language of Science', which although numbering only XVII were treated with an extensive commentary. (Scientific nomenclature was a field in which Whewell made important contributions, being indeed the first recorded person to use the English terms 'scientist' and 'physicist'.)

Only after these aphorisms were completed did the main text begin. It was continued all the way through both volumes, which were divided, as with the previous *History of the Inductive Sciences,* into a number of 'books'. In the course of these various 'books' the first two sections of aphorisms were expanded into discursive accounts, in the first and second volumes respectively.

★

The text of the first volume had the general title 'Of Ideas'. Its first 'book' was headed 'Of Ideas in General'.

Among the several chapters in this 'book' was one on 'The Fundamental Antithesis of Philosophy', a theme central to Whewell's epistemological position. And a reader who continues to bear in mind the statements in his preface to the effect that the great masters of the philosophy of science, Bacon, Cuvier and even Newton himself, would upon maturer consideration have been led to those doctrines and precepts which the author preferred to theirs, and that if Bacon himself had had unfolded before him the great theories established since his time he would have acquiesced in the contemplation of them and readily proclaimed the real reason for aiming at the knowledge of such truths to be that they are *true*, may well ponder over a section in this chapter headed 'Subjective and Objective'.

This section opened as follows:

> The Fundamental Antithesis of Philosophy of which I have to speak has been brought into great prominence in the writings of modern German philosophers, and has conspicuously formed the basis of their systems. They have indicated this antithesis by the terms *subjective* and *objective*. According to the technical language of old writers, a thing and its qualities are described as *subject* and *attributes*; and thus a man's faculties and acts are attributes of which he is the *subject*. The mind is the *subject* in which ideas inhere. Moreover, the man's faculties and acts are employed upon external *objects*; and from objects all his sensations arise. Hence the part of a man's knowledge which belongs to his own mind is *subjective*; that which flows in upon him from the world external to him is *objective*. And as in man's contemplation of Nature there is always some act of thought which depends

upon himself, and some matter of thought which is independent of him, there is in every part of his knowledge a subjective and an objective element. The combination of the two elements, the subjective or ideal, and the objective or observed is necessary in order to give us any insight into the laws of Nature. But different persons, according to their mental habits and constitution may be inclined to dwell by preference upon the one or the other of these two elements. It may perhaps interest the reader to see this difference of intellectual character illustrated in two eminent men of genius of modern times, Göthe and Schiller.

Göthe himself gives us the account to which I refer, in the history of the progress of his speculations concerning the metamorphosis of plants, a mode of viewing their structure by which he explained, in a very striking and beautiful manner, the relations of the different parts of a plant to each other, as has been narrated in the *History of the Inductive Sciences*. Göthe felt a delight in the passive contemplation of Nature, unmingled with the desire of reasoning and theorizing; a delight such as naturally belongs to those poets who merely embody the images which a fertile genius suggests, and do not mix with these pictures judgments and reflexions of their own. Schiller, on the other hand, both by his own strong feeling of the value of a moral purpose in poetry, and by his adoption of a system of metaphysics in which the subjective element was made very prominent, was well disposed to recognize fully the authority of ideas over external impressions.

Göthe for a time felt a degree of estrangement towards Schiller, arising from this contrariety in their views and characters. But on one occasion they fell into discussion on the study of natural history; and Göthe endeavoured to impress upon his companion his persuasion that Nature was to be considered not as composed of detached and incoherent parts, but as active and alive, and unfolding herself in each portion, in virtue of principles which pervade the whole. Schiller objected that no such view of the objects of natural history had been pointed out by observation, the only guide which natural historians recommended, and was disposed on this account to think the whole of their study narrow and shallow. 'Upon this,' says Göthe, 'I expounded to him, in as lively a way as I could the metamorphosis of plants, drawing on paper for him, as I proceeded a diagram to represent that general form of a plant which shows itself in so many and so various transformations. Schiller attended and understood; and accepting the explanation, he said, "This is not observation, but an idea." I replied,' adds Göthe, 'with some degree of irritation; for the point which separated us was most luminously marked by this expression: but I smothered my vexation, and merely said I was happy to find that I had got ideas without knowing it; nay, that I saw them before my eyes.' Göthe then goes on to say that he had been grieved to the very soul by maxims promulgated by Schiller that no observed fact ever could correspond with an idea. Since he himself loved best to wander in the domain of external observation, he had been led to look with repugnance and hostility upon anything which professed to depend upon ideas. 'Yet,' he observes, 'it occurred to me that if my observation was identical with his idea, there must be some common ground on which we might meet.' They went on with their mutual explanations, and became intimate and lasting friends. 'And thus,' adds the poet, 'by means of that mighty and interminable controversy between *object* and *subject*, we two concluded an alliance which remained unbroken, and produced much benefit to ourselves and others.'

The general diagram of a plant, of which Göthe here speaks, must have been a combination of lines and marks expressing the relations of position and equivalence among the elements of vegetable forms, by which so many of their resemblances and differences may be explained. We shall hereafter see, according to the phraseology which we shall explain in the next chapter, how such a diagram might express the *ideal conception* of a plant.

The antithesis of *subjective* and *objective* is very familiar in the philosophical literature of Germany and France. Nor is it uncommon in any age of our own literature . . .

The further 'books' in this first volume were headed: 'The Philosophy of the Pure Sciences', 'The Philosophy of the Mechanical Sciences', 'The Philosophy of the Secondary Mechanical Sciences', 'Of the Philosophy of the Mechanico-Chemical Sciences', 'The Philosophy of Chemistry', 'The Philosophy of Morphology, including Crystallography', 'The Philosophy of the Classificatory Sciences', 'The Philosophy of Biology' and 'The Philosophy of Palaetiology'.

The second volume had the general title 'Of Knowledge'. This had only three 'books', relatively larger in content. They were headed: 'Of the Construction of Science', 'Review of Opinions on the Nature of Knowledge, and the Method of Seeking it' and 'Of Methods Employed in the Formation of Science'.

Sur le Sommet des Cordilleras

The 46-year-old William Whewell sent a copy of *The Philosophy of the Inductive Sciences* to the 70-year-old Alexander von Humboldt. The latter replied:

A Sans Souci près Potsdam,
ce 14 Août, 1840.

Monsieur,

J'ai été extrêmement sensible, Monsieur, à l'honneur que vous m'avez fait de m'envoyer votre grand et important ouvrage de 'Philosophie des sciences

Alexander von Humboldt

> exactes'. Je n'ai pu mériter cette distinction que par la vive admiration que depuis bien des années j'ai marqué pour votre *History of the Inductive Sciences*. Je vous ai lu non dans la pâle traduction de M. Littrow, mais dans la langue dans laquelle on aime à lire ceux qui ont la puissance de la parole. Je savois que vous nous prépariez la jouissance d'un ouvrage philosophique propre à apprécier la sûreté des méthodes et la certitude sur laquelle reposent nos connoissances du monde intérieur; j'en avais parlé avec chaleur au Silurien M. Murchison, et comme nous respectons en lui, et dans l'excellent et respectable M. Sedgwick un ami commun, je suis tout satisfait de la bienveillance avec laquelle M. Murchison vous aura révélé la curiosité dont j'ai été tourmenté...

The reference was to the Scottish geologist Roderick Murchison, author in 1838 of a monograph on *The Silurian System*.

> ...J'aime à me rappeler de plus une soirée bien agréable que nous avons passée ensemble chez l'illustre Cuvier, dont l'esprit étoit plus logique que philosophique et qui blâmoit un peu trop tout ce qui tendoit au delà 'de mettre de l'ordre dans les idées'...

A fine characterization of the great French naturalist. Whewell was indeed an admirer of Cuvier, and Humboldt was gently advising the Englishman to keep his admiration in perspective.

> ... Vous ne me rendez pas justice, Monsieur, si vous craignez que j'appartienne à cette secte de mes compatriotes qui dédaignent Bacon et le trouvent un peu *rococo*. Je suis innocent de ce dédain et aucun de mes travaux (si toutefois ils en existent) montre de l'indifférence pour le *Novum Organum*. J'ai dû commencer par me justifier devant celui qui honore de nos jours par son nom le 'collège de Bacon et de Newton'. Quant à l'ensemble de votre vaste ouvrage, Monsieur, il m'est pour le moment impossible d'entrer dans des discussions partielles. Je vous écris ces lignes du haut d'une petite 'colline historique', dont le nom peut vous rappeler bien des distractions et des devoirs de position qui ne sont pas tout à fait littéraires. Je ne connois pas d'ouvrage depuis 10 ans qui excita à un plus haut degré mon vif intérêt. Les chapitres 'Philosophy of the Pure Sciences', la morphologie, les forces vitales (un des mythes nombreux de nos physiologies), la mer ténébreuse des traditions palaetiologiques que vous avez navigué avec une noble indépendance de l'esprit, les méthodes d'induction et le résumé historique que vous avez donné Vol. ii pp. 283 ... 469, m'ont offert des lectures pleines d'intérêt et de charme dans les jardins de Sans Souci! Après vous avoir suivi dans vos ingénieuses recherches sur les mouvements de l'océan, on aime à vous suivre à travers ces fluctuations de l'intelligence, variées selon l'espace et le temps et soumises cependant à des retours periodiques. Lorsqu'on voit les choses de si haut, comme vous Monsieur, on permet le doute à ceux, qui comme moi, ne savent que glaner dans les spécialités. Je n'ai encore vu votre grande composition que comme ces forêts vierges (sylvas sylvarum) dont on découvre la surface ondoyante lorsqu'on est placé sur le sommet des Cordilleras ...

The allusion in parentheses was to Bacon's natural history *Sylva Sylvarum*—published straight after the author's death in 1626 by his chaplain and literary executor William Rawley.

The associated geographical reference was to Humboldt's own travels across the Andean mountain-ranges during his explorations of South America at the beginning of the nineteenth century, and especially to his attempt to scale Mount Chimborazo in Ecuador, which on 23 June 1802 had taken him up to 18,000 feet, only 2000 feet from the cloud-capped summit.

> ... Je n'ai encore pu jouir que du coup d'oeil général, mais votre grand ouvrage m'accompagnera sous peu vers le nord, devant suivre le Roi à la prestation des hommages à Königsberg, où je trouverai deux savans illustres bien dignes de vous lire, M. Bessel et le grand géomètre M. Jacobi.
>
> Je saisis avec empressement cette occasion, Monsieur, pour vous renouveler l'hommage de ma haute et respectueuse considération.
>
> Le Bn. de Humboldt.

> Veuillez bien excuser mon écriture illegible. J'ai un bras malade des exhalaisons des forêts du Cassiguiaré.

The scholars referred to were teachers at Königsberg University: Friedrich Wilhelm Bessel, Professor of Astronomy, and Carl Gustav Jacob Jacobi, Professor of Mathematics.

So Humboldt, who must have noted the statement in Whewell's preface that he had 'adopted Kant's reasoning respecting the nature of space and time', was shortly taking this book up to the very town on the Baltic associated with that 'acute metaphysician' from whose views on other subjects Whewell 'differed widely'. It was in Königsberg, where Kant lived all his life from 1724 until 1804, that the edifice of Kantian philosophy was erected which then became so dominant in the whole of European thought.

Blest Reality

The translator into German of William Whewell's *History of the Inductive Sciences*, Joseph Johann von Littrow, died in Vienna on 30 November 1840, aged 59. His translation of the third volume of *Die Geschichte der Induktiven Wissenschaften* came out posthumously in 1841.

Another of Whewell's publications now rendered into German was his first textbook from 1819, *An Elementary Treatise on Mechanics*, which had since gone into six editions and been entirely rewritten. *Elementar-Lehrbuch der Mechanik* appeared in 1841 at Braunschweig. In England, meanwhile, Whewell was publishing a further tome on the subject, *Mechanics of Engineering*, described by one contemporary as 'a most useful and much-needed treatise on the practical application of mechanical principles to questions of construction and machinery'. It played an important part in popularizing a new approach to mechanics among working engineers.

Whewell presided at the meeting of the British Association held that year at Plymouth. In the course of his published *Address at the Opening of the British Association* he remarked that there was scarcely 'any subordinate office of labour or dignity' in the body which he had not discharged at one or other of its meetings.

★

Describing her uncle William Whewell, his niece Janet Stairs Douglas wrote:

> The same ardour which distinguished his intellectual temperament belonged in an even greater degree to his affections. They bound him with

filial fondness to his remote Lancashire home, to his family, to the picturesque town of Lancaster itself, to his old schoolmaster Joseph Rowley. They bound him with great tenacity and appreciative esteem to persons from whom he differed in opinion on almost every point. They bound him with most indulgent tenderness to younger relations who could contribute nothing but love and gratitude to the unequal friendship. And they bound him also with a loyalty and fidelity which no shock of disagreement, no strain of separation could permanently impair, to the 'friends of a lifetime', as he delighted to call Herschel, Jones, Sedgwick, Worsley, Peacock, Kenelm Digby, Airy, Henslow, Forbes and others, whose friendship he reckoned amongst the greatest blessings of his life.

In reminiscences of Whewell one of these named persons, Kenelm Digby, recorded:

> During our long friendship I never remember him speak unkindly of anyone behind his back, though he was free enough and bold enough spoken when he had you face to face. He was wonderfully fond of his friends, whom he never forgot. I remember his having made one of them sit for his picture to Lonsdale, and then his having given the portrait, which he paid for, to a third party, a mutual friend. But it would be endless to tell instances of his generous spirit. And in fact it was that no doubt which gained him the friendship of so many who were incompetent to profit by his extraordinary intellectual powers . . .

Whewell's relation to another of the named persons found expression in 1841 in a short work entitled *Two Introductory Lectures to two Courses of Lectures on Moral Philosophy*. It opened with a dedicatory letter:

TO THE
REVEREND THOMAS WORSLEY, M.A.
MASTER OF DOWNING COLLEGE

My dear Worsley,

I think you already know that in my opinion one of the greatest pleasures which the writing of books brings is that we may make them memorials of our most cherished friendships. The few pages now before you I have peculiar and paramount reasons for dedicating to you. It is through your kindness that I hold the Professorship in virtue of which these lectures were delivered; for the encouragement which you gave me when the vacancy occurred, you being as Vice-Chancellor one of the electors, principally induced me to offer myself as a candidate for the office. Yet the subject which the Professorship embraces was one which had occupied your own thoughts so much that the vacancy might readily have suggested other wishes to a person who thought more of himself and less of others. To yourself and the other excellent and valued friends who concurred in my election, my acknowledgments are due for the good opinion implied in your suffrages. As the present publication may serve to show, I have endeavoured to make the appointment effective towards the furtherance of the study of Moral Philosophy among us.

I reflect with the more pleasure on this act of kindness on your part, because it is only one among many manifestations of a friendship which it has been my happiness to enjoy during almost the whole course of my university life; which is still a constant source of gratification to me; and which will, I trust, never be interrupted.

With all cordial wishes believe me,

My dear Worsley,

Affectionately yours,

W. Whewell.

★

Not that the affections of William Whewell were confined to his own sex. For in June of this year, at the age of 47, he became engaged to Cordelia Marshall. One occasion related in verse describes them watching a summer sunset together from the summit of England's highest peak, the 3118 feet high Helvellyn.

As a love-token Cordelia sent her betrothed a braid of her hair. William, always a lover of words—he was in that year among the founders of the Philological Society—responded by a poem, in octosyllabics with alternate rhyme:

Beloved Cordelia, kind and dear,
And now my own while life endures,
Would you the wonted language hear
Of him whose every thought is yours?
In boyish days, in youthful hours,
And e'en in manhood's graver time,
He oft has gathered Fancy's flowers
And strung them in some idle rhyme.
And now a chain, of tresses wove,
Your earliest gift, behold is mine!
Your gift, your chain, your locks, my love,
May claim at least one little line.
And yet to give it meaning due
I need not ask Invention's aid;
Your own sweet fancies, bright and true,
May fitliest grace the simple braid.
You bid it say, our hopes, our vow,

The mutual trust 'tween you and me,
Are no past vision, vanisht now,
But firm and blest reality.
Such as your gift, your love, you own,
More truly strong than seeming fair;
Though shown to few, yet given to one
Who well may know that it is there.
Woven of that which tells a tale
Of emblematic mystery;
The woman's glory yet her veil;
Grace shrouding round her modesty;
Full many a fine weak-seeming hair,
Slight bonds, save in their mingled twine,
In settled order twisted there
Make up a strong enduring line.
And so it seems, my love, to you—
To you when Fancy loves to play—
That many a service slight to view,
Brief tasks of love from day to day,
Small duties, trials, charities,
In growing union, kindly strife,
Form love's most firm and lasting ties
And bind us heart to heart for life.
So be it. Hoping, trusting so,
Close to my heart your chain I wear;
And think the days and hours run slow
Till I may press the giver there.

W.W.

Trinity College: June 27, 1841

The days and hours may have run slow, but they ran nevertheless, and some four months later, on 12 October, William Whewell was finally married to Cordelia Marshall in the church at Watermillock, on the fellside above Ullswater in Cumberland.

The Drama of My Life

At this very point the Master of Trinity College Cambridge, the 67-year-old Christopher Wordsworth, decided to retire to a country living. On 12 October 1841—the same day when William Whewell and Cordelia Marshall were married in distant Cumberland—he announced his resignation as Master of the College.

The news was sent to Whewell, who was still on his honeymoon in the Lake District. The appointment to the Mastership lay in the gift of the monarch, and the Prime Minister, Robert Peel, had already heard enough about Whewell's abilities to have him put him forward for the post. So on 17 October—only five days after his wedding—Whewell received a request from Peel to accept nomination from the young Queen Victoria as Master of Trinity College. He accepted the next day.

Shortly afterwards, Whewell wrote to his sister:

> What you said about my appointment to the Mastership was most truly and rightly said. It is a very serious and solemn consideration to think that I am now about to take the position which I must occupy for the rest of my life, and that I have nothing better nor higher to wish or pray for than that I may have strength and virtue given me to discharge the duties of the office I am now to occupy, and may find my happiness in that employment and in the comfort of my married life. You will give me your prayers as well as your good wishes, and I shall go on hoping for the blessing of God through these and other good influences.

Whewell's tenure of the Mastership was indeed to last for the remainder of his life, almost 25 years. Although at first retaining his professorial chair and continuing to deliver lectures, he also became deeply engaged in both collegial and university administration. One commentator stated that

> . . . During his tenure of the mastership he was incomparably superior to any of the other heads of college, very few of whom had any reputation outside Cambridge, while none showed any intellectual power of at all the same order. Whewell's force of character, as well as his knowledge and ablities, soon gave him the most prominent position in the university . . .

And with regard to his own college, it may be noted that in March 1842, only five months after taking up his post, the new Master proposed to the governing body the erection in the college antechapel of a statue of Francis Bacon.

★

Whewell's new status at Cambridge University gave cause for celebration in his home town in the north. In September 1842 he and his childhood acquaintance Richard Owen were entertained at a public dinner given in their honour in Lancaster.

During his speech on this occasion the Master of Trinity referred to the polarity in his life formed by Lancaster and Cambridge:

> The early scenes of youth—the castle towers, the waters of the Lune—have haunted me when absent, and been a source of especial pleasure to me when

present. My heart has leaped up when I revisited them, with a delight wholly different from that which other scenes, not devoid of enjoyment, have brought to me. We owe to the early years of our boyhood influences which remain with us through all the years of succeeding life. The poet Wordsworth, with whom I have in the last few days had the advantage of associating, says

> The child is father of the man

and

> I could wish my days to be
> Bound each to each by natural piety.

So I feel that the boy is indeed the father of the man, that the early sympathies he may enjoy—the love of poetry among schoolfellows, the facilities he meets with in the prosecution of his favourite studies and pursuits—have more power than when his nature is more matured and his mind more expanded. His must be a hard nature indeed who does not feel this 'natural piety' on reverting to the scenes of his boyhood. I feel it with joy every week of my life. I am grateful to you for having now connected the past with the present—for having called up the days of boyhood with their charms of sunshine, and their thousand tender associations, and connected them with the experience of middle life, in a unity in which nothing is disjointed and incoherent.

In the drama of my life there are but two scenes—Lancaster and Cambridge; and the early scenes of Lancaster have been enhanced by the transition from one to the other. If ever a man had cause to love an English University it is I, who owe so much to one. To me has been given all that the mind of man could desire—the means of prosecuting studies which were the dream of my early youth, the opportunity of mingling with and enjoying the friendship of the greatest men and most lofty intellects of my time, at once the most modest and most profound thinkers, worthy representatives of the soul and mind of their age.

Natural Philosophy

The many details of William Whewell's administrative work at Cambridge University belong rather to that body's internal history. Here it may only be mentioned that during the academic year 1842–3 he held the post of Vice-Chancellor. In this capacity he had personal communication with Queen Victoria and her German husband Prince Albert, who together made a royal visit to Cambridge in 1843.

★

In the following summer of 1844 there took place another royal visit to Cambridge, but this time the royalty in question came from a foreign country. Frederick Augustus II, King of Saxony, was undertaking a tour of the whole of Britain, and included Cambridge in his itinerary.

The king was accompanied on this tour by his personal physician Carl Gustav Carus,[9] a prominent doctor and gynaecologist—previously Professor of Obstetrics at the Institute for Medicine and Surgery in Dresden.

Carus was also a pioneering Goetheanist, having published in 1843, just a year before this British tour, the book *Göthe: zu dessen näherem Verständnis*, which reproduced a series of Goethe's letters. Their correspondence had begun in 1818, when he had sent Goethe a copy of his *Lehrbuch der vergleichenden Zootomie*, a work with an epigraph taken from Goethe's hexametric poem 'The Metamorphosis of Plants':

> Alle Gestalten sind ähnlich und keine gleichet der andern
> Und so deutet das Chor auf ein geheimes Gesetz . . .

These very same lines were found 19 years later in the part of Goethe's poem translated into English hexameters by William Whewell in that footnote to the third volume of his *History of the Inductive Sciences*:

Carl Gustav Carus in 1844

All the forms resemble, yet none is the same as another;
Thus the whole of the throng points at a deep hidden law...

Although Carus actually met Goethe only once, on a visit to Weimar in 1821, their correspondence was continued until 1831, only a few months before Goethe's death in the following spring.

Another notable figure among the circle of Carus's friends was Ludwig Tieck. From 1824 onwards he had regularly attended Tieck's famous evening readings at the old market place in Dresden, and they still remained befriended after the poet's move to Potsdam in 1842.

★

Carus kept a detailed diary of the royal journey to Britain, which in 1845 he went on to publish as a book, *England und Schottland*—actually the tour included Wales as well—*im Jahre 1844*. Already in 1846 it was to appear in an English translation by S.C. Davison.

After a dedication to the king, the work opened with a preface, which *inter alia* stated:

> A reader must not expect here complete statistical notices, extensive geographical or historical descriptions, and still less far-reaching political reflections, but may in a certain sense take part in a journey favoured in every respect, through an important country favoured in every respect, and among so many persons who exercise a remarkable influence upon the history of our times.

The main text began by narrating the journey from Dresden to Belgium, where the royal party caught a ferry from Ostend taking them across the Channel.

Carus then interrupted the narrative of their journey with a chapter on 'England' which proceeded to give a general account of Britain. It described briefly the island's geography, climate, geology, botany, zoology, anthropology, architecture and general national character. Towards the end came this passage:

> ...Even the sciences are not in any way popular in and of themselves, and least of all in their freest researches and endeavours within the domain of more profound philosophical thinking, but are only cultivated...

Davison in his translation added: '...zealously and effectually...'

> ...in so far as they are useful to foster the immediate purposes of life. In England, *natural philosophy* is by no means the *Naturphilosophie* of the Germans, but consists of a combination of mathematics and physics, and is tolerated only as such, while every truth is decidedly repulsed which could

promote such free spiritual activity as might in the remotest degree interfere with or destroy any political or orthodox ecclesiastical rule.—By and by an incipient awakening even in England of a finer scientific trend regarding physiology and comparative anatomy will pave a little the way for a more general and truthful consideration of Nature. But it will still be a long time until this goal is attained.

★

King Frederick Augustus and his retinue landed at Dover and began their British tour by making their way westwards through the English countryside. They passed through various places described in detail by Carus, including Brighton, where they visited the Royal Pavilion, 'the most wonderful building which can possibly be conceived'. On reaching Southampton they boarded a train taking them up the recently built railway-line to London. Here they were met at the station by Prince Albert, who conducted them to Buckingham Palace and introduced them to the Queen.

The following days were spent in London, and included visits to the British Museum and also to the Hunterian Museum of the Royal College of Surgeons, where they were shown around by its curator, Professor Richard Owen, described as

> . . . a sensible, able man, deeply versed in what is old, and ready to receive what is new, who has with great propriety been recently characterized as the Cuvier of England.

They looked at the museum's exhibits and, according to Carus,

> . . . during the inspection of these objects, and our conversation about them, Cuvier was necessarily often present in our minds . . .

Owen took Carus to Regent's Park for a tour around the zoo, after which the latter hurried back to the Palace for royal dinner in company of the Tsar of Russia, the Duke of Wellington, and the Prime Minister Sir Robert Peel.

After a few days spent at Windsor and the Ascot races, the Saxon royal party soon came back again to London. There was sightseeing in plenty to places of interest: the Houses of Parliament, Westminster Abbey, the Haymarket, St Paul's, the Monument, a steamer trip on the Thames, Lambeth Palace, Kew Gardens, Hampton Court, the Tower, Goldsmith's Hall, the Mansion House, as well as visits to theatrical and operatic performances.

At the Royal Academy Carus saw exhibited

> ... some sea-pieces by J.M.W. Turner. If a brightly coloured sea-picture painted on a wax tablet were to be melted and the colours mixed up together, it would look somewhat like that! I would give something to know *how* this painter sees Nature, and what there is in his eyes which causes him to see Nature thus ...

Besides cultural attractions, Carus also viewed practical scenes of daily life. He attended a court case at the Old Bailey, and inspected the internal workings of the General Post Office. He visited both Bridewell and Pentonville Prisons, as well as five separate hospitals: Bethlehem, St George's, St Luke's, St Thomas's and Guy's. Together with the king he also drove out to the East End, where Brunel showed them the plans of the tunnel then being constructed under the Thames.

Although it is understandable that Owen, whom he visited three times, was the person Carus was most interested to meet, he was also introduced at a royal soirée to Sir John Herschel, and on another occasion

> ... found time to pay a visit to the excellent physicist Faraday, to whom we also in Germany are indebted for many teachings. I found in him a man of vitality, of middle size and a rather broad form of head corresponding to his knowledge. He received me with courtesy and vivacity ...

A Still Spirit of Knowledge

Having spent a fortnight in London, King Frederick Augustus and his retinue left the capital on the next stage of their tour around other parts of Britain. They first made their way north-east and visited Hatfield House.

At this point the account written by Carl Gustav Carus in the evening of 20 June 1844 continues:

> On rising from table we left at once, and drove through the village of Hatfield and across wide expanses of fields, under a continually brighter sky, through Stevenage towards Cambridge.
>
> It had become quite a cheerful and beautiful evening as we passed through the green parks surrounding the town. After the noise of the streets of London, it is pleasant to feel the quietness of a place of only 20,000 inhabitants. There seems to breathe around here a still spirit of knowledge!
>
> Immediately on entering one first passes a new and still not quite completed art museum in the style of a Greek temple, built from a bequest. (Besides his art collection, the legacy of Viscount Fitzwilliam, who died in 1816, amounted to the sum of £100,000 sterling.) Several old colleges next presented their grey walls with battlements and delicate Gothic turrets, and we could make out the slender Gothic church of St. Mary's. We drove

> through quiet streets, illumined by the evening sun, and arrived at last in Trinity College, the foremost and richest of the colleges. Here, ever since the time of Queen Elizabeth, monarchs on their travels have been accustomed to stay with the principal (the Master, at present Dr. Whewell).

William Whewell had in this very year been awarded the degree of Doctor of Divinity.

> Scarcely had we been shown our rooms than we were straightaway following our friendly host to obtain the clearest possible idea of the buildings and arrangements in this famous, old and remarkable teaching establishment. The whole spacious court of Trinity College, with its yellowish-coloured stone and lofty old Gothic architecture, produces a splendid effect. It was originally founded in 1546 by Henry VIII. (Cambridge is in general so old as to have been already once destroyed by the Danes in the 9th Century.) The college contains about 400 students. The gate especially is in beautiful style—lofty, castellated, with two turrets crowned with battlements . . .

Unlike his friendly host, Carus was not a mathematician. The number of turrets forming part of the Great Gate of Trinity College is actually four: one at each corner.

The Great Gate of Trinity College, Cambridge

> ... The adjacent buildings, which are only very little lower, harmonize with it admirably. A delicate Gothic fountain, in the open space within, makes the best of effects.
>
> The arrangement of these colleges is moreover very peculiar. There are no less than seventeen of them, of which the oldest, St. Peter's, was founded as early as 1257. In all, between 1,700 and 1,800 students reside within their walls. Each college has its own endowments and is governed in its own way, and through its teachers, called fellows, trains its young men in ancient languages, mathematics and theological morals, while all together may attend and actually do attend the lectures of university professors in separate faculties, according to their departments and their purposes in life.
>
> Actually it was vacation, and there were few students present. They all wear black gowns and mortar-boards, the fellows and masters a black robe (almost like our clergy) and black mortar-board, in form of a tasselated round cap sitting on the head, ending on top in a wide, flat, square cover. Between individual colleges there are supposed to be jealousies and squabbles, and I myself heard for instance that one of the fellows compared the relationship between Trinity and St John's to that between Athens and Sparta.
>
> We visited the gardens behind Trinity, and under some beautiful trees found the pretty, clear and wide course of the river Cam, which runs into the Ouse and connects Cambridge with the sea. It gives students here a splendid opportunity to practise punting and boat-racing, which are done with passion ...

In his English translation Davison proudly added '... and the young men become adepts in the art'.

> Then back into the college buildings, to view also the hall and library. The college is proud to have once had Newton among its fellows. A marble statue and a portrait of Newton ...

Davison has here '... a portrait of the great philosopher ...'

> ... are to be found in the hall, and various relics of his in the library. Some of his hair, manuscripts and instruments were exhibited, including the earliest and imperfect form of his refractor. Among the manuscripts there were also letters to Newton from foreign scholars, even a letter to him from Voltaire written in almost totally correct English. The college is no less proud of Bacon of Verulam, whose portrait hangs beside that of Newton; the naturalist John Ray, Dryden, Barrow and other notabilities of England were once students here, and Richard Bentley was once Master.
>
> Indeed the present Master, Dr. Whewell, is also a thoroughly educated man, and among other things so well versed in the German language as to have given his countrymen a fluent translation of *Hermann und Dorothea*, without being deterred by the difficulty of attempting English hexameters.

Through shortage of time, only few of the remarkable things in the library besides those mentioned could be examined. There is however a very old gospel-book, important for art history, with pictures in Byzantine mosaic-style. Waagen reckoned its date to the 8th Century. We were then shown some manuscripts of Milton—letters and so on. Most interesting was the first sketch of his *Paradise Lost*—and in the form of a drama.

But evening was advancing, and it was time to dress for dinner.

Sweet, Dry and Highly Baked

So on the evening of 20 June 1844 Carl Gustav Carus dressed for dinner at Trinity College Cambridge, and took his seat at table in the dining-room of the Master's Lodge.

His account continues:

> After the numerous state-dinners in London, this present one in a circle of scholars and some educated ladies gave me quite special refreshment. Master Whewell had invited several fellows, Dr. Paget, a physician, and Dr. Clark, the Professor of Anatomy . . .

George Edward Paget, Fellow of Caius College, was Physician at Addenbrooke's Hospital. William Clark, Fellow of Trinity (and former friend of Byron) was Professor of Anatomy, and author of an *Analysis of a Course of Lectures on the Anatomy and Physiology of the Human Body.*

> . . . The conversation was lively, and there was much which was original in the order of the meal itself. Here I first saw properly practised the system of serving customary in England at every smaller dinner, where several dishes are set out simultaneously and whoever has them in front of him offers them to other guests and helps them. For me, however, it was almost something Oriental when after the courses were all finished, a large silver bowl with rosewater and a big silver spoon were then set out and passed around over the tablecloth, allowing each person to take some onto a small saucer, so as to dip his napkin and clean his mouth . . .

In his English translation Davison said nothing about 'clean his mouth', but rather that the napkin was 'for the purpose of refreshing the face and hands'!

Be that as it may, Carus continued:

> . . . After this procedure the tablecloth was removed, and onto the middle of the beautiful polished table was placed a silver tree-shaped service, hung with all kinds of bowl filled with confectionery and the like. In addition there were dried fruits, fresh fruit, cakes and sugarwork.

> Among the cakes attention was especially drawn to a piece of the national bride-cake. It came from the wedding of the Master with his very agreeable lady, and was particularly sweet, dry and highly baked. They are often preserved for years, repeatedly brought out on festive occasions and a portion consumed.

The bride-cake of William and Cordelia Whewell, brought to Cambridge all the way from the Lake District, was by this time over two and a half years old.

> The ladies now withdrew, and Master Whewell took the seat of the lady of the house beside His Majesty the King. A small silver wagon with cut decanters filled with sherry and claret was put into circulation on the smooth table, always from right to left, allowing people to help themselves according to their pleasure. Finally the gentlemen too rose from table, followed the ladies into the drawing-room, and found in an adjoining room a sideboard with coffee and tea, so that a complete and genuine English dinner was then concluded.
>
> As I have said, I felt particular pleasure in being once again in the mere company of scholars, and all the more so on discovering that I was myself already quite well known here through my works. It was not only the doctors who had studied my physiology and comparative anatomy...

Carus was referring respectively to his *Von den Ur-Theilen des Knochen und Schalengerüstes* of 1828, and his *Lehrbuch der vergleichende Zootomie* of 1818 as headed with the Goethean epigraph.

> ...With a Mr. Worceley, a lively young man and fellow of Trinity, who knew these things quite well, I had at the same time opportunity to converse about other important literary publications...

About eight years younger than the 55-year-old Carus, Whewell's friend Thomas Worsley (b. 1797) was a former student but not a fellow of Trinity. He was Master of Downing College.

> ...He had for instance read Tieck's *Vittoria Accorombona*, and held it in high regard.

The reference was to a historical novel published by Tieck in 1840.

> Moreover, just as I was engaged in lively discussions with Paget and Clark about the nervous system and the stream of innervation, I was introduced to a second Carus.

This was William Carus, Fellow and Dean of Trinity College.

> He was a theologian—also a fellow—and had already been in the college for 17 years. I learned on this occasion that apparently several families of this

> name live in the north of England. Curiosity was expressed to hear how my name was pronounced—the English Carus is pronounced 'Käros'. Probably they too derive from Roman stock. Which of us descends from the Emperor Carus would be hard to determine. Perhaps I might sooner establish descent from the nature-poet Titus Lucretius Carus.
>
> We only separated quite late.

Despite the lateness of the hour, the German guest still wrote down that same evening, like a kind of *Rückschau*, this diary account of the day's events.

A More Festive Impression

Carl Gustav Carus composed the next instalment of his account, which described the happenings at Cambridge on June 21, during the evening of that day at the safe distance of Woburn Abbey:

> We lingered in Cambridge until midday, and I have experienced and seen there much which appears to me to proclaim the start of a fresher impulse in this otherwise also somewhat antiquated establishment. Means of study are not lacking: the place's quietness, the rejection of all plays, and the non-existence of factories and trade are very inviting to undisturbed work on one's own behalf. May the genuine spirit of free science more and more there throw off those chains which a Puritan theology still holds altogether very strictly drawn over England!
>
> In Master Whewell's house I witnessed a characteristic scene at the usual house service before breakfast. It is customary for the whole household to come together; all the servants enter as well and take their places on a row of seats by the windows. The master of the house sits down at a small table with Bible and prayer-book. He reads out a prayer and a couple of chapters from the Bible, and then, while everyone kneels down, a long long litany, corresponding in most of its parts to that of the Catholic Church!
>
> Everyone then rises up, the servants leave, and only now is served breakfast, which in England, as is known, is very rich and complex.
>
> To me the scene was interesting for *once*! As a matter of daily usage it must lose any effect, and presumes much time to spare!
>
> After breakfast Master Whewell escorted the king and us towards St. John's College, which contains about 300 students and has recently been rebuilt. Part of the buildings lie across the Cam, and a covered bridge, constructed entirely as a Gothic corridor with glass windows, connects the two buildings . . .

The tour continued to the University Library, and then to King's College, where the party visited the chapel. In his youth Carus had once made a drawing of this building after a copper-plate engraving, and inserted into his published account a sketch of the end-elevation.

On entering the chapel, the visitors were met by organ-tones, and sunlight streaming in through the stained-glass windows. They climbed one of the towers, and came out onto the roof.

> In the pure sunlight the view over the town with its many Gothic buildings and pleasant surroundings was very beautiful. The stone vault beneath us, the blue firmament—the highest dome—above us, and this wealth around, made a more festive impression on me than the litany of this morning!

From King's College they proceeded to the mineralogical and geological collection assembled by Whewell and Sedgwick (now the Sedgwick Museum of Geology), then housed in the Cockerill Building on King's Parade. Carus noted two large fossil exhibits: a giant deer (*Megaceros giganteus*) from Ireland, with an enormous antler-span, and a 'splendidly preserved' plesiosaur from Yorkshire, nine feet in length. He was also interested in the specimens of 'spiriferae' fossil shells.

After a walk around the new Botanical Garden created by Henslow, the party divided. The king went on to the Observatory, while Carus made his way to the museum of comparative and pathological anatomy. Here he found a specimen of *Graviditas uterotubaria*, a pathological preparation 'whose importance had till then completely escaped even Dr. Clark', and in his published account added a footnote about it. Maybe he showed particular interest in some skulls of savages, for he was presented with one of a New Zealander, which then accompanied him 'as an anatomical vademecum' on the rest of his British tour.

He rejoined the King for lunch at St Peter's College, after which they were soon on their way towards Woburn Abbey.

★

A few days later, on the 26th, Whewell wrote to his sister:

> You will have seen that we have had another royal visit, for I think Cordelia sent you the newspaper which contained the account of our receiving the King of Saxony. He came here *incognito*; that is, though everybody knew who he was and called him 'Your Majesty', he did not keep up the forms of royalty. He himself does not talk much, though he is very good-humoured and laughs readily. He brought with him a distinguished German physiologist, Dr. Carus, whom I introduced to our Mr. Carus. They were both amused at finding namesakes in foreign lands without any known connection.

A Noble Work of Art

In 1845 William Whewell's book *On the Principles of English University Education* was published in a German translation entitled *Über die Grundsätze der englischen Universitätsbildung*. One may perhaps wonder whether the German version was ever perused by Carl Gustav Carus.

Be that as it may, in the same year Whewell brought out a further work on the same subject, which—as if to contradict Carus's view that at Cambridge 'the free spirit of science' had to 'throw off the chains which a Puritan theology still holds altogether very strictly drawn over England'—was headed *Of a Liberal Education in General, with particular reference to the Leading Studies in the University of Cambridge.*

The work opened with a dedicatory letter:

TO
GEORGE BIDDELL AIRY, ESQUIRE
ASTRONOMER ROYAL

My dear Airy,

It gives me great pleasure to make the present volume the memorial of a long and valued friendship by dedicating it to you. But even without such a

George Biddell Airy

motive, I might fitly have placed your name in the front of my book on account of its subject; for though it is now several years since you were called from a sphere of academical to one of more direct national influence, we still enjoy the benefit, both in our scientific activity and in our educational methods, of the paths which you traced for us, and of the spirit which you diffused among us. I know too that you continue to take a lively interest in the proceedings and character of your ancient home. I will further add, as another reason for offering my reflections to you, that with regard to the kind of mathematical studies most suited to the University, and especially with regard to the destructive effect of mere analysis upon the mind, I know that your views agree with my own.

That you may long continue your noble career of scientific distinction and national usefulness is the hearty wish and prayer of

My dear Airy,

yours most truly,

W. Whewell.

Trinity Lodge,
Oct. 10, 1845.

Of a Liberal Education in General soon went into a second edition enlarged by a 'Part II', later supplemented by a 'Part III' published separately.

★

In his inaugural lecture of 1839 in the chair of Moral Philosophy, Whewell had expressed the hope of bringing before his hearers 'the results of a longer course of labour employed on this study'. These results were finally produced in 1845 in the form of a systematic textbook in two volumes, *Elements of Morality, including Polity*.

To counter the effect of a well-selling but controversial work on 'the natural history of creation' put out anonymously by a Scottish publisher, Whewell also assembled in the same year a small volume headed *Indications of the Creator*, which reprinted extracts of theological import from *The History* and *The Philosophy of the Inductive Sciences*.

★

Now on his visit to Trinity College in the previous year, Carl Gustav Carus learnt not only that Newton had once been among the Fellows, but also that 'the College is no less proud of Bacon of Verulam'. Almost certainly this reproduces a remark made to the German royal party by Whewell, who at the time was still awaiting completion of the statue of Bacon commissioned for the antechapel.

In 1845 the statue—an exact replica of the famous effigy erected over

Statue of Francis Bacon

Bacon's grave in St Michael's Church at Gorhambury by his former secretary Sir Thomas Meautys—was at last ready. It was positioned on the south side of the antechapel, towards the chapel end.

At the front of the pedestal is an inscription, composed by Whewell:

FRANCISCVS BACON
BARO DE VERVLAM Sti ALBANI VICECOMES
SEV NOTORIBVS TITVLIS
SCIENTIARVM LVMEN FACVNDÆ LEX
SIC SEDEBAT.
QVI POSTQVAM OMNIA NATVRALIS SAPIENTIÆ
ET CIVILIS ARCANA EVOLVISSET
NATVRÆ DECRETVM EXPLEVIT
COMPOSITA SOLVANTVR
ANo DNi M. DC. XXVI
ÆTATs LXVI

On the western side of the pedestal is a further inscription:

> FRANCISCUS Baro de Verulamio, Vicecomes Sancti Albani, percelebri collegio SANCTÆ et INDIVIDUÆ TRINITATIS in Cantabrigia salutem.
>
> RES omnes earumque progressus initiis suis debentur. Itaque cum initia

scientiarum e fontibus vestris hauserim, incrementa ipsarum vobis rependenda existimavi. Spero itidem fore, ut hæc nostra apud vos, tamquam in solo nativo, felicius succrescant. Quamobrem et vos hortor, ut salva animi modestia, et erga veteres reverentia, ipsi quoque scientiarum augmentis non desitis: verum ut post volumina sacra Dei et Scripturarum, secundo loco volumen illud magnum operum Dei et creaturarum, strenue et prae omnibus libris (qui pro commentariis tantum haberi debent) evolvatis. Valete.

A reader will recognize here Bacon's letter to the College as quoted in English translation in Whewell's sermon of 1828. The original letter is preserved to this day in the college library.

On the opposite, eastern side of the statue is a modest signature by the sculptor:

H. Weekes, SC.
1845

Underneath on the pedestal is another inscription:

POSVIT W. WHEWELL
COLLEGII HVJVS SS. TRINITATIS MAGISTER
A.D. M. DCCC. XLV.

★

Adam Sedgwick wrote to Whewell:

My dear Master,

The enclosed letter, though dated Nov. 1, only reached me on Wednesday evening, and I employ my first moment of leisure in complying, as far as I am able, with the united wishes of the resident Fellows of the College.

I may say with truth that a more delightful task could not have been imposed upon me, for I feel in common with every good member of the College that the noble monument with which you have adorned our chapel entitles you to our heartfelt thanks, and the expression of our deepest personal gratitude.

I am sure that you have given us credit for such sentiments, and it is in no hope of convincing you that we entertain them that we now address you; but we do so to satisfy our feelings, and to perform a positive duty we owe to ourselves and the College.

I have often longed to see a statue of Bacon erected in our chapel, and it is a matter of most honest and heartfelt exultation to see one now, worthy, as far as any sculptured stone can be, of that illustrious philosopher, given to us by one who has spent the best years of his life as our brother, who has drunk deeply from those fountains from which Bacon and Newton drew their strength, and whom Providence has placed at the head of this Society.

When the heart is full a few words will best tell its meaning, but I hope you will allow me to add a few words more on my own account. Let me then congratulate you on having so well completed an object you have long earnestly wished for. The statue you have erected is a noble work of art, combining as it does the severity of the old monument with the grace and freedom of more modern sculpture. It is in this respect worthy of a place by the side of our glorious statue of Newton. It represents Bacon as we may figure him to ourselves in his latter days, when he had fallen from his high worldly estate, and when his life was most truly great and glorious.

Our College history is our best inheritance. You, my dear Master, by your example, your great intellectual labours, and your munificence, have done your utmost to keep in our minds this goodly inheritance, and to make us worthy of it; and I trust that under Providence you will be permitted (to whatever station you may be called) to enjoy the happy fruits of your long-continued services in the great cause of sound academic learning.

It delights us all to think that there is a moral fitness in having the sculptured figures of Bacon and Newton in our house of daily prayer; one represented in the repose of philosophic age, the other in the vigour of life, gazing towards the heavens under the inspiration of some great discovery.

The philosophic labours of these men were not carried on to exalt themselves; they bowed before a power above all material nature, and they had an aim far above this world's knowledge and all the honours it could bring them. They laboured honestly to erect a rich storehouse at once to the glory of the Creator, and the good of the human race. It is a high privilege to have contributed as you have done to keep alive such remembrances as these, both among the older and the younger members of our Society. And I trust that the sobering as well as the exalting influence of these sentiments will continue to be felt among us and those who follow us so long as England shall last as a nation, and its institutions and monuments be the admiration of wise and good men. Pray accept the expression, however feeble, of my hearty goodwill and gratitude, and believe me, my dear Master,

Affectionately and gratefully yours,

Adam Sedgwick,
Vice-Master

Whewell replied:

Trinity Lodge
Nov. 8, 1845.

My dear Vice-Master,

I have to acknowledge a letter which you have sent me, addressed to you by the resident Fellows, and a letter from yourself, both of them containing expressions most gratifying to me relative to the statue of Bacon which has recently been placed in the antechapel. The acknowledgement of my share

William Whewell in 1845, aged 50

in this work, and the accompanying expressions of goodwill both from yourself and from them are deeply grateful to my feelings, but are, I fear, beyond my just merits, as they certainly are far beyond my highest expectations. I look upon myself as having had a great privilege conferred upon me in being allowed to erect the statue of Bacon near the place where my predecessor erected the statue of Newton. It has long been one of my heart's desires to see such a memorial among us; and when I was placed by Providence in a situation which seemed to justify me in asking to be allowed to fulfil this desire, I did not delay to do so. I feel grateful to yourself and to the other Seniors for indulging me in this matter.

In executing the design I could not hope to obtain a work of art which could rival the noble monument already erected; although if my lamented friend Chantrey had lived to whom I had already mentioned my hopes, we should have seen what the power of genius so inspired could do. But I trust that Mr. Weekes's work, borrowing interest, in addition to its own merits, from the resemblance which the philosopher's friends and disciples loved to dwell upon and to perpetuate, and from the burial-place which he himself selected, may always be looked upon with satisfaction. I hope, too, it may serve to keep alive among us and among our successors who worship in that edifice the spirit and the sentiments you, Mr. Vice-Master, so well describe:

the spirit of a vigorous yet reverent philosophy, the sentiment of gratitude for the great and good men who have adorned our land. And I trust that by God's blessing upon such dispositions, the College may continue to prosper and flourish in our time, and for long ages after us.

For myself, Mr. Vice-Master, I will only thank you and the other Fellows in whose name you have spoken; and I thank you from the bottom of my heart for your kind expressions and good wishes. I beg you to believe that I am deeply grateful for this your kindness, and I wish to each of you all happiness and all blessings, both while each of you continues a member of our family, and after he may have been called to other conditions. I am, my dear Mr. Vice-Master,

Your faithful and obliged friend and servant,

W. Whewell

And from this time onward for the remaining 21 years of his life, whenever he entered the college chapel to go to a service, or came out again from the chapel when the service was over, Whewell would have passed by—and no doubt gazed proudly upon—this statue he had erected of Francis Bacon.

True to the Tones of the Heart

In 1846 William Whewell brought out a second impression of his *Indications of the Creator*, which also appeared in German as *Spuren der Gottheit.* Besides editing in the original Latin the first three sections of Newton's *Principia*, with explanatory notes and references, he also published a study on *Conic Sections, their Principal Properties Proved Geometrically*—later reissued in improved editions—as well as a volume of *Lectures on Systematic Morality* complementing his previous textbook.

In 1847 he republished in revised editions both *The History* and *The Philosophy of the Inductive Sciences.* The former now included references, sometimes appreciative but at other times dissenting, to the notes by 'my accomplished German translator, Littrow'.

Such publications did not lessen Whewell's continued involvement in the regular course of university affairs. When in that year the chancellorship of Cambridge University fell vacant, it was he who proposed the election of Prince Albert, which was successfully accomplished.

⋆

Another book which Whewell assembled in 1847 was a collection of 22 of his own *Sermons preached in the Chapel of Trinity College, Cambridge.* It opened with a dedicatory letter:

TO THE
REVEREND WILLIAM CARUS, M.A.,
SENIOR DEAN OF TRINITY COLLEGE

My Dear Dean,

There is no-one to whom I can dedicate these sermons with so much propriety as to you. You were present at most or all of the occasions on which they were delivered; and if there be in them any thoughts and words suited to those occasions, no-one will appreciate such passages more quickly and more kindly than you will do.

I rejoice to think that these sermons, delivered in our college chapel, are likely to call up in your mind gratifying and thankful recollections of the devout demeanour of the congregation, and of the religious thoughtfulness which, so far as the human eye can judge, all, young and old alike, bring to such acts of worship. I know how much you have always had such a result at heart; and I know that, like myself, you look back upon the long course of improvement in such matters which we have witnessed, and have perpetually endeavoured to forward, with feelings of gratitude to God, and of hope for His further blessing on our ordinances and institutions.

We are now, my dear Dean, very old fellow-labourers in the service of our beloved College; and I rejoice to have an opportunity of expressing to you my gratitude—a feeling in which the whole College shares—for your unwearied exertions in the promotion of piety, virtue and sound learning among us.

That you may long enjoy the satisfaction of seeing us make still further progress in those respects is the earnest wish and prayer of one who is,

My dear Dean,

Your affectionate Friend

W. Whewell

Among the sermons in the volume was that preached on Commemoration Day 19 years previously, 17 December 1828.

⋆

During this same year 1847 Whewell brought out three further publications, in the field of poetry. One was a collection of his *Sunday Thoughts, and other Verses*. The title came from an opening series of poems on religious subjects. Also included were the prize-winning *Boadicea*, the *Nugae Bartlovianae* (with a supplementary eclogue headed 'Nugarum Bartlovianarum Epilogus'), the *Isle of the Sirens*, and other pieces in varying styles composed on divers occasions down the years, together with translations of 33 fables from a German collection.

⋆

The second was a volume of his *Verse Translations from the German*, which presented renderings of lyrical and narrative poems by Bürger, Schiller and Goethe. A preface, written on 23 April—St George's Day—began:

> English admirers of German poetry cannot help requiring that translations of their favourite poems should unite several very various merits. The relation of the two languages and of their literature naturally suggests this expectation: for the languages have the same original stock, the same rhythm, in a great measure the same familiar constructions; and modern German poets have caught their style and manner (except in their hexameters and elegiacs) from the same models as the English. No translation of a German poem into English quite satisfies us which does not present to us all that the original contains, and no more, with a similar character of style, a similar movement of versification, and along with all this, a freedom of expression as complete as if it were not a translation, but an original.
>
> These are severe requirements, and it is not hoped that they are attained in the following attempts. But that we cannot help looking for such translations is a reason why new attempts of this kind may be received with indulgence . . .

The poems were in differing metrical forms corresponding more or less to those of the originals, extracts from some of which were also included in historical notes at the back.

★

The third was an anthology of *English Hexameter Translations from Schiller, Goethe, Homer, Callinus and Meleager*, of which Whewell was the unnamed editor.[10] This work opened with an editorial note:

> The following English hexameters and elegiacs have been written by several persons, and at various times; and there are therefore probably some discrepancies in the versification of various parts. It is believed, however, that these are slight; for all the pieces are executed with the intention that the lines, being read according to the natural and ordinary pronunciation, shall run into accentual hexameters or pentameters. If this point be gained, such verses may be no less acceptable to the English than they have long been to the German poetical ear, and may be found suited, in our language, as well as in its sister speech, to the most earnest and elevated kinds of poetry.
>
> To some of the translations the original is appended, both to give a scale of their fidelity (for the others are no less faithful) and also to suggest the tone of classical compactness and purity at which this kind of verse ought to aim. In other pieces the original has been omitted; and the reader will thus be better able to judge whether these essays have any of the charm of poetry, besides that which their closeness to the beautiful originals reflects upon them.

A list of contents gave beside each piece the initials of its translator. It began with poems from Schiller: 'The Walk', J.F.W.H.; 'The Dance', W.W.; 'The Sexes', W.W.; 'Epigrammata: Columbus', W.W.; 'Odysseus', W.W.; 'Further Epigrammata', J.C.H. Then came a list of poems from Goethe: 'Herman and Dorothea', W.W.; three poems rendered by J.C.H.; and 'The Metamorphosis of Plants', W.W.

These initials are recognizable as those of John F.W. Herschel, William Whewell and Julius C. Hare. Passages from Homeric epics and some poems from Callinus and Meleager were initialled by other translators.

After the list of contents, and on a page of its own heading the whole anthology, was an anonymous epigraph in elegiacs (alternating hexameters and pentameters):

> Art thou a lover of Song? Would'st fain have an utterance found it
> True to the ancient flow, true to the tones of the heart,
> Free from the fashions of speech which tinsel the lines of our rhymesters?
> Lend us thy listening ear: lend us thy favouring voice.

All poems by Schiller were printed in both German original and English translation. For those by Goethe, 'Herman and Dorothea' reproduced only Whewell's English rendering, but the rest were also in original and translation on facing pages. 'The Metamorphosis of Plants', the opening of which had already appeared in that footnote to the third volume of *The History of the Inductive Sciences*, was now both presented and translated in its entirety.

All the Rich Wealth of the World

Towards the end of 1847 William Whewell resumed once again his foreign travels, making in December a further visit to Paris.

In 1848 he was responsible for creating triposes at Cambridge University in both the Moral and Natural Sciences. His continued engagement in each of these fields received further expession in 1849 when he edited *Six Sermons on Moral Subjects* by the eighteenth-century theologian Joseph Butler, and also published a work of his own replying to an attack on his scientific opinions made some years previously by John Stuart Mill: *Of Induction, with special reference to Mr. J.S. Mill's 'System of Logic'.*

★

By this time Whewell had conceived the idea of founding at Cambridge a chair of International Law, as well as scholarships on this subject. To realize such a project, however, funds had to be raised for an endowment. As Master of Trinity College he himself received a good income, while his wife Cordelia was in her own right well off. In 1849, noticing some properties for sale opposite the Great Gate of Trinity—whose four turrets had been miscounted by Carl Gustav Carus—they bought the properties themselves, and gifted them to the college.

Whewell hoped that in due course Trinity College would be able to erect on the acquired site a new building for students, the rents of which could then be devoted to the intended endowment. He laid this plan before the college, and over the following years made various proposals about it.

⋆

In the summer of 1849 the Whewells crossed over to the Continent, where William was being made an Associate of the Académie Royale de Belgique. The main reason for this journey was however that Cordelia's health was starting to decline, and proceeding into Germany they made for the spa at Bad Kreuznach, south-west from Mainz. William himself went on an excursion downstream to revisit Cologne Cathedral, described in a letter to his sister as 'the finest building in the world'.

In the next year, 1850, the Whewells made another visit to Bad Kreuznach and, leaving Cordelia to take the waters, William travelled further south into Switzerland. He took with him a book which he had probably just come across. It was the second volume, published in 1849, of the *Schwarzwälder Dorfgeschichten* by Berthold Auerbach—the very writer to whose *Volkskalender* Edmund Reitlinger was later to contribute various articles, and who was to give him in 1874 the title for his article 'Into the Interior of Nature'!

Whewell must have enjoyed reading one story in Auerbach's collection called 'Die Frau Professorin', for he decided to translate it into English. Several pages of his version were completed in the mountain hotel on the summit of the Faulhorn, east of Interlaken, at a height of 8000 feet—looking out over the glorious panorama of the Bernese Alps.

When *The Professor's Wife* by Auerbach was published in England within that same year, its translator's name was not given. But there was no anonymity in the following year in Switzerland about Whewell's election to the Societas Naturae Scrutatorum Helvetorum.

⋆

One of the foremost achievements of Queen Victoria's husband Prince Albert was the part he played in organizing the Great Exhibition of 1851 held in London in the Crystal Palace erected for the occasion over nearly 20 acres of Hyde Park. Prominent British scientists of the time, such as Michael Faraday, Sir John Herschel and Richard Owen, were also involved in the preparations.

The exhibition was visited by several million people (including for instance Charles and Emma Darwin and their family, numbering by this time six children).[11] There were literally miles of stands, the eastern half of the Palace being filled with sumptuous displays from foreign countries, and the western half with products from Britain and the Empire, both artistic objects as well as the latest scientific and technological inventions.

At the close of the Exhibition in November, an inaugural lecture for a course at Cambridge University was given at Prince Albert's suggestion by the Master of Trinity College. Published as *The General Bearing of the Great Exhibition on the Progress of Art and Science*, it attempted to draw out the most valuable lessons derived from the Exhibition by contrasting the case of a traveller who spent his life examining the arts in various countries of the world with the inspection of the whole simultaneously which the Exhibition had rendered practicable.

★

Another work brought out by Whewell in 1851 was an edition of *Praelectiones Decem* by the seventeenth-century casuist Robert Sanderson, with notes and an abridged translation. A related volume in 1852 presented Whewell's own *Lectures on the History of Moral Philosophy*. Meanwhile,

William Whewell in 1851, aged 56

another controversy with a contemporary philosopher, Henry Mansel, inspired Whewell to compose *A Letter to the Author of Prolegomena Logica.*

Many years previously Whewell's friends Julius Charles Hare and Connop Thirlwall had brought out an English version of the first two volumes of Niebhur's *Römische Geschichte.* This was followed in 1852 by a translation of the biographical study *Lebensnachrichten über Barthold Georg Niebuhr.* Ancillary material assembled in the volume included an essay by Niebhur on the history of Rome, with a couple of footnotes reproducing medieval Latin elegies. To provide English renderings for these verses, the translator, Susanna Winkworth, approached Whewell, who duly turned them into suitable elegiacs.

Here is Whewell's version of a twelfth-century elegy by Hildebert of Mans:

Rome! even now unequall'd, ev'n now, when beheld as a ruin:
  Here in thy fragments we see how thou wast great as a whole.
Time has humbled thy pomps, and levell'd the walls of thy Caesars,
  Yea, and the fanes of thy gods cumber the slimy morass.
Fallen are the works of thy power, the works on which distant Araxes
  Trembled to gaze as they stood, mourns to reflect in their fall...
Weigh we now thy treasures, thy leaders, thy fame and thy fortunes,
  All the bright glories of art, all the rich wealth of the world;
Weigh we this, and then say—but what can we say that is worthy?
  What can we say but this—Rome was, and this now is Rome!
But not even long ages, nor flame, nor the swords of thy foemen,
  Quite have availed to destroy, quite to extinguish thy grace.
So much is left, so much still falling, that man is unable
  That to match which remains, that to restore which is gone...
Thus the labours of ages have raised a Rome which may not be
  (Made by the hands of men), marr'd by the pow'r of the gods.
Here the forms of celestials, celestials marvel to gaze at,
  Yea, they would willingly be such as they see themselves here.
Nature herself is poor to produce a presence so godlike,
  Such a presence as here sprang from thy formative hand;
Such a presence as draws devotion, which follows and worships
  Rather the art so divine, than the divinity's self.
Happy thou as a city, if either now were thy masters,
  Or if thy masters could know that it is base to deceive.

Our Paths and our Portions

In the summer of 1852 William and Cordelia Whewell travelled once again over to Germany. Cordelia stayed as before at Bad Kreuznach, while

William went on to Berlin. On returning to Kreuznach, he wrote to his sister on 7 August:

> I have just returned from an excursion to Berlin, where I have not been since, I think, 1825. The railroads now make that an easy and short journey which used to be a long and laborious one. I was there for a week, and saw several persons whom I was very glad to meet, especially some old friends. Of the persons I was with there whom you will care most to hear about are Ranke,[12] who wrote the *History of the Popes*, and Humboldt, the great traveller, whom I had often before seen, and who was friendly enough to come all the way from Potsdam, an hour by railway, to see me, though he is eighty-two at least.
>
> Berlin is grown to be a very fine city since I saw it, and I should think is now next in splendour to London and Paris.

★

In 1853 Whewell brought out an edition in three volumes of the legal treatise *De Jure Belli et Pacis* by Hugo Grotius, with an English translation.

After consulting literary friends he also published a carefully composed 'essay', written in the previous year at Bad Kreuznach, *Of the Plurality of Worlds*. This proved quite a success, already reappearing in 1854 in an enlarged edition, which later went into two further impressions—all of them, like the first edition, anonymous.

Among those who knew the author's identity was the now 84-year-old Alexander von Humboldt, who on receiving a copy sent Whewell a letter of thanks from Berlin, dated 21 February 1854:

> Je ne saurois vous exprimer assez vivement, Monsieur illustre ami, combien j'ai été touché de votre aimable souvenir en m'adressant, signé de votre main, l'important ouvrage sur La Pluralité des Mondes. Vous avez attaqué, avec cette puissance que donne une vaste étendue de connoissances et cette sagacité dans les vues dont brille votre admirable Histoire des Sciences Inductives, un problème souvent dénaturé. On l'a rendu presque dangeureux à traiter, en craignant d'empiéter sur la liberté d'une imagination toute poétique ou de mêler trop directement à la discussion des intérêts élevés de la religion positive. Je tiens beaucoup aux premières impressions d'une lecture rapide mais pourtant très instructive. Tout ce qui a rapport au système solaire et aux nébuleuses est rempli d'idées grandioses et souvent très neuves. L'aperçu géologique, 'The Theory of the Solar System', le 11me et surtout le 12me chapitre, 'Unity of the World', m'ont paru pleins d'attraits. C'est un désir bien doux à remplir que de vous offrir, Monsieur, le respectueux hommage de ma reconnaissance . . .

★

(top) Faraday at work in the Chemical Laboratory; (bottom) Faraday lecturing at the Royal Institution in 1855

In the spring of that year the Royal Institution organized a lecture series in London where Michael Faraday spoke 'On Mental Education' and Whewell 'On the Influence of the History of Science upon Intellectual Education'. The latter also published a related work *On the Material Aids of Education*.

In 1855, after 17 years in the post, Whewell finally retired from the chair of Moral Philosophy at Cambridge University, but served again as Vice-Chancellor in 1855–6. During this time he made a further visit to Paris.

★

At the beginning of 1855 two long-standing friends passed away. Julius Charles Hare died on 23 January, Richard Jones just three days later, on the 26th.

And towards the end of the year, Whewell suffered an even closer loss with the death on 18 December of his own wife Cordelia. Soon afterwards, he composed a series of eleven poems, printed privately under the simple title *Elegiacs*. One copy was sent to a friend with an accompanying letter, stating:

> You will not be surprised that I have had a desire to put some of my memories of my beloved one in a distinct form. I think that the kind of verse I send you is best for the purpose. It enables the writer to shake off entirely the encumbrance of poetical phraseology and the vagueness of conventional modes of presentation of thought, and is, to my feelings, as earnest as prose can be, while many of the things said derive force from the symmetry of structure which this kind of composition favours. Whether this may be so for others I cannot tell; but I can say for myself that I could not have written what I have written more solemnly and earnestly in any other form.

Here is a passage from the opening poem, 'The First Sabbath after the Burial':

> Blessed beyond all blessings that life can embrace in its circle,
>   Blessed the gift was when Providence gave me to thee:
> Gave thee, gentle and kindly and wise, calm, clear-seeing, thoughtful,
>   Thee to me as I was, vehement, passionate, blind;
> Gave me to see in thee, and wonder I never had seen it,
>   Wisdom that shines in the heart clearer than intellect's light:
> Wisdom that sees its way to the good so simply and clearly
>   That it might seem to be skill, only that skill is too blind:
> Gave me to find in thee, when oppressed by loneliness' burden,
>   Solace for each dull pain, calm from the strife of the storm.
> For O, vainly till then had I sought for peace and contentment,
>   Ever pursued by desires—yearnings that could not be stilled;
> Ever pursued by desires of a heart's companionship, ever
>   Yearning for guidance and love such as I found them in thee.
> Vainly till then had I mov'd in the cities of men with their millions,
>   All was solitude still, all was a waste to the soul;
> Vainly till then had I roved the land from mansion to mansion,
>   Pleasure and kindness I found; found not the love that I sought.

Vainly had I explored the long-flowing river of Science,
   Back to its fountain-heads, down to its glittering sea;
Vainly had striven with the Sphinx of Philosophy, reading her riddles,
   Bidding her mark me the path up to the cavern of Truth.
Vainly had wandered oft in the flowery fields of the Muses;
   They stirred up in the breast thoughts that they could not appease.
Vain, to bring the heart's peace, even prayer and loftiest musing;
   Prayer and musing had oft need of a sympathy's charm.
E'en on the Sabbath the trouble return'd with a drearier anguish;
   Lonely the Sabbath was then. Lonely again it is now!
Devious while thus was I driv'n by the blasts of an objectless craving,
   Blind, while vain of my sight; shallow, though proud of my depth;
Found I in thy clear eyes the lode-star, the mark of my wand'ring,
   Found I in thy serene bosom my haven of rest.
Golden then was the calm that soothed the storm of my being,
   Golden then was the light shed on the gloom of my soul...

After further passages describing in turn their initial seven years of married happiness, and the next seven years of increasing anxiety as Cordelia's illness first became apparent and then gradually worsened, the poem ended:

Ever by me be remember'd the words that cheer'd thy departure,
   Cheer'd thee utterèd then, utterèd often before:
'Grant, O Lord, that as we are buried with Thee in our baptism,'
   —When Death over her hung this was the pray'r that she pray'd—
'So through the grave, the Gate of Death, we may pass to our rising,
   Ris'n to a joyfuller life—Thy Resurrection may share.'
And so passed away the blessed soul to her Maker;
   Passed away to her God; follow'd her Saviour's path.
Thus we parted. Diverse, how far! our paths and our portions,
   She to the Saviour's embrace, I to the wearisome world.
I to the wearisome world, to toil all lonely and helpless,
   Yet not lonely quite, her since I bear in my heart:
Yet not helpless quite, for thy companionship, dear one!
   Still shall lend me its help, guiding and raising me still.
And if spirits of the just made perfect, and hov'ring as angels,
   Still may watch o'er our ways, bending benignant their eyes,
Haunt me and soothe me daily, O gentle spirit, till *I* may
   Rising from this dead world, live in The Presence with *thee*.

In Later Years

In mid-December of 1856 William Whewell embarked again on a ferry crossing over the Channel, and after reaching France travelled south to

Marseilles, where he took another ferry down the Italian coast as far as Civitavecchia. He then completed by land the remainder of his journey, arriving in Rome at 9 p.m. on Christmas Eve. Making his way through the darkened city towards St Peter's and the adjacent Vatican, he was able to attend midnight service in the Sistine Chapel.

The source of this information is a letter to a friend. The deceased Cordelia was not mentioned in the letter, but a reader may nonetheless reflect that the first anniversary of her death had taken place just one week previously. And it was 17 years since William had last set foot in Italy, before his marriage.

He stayed on in Rome throughout the Holy Nights and indeed until the middle of January. Naturally he viewed many of the sights extolled in the poem by Hildebert of Mans which he had rendered into English elegiacs four years previously. Although nearing the age of 63, he also spent his time improving his knowledge of Italian, 'taking lessons and writing exercises like the veriest schoolboy'. The return journey northwards took him overland via Siena and Florence, with visits in both towns to the picture galleries.

His niece later stated:

> The visit to Rome restored Dr. Whewell to a far greater degree of cheerfulness than he had been able previously to attain, and he always afterwards enjoyed recurring to the memories connected with that time. It had revived his interest in many subjects which had engaged his attention in past years, and it showed him, by the enjoyment with which he turned to fresh ones, that elasticity of mind was not gone.

★

In 1857, Whewell was elected Correspondent in the department of Moral and Political Sciences of the Académie Française, and also an Honorary Member of the Kaiser-königliche Geographische Gesellschaft in Vienna.

He brought out a third enlarged edition of the three-volumed *History of the Inductive Sciences*, later reprinted in America. He also revised the two-volumed *Philosophy of the Inductive Sciences*, expanding it so much that it was redesigned in three volumes as well. These were now published individually under new titles, with the previous title retained as a common subtitle. The first two volumes appeared in 1858, comprising the original first volume, re-titled *The History of Scientific Ideas*, and the first and third 'books' in the original second volume together with their sets of aphorisms, under the quasi-Baconian title *Novum Organon Renovatum*.

★

The *Dictionary of National Biography* describes Whewell at this time:

> In later years, age made him conspicuously milder, and the object not only of the pride but of the warm affection of the university. Though rough at times, he was from the first magnanimous. He never cherished resentment and admitted defeat frankly, and received the opinions of young and insignificant persons with remarkable courtesy. Few men, too, have had more friends, or retained their friendships more carefully. He had many controversies, but no personal quarrels. His domestic life was perfect, and he always respected and attracted women.

On 1 July 1858, some two and a half years into his widowhood, William married for a second time. His new bride, Everina, was the sister of Robert Leslie Ellis—Fellow of Trinity and co-editor of a Victorian edition of the *Works* of Francis Bacon—and widow of Sir Gilbert Affleck, and continued even after her remarriage to be called Lady Affleck. She was described as 'a lady whose sweet disposition and engaging manners rendered her universally beloved'.

For both widowed partners this second marriage was thoroughly happy.

⋆

During that same year Whewell of course travelled up to Linconshire to represent Trinity College at the unveiling of the bronze statue of Isaac Newton on St Peter's Hill in Grantham, the town where the famous scientist had once attended the Grammar School.

And in Trinity College itself Whewell celebrated another long-deceased luminary. Alongside the statue of Francis Bacon on the south side of the antechapel he erected another statue, this time of Isaac Barrow, Newton's teacher and later Master of the College. For the pedestal he composed another laudatory Latin inscription.

⋆

In 1859 Whewell brought out as a posthumous tribute the *Literary Remains* of his deceased friend Richard Jones.

He also began on a trilogy of translations from Ancient Greek, *Platonic Dialogues for English Readers*, the first volume of which was published that year. It had the subtitle 'Dialogues of the Socratic School, and Dialogues referring to the Trial and Death of Socrates'. The former comprised *Laches*, *Charmides*, *Lysis*, *The Rivals*, *First Alcibiades*, *Second Alcibiades*, *Theages* and *Clitophon*, and the latter *Meno*, *Euthyphro*, *The Apology*, *Crito* and *Phaedo*. These translations were interlinked with substantial commentary.

⋆

Whewell's plan that Trinity College should erect on the land gifted by himself and his first wife a building for students which would serve to endow a chair of International Law had not in the interim moved any further. On her death in 1855 Cordelia Whewell left in her will a large sum of money to be applied according to her husband's directions for the benefit of the college, and William had devoted its income to the augmentation of small livings. But he and Lady Affleck, who in her turn was also quite wealthy, now further resolved to carry out the plan of erecting a new 'hostel for students' at their own personal expense. The college accepted this proposition, and thus in 1859 a whole quadrangle began to be erected on the previously donated site. It was completed in the following year, and immediately occupied.

With More Pain Than Pleasure

Meanwhile, in late 1859, Charles Darwin finally brought out *The Origin of Species*.

At the front of this work, opposite the title page, was a facing page presenting two epigraphs:

> 'But with regard to the material world, we can at least go so far as this—we can perceive that events are brought about not by insulated interpositions of Divine power, exerted in each particular case, but by the establishment of general laws.'
>
> W. WHEWELL: *Bridgewater Treatise.*
>
> 'To conclude, therefore, let no man out of a weak conceit of sobriety, or an ill-applied moderation, think or maintain that a man can search too far or be too well studied in the book of God's word, or in the book of God's works; divinity or philosophy; but rather let men endeavour an endless progress or proficience in both.'
>
> BACON: *Advancement of Learning.*

Down, Bromley, Kent.
October 1st, 1859.

The book was published in London on 24 November.

Exactly one month later, on 24 December—Christmas Eve!—Adam Sedgwick wrote from Cambridge a lengthy letter to Darwin condemning the work. Here is the main passage:

If I did not think you a good-tempered and truth-loving man, I should not tell you that (spite of the great knowledge, store of facts, capital views of the correlation of the various parts of organic Nature, admirable hints about the diffusion, through wide regions, of many related organic beings, &c, &c.) I have read your book with more pain than pleasure. Parts of it I admired greatly. Parts I laughed at till my sides were almost sore. Other parts I read with absolute sorrow, because I think them utterly false and grievously mischievous. You have deserted—after a start in that tram-road of all solid physical truth—the true method of induction, and started us in machinery as wild, I think, as Bishop Wilkins's locomotive that was to sail with us to the Moon. Many of your wide conclusions are based upon assumptions which can neither be proved nor disproved. Why then express them in the language and arrangement of philosophical induction? As to your grand principle—natural selection—what is it but a secondary consequence of supposed or known primary facts? Development is a better word, because more close to the cause of the fact? For you do not deny causation. I call (in the abstract) causation the will of God, and I can prove that He acts for the good of His creature. He also acts by laws which we can study and comprehend. Acting by law, and under what is called final causes, comprehends, I think, your whole principle. You write of 'natural selection' as if it were done consciously by the selecting agent. 'Tis but a consequence of the presupposed development, and the subsequent battle for life. This view of Nature you have stated admirably, though admitted by all naturalists and denied by no-one of common sense. We all admit development as a fact of history. But how came it about? Here, in language, and still more in logic, we are point-blank at issue. There is a moral or metaphysical part of Nature as well as a physical. A man who denies this is deep in the mire of folly. 'Tis the crown and glory of organic science that it does through final cause link material and moral; and yet does not allow us to mingle them in our first conception of laws, and our classification of laws, whether we consider one side of Nature or the other. You have ignored this link; and, if I do not mistake your meaning, you have done your best in one or two pregnant cases to break it. Were it possible (which, thank God, it is not) to break it, humanity in my mind would suffer a damage that might brutalize it, and sink the human race into a lower grade of degradation than any into which it has fallen since written records tell us of its history ...

Later on during the Holy Nights, Whewell too wrote to the author, but more briefly:

Trin. Lodge
Jan. 2. 1860

My dear Mr. Darwin,

I have to thank you for a copy of your book on the 'Origin of Species'. You will easily believe that it has interested me very much, and probably you will not be surprised to be told that I cannot, yet at least, become a convert. But there is so much of thought and of fact in what you have written that it is not to be contradicted without careful selection of the ground and manner of the dissent, which I have not now time for. I must therefore content myself with thanking you for your kindness.

Believe me

Yours very truly

W. Whewell

So Sudden and Luminous

Several months later, in June 1860, there took place at Oxford a famous stormy meeting of the British Association. Although Charles Darwin himself did not attend, it was his newly published book that was the cause of all the tumult.

Many different reports of this meeting are extant. In the second volume, *The Power of Place*, of her biography *Charles Darwin*, Janet Browne gives a detailed account:

> At Oxford evolution was an issue from the first evening. Darwin's book and the stream of comments and reviews published over the previous six months ensured everyone had something to say. Lord Wrottesley's opening address, as bland and all-encompassing as these functions require, was charged with emotion in his call not to forget the wonders of God's creation.
>
> The initial papers the next day did not disappoint. The usual crowd-pullers of geology and geography lost some of their customary attraction as attention lurched decisively towards the life sciences. All the rising young men of science and those members of the public who hoped for controversy followed Huxley, Hooker and Owen into Section D, held in the new Natural History Museum, a relatively arcane division usually devoted to dull talks on botany, zoology and physiology, over which the aged Henslow presided. Any fireworks would be here, the youngsters thought, Huxley and Owen on the platform together.
>
> Audiences were an essential part of British Association meetings, particularly at Oxford. Shared events like these thrived on spectacle, gossip and controversy. In a very real sense, participants demanded something different every time, and local organizers would strive to produce for them increasingly striking occasions year by year, offering outings to technological marvels like Clifton Suspension Bridge in Bristol, candlelit caves in Derbyshire, artillery displays at Portsmouth, or yachting excursions to the Isle of Wight. The press regularly attended and reported these events. In return, visitors required scientific celebrities to do what was expected of them—to declaim, smoulder, preach or shock. As a result British Associa-

tion meetings were very much led by the audience, an unusual phenomenon that rarely occurred in the nation's other scientific societies.

Speakers were quick to establish where they stood on the *Origin of Species*. Charles Daubeny, chief local organizer of the meeting and Henslow's counterpart as Professor of Botany at Oxford, as well as a vice-president of the Association, introduced the topic directly, cautiously dissenting from Darwin's thesis. There ensued some light-hearted talk about monkeys, upon which Richard Owen jumped to his feet and elaborated on the anatomical differences between man and apes. He for his part received a critical rejoinder from another member of the audience, Thomas Henry Huxley ('Darwin's bulldog'), who insisted that the anatomical differences were not that large, adding the facetious comment that churchmen would have little to fear 'even if it were shown that apes were their ancestors'.

The rest of the meeting continued on the following day, Saturday, 30 June:

> Irresistibly drawn by the prospect of heated exchanges about monkeys and the heavenly host, an unusual number of people arrived at the museum along with Huxley, including a noisy posse of undergraduates staying on through the holidays, so many that the organizers felt obliged to move the session to a much larger room on the west end of the building (which later became the library). The *Athenaeum* said the audience was immense, and other reports put the figure somewhere between four and seven hundred. Hooker thought there were nearly a thousand people present.

John William Draper, head of the medical school at the City University of New York, gave a lecture 'On the Intellectual Development of Europe, Considered with Reference to the Views of Mr. Darwin'. Draper was already well known for his dislike of organized religion, and the main thesis of his lecture was that human progress depended on science vanquishing theology.

Among the audience at this lecture were Samuel Wilberforce, Bishop of Oxford—reportedly the model for Archdeacon Grantly in the satirical novel-series by Anthony Trollope—and Admiral Robert Fitzroy, 23 years previously captain of the *Beagle*.

Draper's lecture lasted about an hour and a half. Janet Browne describes the sequel:

> Henslow, as chairman, let one or two members of the public ask questions before raising an inquiring eyebrow at Huxley. Would he like to comment? A few unruly spirits at the back were already chanting 'Mawnkey, mawnkey!' Huxley shook his head. The eyebrow moved to Wilberforce.

This was the moment Wilberforce was waiting for. Theatrically rising to his feet, he took control of the meeting. He discoursed eloquently for thirty minutes or more, powerful, argumentative and amusing, his voice filling the hall with confident assertions and making good use of the witticisms he felt constrained to omit when in the pulpit. Draper was forgotten as Wilberforce transformed his still-unpublished review of the *Origin of Species* into his text for the day. It was one of his best secular sermons, carried along by peals of laughter from the students and punctuated by attentive silences. Darwin's facts, Wilberforce proclaimed, did not warrant his theory. Evolution by natural selection was unphilosophical. The line between humanity and animals was obvious and distinct. There was no tendency on the part of lower organisms to become self-conscious intelligent beings. 'Is it credible that a turnip strives to become a man?'

Perhaps it was the laughter that loosened Wilberforce's grip. At some point he turned with a flourish to Huxley and alluded to the remarks made the day before. Was Huxley related on his grandfather's or grandmother's side to an ape?

In truth, no-one could afterwards remember exactly what Wilberforce did say. One witness, possibly no more reliable than the rest, recorded that Wilberforce expressed the 'disquietude' he should feel if a 'veritable ape' were shown to him as his ancestress in the zoo. These words have the ring of a Victorian bishop about them. Still, the literal words were not important. Wilberforce used the age-old formula of delivering an insult disguised as a friendly jest. The gibe was understood by every member of the audience. They smelled blood. So did Huxley. 'The Lord hath delivered him into mine hands,' he apparently whispered to Benjamin Brodie on the bench beside him. As the audience fell silent, Huxley stood up on the platform.

He kept them waiting until the end. First, he repudiated the arguments Wilberforce employed. It was clear to him that most of the biological points were derived from Owen. So he stated that brains do not differ very much across the animal-human divide. He commended the way Darwin's theory organized the chaotic data of natural history. When the riposte came, it was so quick that only a few people towards the front can have possibly heard. Like Wilberforce's sally, the form of words was almost immaterial.

'If I would rather have a miserable ape for a grandfather or a man highly endowed by nature and possessed of great means and influence and yet who employs those faculties for the mere purpose of introducing ridicule into a grave scientific discussion—I unhesitatingly affirm my preference for the ape.'

With this, the accumulated force of the theological, scientific and social upheavals of the previous twenty or thirty years came to a head. Ever afterwards, Huxley was credited with having said that he would rather be a monkey than a bishop.

One by one, Hooker, Henslow, and John Lubbock rose to speak over the clamour of the crowd. Their arguments in defence of Darwin were just as powerful as Huxley's, perhaps more so; and each man felt afterwards that he had personally made the best points of the day. Undergraduates waved their programmes and cheered, people pushed in and out of the hall, the heat rose, bonnets bobbed and weaved, and one over-stretched scientist's wife in the early months of pregnancy gave up completely and fainted. Many people felt that the bishop had been ill-treated—that Huxley was much too vulgar in his reply. Somewhere in the audience, young Henry Tristram, who had already published one of the first articles to use natural selection as an explanation for biological problems, changed his mind about Darwin and declared to Alfred Newton, who was sitting next to him, that he was from now on an anti-Darwinian. He said he objected to seeing a guardian of the nation's soul shouted down by a mob hailing 'the god Darwin and his prophet Huxley'.

Also in the audience, Robert Fitzroy tried to make himself heard. It must have seemed to him that he was personally responsible for this confrontation between faith and science, between God and his former shipmate. Hepworth Dixon, editor of the *Athenaeum*, was one of the few who caught what he said. Fitzroy shouted that he 'regretted the publication of Mr. Darwin's book, and denied Professor Huxley's statement that it was a logical arrangement of facts...' He waved a copy of the Bible aloft—a futile exercise noticed by the distinguished mathematical physicist George Johnstone Stoney, and recorded by him in an account written many years after the event. According to Stoney, Fitzroy declared he had 'often expostulated with his old comrade of the *Beagle* for entertaining views which were contradictory to the first chapter of Genesis', and implored the British Association audience to believe God's holy word rather than that of a mere human on the question of creation. The scene was corroborated by Julius Carus, the biologist who afterwards translated many of Darwin's books into German. 'I shall never forget that meeting...'

★

Now William Whewell also attended this famous meeting of the British Association, though no comment of his about it seems to be on record. But he had other plans for the summer as well, and only a week afterwards was already crossing over the Channel and travelling away south-west, down towards Spain.

On his return journey he wrote on 24 July from Bayonne to his Scottish friend James David Forbes—now Principal of the United College at St Andrews—with whom he must have spoken at the Oxford meeting:

> I think I did not tell you that Lady A. and I had made up our minds to go to Spain to see the eclipse of the 18th in its totality. We did so, and saw it very

well from a range of hills near Orduña, south of Bilbao. The effect was very striking, above all things the corona, which shone out as soon as the eclipse was total. I had not imagined anything so sudden and luminous. You will probably hear and read a good deal about it, for there were many English observers scattered about the country, and Leverrier with bodies of French and Spanish ones further south. To me, I may say I think to all at our station, the corona appeared to consist of white light with *radial* rays at various points; but other observers whom I have seen speak of the diverging rays being curved in various ways. Galton who was, I believe, at Miranda, has made a wonderful picture with curved and tangential rays. We saw an extraordinary saffron dawn in the horizon, when all was very dark about us. Altogether the phenomena were quite a thing to see in one's lifetime, if possible . . .

★

During this year Whewell edited the *Mathematical Works* of a predecessor in Trinity College Cambridge, Isaac Barrow. He also published the third volume in the new edition of *The Philosophy of the Inductive Sciences*, comprising the second 'book' of the original second volume expanded by further material. It was entitled *On the Philosophy of Discovery*.

William Whewell, c. *1860, aged about 66*

In addition he brought out a second volume of *Platonic Dialogues for English Readers*, containing *Protagoras*, *Greater Hippias*, *Lesser Hippias*, *Ion*, *Euthydemus*, *Gorgias*, *Phaedrus*, *Menexenus* and *Philebus*. It was subtitled 'The Anti-Sophist Dialogues'.

Deep Gratitude

In the spring of 1861 John Henslow, suffering from a terminal illness at his home in Ipswich, sent to William Whewell in Cambridge a message of farewell.

Whewell replied:

April 14, 1861

My dear Henslow,

I am much touched by your kind recollection of me in your situation. If you are really on the point of making the great voyage which we must all make in our turn, may God be with you, and comfort and support you through the passage, and receive you into His paternal and redeeming arms when it is over.

If this reaches you while you are still among us, I should like you to know the deep gratitude I have to you for all that I have received and learnt from you. I never was with you, even for a short time, without thinking that I was the better and wiser for you; and it has been one of the sorrows of my later life that I saw less of you than I wished to do.

But all these regrets will soon be over; for you are going, in a few days as it seems, and I in a few years, where we shall know even as we are known.

God bless and support you, my dear Henslow, and believe me

Yours most affectionately,

W. Whewell

In the event Henslow lingered on for a few more weeks, dying on 16 May.

This considerate letter from Whewell, which must have reached and no doubt comforted Henslow during the last weeks of his earthly life, stands in striking contrast to the behaviour shown by Charles Darwin. In her aforementioned biography, Janet Browne states:

> Henslow was aged only sixty-four (a year older than Lyell), and his death was unexpected, at least to his scientific acquaintances. A month beforehand, he had published an animated note in *Macmillan's Magazine* correcting a misapprehension about his views on species and defending Darwin . . . For him to fail so suddenly was a great surprise. But there was time enough for Hooker and his wife Frances (Henslow's daughter) to travel from Kew to

Ipswich to be at Henslow's bedside; time enough for Jenyns to get over from Bath to say a fond farewell (Henslow was married to Jenyns's sister) and time enough for frail and elderly Sedgwick, Henslow's devoted old university colleague, to arrive by railway train from Cambridge, a long journey across country, to make his adieus. Sedgwick was moved to tears by the occasion and whispered words of faith into Henslow's ear, not knowing if they were heard. Hooker asked Darwin if he would come as well.

After an embarrassing misunderstanding in which Darwin thought Henslow was already dead, Darwin made his excuses and declined.

'If Henslow . . . would really like to see me I would of course start at once. The thought had at once occurred to me to offer, & the sole reason why I did not was that the journey, with the agitation, would cause me probably to arrive utterly prostrated. I shd. be certain to have severe vomiting afterwards, but that would not much signify, but I doubt whether I could stand the agitation at the time. I never felt my weakness a greater evil. I have just had a specimen, for I spoke a few minutes at Linnean Society on Thursday & though extra well, it brought on 23 hours vomiting. I suppose there is some inn at which I could stay, for I shd. not like to be in house (even if you could hold me) as my retching is apt to be extremely loud.'

He felt guilty for months afterwards. He had never before used illness in such an obvious way to avoid personal obligations. By rights, he should have made every conceivable effort to attend Henslow's deathbed. Henslow had made him what he was, not only by giving him the chance of a lifetime with the invitation for the *Beagle* voyage, but also by his kindly attentions and support thereafter. The refusal was seemingly grounded in the same inner tightening Darwin had felt on his father's death in 1849, not as intense as the despair occasioned by the children's deaths, yet involving other disturbing feelings of emotional debts unpaid. Henslow's demise ended another chapter in his life. Yet his absence was a poor return for Henslow's friendship.

★

During this year Whewell republished in an expanded edition his *Lectures on the History of Moral Philosophy*, and also brought out a final third volume of *Platonic Dialogues for English Readers*, subtitled 'The *Republic* and the *Timaeus*'.

In the summer he travelled again over to Switzerland. After returning to Cambridge he delivered in the autumn term a course of lectures on political economy, attended by the young Prince of Wales, then resident in the College. This course was requested by the Prince's father, Albert Prince Consort, who himself died a few months later, in December. In 1862 Whewell printed privately the resultant volume, *Six Lectures on Political Economy*.

Since the widowed Queen Victoria continued as monarch for the remainder of her life, another 40 years were to pass before the Prince of Wales came at the age of 59 to the British throne, on which he sat as King Edward VII from 1902 to 1910.

A Great Event

In 1862 the British Association met again at Cambridge. This was the last time when William Whewell attended, in a now changing scientific climate. Although Richard Owen delivered two anti-Darwinian lectures, their content was ferociously attacked by Thomas Huxley and his friends. Details of the dispute were satirized by Charles Kingsley in his children's story *The Water Babies*.

During the summer Whewell travelled yet again to the Continent, to set eyes once more on Mont Blanc, and climb among the Swiss glaciers.

⋆

Of greater interest in the context of the present work, however, are Whewell's further continental journeys in the following year. Evidence for them is contained in a letter he wrote to the Revd Dr Thomas Mackreth. The only surviving information about this correspondent records that he went early into the Church, being ordained deacon in 1812 and priest in 1813. He then matriculated at Trinity College in 1817—just when Whewell was appointed to his fellowship—and after gaining his degree became in 1825 rector of Halton in Lancashire, where he remained for the rest of his life. Quite a number of Whewell's letters are addressed to him. Since Halton lies only three miles north-east of Lancaster, it seems reasonable to suppose that he was originally a schoolfriend of Whewell's from the first decade of the nineteenth century.

An extant letter written by William Whewell from Cambridge on 8 October 1863 to Thomas Mackreth opens with this paragraph:

> I think you will be glad to hear of us, now that our summer wanderings are over, and we are once more settled in our regular abode. We had a very pleasant tour of about three months, reaching as far as Venice and Trieste in one direction, and Zurich and Lausanne in another. We visited also many of the old German towns which I had visited before when I was following German architecture with great zeal from province to province. We had very fine weather and were carried by the railroads with wonderful rapidity over vast spaces. Indeed, the railroads themselves are among the most noticeable things when they are carried through mountainous country. The

> railway from Vienna to Trieste and Venice is quite one of the wonders of the world, and very beautiful as well as wonderful.

This last reference is to the Semmering line.

It seems therefore justifiable to picture the scene in the summer of 1863 when the train carrying William Whewell and Lady Affleck on the line south from Vienna towards the Semmering Pass and over to Trieste and Venice was passing through the little station at Pottschach.

Referring in his autobiographical lecture to the Pottschach years, Rudolf Steiner stated that 'the arrival of a train was a great event'.

In the autobiography he elaborated:

> At the little station all interest was centred on the operation of the railway. In those days, indeed, trains ran only at long intervals. But when they came, a number of people from the village who had time would mostly gather at the station to bring some diversion into life, which they otherwise seemed to find monotonous.

Since Steiner went on to list the people concerned (with further details given in the autobiographical fragment and the lecture), a reader may visualize the gallery of characters lined up on the platform at Pottschach station in the summer of 1863 to await the passage of the train: the ageing schoolmaster; the funny little parish priest, Ignaz Artner; the accountant from the mansion of the Lichtenstein estate; the mayor; the manager of the spinning factory, with his fixed gaze and hoarse voice, covered on many places of his body with white fluff; and above all the robust, broad-shouldered Cistercian from the neighbouring village of St Valentin, Robert Andersky, who was 'interested in observing the trains which passed by'.

Add to these the good-willed if temperamental stationmaster Johann Steiner, recently posted to Pottschach, his wife Franziska, and their two-and-a-half-year-old child, and the picture is complete.

One may then surely be forgiven for venturing to imagine how the event might have been. As soon as Johann Steiner had received a telegraphic message from Ternitz, the next station down the line, that the Trieste express had just passed by and was now approaching Pottschach, he would have emerged from the station-master's office and announced this news to all the characters on the platform who were eagerly awaiting the 'great event', telling them that the train was coming and warning them to stand well back from the platform edge.

Father Andersky might have instructed them all to wave as the train went by.

The loving Franziska would have hurried protectively towards her precious little Rudl—still her only child—and lifted him up into her arms.

Pottschach station, a period photo

Everyone gazing expectantly north-eastwards down the railway line towards the Ternitz bend would then suddenly have seen in that summer's 'very fine weather' the small but distinct silhouette of an oncoming train, smoke puffing up from the locomotive chimney, rounding the bend and charging at full steam ahead up the line towards them. The exultant Andersky would have shouted with joy, and already have begun to wave. Quite soon the express came thundering its way 'with wonderful rapidity' through the little station at Pottschach, while all the adults on the platform were excitedly waving, and even little Rudl—in whom imitative forces were still strong—waving too. And as the train hurtled by, the onlookers might just have caught a fleeting glimpse of an elderly couple waving back at them through the window of the first-class carriage. Seconds later, the sight and noise of the train had completely passed by, only its rear end being still visible, disappearing up the line and far away into the mountainous distance.

That elderly couple in the first-class carriage was none other than William Whewell, then in his seventieth year, sitting at a window-seat on the platform side of the train, with Lady Affleck opposite, so that both could gain the best possible view of the 'very beautiful as well as wonderful scenery'.

Karma had been made . . .

The Argument from Design

By this time the influence on general consciousness exerted by Charles Darwin's *The Origin of Species* was spreading far and wide. A German translation had already come out in 1860. When in the following year the English original went into a third edition in a print-run of two thousand copies, the title page indicated that the total number printed was now already seven thousand. In 1862 appeared a French translation. And in 1863 all kinds of related works followed both at home and abroad. Sir Charles Lyell published *The Geological Evidences of the Antiquity of Man with Remarks on Theories of the Origin of Species by Variation*, which sold out immediately and was reprinted three times that same year. Thomas Huxley published his provocative *Evidence as to Man's Place in Nature*, the argument of which was sufficiently explained by a frontispiece showing the skeletons of gibbon, orang-utan, chimpanzee, gorilla and man standing in one line. In France, Pierre-Jean-Marie Flourens brought out an *Examen du livre de M. Darwin sur l'Origine des Espèces*, while in Germany Friedrich Rolle and August Schleicher published *Die Darwinische Theorie und die Sprachwissenschaft*, followed in 1864 by Fritz Müller's *Für Darwin*. There was simply no stopping the ever-spreading impulse emanating from Down House.

And at the front of *The Origin of Species*—in whatever language it might be read—stood as first epigraph that quotation from the Bridgewater Treatise by William Whewell.

★

In 1864 Whewell brought out a new edition of this Bridgewater Treatise *Astronomy and General Physics*—first published back in 1832. For this seventh and final edition the author composed a new preface, which will here be reproduced in its entirety.

The preface opened as follows:

> The Bridgewater Treatises, of which this was the first published, were intended to explain and recommend to general readers the proofs of the being and providence of God as shown in the arrangement of the world—the argument from Design, or from Final Causes, as it is sometimes termed. This argument from Design first appears, *as an argument*, in Xenophon's report of the conversations of Socrates. Doubtless many expressions of admiration for the wonderful works of God as shown in the creation may be found in earlier times, for instance in the Book of Psalms and in the Book of Job. But as arguments employed to convince a gainsayer, the exposition of the skill and goodness of the Creator as shown in works of the creation appears for the first time in the discussions recorded as held by Socrates. As from that time to the present day this argument has had a strong interest for all thoughtful readers, it may be not improper to give a specimen of Socrates's mode of speaking on this subject.
>
> His attention was drawn, Xenophon tells us (*Mem.*b.i.c.iv.), to one

Aristodemus, who was reported to him as not acknowledging the gods by prayer or sacrifice, or in any other way. He proceeded, as his manner was, to lead him to conversation by arguing from acknowledged cases to similar cases in question. He said:

'Tell me, Aristodemus, are there any among men whom you admire for their skill?' 'Yes,' said he, 'there are.' 'Tell me their names,' said Socrates. 'I,' he added, 'have been accustomed to admire Homer as the most skilful epic poet, Melanippides as a dithyrambic poet, Sophocles as a tragic poet, Polyclitus as a statuary, Zeuxis as a painter. Now do those who make images without sense and motion appear to you to be more worthy of admiration for their skill, or those who make living and sensible creatures?' Aristodemus answers with caution: 'Certainly those who make living creatures, if they are made not by chance but by design.'

Of course the inference to which Socrates points is that the Creator who made Homer and Melanippides and Sophocles and Polyclitus and Zeuxis is animated by a more admirable principle of design than the poet, the sculptor or the painter, who merely produce images of living things. But Socrates goes on to point out some examples of design in the human frame, which even now are constantly referred to as manifestations of the principle of Final Causes.

'In considering those things,' Socrates says, 'of which it is not clear what their purpose is, and other things which have an evident useful purpose, which of the two do you reckon as works of chance, and which as works of skill?' Aristodemus answers that those which have an evident usefulness must be reckoned as works of skill.

Socrates then proceeds to the application of this.

'Does it not appear to you that He who in the beginning made man added to his frame the organs of each sense of perception—eyes to see what is visible; ears to hear what is audible? Of what use would smells be if we had not noses? What sense could we have of sweet and sour, and other tastes of things which come into the mouth, if the tongue were not put in the mouth to let us know this? And again, does not this appear to you like a work of design, that inasmuch as the eyes are a tender organ, they should be protected by the eyelids, which are opened when the eyes are to be used, but are closed when we are asleep? That the eyes may be protected even from the wind, they have the eyelashes as a screen. Above the eyes is a projection, the eyebrows, that the sweat running down from the forehead may not harm them. And again, such facts as these: that the ears receive all sounds and are never filled up with them; that the front teeth in all animals are fit for cutting, the hinder teeth for grinding what is passed to them by the front teeth; that the mouth by which what each animal devours is taken into the body, is near the eyes and nostrils, but the excretions being unpleasant to the senses, the passages of them are removed away from the organs of sense—

when all these things are arranged so thoughtfully, do you doubt whether they are works of chance or of design?'

'No, truly,' says Aristodemus; 'when I consider the matter so, all this is like the work of some skilful and benevolent worker.'

Other evidences of design are touched of in the same manner: instincts of generation; of the love of offspring; of the fear of death. And again it is urged: *you* are intelligent; where did you get your intelligence if there is no intelligence in the universe?

To this are added arguments drawn from the especial endowments of man: his upright attitude; his being able to articulate, and to worship the gods; his having hands to use and intelligence to use them; for, it is argued, neither hands without intelligence nor intelligence without hands would have sufficed.

These and other arguments are urged in a striking manner, and have often since been repeated. One of the most conspicuous examples of such repetition is that afforded by Cicero in his treatise 'On the Nature of the Gods'. In the second book of that treatise, he states many evidences of design found in the structure of the universe. In many of his exemplifications he follows Socrates, as was natural. One noticeable passage I may introduce (*De Nat D.* ii. 34).

'How is it reasonable when you see a statue or a picture to acknowledge that art has been employed, when you see the course of a ship at a distance to have no doubt that it is moved by reason and skill, when you see a water-clock to understand that it tells the hours by design not by chance; and yet to think that the world, which includes these arts and those who practise them, and everything else, is destitute of intelligence and contrivance?

If anyone were to carry into Scythia or *into Britain* that sphere which our friend Posidonius lately constructed, in which the Sun and the Moon and the five planets revolve by machinery in the same manner as they do in the sky in reality, who in those barbarous regions would doubt whether that sphere were constructed by intelligence? And do our opponents doubt concerning the world, in which all things originate and happen, whether it was produced by chance or by some necessity, or by intelligence and mind? Do they think that Archimedes showed more skill in imitating the revolutions of the sphere than Nature did in producing them, especially when that original is many times more perfect and skilful than that copy?'

Among the ancients, the doctrine adverse to the belief in an Intelligent Creator was the doctrine promulgated by Democritus and others, that the world was produced by a fortuitous concourse of atoms. It was held by the maintainers of this doctrine that the whole universe consisted of atoms; that is, of solid separate particles, which had a certain tendency to move and which, meeting one another and clinging together, formed by their combinations all bodies which exist in the world. Against this doctrine also

> Cicero argues in the work which I have just quoted. He says (*De Nat D.* ii. 37): 'If anyone can persuade himself that this world, so fair and beautiful, has been produced by the fortuitous concourse of such atoms, I do not see why the same man should not hold that if anyone were to have innumerable alphabets of letters, made of gold or anything else, and throw them upon the ground, they might produce the *Annals* of Ennius, or any other book, in a legible form.'
>
> These trains of thought, thus ascribing the structure of the world to design and not to chance, have been constantly dwelt upon and continued to modern times, as I have said; and it was intended, as the business of the Bridgewater Treatises, to enforce such reflections, and accommodate them in their details to the state of knowledge as it now exists. And for this purpose I may notice the form which some of the arguments *against* Design have assumed in modern times.
>
> Are there any persons who, in modern times, assert that the world was produced by a fortuitous concourse of atoms?
>
> There is a near approach to this doctrine in those who maintain, in its extreme form, the Nebular Hypothesis, of which an account is given in Chap. vii of Book II. of the following work, and I have in that chapter stated the arguments which appear to me to refute that and any similar hypothesis, when put in opposition to the belief of an Intelligent Creator of the universe.

Whewell had further developed these arguments in 1853 in his anonymously published *Of the Plurality of Worlds*, which Alexander von Humboldt described as 'votre important ouvrage'. Indeed Chapter XI, 'The Argument from Design', was among those Humboldt singled out as 'pleins d'attraits'.

Humboldt, however, had died on 6 May 1859. He did not live to see the publication six months later of *The Origin of Species* by Charles Darwin.

A Few Words

The preface to the seventh edition of William Whewell's Bridgewater Treatise then continued:

> The arguments for Design may be distinguished into two kinds, as stated in the ensuing Treatise—arguments from cosmical arrangements (including terrestrial arrangements), and arguments for the adaptation of organic creatures (animals and vegetables) to their purposes. Of these kinds of arguments the former is more especially the main subject of the present volume, as described in the phrase 'Astronomy and General Physics'; but I have found it natural, in connection with this subject, to say something of

the history of the argument from Design and the doctrine of Final Causes in general (Book III, Chap. v. vi. vii.). I may offer a few words as to the controversy on this subject also, which has occurred in recent times.

In opposition to the view of the Design shown in the structure of animals, as manifested by the adaptation of their parts each to its purpose, it has been asserted that the structure of animals has become what it is by the operation of external circumstances and internal appetencies. And very recently great stress has been laid upon the argument that all those structures of animals which are less adapted to the mode of their life cease to be continued in the species, precisely because of this want of adaptation, and thus no structures remain for us to consider, besides those in which the organization answers the purpose of life perfectly.

This doctrine, again taking the extreme form of it, makes the universe to be the result of an infinite number of trials, the failures being constantly rejected by the fact of their being failures. It would thus, in its extreme form as I have said, assert the world to be the work of chance.

But the same arguments which I have urged against the Nebular Hypothesis would also, I conceive, refute this hypothesis in this form; namely the argument that the structure of animals at every stage of the world's history being thus derived by necessary causation from a previous state of the animal world, there must have been in that previous state the germs of the adaptations which were afterwards produced; and that these germs and possibilities of adaptation must in reality contain evidences of design. The past state of the animal world, out of which our present animal world was developed by natural causation, must contain evidence of design, just as the egg contains evidence of design no less than the animal. And this must be true, however far we go back in the history of the world, and however different the germs which we suppose to have existed in the womb of the past differ from the existing organized world—however much the egg differs from the animal.

In attempts which have been recently made to show that the organs of animals as they now exist, with at least a seeming adaptation to their purpose, may have been derived by necessary causation from a state of things in which there was no such adaptation, it seems to me that there are two enormous assumptions which deprive the reasoning of all force, and make these speculations a mere work of fancy.

First, it is assumed that the mere possibility of imagining a series of steps of transition from one condition of organs to another is to be accepted as a reason for believing that such transition has taken place.

And next, that such a possibility being thus imagined, we may assume an unlimited number of generations for the transition to take place in, and that this indefinite time may extinguish all doubt that the transitions really have taken place.

> I think it is well worth the consideration of thoughtful men whether systems founded on such assumptions as these do not belong to the domain of fancy rather than of reason.
>
> How far modern speculators carry this assumption—that the mere possibility of imagining a series of transitions by which an organ may have been formed is a reason for believing that the organ has been so formed—may be seen in a very remarkable instance.
>
> The eye of man and of other animals is, to common apprehension, one of the most evident examples of design; so much so, indeed, that it has been considered as by itself sufficient to convince the most incredulous. We see in the ensuing pages (Book III, Chap. vii.) that the Epicurean poet Lucretius, who does not allow that there is design in the scheme of the world, thinks it necessary to exhort his readers to vehement effort to avoid this error, as he calls it . . .

The full name of the Latin poet referred to was Titus Lucretius Carus. Twenty years previously, on his visit to the Master's Lodge in Trinity College Cambridge, Carl Gustav Carus had considered this poet as a possible ancestor of either himself or his namesake William Carus, to whom he was introduced by Whewell.

The subsequent destinies of the two namesakes were quite different. In 1864 Carl Gustav Carus was still engaged in medical practice in Dresden. William Carus, however, on appointment some years previously as Canon of Winchester had resigned from Trinity College, and left Cambridge altogether.

Whewell's preface continued:

> . . . Yet, by the aid of this assumed principle of possible generation equivalent to actual progress, the modern philosopher can believe that the eye was not made for seeing, but produced by a series of transitions from blind matter. The following is the remarkable passage to which I refer.
>
> 'To suppose that the eye, with all its inimitable contrivances for adjusting the focus to different distances, for admitting the different amounts of light, and for the correction of spherical and chromatic aberration, could have been formed by natural selection, seems, I freely confess, absurd in the highest possible degree. Yet reason tells me that if numerous gradations from a perfect and complex eye to one very imperfect and simple, each grade being useful to its possessor, can be shown to exist; if, further, the eye does vary ever so slightly, and the variation be inherited, which is certainly the case; and if any variation or modification in the organ be ever useful to an animal under changing conditions of life, then the difficulty of believing that a perfect and complex eye could be formed by natural selection, though insuperable to our imagination, can hardly be considered real. How a nerve

> comes to be sensitive to light hardly concerns us more than how life itself originated: but I may remark that several facts make me suppose that any sensitive nerve may be rendered sensitive to light, and likewise to those coarser vibrations of the air by which sound is produced.'
>
> After some remarks on the eyes of different kinds of animals, this writer adds:
>
> 'It is scarcely possible to avoid comparing the eye to a telescope. We know that this instrument has been perfected by the long continued efforts of the highest human intellects; and we naturally infer that the eye has been formed by a somewhat analogous process. But may not this inference be presumptuous? Have we any right to assume that the Creator works by intellectual powers like those of man?'
>
> I may remark that this is not very exactly said. Though the telescope has been *perfected* by successive intellectual efforts, it was *invented* by the intellectual effort of a single mind; and all telescopes, however improved, contain in them the principle of the invention; they have an object glass (or object mirror), and an eye-piece. And so the eye, to be an eye, must contain the principle of an eye; which is, I conceive, that it forms an image on a nerve sensible to light; nor can any series of gradations prevent thoughtful men from regarding such an arrangement as a manifestation of intelligence.
>
> When it is asked 'Have we any right to assume that the Creator works by intellectual powers like those of man?' we may reply that we must assume that the powers by which the Creator works *are* intellectual; that they imply *intelligent* working; that the arrangements which we cannot describe except as *contrivances*, cannot be the work of blind chance. The mere possibility of *imagining* a series of steps by which the eye should acquire each of its distinct contrivances—if this were possible, which it does not appear that it is—would not make the contrivances cease to be contrivances.

Whewell nowhere gave his readership either the title of the book containing the 'remarkable passage' being criticized, or the name of its author. But anyone with knowledge of the book in question will recognize the quoted passage. It is taken from the sixth chapter, 'Difficulties on Theory', of *The Origin of Species* by Charles Darwin.

Whewell's preface ended:

> It may be said, perhaps, that some of the steps of this argument from gradation are facts; for instance, the occurrence of change in some degree in organs of animals, and the perpetuation of this change by natural descent. In this way, it may be said, personal differences are produced in animal races.
>
> But if we refer to observations for this fact, we must also refer to observations in order to know how far the fact goes. What amount of permanent difference in the races of animals has been produced by variations perpetuated by descent? Here our modern speculators have no new

facts of any large bearing to tell us, and yet they go very far beyond those who in the last generation studied the subject most completely. Cuvier held that among the animals which have been contemporaries of man upon the earth, the species have not changed from the earliest times; those which we find in the ancient sepulchres of Egypt, for example, being the same species as those who now exist. Nevertheless our modern speculators teach us that all the existing variety of species has probably been produced by changes of former species perpetuated by natural descent; and that though the steps of such a derivation are not visible, they might become real and important in the course of the innumerable generations which we must suppose to have elapsed.

We thus have, as I have said, a second assumption of the effect of innumerable generations, to complete the first assumption of the actual existence of gradations because imaginable. The first assumption allows us to devise any possible change in the structure of animals, the second assumption allows us to reject all doubt of such changes founded on the ground that we do not see them in Nature. Imagination gives us our starting-point, and every deviation from the actual state of things is covered with the veil of Infinity.

I cannot think that a philosophy of the world thus constructed can supersede the ancient doctrine of Final Causes, which, as I have said, has so long had so strong a hold upon men's minds; and which, as I have shown elsewhere, has been the occasion of men making many of the most important discoveries in the structure of man and of animals.

I have further described the history and operation of this principle of Final Causes, and the controversies which have taken place respecting it, in other works; namely *The History* and *The Philosophy of the Inductive Sciences*. Passages in those works which especially bear upon the present question I have collected and published in a small work, which I have entitled *Indications of the Creator*.

Trinity Lodge,
Feb. 13, 1864.

This unsigned, but located and dated ending could even be taken to mirror that located and dated page of epigraphs prefaced to *The Origin of Species* by Charles Darwin!

The latter's son Francis Darwin—who a few years later was to study at Trinity College—eventually went on to include in his work *The Life and Letters of Charles Darwin* a footnote quoting from Whewell's letter to his father of 2 January 1860, and added the comment:

> ... Dr. Whewell dissented in a practical manner for some years, by refusing to allow a copy of the *Origin of Species* to be placed in the library of Trinity College.

The Striking of the Clock

Later in 1864, William Whewell brought out an enlarged edition of his textbook *The Elements of Morality*. He also printed privately, as a posthumous tribute, the poems of his sister Martha Statter, deceased in the previous year.

★

Another person close to Whewell whom he lost at this time was his own wife, Lady Affleck, who died on 1 April 1865.

After this sad event, the twice widowed septuagenarian set out once again during that summer on what proved to be the last of the 21 continental journeys (not counting the first shipwrecked attempt of 1819) which he made in his life.

He was accompanied by Janet Stairs Douglas, a niece by his first marriage. She later recorded the three sights on this tour which moved her uncle most: the cathedral at Amiens, the Rhine at Basel, and the Rhine falls at Schaffhausen.

★

Janet Stairs Douglas further described how on returning to Cambridge her uncle began to relate to other people in an intensified way:

> He perpetually expressed the comfort and gratitude with which he recognized that all love was not taken from him, though that of his wife was removed out of sight. The softening influences of suffering were visible in nothing more than in the singular gentleness and alacrity with which he accepted and appreciated every effort to give him pleasure, especially welcoming every opportunity of doing a kindness, or expressing sympathy with those who were in sickness, sorrow, or anxiety. His interest in external things was returning. Plans connected with the college were dwelt upon and matured. His mind began to flow again in the long-accustomed channels, with much of its old vigour and activity, but in all these things a difference was discernible. His affections and sympathies were quickened and enlarged. He had been very much touched and affected by the sympathy with him in his sorrow which had been felt and universally expressed, and it almost seemed as if this had produced a sort of revolution in his relations with his friends in general, and left him united to them all by warmer, kindlier ties than before. These he seemed to desire to draw closer and closer, almost as if he knew how short was the time that remained to him in which to show them his good will . . .

Having inherited Lady Affleck's estate, the old man decided to spend the lot. Towards the end of 1865 he completed a series of property purchases along the street running behind the quadrangle he had erected five years before. All the new land thus acquired he then gifted to his college. In early February 1866 he signed a contract with builders for the erection on this larger plot of another quadrangle, adjoining the first and about twice the size.

★

On 11 February Whewell preached his last sermon in the chapel of Trinity College, taking as his text Apocalypse 1:8: 'I am the Alpha and the Omega—thus speaks the Lord our God, who is, who was, and who is coming, the divine ruler of the world.'

★

Now 21 years previously in his work *Reise durch England und Schottland im Jahre 1844* Carl Gustav Carus had included in the chapter on 'England' an account of the island's zoology. After giving descriptions of birds, deer, sheep and cattle he continued with the following passage:

> . . . But in order to bring under a general overview the culture of horses in England, where should one start and where end?—In England, where such a great multitude of horses are used especially for the saddle, where boys and ladies often ride like men, and greyheads 70–80 years old do not abandon this beloved exercise! . . .

The 72-year-old William Whewell indeed did not abandon this beloved exercise. On 24 February 1866 he went out riding over the Gogmagog Hills. And on that day his old injury from falls in slippery weather hindered his control of a horse which had already thrown him twice before. The horse bolted away, and for a third time threw him heavily to the ground.

Whewell lay there concussed. He was brought back to the Master's Lodge in Trinity College. But although his consciousness soon returned, the injury to his physical frame had set in train a process of paralysis.

He survived for a further ten days. During this time he was attended by Dr Paget—who 22 years previously had dined with him in the Master's Lodge in company with Carl Gustav Carus.

The subject of Plato kept recurring to the mind of the dying man, in connection with a review he had just written—it was to appear posthumously—of George Grote's recently published trilogy *Plato and the other Companions of Socrates*.

Whewell's niece concluded:

> As days passed, and he became both weaker and more restless, the faces about him could not but indicate extreme anxiety, gradually changing into a more mournful certainty. He drew his own conclusions, and faced the end

> with simple, reverent faith and courage. His utterance, somewhat affected from the first, became more and more imperfect, but we could almost always understand it, and the passages of Holy Scripture he asked for, the hymns he endeavoured to repeat, were read to him as the wish for them occurred.
>
> He received Holy Communion from the hands of Dr. Lightfoot on Monday the 5th of March, and on the 6th he died. Whilst life was ebbing fast away on that last morning, blinds and curtains were drawn wide apart in compliance with his wish that he might see the Sun shine on the Great Court of Trinity, and he smiled as he was reminded that he used to say the sky never looked so blue as when seen fringed with its turrets and battlements...

The sixteenth-century Great Court of Trinity—the largest quadrangle of any Cambridge college—had been familiar to Whewell now for over 53 years. And his final utterance was made at the very striking of what the poet William Wordsworth named 'Trinity's loquacious clock':

> ...Almost to the last he was conscious, and the last words intelligibly uttered, when the striking of the clock roused him as day dawned, were 'The eternal God is thy refuge, and underneath are the everlasting arms.'

The quotation is from the final blessing by Moses, just before his death, of the twelve tribes of Israel.

The Great Court of Trinity College, Cambridge

The Foremost Place

The funeral of William Whewell took place in Trinity College four days later, on 10 March, with an immense attendance. An address was given by the theologian Joseph Lightfoot, which included this passage:

> We may fairly say that as a Master of the college he stands out pre-eminent in the long list of three centuries; as a man of letters, greatest of all since Bentley; as a munificent and patriotic ruler, greatest of all since Nevile; but as uniting in himself many and various qualities which, combined, go far towards realizing the ideal head of a religious and learned foundation, the just representative of a famous academic body, greater than these or any of his predecessors. Vast and varied mental powers, untiring energy and extensive knowledge, integrity of character and strictness of example, a wide and general munificence, a keen interest in university progress, an intense devotion to his own college, a strong sense of duty, a true largeness of heart, a simple Christian faith; the union of all these qualities fairly entitles him to the foremost place among the Masters of Trinity.

Whewell was buried in the college antechapel, where he had himself worshipped for so many years. His grave lies exactly in the centre. It is thus aligned at the east with the entrance to the chapel, and at the west with Roubilliac's statue of Isaac Newton.

The stone bears a simple inscription. (The initials in the first line stand for 'Hic sepultus est'.)

H S E
GVILIELMVS WHEWELL
HVIVS COLEGII MAGISTER
NATVS EST XXIV DIE MAII
MDCCXCIV OBIIT VI DIE
MARTII MDCCCLXVI

★

A lengthy obituary of Whewell in the *Proceedings of the Royal Society* was written by Sir John Herschel. It gave a detailed and intimate account of his life and achievements. Herschel even stated that

> ... A more wonderful variety and amount of knowledge in almost every department of human enquiry was perhaps never in the same interval of time accumulated by any man ... and that not by merely a general and superficial acquaintance, but one which an exact and conscientious application such as most men devote to some favourite branch of study, alone can give ...

Later in the year Herschel made a more personal tribute on publishing his own version of *The Iliad of Homer, translated into English accentuated hexameters*. For this work he wrote an extensive preface, which ended as follows:

> It was the translator's wish and intention to have associated his work, through the medium of a dedication, with the name of one, endeared by the remembrance of long and uninterrupted friendship—the late lamented Master of Trinity College, Cambridge. The melancholy event which cut short so noble a career, and robbed the science and literature of his country of so bright an ornament, has deprived him of that gratification. It is only the more incumbent therefore to acknowledge here the benefits derived from his sound and valuable criticism during the whole progress of the work down to its final completion: resulting in the correction of innumerable blemishes in the versification and no small number of misrenderings of particular and delicate turns of expression in the Greek, which his perfect knowledge of that language enabled him to point out. That it was ever completed at all indeed has been mainly owing to his encouragement and advice, such not having been the intention with which it was commenced.

On the very next page, Herschel's translation then began:

> Sing, celestial Muse! the destroying wrath of Achilles,
> Peleus's son; which myriad mischiefs heaped on the Grecians,
> Many a valiant hero's soul dismissing to Hades;
> Flinging their corses abroad for a prey to dogs and to vultures,
> And to each bird of the air. Thus Jove's high will was accomplished.
> Ev'n from that fateful hour when opposed in angry contention
> Stood forth Atreides, King of men, and godlike Achilles . . .

★

In due course, a fine statue of Whewell by Thomas Woolner was erected near his grave in the antechapel of Trinity College, on the north side. The pedestal bore the following inscription. (The initials in the second line stand for 'Sacrae Theologiae Professor' and 'Regalis Societatis Sodalis'.)

IN MEMORIAM
GVILELMI WHEWELL S.T.P, R.S.S.
VIRI INGENIO SAPIENTIA ANIMI ROBORE ET MAGNITVDINE
INTER AEQVALES CONSPICVI
SCIENTIARVM QVOTQVOT FVERVNT INTERPRETIS DISERTI
VERITATIS INDIGATORIS STRENVI VINDICIS IMPIGRI
MAGISTRI DENIQVE OPTIMI
HANC STATVAM PONENDAM CVRAVIT
BENEFICIORVM MEMOR COLLEGIVM

William Whewell

OBIIT A.S. MDCCCLXVI. AETATIS LXXII
PRAEFECTVRAE XXV

This statue of Whewell on the north side of the antechapel is placed in such a way that the head, turned slightly aslant, gazes straight across to the opposite southern side at that other statue—which he had himself erected—of Francis Bacon.

Child as He Came

The full possession of his mental faculties which William Whewell maintained right up to the last moments of his earthly life stands in vivid contrast to the case of Michael Faraday, who eventually declined into senility.

After retiring from the Royal Institution, Faraday spent his last years in a grace-and-favour house on the Green at Hampton Court, given by Queen Victoria. The last chapter of James Hamilton's biography *Michael Faraday* relates:

... One member of his family wrote that in his final years Faraday was 'quite like a little child'. At Hampton Court he sat under the limes, watched the sunset and the lightning when it came, standing, as Margery Reid wrote, 'at the window for hours, watching the effects and enjoying the scene. I shall also always connect the sight of the hues of a brilliant sunset with him, and especially he will be present to my mind while I watch the fading of the tints into the sombre grey of night. He loved to have us with him, as he stood or sauntered on some open spot, and spoke his thoughts perhaps in the words of Gray's "Elegy", which he retained in memory clearly, long after many other things had faded quite away...'

By the summer of 1866, Faraday's creeping senility had almost wholly overcome him. He had made one of his periodical trips back to the Royal Institution apartment when Henry Roscoe, who was giving a lecture in June 1866 on the opalescence of the atmosphere, tried to find in the laboratory samples of gold film that Faraday had prepared some years before. They were nowhere to be seen, so Roscoe climbed upstairs to ask the Professor if he could remember where the gold had been put. 'Don't you remember those beautiful gold experiments that you made?' Roscoe asked Faraday. 'Oh yes,' the old man replied feebly, 'beautiful gold, beautiful gold.'

During his last few years Faraday was under the care of Dr. Henry Bence Jones. Jane Barnard wrote an account of a visit Bence Jones made to Hampton Court in July 1866:

'My dear Uncle showed more interest & therefore more excitement at the interview than he has done at any meeting of a friend since this illness began. He remembered, he said, something about a book & we knew he referred to an old copy of Shakespeare that we had been speaking of yesterday as being a suitable gift for the doctor. After a while Uncle turned to the doctor & said "I am waiting, just waiting." The doctor replied "Yes, you are waiting..." & Uncle looking wistfully at him said "And you? Are you waiting?" & the tears ran down his cheeks. The doctor seeing he was getting agitated tried to turn it off by saying, "Yes, I am waiting. We are all waiting." ... I then told him how in the course of the week, after my Uncle had repeated the first verse of the 46th Psalm, he turned to me & said "Who is Dr. Bence Jones's refuge & strength?" The doctor seemed quite touched. My Uncle has spoken oftener of him than of anyone... Now he is touchingly patient, quiet & happy, like a little child, so trusting, but shewed very little interest until this afternoon.'

As Faraday waited for death, sitting in his chair or up in bed, he was surrounded by the comforts and securities of his religion. Over his bed at Hampton Court he had these verses from the Book of Psalms written up on a card:

'Remember me, O Lord, with the favour that thou bearest unto thy people: O visit me with thy salvation;

That I may see the good of thy chosen, that I may rejoice in the gladness of thy nation, that I may glory with thine inheritance.

Psalms CVI, 4, 5.'

Bence Jones returned regularly to Hampton Court to see Faraday. In the second week of August 1867 he called as usual, and then went off on holiday to Spa in Germany. Within a fortnight, however, Faraday became noticeably weaker, he spoke little, and during the afternoon of Sunday, 25 August 1867, sitting in his chair in his study, he died.

The simple funeral that he had insisted upon took place five days later. From Hampton Court Faraday's body was taken to the Royal Institution, where the carriages paused momentarily. Making their way north they crossed Oxford Street, and passed up through the Portland estates, a stone's throw from 18 Weymouth Street, where Sir Humphry Davy's carriage had once clatttered up to the door. Slowly the funeral party made its way up the hill to Highgate Cemetery, where a grave was waiting.

★

Hamilton then adds to his account an 'epilogue':

Very soon after Faraday's death, perhaps within weeks, a small cottage industry established itself to keep his memory untarnished. In his lecture 'Michael Faraday: Philosopher and Christian', given in October 1867, Revd. Samuel Martin, the Congregational Minister of Westminster, dwelt on the seven 'bright points' of Faraday's character. These he defined as diligence and conscientiousness; a sincere desire to live a life of godliness; supreme satisfaction in established truth; humility and modesty; patience; the high value of sure and certain knowledge; and Faraday's determination to live the life of a true Christian while engaged in the pursuits of an experimental philosopher. This is a grand model to attempt to emulate, and such stirrings of uncritical praise reached their apogee thirty years later when the poet and art critic Cosmo Monkhouse wrote a three-verse poem 'On a Portrait of Faraday', first published in 1898 as the epigraph to Silvanus Thomson's biography *Michael Faraday: His Life and Work*. The poem was later set to music by Harriet Grant; presumably an audience has heard it sung:

Was ever man so simple and so sage,
So crowned and yet so careless of a prize!
Great Faraday, who made the world so wise,
And loved the labour better than the wage.

And this you say is how he looked in age,
With that strong brow and these great humble eyes
That seemed to look with reverent surprise
On all outside himself. Turn o'er the page,
Recording Angel, it is white as snow.

Michael Faraday in old age

Ah God, a fitting messenger was he
To show Thy mysteries to us below.
Child as he came has he returned to Thee.
Would he could come but once again to show
The wonder-deep of his humility.

To Extinguish War Between Nations

The new quadrangle across the street from Trinity College Cambridge which had begun to be erected under the instructions of William Whewell continued to be built in accordance with his plans, and paid for out of his estate. It was finished in 1868, forming a complex with the previous quadrangle. For generations of dons and students ever since, this resulting complex, known as Whewell's Court, has substantially increased the college's residential facilities.

The first Professor of International Law at Cambridge was appointed in 1869. The incumbent has to give a certain number of lectures, and under a specific directive in Whewell's will must

> . . . make it his aim in all parts of the treatment of his subject to lay down such rules and to suggest such measures as may tend to diminish the evils of war, and finally to extinguish war between nations.

★

In the spring of 1869 the 60-year-old Charles Darwin, while riding through his own village of Down in Kent, fell off his horse. He hurt his leg quite badly, and the accident put him out of action for weeks.

He decided never to go riding in his whole life again.

★

The 80-year-old Carl Gustav Carus died in Dresden that summer, on 28 July. And a couple of months later, on 15 September, he was followed into the spiritual world by William Clark, still Professor of Anatomy at Cambridge, with whom he had once dined and conversed in the Master's Lodge of Trinity College.

★

In May 1870, Charles and Emma Darwin paid a visit to Cambridge to see their son Francis in his final year as an undergraduate at Trinity College.

Janet Browne in her biography relates:

> During the same Cambridge visit, Darwin plodded off to see his old Professor of Geology, Adam Sedgwick, in Trinity College. Sedgwick had lost none of his animation. Well into his eighties, he walked and talked Darwin into the ground while disclosing that he had found it impossible to forgive his former pupil when *The Origin of Species* was published.
>
> 'On Monday I saw Sedgwick who was most cordial & kind: in the morning I thought that his mind was enfeebled; in the evening he was brilliant & quite himself. His affection & kindness charmed us all. My visit to him was in one way unfortunate; for after a long sit he proposed to take me to the Museum; & I could not refuse, & in consequence he utterly prostrated me; so that we left Cambridge next morning, & I have not recovered the exhaustion yet. Is it not humiliating to be thus killed by a man of 86, who evidently never dreamed that he was killing me.—As he said to me "Oh, I consider you as a mere baby to me." '

So in 1870 Darwin visited the same Museum which Carus had visited in 1844.

By Trinity Chapel

Sir John Herschel died in 1871, and was buried in London at Westminster Abbey, beside the grave of Isaac Newton.

Adam Sedgwick died in 1873, and was buried at Cambridge in the antechapel of Trinity College, beside the grave of William Whewell.

★

Another famous scientist of the time, Sir Charles Lyell, died in 1875. In her biography of Charles Darwin, Janet Browne writes:

> As President of the Royal Society, Hooker arranged for Lyell to be buried in Westminster Abbey, as much a tribute to the man himself as any propaganda for the new order of things. Katherine Lyell, Lyell's sister-in-law, asked if Darwin would join Hooker, Huxley and others as a pall-bearer. Darwin refused. He said he 'dared not', for he would 'so likely fail in the midst of ceremony and have my head whirling off my shoulders'. Nor did he attend the funeral. According to Emma's diary, he sent Bessy, Francis, and Francis's wife Amy. It was a sorry end to a remarkable friendship, at root surely reflecting the same form of selfishness, the same self-indulgence, that had tainted his response to John Stevens Henslow's death, the other man who had made him who he was and who had given him just as much dedicated assistance as Lyell. Darwin could be ruthless in cutting himself off from those to whom he owed the greatest debts...

★

In the following year, 1876, Isaac Todhunter published the work *William Whewell, D.D.: an Account of his Writings, with Selections from his Literary and Scientific Correspondence*. It was in two volumes, each running to over 400 pages. The first volume discussed Whewell's major writings, going into extensive details of the complicated changes made by frequent remodelling of his books in successive editions. Interwoven with this account, if rather submerged under it, was also a fair amount of biographical information. The second volume presented a selection of Whewell's letters on literary and scientific matters to many different correspondents from all periods of his life.

But in neither volume was there any mention whatsoever of Charles Darwin.

★

As the Gabriel Age moved towards its end, it was nonetheless Darwin's writings which were gaining ever-increasing influence. By this time *The Origin of Species* had gone into six editions, and been translated not only into German and French but also into Dutch, Russian and Italian, had given rise to a host of commentaries, criticisms or supporting texts, and brought its author unparalleled international fame.

Janet Browne describes an interesting event of the year 1877:

That same November, Darwin was awarded an honorary degree of Doctor of Laws (LL.D.) from Cambridge University, his alma mater. George was the first to tell him the news, writing directly from Trinity College with the result of the vote. Darwin accepted the honour with alacrity—he valued it highly, probably more than any other in his lifetime...

The degree was conferred at a special ceremony held for Darwin alone on Saturday 17 November 1877 in the Senate House in Cambridge. At first Emma doubted whether Darwin would cope with the ceremony, a two-hour haul topped off with a procession. He would be decked out in heavy red robes, followed by a deal of bowing and smiling to be got through. She underestimated her man. He was perfectly capable of effort when it was needed. 'I thought he would be overcome, but he was quite stout and smiling.'

However, they were astounded by the noise. The senate house was crammed with members of the university and their ladies, as the *Cambridge Chronicle* noted. Darwin's sons were there too, George, Horace and Francis. The gallery throbbed with undergraduates cheering and shouting. As soon as Darwin appeared in his robes, a stuffed monkey was dangled from the ceiling dressed in a miniature degree gown and mortar-board.

'His appearance was the signal for a flattering ovation, and partial silence had scarcely ensued when cheers were given for "the primeval man"... A couple of chords stretched from either gallery now became visible and presently there were affixed to them the effigy of a monkey in academicals, and an object to illustrate the "missing link" hung over Darwin's head.'

When the words could be heard above the rumpus, the Latin oration conferring his degree was elegantly incomprehensible. Darwin asked George to send him the Cambridge newspapers afterwards in case a translation appeared. All his works in biology and geology were mentioned, albeit in Latin, from 'all that flies, or swims, or creeps' to the 'tiny tendrils of the vine'. The weekend closed with a sociable lunch hosted by George in his rooms in Trinity. 'J.W. Clarke not pleasant,' Emma said of the Zoology Department's Superintendent, 'but he did me a good turn as I followed his lead in tasting Gallantine which is v. superior... Now we are expecting F. Galton & Fawcett for an evening call & we mean to wind up by Trinity chapel—which I can't believe F. will be up to. F. has been throughly pleased by the cordiality of everyone.'...

Inside his own family Darwin was habitually referred to as 'F.', standing for 'Father'.

...Whether by design or oversight, they missed the Sunday-morning sermon in Great St. Mary's in which Dr. Wordsworth, the university preacher, reminded his congregation to approach the facts of Nature in a properly reverential spirit.

The irony of a university full of ordained fellows and teachers honouring Darwin did not go completely unnoticed. An editorial in the *Rock*, an Anglican journal, commented: 'No doubt the affair has its ludicrous side, though a believer will scarcely regard the honour paid to the apostle of evolution as by any means a laughing matter.'

The *Manchester Weekly Times and Examiner* was more urbane:

'Mr. Darwin has made considerable havoc in the groundwork of Christianity . . . I can only wonder how the Cambridge Doctors of Divinity and official guardians of orthodoxy will manage to square accounts with Mr. Darwin. Perhaps it is believed that a niche may be found for him in some sequestered corner of the Christian fabric.'

By separating the man from his theory it evidently proved possible for Cambridge University, and then nearly all elements of the British establishment over the next several decades, to greet the new regime of evolutionary biology with relative equanimity. Even the Church of England acknowledged Darwin's personal integrity and quest for truth. Perhaps it was merely traditional British hypocrisy, or the spirit of compromise and adaptibility in face of what increasingly appeared to be a scientific truth . . .

A Greater Impulse

A couple of years later, in the autumn of 1879, the Michael Age began.

With hindsight it is understandable that many of the older incarnated souls at the time were still looking back in nostalgia to the preceding Age of Gabriel. During the very next year, 1880, Kenelm Digby wrote a letter to Aubrey de Vere setting down some reminiscences of William Whewell. They included these remarks:

> I had reason to regard Whewell as one of the most generous, disinterested and noble-minded men that I ever knew. I remember circumstances that called for the exercise of each of these rare qualities, when they were met in a way that would now seem incredible, so fast does the world seem moving from all ancient standards of goodness and moral grandeur.

In the newly beginning Michael Age, standards of goodness and moral grandeur such as Whewell had both practised in his own life and further taught to others in his lectures and writings on morality could no longer be taken over from the ancient world, but had to be created afresh. A suitable type of creativity here was both practised and taught by Rudolf Steiner—whose path of destiny had 16 years previously intercrossed with Whewell's path at the railway station in Pottschach.

During the time in 1881 when Steiner as a 20-year-old student was listening in Vienna to Edmund Reitlinger quoting Whewell's work on inductive science, there appeared in London *The Life and Selections from the Correspondence of William Whewell*, edited by his niece Janet Stairs Douglas. This work presented a selection of further letters to many kinds of correspondent, interlinked with biographical commentary. An appendix republished the *Elegiacs* composed on the death of the editor's aunt Cordelia.

Once again, however, although the book ran to over 500 pages, it nowhere contained even the slightest mention of Charles Darwin.[13]

★

Another work published in London during that same year 1881 was Katherine Lyell's *The Life, Letters and Journals of Sir Charles Lyell*. This was in two large volumes, and included among other material much correspondence written to all kinds of people.

One letter, however, was not included, and to the best of the present writer's knowledge has never been published in full. An extract from it had however been quoted in the course of Todhunter's compilation of 1876 about Whewell. According to Todhunter, Lyell sent to Whewell 'not long before publication of the *History of the Inductive Sciences*' a letter including the following statement:

> There was a time when I used to regret that you had not concentrated your powers on some one department of physical science and become a giant in that, or at least that you had been satisfied with some two or three of the arts and sciences, but I have for some years come round to the belief that you have been exercising the calling for which Nature intended you, and for which she gave you strength and genius, and that you have given a greater impulse to the advancement of science among us by being a universalist, and by mastering so much of chemistry, mineralogy, astronomy, geology and other branches, than you would have done if restricted to the perfecting of one alone.

Any reader of this statement will readily understand how appropriate it was for Edmund Reitlinger, whom Steiner described as a universal thinker (*ein universeller Denker*) to have been fond of quoting from the work of a universalist like William Whewell.

4
WHEWELL'S BOOK ON INDUCTIVE SCIENCES

The Basis for a Spiritual World-conception

The 'documents de Barr' include a paragraph about Rudolf Steiner's years at the Technical College in Vienna in the early 1880s:

> Official studies were geared towards mathematics, chemistry, physics, zoology, botany, mineralogy and geology. These studies offered to lay the basis for a spiritual world-conception of much greater security than for instance history or literature, which supplied no particular method, nor significant outlooks over German scientific activity of the time.

It is here made evident that the laying of a secure 'basis for a spiritual world-conception'—later given out as anthroposophy—was offered to Steiner by the scientific subjects he was studying at the Technical College.

And yet the two other subjects, history and literature, named as examples of studies which by contrast did not offer much real security as 'the basis for a spiritual world-conception' were nonetheless both also being studied by him. The autobiographical lecture recounts that during his student years he attended lectures given in Vienna University by the historian Ottokar Lorenz. And he was continuously attending lectures given at the Technical College by the literary specialist Karl Julius Schröer. Both history and literature therefore also formed part of the young Steiner's studies.

But neither Lorenz nor Schröer were able to supply any 'significant outlooks'—or probably indeed any outlooks at all—'over German scientific activity of the time'. Their professional fields were not as such scientific, but humanistic. By the general course of his previous education, however, Steiner had already been to a large extent set onto a scientific path, and was hoping to find outlooks, preferably significant, over various fields within the scientific realm then being researched by German-speaking persons like himself.

★

Steiner's 'official studies' at the Technical College enabled him in particular to gain a number of outlooks over the science of physics. In a preface written in December 1909 to his work *Die Geheimwissenschaft* (translated into English as *Occult Science*) which traces the evolution of the world backwards in time to warmth-processes of a state of existence termed 'Old Saturn', he explained that

> ... the author ... would quite certainly never have undertaken to publish everything stated in this book regarding for instance processes of warmth, if he were not able to assert the following. Thirty years ago he was in a position to make a thorough study of physics, ramifying into various realms of this science. In the domain of warmth-phenomena what then stood at the centre of study were explanations belonging to the so-called 'mechanical theory of heat'. And to him this 'mechanical theory of heat' was actually of quite particular interest. He was continuously studying the historical development of relevant explanations, then linked to names like Jul. Robert Mayer, Helmholtz, Joule, Clausius and so on ...

The physicist James Joule was of course English, but the other three named persons were German. At the time Steiner was studying in Vienna two of them were still alive: Hermann von Helmholtz, a pioneer in several scientific fields, and Rudolf Clausius, founder of the mechanical theory of heat. The work undertaken by these two researchers offered precisely an area of study where Steiner could find 'significant outlooks over German scientific activity of the time'.

Helmholtz was indeed mentioned in the article 'Into the Interior of Nature' in Edmund Reitlinger's book *Freie Blicke*. So too was Julius Robert Mayer, who discovered the law of the conservation of energy. Mayer died in 1878, a year before Steiner's arrival in Vienna, but as some of his writings only came out posthumously his work in effect still formed a significant part of contemporary German science. In his autobiography Steiner specified:

> I was at the time stimulated to read almost all writings by Julius Robert Mayer; and it gave me really great pleasure to be often allowed to speak orally with Reitlinger about their content.

⋆

Now besides 'significant outlooks over German scientific activity' there was according to the above-quoted passage from the 'documents de Barr' also another element impliedly being provided by the official studies at the Technical College which in Steiner's eyes 'offered to set the basis for a spiritual world-conception'. This other element was denoted as a 'particular method'.

Here again, Steiner did not find this element provided by his studies in either history or literature, as is apparent from the descriptions of his teachers in these two subjects. In the autobiographical lecture he stated that:

> ... Lorenz was certainly a character who could make an impression on quite young men. In his lectures he would really utter the harshest of words, laying in as historian with many pieces of evidence against what was being laid into ...

And in his autobiography Steiner wrote that

> Schröer was a person who cared nothing for systematizing. He thought and spoke out of a certain intuition ...

In utterly different ways, both Lorenz and Schröer perceptibly affected the young student. The effect of Lorenz was probably minimal, while that exerted by Schröer was certainly enormous. But however interesting the content of their historical or literary teaching, neither Lorenz's attacking style nor even Schröer's intuitional approach could offer Steiner a 'particular method' whereby to lay the basis for a spiritual world-conception of which he felt secure.

The 'particular method' he considered suitable for laying such a basis was one to which he had already grown accustomed during his years at the *Realschule* in Wiener Neustadt and which he then also found practised in Vienna in his official studies at the Technical College—mathematics, chemistry, physics, zoology, botany, mineralogy and geology. The method referred to may simply be termed the method of modern science.

Naturally this method had its variations in each particular scientific discipline, and of the seven here named, Steiner in his autobiography mentioned directly only two: mathematics and physics.

These two subjects had always been central to his educational development. Steiner described how already at Pottschach 'it was especially the lawfulness of Nature which attracted me, just in its small outliers', so that when supposed to be learning how to write he was actually much less interested in doing so than in making 'physical studies of the elasticity of quill material'. After moving to Neudörfl, he was soon captivated by the geometry-book of Franz Mocnik; and when Franz Maráz explained the Copernican system of the universe he embarked on further physical studies in the wider field of astronomy.

During Steiner's first years at the *Realschule* in Wiener-Neustadt he became absorbed by writings of the then headmaster, Heinrich Schramm, about physical nature-processes. 'Wherever I could get hold of mathematical and physical books, I used the opportunity.' All through his teenage years he had as class-teacher the beloved Laurence Jelinek, an excellent teacher of mathematics and physics. And as teacher in geometrical drawing and descriptive geometry he had the remarkable Georg Kosak—who from 1875 onwards marked him as 'outstanding', a mark never before given in that school. Discovering books by Lübsen on self-instruction in mathematics, Steiner then acquired for himself further knowledge of precisely this subject.

For the final physics examination in the summer of 1879 Jelinek set Steiner to explain the telephone—the most modern physical apparatus of that time. On the school-leaving certificate he marked his pupil as 'excellent' in both physics and mathematics. Kosak too marked him as 'excellent' in geometry.

Steiner's chief private interest during these years had to a large extent become philosophy, but mathematics and physics still remained his core academic subjects. The 'particular method' referred to in the 'documents de Barr' must therefore come to direct or indirect expression in what he had to say about his studies at the Technical College in these two subjects.

With regard to mathematics, described by Steiner as the 'basis of my whole striving for knowledge', it was ironic, if also karmically appropriate, that having decided not to study descriptive geometry at the Technical College—because it would take up too much time—he then made an exciting discovery during a mathematical lecture by learning about synthetic geometry. This recently elaborated mathematical discipline provided a conceptual and methodic tool which he was later to metamorphose into other areas of thought and life.

All the more surprising is it that Steiner did not bother to give the name of the teacher in whose lecture this exciting discovery was made! His silence on the matter stands in striking contrast to the description of his physics studies, where he specifically named Edmund Reitlinger as 'a person whom I quite exceptionally revered'.

And his description went on to state that Reitlinger was

> ...a man with a strictly inductive way of research; for everything methodical in physics he was fond of quoting Whewell's book on inductive sciences.

It may then be deduced that with regard to physics the 'particular method' employed in the official scientific studies which 'offered to lay the basis for a spiritual world-conception' must have been brought to expression for Steiner in Reitlinger's quotations from the work of William Whewell.

Fond of Quoting

When in his autobiography Rudolf Steiner stated that 'for everything methodical in physics' Edmund Reitlinger 'was fond of quoting Whewell's book on inductive sciences', he did not specify the book's title. So the question immediately arises: which of Whewell's two works on this subject was meant?

The work in question, as correctly stated in the index to current editions of Steiner's *Lebensgang*, was quite certainly *The Philosophy of the Inductive Sciences*, which contains numerous observations by Whewell on the subject of scientific methodology, both physical and otherwise.

Reitlinger's quotations—as heard by Steiner—must then have been in the original English, since no German translation of this work existed.

In order that readers may gain an impression of the kind of quotations Reitlinger might have made, it seems appropriate to bring forward from Whewell's book some examples of quotable passages.

★

Already at the beginning of the first volume of *The Philosophy of the Inductive Sciences*, among the 'Aphorisms Concerning Science' may be found these:

XXVII.

> The Methods by which the construction of Science is promoted are *Methods of Observation*, *Methods of obtaining clear Ideas*, and *Methods of Induction*.

XXVIII.

> The Methods of Observation of Quantity in general are *Numeration*, which is precise by the nature of Number, the *Measurement of Space* and *of Time*, which are easily made precise; the *Conversion of Space and Time*, by which each aids the measurement of the other; the *Method of Repetition*; the *Method of Coincidences* or *Interferences*. The measurement of Weight is made precise by the *Method of Double-weighing*. Secondary Qualities are measured by means of *Scales of Degrees*; but in order to apply these scales the student requires the *Education of the Senses*. The Education of the Senses is forwarded by the practical study of *Descriptive Natural History*, *Chemical Manipulation*, and *Astronomical Observation*.

XXIX.

> The Methods by which the acquisition of clear Scientific Ideas is promoted are mainly two: *Intellectual Education* and *Discussion of Ideas*.

Further aphorisms were then given on 'Methods of Induction', the 'Method of Gradation', and the 'Method of Natural Classification'.

If Reitlinger in his lecture courses at the Technical College quoted as much as a single sentence from any such aphorism, he would already have taught Steiner more English than ever had Father Schmeisser in Wiener-Neustadt!

★

Whewell expanded all these aphorisms in the main text of the second volume, in the 'book' entitled 'Of Methods Employed in the Formation of Science', from which Reitlinger might also have quoted. A couple of examples may therefore be given of passages containing memorable phrases.

Since Steiner was working under Reitlinger 'in the physics laboratory in many fields', and also attending his lectures on 'physics for chemists', it seems at least possible for one of those fields to have involved chemical experimentation. At a suitable point Reitlinger might have referred to the chapter in this 'book' on 'Methods of Observation', and quoted from the section on 'Manipulation':

> The process of applying practically methods of experiment and observation is termed Manipulation; and the value of observations depends much upon the proficiency of the observer in this art. This skill appears, as we have said, not only in devising means and modes of measuring results, but also in inventing and executing arrangements by which elements are subjected to such conditions as the investigation requires: in finding and using some material combination by which Nature shall be asked the question which we have in our minds. To do this in any subject may be considered as a peculiar art, but especially in chemistry; where 'many experiments, and even whole trains of research, are essentially dependent for success on mere manipulation' (Faraday's *Chemical Manipulation*, p. 3). The changes which the chemist has to study—compositions, decompositions and mutual actions, affecting the internal structure rather than the external form and motion of bodies—are not familiarly recognized by common observers as those actions are which operate upon the total mass of a body: and hence it is only when the chemist has become to a certain degree familiar with his science that he has the power of observing. He must learn to interpret the effects of mixture, heat, and other chemical agencies, so as to see in them those facts which chemistry makes the basis of her doctrines. And in learning to interpret this language, he must also learn to call it forth—to place bodies under the requisite conditions, by the apparatus of his own laboratory and the operations of his own fingers . . .

★

Now Steiner also described as 'of special importance to me' Reitlinger's lectures on the history of physics.

Reitlinger could suitably have quoted from the following chapter in the same 'book', entitled 'Of Methods of Acquiring Clear Scientific Ideas; and first of Intellectual Education'. For in the opening paragraph of a section headed 'Idea of Space', Whewell made specific historical references to both Thales and Kepler—the latter in regard to conic sections, one of the subjects which as a teenager the author had studied at Kendal in 1811–12 under the blind John Gough.

> It is easily seen that education may do at least something to render our ideas distinct and precise. To learn geometry in youth tends manifestly to render our idea of space clear and exact. By such an education all the relations, all the consequences of this idea come to be readily and steadily apprehended; and thus it becomes easy for us to understand portions of science which otherwise we should by no means be able to comprehend. The conception of *similar triangles* was to be mastered before the disciples of Thales could see the validity of his method of determining the height of lofty objects by the length of their shadows. The conception of *the sphere with its circles* had to become familiar before the annual motion of the Sun and its influence upon the lengths of days could be rightly traced. The properties of circles, combined with the *pure doctrine of motion* (see Book II, c. xiii.) were required as an introduction to the theory of epicycles: the properties of *conic sections* were needed as a preparation for the discoveries of Kepler. And not only was it necessary that men should possess a *knowledge* of certain figures and their properties; but it was equally necessary that they should have the *habit of reasoning* with perfect steadiness, precision and conclusiveness concerning the relations of space. No small discipline of the mind is requisite in most cases to accustom it to go with complete insight and security through the demonstrations respecting intersecting planes and lines, dihedral and trihedral angles, which occur in solid geometry. Yet how absolutely necessary is a perfect mastery of such reasonings to him who is to explain the motions of the Moon in latitude and longitude! How necessary, again, is the same faculty to the student of crystallography! Without mathematical habits of conception and of thinking, these portions of science are perfectly inaccessible. But the early study of plane and solid geometry gives to all tolerably gifted persons the habits which are thus needed. The discipline of following the didactic works on this subject till we are quite familiar with them, and of devising for ourselves reasonings of the same kind (as for instance the solutions of problems proposed) soon gives the mind the power of *discoursing* with perfect facility concerning the most complex and multiplied relations of space, and enables us to refer to the properties of all plane and solid figures as surely as to the visible forms of things. Thus we have here a signal instance of the efficacy of education in giving to our conceptions that clearness which the formation and existence of science indispensably require.

★

Indeed much of the main text of *The Philosophy of the Inductive Sciences* may be said to have a peculiarly quotable character. When the work was reprinted in 1967, its twentieth-century editor ended his introduction by stating:

Finally, one of the greatest and most obvious merits of Whewell's book is the large number of brilliant passages and phrases, often of a descriptive or metaphorical nature, which perhaps allow us to catch something of the brilliance of Whewell's living speech. Some of these passages have already been given, but many more could be quoted, such as: 'physical discoverers have differed from barren speculators not by having *no* metaphysics in their head, but by having *good* metaphysics while their opponents had bad'; or 'truth is consistent and can bear the tug-of-war; error is incoherent, and falls to pieces in the struggle' . . .

★

On introducing the figure of Reitlinger into his autobiography Steiner observed that

. . . when I became his pupil he was already suffering from an advanced disease of the lungs . . .

A reader who pictures this tuberculous lecturer quoting from Whewell's work on inductive sciences may then also recall Steiner's further statement:

. . . One felt he spoke in such a way that because of his illness every word was difficult. And yet his lectures were in the best sense inspiring . . .

Every word in the English quotations from *The Philosophy of the Inductive Sciences* spoken by Edmund Reitlinger in this difficult way must have contributed its share towards that inspiration.

Scientific Hypotheses

After stating in his autobiography that Edmund Reitlinger 'was fond of quoting Whewell's book on inductive sciences', Rudolf Steiner added:

. . . From historical observation of physical problems he would always proceed to general perspectives of cultural history. In a lecture on natural science there would indeed appear quite general philosophical ideas. He would go into optimism and pessimism, and speak in an extremely stimulating way about the justification of forming scientific hypotheses. His presentation of Kepler and characterization of Julius Robert Mayer were masterpieces of scientific lecturing.

Readers of William Whewell's *Philosophy of the Inductive Sciences* will be aware that in course of this work very clear expression is given to the justification of forming scientific hypotheses.

Already at the beginning of the first volume, the 'Aphorisms Concerning Science' included these:

VIII.

The conceptions by which facts are bound together are suggested by the sagacity of discoverers. This sagacity cannot be taught. It commonly succeeds by guessing; and this success seems to consist in framing several *tentative hypotheses* and selecting the right one. But a supply of appropriate hypotheses cannot be constructed by rule, nor without inventive talent.

IX.

The truth of tentative hypotheses must be tested by their application to facts. The discoverer must be ready carefully to try his hypotheses in this manner, and to reject them if they will not bear the test, in spite of indolence and vanity.

X.

The process of scientific discovery is cautious and rigorous, not by abstaining from hypotheses, but by rigorously comparing hypotheses with facts, and by resolutely rejecting all which the comparison does not confirm.

XI.

Hypotheses may be useful, though involving much that is superfluous, and even erroneous; for they may supply the true bond of connexion of the facts; and the superfluity and error may afterwards be pared away.

The argument of these aphorisms was expanded by Whewell in the main text of the second volume, in the 'book' entitled 'Of the Construction of Science'. Its fifth chapter, 'Of Certain Characteristics of Scientific Induction', contained several sections discussing the matter.

In one of these sections there comes again a mention of Kepler, such as might also have been adduced by Reitlinger:

> Yet still, we may do something in tracing the process by which such discoveries are made; and this it is here our business to do. We may observe that these, and the like discoveries, are not improperly described as happy guesses; and that guesses, in these as in other instances, imply various suppositions made, of which some one turns out to be the right one. We may, in such cases, conceive the discoverer as inventing and trying many conjectures, till he finds one which answers the purpose of combining the scattered facts into a single rule. The discovery of general truths from special facts is performed, commonly at least, and more commonly than at first appears, by the use of a series of Suppositions, or *Hypotheses*, which are looked at in quick succession, and of which the one which really leads to truth is rapidly detected, and when caught sight of, firmly held, verified, and followed to its consequences. In the minds of most discoverers this process of invention, trial, and acceptance or rejection of the hypothesis goes on so rapidly that we cannot trace it in its successive steps. But in some instances we can do so; and we can also see that the other examples of discovery do

not differ essentially from these. The same intellectual operations take place in other cases, although this often happens so instantaneously that we lose trace of the progression. In the discoveries made by Kepler, we have a curious and memorable exhibition of this process in its details. Thanks to his communicative disposition, we know that he made nineteen hypotheses with regard to the motion of Mars, and calculated the results of each, before he established the true doctrine that the planet's path is an ellipse . . .

⋆

In the first volume of Christoph Lindenberg's *Rudolf Steiner*, the biographer describes the initial years at the Technical College, and summarizes the effect made on Steiner by his physics teacher:

> . . . he heard Reitlinger give two lecture courses on the history of physics. This genetic introduction into physical problems and methods, presented with great vividness by Reitlinger, was especially stimulating for Steiner because in this way he came to know the decisive points of physical thought-formation and the mostly forgotten alternatives of physical thinking . . . He admired the universal manner with which Reitlinger, already fatally ill, presented the evolution of physical research by everywhere opening out perspectives of cultural history . . .

The first course on the history of physics to be given by Reitlinger during Steiner's time at the Technical College was chronologically the later part, 'From Newton to modern times'. It took place during the first term of Steiner's second year at the Technical College, from autumn of 1880 over the winter and into the next spring. On 18 March 1881 Steiner was examined in the subject by Reitlinger and marked 'excellent'.

At the end of the following summer term Steiner took further exams. On 1 July he was examined by Karl Julius Schröer on the history and grammar of New High German, and marked 'excellent'. On the 4th he was once more examined by Reitlinger, this time on the mechanical theory of heat, and again marked 'excellent'.

Decisively Rejected

After describing Edmund Reitlinger in his autobiography, Rudolf Steiner went on:

> Through the mechanical theory of heat and the wave theory of manifestations of light and effects of electricity I was forced into epistemological studies. At the time the physical outer world was presented as processes of motion in matter. Sense-impressions seemed to be only subjective experi-

> ences, like effects on the human senses of mere processes of motion. Out there in space the material processes of motion are taking place; if these processes encounter the human sense of warmth, man experiences sensations of warmth. *Outside* man are wave-processes in the ether; if these encounter the optic nerve, sensations of light and colour will arise *in* man.
>
> This point of view I met with everywhere. It caused my thinking unspeakable difficulties. It drove all spirit out from the objective outer world. I held in my mind the idea that if observation of natural phenomena did lead to such assumptions, one could not approach *these* assumptions with a view of the spirit. I saw how seductive these assumptions are for the trend of thought then cultivated by science. Even now I could not yet decide to set a personal way of thinking, even just for myself, against what then prevailed. But precisely this caused difficult interior struggles. Again and again the easily conceivable critique of this trend of thought had to be inwardly suppressed, in order to wait for a time when further sources and paths of knowledge would provide greater certainty.

In his previously quoted article, Walter Johannes Stein continued his account of the relation between Rudolf Steiner and Karl Julius Schröer:

> The path taken by Herman Grimm of praising Goethe's *Doctrine of Colours* as a stylistic masterpiece, while disregarding the content, Schröer could not follow. At this moment his glance fell on the youthful Rudolf Steiner, who was grasping humanist and realist sides of knowledge in a similar manner . . .

In his autobiography Steiner himself recorded:

> My experiences at that time were strongly bound up with my relation to Karl Julius Schröer. But above all else I was striving to come into an inner debate with the sciences, which to him were more remote. I also wanted to recognize my 'objective idealism' as in harmony with knowledge of Nature.
>
> At the time of my most vital intercourse with Schröer the matter of the relation between the spiritual and natural worlds came before my mind in a renewed manner. To start with, this happened quite independently from Goethe's scientific way of thinking. For even Schröer could tell me nothing definite about this area of Goethe's creativity. It pleased him when he found that one or other scientist gave favourable acknowledgement to Goethe's observations about the beings of plants and animals. But he found that scientifically educated people everywhere decidedly rejected Goethe's teaching on colours. So he did not develop any particular opinion on the subject.

Favourable acknowlegement to Goethe's observations about the beings of plants and animals was for instance given by William Whewell in the third volume of his *History of the Inductive Sciences*—also available in a German translation by Johann Joseph von Littrow published in Vienna.

Rudolf Steiner, c. 1881, aged about 20

But if Schröer ever opened the second volume of Littrow's rendering he would have read (in German) Whewell's decisive rejection of Goethe's teaching on colours:

> . . . and since that time, the soundness of the Newtonian law of refraction has hardly been questioned among physical philosophers.
>
> It has however in modern times been very vehemently controverted in a quarter from which we might not readily have expected a detailed discussion on such a subject. The celebrated Göthe has written a work on *The Doctrine of Colours* (*Farbenlehre*; Tübingen, 1810), one main purpose of which is to represent Newton's opinions and the work in which they are formally published (his *Opticks*) as utterly false and mistaken, and capable of being assented to only by the most blind and obstinate prejudice. Those who are acquainted with the extent to which such an opinion, promulgated by Göthe, was likely to be widely adopted in Germany, will not be surprised that similar language is used by other writers of that nation. Thus Schelling (*Vorlesungen*, p. 270) says 'Newton's *Opticks* is the greatest proof of the possibility of a whole structure of fallacies, which in all its parts is founded upon observation and experiment.' Göthe, however, does not concede even so much to Newton's work. He goes over a large portion of it, page by page, quarrelling with the experiments, diagrams, reasoning and language,

without intermission; and holds that it is not reconcilable with the most simple facts. He declares (*Farbenlehre*, vol. ii. p. 678) that the first time he looked through a prism he saw the white walls of the room still look white, 'and though alone, I pronounced, as by an instinct, that the Newtonian doctrine is false'. We need not here point out how inconsistent with the Newtonian doctrine it was to expect, as Göthe expected, that the wall should be all over coloured various colours.

Göthe not only adopted and strenuously maintained the opinion that the Newtonian theory was false, but framed a system of his own to explain the phenomena of colour. As a matter of curiosity, it may be worth our while to state the nature of this system, although undoubtedly it forms no part of the *progress* of physical science. Göthe's views are in fact little different from those of Aristotle and Antonio de Dominis, though more completely and systematically developed. According to him, colours arise when we see through a dim medium ('ein trübes mittel'). Light in itself is colourless; but if it be seen through a somewhat dim medium, it appears yellow; if the dimness of the medium increases, or if its depth be augmented, we see the light gradually assume a yellow-red colour, which finally is heightened to a ruby-red. On the other hand, if darkness is seen through a dim medium illuminated by a light falling on it, a blue colour is seen, which becomes clearer and paler, the more the dimness of the medium increases, and darker and fuller, as the medium becomes more transparent; and when we come to 'the smallest degree of the purest dimness' we see the most perfect violet. (*Farbenlehre*, 150, p. 151). In addition to this 'doctrine of the dim medium' we have a second principle asserted concerning refraction. In a vast variety of cases, images are accompanied by 'accessory images', as when we see bright objects in a looking-glass. (ib. 223.) Now when an image is displaced by refraction, the displacement is not complete, clear and sharp, but incomplete, so that there is an accessory image along with the principal one. (ib. 227.) From these principles, the colours produced by refraction in the image of a bright object on a dark ground are at once derivable. The accessory image is semi-transparent (ib. 238); and hence that border of it which is pushed forwards is drawn from the dark over the bright, and there the yellow appears; on the other hand, where the clear border laps over the dark ground, the blue is seen (ib. 239); and hence we easily see that the image must appear red and yellow at one end, and blue and violet at the other.

We need not explain this system further, or attempt to show how vague and loose, as well as baseless, are the notions and mode of conception which it introduces. Perhaps it is not difficult to point out the peculiarities in Göthe's intellectual character which led to his singularly unphilosophical views on this subject. One important circumstance is that he appears, like many persons in whom the poetical imagination is very active, to have been destitute of the talent and the habit of geometrical thought. In all probability he never apprehended clearly and steadily those relations of position on which the Newtonian doctrine depends. Another cause of his inability to accept the doctrine probably was that he had conceived the 'composition' of colours in some way altogether different from that which Newton understands by composition. What Göthe expected to see, we cannot clearly collect; but we know from his own statement that his intention of experimenting with a prism arose from his speculations on the rules of colouring in pictures; and we can easily see that any notion of the composition of colours which such researches would suggest would require to be laid aside before he could understand Newton's theory of the composition of light.

Astonishingly Wide Reading

The fourth chapter of Rudolf Steiner's autobiography is largely taken up with descriptions of five different friends whom he made during his years at the Technical College. But none of them are there named.

Only one of these friends was still alive when Steiner was writing his autobiographical articles in 1924, and indeed he also outlived Steiner. This was the last one described. According to Steiner he had also been to the *Realschule* at Wiener Neustadt, though a year below himself, and first went on to the Technical College at Vienna in the autumn of 1880, commuting every day from Wiener Neustadt. At this time he opposed Steiner's spiritual views, and one day their animated debate on materialism reached a kind of culmination at the *Südbahnhof* in Vienna five minutes before departure of the train taking this friend back to Wiener Neustadt.

Steiner remarked:

> ... Later in life I experienced how close this friend was to my state of soul even then, but at the time he would not allow this inner being to emerge at all.

In the light of this remark it is interesting that they both had the same Christian name. The friend was called Rudolf Schober, and from the brief account in the autobiography one would never be able to guess that until Steiner left for Weimar ten years later he was meeting Schober almost every day. On Steiner's subsequent return visits to Vienna, Schober was always kept informed.

After Steiner's death in 1925, Rudolf Schober provided identifications of other friends from these Viennese years.

★

The second of the five friends described by Steiner, the poetry enthusiast who could make no other connection to existence, was named Rudolf Ronsperger—there were plenty of Rudolfs at the Technical College. Although Ronsperger was about a year younger than Steiner, the intensity of their relationship is shown by the survival of nine letters from Steiner addressed to him, all written within the space of a single month during the summer holidays of 1881, and covering no less than 30 pages in the *Gesamtausgabe* edition of the *Briefe*.

These letters to Ronsperger were written from Oberlaa, a village about a mile to the east of Inzersdorf. So although Steiner's father continued to work at Inzersdorf station, if his family ever lived in that tiny building they only did so for a couple of years at most, before finding in the neighbouring village a more congenial domicile.

★

In his biography of Steiner, Christoph Lindenberg remarks that 'the early letters already give evidence of astonishingly wide reading in the philosophical and literary field'.

Most writers named in Steiner's letters to Ronsperger were German, but that written on 11 August includes a paragraph referring to two well-known figures from English literature:

> I don't wish to doubt that the choice of material for your new tragedy is a fortunate one. You say you don't find in German history any suitable material for a tragedy. This I can quite understand. If I were briefly to provide the reason, I'd say that with German heroes there's a catastrophe but in most cases *no* guilt. But more of this another time. I'll soon be reading M's Milton.

The editorial apparatus in the *Briefe* indicates that 'M' stands for Macaulay. Since the abbreviation shows that Steiner expected his friend to know who was meant, it is possible that Ronsperger had directed him towards this author, or even sent him a copy of the publication referred to.

At this time the Weidmann publishing firm in Berlin had launched a series of Macaulay's *Ausgewählte Essays zur Geschichte der englischen Literatur* in separate little booklets, of which that on Milton had come out in the previous year, 1880. Probably Steiner had in his hands a copy of this booklet.

The Epigone Times

Macaulay's essay on Milton opens with some comments on the latter's prose treatise *De Doctrina Christiana*, recently discovered in his time. It then embarks on a discussion of poetry in general, in relation to the ongoing progress of civilization:

> It is by his poetry that Milton is best known; and it is of his poetry that we wish first to speak. By the general suffrage of the civilized world, his place has been assigned among the greatest masters of the art. His detractors, however, though outvoted, have not been silenced. There are many critics and some of great name, who contrive in the same breath to extol the poems and to decry the poet. The works, they acknowledge, considered in themselves, may be classed among the noblest productions of the human mind. But they will not allow the author to rank with those great men who, born in the infancy of civilization, supplied by their own powers the want of instruction, and though destitute of models themselves, bequeathed to posterity models which defy imitation. Milton, it is said, inherited what his predecessors created; he lived in an enlightened age; he received a finished education; and we must therefore, if we would form a just estimate of his powers, make large deductions in consideration of these advantages.
>
> We venture to say, on the contrary, paradoxical as the remark may appear, that no poet has ever had to struggle with more unfavourable circumstances than Milton. He doubted, as he has himself owned, whether he had been born 'an age too late'. For this notion Johnson has thought fit to make him the butt of much clumsy ridicule. The poet, we believe, understood the nature of his art better than the critic. He knew that his poetical genius derived no advantage from the civilization which surrounded him, or from the learning which he had acquired; and he looked back with something like regret to the ruder age of simple words and vivid impressions.
>
> We think that, as civilization advances, poetry almost necessarily declines. Therefore, though we fervently admire those great works of imagination which have appeared in dark ages, we do not admire them the more because they have appeared in dark ages. On the contrary, we hold that the most wonderful and splendid proof of genius is a great poem produced in a civilized age. We cannot understand why those who believe in that most orthodox article of literary faith, that the earliest poets are generally the best, should wonder at the rule as if it were the exception. Surely the uniformity of the phenomenon indicates a corresponding uniformity in the cause.
>
> The fact is that common observers reason from the progress of the experimental sciences to that of the imitative arts. The improvement of the former is gradual and slow. Ages are spent in collecting materials, ages more in separating and combining them. Even when a system has been formed, there is still something to add, to alter, or to reject. Every generation enjoys the use of a vast hoard bequeathed to it by antiquity, and transmits that hoard, augmented by fresh acquisitions, to future ages. In these pursuits,

therefore, the first speculators lie under great disadvantages, and even when they fail are entitled to praise. Their pupils, with far inferior intellectual powers, speedily surpass them in actual attainments. Every girl who has read Mrs. Marcet's little dialogues on Political Economy could teach Montague or Walpole many lessons in finance. Any intelligent man may now, by resolutely applying himself for a few years to mathematics, learn more than the great Newton knew after half a century of study and meditation.

But it is not thus with music, with painting, or with sculpture. Still less is it thus with poetry. The progress of refinement rarely supplies these arts with better objects of imitation. It may indeed improve the instruments which are necessary to the mechanical operations of the musician, the sculptor, and the painter. But language, the machine of the poet, is best fitted for his purpose in its rudest state. Nations, like individuals, first perceive, and then abstract. They advance from particular images to general terms. Hence the vocabulary of an enlightened society is philosophical, that of a half-civilized people is poetical.

This change in the language of men is partly the cause and partly the effect of a corresponding change in the nature of their intellectual operations, of a change by which science gains and poetry loses. Generalization is necessary to the advancement of knowledge; but particularity is indispensable to the creations of the imagination. In proportion as men know more and think more, they look less at individuals and more at classes. They therefore make better theories and worse poems. They give us vague phrases instead of images, and personified qualities instead of men. They may be better able to analyse human nature than their predecessors. But analysis is not the business of the poet. His office is to portray, not to dissect. He may believe in a moral sense, like Shaftesbury; he may refer all human actions to self-interest, like Helvetius; or he may never think about the matter at all. His creed on such subjects will no more influence his poetry, properly so called, than the notions which a painter may have conceived respecting the lacrymal glands, or the circulation of the blood, will affect the tears of his Niobe, or the blushes of his Aurora. If Shakespeare had written a book on the motives of human actions, it is by no means certain that it would have been a good one. It is extremely improbable that it would have contained half so much able reasoning on the subject as is to be found in the Fable of the Bees. But could Mandeville have created an Iago? Well as he knew how to resolve characters into their elements, would he have been able to combine those elements in such a manner as to make up a man, a real, living, individual man?

★

A further letter from Steiner to Ronsperger written just a week after his previous one, on 18 August, ended with this paragraph:

I'll be writing and sending off without delay a continuation of the present letter. It will answer the questions you've raised, and also contain something about M's Milton, which I've just read.

I remain meanwhile

Your ever faithful

Rudolf Steiner

Steiner's next letter to Ronsperger was written on the very next day, 19 August. Although he made no explicit reference to Macaulay's essay on Milton, the theme explored in the early part of this essay was in a sense developed in the course of the following paragraph:

> But since we have thus already come onto the problem of 'standing at the peak of the time', I want to tell you my opinion of it. I believe that what people usually understand by 'standing at the peak of the time' is being acquainted with the spirit's most important present-day activities and working in harmony with its achievements. It is however clear that not every time is especially rich in fundamental thoughts, but often centuries are needed to spin out the length and breadth of once validated viewpoints. Such are the epigone times and we're now living in one of these. Since spiritual activities in such times remain pretty well at the same level and no deed towers above any other, a 'standing at the peak of the time' in such periods will require 'living into' a great deal, though sometimes, observed from a general human standpoint, into highly unimportant matters. Such training of course demands a great amount of application and memory-work, and no wonder if originality be then lost. You seem at first to be thinking of such periods by saying that not everyone can wrest their bit of talent through the desert of scholarly training. But since spiritual actions at such times have only a secondary nature, I don't in any way believe a poet needs that wresting process. It's quite different with thoughts which move the world, such as come to effect in classical epochs. These absolutely belong to a higher training and a poet has not to learn but *to experience* them. A poet who wants to create not for time but for eternity must however be acquainted with those common human driving-wheels...

Christoph Lindenberg in his biography quotes a couple of sentences from this paragraph as showing the influence on Steiner of Karl Julius Schröer, who lived in the past atmosphere of German classic writers. Without in any way minimizing such an influence, one may however add that connections in the letter may also be perceived with the thought of Thomas Babington Macaulay.

Occult Power

Since on 18 August 1881 Rudolf Steiner stated in his letter to Rudolf Ronsperger that he had read Macaulay's essay on Milton, he must also have read in that essay these further paragraphs:

> The most striking characteristic of the poetry of Milton is the extreme remoteness of the associations by means of which it acts on the reader. Its effect is produced not so much by what it expresses as by what it suggests; not so much by the ideas which it directly conveys, as by other ideas which are connected with them. He electrifies the mind through conductors. The most unimaginative man must understand the *Iliad*. Homer gives him no choice, and requires from him no exertion, but takes the whole upon himself, and sets the images in so clear a light that it is impossible to be blind to them. The works of Milton cannot be comprehended or enjoyed unless the mind of the reader co-operate with that of the writer. He does not paint a finished picture, or play for a mere passive listener. He sketches and leaves others to fill up the outline. He strikes the key-note, and expects his hearers to make out the melody.
>
> We often hear of the magical influence of poetry. The expression in general means nothing: but applied to the writings of Milton, it is most appropriate. His poetry acts like an incantation. Its merit lies less in its obvious meaning than in its occult power. There would seem at first sight to be no more in his words than in other words. But they are words of enchantment. No sooner are they pronounced than the past is present and the distant near. New forms of beauty start at once into existence, and all the burial-places of the memory give up their dead. Change the structure of the sentence; substitute one synonym for another, and the whole effect is destroyed. The spell loses its power; and he who should then hope to conjure with it would find himself as much mistaken as Cassim in the Arabian tale, when he stood crying 'Open Wheat', 'Open Barley', to the door which obeyed no sound but 'Open Sesame'. The miserable failure of Dryden in his attempt to translate into his own diction some parts of the *Paradise Lost* is a remarkable instance of this.
>
> In support of these observations we may remark that scarcely any passages in the poems of Milton are more generally known or more frequently repeated than those which are little more than muster-rolls of names. They are not always more appropriate or more melodious than other names. But they are charmed names. Every one of them is the first link in a long chain of associated ideas. Like the dwelling-place of our infancy revisited in manhood, like the song of our country heard in a strange land, they produce upon us an effect wholly independent of their intrinsic value. One transports us back to a remote period of history. Another places us among the novel scenes and manners of a distant region. A third evokes all the dear

classical recollections of childhood, the school-room, the dog-eared Virgil, the holiday, and the prize. A fourth brings before us the splendid phantoms of chivalrous romance, the trophied lists, the embroidered housings, the quaint devices, the haunted forests, the enchanted gardens, the achievements of enamoured knights, and the smiles of rescued princesses.

In none of the works of Milton is his peculiar manner more happily displayed than in the 'Allegro' and the 'Penseroso'. It is impossible to conceive that the mechanism of language can be brought to a more exquisite degree of perfection. These poems differ from others, as atar of roses differs from ordinary rose water, the close packed essence from the thin diluted mixture. They are indeed not so much poems, as collections of hints, from each of which the reader is to make out a poem for himself...

Might these paragraphs perhaps have led the 20-year-old Austrian student in 1881 to read 'Il Penseroso' as written in 1631 by the 22-year-old English poet?

> ...But first, and chiefest, with thee bring
> Him that yon soars on golden wing,
> Guiding the fiery-wheeled throne,
> The Cherub Contemplation,
> And the mute Silence hist along,

John Milton in 1630, aged 21

Less Philomel will deign a song,
In her sweetest, saddest plight,
Smoothing the rugged brow of night,
While Cynthia checks her Dragon yoke,
Gently o're th'accustomed Oke;
Sweet bird that shunn'st the noise of folly,
Most musical, most Melancholy!
Thee Chauntress oft the Woods among,
I woo to hear thy Even-Song;
And missing thee, I walk unseen
On the dry smooth-shaven Green,
To behold the wandring Moon,
Riding neer her highest noon,
Like one that had bin led astray
Through the Heav'ns wide pathles way;
And oft, as if her head she bow'd,
Stooping through a fleecy cloud,
Oft on a Plat of rising ground,
I hear the far-off Curfeu sound,
Over some wide-water'd shoar,
Swinging slow with sullen roar;
Or if the Ayr will not permit,
Som stil removed place will fit,
Where glowing Embers through the room
Teach light to counterfeit a gloom,
Far from all resort of mirth,
Save the cricket on the hearth,
Or the Belmans drowsie charm,
To bless the dores from nightly harm:
Or let my Lamp at midnight hour,
Be seen in some high lonely Towr,
Where I may oft out-watch the Bear,
With thrice great Hermes, or unsphear
The spirit of Plato to unfold
What Worlds, or what vast regions hold
The immortal mind that hath forsook
Her mansion in this fleshly nook . . .

About Stars, About Sun and Moon

The most famous piece of research into Rudolf Steiner's early life was the discovery by Emil Bock in autumn 1958 of the identity of the herb-gatherer described in the autobiography, as related in Bock's posthumously published *Rudolf Steiner: Studien*. On a visit to Austria made at the age of 63, little more than a year before his own death, Bock finally succeeded in penetrating the herb-gatherer's previous 'mythical halo' by tracking down his surname and other relevant details in the village of Trumau where—as had just come to light through publication of a pedagogical seminar in which Steiner mentioned him as the prototype of 'Felix Balde'—he had been resident. He was named Felix Koguzki, and had had a large family of five sons.

Bock soon located and went on to visit the still living fourth son, aged 76, Richard Koguzki. On the following day the latter took him to meet his nephew Anton, fathered by the similarly named second son. Anton junior had inherited his grandfather's diary, in which Bock was able to read the following entries:

> Nr. 41 'Herr Steiner jun., studiosus, living at Inzersdorf, visited me on Sunday the 21st of August a. D. 1881; unfortunately I was not at home.'
> Nr. 42 'H. St. came to visit me a second time on Friday the 26th o. t. m. a. y.' ('of this month and year').

So the exact date was revealed on which the 20-year-old Viennese student had visited Felix Koguzki in his Trumau home 77 years previously.

★

Rudolf Steiner, after describing the herb-gatherer in his autobiography, added these sentences:

> And yet this person stood worlds apart from anything effusive. On entering his home, one was in a circle of the most sober and simple country family . . .

Bock's researches allow a reader to picture the family constellation at the time of Steiner's visit. Felix himself had a few weeks previously reached the age of 48, while his wife Johanna, younger by 18 years, was aged 30. Their eldest son, named Felix after his father, was aged four, and their second son Anton, known as 'Toni', two years old.

Steiner continued:

> . . . Above the door of his house stood the words '*In Gottes Segen ist alles gelegen*'. One was given refreshment, as with other villagers. I always had to drink coffee, not out of a cup, but out of a '*Häferl*' holding nearly a litre; I also had to eat a piece of bread of gigantic dimensions . . .

The adverb 'always' may in this passage seem problematic. For before writing his autobiography Steiner had previously described the herb-gatherer's house in a lecture given on 22 June 1919 in Stuttgart, where he had stated that

> ... I myself was only in this little house one single time during my youth ...

The solution to the discrepancy must presumably be that when on his first visit on 21 August 1881 Steiner found the herb-gatherer not at home, he was given refreshment as described 'with other villagers' who already then plied him with coffee and bread in Trumau size and style.

Indeed in describing the herb-gatherer Steiner went on to make further reference to these same villagers:

> ... Nor did the villagers consider the man effusive. The way he behaved in his home environment beat off any ridicule. He also had a healthy sense of humour, and on meeting any young or old person in the village knew how to speak in such a way that people were cheered by his words ...

With reference to 'any young ... person' one may reflect that the 93-year-old Steinhauser who in the autumn of 1958 could still inform Bock about Felix's surname would in the summer of 1881 have been aged about 16.

Five days after his first visit, Steiner reappeared in Trumau and made his only entrance into the Koguzki household. On this occasion it was of course there that he was again obliged to drink the '*Häferl*' of coffee and eat the gigantic hunk of bread. So although he may only have gone to Trumau twice in his whole life, it was quite correct to say that he had 'always' had a near-litre of coffee on his visits to that village.

On first leaving school at the age of twelve Felix Koguzki had initially been apprenticed to a baker. On this basis, it seems possible that the enormous piece of bread eaten by Steiner on 26 August 1881 might well have been home-baked.

*

The precise topics of that day's conversation are nowhere recorded. But in an esoteric lesson held at 8.30 a.m. on 30 December 1923 during the Christmas Foundation Meeting of the General Anthroposophical Society, Steiner referred to the part played in his life by

> ... the herb-gatherer who would speak in words going right into one's heart about plants, about stones, about animals, about stars, about Sun and Moon ...

Not that the whole day was necessarily taken up by talking. The old Trumau villagers who could still remember him in 1958, 49 years after his death, recalled that the herb-gatherer also played the accordion. Indeed Richard Koguzki informed Bock that his father used to sing both merry and serious songs, having a wonderfully fine and very powerful baritone voice. He described a warm evening inside their home with his father playing on a well-sounding accordion with three keyboards, and passers-by stopping with approving looks at the open window and giving loud applause at the end . . .

★

Another detail discovered by Bock was this:

> . . . The father was very devout. The children had to pray before meals and before going to bed . . .

Steiner must still have been present when Felix junior said his evening prayers and perhaps Toni tried to imitate him. For in the previously mentioned lecture on 22 June 1919 at Stuttgart the description of the herb-gatherer began:

> In Lower Austria, at a place from which on looking south one overviews mountains which are particularly beautiful in the red evening sky—the Lower Austrian Schneeberg, the Wechsel, mountains forming the northern edge of Styria—there is a small, very unprepossessing little house . . .

The 'red evening sky' indicates sunset—which on 26 August comes at about 7.20 p.m. At that time Steiner would have taken his leave from the Koguzki household, and set off again on the hour's walk along the country lane from Trumau to Münchendorf.

Felix himself may have accompanied him. When in 1950, at an earlier stage of his researches, Bock made enquiries in Münchendorf from a 90-year-old widow—who in 1881 would have been aged 21—she remembered the herb-gatherer at once, though she was unsure where he lived, and stated that he often came over to Münchendorf in the evening and ate with the villagers in the pub.

After taking his leave from Felix at Münchendorf, Steiner caught the train taking him back to Inzersdorf, three stops up the line. By the time he arrived there, darkness would long have fallen. Possibly his father was on duty that evening at the station, and greeted him with the latest political news.

There was then another half-hours's walk back to Oberlaa, so it could hardly have been before 9.30 p.m. by the time he reached home. No doubt his mother was pleased to see him, having been left all day to cope with Poldi and Gustav, both of them now teenagers . . .

★

On his return Steiner probably found waiting for him a letter from Rudolf Ronsperger. At any rate, when he sat down that same evening and wrote a very long letter in reply—covering over five pages in the *Briefe*—he stated that he had only received Ronsperger's last one to him that same day, '26. VIII'. His own lengthy letter was chiefly devoted to literary and philosophical matters.

The letter included this paragraph:

> I've just come from Münchendorf, doing the journey from there to Trumau and back on foot; an hour's walk there and the same back again. In this way I'm getting to know the folk of Lower Austria, and growing fond of them too. These people come towards one with astonishing attentiveness and soon become quite trustful. So I'm tired, and today can only add a little about your remarks on the materialism I hate from the foundations up . . .

Although claiming to be tired, Steiner had consumed on that day almost a whole litre of coffee, so his thoughts were still quite logical.

> . . . Summarizing your words, what emerges is this. Since there are human beings in existence who absolutely don't understand truths of higher philosophy and are simply incapable of seeing anything else than what has <u>sensorial</u> reality, and also people who out of incomprehension, vanity and malice are unable to describe anything else, these latter created for themselves materialism. The most important truth for these 'corner philosophers' is that a head without a brain can't think. We can certainly assure that type of people that we're aware of this without their materialistic science, but that saying such a thing would to us seem petty. This however is an <u>explanation</u> of cursed materialism, but no <u>justification</u>. You'll forgive my words, but in this matter my writing is aroused by real passion. In philosophy there shouldn't be any corner-scholars; these profane people should occupy themselves with other matters created for that kind of weak understanding, but not with philosophy. Here, where Schiller, Fichte, Schelling and Hegel have been at work, it's an unjustifiable crime for such corner-philosophers to stick themselves into the same subject. Philosophy is conceivable for every human being who has eagerness and good will; but precisely these last virtues depart from all materialists. Upright and *real* scientists are never materialists. A geologist and botanist in Wiener Neustadt known to me in person and whom I highly esteem, Dr. med. Lorenz, is a determined opponent of materialism, and Prof. Hyrtl decisively rejects it, <u>because it insults a man's higher feelings</u>. These are generally recognized natural scientists, and if I may continue, Kepler only made his great discoveries because he was an idealist, because he believed that there was reason in the arrangement and movement of the heavenly bodies. Before such things all materialistic stirrings finally fall silent.

This reference to Kepler will remind one of Edmund Reitlinger's deep interest in that astronomer. For it was in respect to Reitlinger that Steiner stated:

> ... In a lecture on natural science there would indeed appear quite general philosophical ideas ...

Now Reitlinger was also fond of quoting from *The Philosophy of the Inductive Sciences* by William Whewell. And in his previous term at the Technical College, Steiner had been attending Reitlinger's course on the mechanical theory of heat. A reader who therefore opens the first volume of Whewell's work and examines the 'book' entitled 'Of the Philosophy of the Mechanico-Chemical Sciences' will find a chapter headed 'Of the Connexion of Polarities' which includes a passage containing just such a general philosophical idea:

> Thus we find that the connexion of different kinds of polarities, magnetic, electric, chemical, crystalline and optical, is certain as a truth of experimental science. We have attempted to show further that in the minds of several of the most eminent discoverers and philosophers, such a conviction is something more than a mere empirical result: it is a principle which has regulated their researches while it was but obscurely seen and imperfectly unfolded, and has given to their theories a character of generality and self-evidence which experience alone cannot bestow.
>
> So far, indeed, as this persuasion of a connexion among apparently different kinds of agencies impels men engaged in the pursuit of knowledge to collect observations, to multiply, repeat and vary experiments, and to contemplate the result of these in all aspects and relations, it may be an occasion of the most important discoveries. Accordingly we find that the great laws of phenomena which govern the motions of the planets round the Sun were first discovered by Kepler in consequence of his scrutinizing the recorded observations with an intense conviction of the existence of geometrical and arithmetical harmonies in the solar system ...

Mediated through Reitlinger's lectures, notions from Whewell's book can be perceived in Steiner's mind on the very day when the herb-gatherer may have been speaking to him

> in words going right into the heart ... about stars, about Sun and Moon.

Some Account of These Doctrines

After the summer vacation, Rudolf Steiner resumed his studies at the Technical College in autumn 1881. He now began to attend the other part—chronologically earlier—of Edmund Reitlinger's lectures on the history of physics: 'From ancient times to Newton'.

It has been seen that Reitlinger, who 'was a man with a strictly inductive way of research', held lecture courses on physics which included verbal quotations and may well have contained other influences from *The Philosophy of the Inductive Sciences* by William Whewell. He must also have been acquainted with the same author's related work *The History of the Inductive Sciences*, available indeed in the German translation brought out in Vienna by Johann Joseph von Littrow.

An interested reader may therefore feel justified in examining a particular topic presented in the first volume of this latter work which may well have been treated in the first part, 'From ancient times to Newton', of Reitlinger's lectures on the history of physics.

★

The very first 'book' in the first volume, 'The History of Greek School Philosophy with reference to Physical Science', consisted of three chapters. The second, entitled 'The Greek School Philosophy', included a section on 'The Aristotelian Physical Philosophy' which entered into discussion of the *Physics* and other related works by Aristotle.

> Another mode of reasoning, very widely applied in these attempts, was the doctrine of contrarieties, in which it was assumed that adjectives or substantives which are in common language or in some abstract mode of conception opposed to each other must point at some fundamental antithesis in Nature, which it is important to study. Thus Aristotle says that the Pythagoreans, from the contrasts which number suggests, collected ten principles—limited and unlimited, odd and even, one and many, right and left, male and female, rest and motion, straight and curved, light and darkness, good and evil, square and oblong. We shall see hereafter that Aristotle himself deduced the doctrine of four elements, and other dogmas, by oppositions of the same kind.
>
> The physical speculator of the present day will learn without surprise that such a mode of discussion as this led to no truths of real or permanent value. The whole mass of the Greek philosophy therefore shrinks into an almost imperceptible compass when viewed with reference to the progress of physical knowledge. Still, the general character of this system, and its fortunes from the time of its founders to the overthrow of their authority, are not without their instruction, and it may be hoped not without their interest. I proceed therefore to give some account of these doctrines in their most fully developed and permanently received form, that in which they were presented by Aristotle.
>
> The principal physical treatises of Aristotle are the eight books of *Physical Lectures*, the four books *Of the Heavens*, the two books *Of Production and Destruction*: for the book *Of the World* is now universally acknowledged to be spurious; and the *Meteorologics*, though full of physical explanations of natural phenomena, does not exhibit the doctrines and reasonings of the

school in so general a form; the same may be said of the *Mechanical Problems*. The treatises on the various subjects of natural history, *On Animals, On the Parts of Animals, On Plants, On Physiognomics, On Colours, On Sound*, contain an extraordinary accumulation of facts, and manifest a wonderful power of systematizing, but are not works which expound principles, and therefore do not require to be here considered.

The *Physical Lectures* are possibly the work concerning which a well-known anecdote is related by Simplicius, a Greek commentator of the sixth century, as well as by Plutarch. It is said that Alexander the Great wrote to his former tutor to this effect: 'You have not done well in publishing these lectures; for how shall we your pupils excel other men, if you make that public to all which we learnt from you?' To this Aristotle is said to have replied: 'My lectures are published and not published; they will be intelligible to those who heard them, and to none beside.' This may very easily be a story invented and circulated among those who found the work beyond their comprehension; and it cannot be denied that to make out the meaning and reasoning of every part would be a task very laborious and difficult, if not impossible. But we may follow the import of a large portion of the *Physical Lectures* with sufficient clearness to apprehend the character and principles of the reasoning; and this is what I shall endeavour to do.

The author's introductory statement of his view of the nature of philosophy falls in very closely with what has been said, that he takes his facts and generalizations as they are implied in the structure of language. 'We must in all cases proceed,' he says, 'from what is known to what is unknown.' This will not be denied. But we can hardly follow him in his inference. He adds: 'We must proceed, therefore, from universal to particular. And something of this,' he pursues, 'may be seen in language; for names signify things in a general and indefinite manner, as "circle", and by defining we unfold them into particulars.' He illustrates this by saying: 'Thus children at first call all men "father", and all women "mother", but afterwards distinguish.'

In accordance with this view, he endeavours to settle several of the great questions concerning the universe which had been started among subtle and speculative men, by unfolding the meaning of the words and phrases which are applied to the most general notions of things and relations. We have already noticed this method. A few examples will illustrate it further. Whether there was or was not a void, or place without matter, had already been debated among rival sects of philosophers. The antagonist arguments were briefly these:—There must be a void, because a body cannot move into a space except it is empty, and therefore without a void there could be no motion. And on the other hand, there is no void, for the intervals between bodies are filled with air, and air is something. These opinions had even been supported by reference to experiment. On the one hand, Anaxagoras and his school had shown that air when confined resisted compression, by squeezing a blown bladder, and pressing down an inverted vessel in the water. On the other hand, it was alleged that a vessel full of fine ashes held as much water as if the ashes were not there, which could only be explained by supposing void spaces among the ashes. Aristotle decides that there is no void, on such arguments as this:—In a void there could be no difference of up and down; for as in nothing there are no differences, so there are none in a privation or negation. But a void is merely a privation or negation of matter. Therefore, in a void, bodies could not move up and down, which it is in their nature to do. It is easily seen that such a mode of reasoning elevates the familiar forms of language and the intellectual connections of terms to a supremacy over facts; making truth depend upon whether terms are or are not privative, and whether we say that bodies fall 'naturally'. In such a philosophy every new result of observation would be compelled to conform to the usual combinations of phrases, as these had become associated by the modes of apprehension previously familiar.

A Complete Failure

The content of the third, final chapter of the 'book' in William Whewell's *History of the Inductive Sciences* on 'The History of Greek School Philosophy with reference to Physical Science' was sufficiently explained by its title: 'Failure of the Physical Philosophy of the Greek Schools'.

The first section, headed 'Result of the Greek School Philosophy', began as follows:

> The methods and forms of philosophizing which we have described as employed by the Greek Schools failed altogether in their application to physics. No discovery of general laws, no explanation of special phenomena, rewarded the acuteness and boldness of these early students of Nature. Astronomy, which made considerable progress during the existence of the sects of Greek philosophers, gained perhaps something by the authority with which Plato taught the supremacy and universality of mathematical rule and order; and the truths of Harmonics, which had probably given rise to the Pythagorean passion for numbers, were cultivated with much care by that school. But after these first impulses, the sciences owed nothing to the philosophical sects; and the vast and complex accumulations and apparatus of the Stagirite do not appear to have led to any theoretical physical truths.
>
> This assertion hardly requires proof, since in the existing body of science there are no doctrines for which we are indebted to the Aristotelian School. Real truths, when once established, remain to the end of time a part of the mental treasure of man, and may be discerned through all the additions of later days. But we can point out no physical doctrine now received of which we trace the anticipation in Aristotle, in the way in which we see the

Copernican system anticipated by Aristarchus, the resolution of the heavenly appearances into circular motions suggested by Plato, and the numerical relations of musical intervals ascribed to Pythagoras. But it may be worthwhile to look at this matter more closely.

Among the works of Aristotle are thirty-eight chapters of *Problems*, which may serve to exemplify the progress he had really made in the reduction of phenomena to laws and causes. Of these problems, a large proportion are physiological, and these I here pass by, as not illustrative of the state of physical knowledge. But those which are properly physical are for the most part questions concerning such facts and difficulties as it is the peculiar business of theory to explain. Now it may be truly said that in scarcely any one instance are the answers which Aristotle gives to his questions of any value. For the most part, indeed, he propounds his answer with a degree of hesitation or vacillation which of itself shows the absence of all scientific distinctness of thought; and the opinions so offered never appear to involve any settled or general principle.

We may take, as examples of this, the problems of the simplest kind, where the principles lay nearest at hand—the mechanical ones.

Whewell went on to give six quotations, of which the first four were taken from the work now known as *Mechanics*, and the last two from what is now comprised in *Problems*. His footnotes—in the present work incorporated into the text—gave numerical references to editions of his time. They are here altered to accord with numeration found in present-day editions of Aristotle's works.

'Why,' he asks, 'do small forces move great weights by means of a lever, when they have thus to move the lever added to the weight? Is it,' he suggests, 'because a greater radius moves faster?' (*Mechanics*, 3.) 'Why does a small wedge split great weights? Is it because the wedge is composed of two opposite levers?' (*Ib.*, 17.) 'Why, when a man rises from a chair, does he bend his leg and his body to acute angles with his thigh? Is it because a right angle is connected with equality and rest?' (*Ib.*, 30.) 'Why can a man throw a stone further with a sling than with his hand? Is it that when he throws with his hand he moves the stone from rest, but when he uses the sling he throws it already in motion?' (*Ib.*, 12.) 'Why, if a circle be thrown on the ground, does it first describe a straight line and then a spiral, as it falls? Is it that the air first presses equally on the two sides and supports it, and afterwards presses on one side more?' (*Problems*, 16:11.) 'Why is it difficult to distinguish a musical note from the octave above? Is it that proportion stands in the place of equality?' (*Ib.*, 19:14.) It must be allowed that these are very vague and worthless surmises; for even if we were, as some commentators have done, to interpret some of them so as to agree with sound philosophy, we should still be unable to

> point out in this author's works any clear or permanent apprehension of the general principles which such an interpretation implies.
>
> Thus the Aristotelian physics cannot be considered as otherwise than a complete failure. It collected no general laws from facts; and consequently, when it tried to explain facts, it had no principles which were of any avail.

In his third and final edition of 1857, Whewell added to this chapter a whole new section, entitled 'Francis Bacon's Remarks'. The section began:

> Though we do not accept as authority even the judgments of Francis Bacon, and shall have to estimate the strong and weak parts of his, no less than of other philosophies, we shall find his remarks on the Greek philosophers very instructive. Thus he says of Aristotle (*Nov. Org.* I. Aph. lxiii):—
>
> 'He is an example of the kind of philosophy in which much is made out of little; so that the basis of experience is too narrow. He corrupted natural philosophy by his Logic, and made the world out of his Categories. He disposed of the distinction of "dense" and "rare", by which bodies occupy more or less dimensions or space, by the frigid distinction of "act" and "power". He assigned to each kind of body a single proper motion, so that if they have any other motion they must receive it from some extraneous source; and imposed many other arbitrary rules upon Nature, being everywhere more careful how one may give a ready answer, and make a positive assertion, than how he may apprehend the variety of Nature.
>
> And this appears most evidently by the comparison of his philosophy with the other philosophies which had any vogue in Greece. For the "homoiomeria" of Anaxagoras, the atoms of Leucippus and Democritus, the heaven and earth of Parmenides, the love and hate of Empedocles, the fire of Heraclitus had some trace of the thoughts of a natural philosopher, some savour of experience and Nature, and bodily things; while the Physics of Aristotle, in general, sound only of logical terms.'

Empty, Barren and Worthless

Edmund Reitlinger might have quarried suitable material for incorporation into his lecture course on the history of physics not only from William Whewell's work *The History of the Inductive Sciences* but of course also from Whewell's related work—which indeed, according to Rudolf Steiner, he was even fond of quoting—*The Philosophy of the Inductive Sciences*.

An interested reader may therefore consider another historical topic found in this latter work, in a 'book' in the second volume entitled 'Review of Opinions on the Nature of Knowledge, and the Method of Seeking It'.

★

Among the several chapters of this 'book' is one headed 'Innovators of the Middle Ages', which includes a section on 'Raymond Lully'. Here is this section in its entirety:

> Raymond Lully is perhaps traditionally best known as an alchemist, of which art he appears to have been a cultivator. But this was only one of the many impulses of a spirit ardently thirsty of knowledge and novelty. He had, in his youth, been a man of pleasure (Tenemann, VIII. 830), but was driven by a sudden shock of feeling to resolve on a complete change of life. He plunged into solitude, endeavoured to still the remorse of his conscience by prayer and penance, and soon had his soul possessed by visions which he conceived were vouchsafed him. In the feeling of religious enthusiasm thus excited, he resolved to devote his life to the diffusion of Christian truth among heathens and Mahomedans. He breathed earnest supplications from above; and these were answered by his receiving from heaven, as his admirers declare, his *Ars Magna*, by which he was able without labour or effort to learn and apply all knowledge. The real state of the case is that he put himself in opposition to the established systems, and propounded a new Art, from which he promised the most wonderful results; but that his Art really is merely a mode of combining ideal conceptions without any reference to real sources of knowledge, or any possibility of real advantage. In a treatise addressed in A.D. 1310 to King Philip of France, entitled *Liber Lamentationis Duodecim Principiorum Philosophiae contra Averroistas*, Lully introduces Philosophy, accompanied by her twelve principles (Matter, Form, Generation, &c.) uttering loud complaints against the prevailing system of doctrine; and represents her as presenting to the king a petition that she may be upheld and restored by her favourite, the Author. His *Tabula Generalis ad omnes Scientias applicabilis* was begun the 15th September 1292, in the harbour of Tunis, and finished in 1293, at Naples. In order to frame an Art of thus tabulating all existing sciences, and indeed all possible knowledge, he divides into various classes the conceptions with which he has to deal. The first class contains nine 'Absolute Conceptions': Goodness, Greatness, Duration, Power, Wisdom, Will, Virtue, Truth, Majesty. The second class has nine 'Relative Conceptions': Difference, Identity, Contrariety, Beginning, Middle, End, Majority, Equality, Minority. The third class contains nine 'Questions': Whether? What? Whence? Why? How great? How circumstanced? When? Where? and How? The fourth class contains the nine 'Most General Subjects': God, Angel, Heaven, Man, 'Imaginativum', 'Sensitivum', 'Vegetativum', 'Elementativum', 'Instrumentativum'. Then come nine 'Praedicaments', nine 'Moral Quailities', and so on. These conceptions are arranged in the compartments of certain concentric

moveable circles, and give various combinations by means of triangles and other figures, and thus propositions are constructed.

It must be clear at once that real knowledge, which is the union of facts and ideas, can never result from this machinery for shifting about, joining and disjoining, empty conceptions. This and all similar schemes go upon the supposition that the logical combinations of notions do of themselves compose knowledge; and that really existing things may be arrived at by a successive system of derivation from our most general ideas. It is imagined that by distributing the nomenclature of abstract ideas according to the place which they can hold in our propositions, and by combining them according to certain conditions, we may obtain formulae including all possible truths, and thus fabricate a science in which all sciences are contained. We thus obtain the means of talking and writing upon all subjects, without the trouble of thinking: the revolutions of the emblematical figures are substituted for the operations of the mind. Both exertion of thought, and knowledge of facts, become superfluous. And this reflection, adds an intelligent author (Degerando, IV. 535), explains the enormous number of books which Lully is said to have written; for he might have written those even during his sleep, by the aid of a moving power which should keep his machine in motion. Having once devised this invention for manufacturing science, Lully varied it in a thousand ways, and followed it into a variety of developments. Besides synoptical tables, he employs genealogical trees, each of which he dignifies with the name of the Tree of Science. The only requisite for the application of his system was a certain agreement in the numbers of the classes into which different subjects were distributed; and as this symmetry does not really exist in the operations of our thoughts, some violence was done to the natural distinction and subordination of conceptions, in order to fit them for the use of the system.

Thus Lully, while he professed to teach an Art which was to shed new light upon every part of science, was in fact employed in a pedantic and trifling repetition of known truths or truisms; and while he complained of the errors of existing methods, he proposed in their place one which was far more empty, barren, and worthless, than the customary processes of human thought. Yet his method is spoken of with some praise by Leibnitz (*Opera*, V. 16), who indeed rather delighted in the region of ideas and words than in the world of realities. But Francis Bacon speaks far otherwise and more justly on this subject (*Works*, VII. 296). 'It is not to be omitted that some men, swollen with emptiness rather than knowledge, have laboured to produce a certain method, not deserving the name of a legitimate method, since it is rather a method of imposture: which yet is doubtless highly grateful to certain would-be philosophers. This method scatters about certain little drops of science in such a manner that a smatterer may make a perverse and ostentatious use of them with a certain show of learning. Such was the Art of Lully, which consisted of nothing but a mass and heap of the words of each science; with the intention that he who can readily produce the words of any science shall be supposed to know the science itself. Such collections are like a rag shop, where you find a patch of everything, but nothing which is of any value.'

On a Path Towards Truth

When describing in the course of the autobiographical lecture his early years in Vienna, Rudolf Steiner stated:

> Besides various other persons making an impression on the youth at the time, one excellent man may be mentioned, who soon however died. The youth heard lectures from him at the Viennese Technical College on the history of physics. It was Edmund Reitlinger, who also collaborated on the life of Kepler, and could present in an excellent way the progress of physics through the ages.

Reitlinger had indeed authored the first volume, *Johannes Kepler*, of a collaborative three-volume biography of the great astronomer. This first volume was published at Stuttgart in 1868. The work opened with an introduction, which began:

> Kepler was one of the most remarkable persons of all countries and times. Astronomers call him the immortal law-giver of planetary movement. Those who write the history of 'strange and riddling men' cannot miss him from their list. One science whose significance can only be fully appreciated since a few decades ago, indeed it might be said only since today, physiological optics, owes to him its first foundations. And yet he also clothed moribund astrology with a last deceptive shimmer of truth. The ancient wisdom of the Pythagoreans celebrated a fleeting resurrection through his harmony of the world, two millennia after Pythagoras, while his inductive method allows him to be recognized as the earliest natural scientist in a modern sense, in the sense of the present. Even before Bacon recommended this method, Kepler was already using it. Though he became a martyr to his Protestant confession of faith, he did not regard the words in the Bible but rather the works of Nature as God's most direct and glorious revelation. He was twice married, and both the imposing Barbara von Mühleck and the charming Suschen from Efferdingen were surrounded by a poetic charm lent by beauty and youth. But the great fortune given him by his two beloved wives was more than offset by the dreadfully tragic disaster which overtook him in the witch-trial of his seventy-year-old mother. Historians

find him at the court of Rudolf II as a respected mathematician of imperial majesty, and later meet him near the then mighty army commander, the Duke of Friedland. Nonetheless he dies in such distress that folklore long believed it was by starvation. In such an eventful and changing destiny he gained the evergreen laurel of posthumous fame not in any '*Tatensturm*', but rather in a scholar's lonely study, making calculations and researches with iron industry and tireless persistence.

Kepler epitomizes the turning-point of modern, as Socrates that of ancient spiritual development. Socrates thought the gods to have jealously concealed from man the secret of planetary movement. He therefore warned people away from 'idle' speculations of natural philosophy in the Italic and Ionic schools, and directed philosophy 'from Heaven to Earth'. Unable however to conceive of Nature, he cried out to man with the Delphic oracle: 'Know thyself'. But what a human being finds inconceivable he also soon considers foreign or even hostile to him. Christianity regarded Nature as man's opponent. Over mankind there broke that disastrous millennium and a half where besides *enjoyment of the world* was only *renunciation of the world*, without higher mediation through *knowledge of the world*. By means of his three famous rules, however, Kepler succeeded in unveiling the secret of planetary movement, which Socrates held the gods to have reserved to themselves. So he later justified the boldness by which he had already prefaced his first piece of writing in the words

> Was ist die Welt? Und warum und nach welcherlei Plane erschuff sie
> Gott? Wie fand er die Zahl, das Gesetz so gewaltiger Massen?

If Socrates directed philosophy from Heaven to Earth, Kepler led it back from Earth to Heaven—but a Heaven including the Earth, the Heaven of Copernicus. Inside this latter, the Earth circled with all other planets around the Sun. Thus the Universe was no longer simply the dwelling-house of man, rather man was only the inhabitant of a little clod of heavenly ground. Could a human being now hope for *self-knowledge* without *knowledge of the world*? Whoever wanted to grasp a part of the part had to strive to investigate the whole. But why should one any longer despair of knowing the world when Kepler, using the Earth's course around the Sun as proclaimed by Copernicus, succeeded in unravelling the much-entwined paths of the planets? He penetrated into light-filled clarity and certainty where all ancient philosophers harboured only fantastic conjectures and Socrates sought a most forceful proof for the futility of natural philosophic speculations. Kepler's 'three laws' gave the lie to the 'learned ignorance' of Socrates, for they unveiled the planets' elliptical courses and showed a remarkable connection between their distances and orbiting periods, all of which subjects Socrates had declared unresearchable. Kepler's fortunate success allowed a new race of thinkers to arise, who no longer drew back from the task of fathoming Nature. In place of the cautious motto 'Know thyself' they set the bold question 'What is the world?', and directed all their fervent endeavours to answering it. Whether one calls them like the Germans '*Naturforscher*', or like the English 'philosophers', it is they who in the last three centuries led mankind on a path towards truth, and the continuous progress distinguishing modern times from all former historical periods is the product of their inventions and discoveries.

In *The Philosophy of the Inductive Sciences*, which Reitlinger was fond of quoting, William Whewell often referred to physicists as 'physical philosophers'.

The Joint Deed of Copernicus and Kepler

Edmund Reitlinger's introduction to his biography of Kepler continued:

If we attribute a similar importance to Kepler for modern spiritual progress as to Socrates for ancient, this is not in any way done in order to isolate him from his precursors and from those striving alongside. No Hercules on his own could cleanse the Augean stables of medieval prejudices. The finest minds had to join together on an expedition of Argonauts, to liberate the golden fleece of truth from the power of those fiends guarding it at the midnight strand of superstition, and lead it into the sunny land of reason. But least of all is it our intention to upraise Kepler at the cost of Copernicus. In the preface to the Rudolfine tables Kepler says that Copernicus was a man of the greatest intellect and, most importantly with such researches, free cast of mind. In his fine posthumous allegorical tale *Der Traum vom Monde* Kepler has the Genius of Astronomy conjured up by a magic spell in 21 letters, 'Astronomia Copernicana', and so too his own genius was stimulated and instigated to all his great discoveries through the Copernican hypothesis. But the reformation of star-lore begun by Copernicus, just like the simultaneous ecclesiastical Reformation, at first awakened only discord and strife. A majority of philosophers declared the hypothesis of a moving Earth improbable and absurd. With both Reformations only Heaven could definitely decide, and establish among the parties fighting against each other unity and peace. Kepler showed how eternal laws derive from the material sky vaulting above us, and from its stars. He thereby provided a model for the modern inductive method of natural science, and gained victory for the Copernican system. His discoveries made people stop talking about different world-systems, and regard the Copernican alone as the 'true' one. Even today we wait in vain for someone who possesses the same art of asking questions from a religious heaven, and manages so to fathom the stars in our breast that, just as among human beings there is only *one* astronomical knowledge, so too there be only *one* faith.

Despite the great service of Copernicus and his overwhelming contribution to discovering the 'true' world-system named after him, the story that he is the one and only discoverer of a true system of the world must nonetheless be described as an admittedly conventional but erroneous one in the history of astronomy. Apelt already states this in his *Epochen der Geschichte der Menschheit* (Vol. 1, p. 239), adding that Copernicus in fact only laid the foundation-stone of this building, and its further erection is the work of Kepler's great genius. In the *Kosmos* (Vol. 2, p. 353) Humboldt expresses himself in the same sense: 'Kepler's great discovery that all planets move around the Sun in ellipses and that the Sun lies in one focus of these ellipses finally liberated the original Copernican system from eccentric circles and all the epicycles. The universe's planetary structure now appeared objective, as it were architectonic in its simple greatness.' Although Copernicus knew how to overcome the sensory illusion of a resting Earth, he did not dare to raise the slightest doubt of a prejudice harboured for centuries that the planets must move uniformly in circles. But according to Bailly, the opinion of uniform movement of stars in circles is the characteristic feature of antiquity. Only with its disappearance does modernity begin. Not with Copernicus, nor even with Tycho—Bailly therefore expressly states—but with Kepler does the superiority of modern over ancient astronomy take its start. Kepler, who discovered the true elliptical planetary courses, is the actual founder of modern astronomy—'a present given to Europe by Germany'. (Bailly: *Histoire de l'astronomie moderne*, Vol 2, p. 5.) Here some will contradict Bailly, and hold the view that Copernicus, by making the dream of Archimedes into a reality, and like a Titan moving the Earth from its place, surpassed Kepler. But it cannot be doubted that discovering the true system of the world must be regarded as the joint deed of Copernicus and Kepler, an epoch-making deed with few parallels, setting being in place of semblance, experience in place of prejudice. The sensory illusion of a resting Earth was abandoned through Copernicus, the preconceived opinion of uniformly circular movement of stars through Kepler. The two enemies which had so long prevented knowledge of the world's true constitution were thus overcome: sensory appearance and preconceived opinion, clouding of the bodily or of the spiritual eye. It can hardly be possible to judge whether greater spiritual power was needed to destroy the first deception like Copernicus, or the second like Kepler. Suffice that they share the immortal fame of discovering the true world-system. For if Copernicus discovered *that* the Earth and planets move around the Sun, yet Kepler first ascertained *in what orbits* this happens. But with regard to the question whether Copernicus or Kepler be greater, we would like to recall words by Goethe. Conflicts of German critics as to whether he or Schiller were greater led him to exclaim that Germans should be glad to possess two such men. A historian too, when looking more closely at the discovery of the Copernican system of the world, fares like an astronomer who points a telescope at a double star. Where he saw only one star, he now perceives *two Suns*.

Rules Erroneously Exemplified

Now in the course of his article in *Freie Blicke* on 'Doctor Faust and Natural Science'—written in 1866, the year of the death of William Whewell—Edmund Reitlinger remarked that Kepler

> ... put forward instances of induction crowned with the highest success, where Bacon later set down rules erroneously exemplified...

This allusion to Bacon is reminiscent of a certain passage from a work which Reitlinger was fond of quoting, namely Whewell's *Philosophy of the Inductive Sciences*. The passage is found in the introduction to the first 'book', entitled 'Of Ideas in General':

> The design of the following work... is to form a Philosophy of Science, by analysing the substance and examining the progress of the existing body of the sciences. As a preliminary to this undertaking, a survey of the history of the sciences was necessary. This, accordingly, I have already performed; and the result of the labour thus undertaken has been laid before the public as a *History of the Inductive Sciences*.
>
> In that work I have endeavoured to trace the steps by which men acquired each main portion of that knowledge on which they now look with so much confidence and satisfaction. The events which that *History* relates, the speculations and controversies which are there described, and discussions of the same kind, far more extensive, which are there omitted, must all be taken into our account at present as the prominent and standard examples of the circumstances which attend the progress of knowledge. With so much of real historical fact before us, we may hope to avoid such views of the human mind as are too partial and limited, or too vague and loose, or too abstract and unsubstantial, to represent fitly the real forms of discovery and of truth.
>
> Of former attempts, made with the same view of tracing the conditions of the progress of knowledge, that of Bacon is perhaps the most conspicuous: and his labours on this subject were opened by his book on the *Advancement of Learning*, which contains among other matter a survey of the then existing state of knowledge. But this review was undertaken rather with the object of ascertaining in what quarters future advances were to be hoped for, than of learning by what means they were to be made. His examination of the domain of human knowledge was conducted rather with the view of dis-

covering what remained undone, than of finding out how so much had been done. Bacon's survey was made for the purpose of tracing the boundaries, rather than of detecting the principles of knowledge. 'I will now attempt,' he says (*Advancement of Learning*, b.i. p.74), 'to make a general and faithful perambulation of learning, with an inquiry what parts thereof lie fresh and waste, and not improved and converted by the industry of man; to the end that such a plot made and recorded to memory, may both minister light to any public designation, and also serve to excite voluntary endeavours.' Nor will it be foreign to our scheme also hereafter to examine with a like purpose the frontier-line of man's intellectual estate. But the object of our perambulation in the first place is not so much to determine the extent of the field, as the sources of its fertility. We would learn by what plan and rules of culture, conspiring with the native forces of the bounteous soil, those rich harvests have been produced which fill our garners. Bacon's maxims, on the other hand, respecting the mode in which he conceived that knowledge was henceforth to be cultivated, have little reference to the failures, still less to the successes, which are recorded in his review of the learning of his time. His precepts are connected with his historical views in a slight and unessential manner. His philosophy of the sciences is not collected from the sciences which are noticed in his survey. Nor in truth could this, at the time when he wrote, have easily been otherwise. At that period, scarce any branch of physics existed as a science, except astronomy. The rules which Bacon gives for the conduct of scientific researches are obtained as it were by divination, from the contemplation of subjects with regard to which no sciences as yet were. His instances of steps rightly or wrongly made in this path are in a great measure cases of his own devising. He could not have exemplified his aphorisms by references to treatises then extant on the laws of Nature; for the constant burden of his exhortation is that men up to his time had almost universally followed an erroneous course. And however we may admire the sagacity with which he pointed the way along a better path, we have this great advantage over him—that we can interrogate the many travellers who since his time have journeyed on this road. At the present day, when we have under our notice so many sciences, of such wide extent, so well established, a philosophy of the sciences ought, it must seem, to be founded not upon conjecture, but upon an examination of many instances; should not consist of a few vague and unconnected maxims, difficult and doubtful in their application, but should form a system of which every part has been repeatedly confirmed and verified.

The High Point of Physical Research

It has been seen that in course of another article in *Freie Blicke*, namely that on 'Galileo Galilei', Edmund Reitlinger pointed out that the Italian scientist died in the same year in which Newton was born. He further stated that from the union of Galilei's mechanics with the laws of Kepler could be said to have arisen Newton's doctrine of gravitation.

A reader who has become aware of the influence exerted on Reitlinger by the writings of William Whewell will therefore turn to the first volume of *The History of the Inductive Sciences*, and in the 'book' on 'The History of Physical Astronomy' examine the chapter entitled 'The Inductive Epoch of Newton'.

The text of the original 1837 edition reads:

> Such, then, is the great Newtonian Induction of Universal Gravitation, and such its history. It is indisputably and incomparably the greatest scientific discovery ever made, whether we look at the advance which it involved, the extent of the truth disclosed, or the fundamental and satisfactory nature of this truth. As to the first point, we may observe that any one of the five steps into which we have separated the doctrine would of itself have been considered as an important advance—would have conferred distinction on the persons who made it, and the time to which it belonged. All the five steps made at once formed not a leap but a flight, not an improvement merely but a metamorphosis, not an epoch but a termination. Astronomy passed at once from its boyhood to mature manhood. Again, with regard to the extent of the truth, we obtain as wide a generalization as our physical knowledge admits, when we learn that every particle of matter, in all times, places and circumstances, attracts every other particle in the universe by one common law of action. And by saying that the truth was of a fundamental and satisfactory nature, I mean that it assigned not a rule merely, but a cause for the heavenly motions; and that kind of cause which most eminently and peculiarly we distinctly and thoroughly conceive, namely mechanical force. Kepler's laws were merely *formal* rules, governing the celestial motions according to the relations of space, time and number; Newton's was a *causal* law, referring these motions to mechanical reasons. It is no doubt conceivable that future discoveries may both extend and further explain Newton's doctrines—may make gravitation a case of some wider law, and may disclose something of the mode in which it operates; questions with which Newton himself struggled. But in the meantime few persons will dispute that both in generality and profundity, both in width and depth, Newton's theory is altogether without a rival or neighbour.

Twenty years later, in the final third edition of 1857, Whewell added a footnote:

> The value and nature of this step have long been generally acknowledged wherever science is cultivated. Yet it would appear that there is, in one part of Europe, a school of philosophers who contest the merit of this part of

> Newton's discoveries. 'Kepler,' says a celebrated German metaphysician (Hegel, *Encyclopædia*, § 270) 'discovered the laws of free motion; a discovery of immortal glory. It has since been the fashion to say that Newton first found out the proof of these rules. It has seldom happened that the glory of the first discoverer has been more unjustly transferred to another person.' It may appear strange that anyone in the present day should hold such language; but if we examine the reasons which this author gives, they will be found, I think, to amount to this: that his mind is in the condition in which Kepler's was; and that the whole range of mechanical ideas and modes of conception which made the transition from Kepler to Newton possible are extraneous to the domain of his philosophy. Even this author, however, if I understand him rightly, recognizes Newton as the author of the doctrine of perturbations.
>
> I have given a further account of these views in a memoir 'On Hegel's Criticism of Newton's *Principia*', Cambridge Transactions, 1849.

The reference was to the *Transactions of the Cambridge Philosophical Society*. The main text continues:

> The requisite conditions of such a discovery in the mind of its author were, in this as in other cases, the idea, and its comparison with facts—the conception of the law, and the moulding of this conception in such a way as to correspond with known realities. The idea of mechanical force as the cause of celestial motions had, as we have seen, been for some time growing up in men's minds—had gone on becoming more distinct and more general; and had, in some persons, approached the form in which it was entertained by Newton. Still, in the mere conception of universal gravitation, Newton must have gone far beyond his predecessors and contemporaries, both in generality and distinctness; and in the inventiveness and sagacity with which he traced the consequences of this conception he was, as we have shown, without a rival, and almost without a second. As to the facts which he had to include in his law, they had been accumulating from the very birth of astronomy; but those which he had more peculiarly to take hold of were the facts of the planetary motions as given by Kepler, and those of the Moon's motions as given by Tycho Brahe and Jeremy Horrox.
>
> We find here occasion to make a remark which is important in its bearing on the nature of progressive science. What Newton thus used and referred to as facts were the laws which his predecessors had established. What Kepler and Horrox had put forth as 'theories' were now established truths, fit to be used in the construction of other theories. It is in this manner that one theory is built upon another—that we rise from particulars to generals, and from one generalization to another—that we have, in short, successive steps of induction. As Newton's laws assumed Kepler's, Kepler's laws assumed as facts the results of the planetary theory of Ptolemy; and thus the

> theories of each generation in the scientific world are (when thoroughly verified and established) the facts of the next generation. Newton's theory is the circle of generalization which includes all the others; the highest point [in Littrow's translation *der höchste Punkt*] of the inductive ascent; the catastrophe of the philosophic drama to which Plato had prologized; the point to which men's minds had been journeying for two thousand years.

Describing Reitlinger in his autobiography, Rudolf Steiner stated:

> ... Newton represented for him the high point [*der Höhepunkt*] of physical research ...

★

On 3 March 1882 Steiner took an exam on the history of physics 'from ancient times to Newton', and was marked by Reitlinger as 'excellent'.

5
THE SCHRÖERIAN MISSION

Inner Release

In the course of his autobiography Rudolf Steiner went on:

> My relation to science during this period of my life was not influenced by Goethe, although in contact with Schröer I was coming close to Goethe's spiritual life. The relation was built up much more by the difficulties I encountered when having to think about optical facts in the way done by physicists.
>
> I found that in scientific observations light and sound were thought of with an analogy which is inapplicable. People spoke of 'sound in general' and 'light in general'. The analogy was as follows: individual tones and sounds are seen as specially modified aerial vibrations, and sound itself—apart from human experience of a sonar sensation—as a vibratory condition of the air. Light was thought of in a similar manner. What takes place outside man if he perceives a phenomenon caused by light was defined as a vibration in the ether. Colours are then specially formed ether-vibrations. In my mental life this analogy was at the time really torturing. For I believed myself to be quite clear that the concept 'sound' is merely an *abstract* combination of individual occurrences in the sounding world, while 'light' presents in itself something concrete as against manifestations in the illuminated world.—'Sound' was for me a collective abstract concept, 'light' a concrete reality. I told myself that light is not sensorially perceived at all; 'colours' are perceived *through* light, which is revealed everywhere in colour-perceptions, but is itself not sensorially perceived. 'White' light is not light, but already a colour.
>
> Light thus became for me an actual reality *in the sense-world*, but which is itself extrasensory. The opposition between Nominalism and Realism as this developed within Scholasticism now arose before me. Realists maintained that concepts are an essentiality living in things and only drawn out of them by human cognition. Nominalists on the other hand held concepts to be only names devised by men to sum up the manifold qualities of things, but having no existence within them. I felt that sound-experiences should be regarded in a Nominalist way and experiences made through light in a Realist one.
>
> With this orientation I approached the optics of the physicists. Much of this I had to reject. Here I acquired views which paved the way for me to Goethe's teaching on colours. It was from this direction that I opened the

door to Goethe's scientific writings. At first I brought Schröer some short accounts written out of my scientific views. He could not make much of them. For they were not yet worked out from Goethe's way of viewing things, though towards the end I had just made a brief remark that only when people came to think about Nature as I had presented it would Goethe's research into Nature be given credit in science. Schröer was inwardly pleased when I expressed such views; but beyond that, nothing at first occurred. The following instance well characterizes the situation in which I found myself. One day Schröer told me that he had been speaking with a colleague who was a physicist. Well, said the latter, Goethe opposed Newton, and yet Newton was 'such a genius'. Upon which he, Schröer, rejoined that Goethe had been 'a genius too'. So once more I felt myself wrestling, entirely alone, with a riddling question.

The anecdote recalls the punning inscription at the base of Roubiliac's statue of Newton in the antechapel of Trinity College Cambridge:

NEWTON
Qui genus humanum ingenio superavit

Steiner went on:

The views I reached on physical optics seemed to me to build a bridge from insights into the spiritual world towards those deriving from scientific research. At the time I felt a need to arrange on my own certain optical experiments so as to test through *sensory experience* the *thoughts* I had elaborated about the nature of light and colour. It was not easy for me to purchase things needed for such experiments. For what I earned by private tutoring was little enough. I did everything possible to make experimental arrangements for the doctrine of light which would really lead to unprejudiced insight into the facts of Nature in this field.

How these tests were usually carried out by physicists was known to me from my work in Reitlinger's physics laboratory. I was familiar with the mathematical treatment of optics, having made intensive studies in this very field.—Despite all objections raised by physicists against the Goethean doctrine of colours, my own experiments drove me increasingly away from the normal physical view and towards Goethe. I became aware that all this kind of experimentation merely posits facts 'onto light'—to use a Goethean expression—but is not experimenting 'with light' itself. I said to myself: colour is not drawn out of light according to a Newtonian way of thinking, but becomes manifest if light is confronted with obstacles to its free expansion. It seemed to me that this could be read directly from experiments.

But for me *light* had thus left the series of actual physical entities. It presented a midway stage between entities comprehensible to the senses and those perceptible in spirit.

I was disinclined merely to live in philosophical thought-processes about these matters. But I laid very great value on *correctly reading* the facts of Nature . . .

The italics are Steiner's. His metaphor recalls the initial 'Aphorisms concerning Ideas' in the first volume of William Whewell's *Philosophy of the Inductive Sciences*:

I.

Man is the interpreter of Nature, science the correct interpretation.

II.

The *Senses* place before us the *Characters* of the Book of Nature, but these convey no knowledge to us, till we have discovered the Alphabet by which they are to be read.

III.

The *Alphabet*, by means of which we interpret phenomena, consists of the *Ideas* existing in our own minds; for these give to the phenomena that coherence and significance which is not an object of sense.

Steiner continued:

. . . It became ever clearer to me that light itself does *not* enter the realm of what is sensorially perceptible; rather it remains beyond that realm, while colours appear if something sense-perceptible is brought into the realm of light.

I now felt impelled to approach scientific knowledge anew from the most diverse sides. I was again led towards the study of anatomy and physiology, and observed the members of human, animal and plant organisms in their structures. Thus I arrived in my own way at the Goethean doctrine of metamorphosis. I became increasingly aware that the picture of Nature perceptible to the senses presses towards what was perceptible to me in a spiritual way.

If I observed in this spiritual way the mobility of the human soul, of thinking, feeling and willing, a 'spiritual man' took shape for me to the extent that it could be seen pictorially. I could not remain in the abstractions commonly thought of when thinking, feeling and willing are usually discussed. In these inner manifestations of life I saw creative forces which placed before me in the spirit 'man as spirit'. When then looking at man's sensory appearance, I observed it as supplemented by a spiritual form holding sway in the sense-perceptible.

I arrived at the *sensible-supersensible form* spoken of by Goethe, which for a truly natural observation as well as for a spiritual one inserts itself between what is grasped by the senses and what is perceived spiritually.

Anatomy and physiology were pressing step by step towards this sensible-supersensible form. And in this process I observed, at first in a quite imperfect way, the threefoldness of man's nature. Only when I had been studying it for thirty years did I begin to speak about it publicly in my book *Von Seelenrätseln*. It first became clear to me that in the part of a human organism where the structure is mostly oriented towards the system of nerves and senses the sensible-supersensible form is also imprinted most strongly into the sensorially perceptible. The organism of the head seemed to me the one where the sensible-supersensible also comes most strongly into view in sensory form. By contrast, the organism of the limbs I regarded as the one where the sensible-supersensible is most concealed, so that within it forces active in extra-human Nature are extended into human formation. Between these poles of a human organism seems to me to exist all that comes to expression in a rhythmic way, the organism of breathing and circulation, etc.

I did not at the time find anyone to whom I would have been able to speak about these views. When here or there I hinted at them, they were regarded as the result of a philosophical idea. But I was certain that they had become manifest to me from unprejudiced experiential knowledge of anatomy and physiology.

In the mood weighing upon my mind through isolation with these views I only found inner release by repeatedly reading the conversation between Goethe and Schiller as they went away together from a meeting of the Society for Scientific Research at Jena. They were both in agreement that Nature ought not be treated in such piecemeal fashion as was done in the lecture they had heard by the botanist Batsch. And with a couple of strokes Goethe sketched out before Schiller's eyes his 'archetypal plant'. It represented in a sensible-supersensible form the plant as a whole, out of which leaf, blossom, etc. are shaped, reproducing the totality in the details. Schiller, having not yet overcome his Kantian standpoint, could see in this 'totality' only an 'idea', formed by human reason through observing details. Goethe would have none of this. He 'saw' the totality spiritually as he would see a detail sensorially. And he admitted no fundamental difference between spiritual and sensory perception, but only a transition from one to the other. It was clear to him that both raise a claim to be standing in experiential reality. However, Schiller could not but maintain that the archetypal plant is not an experience, but an idea. Goethe, in accordance with his way of thinking, then rejoined that he saw his ideas before him with his eyes.

I believed I had penetrated into these words of Goethe's, and what I gained by understanding them brought to calm a lengthy mental struggle. Goethe's view of Nature presented itself to my mind as one in accordance with the spirit.

Thus Steiner found confirmation for his insight into Goethe's view of Nature through repeated rereading of the same passage from the latter's writings which seven years earlier had been recounted for German readers in *Freie Blicke* by Edmund Reitlinger, and 40 years earlier for English readers in both *The History* and *The Philosophy of the Inductive Sciences* by William Whewell.

English and French

The first of the five friends described by Rudolf Steiner in the fourth chapter of his autobiography—the blond-haired, blue-eyed Wagner enthusiast who soon became a newspaper correspondent in a provincial town—was Emil Schönaich. The town was Troppau, and the newspaper was the *Freie Schlesische Presse*.

Steiner's first published articles are known to have appeared in this paper. But unfortunately no back-numbers from these years have survived, nor have any letters from Steiner to Schönaich.

Several letters have however survived from Schönaich to Steiner. One dated 5 January 1882 included this passage:

> ... So you've still been rather polishing your work and not spared any trouble to complete it properly, but now don't lose any time at all in making the little ship you've filled with your spirit go out onto the sea of dangers. The good subject-matter, to which it should be like a tiller, will itself be steering it, that it enter safely into haven ...

The first article of his own mentioned by Steiner in his autobiographical lecture was '*Auf der Höhe*'—the title of a novel by Berthold Auerbach.

⋆

In his biography of Karl Julius Schröer, Walter Beck includes this passage:

> At the Technical College too Schröer treated dramatic themes as well as themes from the life of Goethe; in the 1881/1882 term he held courses on 'Shakespeare in Germany' and 'Goethe's Life and Writings'; themes therefore which formed part of his research work.
>
> During the General Meeting of the Viennese Goethe Society on the 29th of January 1882 an annual report was presented, with Schröer named among the Vice-Presidents. The meeting discussed *inter alia* the erection of a Goethe Memorial, so besides a literary committee there was also founded a memorial committee.
>
> Thus began the long history of the Goethe Memorial, instigated by Schröer and lived through by him with such great intensity.

A little later, Beck goes on:

> To all those familiar with Goethe the year 1882 called to memory a significant event in the history of the 19th century: Goethe's death on 22

March 1832. The Viennese Goethe Society, along with the Concordia and with participation from the Male Voice Choir, arranged a big memorial celebration in the large hall of the Musikveriengebäude, with Heinrich Laube, Director of the Hofburgtheater, giving an opening address.

Schröer treated the central theme in his lecture 'After 50 Years', which was reported on 29 March in the *Neue Freie Presse*:

'Fifty years have passed since Goethe's death, and it almost seems to us as if he now stands more truly and livingly before our eyes than before those of his contemporaries of fifty years ago . . .

'Now the public he had in mind were men of high standing. Here also lies the great benefit which education draws from his works: they elevate us to the spiritual Monserrat of highest culture.'

In the concluding part of his lecture Schröer voiced a future expectation:

'I can here only indicate that Goethe—it seems to me—must again come to active expression in the evolutionary history of knowledge when the dominant stream of natural science emanating from England and France, which has toppled Philosophy from her throne without knowing her, will have exhausted its power of flight.'

No doubt there was much truth in Schröer's 'future expectation', and a reader can anyway understand what he meant. It may however also be added that there was a further interesting background to his statements—namely the totality of cultural affiliations within his own family.

Karl Julius Schröer and his wife Hermine had a large family, of five children. The eldest was a daughter, Lili, probably named after the figure in Goethe's *Märchen*. There was also a younger daughter, Ida.

Many years previously, in 1869, Schröer had engaged a lady friend, Nina Matscheko, to give these two daughters—then aged respectively 14 and nine—private tuition in English and French. This tuition may have included certain musical aspects, for in May 1871, when Lili was 16, her father reported in a letter to a friend that:

> Hermine is weak and should take it easy, so Lili is active caring from morning to evening . . . and always meanwhile occupied with English and French piano exercises . . .

Five months later, in October of that year, when Lili was staying with his niece in Pressburg, her father wrote to this niece:

> . . . I'm keen to know how Lili has being doing in the elements of both languages, English and French—in both of which she's still weak . . .

One may perhaps wonder whether Lili managed to improve her knowledge of Western languages during the subsequent years of her education. Be that as it may, four years later in 1875 Lili Schröer—just a couple of months after celebrating her twentieth birthday—became engaged to a scientist. This was Dr August von Mojsisovics, formerly a student at Jena under the great Darwinian Ernst Haeckel, and now a lecturer at the Zoological Institute in Graz. August could be described as a devoted exponent of precisely what Schröer went on to term 'the dominant stream of natural science emanating from England and France'.

August and Lili were married in 1876, and lived happily ever after.

⋆

Meanwhile, over in England—just a few weeks after Schröer's speech in Vienna about 'the dominant stream of natural science emanating from England and France'—the 73-year-old Charles Darwin finally died at Down House in the afternoon of 19 April 1882.

In the final section of her biography, Janet Browne relates the aftermath:

> Before the day was through, John Lewis creaked up the road with a coffin on his cart and laid Darwin out, as old country tradition required. Emma knew that Darwin expected to be buried in Downe churchyard, alongside Erasmus and the Darwins' two dead babies, 'the sweetest place on Earth,' he had once remarked to Hooker. He no doubt imagined that Emma would be buried there in the future. He had made his life, and his books, on that spot. But science claimed him, as it always had. News of his death went directly from Francis Darwin that evening to Huxley, Hooker, Galton and the rest. The next day Galton hurried to William Spottiswoode, President of the Royal Society, to request that Darwin be interred in Westminster Abbey, as a fitting memorial for a great man.
>
> Dying was the most political thing Darwin could have done. As Huxley and others were aware, to bury him in Westminster Abbey would celebrate both the man and the naturalistic, law-governed science that he, and each member of the Darwinian circle, had striven, in his way, to establish. Such an accolade suited Huxley down to the ground. His affection and admiration for his friend meshed seamlessly with elevated regard for modern science. Before long Lubbock was able to send to the Dean of Westminster a document stating that 'it would be acceptable to a very large number of our countrymen of all classes and opinions that our illustrious countryman, Mr. Darwin, be buried in Westminster Abbey'. Twenty Members of Parliament had signed it. Lubbock was confident that Dr. Bradley (the Dean) and Gladstone (the Prime Minister) would give their consent.
>
> The funeral at Westminster Abbey was held on Wednesday 26 April, a week after Darwin's death. The ceremony was overwhelming in size and content, a chance for science to show its strength as well as render formal acknowledgement of Darwin's place in history. The original Kent coffin

was changed for a sumptuous velvet-draped affair. Philosophers, scientists, naturalists, admirals, museum superintendents and civic dignitaries attended, 'together with a host of lay celebrities', all keen to pay their last respects to the man and the achievement. There were a few absences—Gladstone was busy in Downing Street ('off to Windsor at 5. Grand dinner in the Waterloo gallery'), and the Archbishop of Canterbury was indisposed. It is not known how far these may have been tactical . . .

'Happy is the man that findeth wisdom and getteth understanding' sang the choir from Proverbs 3. Two dukes and an earl were among the men who carried his coffin to the grave—the Duke of Argyll, the Duke of Devonshire, and the Earl of Derby—accompanied by the American ambassador, J. Russell Lowell, and William Spottiswoode, representing English science as President of the Royal Society. The other pall-bearers were equally eminent, the four men whose lives had intertwined so intimately with his own and whose rise to public position had matched the growing acceptance of his theories: Hooker, Wallace, Huxley and Lubbock . . .

Darwin's grave was in the nave, near Sir John Herschel and Isaac Newton, an honourable place but not as close to Lyell as Emma had hoped. The stone was inscribed with his name and dates, and only later did the Royal Society organize a fund to add a bronze tablet that described his contribution to science. As the *Pall Mall Gazette* declared, well-wishers believed they were laying there 'the greatest Englishman since Newton', one who had given 'the same stir, the same direction to all that is most characteristic in the intellectual energy of the nineteenth century, as did Locke and Newton in the eighteenth'. No one, said the *Times*, has 'wielded a power over men and their intelligences more complete than that which for the last twenty-three years has emanated from a simple country house in Kent'.

Emma remained at home. Unexpectedly, Francis had to put down Darwin's dog Polly a few days afterwards, and he buried her under the Kentish Beauty apple tree in the orchard.

And Darwin himself slipped into legend.

Popular, Popular

On 4 June 1882 Karl Julius Schröer in Vienna wrote to Professor Joseph Kürschner, literary director of the Spemann publishing firm in Stuttgart, who was bringing out Schröer's edition of Goethe's plays in his book-series *Kürschners Deutsche National-Litteratur*, and was on the lookout for someone to edit in this same series Goethe's scientific writings.

In course of his letter Schröer stated:

> A student in the upper terms reading physics, mathematics and philosophy, but who has for years also been attending my lectures, is intensely concerning himself with Goethe's scientific writings. I've given him the stimulus to try out a popular 'Article on Goethe and Newton' and send it to your journal. If this article were to succeed, we'd have the right man to edit the natural scientific writings. I'm not telling him anything of my thoughts, nor do I know how he writes. But from discussions I observe that he has a mastery of the subject, and has gained an independent view which seems to me correct. He's called Steiner.

★

On 21 June, the student's father, Johann Steiner, was transferred from the railway station at Inzersdorf to that at Brunn am Gebirge, and brought his family with him to this new abode.

Ten days later, on 1 July, the student himself took an examination in 'physics for chemists' under Edmund Reitlinger, who marked him as 'excellent'.

★

Another early article mentioned by Rudolf Steiner in his autobiographical lecture was 'about parallels between Shakespeare and Goethe'. In a lecture given at Dornach on 7 October 1914 he provided further details:

> As you know, I only mention personal matters when there is a factual reason. When directing my thoughts onto the evolution of mankind, I am now often obliged to remember a feeble attempt which I made as a quite young man. This piece of writing was the second one by me which was printed at all. I was at the time attempting—in a childish way of course, for I was only twenty-three or twenty-four years old—to make clear to myself the progression from Shakespeare's figures to Goethe's Faust.

If, as seems probable, the article concerned was written in the spring of 1882, Steiner was in fact aged only 21.

The lecture continued:

> Shakespeare created something needing to be created in precisely his age, when men could only be presented as human types, so that the manner of presenting them illustrates directly a development in their inner soul-forces. The progress in the Goethean *Faust* lies in the fact that Goethe did not put forward his individual figures as individual types—like Hamlet, Lear, Macbeth and so on in Shakespeare—but put forward Faust as the human being of our time. Only once can Faust be put forward in a poem. What Shakespeare had to give could be put before people in many human types. In every age it is precisely the characteristic expression of the age which has

Title page of the first folio of Shakespeare's works

to happen, so that the manifold nature of human spiritual life in course of evolution can be appreciated.

The article setting out this argument may have been referred to by Steiner's friend Emil Schönaich in a letter on 25 July 1882, where he stated *inter alia* that he himself had just written an article about Defoe. His letter included this passage:

> ...Don't be angry with me for not yet sending the issue with your article, which was everywhere well received. It was no longer available in the shops, so I can only find out at the press, where repairs are being done and the resultant disorder makes any search for later issues impossible. Perhaps I can send it to you tomorrow...

A fortnight later, on 8 August, Schönaich wrote again. His letter began:

> I'd prefer to have gone to work in replying at once to your friendly letter. Every line of it pleased me, and gave me a wealth of matter to think about. You don't know how warm it gets around my heart when I think that we're united in friendship and that this rests on quite different things than ordinary friendships are based on.

After discussing some other subjects, Schönaich remarked, 'I'm always pleased to hear that you're still repeatedly sticking to *Faust II*,' and then turned to the topic of music, chiefly that of Wagner, and its capacity to express feelings. The discussion ended:

> ...You'll perhaps find something about it in my article in the Fr. Schl. Pr., where I speak more clearly.
>
> I must still tell you about this paper, since you need this information as you're its obliging co-worker. The circle of readers before one which is being addressed must always be known. The circle of Fr. Schl. Pr. readers is according to provincial circumstances here what may be called moderately

> educated; a third of the subscribers are indeed educated people, the other sections are manual workers and dwellers in the country. This majority has very much to be considered if the paper wants to keep them. Recently I wanted to start in the paper a permanent column on literature and art, but the publishers thought many readers wouldn't be interested! Zitter's work can't be printed as it offers absolutely nothing which people find interesting. This discovery didn't give me the slightest pleasure. What subjects don't people find interesting???? . . .

Moritz Zitter was the third of the five friends described by Steiner in his autobiography—the one from Transylvania.

> . . . Bring out something for our paper very soon, but popular, popular. That's what the editor recently cried out to me. And now enough. Intimate greetings from your sincerely true friend
>
> Emil Schönaich

What the editor of the *Freie Schlesische Presse* wanted was something which, as expressed in Schönaich's previous letter, would be 'well received everywhere'—like the article 'about parallels between Shakespeare and Goethe'. . .

This Chain of Actions

The fourth of the five friends described by Rudolf Steiner in his autobiography—the reserved one who lived in his dreams, but also had literary interests—was Joseph Köck.

Unlike all the other friends, Köck was not a student at the Technical College. Rudolf Schober described his background:

> He came from very humble circumstances. His father was a so-called 'shunter' in the Wiener Neustadt goods depot. Köck was highly gifted, but very hard of hearing and consequently reserved and shy of people. We were in the same class and close friends. Owing to the small number of pupils in the two upper classes our gymnastic lesson was held in common, so occasion arose to become acquainted with Rudolf Steiner, who was about a year older. Moroseness towards the world, as well as unrequited love and perhaps also the influence left on him by the unhappy fate of an intimate friend made him at the end of the school year commit the folly of volunteering for the army. Owing to his hardness of hearing he had a very bad time there. He also made two attempts to poison himself, and was then allocated to an office of the munitions factory at Möllersdorf next to Wiener Neustadt. When he left the army, he wanted to complete the final class in the *Realschule* as a private pupil. But the three years of military service had brought

> him too far off the track, and after half a year he realized that his aim was impracticable. Luckily he then obtained an official position which had just become vacant in the Wiener Neustadt post office. Later he was assigned to postal service on the Vienna–Triest railway line . . .

If at the *Realschule* Köck was in the class below Steiner's, but left the school without completing the final year, he must have left at the same time as Steiner. His three years in the army would then have been from 1879 to 1882. In his autobiography, Steiner stated:

> He only came close to me in Vienna, where he first often visited me and later lived as an official.

Köck's first visits to Vienna were probably made in company of his close friend Schober after the latter started attending the Technical College in autumn 1880. Since a recently recruited soldier would not be given much leave, it may be supposed that if he managed to visit Steiner 'often' this must have been after he had been withdrawn from field service as a result of his suicide attempts and re-allocated to the munitions factory.

When was this? There is some evidence in Steiner's first letter to Köck, which is indeed his earliest surviving letter to anyone at all. It was written on 13 January 1881—a time therefore when Köck had been in the army for about a year and a half. Although the letter is not explicit on the point, it may be deduced from the content that Steiner wrote it as soon as he came to hear about one of Köck's suicide attempts.

Steiner's second letter to Köck was written from Vienna six months later, on 27 July 1881, a time when the recipient would have been in the army for about two years. Köck's state of mind may be deduced from the fact that in the course of this letter Steiner advised him not to curse people much, and not to be a pessimist.

Steiner's third letter to Köck is undated, but on the basis of letters from Köck to Steiner the editors of the latest edition of the *Briefe* have assigned it to 1882–3. This then was the time when Köck had finally come out of the army and returned to the *Realschule* at Wiener Neustadt intending to complete his lost final year.

The letter is entirely devoted to literary matters. It is reproduced here in full because it includes a reference to Shakespearean drama and in particular to the figure of Hamlet.

⋆

Now Hamlet—if alliteration on 'p' be permitted in order to emphasize the point—is the protagonist of a play in whose plot a particularly prominent part is played by poison.

After meeting in Act I the ghost of his father, poisoned 'with juice of cursed hebenon in a vial', the prince delivers in Act III his famous monologue about suicide, 'To be or not to be, that is the question . . .'

He goes on to arrange the performance of a play about a duke poisoned—in Vienna!—by his nephew Lucianus, who at the moment of administering the potion recites this speech:

> Thoughts black, hands apt, drugs fit, and time agreeing,
> Confederate season, else no creature seeing,
> Thou mixture rank, of midnight weeds collected,
> With Hecate's ban thrice blasted, thrice infected,
> Thy natural magic and dire property
> On wholesome life usurps immediately.

Later, in the tense finale of Act V, Hamlet, mortally wounded by the poisoned rapier of Laertes, with the same rapier mortally wounds him in return and, after seeing his own mother die from having drunk a poisoned cup intended for himself, uses the same poisoned rapier to dispatch his own uncle.

He then finally also expires after stating:

> The potent poison quite o'ercrows my spirit.

★

Whoever considers the related ideas expressed by the play's characters in lines such as these will also understand the hidden significance in Steiner's third letter to the literary-minded Köck—a friend who on two separate occasions within the three or four preceding years had tried to commit suicide by poisoning himself—of a reference to Shakespearean drama and especially to the figure of Hamlet.

This letter reads:

> Dear friend,
>
> Let the paper on which I'm now writing in order to go deep enough into my dear, dear Goethe then be put aside. It's true, I'm not promising or holding to anything, and yet at the same time be assured I wouldn't promise anything if I didn't have the best will to hold to everything. But I feel myself called on to spread around enlightenment about part of the Goethean spirit. I feel it in a way that I'd have to call it criminal if I didn't often take up my pen at the right time. Dear friend, you can to some extent disregard the prejudice many straightaway have if everything can't be made right for them. I believe I'll have read all your items in a week. I've already read some, there's a lot to say about them, and even more to think. One thing in general. For you I believe it's always more of a fundamental idea which a poem etc. carries than the roaring flow of events. The action or task is so to

speak only discovered in order to express a thought. For someone who has once recognized that fundamental thought, the clothing as such then loses its interest. I'm taking the story 'The Old and New Faith'. The fundamental thoughts are extremely true, grandly thought out and very significant. But the story has only little interest. I'd have been glad to see you soon emerging with your pieces into publicity, first perhaps without collecting any royalty. I believe it anyway a matter of course to use the 'Old and New Faith' itself, but the editor would say: what ought to be said should be said in another form as a prose article, and what's really being said leaves readers without interest. With something like this the plot itself must be interesting. Did Shakespeare in any of his plays express a fundamental idea? Nowhere! Where in that Hamlet, in that fine prince, in the senseless ghost stories and unnatural complications might there be any fundamental thought, except at the most that it's all thoughtless? And yet! What interest in this chain of actions! Ideas don't belong in poetry, nor in art at all, but only in philosophy. The model is and remains Greek art, not Goethe's or Schiller's. Wherever did Homer, Aeschylus, Sophocles, or Euripides ever want to express a fundamental idea, or where did Phidias want to incarnate ideas in his statues? Art is art all the more, the more it moves in pictures, not in thoughts (ideas). The second part of Faust has only been enjoyed in its true greatness since people started, under guidance from Loeper, to find there not ideas or allegories but a row of dreamy pictures; allegories are just wooden. I'm therefore advising you, dear friend, not to garb your thoughts in poems, but rather in prose articles, and only clothe in poetic garb what's obviously real. Art isn't merely the divine as such, but what has sensory nature. And it's the latter as such which must be pleasing, not the divine.

We want to talk about this as soon as we can. When I've read everything, you'll be getting a letter again. Don't be angry with me for my negligence.

Your unchangeable

Rudolf Steiner

The Essence of Freedom

On 3 September 1882—still during the summer vacation at the Technical College—the tuberculous Edmund Reitlinger finally died, aged 52.

During the previous term Rudolf Steiner had attended Reitlinger's course on 'physics for chemists', a subject which may have included further matter on the mechanical theory of heat. At any rate he recalled in his autobiography:

> It was a great sorrow for me when, a few weeks after I had sat under Reitlinger for my final examination in the mechanical theory of heat, this beloved teacher succumbed to his severe illness. Shortly before his end, like

> a legacy, he had still given me recommendations to persons who could provide me with pupils for private tutoring. This had very good results. I had to thank the dead Reitlinger for no small part of the income I earned to support myself in the following years.

At the time of Reitlinger's death almost two more years were to pass before Steiner found permanent work.

⋆

Towards the end of the same month, on 28 September—Michaelmas Eve—Steiner wrote to Joseph Kürschner stating that he was ready to undertake the project of editing Goethe's scientific writings.

Walter Johannes Stein continued in his article:

> I would here like to present what Rudolf Steiner experienced through this task, and how his acceptance of the commission became for him a turn of destiny. Rudolf Steiner recognized that it was not *his* destiny, it was *Schröer's* destiny to transmit a newly enlivened Goethean scientific view to the closing nineteenth century.
>
> In his *Course of my Life* Rudolf Steiner says: 'In my relation to the Goethe work I could quite vividly perceive how karma works in human life. Destiny is made up of two factual configurations growing together into unity. One of them streams out from the soul's inner longing; the other comes towards man from the outer world. The inclinations of my own soul were directed towards conceiving the spiritual; the outer spiritual life of the world brought me the work on Goethe. Both of these two streams, which met in my consciousness, I had to bring into harmony...'
>
> So Rudolf Steiner took over in his soul the inner work on a world-conception which Schröer had to carry out. But Schröer could not make the step into science. The age did not provide the necessary bridge.
>
> At the time science itself stood at a turning point. The question was whether the age had to divide art, science and religion... In the incapacity into which the literate Schröer felt himself put by Goethe's scientific works, Rudolf Steiner saw before him the suffering of the age... Something had to happen for mankind, which had to happen through Schröer, but could not.
>
> And so in Rudolf Steiner's youthful soul, where the suffering and purpose of mankind already then lived in pictures, a decision was formed to bring a sacrifice. Rudolf Steiner said: 'I then decided to live Schröer's destiny as my own, by renouncing my own path of destiny.' He was brought back to this only in 1923 at the re-foundation of the Anthroposophical Society, while everything lying in between resulted to an outstanding extent from taking on paths of destiny which it was for Schröer to tread.
>
> In his *Course of my Life* Rudolf Steiner says that his own path of destiny led

towards a spiritual conception. What carries on as destiny from one earthly life to another stood before his soul. To work this out in detail was *his* mission. But the world first required from him something different, namely the transformation of scientific thinking. The seeds found in Goethe had first to be brought to life. This however was in truth the task of Schröer, and not his own. So he decided first to put aside his own mission, and do what was needed by the world: he took over the Schröerian mission.

'By then making this decision, I experienced the essence of freedom. I was able to write my *Philosophy of Freedom* because I had experienced what freedom is.'

At the time, Steiner had of course no idea at all of the consequences of his decision. Clear evidence for this is given by a further letter to Kürschner written some three weeks later, on 21 October 1882, which shows Steiner to have then believed that the entire work of editing Goethe's scientific writings would be finished in little more than five months, by the end of the following March.

★

Ferdinand Hochstetter had now retired from the Technical College as Professor of Geology and Mineralogy. From autumn 1882 Steiner attended further lectures on these subjects given by his successor, a former student of the college named Franz Toula—an expert on the geology of the Balkans and a prolific cartographer.

In course of the karma lecture given at Torquay on 12 August 1924 Steiner made these observations:

> . . . I myself grew up in such a way that I never actually had difficulties in grasping the spiritual world. What the spiritual world brought me entered my mind, shaped itself out to ideas, could be formed in thoughts. What was so easy for other human beings was for me difficult. I could grasp scientific connections rapidly, but single facts did not want to stay in the memory, did not go in. I could grasp with ease the theory of undulation, the views of mathematicians, physicists and chemists. A mineral, by contrast, I did not, like some, have to see once or twice in order to recognize it when it reappeared before me, but this had to happen thirty or forty times . . .

Professor Toula was a known collector of geological and mineral specimens.

★

In November 1882 Karl Julius Schröer's younger daughter Ida, aged 22, followed the example which her elder sister Lili had set four years earlier by getting married. And in her case too, the bridegroom came from the scientific world: Carl Revy, by profession an engineer.

The Banners of France and England

In late 1882 Rudolf Steiner speedily set to work on his edition of Goethe's scientific writings. Taking most of the text from a version published some years previously by Salomon Kalischer, and also consulting a large amount of relevant secondary literature, he composed under Schröer's guidance an extensive introduction and footnotes for his first volume.

But he soon began to learn how slowly affairs tend to move in the publicational world. On 22 February 1883 he wrote to Kürschner telling him that the manuscript of his first volume was ready. In the event, however, owing to a prolonged sequence of contractual complications, the manuscript was not sent to Kürschner until 15 September, almost half a year after Steiner had originally supposed that the entire project would be finished and done with!

And indeed under the written contract the texts for all three then projected volumes were still meant to be in Kürschner's hands by 1 October. But by the time that deadline had come and gone it was quite obvious that the originally proposed timescale for the project was already a complete and utter dead letter.

★

On 18 October Steiner formally left the Technical College, without bringing his studies there to a proper end or taking any final examination. For to him these affairs no longer held any interest. He was now totally engaged in completing his editorial project.

Further letters passed back and forth with Kürschner, who forwarded the proofs of the first volume for correction. And not until five months later did this first volume finally come out, on 8 March 1884.

In his biography *Karl Julius Schröer*, Walter Beck recounts:

> As a result of intense prelimininary work there appeared two instructive new publications: the first volume of Goethe's *Naturwissenschaftlichen Schriften* by Rudolf Steiner and the first volume of *Dramen Goethes* by Karl Julius Schröer, both coming out in Kürschner's collected series *Deutsche Nationalliteratur*. Schröer prefaced the volume of Goethe's *Naturwissenschaftlichen Schriften* with a foreword composed that summer during his stay in Hungary, to which he added the date of Goethe's birthday, 28 August (1883).

Goethes Werke

Dreiunddreißigster Teil

Naturwissenschaftliche Schriften

Erster Band

Herausgegeben

von

Rudolf Steiner

Mit einem Vorworte von Prof. Dr. K. J. Schröer

Berlin und Stuttgart,
Verlag von W. Spemann

Title page of the first volume of Goethe's scientific writings

In this foreword Schröer refers to the development of natural sciences in the middle of the nineteenth century:

'Those who completed their studies in Germany before 1848 will certainly still recall the time of idealism, when the study of philosophy dominated every circle and could be felt in every science. It was a time when a great upswing in our folk was brought to culmination. Meanwhile a stream has set in where, instead of philosophy, natural sciences have taken on a leading role, under the banners of France and England. Older people . . . are now confronting a world where scarcely any further trace of that idealism may be perceived.'. . .

Now the banners of France and England—to continue Schröer's metaphor—were in the world at large chiefly being carried into what the deceased Edmund Reitlinger in the penultimate paragraph of *Freie Blicke* had termed 'the great cultural battle of the present' by people speaking the very languages for which Schröer himself had 14 years previously arranged private tuition for his own two daughters Lili and Ida. And both those daughters had gone on to marry persons who followed 'the leading role' of the natural sciences.

The irony of this situation was further compounded inside Schröer's family by another of his children. His second son, Arnold, followed his father's example by entering the educational profession, gaining a post in Vienna as a teacher at the Schottenbastei *Oberrealschule*. His subject was languages. One was his native tongue: German. And the other two were foreign: French and English.

The Task I Set Myself

Rudolf Steiner's introduction to the first volume of Goethe's scientific writings in the Kürschner edition was divided into several parts. The first part set out some brief preliminaries.

The second part, 'Origin of the Doctrine of Metamorphosis', embarked on a detailed account of the historical development of Goethe's thoughts on this subject from his earliest years.

One passage, recounting the autumn of 1786, reads as follows:

> ... Now it was above all a question of developing the details of what is lasting and continuous, that primal form with which Nature as it were plays, into a picture which could be grasped. An opportunity was needed to separate what is really constant and permanent in the plant-form from what is changing and incontinuous. Goethe had investigated too small a domain for observations of this kind. He had to observe one and the same plant under different conditions and influences; for only thus can what is variable be properly perceived. In plants of different kinds it strikes us less. The fortunate journey to Italy, which he began from Karlsbad on the 3rd of September, brought all this to him. Various observations were already made on the flora of the Alps. He found here not only new plants which he had never seen before, but also ones which he already knew, *but changed*. 'While in the more low-lying region branches and stems were stronger and fatter, with eyes closer to each other and broad leaves, up in the mountains branches and stems became more delicate, eyes were spread out at wider intervals so that there was a bigger space between node and node, and leaves were more lanceolate in shape. I noticed this in a willow and a gentian, and became convinced that it was not for instance a matter of different species. At the Walchensee too I noticed longer and more slender rushes than in the lowlands.' (*Italian Journey*, 8th of Sept. 1786.) Similar observations were repeatedly made. At the seaside in Venice he discovers different plants, showing characteristics which only the old salt on the sandy soil, but still more the salty air, could give them. He found there a plant appearing to him like our 'innocent coltsfoot, but armed here with sharp weapons and with leaves like leather, as were the seed pods and stalks, everything fleshy and fat.' (*Italian Journey*, 8th of Oct. 1786). Goethe saw here all the plant's outer features, everything on it which belongs to appearances and is transitory and changing. From this he concludes that the essence of a plant does *not* lie in these characteristics, but must be sought deeper. Darwin too, when stating his doubt about constancy in outer forms of genera and species, proceeded from observations similar to these of Goethe. But the results at which the two of them arrive are utterly different. While Darwin holds the essence of an organism to be actually expended in those characteristics, and from their variability concludes that in plant life there is thus nothing constant, Goethe goes deeper and concludes that if those characteristics are not constant, what is constant must be sought in something else underlying those variable externalities. Goethe's aim is developing this latter, while Darwin's endeavours are directed towards investigating and explaining in detail the causes of that variability. Both methods of observation are necessary and

complement each other. One would go completely awry in believing Goethe's greatness in organic science were found by seeing in him the mere precursor of Darwin. His method of observation is a much broader one. It embraces two sides: 1. the type, i.e. the regularity manifesting in the organism, the animality in the animal, the life arising out of itself, which through potentialities lying within it has the power and capacity to develop itself in manifold outer forms (species, genera). 2. the interaction of the organism with inorganic nature and of organisms with each other (adaptation and struggle for existence). Darwin developed only this latter side of organic science. So one cannot say that Darwin's theory is a development of Goethe's fundamental ideas, rather it is just the development of one side of them. It only looks at those facts which cause the world of living beings to develop in a certain way, but not at that 'something' onto which those facts have a determinant effect. If only one side is pursued it is also utterly unable to lead to a complete theory of organisms. It must be pursued essentially in Goethe's spirit, must be supplemented and deepened by the theory of the other side. A simple comparison will make the matter clearer. Take a piece of lead, by heating it make it liquid and then pour it into cold water. The lead has gone through two successive stages of its condition, the first caused by the higher temperature, the second by the lower. How the two stages take form depends not only on the nature of warmth but also quite essentially on that of the lead. Another substance, subjected to the same influences, would manifest quite different conditions...

This comparison may well have been drawn from an experiment demonstrated by Edmund Reitlinger in the physics laboratory during his course on the mechanical theory of heat.

...Organisms too are subject to surrounding influences; they too, affected by the latter, take on different conditions in complete accordance with their nature, in accordance with that essential being which makes them organisms. And this essential being is found in Goethe's ideas. Only someone equipped with an understanding of this essential nature will be in a position to grasp why organisms respond (react) to particular causes in precisely one such way and no other. Only he will be in a position to make correct mental pictures about the variability in the manifest forms of organisms and about the related laws of adaptation and struggle for existence.

At this point Steiner added a footnote:

It is probably unnecessary to say that no doubt of any kind is being thus cast on the modern theory of evolution, nor its claims thereby restricted. On the contrary, only in this way is a sure basis created for them.

After this second part of the introduction tracing Goethe's botanical studies, the corresponding third part went on to examine 'Goethe's Thoughts on the Morphology of Animals'.

★

The fourth part of Steiner's introduction was entitled 'On the Nature and Significance of Goethe's Writings on Organic Morphology'. It presented general conclusions applicable to both the botanical and zoological fields. Here is one passage:

> With these ideas Goethe established a theoretical basis for organic science. He discovered the being of the organism. One can easily misjudge this by demanding that the type, that principle which shapes itself out of itself (entelechy), should itself be explained through something else. But this is an unfounded demand, because the type, apprehended in intuitive form, explains itself. For every person who has grasped that 'forming itself according to itself' of the entelechial principle, this constitutes the solution to the riddle of life. Another solution is impossible, because that one is the essence of the thing itself. If Darwinism is compelled to postulate a primal organism, it can then be said of Goethe that he discovered the essence of that primal organism . . .

At this point came a footnote:

> By primal organism is usually understood in modern teaching on nature a primal cell (primal cytode), i.e. a simple entity standing at the lowest stage of organic development. This envisages a quite definite, real, sense-perceptible actual being. That is not what is envisaged when speaking about a primal organism in the Goethean sense, but rather the essence, the formative, entelechial principle which makes that primal cell into an organism. This principle manifests in the simplest organism as in the most perfected, only differently developed. It is the animality in the animal, what makes a being into an organism. Darwin presupposes it from the start; it is there, is introduced and he then says that it has reacted to influences of the outer world in this or that way. With him it is an indefinite X. Goethe seeks to explain this indefinite X.

The main text continued:

> . . . It was Goethe who broke with the mere classifying of genera and species and carried out a regeneration of organic science according to the nature of the organism. While the pre-Goethean system required just as many different concepts (ideas) as there are outwardly differentiated genera, between which no link could be found, Goethe declared that all organisms are the same in idea, and just different in appearance; and he explained why they are so. Thus a philosophical basis was created for a scientific system of

organisms. It was only a question of elaborating it. That all real organisms are just revelations of an idea would have to be demonstrated, and *how* they are revealed in a particular case.

The great deed thus accomplished for science was also given multifarious recognition by more deeply educated scholars. The younger d'Alton writes to Goethe on 6th of July 1827: 'I would consider it the finest reward if Your Excellency—to whom natural science is indebted not just for *a complete transformation in magnificent perspectives and new views* for botany, but also for splendid enrichments in the domain of osteology—were to recognize in the accompanying pages an endeavour worthy of applause.'...

At this point came another footnote with a bibliographical reference to the *Naturwissensch. Korr.*—the book Reitlinger had reviewed nine years previously in *Freie Blicke*. And in the main text the citation from d'Alton was followed by a couple of further citations also taken from the same book.

*

Somewhat later in this part, Steiner continued:

In Goethe's ideas we also receive an ideal explanation for the fact discovered by Darwin and Haeckel that the developmental history of an individual represents a repetition of the history of the race. For what Haeckel here puts forward cannot be taken as more than an unexplained fact. It is the fact that each individual passes in abbreviated form through all those developmental stages which at the same time palaeontology shows us as separated organic forms. Haeckel and his followers explain this by the law of heredity. But the latter is no more than an *abbreviated expression* for the given fact. The explanation is that those forms, just like each individual, are the phenomenal forms of one and the same archetype, which over successive periods of time unfolds the shaping forces lying within it as possibilities. For each higher individual is more perfected by not being hindered through the favourable influences of its environment from developing itself quite freely according to its inner nature. If on the contrary an individual is obliged by various influences to remain on a lower level, only some of its internal forces will manifest, and what for such an individual is then a totality is for that more perfected individual only part of a totality. In this way the higher organism appears in its development to be composed of lower ones, or lower ones appear in their development as parts of a higher. We must therefore again discern in the evolution of a higher animal the evolution of all lower ones (biogenetic law). Just as a physicist is not satisfied by merely stating and describing facts, but searches after their *laws*, i.e. after the concepts of phenomena, so too whoever wants to penetrate into the nature of organic beings cannot be satisfied merely by referring to heredity, struggle for

> existence, etc., but wants rather to recognize the ideas underlying these things...

With regard to the analogy of a physicist searching after '*laws*, after the concepts of phenomena', Steiner in his autobiography observed of Reitlinger that

> ... For everything methodical in physics he was fond of quoting Whewell's book on inductive science...

The second volume of Whewell's *Philosophy of the Inductive Sciences* contains in its first 'book', 'Of the Construction of Science', a section entitled 'Of Laws of Phenomena and of Causes'. This begins:

> In the first attempts at acquiring an exact and connected knowledge of the appearances and operations which Nature presents, men went no further than to learn *what* takes place, not *why* it occurs. They discovered an Order which the phenomena follow, Rules which they obey; but they did not come in sight of the Powers by which these rules are determined, the Causes of which this order is an effect. Thus, for example, they found that many of the celestial motions took place as if the Sun and stars were carried round by the revolutions of certain celestial spheres; but what causes kept these spheres in constant motion they were never able to explain. In like manner in modern times Kepler discovered that the planets describe ellipses, before Newton explained why they select this particular curve and describe it in a particular manner. The laws of reflection, refraction, dispersion and other properties of light have long been known; the causes of these laws are at present under discussion. And the same might be said of many other sciences. The discovery of *the Laws of Phenomena* is, in all cases, the first step in exact knowledge...

Steiner continued:

> This is what Goethe was striving for. What Kepler's three laws are to a physicist, Goethe's thoughts about the type are to an organic scientist. Without them the world is for us a mere labyrinth of facts. This was often misunderstood. It is claimed that the concept of metamorphosis in Goethe's sense were a mere *picture*, which has basically just been formed in our understanding through abstraction, and that it was unclear to Goethe that the concept of leaves changing into organs of blossom only had meaning if the latter, e.g. the stamens, had once actually been leaves. Just this places Goethe's view on its head. A sense-perceptible organ is made into the principal first one and the other derived from it in a sensory manner. Goethe never intended it that way. With him what comes first chronologically is not at all also primary according to idea, to principle. Not because stamens were once true leaves are the latter today related; no, rather do they appear

> once as true leaves because they are related ideally, according to their inner being. The sensory transformation is only a consequence of the ideal relatedness and not the other way round. The empirical matter of fact that all lateral organs of a plant are identical is today established, but why are they called identical? According to Schleiden, because they *all* develop on the axis by being pushed out as lateral protuberances, in such a way that lateral cell-formation continues only on the original body and no new cells are formed at the tip which was formed first. This is a purely external relation, and the idea of identity is regarded as its consequence . . .

Matthias Schleiden was a recently deceased author of various botanical textbooks.

> . . . Again, with Goethe the matter is different. According to him lateral organs are identical according to their idea, to their inner being; they therefore also *appear* on the outside as identical formations. The sense-perceptible relatedness is for him a consequence of the inner ideal one. The Goethean perspective differs from the materialistic view by the questions asked; they do not contradict but complement each other. Goethe's ideas form a basis for the materialistic view. They are not just a poetical prophesying of later discoveries, but independent theoretical discoveries still not nearly enough appreciated, and from which natural science will for a long time draw sustenance. Through more exact and detailed research the empirical facts he used may be quite superseded, partly even disproved. But the ideas he established are once and for all fundamental to organic science, since they are independent from those empirical facts. Just as every newly discovered planet must in accordance with Kepler's laws orbit its fixed star, so every process in organic Nature must take place in accordance with Goethe's ideas. Long before Kepler and Copernicus, processes in the starry heavens were being seen. But these men were the first to discover the laws. Long before Goethe, the realm of organic Nature was being observed, but Goethe discovered its laws. *Goethe is the Copernicus and Kepler of the organic world.*

This—italicized—characterization of Goethe combines the two named astronomers in the way done by Reitlinger when stating in the introduction to his work *Johannes Kepler* that '. . . discovering the true system of the world must be regarded as the joint deed of Copernicus and Kepler'.

Steiner continued:

> The nature of the Goethean theory can also be made clear in the following way. Besides ordinary empirical mechanics, which only assembles facts, there is also a rational mechanics, which deduces *a priori* laws from the inner nature of basic mechanical principles. Just as the former stands to the latter, so do the theories of Darwin, Haeckel, etc. stand to Goethe's rational organic science . . .

In the article on 'Galileo Galilei' in *Freie Blicke* Reitlinger had stated that Galilei 'laid down the immortal foundations of rational mechanics'. And indeed, that Steiner had Galilei in mind is shown in the final fifth part of his introduction, 'Concluding Remarks about Goethe's Morphological Views', where after admitting that Goethe sometimes made factual mistakes, he added:

> In principle, however, he arrived at basic views which have the same significance for organic science as do the basic laws of Galilei for mechanics.
>
> This was the task I set myself to establish.

To sum up, Steiner's first task in embarking on the Schröerian mission was to compose a proper account of Goethe's views on organic science. Although it was fundamental to these views that they were quite different from those relating to the inorganic realm, in carrying out this task Steiner nonetheless made good use of appropriate analogies in that latter realm taken from his own training in physics at the Technical College under Reitlinger.

Through All its Succession of Changes

After Rudolf Steiner's introduction, the actual content of this first volume in the Kürschner edition of Goethe's scientific writings consisted of a number of pieces brought together by Goethe himself under the title *Bildung und Umbildung organischer Naturen*. As noted by Edmund Reitlinger in his article 'Into the Interior of Nature' in *Freie Blicke*, Goethe placed at the front of this collection the motto:

> See, he goes over me before I am aware, and changes before I notice.

Steiner added an editorial footnote:

> This motto, from Job 9:11, was—slightly changed—written by Goethe on the 21st of April 1830 into Eckermann's album before the latter's journey to Italy with August von Goethe.

Fourteen years later, in 1844, Karl Julius Schröer as a 19-year-old student at Halle University had made his first visit to neighbouring Weimar and still been able to meet the then ageing Eckermann—during the very same year when Carl Gustav Carus had visited Cambridge University and met with William Whewell.

★

The collection opened with Goethe's short pieces 'The Enterprise Is Excused', 'The Purpose Introduced' and 'The Content Approved'. There then followed the *Metamorphosis of Plants* and a related biographical account entitled *Geschichte meines botanischen Studiums*.

The remainder of the volume consisted of a large number of shorter pieces gathered together under the title 'Pursuance'. Among these pieces was 'Destiny of Printed Writings'. This began:

> Anyone who is quietly occupied with a worthy object, striving in all earnestness to grasp it, forms no conception that human beings living at the same time are accustomed to think quite differently from himself. This is lucky for him, for he would lose faith in himself unless he were able to believe that things could be shared. But if he comes out with his own view, he soon notices that in the world different kinds of ideas struggle against each other, and confuse scholars as much as laymen. The day is always divided into factions, which know themselves as little as their antipodes. Every person does passionately what he can, and succeeds in so far as success arrives.
>
> I too, therefore, even before public judgement was made upon me, was quite wondrously moved by a piece of private news. In an imposing German town there had formed a union of scientific men, who together had established various good things in theoretical and practical ways. My little booklet was eagerly read in this circle as a peculiar novelty . . .

The reference was to the *Metamorphosis of Plants*.

> . . . But everyone was dissatisfied with it, and all were sure that what it might mean could not be made out. One of my Roman artist friends, who loved me and trusted me, felt it bad to hear my work so censured and indeed rejected, since in long continued dealings he had heard me speaking on manifold subjects quite reasonably and consequentially . . .

Steiner added a footnote:

> According to Riemer's *Mitteilungen* (II, 315) this Roman artist friend is Tischbein.

Goethe continued:

> . . . So he read the booklet attentively and, although not himself really knowing what my purpose was, grasped the content with kindness and artistic sense by giving the argument an admittedly strange but yet ingenious meaning.
>
> The author, he said, has his own hidden intention, which I however perceive quite clearly. He wants to teach an artist how to discover burgeoning and entwining floral embellishments, in continuous movement according to the manner and fashion of the ancients. A plant must arise from the simplest leaves, which by stages become manifold, divided, multiplied, and by pushing forward ever more shapely, thinner and lighter, until they

gather into their greatest abundance in a flower, and either shake out their seed or even start again on a new course of life. Marble pillars, embellished in such a way, can be seen in the Villa Medici, and only now do I understand what that means. An endless wealth of leaves is finally topped by a flower, and instead of seeds there finally spring forth animal figures and genii, without being found—after the preceding splendid evolutionary sequence—improbable in the slightest. I now rejoice to discover for myself many embellishments in this given way, having before been copying unconsciously from the ancients.

In the present case, however, this was not a good sermon for scholars. They let the explanation pass, but believed that if nothing more were in mind than art, and that what was intended were decorations, one should not act as if one were working for the sciences, where validity was not permitted to such fantasies.

Steiner added a footnote:

In the year 1850 similar claims are still expressed by Schleiden in Volume II of his *Botanik als induktive Wissenschaft.*

Goethe continued:

... The artist later assured me that as a result of the laws of Nature I had expressed, he had managed to unite the natural to the impossible and produce something delightfully probable. However, he was not permitted to wait upon those gentlemen again with his explanations.

From other quarters I heard similar sounds. Nowhere would people admit that science and poetry might be united. That science had developed out of poetry was forgotten. People did not consider that after a change of times both of them might quite well meet again as friends on a higher level, to mutual advantage.

Steiner added a footnote:

That science and poetry might well be united was stated by A. v. Humboldt.

Goethe continued:

Lady friends, who already before would have willingly drawn me away from lonely mountain ranges and observation of rigid cliffs, were also not in any way satisfied by my abstract gardening. Plants and flowers were to be distinguished by shape, colour and scent; but they then vanished into a ghostly scheme. I then tried to lure these well-wishing minds into participation through an elegy. May a place for it be granted here. It should become more comprehensible when related to scientific presentation than if inserted into a sequence of tender and passionate poems.

Steiner added a footnote:

The following elegy was composed in the year 1798 (*Goethes lyrische Gedichte*, elucidated by Dünker). Karl Rosenkranz sees here the genuine speculative development of Goethe's 'ideas on the formation of plants'. (Cf. his book *Goethe und seine Werke* p. 78). It is addressed to Christiane Vulpius.

And here it is translated by William Whewell:

> Thou, my love, art perplext with the endless seeming confusion
> Of the luxuriant wealth which in the garden is spread;
> Name upon name thou hearest, and in thy dissatisfied hearing
> With a barbarian noise one drives another along.
> All the forms resemble, yet none is the same as another;
> Thus the whole of the throng points at a deep-hidden law,
> Points at a sacred riddle . . .

Steiner added a footnote:

> *Sacred riddle*. Already in Italy Goethe calls the idea of metamorphosis a secret. Cf. Goethe to Herder, Naples 17th of May 1787. 'I must further confide to you that I am quite near the secret of the procreation and organization of plants.' Despite his deep insights into Nature Goethe nonetheless always retained a sacred timidity before her, and on the 15th of July 1831 says to Eckermann (*Gespräche*, p. 245): 'Her secrets are of unfathomable depth. But man is allowed to gain ever deeper insights.' So here too he calls the riddle *sacred*.

Whewell's translation continues:

> . . . O could I to thee, my belov'd friend,
> Whisper the fortunate word by which the riddle is read!
> Come then, trace we the plant through all its succession of changes,
> As its inherent pow'r forms it to blossom and fruit.

Steiner added a footnote:

> Organic bodies cannot be understood by looking at them as finished self-contained forms; rather must one observe how in member upon member they develop from their essential nature, how they come into being. Cf. Goethe's *Sprüche in Prosa* Nr. 940: 'Reason rules over the living alone, the produced world treated by geognosy is dead,' and Nr. 896: 'Reason applies to what is becoming, understanding to what has become.'

A further footnote stated that the next section of the poem

> . . . Contains in poetic form the whole development of the plant, which is also contained in the 1790 essay. Cf. here: to lines 11–20 §§.10–18; to 21–32 §§.19–28; to 33–44 §§.29–38; to 45–48 §§.39–45; to 49–56 §§.46–73; to 57–58 §§.74–83.

Whewell's translation continues:

Out of the seed unfolded it comes, as soon as the silent
Nourishing womb of the Earth sends it to life and to light.
Holy Light, ever active, which makes the forms that it shines on,
Broods o'er the delicate leaves, e'en as they burst from their cell.
—Slept in the seed such power; an inborn type of the future
Lay, wrapt fold within fold, deep in the heart of the mass—
Leaves, and the root, and the bud, as yet unformed and uncoloured;
So the dry kernel holds, stilly, the springs of a life.
Then the young birth breaks forth, confides in the genial moisture,
Gathers and lifts itself up, out of the chaos of night.
Simple at first is the form, and plain and unvaried its aspect;
Simple is childhood still; now as a child is the plant.
Upwards straining again and again, the formative impulse
Thrusts forth, stage above stage, shapes that are like to the first;
Like, and yet different still: for lo, still higher and higher,
Multiform more does the leaf show us the working of change.
Spreading and notcht and carved with varied and multiplied members,
Which, all merged in a mass, dwelt in the stages below.
And thus reaches at last the leaf its fullness of fabric,
Which in full many a kind much thy astonishment moves,
Ribb'd and indented about, and in rich convexity swelling—
Seems as the impulse of growth freely and boundlessly wrought.
But at this point arriv'd, the expanding urgency Nature
Checks with her mighty hand—guides to a loftier plan—
Tames the flow of the juices—contracts the vessels—and straightway
Finer workmanship shows in the refinement of form.
Back to the centre retreats the expanding thrust of the margin:
Fuller the leafy rib gathers itself in the midst.
Leafless and smooth, a more delicate stalk springs rapidly upwards,
And a marvellous show meets the contemplative eye.
Close ranged round the stalk—or fixed in number or boundless—
Leaflets, each like each, gather themselves in a ring.
Here, with protesting circle, the calyx girdles the axis,
And in the fairest forms lovely-hued coronets wears.
Nature thus stands forth in her pride, refined and exalted;
Member on member imposed—fullness and symmetry joined.
And with wonder thou seest the flow'r, as it waves on its footstalk,
Over the changeful leaves—scaffolding, these, of the flow'r.
Yet does this splendour all but announce new formative changes:
Yet does the petal again yield to the pow'r which transforms.
See—it contracts to the slenderest shapes, which, higher aspiring,
Twofold show in their forms—double, yet made to unite.

> Each confiding in each, the lowly pairs, as they gather
> Numerous, orderly stand circling the altar of Love.
> Hymen hovers above, while around, a deliciöus fragrance,
> Breathed from each to each, floats with a life-giving pow'r.
> And now, separate all, the buds in the motherly shelter
> Each of its swelling fruit, rip'ning, innumerous, swell.
> And thus Nature rounds the eternal ring of her working,
> There where it seems to end, ever beginning again . . .

Steiner added a footnote:

> In seed-formation Nature completes the forming of a plant, in order at the same time to make the beginning of a new one. A seed is both the end of a process of plant-formation, and the start of a new one.

Whewell's translation continues:

> Thus is the chain prolonged through the endless circuit of ages;
> Thus, as each thing has a life, is there a life in the whole . . .

Steiner added a footnote:

> The thought that the whole is alive like the part, i.e. that the whole being of the plant is potentially contained in each separate organ, is Goethe's fundamental thought.

Whewell's translation ends:

> And now turn, O belovéd! thy glance to the motley assembly
> Troubling thy mind no more, now, with its manifold show.
> Now does each plant proclaim the eternal law of its being;
> Every plant as it blows speaks to thee clearly and plain.
> But if thou here canst decypher the sacred letters of Nature,
> See them ev'rywhere stampt, though in a varying form.
> See how the grub creeps low, till the butterfly flutters expanded;
> See even man himself changed by the formative pow'r.
> And O! then reflect how in us too the bud of acquaintance,
> Opening day by day, grew to the sweetness of use.
> How then friendship next disclosed its pow'r in our bosoms;
> How Love came at last—came with his flow'rs and his fruits.
> Think how many a shape, each springing out of another,
> Nature, unfolding our hearts, unto our feelings has given.
> Joy with me in the thought of today—when Love, in its yearning,
> Seeks Love's fairest of fruits—seeks a communion of thought;
> Seeks a oneness of view in the pair, that, harmoniously musing,
> Heart may, united to heart, rise to a loftier world.

6
THE VIENNESE CONTINUATION

In the Affirmative

After publication in 1884 of the first volume of Goethe's scientific writings in the Kürschner edition there was a long pause in this whole project. The second volume did not appear for another three and a half years, until the late summer of 1887.

A further three years then elapsed before a third volume came out in 1890, by which time it was clear that the work would still need another two volumes in order to reach completion: these fourth and fifth volumes only appeared in 1897, when Steiner had also concluded the editing of a large part of Goethe's scientific writings from primary sources in six volumes of the great Weimar edition.

So the edition in Kürschner's series, which Steiner had once thought would only take six months to complete, turned into a publicational project which in the end spread out over no less than 13 years.

★

The immediate reason why the second volume of Goethe's scientific writings in Kürschner's series did not soon follow on the first was that further work on the second volume was interrupted by the unexpected emergence of a completely different literary project suggested by the publisher himself.

For only six weeks after the first volume had come out, when Steiner was still busy sending copies to various influential scholars, he received this letter:

Stuttgart,
24th of April 1884

Most Honourable Sir,

Allow me today in a private matter also once to turn to your kindness. I am intending soon to publish a kind of practical handbook, to which I am thinking of giving an appendix orienting the reader in the tersest possible form about what is most worth knowing. A series of quite short articles from the field of mineralogy are to find inclusion in the same and if you were disposed to edit this domain you would oblige me to exceptional gratitude. It is, as stated, a matter of quite brief articles, without particular stylistic connection, just sufficiently explaining the headword by providing factual content. Unfortunately, however, I am not in a position to pay any exceptionally high royalty, as I myself only receive very little, but I also believe that the work will occasion extremely little trouble.

I would then forward a list of articles and put all further details in writing.—Should you yourself not be disposed or in a position to take on the work, perhaps you would nonetheless be able to give me the name of some person disposed to do so.

Hoping soon to hear good things from you,

Your fullest of high esteem and devoted

Kürschner

⋆

Three days later, Steiner sent Kürschner a long reply, still largely devoted to his Goethe edition and related matters, but also including a paragraph which began:

> I come now to your friendly request about editing the mineralogical part of the book which Your High Wellbornship has described. I am quite well able to take on such a work, thereby answering your kind question in the affirmative. I would therefore like to ask you to forward to me the list of articles you mentioned and let me know more about your book's tendency and conception. In any case I also request information about the approximate spatial length of the articles. I give you my best thanks, most honourable Herr Professor, for having thought about me on this occasion and assure you that it would give me much pleasure if I were to succeed in gratifying you . . .

Further letters passed back and forth about the details, and little more than a month later, on 30 May, Kürschner asked Steiner not only to forward all the articles he had so far written on mineralogy, but also to write some others on the subject of mining. His firm would begin to set up the work in print in the middle of the following week.

⋆

In the meantime, on 6 June, the Viennese *Deutsche Zeitung* published an article by Steiner on 'Goethe's Rights in Natural Science'. This may have been the 'Article on Goethe and Newton' referred to by Karl Julius Schröer in his letter to Kürschner two years previously—and later sent to him for publication in a German journal which however had by then been discontinued.

The article included the following paragraph about Goethe's relation to Newton's theories on light and colour:

> Only to begin with was the battle with Newton the chief thing for Goethe; it was merely the starting point, not the aim of his optical work. The aim

was nothing else than tracing the rich manifoldness of the world of colours into a systematic whole, so that every colour-phenomenon from this whole would be as comprehensible for us as any relationship of spatial sizes from a mathematical system. The structure of mathematics outlasting the centuries, well divided and self-supporting, stood as an ideal before Goethe's eyes when he built up his teaching on colours. One awakens from the outset only misunderstandings by overlooking this lofty purpose and placing into the foreground the battle with Newton. The matter then gains the appearance of Goethe having fought against a fact discovered by Newton, while his endeavours had nothing else in view than to correct a method which misunderstood itself, a hypothetical explanation of a fact. That the contrast in question, thus considered, gains a quite different meaning from the one usually attributed to it was repeatedly recognized by stimulating thinkers like Joh. Müller or Karl Rosenkranz. Newton's assertions actually bear in themselves the character of aphorisms. They extend over only part of the teachings on colour, over colours arising from the refraction of light. They are straightaway modified by themselves if inserted into a system treating the totality of colour phenomena. What is difficult to see here is only in fact that assertion does not stand against assertion, but a totality against a particular chapter. In any harmony a whole must not just be mechanically put together out of its parts, but the parts are also determined by the nature of the whole.

A Time of Retardation

In his biography of Rudolf Steiner, Christoph Lindenberg characterizes the subsequent Viennese years:

> The retardation of Steiner's strivings was of the very greatest importance for his own course of progress. Up to the year 1897 the deceleration of his progress was bound up with the Goethean work. In retrospect Rudolf Steiner acknowledges the purpose for his development of the apparent delays through his work on Goethe: 'This development went more slowly than would have been the case if the Goethe task had not been placed as a matter of destiny into the course of my life. I would then have pursued my spiritual experiences and presented them just as they appeared before me. I would have been swept more rapidly into the spiritual world; but would have found no reason for struggling to submerge myself into my own inner being . . . At the time when I was working out my interpretation of Goethe I always had him beside me in spirit as an admonisher, incessantly calling out to me: Whoever goes forward too fast along spiritual pathways can certainly attain a narrowly circumscribed experience of the spirit; but he steps out from the wealth of life impoverished in respect to the content of reality.'

> The Viennese time from 1884 to 1890 was in especial measure a time of retardation, for the applause Rudolf Steiner had gained with his first Goethe volume remained without consequences for his daily life. His scientific success did not open up for him any academic career. So Steiner had to find a post as a private tutor, or in the expression then still current, as a *hofmeister*. In this period of private tutoring he not only had to fulfil his pedagogical tasks, but had enough time to pursue his Goethean studies...

In mid-June 1884, through recommendation from Karl Julius Schröer to an intermediate party, Steiner was engaged as private tutor to the four sons of Ladislaus and Pauline Specht. At that time the Specht family were resident in Vöslau, just south of Baden, and for over a year Steiner either stayed in Vöslau or sometimes commuted there from his own family home in Brunn am Gebirge.

A few weeks after Steiner's death, on 26 April 1925, the eldest son Richard Specht published some reminiscences in the *Neues Wiener Journal* recalling this time, when he himself was aged 14:

> I do not want to speak about the world-famous anthroposophist, who became and remained a stranger to me. But I would like to tell about the friend of my youth who was for many years our fellow lodger and remained faithful to our family till the end of his life...
>
> Already then he looked just as in later years, already then had his pale, slightly creased ascetic face with brown eyes behind sharp spectacles. His long, smooth, black hair, his gaunt neck with the big Adam's apple, his tall figure wrapped around by jacket and tails, having about him something of a clergyman, something of a philosopher and something of a self-opinionated pedant. Already then he had his own manner of talking—since experienced by thousands upon thousands—with the piercing upleaping accents of his never resonant, always a little sermonizingly lecturing and at the same time childishly questioning voice. There was a strange mixture in him of scholarly seriousness, boyishness and rhodomontade, also something enormously strong-willed, something pedantic and at times even something casually idle, which however would repeatedly change into a fanaticism for work. He was such a bodily weakling that if one of us boys in a fit of love or high spirits wanted to hang around his neck he would at once collapse to the ground. Mentally he was nonetheless of the greatest energy. How often when I too was sitting at the table by night could I watch him battling against sleep and often succumbing to it. But he would never give up, was never persuaded by me to go to bed, and found help in black coffee...

★

By the time he took up his tutoring post in the Specht family on 10 July 1884 Steiner had already sent Kürschner most of the requested entries on mineralogy and mining for the projected handbook. In the late summer and autumn he brought to completion the rest of his entries and sent them off as well.

At the end of October the handbook was duly published in Stuttgart under the title *Kürschners Taschen-Konversations-Lexicon.*

A Free View

On 6 and 15 November Rudolf Steiner published in the *Deutsche Lesehalle für alle Stände*—a Transylvanian journal edited by his friend Moritz Zitter—a sequence of two articles (here combined) entitled 'Ein Freier Blick in die Gegenwart' ('A Free View into the Present').

This title was of course adapted from the title of *Freie Blicke* by Edmund Reitlinger.

> At the beginning of this century a mighty spiritual endeavour arose among the German people and sought to penetrate into the deepest secrets in the edifice of the world through the power of human thinking. There developed an original knowledge which was emancipated from every practical activity and, hovering in the highest spheres of idealism, wanted to satisfy only the needs of the spirit. This striving was ensouled by a deeply earnest German impulse, imbued with high moral sense.
>
> On considering German poetry of that time we have to say that it too is filled with a magic juice, welling up for German thinkers out of their striving towards an innermost brotherhood with the spirit of the world. In this respect both research and artistic creativity had a religious impulse, since they fulfilled the first basic requirement of religion: to raise men above the day-to-day and the ordinary into a higher, purely spiritual region.
>
> This was a break with ancient traditions, but a break of *different* kind than the almost simultaneous one of the French Revolution. Germans rose up against things from olden times—against outmoded forms of religion, art and science—because a new world was opening inside them, and genuineness and inner truth were driving semblance out. With Frenchmen after all it was nothing but clever understanding, the vacuity of enlighteners, for whom old things did not suffice, and for this very reason the liberality of the French turns so easily into frivolity.
>
> That cultural height on which Germans once stood appears to us today only as something bygone, and we disciples look back with nostalgia to that better time. For us indeed nothing seems to remain but the little comforting task of being gravediggers and memorial-raisers to those great minds who brought that tremendous epoch about.
>
> What are we bringing about which could even be remotely compared to

those achievements? The power of creating anything original seems to have long disappeared, and our whole art to consist in making biographies of our great ancestors and commentaries on their works. Where is the German power which once conceived Lessing, Schiller, Goethe, Fichte, Schelling, Hegel and Jean Paul?

The mighty Germanic giant in mid-Europe could almost appear to be asleep. But on looking more closely, this gloomy picture vanishes before one in a still highly gratifying manner. We gain a conviction that we do not need at all to despair of the present, but in many repects may be pleased with it.

If we consider the spiritual life of Europe, it is like a system of threads in many ways intertwined. Whichever of these threads is followed, we come *even today* to Germany as a crossing-point where they all meet. The scientific, artistic, economic and social life of Europe is a connection of forces all having their centre in Germany.

If we want to prove the truth of this statement, we need only look at two distinct interests. One dominates the scientific, the other the economic and social striving of the present.

By the first point we mean Darwinism, the scientific doctrine that all animal forms now living are just descendants of some or of a single basic form, which in course of very long periods of time has perfected itself; that man is just the most perfect, most developed animal form, and his ancestors are to be sought in no other place than where those of other mammals may also be found. This teaching is of English origin. But the way it emerged from the head of the Englishman Darwin around the middle of our century made it into a hazy view, in itself unclear. Neither were the moral consequences drawn, nor was the necessary all-round scientific extension available. At the centre were a number of observations, experiences and undoubted truths, but start and finish were completely wrapped in mist.

At the beginning of the sixties German scholars took this view over. German profundity, thoroughness and deep moral earnestness struck like lightning into the confused web. By applying all powers of mind, the whole subject was thought through and penetrated into its final consequences, and under the care of German researchers there soon arose a scientific building, firmly situated and founded in all its parts. What had been indicated by the Englishman Darwin was completed in a superb monumental way by the German Haeckel. The latter has created a complete mental edifice, set out in all details with admirable astuteness. In England a mysterious document of Nature had been found, but over it lay a thick veil. A German then came and tore the veil away, and the world henceforth knew what stood on the mysterious piece of writing. But matters did not remain there. The lofty ethical sense of Germans also had to weigh up the new doctrine's necessary consequences for morality and public life. Numerous are the writings of

German researchers who wanted to show with more or less success either the harmony of Darwinism with pure morality, or the danger to the latter through the former. The highlight of German culture was thus also recalled: German idealism and its great representative Goethe. The ideas of this great genius needed to be brought into harmony with the new teachings. No little suggestion is made by saying the following: any German is so permeated by that ideal world that every disharmony of new conceptions with this world is painful to him. The striving by German scholars to bring the results of a modern world-conception into harmony with Goetheanism is a reaction of the German conscience to the trend of scientific fashion. The will of Germans that only *the ideal* may find entry into life is ultimately a belief that idealism must be *true*.

It is a specifically German phenomenon for pessimism in its deepest form to present itself as a consequence of Darwinism. There is no small number of inward, thoroughly good and highly gifted souls whom the new doctrine brings to despair of the world and of life. If one has such deep feeling as a German, is as distant as he from every kind of frivolity and foolishness, and possesses *his* striving towards the *divine*, one will not easily escape from pessimism when completely thinking through the nullity of man and his race which follows if Darwinism be in its full extent upheld. This arouses a series of thoughts which certainly may still be long extended, since as we have seen the most tremendous power moving the scientific world today points us towards Germany. The West has thrown up a problem, Germany attempts to solve it. And if redemption from the spell of the enormous one-sidedness of the modern world-view should *ever* come, it can only come from Germany. The power of the German mind will show what is true in Darwinism, and at the same time show that Darwinism, applied beyond a certain point, is inwardly untrue, superficial and shallow. This power will *overcome* Darwinism, by *limiting* the domain of its might, by *understanding* it.

The second phenomenon to which we wish to refer is the striving of European peoples to find that form of state where the moral dignity and freedom of every individual citizen comes to fullest effect. Again it was the West, France and England, where this striving first became manifest. Necessary reason had to appear instead of caprice, equal entitlement instead of prerogative, freedom instead of unfreedom. But it is probably not too daring to claim that the first seeds really capable of life, of setting up instead of a state ruled by chance and subjective caprice one where *reason* holds the uppermost regency, are just now being laid in Germany. The state must take care that an individual's fortune does not depend on chance or caprice, but that a totality erected according to principles of reason so far ensures his welfare that he can develop himself freely in a physical and mental direction. The state cannot make men free, only education can. But the state certainly has to take care that each person find a basis on which his freedom may thrive. For progress here from the steps of a throne once occupied by Frederick the Great this password is today being given: in Germany state guidance lies in the hands of a man deeply permeated by that state mission. History will one day record this as one of the greatest of its political facts.

Now one thing more. Germans do exist who are not called on to take part in the great work which German people today are in a social respect fulfilling. We are indeed here speaking to a great number of such Germans, but do not wish to describe it as unfortunate that this is the case. For maybe an important part of the common cultural work of our people devolves today upon precisely *these* Germans. We accept present-day conditions with unfeigned resignation, asserting the circumstance that it is to a high degree desirable for things to be as they are. We may not forget that through the great economic problems of the present the German people have today lost an ideal momentum for higher *spiritual* matters. Nor may we leave out of consideration that even German youth—once the proven guardian of German idealism—forgets the latter for social and reformatory thoughts. We shall perceive that the German being in its finest development needs a refuge in precisely such Germans as live outside the German fatherland.

A fine perspective opens here for these latter German peoples. We know one folk which has always held to this principle, and is therefore equal to all German peoples—in many repects ahead of very many in both culture and education—the Saxons in Transylvania! May this journal contribute to further growth of their culture and education, and succeed in the sense referred to in speaking to a German people in a non-German land.

Able and Willing

On 20 November Joseph Kürschner sent Rudolf Steiner from Stuttgart a complimentary copy of the newly published *Taschen-Konversations-Lexicon*, asking him also to bring out somewhere a few friendly words about it.

Steiner replied on 1 December, promising to give the book a suitable review, and at the same time asking whether the Spemann firm might be able to publish a brochure of 6–8 sheets entitled 'Erkenntnistheorie auf Grund der Goethe-Schillerschen Weltanschauung und des deutschen Idealismus'.

A few days later Kürschner gave a favourable reply, also forwarding a royalty of 30 marks for Steiner's work on the lexicon articles.

★

Steiner's review came out on 13 December, in the evening edition of the Viennese *Deutsche Zeitung*:

Kürschners Taschen-Konversations-Lexicon. Berlin and Stuttgart. Publishers W. Spemann.

Assembling on 840 sextodecimo pages what is most needed in all branches of knowledge, as has actually happened here, was probably only made possible by Professor Kürschner's amazing circumspection and dexterity in literary matters. The book is meant to satisfy a twofold need: firstly, allowing a lexicon to be purchased for the modest outlay of three marks by those to whom even the small editions of Meyer and Brockhaus are too expensive; secondly—and this is probably more important—serving the uses of the moment. Looking things up, which in larger works of this kind is often tiresome and time-consuming, can take place here in the shortest conceivable time. So the book will in many cases be of service even to owners of a larger lexicon. The modest compass has not been achieved at cost of content, but by making the greatest possible use of space by understandable curtailments. This little book has come about by employing relatively large resources. Apart from Kürschner there number eighteen collaborators. Greatest care has been laid on completeness of entries. Emphasis may be placed on the fact that apart from entries normally admitted into a lexicon, it contains details on courts of law, insurance companies for life-, fire- and pension schemes, urban quarters of regimental troops, embassies, consulates, and other matters. Brought together with great sacrifice and truly bee-like industriousness, the book should soon enjoy appropriate dissemination.

Interior of Steiner's flat in Brunn am Gebirge

On 18 December, Steiner sent Kürschner an extract from the paper containing this review, and also expressed his gratitude that the Spemann firm were willing to publish his theory of knowledge. He stated that he was currently writing out the manuscript.

Several further months then passed by.

★

In the late spring of the new year, probably soon after the beginning of May, Kürschner must have written again. Although his letter does not survive, its content is deducible from Steiner's historic reply, which one may imagine him composing in the little upstairs flat rented by the family in Brunn am Gebirge.

Brunn am Gebirge,
15th May 1885

Most Honourable Herr Professor,

Allow me herewith to reply to your friendly letter that I am firstly very happy over the fact that a new edition of the little lexicon is already now needed, and am with pleasure ready to attend again to my part in the manner indicated by yourself, most honourable Herr Professor. I therefore very much request you to send as soon as feasible the paper mentioned in your letter, and you may rest assured that I will apply every necessary care. In particular I suggest increasing by one the little illustrations elucidating the article 'Geological Periods', which I shall be sending you at the same time as my manuscript. Should you, most honourable Herr Professor, still be in a position to assign me the Fr. and Engl. translation of my part, I would be able and willing to undertake the same quite well.

Best commending myself to your distant goodwill,

Rudolf Steiner

★

The final sentence of this letter is remarkable. Steiner's assertion that he would be 'able and willing' not only to undertake both stated translations (even underlined!) but even to do so 'quite well' appears to suggest some confidence on his part in his own translational skills. And yet extremely little in the several years which had now elapsed since he received his school-leaving certificate at Wiener Neustadt in 1879 could be said to have indicated any interest—let alone proficiency—in either of the foreign languages referred to.

Most German-speakers in Steiner's position in May 1885, although of course pleased at the prospect of having their carefully composed scientific items translated into other languages, would have been perfectly content, if not indeed fairly grateful, had Kürschner found someone else to take on this wearisome chore, thus leaving them free to pursue further original work of their own which—in so far as it came to linguistic expression—was conducted in the medium of their own mother-tongue. It is therefore most striking how readily Steiner offered to undertake what was for him an unprecedented task, at the cost of delaying not only the book he was then writing on Goethe's theory of knowledge but also the remainder of his edition of Goethe's scientific writings, both of which projects were incomparably more central than Kürschner's little lexicon to the Schröerian mission.

Can Steiner's offer be considered as a part, small maybe but nonetheless significant, of that deliberate retardation which formed such an essential strategic element in the unfolding of his biography? Did he take the task of translation as a challenge to which he decided to respond precisely by reason of his deeply ingrained Germanicity? Or was he trying to smooth out the somewhat ambiguous karmic relationships to Father Lambertz and more especially to Father Schmeisser in Wiener-Neustadt? That Steiner could not at this time speak properly either of the languages in question is certain, but he must nonetheless have acquired—in the case of English chiefly from listening to Edmund Reitlinger quoting Whewell's work on inductive sciences—sufficient basic command of the written forms of their grammar, syntax and vocabulary as was necessary to render his lexicon entries into what were for him largely alien linguistic modes.

Without Delay

The sequel is recorded in a series of letters passing to and fro between Stuttgart and Brunn am Gebirge or Vöslau during the summer months.

Stuttgart,
23rd May 1885

Most Honourable Sir,

Best of thanks for your kind agreement in being willing to undertake a revision of the new edition. You are receiving enclosed a series of articles to be followed at short intervals by others, and I request the most rapid possible completion. The enclosed notes give further information about principles to be observed. Incidentally for minerals etc. it seems to me advisable to leave out the different formulae, which for a reader will remain more or less incomprehensible. On the other hand it seems to me necessary in particular to consider strictly separating the indications of what are minerals from what are crystals. I fear that through using the sign  many mistakes have slipped in. If you will be so kind to enclose the translation straightaway, I shall be under an obligation of special gratitude towards you. With regard to abbreviations I reserve a special statement.

With exceedingly high esteem,

Your most devoted

Kürschner

★

Brunn am Gebirge,
30th June 1885

Your High Wellbornship,
Most Honourable Herr Professor,

In your honoured lines, which you, honourable Herr Professor, added to the consignment of the first series of articles for the little lexicon, you expressly reserved that you would still make some communications to me concerning abbreviations, through which in the 1st edition an unclarity had slipped in. I have not yet received this communication. I am now sending off the first series notwithstanding, and do not believe that confusions can arise, for I have indicated each mineral with  and if it crystallizes have expressly noted this with 'cryst.' I am sending on what follows and the translations without delay.

With exceedingly high esteem,

Rudolf Steiner

★

Brunn am Gebirge,
4th July 1885

Your High Wellbornship,
Most Honoured Herr Professor,

Enclosed the continuation of the articles. I hope the numerous changes I have made are advantageous to the matter. The remainder is following without delay.

Recommending myself to your distant gracious goodwill,

Rudolf Steiner

★

Stuttgart,
24th July 1885

Most Honourable Sir,

As by far the greatest part of the texts of the Fr. & Engl. edition of the lit. lexicon have now already been delivered, and work is progressing on the ordering of the entire alphabet, I see myself obliged to request you again to very much expedite the translation. Above all things I would be concerned to receive the Engl. translation, and am asking you to send me what is ready and have the continuation and conclusion forwarded as promptly as possible.

With exceedingly high esteem,

Your most devoted

Kürschner

★

Brunn am Gebirge,
4th August 1885

Your High Wellbornship,
Most Honourable Herr Professor,

I hereby beg pardon many times for sending these sheets only today. Your friendly card did not find me at home and so to my sincere regret the matter has again been delayed. For subsequent letters I just have to do the index and am forwarding it immediately. I give you an assurance that in a few days now everything will be in your hands and again beg pardon for my delay.

Best commending myself to Your High Wellbornship's distant goodwill,

Rudolf Steiner

★

Stuttgart,
6th August 1885

Honourable Sir,

I confirm receipt with most obliging thanks of the first part of the articles and translations and am very pleased to hear that I shall soon be receiving the conclusion. I am having manuscript paper forwarded to you (wrappers) and also point out that I am at first chiefly interested in the English.

In exceedingly high esteem,

Your most devoted

Kürschner

★

Stuttgart,
11th August 1885

Honourable Sir,

Might I not soon have again a batch of translations? The matter is highly urgent. Please always take first just the English, which is of foremost importance to me, and only then French.

In exceedingly high esteem,

Your most devoted

Kürschner

★

Vöslau
17th August 1885

Most Honourable Herr Professor,

Allow me herewith to report that what is desired for the lexicon I am having still forwarded today.

In exceedingly high esteem,

Rudolf Steiner

★

1885

Most Honourable Herr Professor,

Enclosed with best regards the continuation of the articles for the lexicon. The next ones and translations in the shortest time.

Commending myself to your distant goodwill,

In high and sincere estimation,

Rudolf Steiner

★

Exactly when this last letter was written is not clear, but probably in the autumn.

Apart from his tutoring work in the Specht family, a further reason for Steiner's delays in supplying these revised entries and translations must have been his involvement in other writing. Even apart from continued work on his book about Goethe's theory of knowledge, on 6 September he also published in the *Deutsche Wochenschrift* an extensive review of Richard Wahle's book *Gehirn und Bewustssein*.

He evidently had a guilty conscience about the delays, for in October he wrote again to Kürschner—trying to distract his attention to another subject!

Brunn am Gebirge,
13th October 1885

Your High Wellbornship,
Most Honourable Herr Professor,

Allow me to remit in the enclosure the latest numbers (16 & 17) of the *Österreichischen Literaturzeitung*. It contains an extensive review of the *Naturwissenschaftlichen Schriften Goethes* (p. 17). I shall emphasize the more important passages by a line in the margin. What the reviewer brings forward about the order and the 'formal principle in Goethe's scientific writings' will be set right by me in a rejoinder.

Begging pardon many times for many defaults of which I have recently been guilty towards you, most honourable Herr Professor, I am in exceedingly high esteem

Your most devoted

Rudolf Steiner

In a Consuming Battle

In the autumn of 1885 the Specht family moved from Vöslau into Vienna. So Rudolf Steiner, as tutor to the family's children, returned to Vienna as his place of work.

The 24-year-old had still not finished translating his lexicon articles, and in the bustling Austrian metropolis he soon found other matters to concern him. Some time in the last months of the year he was invited into the home of a friend named Walter Fehr. And here he met the latter's younger sister, the 18-year-old Radegunde—known as 'Gundi'.

In the seventh chapter of his autobiography Steiner described what began to happen:

> A beautiful friendship gradually developed between the younger daughter and myself. She really had about her something of the archetypal picture of a German girl. She brought no learned education in the mind, but presented an original, charming naturalness, with a noble reserve. And this reserve of hers called up a similar one in me. We loved one another and both of us knew this quite certainly and clearly; but neither of us could overcome our shyness and say to each other that we loved one another. And so love was living between the words we spoke with each other, but not *in* them. I felt the relationship of our souls to be most intimate; but it had no possibility of making even a single step beyond the soul-sphere.
>
> I was happy in this friendship; I felt the girlfriend to be like sunshine in my life . . .[14]

His account goes on to speak of 'happy hours spent together'. Maybe those hours in the company of Gundi Fehr took priority over the still unfinished translational work . . .

Anyway, in due course the young man was brought back to his task by receipt of another missive:

> Stuttgart,
> 11th December 1885
>
> Most Honourable Sir,
>
> Allow me herewith to inform you that I am now in most urgent need of the conclusion of the articles on mineralogy, especially for English, as progress on the work here will otherwise come to a standstill. So I beg you to put me in possession of the same as promptly as possible.
>
> With heartfelt gratitude in advance,
>
> Your fullest of high esteem and devoted
>
> Kürschner

Steiner must have hurriedly completed the last batch of his English translations, perhaps even at the same venue where he was now writing his also still unfinished book on Goethe's theory of knowledge: the noisy and smoke-ridden Café Griensteidl on the Michaelerplatz.

He replied to Kürschner a few days later:

> Brunn am Gebirge,
> 15th December 1885
>
> Your High Wellbornship,
> Most Honourable Herr Professor,
>
> Allow me herewith to report that in consequence of your friendly card I shall be straightaway sending off the desired conclusion of the articles, so that within 24 hours the same will be in your hands. Hoping not to hold you up in the proper course of the printing through my delay,
>
> With exceedingly high esteem,
>
> Rudolf Steiner

★

In the late spring of the next year, May 1886—the time when he became acquainted through Karl Julius Schröer with the circle around the poetess Marie Eugenie delle Grazie—Steiner forwarded to Kürschner the finished manuscript of his own book. It was finally published in October, under the title *Grundlinien einer Erkenntnistheorie der Goetheschen Weltanschauung.*

Thirty-seven years later, in November 1923—shortly before the Christmas Foundation Meeting of the General Anthroposophical Society, therefore at a time when the Schröerian mission was finally coming to completion—the author composed a foreword to a forthcoming new edition.

The foreword included this passage:

> In the eighties of the last century I was recommended through Karl Julius Schröer, my teacher and fatherly friend, to whom I am much indebted, to write introductions to Goethe's scientific writings for Kürschner's *National-Literatur* and take on the editing of these writings. During this work I followed Goethe's cognitional life in all domains in which he was active. The fact that my own perception placed me into an epistemology of Goethe's conception of the world became in detail ever clearer to me. And so I wrote this theory of knowledge during the course of the works referred to.
>
> By again placing it before me today, it also seems to me the epistemological foundation and justification for everything which I have later said and published. It speaks about an essential nature of cognition which uncovers the path from the sensory world into a spiritual one.

The initial sentence in this last paragraph is noteworthy. Merely by listing their titles a reader may bring to mind the number and variety of all Steiner's publications between 1886 and 1923: *Wahrheit und Wissenschaft* (1892), *Die Philosophie der Freiheit* (1894), *Friedrich Nietzsche* (1895), *Welt- und Lebensanschauungen im 19 Jahrhundert* (1900), *Die Mystik* (1901), *Das Christentum als Mystische Tatsache* (1902), *Theosophie* (1904), *Wie erlangt man Erkenntnisse der höheren Welten?* (1909), *Aus der Akasha-Chronik* (1909), *Die Stufen der höheren Erkenntnis* (1909), *Die Geheimwissenschaft* (1910), *Die Pforte der Einweihung* (1910), *Die Geistige Führung der Menschen und der Menschheit* (1911), *Die Prüfung der Seele* (1911), *Anthroposophischer Seelenkalender* (1912), *Ein Weg zur Selbsterkenntnis* (1912), *Der Hüter der Schwelle* (1912), *Die Schwelle der geistigen Welt* (1913), *Der Seelen Erwachen* (1913), *Die Rätsel der Philosophie* (1914), *Vom Menschenrätsel* (1916), *Von Seelenrätseln* (1917), *Goethes Geistesart* (1918), and *Die Kernpunkte der Sozialen Frage* (1919). Add to these not only numerous letters, forewords, articles and brochures but also all the transcribed lectures from those years which now fill many volumes of the *Gesamtausgabe*. Even disregarding the similar range of continued work both oral and literary which Steiner went on to produce for the remainder of his life after November 1923, his output up to that point was already enormous.

According to his own statement, the 'epistemological foundation and justification'—the latter term needs to be just as carefully considered as the former—for the entirety of this work was found in his very first book, the *Grundlinien einer Erkenntnistheorie.*

★

In 1889, three years after its publication, the author wrote inside one copy an inscription for the actress Ilma Wilborn-Seiler, beginning:

> What stands in this booklet I have not only written but have lived, when powers of my inner being joined each other in consuming battle; with words I then sought to draw pathways of the struggling spirit . . .

The words in question were of course all German. It is therefore of great interest that for over half a year of this consuming battle from 1884 to 1886, when Steiner was engaged in selecting and arranging suitable German words for a book which he later looked back on as 'the epistemological foundation and justification' for his total output both literary and oral over the next 37 years, his own struggling spirit was also attempting to find and order appropriate English words for the translation of his entries on mineralogy and mining in Kürschner's pocket lexicon.

Invented in England

The *Grundlinien einer Erkenntnistheorie* was divided into several parts, listed alphabetically: A, 'Preliminary Questions'; B, 'Experience'; C 'Thinking'; D 'Science'.

Then came the longest part of the book: E, 'Knowledge of Nature'. It had two chapters: 'Inorganic Nature', which developed the concept of the 'primal phenomenon', and 'Organic Nature', which developed the concept of the 'type'.

One passage in the latter chapter reads:

> The type, as we have seen, is a more complete scientific form than the primal phenomenon. It also presupposes a more intensive activity of our mind than the latter. In reflecting about the things of inorganic Nature sense-perception gives the content into our hand. Here it is our sensory organization which already provides for us what we receive in the organic only through the mind. In order to perceive sweetness, sourness, warmth, cold, light, colour, etc., one only needs healthy senses. There we have to

find *in thought* only the form for a substance. But in the type content and form are closely bound up with each other. Therefore the type does not determine the content purely formally like a law, but permeates it livingly, from within outward, as its own. Our mind is given the task of participating productively in creating the contentual element at the same time as the formal.

A mode of thinking in which the content appears in direct connection to the formal element has always been called *intuitive*.

Intuition repeatedly appears as a scientific principle. The English philosopher Reid calls an intuition our having drawn from perception of outer phenomena (sense-impressions) at the same time a conviction of their *being*. Jacobi held that in our feeling of God not only this itself is given, but at the same time the surety that God *is*. This judgement too is called intuitive. What is characteristic, as one sees, is always that in the contentual element more must always be given than this itself; that a thought-determination is known, *without proof*, just through direct conviction. It is not believed necessary to prove the thought-determinations of existence etc. from the substance of perception, but believed that they are possessed in inseparable unity with the content.

With the type, however, this is really the case...

The reference to the supposed 'English philosopher Reid' was of course to the well-known Scottish philosopher of that name, Thomas Reid.[15] The relevant thesis is found in his work *An Inquiry into the Human Mind*, published in 1764.

★

The final part of Steiner's book was F, 'The Spiritual Sciences'. It included a chapter on 'Psychological Cognition'. In course of the chapter came this passage:

...In all manifestations of the spirit—thinking, feeling, willing—it is a matter of recognizing them in their essence as expressions of the personality. On this psychology rests.

But a human being does not belong to himself alone, he belongs also to society. What is alive in him is not merely his individuality, but at the same time that of the folk-group to which he belongs. What he accomplishes proceeds equally from the full power of his people as from his own. With his mission he fulfils part of that of his folk-kindred. What matters is that his place within his people be such that he can bring the might of his individuality fully to effect. This is only possible if the folk organism is of a kind that the single person can find the place where he can set his lever. It must not be left to chance whether he finds this place.

In his biography of Steiner, Christoph Lindenberg comments:

> Besides the general demand for a form of society founded on reason and knowledge of man, one can also divine in these words an objectivized complaint on Steiner's part. He was probably of opinion that he had not yet first found the place where he could set his lever. It is the complaint of a man who knows himself to be subjected to chance, having to ascribe to the seemingly accidental fact that his father had sent him to the *Realschule* the situation that in Austria he cannot join a university, study philosophy and take up an academic career.

Steiner continued:

> The way to investigate how an individual lives within the community of his people is a matter for the study of peoples and for the science of the state. The folk-individuality is the subject of that science. This has to show what form the organism of the state must assume if the folk-individuality should come to expression within it. The constitution which a people gives to itself must be evolved out of its innermost being. Here too fallacies are current of no small import. The science of the state is held not to be an experiential science. It is believed that the constitution of every people can be set up according to a certain stereotype.

At this point a footnote added:

> This reproach is above all directed at those who believe that the liberal stereotype invented in England can be imposed onto all states.

Thirty-seven years later, for the second edition of 1924, Steiner had this footnote deleted.

The main text continued:

> But the constitution of a people is nothing else than its individual character brought into fixed and determined forms of law. Whoever would draw up beforehand the direction in which a particular activity of a people has to move may not impose upon this anything external: he must simply express what lies unconscious in the character of the people. 'It is not the understanding person who rules, but Understanding; not the rational person, but Reason,' says Goethe.

Both this and the next quotation are taken from Goethe's 'Prose Sayings'.

> To grasp the folk-individuality as rational is the method for the study of peoples. Man belongs to a whole whose nature is the organization of Reason. Here too we may quote again a significant statement by Goethe: 'The rational world is to be considered as a great Immortal Individuality, which cannot be stopped from causing the necessary and thereby makes itself lord even over the fortuitous.'—As psychology must investigate the

being of the single individual, so must study of peoples (psychology of peoples) investigate that 'Immortal Individuality'.

An Exemplary Historical Presentation

In October 1886—the same month when Rudolf Steiner's book *Grundlinien einer Erkenntnistheorie der Goetheschen Weltanschauung* came out—there also began to appear another Goethean publication, as recorded in Walter Beck's biography of Karl Julius Schröer:

> In the committee meeting of the Goethe Society on 12 April 1886, on motion of the newly elected Recorder, governmental adviser Egger von Möllwald—and certainly after previous agreement with Schröer—a resolution was taken to issue a *Chronik*, appearing monthly. The first number was to come out in October, and Schröer was named as publisher and responsible editor.
>
> A decision was thus made which required from Schröer a large output of work, and induced him to intensify his own Goethe research.
>
> Reports were given in this *Chronik* about events in the Viennese Goethe Society, the Goethe Memorial, and everything otherwise connected with Goethe and Goethean work both within Vienna and outside.
>
> The first number, on 17 October 1886, begins with an extensive article by Schröer about the Society's origin, recalling on the very first page the advice of Auersperg that (after the Schiller Memorial) the next one had to be a Goethe Memorial. In conclusion, Schröer presented over several pages the tasks of the Goethe Society . . . After Schröer, as generally second publicist in the *Chronik*, Rudolf Steiner produced a short article about a book which had just come out, *Errinerungen an Moritz Seebeck* . . .
>
> Steiner's article was followed by Goethean notices from Schröer and a brief exposition by Egger von Möllwald, 'Goethe Memorials' . . .

★

Over the winter of 1886/7 Steiner composed his introduction to the second volume of Goethe's scientific writings. This very extensive essay reads in effect like a second version, somewhat different in form, of his book on Goethe's theory of knowledge.

It was divided into several parts. The first three were 'On the Arrangement of the Scientific Writings', 'From Art to Science' and 'Goethe's Epistemology' (contrasted with that of others such as John Stuart Mill).

The fourth and longest part was entitled 'Knowledge and Action in the Light of a Goethean Way of Thinking'. It had several sections, one of which, on 'Ethical and Historical Sciences', included this passage:

> Anthropology and political science must investigate the manner in which the single personality can come within the state to a position corresponding to itself. The constitution must arise from the innermost being of a people. The folk-character expressed in single sentences is the best constitution. A statesman cannot force a constitution upon a people. It is sheer stupidity to believe that all states can be ruled according to the *liberal stereotype* customary in France and England...

When in 1926 Steiner's introductions were gathered together and published as a separate work, this last sentence was omitted, and has never since been restored.

The text goes on:

> ...The leader of a state has to investigate the deep characteristics of his people and through the constitution give the tendencies slumbering in it a direction corresponding to them. It can happen that the majority of a people wants to head into directions going against its own nature. A statesman then has to let himself be guided by the latter and not by chance demands of the majority. In this case he has to represent the *folkhood* as against the people. (*Sprüche in Prosa* 477).
>
> We should add here a word about the *method* of *history*. History must always bear in mind that causes of historical events are to be sought in the individual intentions, plans, etc. of human beings. All derivation of historical facts from plans underlying history is a mistake. It is always just a matter of what goals this or that personality set himself, which paths he entered into etc. History is to be based completely on human nature. *Human* will, human tendencies are to be established.

At this point came a footnote:

> An exemplary historical presentation in our sense may be seen in e.g. the book by Max Koch: *Shakespeare* (Stuttgart 1885) (v. especially its outstanding treatise: IV. The Renaissance).

Once again, Dornach policy has had this footnote omitted from the *Gesamtausgabe* edition.

★

This second volume of Goethe's scientific writings covered general science, mineralogy, geology and meteorology. The work came out in the early autumn of 1887.

A month or so later, in mid-October of that year, Joseph Kürschner wrote to Steiner again, inviting him to contribute articles on mineralogy and geology to another and much bigger encyclopaedic enterprise, a new edition of a work last published some eight years and more previously: the multi-volumed *Pierers Konversations-Lexikon*.

Steiner not only accepted the commission, but asked whether he could contribute articles on other scientific subjects as well. Kürschner therefore also assigned to him the subject of general science.

A Real Boon

By November 1887 Rudolf Steiner had become closely befriended with a writer whom he had met in the previous year, as recalled in his autobiography:

> ... Fritz Lemmermayer, who later became a close friend, I first met at the delle Grazie afternoons. A quite remarkable man, he would speak with inwardly measured dignity about everything which held his interest. In outer appearance he resembled both the musician Rubinstein and the actor Levinsky. He almost worshipped Hebbel. He had certain very firmly held views about art and life, born of a shrewd knowledge in his heart. He wrote the profound and interesting novel *Der Alchymist* and much else of beauty and depth of thought. He was able to endow the smallest things in life with importance. I am thinking of how I once visited him with other friends in his charming little room in a side street of Vienna. He had just prepared his meal himself: two soft-boiled eggs, with bread. While the seething water was boiling the eggs for us, he said with emphasis: 'This will be delicious!'...

Lemmermeyer for his part recalled Steiner in his *Erinnerungen* (1929):

> When in 1887 after a longish stay in Italy I was allowed to greet again my beloved home town of Vienna, the personal intercourse between Rudolf Steiner and myself was at once taken up and in a short time a strong bond of heartfelt friendship had entwined around us.
>
> At the time I was living in an old house in the first district, in the so-called 'inner town', at the corner of Rauhensteingasse and Himmelpfortgasse. My room, called by my friends 'alchemist's cell', was old-fashioned but very pleasant, filled with my own familiar utensils from my mother's house. In his autobiography *Mein Lebensgang* Rudolf Steiner speaks of this dwelling of mine as a 'charming little room in a side-street of Vienna'. And there in that 'charming little room' my medieval novel *Der Alchymist* was composed; and it was graced through Rudolf Steiner who liked to stay in it and drink tea ...
>
> In this little room we spent cheerful and sad times, but also festive times, in youthfully ideal enthusiasm, no domain of spiritual life excluded. There was no question of the day which was not vividly discussed between us, and none of the questions of eternity which did not strike on our souls as if with a silver stave. Rudolf Steiner, then 26, was a spirit-man, and already then

one of extensive knowledge; he was a thinker, a philosopher. With me, about four years older, the forces of feeling and fantasy seemed to be stronger developed or, to speak more modestly and probably more rightly, they emerged more clearly at the time. Literary works from each of us had already appeared.

And so we would sit countless times together in my quiet little room. Not seldom was I joined by other young companions, but was often alone with my friend, many hours long. And there we would debate through many long evenings, especially in winter with a crackling fire and water bubbling for tea. We would argue and battle over every conceivable problem, fervidly eager, in the storm and stress of thoughts and feelings. Rudolf Steiner was a calm, level-headed thinker, not carried away by passion and impulse like me. Our favourite subjects were literature, art and philosophy. And his solar constellation, standing exalted above all, was Goethe, to whom he looked up in never wearying admiration . . .

Though we also did not confront life and the world as strange, we were much more intensely concerned with the being of the spirit and soul and their relationship to the kingdom of God, and this tendency and yearning was a firm bond between us. How often did the Moon rise at midnight and still find us discussing, dreaming and enthusing. The latter was left to me, philosophical matters primarily to my friend. It was a glorious time, for me unforgettable, and also kept in memory by Rudolf Steiner, as is shown by his *Lebensgang* . . .

Many years have since passed by, and difficult years, not lacking in tragic disruptions. But in memory Rudolf Steiner stands before me tangibly near: a figure of medium height, slim, supple. Deep black shiny hair, combed smooth, surrounding his head, which was fine and small. His facial colour was not pink, but mostly of the paleness gained from studying in one's room. Dark and thick eyebrows rose above, falling strongly sideways to right and left. The eyes too were dark, but within them glowed a light which was for me unforgettable, as though coming from eternity. Those eyes could gaze deeply and sink enquiringly into a person's countenance, as if Rudolf Steiner wanted to read in the concealed ground of the soul. And he was able to, for he understood the hieroglyphs of the human psyche. He had a light and yet firm walk. His voice was sonorous, his way of speaking somewhat stately and elevated, as though permeated by the value of language, by the force and importance of speech, which is so much sinned against. And he liked talking. The seed already existed of the future speaker. Though his being was grounded in deep seriousness, as could be read from his thought-filled forehead, he nonetheless loved fun and jokes. At times we played tricks and laughed heartily—among my friends I was specially known for my love of laughter, despite or perhaps because of my tendency to melancholy.

Oh, if only I could hold them fast, the hours we spent together, which did such good to heart and mind!

★

During all this time there must have been further delays in producing the English version of the *Taschen-Konversations-Lexicon*, for after 1885 nothing further had been heard of it.

However, the work did eventually see the light of day, being published in 1888 under the joint imprint of Kürschner in Stuttgart and Sampson Low & Co. in London, as *The Pocket Encyclopaedia, A Compendium of General Knowledge for Ready Reference*. It came out both as an octavo volume—to which the term 'Pocket' was quite incongruous—and in more suitable duodecimo form. This latter numbered 1206 pages, and was priced at 3/6. Sales proved good enough to warrant Samson Low & Co. producing a second impression under their own sole name within the very same year.

The work was headed with a preface:

> Diminutive though this Dictionary is in form, it is the result of much time, labour and thought; and no effort has been spared to render the wide array of facts which it will be found to contain accurate, clear and up-to-date.
>
> The *Pocket Encyclopaedia* had its origin in the author's desire to provide himself with short answers to the thousand and one questions which are daily arising amid the affairs of ordinary life. Works of reference are usually both cumbrous and costly, and are seldom at hand when most required. Many people, moreover, have neither time nor money to spend over them. The author is free to admit that he prepared this book in the first instance for his own use, but was afterwards led to widen its scope, and to make it public under the conviction that his labours would prove welcome and useful to thousands who, for a variety of reasons, are shut off from the resources of a reference library.
>
> It would of course be absurd to expect that a volume of such Lilliputian dimensions can enumerate, even in outline, all the scientific discoveries of our age. But those who examine these pages with the greatest care will probably be the first to admit that enough has been done in this direction to satisfy all common wants and reasonable demands. Specialists in various departments of learning have assisted the author in his task, and though the book does not pretend to be perfect, it can honestly be said that it represents an amount of toil, thought and research which perhaps few at first sight would be inclined to credit.
>
> The author therefore believes that the handy size of the *Pocket Encyclopaedia*, the concise and accurate nature of its contents, and the low price at which it is published will make it a real boon to multitudes of busy people

343 Crusader—Cuckoos. 344

Crusader, person engaged in a crusade.

Crusca, *Academia della C.*, liter. society, Florence; founded 1584 t. purify Ital. langu.; now tog. with 2 oth. societies the "Royal Florentine Academy".

Crustacea, class of articulated animals w. crust-like shell wh. covers body a. legs; includes lobsters, shrimps, a. crabs.

Crypt, 1) subterranean cell or cave, esp. a vault under a church, used f. interment; tomb; 2) subterranean chapel or oratory, esp. under a church; hence, a hiding-place.

Cryptocalvinists, reformers wh. made th. least concessions to th. Reformation; esp. Melanchthon a. his adherents.

Cryptogamia, lowest organizat. o. plants, no flowers, no organs o. fructification; reproduction by spores.

Crystalline humor, s. crystalline lens.

Crystalline lens, white, transparent, firm subst., inclosed i. a membranous capsule, a. situated in a depression of th. vitreous humor o. th. eye; has th. form o. a lens, a. brings the light admitted to the eye in a focus on th. retina; crystalline humor.

Crystals, ⊛, occg in definite geometric forms; 6 systems o. forms based on th. number, situation a. relative lengths o. th. axes: 1) *Cubical*; 3 axes at right angles t. each other, equal in length; octahedron (table XIX, 1), bounded b. 8 equ. equilateral triangles; rhombic dodecahedron (fig. 3), b. b. 12 equ. rhombs; cube (2), b. b. 6 equ. squares; three-faced octahedron (5), b. b. 24 equ. isosceles triangles; is evidently like an octahedron, in wh. 3 planes have been built over each o. th. original; four-faced cube (4), b. b. 24 equ. isosceles triangles; deltahedron (6), b. b. 24 equ. deltoids; six-faced octahedron (7), b. b. 48 irreg. triangles; if cryst. are prod. b. applying planes only t. each alternate set of 3 points, omittg th. others, they are called hemihedral; tetrahedron is th. hemih. form o. th. octahedron (8 a. 9), b. b. 4 equ. equilat. triangles; its faces correspond w. 4 altern. faces o. th. octah.; trigonal dodecahedron (10), b. b. 12 equ. isosceles triangles; deltoiddodecahedron (11), b. b. 12 equ. deltoids; six-faced tetrahedron (12), b. b. 24 equ. scalene triangles; trapezohedron (14), b. b. 24 equ. trapeziums; pentagonal dodecahedron (13), b. b. 12 equ. pentagons. 2) *Th. pyramidal system*: 3 axes at right angles to each oth. but one being shorter or longer than th. other 2; tetragonal pyramid (19), b. b. 8 isosceles triangles; tetragonal prism (20), b. b. 2 equ. squares a. 4 equ. rectangles; there are 2 orders of prisms, differg only in th. positions of th. axes; i. th. pr. o. th. 1st order, th. lat. axes join th. centr. points o. th. vert. edges (20); i. those o. th. 2d order, th. centr. points o. th. lat. planes (24); tetragonal sphenoid, hemiedr. form o. th. tetr. syst. (25); ditetrag. pyr. (21), dit. prism (22). 3) *Rhombic*: 3 axes at right angles to each oth., but all unequ. i. length; either o. these taken f. th. princ. a. placed vert. t. th. longer o. th. oth. 2 is called macrodiagonal, the shorter brachydiagonal; right rhombic pyramid (28), b. b. 8 equ. scalene triangles; right rh. prism (29), b. b. 4 equ. rectangles a. 2 equ. rhombs. 4) *Oblique*; 3 axes, princ., orthodiagonal, a. clinodiagonal; princ. axis is placed vert., orthodiag. is at right angles t. it, clinodiag. at right angles t. th. orthodiag., but incl. t. th. princ.; oblique rhomb. pyramid (34), obl. rh. prism (35), obl. rect. pyr., a. obl. rect. prism, oblique sphenoid. 5) *Anorthic*: 3 axes all incl. a. o. unequ. length. 6) *Hexagonal*; 4 axes, 3 lateral of equ. length, lying i. one plane, inclined t. each other 60°, th. 4th (princ.) variable length placed at right angles to th. oth.; hexag. pyramid (41), b. b. 12 equ. isosc. triangles; hexagonal prism (42), b. b. 6 rect. a. 2 reg. hexagons; dihexag. pyr. (43), b. b. 24 equ. isosc. or scalene triangles; dihexag. prism (44); rhombohedron (45), b. b. 6 equ. rhombs; scalenohedron (46), b. b. 12 equ. scalene triangles.

Csaba, ⊙ o. Hung., *p.* 32616.

Csokanay, Vitez Mich. von, Hung. poet, *1773 Debreczin, †05 Presburg; *Hungarian Muse*, a. o. works, 46, II vol.

Ctesias, Grk [illegible], Persian [illegible] i. ordinary 416|399 b.C.; wrote about Persia.

Cuartilla, Span. meas. f. liqu., abt 1 gal.; for grain, abt 4 gal.

Cuba, largest o. th. Antilles, Span., 45000 s. m., *p.* 1521684; *Climate*: healthy; *Prod.*: sug., tob., coffee, cott., cocoa, indigo, maize, rice, wood; c⊙ Havana; ⊙: Santiago, Trinidad, Porto Principe; ▲: Tarquino Peak; seat o. th. Captain Gen. o Havana; divid. in 3 distr.; discov. [illegible] 1492 by Columbus, orig. named Juana, then Ferdinanda; 1511 settled by Span.; revolutions 51, 68, [illegible].

Cube, 1) (*Geom.*) a regular solid w. 6 equal square sides; hexahedron; 2) (*Arith.*) product o. a numb. multiplied twice into itself.

Cube root, th. numb. wh. produces a cube.

Cubic equation is the highest power of th. unknown quant. o. a cube.

Cubic foot, cubic solid, each side o. wh. is 1 square foot = 1728 cubic inches.

Cubic yard, cubic solid, each side o. wh. is 1 square yard = 27 c. feet = 46656 c. inch.

Cubit, lineal meas. differing i. diff. countries; Rom. 17.47"; Grk 18.20"; Hebrew 21" or 18"; Engl. 18".

Cubus (leather bag), Rom. liqu. measure, [abt 13 gal.

Cuckoos, *Cuculida*, fam. o. climbing birds; common c., *Cuculus canorus*, lays his eggs into the nests of singing birds.

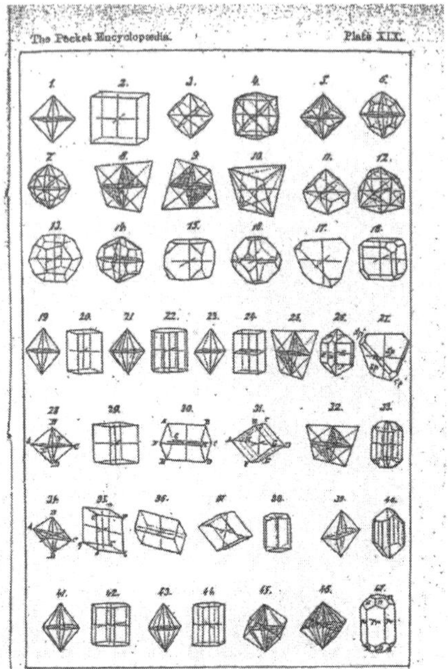

Crystals.
(See fol. 343.)

who hitherto have constantly found themselves at a loss for precisely the kind of information which this little book endeavours to present in an easy and accessible shape.

The entries on mineralogy and mining in this work comprised the earliest writings by Rudolf Steiner to appear in English translation, and the only such brought out in the nineteenth century. The translator was himself.

A Further Burden

By the time *The Pocket Encyclopaedia* was published in Britain, the author-translator of its articles on mineralogy and mining had become involved in his native Austria in another completely different literary enterprise.

In his biography, Christoph Lindenberg records:

> On 1 January 1888 Rudolf Steiner, quite unprepared and overwhelmed, unofficially took over as editor of the *Deutsche Wochenschrift*. We do not know how this came about, or what hopes Rudolf Steiner invested in the matter. He anyway added a further burden to his other duties, which just at that time included collaboration in a lexicon published by Joseph Kürschner.

Possibly Steiner came into contact with the *Deutsche Wochenschrift* through Fritz Lemmermayer, who worked as a literary journalist for both this and other papers and journals of the day.

Be that as it may, from January 1888 onwards for the next six months, Steiner as editor of this weekly composed for every single issue a summary of the current political news, presumably culled from the dailies. Most of his chosen news concerned continental affairs, but from time to time he also added snippets of British interest:

'The Week 30 December 1887–5 January 1888':

> ...We may also think of the jubilee celebrated at New Year by the *Times*. On the 1st of January a hundred years ago it first appeared under its present title. The city paper, the greatest and most influential paper in England and the whole world, could look back with no unjustified pride on the hundred years during which it has been serving public opinion.

'The Week 12–18 January 1888':

> ...Fairly hopeful like the Tsar, but no more definite or decisive, Salisbury also spoke at a Conservative banquet in Liverpool about the development of circumstances on the Continent. He thought the European situation had taken a turn for the better, and peace was anyway assured for the immediate future. Sovereigns and ministers were committing themselves with all their energy to the maintenance of peace. Such expressions have again become typical among statesmen and princes, and might after all be endowed with great trust were it not for the fact that everyone is arming on all sides...

'The Week 8–15 February 1888':

> ...The treaties are to be extended by agreements made between Italy, Austria and England to protect Austrian and Italian coasts against all cases of enemy landings. No official seal has yet been put on these announcements; however, their inner probability has been quite generally accepted. But as far as England is concerned, Under Secretary of State Fergusson explained beforehand in the Lower House that the government had not entered on any agreement unknown to the House which would oblige England to any material action...

'The Week 1–7 March 1888':

> Count Herbert Bismarck, who went off for a time to England, is according to remarks by some papers supposed to have had the secret task of bringing the cabinet of St. James to agree to Russian wishes in the Bulgarian question. But it is hardly vouched that the *Reichskanzler*, who at the Berlin Congress designated himself in grim self-mockery as the fourth Russian pleni-

potentiary, has now also entrusted his son, the German Secretary of State, with the business of a second Russian ambassador in London...

'The Week 18–25 April':

> On the 23rd took place the meeting between Kaiser Franz Joseph and Queen Victoria of England. Extremely sympathetic remarks are devoted to this not only by Austrian, but also by German and English papers. The same applies to the Queen's visit to Charlottenburg and Berlin...

'The Week 3–10 May':

> England is arming too. Minister of War Stanhope has introduced a measure to improve national defence, accepted by the Lower House at its first reading. Everywhere in Europe people are bowing to the iron commandment: *si vis pacem, para bellum*...

'The Week 11–16 May':

> England too has at last emerged from the reserve of a quiet onlooker. On the 14th inst. a deputation of members from among the most respected persons in the land met with Minister of War Stanhope asking him to take necessary precautionary measures for the country's defence. An appeal is currently circulating among merchants, bankers and other leading City circles asking them to take part in a large gathering for the purpose of investigating England's present state of defence on land and sea, since war with a foreign power is in the near future not impossible, and the previous policy on defensive measures cannot further continue.
>
> England however is preparing for the danger of war not so much with Russia as with France, which, if Boulanger once realizes his ambitious plans, would sooner attack the unprepared island realm than the well-armoured German kingdom...

'The Week 23–30 May':

> ...On the 24th there took place in Charlottenburg the marriage of Prince Heinrich with Princess Irene of Hessen, granddaughter of Queen Victoria of England...
>
> ...A British East-African Society, with the aim of further exploring and civilizing Africa, has been founded in England and provided by the government with the right of levying customs and taxes and organizing armed forces.

'The Week 6–13 June':

> An astonishing event is the fall of the Egyptian Prime Minister Nubar Pascha, which even for England, where he used to be seen as the promoter of English interests, appears to have come as a surprise. The immediate cause

> is said to be the reforms demanded by Nubar with respect to land taxes and agriculture, for which Nubar received no support from the English representative Baring, who has long been his opponent...

'The Week 21–27 June':

> On the 18th of June the English Upper House passed Salisbury's bill to reform the Upper House. The bill empowered the Queen to nominate yearly not more than five life peers, of whom three must have had a high state position, and the remaining two public importance. The total number of peers must never exceed fifty.

'The Week 28 June–4 July':

> On the 20th of June the ambassador in London, Count Karolyi, went into permanent retirement...
>
> Salisbury's ministry has happily withstood the storm of opposition. Morley's motion of censure was rejected in the House by 366 votes to 273...

'The Week 5–11 July':

> In the English Lower House Fenwick brought a motion, supported by Gladstone, to reintroduce diets for members. The motion was rejected by 192 votes to 35. Parnell has brought a motion regarding appointment of a committee with the task of investigating accusations brought against Irish leaders. A great number of motions still unresolved will necessitate a Parliamentary session in the autumn...

'The Week 11–18 July':

> The memorandum published on the 10th of July [*Die Krankheit Kaiser Friedrichs III*], composed from official sources by the German doctors Prof. Gerhardt, Shrotter, von Bergmann, Bardeleben is causing an enormous sensation. It forms a serious accusation against Mackenzie, who seems made out as frankly a quack. It is remarkable that this question, which should be examined simply from a medical standpoint, is turned into one of party politics. In their publicational organs liberals are standing up for Mackenzie against German doctors, while national and conservative newspapers find the English doctor's actions decidedly reprehensible. We publish above an extensive article, which deals with the question of how, according to what has now been presented, such actions can happen...
>
> In the English Upper House Argyll brought a motion of confidence in the government for the policy being followed with regard to Ireland. This was unanimously carried...

In his autobiography Steiner concluded the account of his editorship by stating:

> I felt relieved of a heavy burden when this activity came to an end through the fact that the weekly's then owner became involved with its founder in a controversy over the purchase price.

As a result, the *Deutsche Wochenschrift* was towards the end of July suddenly discontinued. So Steiner's budding career as a news editor—at which he seemed to be doing quite well—ended in brusque and no doubt fortunate collapse.

Man's Repeated Earthly Lives

In June 1888—still during his editorship of the *Deutsche Wochenschrift*—Rudolf Steiner, as described in his autobiography, met through mediation of Fritz Lemmermeyer the Carinthian poet Fercher von Steinwand.

> ... I regard the fact that I was privileged to become acquainted with Fercher von Steinwand as among the important events which came towards me in my youth. For the effect of his personality was like that of a sage, revealing his wisdom in genuine poetry.
>
> I had been wrestling with the riddle of man's repeated earthly lives. Many insights in this regard had occurred to me when meeting people who in their living habits and personal stamp manifest without difficulty traces of an essential content which is not to be sought in what they inherited through birth and have experienced since. But Fercher's play of expression and his every gesture revealed to me a soul-being which could only be formed at the time when Christianity was beginning to develop and Greek paganism still affecting this development. Such insight is not gained by considering a person's immediately apparent external traits; rather one feels it stimulated by individual features which seemingly accompany such outer traits, but in reality deepen them to a unlimited degree and turn into intuition. Nor is it gained by searching for it while in the person's company, but only when a strong impression reverberates until it becomes like a vivid memory. Then what is significant in outer life dissolves and the otherwise 'inessential' begins to speak a clear language. Whoever 'observes' people in order to puzzle out their previous earthly lives will quite certainly not reach his goal. One must feel this as an offence towards the person observed before one can hope that a human being's distant past will disclose itself in the present, like an act of Providence coming from the external spiritual world.
>
> During the very time presented here I acquired definite conceptions about man's repeated earthly lives. Previously these conceptions were indeed not far from me, but had not been rounded from indefinite features into sharp impressions. However, I did not form theories about such things as repeated earthly lives in my own thoughts; I accepted them into my mind

> from literature or other communications as something illuminating, but did not myself theorize about them. And only because I was conscious of real insight into this domain could I have the conversation mentioned before with Professor Neumann...

The previously mentioned conversation was about repeated earthly lives.

★

In describing his relationship with Neumann, Steiner had actually mentioned two separate conversations:

> ...I thus had many conversations with this 'ideal' of a scientific man, but at the same time 'true son of his Church'. Here I would only like to mention two. One was about the being of Christ. I expressed my view that Jesus of Nazareth had through extraterrestrial influence received into himself the Christ, and that since the Mystery of Golgotha Christ as a spiritual being is living along with human evolution. This conversation has remained deeply imprinted in my soul. I have often had occasion to recall it, for to me it was deeply significant...

It was recalled by Steiner in regard to philosophical concepts during a lecture given at Dornach on 8 October 1921:

> ...I must confess that a conversation I had with one of the most significant theologians of the Viennese theological faculty about the nature of Christ, which is indeed related to all this, will long remain significant to me. When I tried to develop for him my idea of Christ, the conversation ended by him simply saying: 'We are now coming to a point where I need concepts which I am forbidden to think.'

In somewhat different words, this conversation was recalled by Steiner again in a karma lecture given at Arnhem on 18 July 1924. Here he now revealed that the subject of the conversation had not been strictly confined to Christology, but had also gone on to include another aspect. For clearly if 'Christ as a spiritual being is living along with human evolution', then it becomes absolutely essential to investigate as fully as possible exactly what is signified by that concept of 'human evolution', a concept which may be opened out to include repeated earthly lives.

> I myself had a remarkable conversation, also related in *The Course of My Life*, with a member of the Cistercian Order who was an extremely learned man. We were coming away from a gathering, and speaking about the problem of Christ. I set out my ideas on it, essentially the same as those I am always bringing in my lectures. While I was explaining them, he became uneasy and said: 'We may perhaps hit upon something of the kind. We shall not allow ourselves to think such things.' He would express himself in a similar

> manner on other Christological problems. But we then stopped briefly—the moment stands with great vividness before me—at the point in Vienna where the Schottenring and the Burgring meet, on one side the Hofburg, on the other the Hôtel de France and the Votivkirche. The man said: 'I should like you to come with me. I will give you a book from my library. There is something remarkable in it which relates to what you were just saying.' I went along, and the man gave me a book about the Druses. From the whole link between our conversation and the perusal of this book I realized that when, starting from Christology, I came to speak about repeated earthly lives, this deeply learned man was as if abandoned by his spirit in a quite remarkable way, and when he came to himself, merely recalled that he had a book about the Druses containing something about reincarnation. He knew about it from that one single book. He was a *Hofrat* at the University of Vienna and so learned that he was said to know the whole world and three villages besides. He was so erudite, but knew in his bodily constitution no more than that in a work about the Druses stood something about repeated earthly lives...

While Steiner went away to peruse 'that one single book' from which Neumann knew something about reincarnation, Neumann for his part must have consulted some reference-work about the topic and discovered allusions to other literature. It was perhaps when Steiner returned the book to him that they had a further conversation, as described in the autobiography:

> On another occasion we spoke about repeated earthly lives. The professor then listened to me, and spoke about all kinds of literature in which something concerning this could be found. Often he slightly shook his head, but had certainly no intention at all of examining the content of what to him seemed a peculiar topic. And yet this conversation too became important for me. The discomfort Neumann *felt* about his unspoken opinions regarding my statements has remained deeply engraved in my memory.

★

Now in the Arnhem karma lecture Steiner continued:

> And then came something remarkable, when I was once holding a lecture in Vienna. The same person was there, and after the lecture made a remark which could only be taken to signify that at this moment he had complete understanding for a human being of the present and for the relationship of that human being to his former incarnation. What he said about the connection was right, not false. But he understood nothing at all. He just spoke it out.

After his last visit to England, Steiner expanded this reminiscence in a further karma lecture given at Dornach on 12 September 1924:

> Then I came to Vienna—I have described all this in *The Course of My Life*. After some time I came into the circle gathered around delle Grazie . . .
>
> In order to show you how karma works, I want to refer to one event. I gave a lecture, and had indeed through delle Grazie's *jour-Tage*—in England it's five o'clock teas, in Vienna *jour-Tage*—become very well acquainted with the professors of the theological faculty gathered there, the Cistercians. I was giving a lecture. A priest of the Cistercian Order was there, an especially remarkable man, and when I had ended my lecture he said something quite peculiar, something which I wish only to indicate by saying: he spoke words to me in which was contained his memory of having been together with me in a former earthly life.

The words in question had been related by Steiner in a previous lecture, held at Dornach on 24 May 1920:

> When towards the end of the eighties I was speaking in Vienna in the Viennese Goethe Society on the theme 'Goethe as Father of a New Aesthetics', there was among the listeners a very learned Cistercian. I was explaining how we should think about Goethe's conception of art, and then in those days Father Wilhelm Neumann, a Cistercian, who was at the same time a professor in the theological faculty at the University of Vienna, made the remarkable statement: 'The germs of this lecture which you have given us today are already to be found in Thomas Aquinas.'

The lecture on 'Goethe as Father of a New Aesthetics' was held in Vienna on 9 November 1888. The moment when Neumann made his statement was later described by Emil Bock as 'a moment of the first rank in the history of the world.'

Extremely Interested

In course of his autobiography, when relating events from this period, Rudolf Steiner went on to state:

> At the time when my concrete views about repeated Earth-lives were becoming ever more clearly defined, I came to know about the Theosophical Movement stemming from H.P. Blavatsky. A friend to whom I had spoken about these things put into my hands Sinnett's *Esoteric Buddhism*. This book, the first I came across from the Theosophical Movement, made no impression on me at all. And I was glad not to have read it before forming my own views out of my own life of soul. For to me its content was

> repellent; and my antipathy to this way of presenting the supersensible might well have prevented me in the first instance from making further progress along the path which had been outlined for me.

Steiner's antipathy did not however prevent him from going on to purchase another theosophical work. For in the autobiographical lecture he recorded:

> The person referred to may indicate that he was probably one of the first purchasers of A.P. Sinnett's *Esoteric Buddhism*, as also of the book by Mabel Collins *Light on the Path*. Straight after its publication he brought this book to the bedside of a well-known lady who was very badly ill, and gave her various instructions for understanding the book from her own standpoint. He also brought it to a man whom he was having to prepare for the Austrian officers' examination in integral calculus and mathematics. He lived in the family where the very badly ill lady was housed.

Light on the Path first appeared in German translation in 1888.

★

A decade later, on 29 October 1898, Steiner was to write an article in the *Magazin für Literatur* entitled 'A real "disciple" of Zarathustra'. It began:

> About nine years ago I made the acquaintance in Vienna of a man from whom I anticipated in the future much fine spiritual fruit. He was often named at the time in journals and newspapers. He had recently received a prize from the Berlin Philosophical Society for the best presentation of Hegel's view of the world. Wider circles became interested in him, including such as would have been quite indifferent to a book on Hegelian philosophy were it not turned into a sentimental event by the author's position. For this author composed his work far removed from culture, in the Hungarian hideout of Zombor, where he had been working as a legal clerk. That a man who from early morning to late evening expresses in a corner of the Magyar country what an eminent German scholarly society characterized as the deepest thoughts on the most effective philosophy of the century made him in many people's eyes into a piquant personality.
>
> I was delighted by the germs of the world-conception which this man carried in him and brought with rare eloquence before my eyes on his then visit to Vienna. He had a wealth of ideas with future promise, and set out his views in vigorous language borne up by philosophical enthusiasm. I can still see him before me, sitting with us—the great Austrian poetess Marie Eugenie delle Grazie, the Vienna University professor Laurenz Müllner and myself. An inner gladness flashed through me on feeling that we possess such human beings at the present day.
>
> I am speaking of Eugen Heinrich Schmitt . . .

Lord Byron in Albanian dress

Over two decades after that Steiner continued this reminiscence in the karma lecture given at Dornach on 22 March 1924:

> At a particular moment . . . I began to be extremely interested in the life of Lord Byron. And at that time I became acquainted with people who were extraordinary Byron enthusiasts. Among them was for instance the poetess about whom I shall have a lot to say in the description of my life, Marie Eugenie delle Grazie. During a certain period of her life she was a Byron enthusiast.
>
> Then there was a Byron enthusiast who was a remarkable personality, a strange mixture of all possible qualities, Eugen Heinrich Schmitt. Many of you who have concerned yourselves with the history of anthroposophy will probably have come across his name.
>
> Now Eugen Heinrich Schmitt first became known in Vienna during the eighties, and it was then that I made his acquaintance. He had written his prizewinning work about the dialectics of Hegel, which was published by the Berlin Hegel Society.

Schmitt's work *Das Geheimnis der Hegelschen Dialektik* came out in 1888.

> Eugen Heinrich Schmitt came to Vienna. He was a tall and slight man, and really motivated by forceful enthusiasm, if outwardly in a way tending very

strongly towards ostentation. At times this enthusiasm took on, as I said, very strong forms even outwardly. But he was after all an enthusiast! That perhaps just gave me as it were the required jerk. I thought I would like to do him a kindness, and as he had just then written his enthusiastic article on Lord Byron I introduced him to my other Byron enthusiast, Marie Eugenie delle Grazie. There then began a frightfully enthusiastic Byron discussion. They were actually in agreement, but excitedly discussing. All others sitting around were silent: a whole number of theologians from the Viennese Catholic faculty were gathered there, who came every week. One got to know them very well and I became very friendly with them. We others were all silent. But the two who were conversing about Byron were like this: here was the table, rather lengthy, delle Grazie was sitting here, and Eugen Heinrich Schmitt was sitting there, gesticulating with might and main. All of a sudden his chair slips away from under him, and he falls under the table, his feet stretching right out to delle Grazie. I can tell you, it was a shock for us!

This shock, however, resolved for me a quite particular matter, and I would like to narrate it in a really quite objective historical way. Everything which had been said there about Byron made me feel the keenest need to know what the karmic connections might be in Byron's case! That of course was not so easy. But it is really as if the picture of this conversation stood there with Eugen Heinrich Schmitt and his offensive foot, and this brought me to Byron's foot, which was a club foot, as you know. He dragged his foot, because it was shorter . . .[16]

Particular Care

On 19 February 1889 Rudolf Steiner sent a telegram from Vienna to Joseph Kürschner in Stuttgart:

Pierer articles due tomorrow dispatched definitely today. Steiner.

The articles themselves were accompanied by a letter:

19th February 1889

Most esteemed Herr Professor,

In respect to the enclosed articles 'Darwin' and 'Darwinism' I would very much like to ask you, if at all feasible, to have them printed unaltered. I have taken particular care in the composition.

The others will still follow today.

With specially high esteem,

Most devotedly,

Rudolf Steiner

★

The first of the named articles reads as follows:

> *Darwin, Charles Robert*, natural scientist, grandson o. Erasmus D., son o. the doctor Robert Waring D., b. 12.2.1809 Shrewsbury, d. 19.4.1882 on his Down estate near Beckenham in Kent. Already from early youth full o. interest for Nature a. an eager collector, D. on entering Edinburgh University in 1825 turned to the study of medicine. Since his aversion here to dissecting corpses became a hindrance, he decided to study theology a. in 1827 went to Cambridge, but here soon took up the study o. natural sciences, strengthened in his change of mind by the botanist Henslow. After gaining in 1831 the first academic degree o. bachelor, he joined in the same year the expedition o. Captain R. Fitzroy on H.M.S. *Beagle* as a natural scientist. On this journey around the world lasting five years, which allowed him to conduct scientific studies esp. in Tierra del Fuego, South America, Brazil a. on the islands o. the South Pacific a. collect together a wealth of material, he gathered the first observations a. thoughts for his teaching on the origin of species in the animal a. plant kingdom. Having returned to England in 1836, he gained in 1837 the higher academic degree o. Magister (M.A.) a. was f. then on exclusively concerned with scientific works, as his outer position allowed him complete independence. Since 1842 he lived secluded a. withdrawn on his Down estate, applying himself only to his studies, a. seeking relaxation in his own circle. He was married to his cousin Emma Wedgwood. The first years after his journey were devoted to working over the collected material a. to the composition o. a series o. treatises esp. of geological content, o. which esp. emphasis may be given to the study on the origin o. coral reefs. In 1859 appeared as the product o. years o. work the book: *On the Origin of Species by Natural Selection*, in which D. helped to bring to victory the *theory o. evolution* (q.v.) a. put forward the philosophic nature-system named after him *Darwinism* (q.v.). All his further writings in the zoological a. botanical realm contain only further expositions a. new evidence for the correctness o. his teaching, which called forth a positive revolution in the realm o. natural research a. unleashed a storm going far beyond scholarly circles, esp. as D. in his second main work *On the Descent of Man a. Sexual Selection* also treated the human being a. his family relations to the animal kingdom in the sense of his theory. D. gained the wonderful satisfaction of experiencing the complete triumph o. his teaching. The initially embittered struggle, where the passion o. D's opponents not seldom led them to personal attacks, soon had its sharpness removed, esp. through D's mildness, by which he defended his theory, a. his great a. exemplary objectivity a. merciless strictness towards himself in testing scientific questions a. assessing experiments. In the course o. years opponents became ever fewer and by D's death the basic idea o. his teaching, the 'struggle for existence' and its consequences, had already become everyone's common property. D. was buried in Westminster Abbey. Apart from the above-named works he also

wrote: *Voyage of a naturalist round the world* (Lond. 1844, translated by Carus, Stuttg. 1875); *Zoology of the voyage of H.M.S. Beagle* (Lond. 1840–48, 5 vols; n. ed. as *Natural history and geology. Voyage of H.M.S. Beagle*, ebd. 1884); *Geological observations on volcanic islands* (ebd. 1842); *Geological observations on South America* (ebd. 1846); *Monograph of pedunculated and sessile Cirripedia* (ebd. 1851–53, 2 vols.); *Variation of animals and plants under domestication* (ebd. 1868); *Insectivorous plants* (ebd. 1875), *Cross- and self-fertilization of plants* (ebd. 1876), *The power of movement in plants* (ebd. 1880); *The formation of vegetable mould through the action of worms* (ebd. 1881). His collected works appeared in German translation by Carus (Stuttg. 1875–82, 12 vols.); single ones are also translated by Krause (Lpz. 1886).

Literature: Francis D. (D's son), *Ch. D.* (Lond. 1888, German Stuttg. 1889).

The accompanying article on 'Darwinism' was more than five times as long. Both were published later that year in Volume IV of the new edition of *Pierers Konversations-Lexikon.*

At about the time when that volume was published, Steiner had made his first visit to Weimar and on returning to Vienna gave on 20 November another lecture in the Viennese Goethe Union, entitled 'On the Gain to Goethe Studies from the Weimar Edition in a Scientific Connection'. The text, duly published in the *Chronik des Wiener Goethe-Vereins*, included this paragraph:

> The attempt has been made to present Goethe as a precursor of Darwin. That was the well-meaning conviction of those who see in Darwinism the 'be-all and end-all' of the science of living beings and thus wanted to 'rescue' Goethe's scientific expositions. This view has roused contradiction from natural scientists tending more towards the school of DuBois-Reymond, because countless places in Goethe's writings absolutely cannot be harmonized with the notion of Darwin's teaching that is usual today. Now there is no denying that both of these two parties are able to adduce seemingly important reasons for their assertions. Anyone looking more deeply was of course clear that Goethe could never have been a Darwinist in the customary sense. He did not indeed fail to perceive that all natural beings stand in close connection to each other, that there is nothing unmediated in Nature, but that transitions between living beings of different form must make the whole of Nature appear as a continual sequence of steps. But he looked more deeply than the Darwinism of today. While the latter only researches kindred relationships of organic beings and their connections to their environment, in order thus to gain as complete as possible a family tree of all life on Earth, Goethe insisted on the *idea of the organic*, on its inner nature. He wanted to investigate what an organic being is, in order therefrom to ascertain the possibility of how it can appear in so and so many

manifold forms. Present-day Darwinism seeks the different forms of eternal change. Goethe sought what was lasting in this change. A natural scientist of the present asks: 'What influence of climate or way of life has taken place for this living being to have developed from that one?' Goethe asked: 'What inner laws of organic formation are working in that development?' Goethe stands to a modern natural scientist as an astronomer explaining phenomena in the sky through summarizing cosmic laws stands to an observer fixing by experience the different positions of the stars through a telescope. Goethe's scientific expositions are not just a prophetic anticipation of Darwinism, but rather its ideal preconditions . . .

The English Diploma

In 1890 there followed a further volume of the new edition of *Pierers Konversations-Lexikon*, which contained *inter alia* an article by Rudolf Steiner on 'Geology'. It discussed the work of many pioneers in this field, including several British ones: Martin Lister, Robert Hooke, Edward Elwyd, John Woodward, James Hutton, William Smith, and especially Charles Lyell. A list of textbooks at the end gave first place to Lyell's *Principles of Geology*.

★

During the same year, Steiner drafted a letter to an unnamed person:

Very honoured Herr Director,

With reference to yours of 12th May allow me to forward enclosed a sketch of my life and to transmit the consultation fee by postal order. I am now requesting you to pursue my business further. But I wish again to stress that it is only a matter of the right to be allowed to have a doctor's title socially. If therefore you could in the sense of your letter obtain it for me without examination, that would be valuable to me above everything. I would then somewhat later again request your mediation in order to gain a title based on an exam. Provisionally, as I said, what is important to me is the title. So if you would have the friendliness to let me know about the reservation you mentioned, I would be very bound to you.

Looking forward most soon
to your friendly reply

Rudolf Steiner
Vienna IX Kolingasse 19
Mezzanine

Enclosed the forwarded documents: letter, prospectus, advertisement,
8 fl. by postal order will go at the same time as the letter.
All documents are available <u>at once</u> on request.

On the back of this draft Steiner copied out formulae from an English doctoral diploma:

Kingdom of England.
Royal University
Doctor's Diploma.

The high council of the Royal University of England, on proposal of the president, director of the London faculty of classics, and after being made acquainted with documents identifying and showing the competent person Mr.—

Diploma granted to the above person, by right of laws and state regulations, the title of Doctor of—

In witness hereof the above title has been given to him.

In London on the—188.

Director of the Royal University Chief Secretary

The draft has also survived of a further letter to an unnamed person, perhaps indeed the same one:

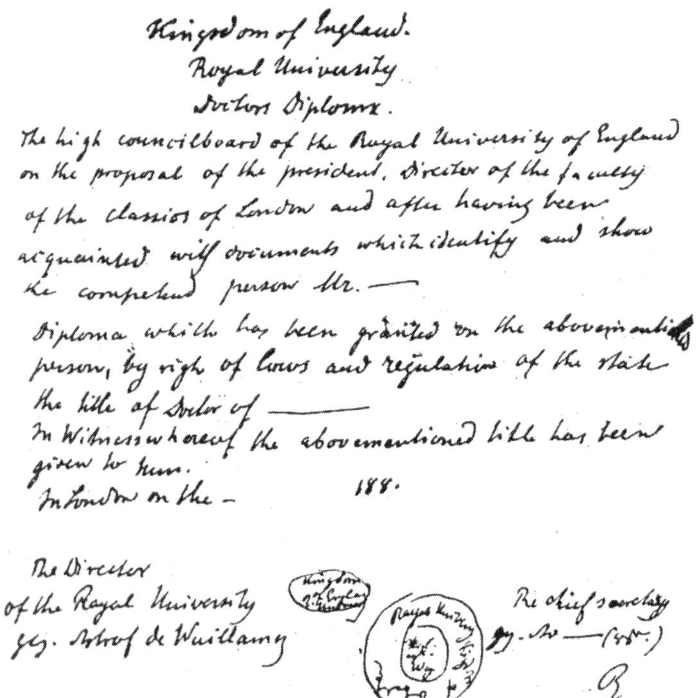
Kingdom of England.
Royal University
Doctors Diploma.
The high councilboard of the Royal University of England
on the proposal of the president, directer of the faculty
of the classics of London and after having been
acquainted with documents which identify and show
the competend person Mr. —
Diploma which has been granted on the abovementioned
person, by righ of laws and regulation of the state
the title of Doctor of ——
In Witness whereof the abovementioned title has been
given to him.
In London on the — 188.

The Directer
of the Royal University

The chief secretary

Express letter

Vienna, 24th June 90

Most esteemed sir,

I was on the very point of writing to you about the English diploma, when there occurred the case of Peratoner, perhaps already known to you from the newspapers, which made me wonder. For this case will have no other result for us than filling officials with heightened mistrust about that doctoral diploma. With an English diploma there are so many more grounds for supposing it to be examined. Now if the diploma had a snag, which indeed you do not exclude, I might come into the most awkward position. I would anyway be exposed to the possibility of having the respected name acquired from my works put at risk. You will understand that this fills me with earnestness. I would therefore ask again urgently for your advice. What shall I do? Meanwhile I am in any case working on an essay about 'Fichte's Doctrine of Science and the *punctum saliens* of all Epistemology. Prologomena to any Future Theory of Science'. It can in any case do no harm for me to have the essay, which—if necessary—can be ready on 5–10 July.

I can only once again repeat that it will be hard for me to sacrifice 600 M. for a diploma of whose genuineness you cannot regard me as convinced. I very much wanted to go along with your suggestion and take the eng. diploma, in order to add the German examinations in the autumn. But I do not know whether after the case of 'Dr.' Peratoner, you yourself would not advise me something different.

Forgive me for plaguing you with these continual reflections and with my hesitancy, but the matter is serious.

Awaiting your decision,

Yours with especially high esteem,

Rudolf Steiner

Whatever advice Steiner may have received, in the course of the following months he abandoned completely the idea of obtaining a doctorate from the University of London, and decided instead to apply to the University of Rostock.

7
THE WEIMAR PROGRESSION

The Breath of Goethe's Spirit

In his biography *Karl Julius Schröer*, Walter Beck recounts that by this time Schröer had made the acquaintance of the Viennese sculptor Victor Tilgner, who like himself was born in Pressburg. A friendship developed between them, and Schröer came to look on Tilgner as being the ideal sculptor to undertake the proposed Goethe Memorial.

In 1890 discussions on this matter took place between the Viennese Goethe Society and the Academy of Plastic Arts. Tilgner's name was put forward as a possible sculptor of the proposed statue. But the name was also put forward of another possible sculptor, Edmund Hellmer.

Beck continues:

> ... The September issue of the *Chronik* announced that Tilgner had made a new design for the Memorial with a *standing* Goethe. At the same time appeared Schröer's article 'Good Wishes for a Goethe Memorial in Vienna', setting out his long-pursued theme: the story of Goethe pictures and Goethe Memorials. With regard to the present he wrote:
>
> 'As far as I can perceive, there are especially two wishes being publicly expressed: that Goethe be presented *standing*, not sitting, and that the *young* Goethe be presented, not always the old one... What we do not want to miss is the breath of Goethe's spirit, which should move, uplift and gladden us. Nowhere is this done in such a manner as in the picture by Tischbein, still ensouled by a youthful spirit. It is expressed in his lofty stance, his fiery royal eye, which *seeks and finds* the ideal in *reality*.—He loves reality, because he knows that within it is hidden the eternal, the ideal.'

Readers may recall here the observations made by Schröer's now long-deceased colleague Edmund Reitlinger in the foreword to *Freie Blicke* about 'the poetry of reality'.

Beck goes on:

> In autumn 1890, on 29 September, Rudolf Steiner left Vienna and on the 30th began his work at the Goethe and Schiller Archive in Weimar.
>
> Steiner's connection to Vienna and Schröer did not however break off. He remained in the Viennese Goethe Society and wrote Schröer informative letters. During Steiner's time in Vienna—by reason of close personal

contact—only few letters were exchanged with Schröer, while of the letters after Steiner's departure from Vienna only few have survived.

A letter of Schröer's to Biedermann from the end of this highly eventful year 1890 gives information about Schröer's further intentions and provides insight into his private life. On 7 November 1890 he wrote:

'In Muse-hours I'm now occupied with the thought of writing a life of Goethe as a commentary to his works, though I don't have courage to hope it will be finished.—I feel myself becoming old and weary, and have also many cares . . .'

Schröer's statement in this letter that he wanted to write a Goethe biography as a commentary to Goethe's works is of interest.

In his lecture on 23 September 1924 Rudolf Steiner reported that towards the end of the eighties Schröer had told him about this intention:

'. . . but never otherwise . . . than that he would say "Goethe is always visiting me in my study" . . .'

This fundamental experience of Schröer's thus continued into later years of his life, acting furthermore as a premise for his Goethe research. It may also be clearly sensed behind his later lectures, reports and articles, as behind his endeavours for the Goethe Memorial.

The Goethe biography did not come about, nor could even fragments be found . . .

The Conflict of These Two Egos

Soon after his arrival in Weimar, Rudolf Steiner wrote to a newly made friend, Rosa Mayreder:

Weimar,
30th November 1890

Highly esteemed and gracious lady,

I would most like to be already writing today with brief news about the fate of your writings. But this I have not yet received. I have provided the things with the stipulated short summaries and sent them to Professor Kürschner, who with his wealth of connections and the big publishing firm of which he is literary director will, I am firmly convinced, do all he can for the matter. I have gained the above conviction from being associated with this man for six years. You will certainly soon come to the view that patience is hardly anywhere more needed than in the literary world.

And now to answer your kind letter, which unfortunately has already remained only too long unanswered. Forgive me for this delay, never again shall I let a reply wait so long. And now straight in mediam rem.

In our case, however, this is your view about materialism. When stating that we may assume two fundamentally different organizations of the human spirit, 'whose cognitional realms are strictly separated', you will certainly always find me on your side. I only demand that one keep this separation always in mind and not put oneself with the organization for the materialistic view into a realm which is only accessible to the opposite organization. Materialism certainly has a limited justification. It is equally true that there must be materialism as it is that matter exists. But it is incorrect and contradictory to carry the materialistic way of thinking into where—I would like to say—the spirit may be grasped. The most bigotted of present-day physiologists, Emil Du Bois-Reymond, once said that if we only knew how matter thinks, we would then be able to solve all the riddles of the world. Although this assertion slaps all healthy thinking in the face, I still want for once to postulate it hypothetically and show how even if we knew that, we would really gain nothing from it. Let us assume: matter thinks, i.e. in other words, matter divides itself, is separated into itself and its product, thought. So we have matter as subject, and thought as object. Now comes the further question: what is the content of thought? Since under this precondition nothing real outside matter has any existence, the content of thought can again only be matter. So we would have arrived at thinking matter again producing matter. Now I ask anybody how to come by this path to any view at all. I have assumed above the division into subject and object. The subject is matter; the object thought, which however only turns out to be again matter. So we have matter as at once subject and object, i.e. we remain sitting inside it. Materialism is just a quite sterile view of the world, and if it still gains a content, the reason is that it borrows this from other ways of conception and interprets it in its own sense.

Now if you say that you are 'entangled in that objective way of observing which Nietzsche derives from erroneous application of historical studies', I would find it unjustified, from precisely the standpoint of this objective way of observing, to agree with such an exclusive view as materialism is. For materialism is at any rate exclusive by simply denying the world of spirit. To idealism such one-sidedness would absolutely not occur. The latter recognizes materiality, since it perceives very well that there is a form of existence reflecting the spirit spatio-temporally by negating the ideational form. Idealism sees in materiality the spirit's necessary correlative, which must accompany it as a shadow does a wanderer. And since it is impossible to retroconstruct from the shadow the object throwing the shadow—namely according to the content not the form (without this insertion Lino would have to accuse me of lamentable ignorance in describing)—just so is it impossible to erect spirit out of matter...

'Lino' was a shortened form of 'Carolino', the Italian version of the forename of Rosa's husband, the architect Karl Meyreder.

...And now I come to the actual Langean theory. According to this our spirit is so organized that it must necessarily explain the world of reality materialistically, i.e. in Lange's case atomistically. I beg you to follow the train of thought with me step by step. Lange says: we can only perceive the world according to the organization of our spirit. Our spirit is so organized that it finally dissolves into the realm of atoms. In consequence it constructs the order of the world atomistically. It explains atomistically all phenomena and finally itself. If anyone were to offer a prize for towering up the most blatant contradictions, Lange's followers would definitely win this prize. The spirit is so organized that it can only be explained materialistically. Well, from wherever then does consciousness of spirit derive? The spirit must see unspiritual things. Where then should it in this world, to which its organization once condemns it, find itself, thus also its own organization? How should a spirit know that it can only explain itself in this way, when it is not organized to perceive the organization of spirit at all but only the constitution of matter? Whoever in the whole world can grasp a spirit which itself perceives that by virtue of its organization it is its own opposite must certainly have a peculiar brain.

I am a man who can only agree to a conception when it can be legitimized at the forum of strict thought. Materialism cannot be, because it can never understand itself.

Most honoured and gracious lady, if you say that materialism has gone on for a long time quietly working and even borne fruits, then I ask you: where are these fruits? Has materialism, propped up by itself, brought forward mankind's scientific or artistic epochs? Have not materialistic epochs in history always been the most unproductive ones? Is the blossom of Greek wisdom epitomized by Plato and Aristotle or epitomized by Democritus? Was it Goethe—who hated materialism to excess—or was it Holbach who rejuvenated the aged humanity of the eighteenth century? You say: 'Does not the certainty that day will again arrive make the night our friend?' I contest the rightness of this comparison. Materialism does not stand to idealism as night to day. I would put the metaphorical question differently. To perceive that a winter coat is advantageous, must I face an hour of icy cold? In further course of your letter you say: 'So I myself confirm what I would nonetheless like to deny: where one wants to be active, working and strong, one may not be objective. I am coming more and more to the insight that striving towards objectivity ends in indifferentism, and reflection finally makes action impossible.' This I cannot admit, for objectivity belongs to observation, action to the will. If I in any way intervene in the order of the world, my action is something quite particular, individualized, dependent on partial regulations of the world-process and not on general unconditioned ones serving as a basis for observation. I can very well perceive that some action—and this applies to any action—is imperfect if considered in relation to the highest principles of existence, and yet be clear that according to individualized preconditions I can only fulfil this action and the latter only thus. This does not detract at all from my freedom. When acting, I am not concerned with general principles of knowledge, but only with my action's antecedences. These principles relate to my action just as laws of the digestive process do to the latter itself. No one can digest according to physiological laws, even if he knew them down to the last detail. We must strictly separate the regulatory bases of our will from principles of ethics. I admit that it is very hard to keep these two things apart.

But yet it must happen, if clarity is to enter the subject. In any other domain this separation is easier, because the scene where laws hold sway is different from that where they appear. When observing the laws of planetary motion, I know exactly that the thing which these laws underlie is outside me in space, but the laws come to appearance in my mind. Here no one confuses thing and concept. With my action it is different. Here thing and cognitional process take place on the same scene inside my consciousness. A human individual who acts is simultaneously the observer of these his actions. But thing and concept must therefore be held apart. For I am not an abstract unity into which everything merges, but the living union of an individual particular ego, alive in a sphere of time and space, and a general reflecting ego which is unbounded, spaceless and timeless. Whoever like Hamlet confuses the two egos does not come firstly to action nor secondly to understanding of himself. The deep tragedy in Hamlet's character lies in the conflict of these two egos. But freedom nonetheless remains entirely present. For I would only be unfree if I came to act in a particular case according to general ethical principles and were unable to do so. But I am never in this position, for my tasks are set me by the time and place I live in, not by ethics. That I am now writing this letter is a result of our having come to know each other, of being friendly towards one another, of your wishing for an exchange of thoughts in this direction, of your having written to me etc. And *because* of all that has preceded, I decide out of free will to write you this letter. Now this way of observing can be applied to *any* human action. But the contradiction which torments you is then completely resolved. For me it is quite impossible to see the matter differently. I ask you *urgently* to write and tell me what doubts you may still have after these rather broadly layered expositions of mine. I shall reply *at once*, for in the circumstance of my knowing exactly that your spiritual direction accords wholly with my own, every difference of opinion worries me. If in any question you have a different view from me, it is not caused by a different spiritual organization, but only by the circumstance that on the relevant point we have not expressed ourselves clearly enough for complete understanding.

You were very wrong to add to your letter the sentence 'and I only refrained from it through not wishing to saddle myself with an appearance of obtrusiveness'. For a moment I did not there understand you. To anyone who knows me such a wish should not occur at all. There are relations between people which no longer have such words as obtrusiveness in their lexicon. For I am so inwardly pleased by any new sign of life. Only do not repay me like for like by making me wait weeks on end for a reply.

It is truly regrettable that your husband has such disagreements with projective geometry. I simply believe he goes too far in conscientiousness. In such a case one must always bear in mind that the greater or lesser perfection of a continuous lecture actually has little consequence to the audience. When you write to me of Lino's misgivings that 'he had not worked out the lectures well, not independently enough', I find these misgivings hypercasuistical. For this is a demand which no one may raise. Do not omit also to write and tell me whether the painful hours this new task has brought him have now already disappeared. Greet him from me most cordially, and greetings to yourself from

Yours,

Rudolf Steiner

You will soon receive my photograph—admittedly a Weimar one.

Great Significance

On the very same day as he composed the above letter to Rosa Mayreder, 30 November 1890, Rudolf Steiner also wrote to Karl Julius Schröer telling him *inter alia* that he had an article ready for the *Chronik des Wiener Goethe-Vereins* and would be sending it off in perhaps three to four days' time.

The article, 'Thoughts on the Handwritten Papers of Goethe's Estate', was several pages long. It ended with this incisive paragraph:

> Anyone following thus on paper the signs which express clearly enough how ideas arise in Goethe by continual intercourse with the world will also be able to understand what is meant by idealism being wholly compatible with experiential knowledge. Idealism is simply nothing else than *complete* experience, the sum of everything it is possible for us to become acquainted with from things, while what empiricists normally make into the object of their science is only *half* the experience, the summand without the total sum. Francis Bacon, the well-known English philosopher, once said that scientific research is a task of addition. But he took it no further than instructions on how to set up individual entries. How to find the sum total remained hidden from him, because he held the senses for the only transmitters of experience, and did not know that reason has the same claim to

this title. Goethe established the latter's rights as well, thereby fulfilling a high mission. The senses are wonderful messengers of the outer world, if the mind understands the declarations they bring towards it according to their ideal meaning. But the strokes of their pen are worthless, if we just stare at what we should be reading. To anyone who claims there be nothing to read, those who have gone to school with Goethe will all reply: 'Do not seek the cause in the things of this world, but rather in yourself.'

★

Early the next year, on 24 January 1891, Steiner published in the *Weimarische Zeitung* a substantial review-article of the book *Zur Geschichte des Erkenntnisproblems* by Eduard Grimm, published in Leipzig during the previous year. This too included an examination of Bacon, but now within the whole context of the English philosophical tradition.

Here is the complete article:

A few weeks ago German philosophy was enriched by a valuable book written in Weimar. The circumstance of its author being Archdeacon Eduard Grimm and the scientific importance attaching to the work is quite enough to justify us in expressing here the inner gratification we derived from reading it. We found one of the most interesting epochs in the development of science discussed in a truly exemplary way. The book sets itself the task of presenting the epistemological teachings of five English philosophers: Francis Bacon (1561–1626), Thomas Hobbes (1588–1679), John Locke (1632–1709), George Berkeley (1685–1753), David Hume (1711–1776). Epistemology is that science concerned with answering the question: how far can man by thinking solve the riddle of the world, and investigate the laws of nature and of life?

The scientific period to which these five thinkers belong is of exceptional significance because it marks one of the most important turning points in scientific life. Medieval wisdom had been content to walk further along paths trodden by the tremendous teacher of Alexander the Great, Aristotle. Both the way he conceived the tasks of the sciences and the aims he set out were still taken as incontestable, even when new observations and experiences could no longer be brought into proper accord with them. But this was a hindrance to all progress, and made impossible the unfettered development of free and independent thought as required by discoveries in the scientific field. Francis Bacon then arrived on the scene. He had the aim of cleansing science from all transmitted prejudices and building it up completely afresh on the basis of the then new achievements. Grimm has a masterly understanding of how to grasp Bacon just where the latter's great significance for the development of European thought most clearly emerges. By keeping to principles belonging to a long past period and which could only have validity and value for life at that time, science had become estranged from life of the immediate present—indeed was totally unusable. But 'all knowledge has arisen from life, and derives therefrom the right and basis of its existence. If knowledge departs too far from its source, life itself with its own direct power inevitably comes into opposition with it and presses towards a reformation of science. In such fashion did Francis Bacon of Verulam confront the science of his day. He accuses it of being like a plant which, cut off from its roots, has no further connection with the body of Nature and thus receives from it no further nourishment.' (Cf. Grimm, *Zur Geschichte des Erkenntnisproblems*, pp. 5–6.) Grimm explains with both thoroughness and real philosophical consideration how by presenting a method of observation and experiment not susceptible to error Bacon wants to bring science onto the right tracks. By going ruthlessly to the core of all prejudices and mistakes, whether by scholars or by all other educated people, he wants to allow entry only to absolutely certain knowledge. Here—as everywhere in the book—we must praise the only historically correct method, which does fullest justice to the thinkers concerned by letting them speak for themselves wherever this seems necessary. The beneficial effect emanating from the book is in no small part to be sought in the circumstance that its author does not, like so many new historians of science, emphasize his own scientific views in judging foreign thoughts. Rather he places personal skill—which to the perceptive is nonetheless everywhere visible—at the service of developing in an all-round objective way the relevant thought-systems.

For all its high significance, the Baconian trend of thought had become guilty of one-sidedly overestimating mere observation of things, at the cost of independent creative thinking within man's own breast. This defect became still greater with Thomas Hobbes, who in thought saw nothing but a capacity transmitted by language. 'Understanding is understanding of words.' (Grimm, p. 87.) Hobbes denies that thinking can of and through itself come to knowledge. 'Sensory perception, imagination and the sequence of our mental pictures, which we call experience, is what Nature has given us.' (Grimm, pp. 85–86.) 'Hobbes denotes as reason that activity by which we associate mental pictures and words.' (Grimm, p. 87.) So according to Hobbes science does not depend on grasping the world in thought, but simply on reasonable use and correct understanding of words. That words transmit ideas and only on these does our knowledge depend is a proposition which for Hobbes does not exist. It is quite understandable that in such circumstances knowledge can have no further independent purpose. Hobbes therefore finds that 'knowledge is there for the sake of doing, mathematics for the sake of mechanics, all speculation for the sake of some work, some action.' (Grimm, p. 99.) Admittedly, knowledge consisting merely of words cannot have an independent value. Hobbes however believed that only by turning science into this direction could what he wanted be attained. What we observe or experience in individual cases has indeed only limited truth. We can never know if it also comes true in all the cases we have not observed. But words we determine arbitrarily; so with them we know exactly how far what they claim has validity. When he established a doctrine for morals and the state, this view of Hobbes became disastrous. For if everything having objective validity rests merely on the caprice of words, there ceases to be any real difference between 'good' and 'bad'. These concepts also become arbitrary creations by human beings. 'There is no general rule about good and bad deriving from the essence of things themselves.' (Grimm, pp. 135–136.) Order in the state cannot be maintained by human beings mastering their urges through reason or free insight, but only by a despotic ruler forcing the observance of arbitrarily established moral laws.

At the centre of Grimm's work stands John Locke. He is indeed 'the first philosopher to place the question of knowledge at the centre of investigation, as a completely independent task existing in itself.' (Grimm, p. 173.) On the Continent René Descartes (Cartesius 1596–1650) is the founder of a new philosophy freeing itself from the bonds of Aristotle. The reason we can come to direct and undoubted knowledge, he sees in the fact that certain ideas are inherent within us. We need only raise these from hidden depths of our soul and place them into the full light of consciousness. To this view Locke now opposed the proposition that we have no inherent knowledge at all, but only an acquired one. According to Locke we bring no knowledge with us into the world, but only a capacity to acquire it. Proceeding from this view, he attempts to examine the sources and validity of our knowledge. He thereby arrives at a proposition which today virtually forms an element of modern consciousness, namely that only mass, form, number and movement are qualities really existing in bodies, while colour, sound, warmth, taste and so on are merely effects of bodies on our senses, not something in the bodies themselves.

Now George Berkeley claims that even the first-named qualities have no existence independent from our conception, but only exist in so far as we conceive them. There is absolutely nothing corresponding to our conceptions. Berkeley denies the existence of a bodily world, and only allows spirits to exist in whom the Divinity calls forth conceptions through His all-controlling power. 'What I perceive, that I must also conceive. Something of which I have no conception whatever can also not be the object of my perception or experience, it does not exist for me at all.' 'Therefore beyond the boundary of conception there is no perception, no existence, no experience.' (Grimm, p. 385.)

Finally, David Hume once more takes up Locke's standpoint that only by observing can we gain all our knowledge. But since by observing we can always gain only information about particular cases, so too do we have only such knowledge relating to particular things and no generally valid cognition. If I see one thing always following on another thing, I then name the latter the cause, and the former the effect. In similar cases I expect the same cause to call forth the same effect. Whether this has to be so, I can never know. All our conviction rests on the habit of always presupposing what we have often found proven. So Hume arrives at complete doubt about all actual cognition.

It was this doubt which, according to his own testimony, tore Kant out of his cognitional slumber and stimulated him to that great work stirring the scientific world in all its depths, the *Kritik der reinen Vernunft*. Hume and his named predecessors—in so far as he is based upon them—thus exercised a decisive influence on German knowledge.

In order to understand recent philosophy it is an absolute necessity to know both the evolution of thought and the significance of the researchers examined by Grimm. Through his book the author has thus gained lasting credit. He shows us with penetrating clarity the threads uniting the five men to one another, and always refers with admirable precision to the page on which each of them developed one and the same fundamental thought. It is actually *one* question they all deal with; only the different light into which they bring it always leads them to other conclusions. All are ensouled by their striving towards satisfactory cognition, and equally convinced that only observing and experiencing provide us with real knowledge. No less excellent than the presenting of how the single presentations depend upon one another is the way Grimm sheds light on the course of development they have undergone. This is especially characteristic for Berkeley and Hume. In clarifying these relationships Grimm proves himself also a master of psychological analysis.

We do not believe to be stating too much by letting our judgement of Grimm's book culminate in these words: for an expert it is a work not to be ignored if he wants to come nearer to the period concerned, and for an educated person an interesting read orienting him on countless questions.

⋆

This orientation was of course applied by Steiner elsewhere. His article 'On the Gain for our Views of Goethe's Work in Natural Science by Publications of the Goethe Archives', appearing that year in the annual *Goethe-Jahrbuch*, includes another reference to Bacon:

> . . . Goethe was driven to a 'theory of observation'. He had to establish how to observe, in order to obtain in the above sense scientifically usable results. In this investigation Goethe had only one predecessor, whose manner of thinking however was quite foreign to his own: Francis Bacon. The latter

showed how to approach Nature's phenomena in order to obtain not incidental or useless facts, as presented to normal naive opinion, but results with the character of *necessity* and *natural law*. In his way Goethe was attempting the same thing . . .

The Town of Classical Mummies

On 1 April 1925 the writer Max Osborn published in the *Vossische Zeitung* an obituary of Rudolf Steiner which began as follows:

> The master of anthroposophists who has just departed from us was not always an effusive mystic accepting with pleasure the reverence of his faithful congregation. When I came to know him in Weimar, where as editor of Goethe's scientific writings he had a considerable part in the Sophie edition, he was especially dear to us younger folk by the fine disrespect with which he expressed himself about everything sacred on the Ilm, about the town, the townsmen, the court, the scholarly colleagues, the venerable traditions and—with appropriate distance—even about Goethe himself. At the same time he was the most lovable, most witty and most stimulating of comrades at the pub table, a particularity of Steiner's which we would conscientiously study. In his company a modest drink with Weimar beer could become the most boisterous symposium. I still see before me the picture of us wild Weimar students and freshly baked Doctors—it was in the year when *Hedda Gabler* came out—plaiting 'fervently and gladly' not vine leaves but young birch sprigs into the then very full black hair of the table chairman Rudi. There was nothing in heaven or earth which this scientist would not laughingly castigate . . .

Hedda Gabler came out in 1890, but Steiner did not arrive in Weimar until autumn of that year. So the telltale 'young birch sprigs' must be taken to denote the spring of the following year, 1891.

★

The paradox of the Weimar years as set out in Chapter XVI of Steiner's autobiography was that of his outer sociability and at the same time inner loneliness. He wrote:

> I was living quite intensively with what others saw and thought; but I could not let my inner spiritual reality flow into the world I experienced. With my own being I always had to remain behind in myself. My world was really cut off from the outer world as if by a thin wall.
>
> With my own mind I lived in a world bordering on the outer world; but I always needed to cross a border if I wanted to have something to do with the outer world. I engaged in the liveliest intercourse, but in every single

case had to enter into this intercourse from out of my world as if through a door. That made it seem to me as if I was paying a visit each time I approached the outer world. This however did not prevent me from giving myself up to whoever I was visiting, with the liveliest participation. I even felt quite at home during such a visit.

★

Some of Steiner's own world was revealed in a further letter to Rosa Mayreder:

Weimar,
20th of May 1891

Highly esteemed and gracious lady,

Answering your letters only today is certainly an unheard-of negligence. But when I am in Vienna if you will hear with what discontent and with what despondency of mind I have to struggle throughout all these weeks, you will perhaps find forgivable even the unforgivable. At the Goethe festivities I was glad to find at last—after eight weeks—a human being who grasps my whole tragic situation here in Weimar. A curate from Würtemburg, who has however gone through the Tübingen seminary—and thus taken on to develop a lofty intellectual capacity on which Germans of a better time still laid value—introduced himself to me at the Goethe dinner and little by little turned out to be an understanding supporter of my circle of ideas . . .

This was Max Christlieb, discussed in Chapter XX of Steiner's autobiography.

. . . Now he also grasped what a tragedy for me it is to have to be outwardly woven into a circle of activity from which inwardly I have already become quite estranged. He said: just the preface to my third Goethe volume shows that I have in my heart come away from this following, towards a quite free manner of treatment. So I see myself all day long in an activity which my 'ego', as it was four or five years ago, would have done with great devotion. In that I today undertake it, I am no longer doing it. Under such circumstances you can probably imagine that the journey to Vienna means much to me, very much. I cannot however leave before completing my volume. We are now printing the 26th sheet . . .

The reference was to the first volume of Goethe's morphological writings in the Weimar edition.

. . . And then I still have a heartfelt wish. I would not like to come to Vienna before I can bring you full and favourable certainty about your writings. And this must now happen to me in the shortest time. Kürschner is probably also somewhat annoyed with me at the moment, as my fourth volume is not advancing with desirable speed. Only when it is ready will everything there too be once again in order. As I said: except for the circumstance that I want at last to cast off the skin organically separated from me two years ago, but still surrounding me like a mere inorganic husk. Otherwise my whole existence is a lie and meaningless; my activity not my own, but that of a wretched puppet, drawn by the strings I spun years ago but which I do not want now even to touch, let alone myself pull. I believe you will understand me. I am estranged and cold towards all the life and bustle here in Weimar, the town of classical mummies. I have no one to whom I could express myself, or who would bring towards me even the least understanding. Please greet your dear husband most heartily from me.

In loyalty and in full friendship

Yours

Steiner

★

A few days later, he penned another but quite different letter:

Oberhof, Thuringia
24th of May 1891

Esteemed and gracious lady,

After the plaintive cry you received from me in these days, I want to send you today a greeting in a more joyful mood. Instead of classical mummies I have for one and a half days been seeing at last the most glorious, delightful Nature.

Please give your dear husband and our whole circle the most heartfelt greeting, which I am sending from a delightful Thuringian spot.

St.

With the Light of his Inner Being

In June 1931, the painter Curt Liebich published in the *Freiburger Zeitung* reminiscences of his student years in Weimar:

When travelling at the time from Dresden to Weimar I went from Dresden station to the Thüringen station with a porter to whom I had given my luggage. The porter was also carrying the luggage of another man, who stepped almost wordlessly on the porter's left and struck me with his jet-black, straggly hair, pale yellow face, dark eyes peering searchingly and self-consciously through spectacles, upright posture, and not so lengthy trousers, as fashion dictated. He took a ticket at the Thüringen station, both of us tipped the porter, and the latter dealt with our luggage. By so-called chance, which played so often into my life, we met one another in the same compartment, after long searches also exchanged some words with each other and both also got out at Weimar. I could come quite close to this companion of my arrival in Weimar. It was Dr. Rudolf Steiner...

After describing some youthful pranks which he played in the town, Liebich continued:

...Through the prank I had quickly become in Weimar a well-known person. The time passed by between work and freedom. Little by little I came together with Dr. Rudolf Steiner almost every midday after lunch, or on winter afternoons, at Kaffee Raumer on the market place, where he would play chess with the opera singer Heinr. Zeller—at the time known through his witty poems in the broadsheets—or myself and then often still go walking with me in the park. At the time Dr. R. Steiner was assigned, with yet another, Dr. Wahle, to the Goethe-Schiller Archives presided over by Prof. Dr. Suphan,[17] all three Austrians. The relation between us, of some distance in age for those years, became ever closer. A day hardly passed when we were not together, and he initiated me more and more into his flight of thought. Since at the time some spiritualists were being talked about in Weimar circles, he also went on the track of this occult science, and I still recall a séance with a medium Schraps in Buttstädt to which we had gone together. I owe him much in the explanation of Goethe, especially his interpretation of *Faust* Part II, and of the *Fairy Tale of the Green Snake and the Beautiful Lily*, of which I still today possess a copy. In brief: he enriched me with the many-sidedness of his eminent being. We would often visit every conceivable pub, where he would study people, and could be a man among men, while always playing the withdrawn observer and on the next day exchanging with me his observations about this or that person. One late evening we were sitting in a little café, having come into a set of people where one person had lost a bet with a large number of round 'Knickebeine'. The result was that I believed I would die that night, having in my stomach thirteen egg yolks with their appertaining liquor. In the morning I had to call a doctor. So I was then lying in bed, while my train to Munich, for which I had a ticket, departed. Yet I was lucky to stay behind, for this train crashed at Eggolsheim...

So sitting up at night with Dr. Steiner was my salvation, albeit with much stomach-pain.

I once angered Dr. Steiner badly: at chess. I was being checkmated and grabbed the chessboard in a fury, shaking it so that all the pieces went flying around. 'You man of a man,' he shouted in his Styrian pronunciation—he would often say this if something in my youthful storminess did not suit him—'Go off, I'm never playing with you, until you're polite again.' He was in a serious rage. One day in really bad weather, after the other players had gone, I stayed at the table alone with him. We had not since then

Rudolf Steiner

spoken a word. Suddenly I said: 'Herr Doktor, I'm polite again.' 'Well,' he replied, 'if it's true, let's have a game.'

He would hardly enter the artists' union; a clique forming there did not appeal to him. In that he was particular. It was made up of young painters, writers and musicians who, incited by a Dutch painter, only did their tour of tricks in top hat, with kid gloves and in the latest fashion. One day I too was among them. When he saw me with them on the street, he ignored me. This was painful to me, but provoked me as well. However, I soon had enough of that genteel activity, and threw top hat and gloves into a corner; and one day when I came ruefully back into the café in a solid bourgeois suit, he said: 'I knew you'd soon think better of it. Go on, that's nothing for you.' The friendship was re-established. One day he sent me his picture, certainly the best snapshot I know of him, by a Weimar photographer, with his dedication:

'To the painter Curt Liebich in friendly memory!

Man sees clearly in the outer world only what he can illuminate with the light of his inner being.

Weimar, 13th of June 1891. R. Steiner.'

Among the Foremost Spirits

A few days later, Rudolf Steiner wrote to the Anglicist scholar Helene Richter, who had published some four years before a German translation of Shelley's *Prometheus Unbound*.

Weimar,
19th June 1891

Most esteemed lady,

I certainly feel it as an injustice not even today to have sent your Shelley article. But in a few days now this neglect will be made up. The 'excesses' of the theatre festival week made me awfully tired, and while it lasted I did not want to engage in a work I can honestly say gives me extremely great pleasure: a closer perusal of your manuscript. The latter you will now in the shortest time be receiving, much spoiled by my marginal comments. If I may make a request about your treatise, it is this: keep to the theme. You have grasped it from a side from which it can be quite specially deepened. Also, you will not easily find material where you can apply your own way of treatment to the extent possible precisely for Shelley. I like this method, letting an individual spirit appear on a broad foundation of his view of life and the world. Perhaps Georg Brandes, despite many weaknesses, can here serve as an example. I just believe that in precisely this respect you would again have to set to work. Indeed I know very well that an author often feels stylistic architecture to be a fetter. But for a reader it is indispensable. From my comments you will gather how in particular I would like to see these general maxims applied. Anyway, you should soon rest convinced that your manuscript has not met the disastrous fate you suppose. One sufficient reason is that since your departure I have not been in the 'artists' pub' at all.

I am extremely pleased you found the ideas represented in my epistemological work not entirely uninteresting. I too hope I shall once be able to talk with you about them. And I too remember the festival week with much pleasure—the finest I have yet spent in Weimar. It is perhaps an easily conceivable egoism to think that I have personally to record two important experiences. By this I mean: firstly my satisfaction in making the acquaintance of someone with such accurate and serious knowledge of Shelley. He is highly revered by me and counted among the foremost spirits. Secondly the pleasure given me by the emergence of Max Christlieb, who judges my view of the world with full understanding. And now today I just want to fulfil the duty of giving Wahle's greetings to you and your sister, and ask you yourself to accept and also kindly give to your sister the best regards

of your wholly devoted

Steiner

★

A couple of months later, Steiner sent Helene Richter a further letter:

Weimar,
29th August 1891

Most esteemed lady,

Your honoured communication on the 20th of this month freed me from worry, for the letter from Franzensbad, according to which I should until the 25th of July send the work to Franzensbad, came much too late to send the manuscript there, and as you do not write where you are first going to, I simply did not know what to do with the thing. It is going off to you now at once, and you will probably receive it at the same time as this letter. I have repeatedly read through it and stand by my opinion that the work is not only no wayward child, but even one which has a quite specially good disposition, and just still needs a little cultivating to count as fairly excellent. You have developed the basic idea of Prometheus in a quite telling way. If anything in your view seems to me questionable, it is the opposition you bring to the figure given to the Prometheus saga by Goethe. With Goethe the humanity embodied in Prometheus does not appear at all as one indignantly rising in unceasing pride against a creator of the world. Rather it appears as one which realizes that it must create from its own self the highest element there can be for it anywhere in the world, and therefore as such rejects any divine principle working onto it from outside. The moment man realizes that the highest potency of existence has surrendered its own self in unending love, so as to come to life again in a human soul and here perform deeds of freedom, he must at that same moment regard any god standing outside him as a pseudo-god, against whose tyranny he must rebel. Basically Shelley's Prometheus too is in agreement with this, for liberation of a chained being through wisdom and love means in the last resort only that chaining ceases the moment the inwardly slumbering highest potency of existence—which is indeed wisdom and love—is released. But a man then

Percy Bysshe Shelley in 1819

also sees that the chains he bore were only the fetters of a pseudo-god, falling from his limbs the moment Zeus, that is the god of a man who has not yet woken to full self-consciousness, dissolves into his nothingness. If Goethe had carried through to the end with his Prometheus, he would doubtless have embodied this fundamental idea. But it cannot be doubted that with increasing age Goethe no longer in the same sense believed in the power of that self-consciousness which would have let him carry the poem to its end. Inside him there took place more of a rapprochement to Jupiter, with which necessarily goes hand in hand a distancing from Prometheus. Whether we should deplore this I do not know. But it seems to me that the deepening absorption in the real world of phenomena which we owe to Goethe's later poetry made necessary such an apotheosis of Nature that the idea of man's absolute self-release becomes inconvenient. I am so keen to miss nothing at all of what Goethe did create that I cannot at all regret his having left some things in consequence unfinished. The way you link on to Prometheus an analysis of the Shelleyan spirit seems to me fairly good, and I admire the wide vision with which you easily survey so much of what to our time is otherwise a book with seven seals. Just for this reason I would again request you in any case to prepare the article for print and then also to publish it. Various things, however, do not seem to me to fit harmoniously into your whole view of the world, as for instance the tremendous reverence you have for Dubois-Reymond. I value this scholar's specialized works, but what he serves up to the nation from time to time as general ideas betrays a philosophical dilettantism which in regard to these things simply prevents me from taking this man seriously. Someone who puts such statements into the world as stand in the 'Grenzen des Naturerkennens' and in the 'Sieben Welträtseln' simply cannot be considered at all with regard to philosophy. And even where giving explanations concerning Dubois-Reymond you by no means seem to me to hit the mark. I hold it completely impossible for a being in whom the world of ideas is present to be unfree. I therefore believe that the whole dispute about freedom or unfreedom of the human will only stems from the disputants not having yet made clear to themselves what freedom of the will means. I hold that dissemination of the ideas put forward by Dubois-Reymond in the 'Grenzen des Naturerkennens' signifies the death of all healthy and especially of all deeper thinking. On this point I would be extremely pleased were you not to deny your agreement with me.

In particular I have allowed myself to make little remarks on the unwritten sides of your pad. If I may take the liberty of advising you about the work, my advice would be to put the work in front of you and write it once again sentence by sentence. For if it does contain mistakes, they lie perhaps especially in a manner of expression which is partly jerky, partly cursory, unpolished. As a whole the work is good, but details leave something to be desired. That is anyway much better than if the opposite were the case. But just for this reason I believe that working further through it would make the subject ready for print. In German literature we need essays such as yours by its whole disposition is, since what we get for this fare are mostly works containing a great deal—a very great deal—of learning and no thoughts whatsoever. I was truly delighted by the end of the treatise, containing your views on art and poetry. At the appropriate point I have ventured to insert for you my article on this matter, about fundamental thoughts of a new aesthetics. It would afford me special gratification if you declared yourself also in agreement with the other ideas expressed by me in regard to art—which indeed, according to what you say at the end of the work, must necessarily be the case.

The final sentence of your letter, 'I solemnly promise to leave the lady totally unenlightened and in peace,' is actually unfair to me and judges me rather too strictly. But I must admit that you have a right to curse, since the few days after expiry of which I wanted to send your work have now become several months. Anyway I beg you a thousand times to excuse me. When I positively wrung the work from you, and you only reluctantly let me see it, I was indeed under all the more obligation to fulfil my promise punctually. But if the warm interest I have for the whole orientation of your mind can reconcile you, let my irresponsible neglect nonetheless be forgiven. Believe me that few people will be as pleased as myself if your work should ever appear. Please give my very best commendations to your sister and equally to Herr and Frau Dr. Friedländer who, I hear, must also be at the Aussee, and best greetings to yourself from your wholly devoted

Steiner

With regard to the content of this letter, here are the closing lines in the final fourth act of Shelley's *Prometheus Unbound*, spoken by Demogorgon:

This is the day, which down the void abysm
At the Earth-born's spell yawns for Heaven's despotism,
  And Conquest is dragged captive through the deep:
Love, from its awful throne of patient power
In the wise heart, from the last giddy hour
  Of dread endurance, from the slippery, steep,
And narrow verge of crag-like agony, springs
And folds over the world its healing wings.

Gentleness, Virtue, Wisdom and Endurance,
These are the seals of that most firm assurance
  Which bars the pit over Destruction's strength;
And if, with infirm hand, Eternity,
Mother of many acts and hours, should free

The serpent that would clasp her with his length;
These are the spells by which to reassume
An empire o'er the disentangled doom.

To suffer woes which Hope thinks infinite;
To forgive wrongs darker than death or night;
To defy Power, which seems omnipotent;
To love, and bear; to hope till Hope creates
From its own wreck the thing it contemplates;
Neither to change, nor falter, nor repent;
This, like thy glory, Titan, is to be
Good, great and joyous, beautiful and free,
This is alone Life, Joy, Empire and Victory.

Spiritual Refinement

At the beginning of the following month, Rudolf Steiner wrote to Pauline Specht:

Weimar, 4th of September 1891

Highly esteemed and gracious lady,

If the feeling of pleasure when news from your house arrives to me were not greater than any other conceivable, worry about my long silence would perhaps hardly have found counterbalance when this morning your dear letter again brought right before my eyes my unblessed dislike of writing. The reports you give me are truly not the best. This time you seem to have had the Berghof full of patients...

The Berghof was the Specht holiday home at Unterach on the Attersee.

...But you say that everything is well again or at least in process of decisive improvement, to which latter I wish with all my heart the most decisive progress.

Part of the letter received from Pauline Specht was concerned with her sister Helene and the latter's son Hans. This part had stated:

...For I desire something from you, namely a favour for my sister. She would be extremely pleased to gain the younger Fehr as teacher and companion for Hans in the afternoons and, if it does not work another way, be satisfied if the young lady wanted to stay from four to seven. Helene believes that if you approve of the matter, it would have more chance and therefore asks you to lend it your approval...

To this Steiner replied:

Now before everything else the subject of dear Hans. I must here state in advance that I have not exchanged a letter with any member of the Fehr family since New Year. You see: through me shines everywhere a 'fear of the pen', even if just in regard to the Fehrs various other things come into account. At any rate I have currently no knowledge of what has been happening there in the past year, nor whether lessons given by Gundi Fehr are thinkable. I would therefore suggest that you wait with this matter for a few days, since I am leaving here between the 10th and 15th of September, going via Frankfurt and will be in Vienna at any rate before the 20th of this month. Hopefully the matter can be arranged in such a way that I can still see Unterach, even if only for a very short time. Please tell your esteemed sister that I will definitely be in a position to speak with Gundi Fehr on her behalf before the 20th of this month. But should she wish the matter dealt with earlier, please let me know. I will then write to the Fehrs at once.

Last month I had the pleasure of being able to greet here in Weimar my good Schröer with his wife and spend a few days with them. They were here from the 12th till the 15th of August. He has certainly suffered greatly under the misfortunes which struck him during last winter. But the journey here visibly refreshed him . . .

The misfortunes striking Schröer during the winter of 1891–2 were the deaths in swift succession of various close relations, all younger than himself—both his sisters, Luise Gubner and Marie Slaby, his sister-in-law and brother-in-law, his own eldest son Robert, and his son-in-law Carl Revi.

Steiner continued:

. . . In the last days Herman Grimm was also a few days here. I was very pleased to come to know him. He is a man who absolutely regards things from lofty points of view, and it does one good to learn that.

In mid-August I was surprised to receive poems by delle Grazie with a friendly letter from Professor Müllner, in which Richard is also thought of. The poems are very important and in high measure characteristic for delle Grazie's particular talent.

Please recommend me to all members of your esteemed dear family. I thank Richard and Otto most heartily for their letters, which I shall be answering as soon as possible.

So until we see each other again, if possible still at Unterach. Written at Weimar, the 4th of September 1891 in the Goethe and Schiller Archives, in ever the same high esteem,

Yours,

Steiner

★

In Chapter XIV of his autobiography Steiner described Grimm as follows:

> Spiritual refinement entered the archive when Herman Grimm appeared. From the point in time when—still in Vienna—I had read his book on Goethe, I felt deeply drawn towards his cast of mind. When for the first time I was privileged to meet him in the Archives, I had read almost everything of his which had till then appeared. Through Suphan I soon became better acquainted with him. Once when Suphan was absent from Weimar and he came to visit the Archives, he invited me to lunch at his hotel. We were alone together. He seemed pleased that I could enter into his way of regarding life and the world, and became communicative. He told me about the idea he carried in his mind of a 'History of German Fantasy'. At the time I had the impression he wanted to write it, but this did not happen. However, he explained to me beautifully how the continuous stream of historical evolution has its impulse in a people's creative fantasy, which he viewed as a living, active, supersensible genius. During this luncheon I was completely absorbed by Herman Grimm's expositions. I believed I knew how supersensible spirituality is working through human beings. And here was someone whose inner gaze reaches as far as creative spirituality, but does not want to grasp cognitively that spirituality's own life, remaining rather in the region where the spirit is expressed in man as fantasy.
>
> Herman Grimm had a special gift for surveying larger or smaller epochs of spiritual history and presenting them in precise, ingeniously epigrammatic characteristics. When depicting a single personality—Michelangelo, Raphael, Goethe, Homer—his presentation always appeared against the background of such a survey. How often have I read the article where he characterizes in striking surveys the Greek period, the Roman period, and the Middle Ages . . .

This article was in Grimm's *Vorlesungen über Goethe* (1876).

> . . . The whole man was the revelation of a uniform style. When he formed his beautiful sentences in oral discourse, it seemed to me that they could stand just like that in one of his articles; and when after coming to know him I read one of his articles, I thought I was listening to him speaking. In oral discourse he allowed himself no laxity; but in composing an artistically written account he had the feeling that one ought to remain the person walking around everyday. But Herman Grimm did not walk around in everyday existence like other human beings. For him it was a matter of course to lead a stylized life.
>
> When Herman Grimm appeared at Weimar and in the Archives, one then felt the depository of the estate as if linked with Goethe by secret spiritual threads . . .

On Shakespeare

Towards the end of the year, Rudolf Steiner wrote again to Pauline Specht:

Weimar,
14th of December 1891

Highly esteemed and gracious lady,

Do not scold me as an eternally dissatisfied person if I again begin my letter by saying how hard, how very hard it is for me to believe in my ability to put up again for an indefinite time with the wretchedness of Weimar. For over a week I have again been seeing better relationships. If the fundamental mood flowing from these relationships were not so powerful, I would be silent about it just in order that my letters were not subjected to the accusation of extreme boredom. For there are certainly no more boring persons than those who are always complaining. But with me it is truly not a matter of this or that small or great trouble. These I would like to put up with. Such troubles are disgruntling for a short time, but one can breathe out again when better moments of life arrive. But it is something different if we are surrounded by circumstances which continuously instil into us a feeling of disgust. That is what I cannot rid myself of when seeing all the wretchedness, pettiness and bigotry surrounding me here. All the greater is the feeling of gratitude I sense towards you and your esteemed husband and which I hereby express for having once again let me belong for some days to your dear circle. I am really not saying too much by confessing that the Viennese days appear to me like a beautiful dream. Admittedly you are obliged to believe me in this, for you could only feel it by knowing also the second of those two opposites, Vienna and Weimar. Admittedly it makes up for a great deal now to have the work on my book, which to me is comfort, uplift and relaxation too. Perhaps Weimar's spiritual desolation will also do what Richard would so much like—give width and expanse to my style. I do not know, and will hardly be seeking it. In any case by Easter I hope to have finished the manuscript. By staying away for just a couple more days I have missed absolutely nothing, for there is as yet no thought of ending the typesetters' strike. It is even questionable whether work will be taken up again on the 1st of January. And I have come just in time to see the management in one of its most wretched steps. I have also just taken part in a postponed Mozart evening (first piece: the quintet in G minor). The second of the lectures in the series arranged by myself was moved from the 7th to the 11th, so I could listen to it as well. So everything is in best order.

But I now still want to tell you that I was especially pleased this time to observe Otto reflecting on his Hamlet essay. He grasps the matter thoroughly and independently, thus giving the best indications for successful progress during student years at a university. I believed I had definitely again perceived a growth of his mind. You know this gives me particular pleasure. While writing this here, I recollect with especial vividness the disputation with Richard and Otto on Shakespeare around half past ten at night. That's exactly correct, since my watch is still going according to Viennese time; I haven't yet changed it.

I shall definitely write to Richard tomorrow. Hopefully he is better again. He gave me great pleasure by keeping me company at the station for the last hour before departure.

Now however I only still ask you to recommend me to your dear family, your mother and your dear husband, and to greet the children from me most heartily. Should you soon send some lines in his suffering and not at the same time forget to remark how the various patients are getting on, you will especially please

your in most exceedingly high esteem
devoted

Steiner

Pondering and Musing

In Chapter XVI of his autobiography, Rudolf Steiner described a particular Weimar circle:

> At that time Hans Olden and Frau Grete Olden were living in Weimar. They gathered around them a convivial circle desiring to live 'in the present', by contrast to everything which regarded a continuation of past life in the Goethe Archives and the Goethe Society as the centre of spiritual existence. I was admitted into this circle, and recall with great pleasure everything I experienced there.
>
> However rigid one's ideas had become in the Archives through experiencing the 'philological method', they had to become free and versatile on entering the Olden house. Here everything set into one's mind that a new way of thinking had to gain ground in mankind was met with interest. So too everything which felt inwardly pained by various old cultural prejudices, and was thinking about future ideals.
>
> Hans Olden is known to the world as the author of light-hearted plays like the *Offizielle Frau*. In his Weimar circle at that time he was living differently. His heart was open to the highest interests then existing in spiritual life. Endless but always stimulating discussions went on in his house about what was living in Ibsen's plays, or what was rumbling inside the mind of Nietzsche.
>
> Gabriele Reuter came to the Olden circle. She was then writing the novel *Aus guter Familie*, which soon stormed her into a literary position. She

> filled the circle with all the serious questions then stirring mankind in regard to the life of women.

Even before Steiner, Gabriele Reuter had already set down her own memories of this time in her book *Vom Kinde zum Menschen*, published in 1921:

> At the beginning of the nineties we were a small circle of people in Weimar, passionately attached to truth. We would ruffle with gladsome pleasure any courtly, scientific and artistic set of empty phrases coming under our fingers until it lost—at least in our eyes—any sparkle and incentive. And it must be said that at Weimar we found incentive enough for practising our work of mental destruction. The only pity was that those on the receiving end noticed it so little, for indeed we were not thereby enlightening the public, but just enjoying ourselves in a circle of initiates with our causticity, uninfluenceability, and clear, cheerful cynicism. We were all at a period in life when the illusions of youth are already gone, and yet no resigned old age told us that truth and lies rule over mankind like day and night in eternal alternation, and that there is no existence and no culture without ceaseless compromises.
>
> We were all fiery and still very impatient.
>
> To me . . . the new friends signified a bath of mental steel. Being together with them was at times like a session in a fencing ground, where fine blades clashed against each other and only with dexterity and alertness does one remain protected from laughable collapse.
>
> We were all individualists of the purest water . . . We believed ourselves, certainly with honesty, to be working for our own most personalized development, while yet only sharing the typical developmental life of our age. Sensitive people as we were, even in remote Weimar we felt the motions of its waves, let ourselves be lifted by them onto glittering heights, which we were glad to have climbed by our own powers . . .
>
> Now Friedrich Nietzsche had become our god, around whom our minds turned like planets round the Sun . . .
>
> What abundant spirit was scattered out during endless debates in the beautiful big house on the Horn, where the Goethe-archivist Eduard von der Hellen lived with his young wife, or on the veranda of the small white house on the Tiefurter Allee, where the clever gracious Grete Olden, recently married to the writer Hans Olden, had her reception day: on Tuesday, when 'an egg was slaughtered'—for more than an egg was not spent, and egg buns were so much more desirable than those with finely cut ham. Each of us was lord of the world and the centre of its existence, and the sovereignty of the individual (after Max Stirner!) was confirmed with the most grotesque reasons and the most daring conclusions. Especially Rudolf Steiner, editing Goethe's scientific writings for the Sophie edition—after-

wards priestly leader of anthroposophists—was great at putting forward baroque and unheard-of premises and then defending them with an amazing application of logic, knowledge, bold instances and paradoxes. How amusing he could be when falling into a state, the then freethinker with the little monk's head graven through by the spirit, and the high shining brow! How excited he would become when opposed by the witty cynicism of Hans Olden with his faun's kindly smile!

We all enjoyed the feeling of having left the bourgeoisie behind us and landed in the country 'beyond good and evil'. But arranging things there was not at all as easy as it seemed, and we ladies sometimes came into terrible conflicts. Steiner struggled with hunger and need . . .

In the evening, often late at night, he would accompany me on the long way home from the Oldens, for we both lived to the west of the town. He would then become serious, and I owe to his outstanding mind and incredibly wide knowledge a wealth of thoughts and stimuli in the philosophical domain. He especially taught me how to come to know Goethe in a quite new way. Till then I had known nothing about the scientific prophet in the poet. One of Steiner's thoughts has followed me a lot: the demand for moral and religious fantasy . . .

★

At one point Steiner himself filled out answers to a questionnaire, of a type enjoying great popularity in literary circles of the time:

Your favourite qualities in a man? *Energy*
Your favourite qualities in a woman? *Beauty*
Your favourite occupation? *Pondering and musing*
Your idea of happiness? *Pondering and musing*
Which calling seems to you the best? *Any by which one can perish of energy*
Who would you certainly like to be, if not yourself? *Friedrich Nietzsche before his madness*
Where would you like to live? *That's all the same to me*
When would you like to have lived? *In times when there's something to do*
Your idea of unhappiness? *Not knowing what to do*
Your main character trait? *That I don't know*
Your favourite writers? *Nietzsche, Hartmann, Hegel*
Your favourite painter and sculptor? *Rausch. M. Angelo*
Your favourite composer? *Beethoven*
Your favourite colour and flower? *Violet. Meadow saffron*
Favourite heroes in history? *Attila. Napoleon I. Caesar*
Favourite heroines in history? *Catherine of Russia*
Favourite character in poetry? *Prometheus*
Your favourite names? *Radegunde. Let the ladies decide this*
Which historical characters can you not stand? *Weak ones*

Which fault would you most readily forgive? *All, if I have grasped them*
Your insurmountable detestation? *Pedantry and sense of order*
Of what are you afraid? *Of punctuality*
Favourite food and drink? *Frankfurt sausages and brandy. Black coffee*
Your temperament? *Changeability*
Place and time: *Weimar, 8th Feb. 92*
Name: *Rudolf Steiner*

According to my Concepts

A week or so later, Rudolf Steiner received the following letter from Joseph Kürschner:

Stuttgart, 15th of February 1892

Very honoured Sir,

You will probably have no difficulty in guessing what matter again obliges me to take my pen into my hand and write to you. It is the lack of manuscript for the *Nationalliteratur* which has set in at the press. You will indeed be easily able to imagine that now, when the undertaking is coming to its end and the number of manuscripts standing available to the press becomes ever smaller, I must receive as fast as possible everything still outstanding, so as to keep the press occupied in such a way that 2 instalments are published weekly. Under no circumstances may we now any more give fewer ones, for subscribers are starting to become impatient in the most frightening way. I can lay before you dozens of letters and cards in which people are taking the publishing firm to task and complaining in the most accusational way conceivable about the immense protraction and delay in finishing; and every such card, every letter brings me into an ever more unpleasant position with regard to the firm.

It will soon be <u>two years</u> since after my <u>repeated</u> reminders I received from you the first telegram

'Manuscript following definitely Saturday'.

Since then 87 weeks have passed by, and in reply to my reminders at least 4 quite similarly sounding telegrams have come to me, but still not a single page of manuscript from the last volume of the scientific writings. Let the cruel game now suffice and put me, please, finally in possession of the last volume, at any rate in course of the next two weeks. Very grateful to you for this will be your

most highly esteeming and devoted

Kürschner

*

The main reason for Steiner's delay was of course his engagement in various other projects, in particular at that time the published version of his doctoral thesis, referred to a month later in a further letter he wrote to Pauline Specht:

> Weimar, 20th of March 1892
>
> Highly esteemed and gracious lady,
>
> It would have been very pleasant for me had the accompanying little piece of writing greeted you on your birthday complete and finished. But since I would like it to reach you on that very day, I am forwarding you the unbound sheets without the foreword, which will only leave the press in the next few days. What stands on page 1 to 46 was in essence the work on the basis of which my doctorate was gained. This piece of writing forwarded to you will have the title: 'Truth and Knowledge. Prelude to a Philosophy of Freedom'. From the content you will perhaps be able to think that what is found on page 47 and 48 was not in my doctoral work. I request you and your dear husband to receive the work in a friendly way even in its still uncompleted form; in a few days it will also appear in its delicate dress. Along with this I give you most heartfelt greetings and friendliest wishes for your birthday, which I shall be celebrating here, united in spirit with your dear family. The lack of immediate presence will not lessen my full participation in your fortunes and those of your family, two years ago on this day I could personally assure you about this.
>
> As said in your last kind letter, for which I heartily thank you, this winter too did not pass without troubles regarding the children's health. How is Richard? I hope to hear about his health also from himself. How is the health of good little Ernst? Has he recovered again?
>
> I was very pleased to read that Dr. Schiff has become a superfluous person in your home. It was time too. Hopefully such ointment-smearers do not again cross so soon over your threshold, i.e. of course only with ointment. Otherwise I have not the least thing against Dr. Schiff, of course.
>
> You write about the 'Mysterium' by Rudolf Lothar and ask me my opinion of it . . .

The reference was to *Der Wert des Lebens. Ein Mysterium in einem Vorspiel und 4 Auszügen* by Rudolf Lothar, pseudonym of R.L. Spitzer.

> . . . I will only get the book in a few days and will then not fail to tell you my view about it. From previous writings I know the author—who lives in Vienna and a short while ago held there a lecture on the game of Tarot—as a highly gifted man. I consider his view of the world, as expressed for instance in his 'Verschleierter König', absolutely right with regard to the negative; I have admittedly less approval for what he wants to set in place of

what he rejects. Anyone who robs a human being of so many ideals as Lothar does with the words:

'Right and might come to you from heaven, you say—(the king is meant). We tell you, heaven is empty! . . . The people then rage: His belief was deception' should not close *merely* with the words: 'I spring from the people just like you, and we are companions in the service of truth.'

I shall be pleased if the 'Wert des Lebens' makes me recognize progress in Spitzer—which is Lothar's name—in a positive sense as well. The time demands with yearningly outstretched arms a view of the world. Anyone who knows how to interpret the gaze, that tired-of-olden-days and yet eager-for-the-future gaze of the time-spirit, must before all things seek after positive content for head and heart. When we have this, then we can well look back upon that prehistory which is now the present.

You ask me why I have set so many plans before myself. Basically I do not know, except this much, that each one of them interests me, and that I want to see each one of them carried out as soon as possible. If from all that one likes one has only work in the immediate present, the latter can be nothing excessive. I also need a mighty counterbalance to the archival work, if I want to stay upright. Since I am collaborating in a Goethe edition with the principles of which I absolutely do not agree, I must carry out another task in order to show how an edition according to *my* concepts should be. Only in this way do I provide evidence that even in the Goethe edition what I am doing appears corrupted not *through me*, but rather through the senseless editorial principles. That is after all the best polemic. It does not destroy, but rather creates.

In your last letter, most treasured gracious lady, you accused me of laziness in writing. I abundantly deserve this accusation. I now see in myself how little human nature is inclined to lay aside even its most unblessed habits. I only ask you not to ascribe my not having written to a cooling of my friendship, which has remained the old one and will never become different. When looking over the sheets I am forwarding to you in print, I must recognize that many a thought arose in the beautiful time I was able to spend in your family; I must then recall how unspeakably much I owe to the good-willed attitude there surrounding me. And whoever knows that such a good-willed attitude is precisely the basis on which natures most like to stand in whose mind the seemingly most impersonal, the thought, struggles for expression, will know what your home means *to me*. But my casualness in writing letters, under which I myself suffer so greatly, has nothing of significance.

I had quite exceptional pleasure from your telegram on my birthday. I send you most heartfelt thanks for having thought about me.

I respectfully beg you to recommend me to your mother, give most heartfelt greetings to your dear husband, the children, your sister, her husband and my dear Hans and gladden me again as soon as possible with a letter.

In ever the same high esteem and gratitude,

Yours,

Steiner

I was pleased by the news that Ignaz Brüll's opera will be performed in Munich.

The History of Sciences

On 17 August 1829, William Whewell, on his way over to Italy, wrote from Realp in Switzerland to his friend Richard Jones:

> ...I shall return by way of Munich, and if possible, both by Weimar and Heidelberg; but I believe this is too wide a project...

So indeed it was. Further letters show that after visiting Milan, Whewell did return by way of Munich and then Nuremberg. At that point he faced a choice between going north to Weimar—residence of the then octogenarian Goethe—or west to Heidelberg to attend the scientific congress. He decided for Heidelberg, and so far as is known never came to Weimar in his life.

★

Some 63 years later, in April 1892, there came out in Weimar Rudolf Steiner's book *Wahrheit und Wissenschaft*, dedicated to Eduard von Hartmann.

The introduction, covering several pages, ends with an extensive bibliography. Here are some of the cited titles:

Eduard Grimm: *Zur Geschichte des Erkenntnisproblems. Von Bacon zu Hume*; Leipzig, n.d. (1890).

Friedrich Heinrich Jacobi, *David Hume über den Glauben oder Idealismus und Realismus. Ein Gespräch*; Breslau 1787.

Matthias Kappes, *Der 'Common Sense' als Prinzip der Gewissheit in der Philosophie des Schotten Thomas Reid*; Munich 1890.

Alexius Meinong, *Hume-Studien*, Volume I: *Zur Geschichte und Kritik des modernen Nominalismus*; Vienna 1877.

John Stuart Mill, *Die induktive Logik. Eine Darlegung der philosophischen Prinzipien wissenschaftlicher Forschung, insbesondere der Naturforschung*; (Original London 1843) German by J. Schiel, Braunschweig 1849.

—*System der deduktiven und induktiven Logik*; German by J. Schiel, Braunschweig 1868.

> Thomas Reid, *Untersuchungen über den menschlichen Geist nach den Grundsätzen des gemeinen Menschenverstandes*; German Leipzig 1782; Original: *An Inquiry into the Human Mind on the Principle of Common Sense*; Edinburgh 1765.

The introduction was followed by an opening chapter, headed 'Preliminary Remarks'. This began:

> Epistemology should be a scientific enquiry into what all other sciences without examination presuppose: *cognition* itself. It is thus granted from the start the character of a fundamental philosophical science. Only through it can we learn the value and significance which insights gained through other sciences possess. In this respect it provides a foundation for all scientific effort. Clearly it can only do justice to this task by being itself without presuppositions, so far as this is possible according to the nature of the human faculty of knowledge. In general this will probably be accepted. By closely examining the better-known epistemological systems one will however find that at the starting point of an enquiry a whole series of presuppositions are already made which then substantially prevent further expositions from having any convincing effect. It will particularly be noticed that even in presenting fundamental problems of epistemology certain hidden suppositions are usually made. But if the questions of a science are misstated, a right solution is unlikely from the outset to be forthcoming. The history of sciences teaches us indeed that countless errors from which whole epochs have suffered may just be traced back to certain problems having been erroneously formulated. To corroborate this sentence we need not go back as far as Aristotle's physics or the Ars magna Lulliana, but can find sufficient examples in more recent times . . .

Both common sense and inductive logic (to use the terms of Reid and Mill appearing in the preceding bibliography) lead towards the conclusion that these last two sentences represent teaching given to the author almost 12 years previously at the Technical College in Vienna by Edmund Reitlinger in the first part, 'from ancient times to Newton', of his lecture course on the history of physics.

Reitlinger had been fond of quoting from Whewell's book on inductive sciences, and Steiner's juxtaposition in a negative context of two such recondite subjects as Aristotle's physics and the Ars magna Lulliana clearly reflects Francis Bacon's disparaging treatment of these subjects as followed by Whewell in his *History* and *Philosophy of the Inductive Sciences*.

★

The last surviving members of the circle of friends around Whewell, all of them now knighted, passed away in course of this very year 1892: the nonagenarian astronomer Sir George Biddell Airy, the Cambridge physician Sir George William Paget, who had once dined with Carl Gustav Carus in the Master's Lodge of Trinity College, and finally the famous naturalist Sir Richard Owen, who would still have been able to remember Whewell from as far back as his own memories reached—to his childhood in Lancaster during the very first decade of the nineteenth century.

8
THE HISTORICAL RELATION

Worthy of Appreciation

One day in the summer of 1892 the following telegram was sent to Rudolf Steiner:

> Stuttgart, 16th of July 1892
>
> Do I receive Goethe volume definitely by Monday? Longer waiting not possible.
>
> Kürschner

Steiner replied a few days later:

> Weimar, 19th of July 1892
>
> Manuscript going now today by express mail.
>
> Steiner

> Weimar, 20th of July 1892
>
> Express mailing gone.
>
> Steiner

The reference was to the main content of the projected 'fourth' volume (comprising two halves, which thus became the fourth and fifth volumes) of Goethe's scientific writings in the Kürschner edition.

For publicational reasons Kürschner did not in the event then bring out these volumes for another five years. But since Steiner's submitted text was as such complete it will be reproduced at the present point.

★

The content of the fourth volume comprised most of the *Geschichte der Farbenlehre*. Goethe's 'Introduction' to this work opened as follows:

> For striving youth, history is more tiresome than pleasant, because it wants to begin a new, perhaps indeed a primal world-epoch from itself. But those progressing in education and age quite often recognize with vivid thankfulness that various good, usable and helpful things were bequeathed to them from their ancestors.

Steiner added a footnote:

> In order really to grasp a truth it needs to arise in our spirit with the same naturalness as in the mind of the one who first recognized it. A younger

> thinker is mostly aware of this naturalness, but not of the historical relation in knowledge which has become clear to him. He then quite often sees as a first discovery what indeed is new *to him*, but otherwise has long been recognized and received into historical development. The *historical* sense, appertaining to recognition of the historically real, awakens in man only late. Goethe held very highly what is passed on historically. See *Spr. in Prosa* saying 1: 'Everything clever has already been thought. One must just try to think it again'; and saying 29: 'A historical human feeling means one formed in such a way that in appreciating contemporary merits and meritabilities it also takes the past into account'; saying 175: 'The most foolish of all mistakes is when good young minds believe they lose their originality by recognizing a truth which has already been recognized by others.' Herbert Spencer regards it as a psychological and historical law that the individual human mind goes through again in shorter sequence the mental periods lived through by its ancestors. Applying thus the fundamental biogenetic law to the development of mankind, it would now be possible to explain the *factual* necessity why we must first ourselves come upon long recognized truths, if we want to understand them completely.

Goethe continued:

> Nothing is at a standstill. For all seemingly backward steps, mankind and science must always progress, even if both were finally to terminate once again in themselves . . .

Steiner added a footnote:

> This is based on the view that for every newly appearing view an analogy will be found in an earlier period of cultural development. Views appear, are lived out in a certain form and disappear, in order to reappear modified in new ages and for other peoples. This view does not correspond to the Schopenhauerian, according to which history brings to the surface nothing but eternal monotony, but rather it sees unity in a process of continual metamorphosis and turns its interest to this multiformity of the particular, convinced that with each new modification a higher step will be climbed on the spiritual ladder.

Goethe's text went on:

> . . . Excellent minds have always been found who wanted to communicate. From this much has come down to us worthy of appreciation; so we can be assured that our ancestors were never lacking in suitable views of Nature.

Steiner added a footnote, quoting from one of Goethe's poems:

Cf. Hempel III, p. 192:

'Das Wahre war schon längst gefunden,
Hat edle Meisterschaft verbunden,
Das alte Wahre, fass es an!'

Goethe continued:

> The circle mankind has to run is definite enough, and despite the great standstill made by barbarism has already more than once completed its course. Even if we also want to ascribe to it a spiral movement, it always returns into that domain which it already once went through. In this way are repeated all true views and all mistakes.
>
> In order to learn about the doctrine of colour, one must at least cross through the entire history of science, and not leave out of account the history of philosophy . . .

Steiner added a footnote:

> According to the particularity of Goethe's view of nature a single branch of natural science *cannot* be fully grasped without considering its relation to the totality of knowledge of Nature. Goethe's doctrine of colour will also only be grasped by one capable of understanding it out of the totality of the Goethean view of Nature. An age or a single scientist have *that* view about colours which is consistent with the rest of their view of the world, if they think consequentially. It was left only to our time of comfortless specialist knowledge to let single branches in the knowledge of Nature go along beside each other.

Goethe went on:

> . . . A packed presentation would have been desirable; but could not be achieved under the given conditions. We therefore decided to supply merely materials for a history of the doctrine of colour, and to that end sift somewhat through what we had heaped up.
>
> It will not be hard to indicate what we understand by that expression. Anyone supplying material for a building will always bring more and less than is required. For so much must often be taken from what is produced, just in order to give it a form; and when starting on a building, one is accustomed to think least about what actually furnishes the last and best decoration.
>
> We have provided extracts, finding ourselves induced to do so by several reasons. The books requiring to be consulted are seldom to be had, if not in large towns and well-furnished libraries, yet certainly in many medium-sized and small places, by whose participating inhabitants and teachers we wanted our work tested and used. Therefore this volume should become a kind of archive, setting down what the most excellent men occupied with the doctrine of colour have declared about it . . .

Examining the Opinions of Predecessors

After a list of contents, the actual text of Goethe's history of the doctrine of colour began with a preliminary part on 'History of Primeval Times'. This part ended as follows:

> The characteristic impression of different colours was quite soon noticed by former peoples, and one can regard the different application in this sense for dyeing and for related weaving, at least sometimes, as intentional and derived from a right feeling.
>
> Thus everything we can observe in earlier times and for undeveloped peoples is practical. The theoretical only meets us in so far as we now proceed to the educated Greeks.

Rudolf Steiner added a footnote:

> Theory can only be evolved when enough has taken place for men's practical needs. For theory can only be a creature of freedom. But the latter only finds an appropriate basis when man's dependence on Nature through compulsion of the same has ceased. Only when man has succeeded in placing natural forces to a certain extent into his service can he devote himself to activities serving his higher needs. It is wrong for Bacon to let all theory have the aim that human beings make Nature serviceable to themselves. True theory rather begins when dependence on Nature is overcome. For man possesses reason for higher purposes than only to use it as a device for that part of his existence which is *not* reason.

Goethe in this part had made no mention whatever of any historical person. But Steiner in his footnote nonetheless found it appropriate to include a negative reference to the views of Francis Bacon.

⋆

The first properly historical part of Goethe's account was on 'Greeks'. It contained sections on Pythagoras, the Pythagoreans, Empedocles, Democritus, Epicurus, Chrysippus and the Pyrrhoneans.

Then came a section on Plato, with Steiner supplying this footnote:

> Plato (b. 429 B.C. in Athens) is the first scientific representative of objective idealism. From his 20th to 28th year he enjoyed instruction from Socrates and was one of his closest friends. After his teacher's death he went with some comrades to Megara; from there he travelled to Cyrene, Egypt, Lower Italy and Sicily. In Italy he became acquainted with Pythagorean philosophy. In Sicily he came to know the elder Dionysius and his brother-in-law Dion, whom he also befriended. As a confidant of Dionysius he brought suspicion onto himself of a behavioural manner

offensive to the ruler and had to return to Athens. Here he gathered around him a circle of pupils, to whom he taught philosophy in a school (the so-called *academy*) outside the town. He then made two more journeys to Sicily, probably in order to bring about with help of the younger Dionysius the ideal state deriving from his fundamental philosophical views. In this respect however he achieved nothing. He died in 347 B.C. Plato's philosophy is one of the sublimest thought-structures ever to have arisen from the mind of humanity. It belongs to the saddest signs of our time that a Platonic way of conceiving is held in philosophy for precisely the opposite of healthy reason. Platonism is the conviction that the purpose of all cognitional endeavour must be to acquire the *ideas* which uphold the world and form its foundation. Someone who cannot in himself awaken this conviction does not understand the Platonic view of the world. Plato was always striving to uncover from the fluctuating phenomena of the sense-world the permeating ideal substance. Plato wanted *not to grasp phenomena*, but rather to penetrate through them to their spiritual basis. Goethe's above quotations are from Plato's *Timaeus*.

Next came a section on Aristotle, with Steiner providing footnotes such as these:

The world-view of Aristotle (384–322 B.C.) does not stand in opposition to that of Plato. The difference lies more in the way the two men are captured by the different sides of reality (world of ideas and of senses). For Plato the sense-world is merely a preliminary stage for reaching the world of ideas; the former only has significance in so far as it serves to attain the latter. With Aristotle the opposite is the case. He wanted to explain the sense-world; this explanation he sought through ideas. It can be said that both philosophers have factually the same view; only their interest is attached to opposites.

Aristotle begins his expositions, as is seen, by subjecting to criticism opinions of his predecessors on the matter treated by him. In this respect he is exemplary for the scientific endeavours of all subsequent time. One seeks to raise oneself to the peak of the time with one's scientific pursuits by examining the opinions of predecessors in the domain to be worked upon. In this way one may avoid their mistakes and make use of whatever has already taken place in the establishment of truth. By proceeding otherwise the possibility arises of falling into an opinion which has been long existing, and perhaps also within historical development already been overcome.

It may from this be seen that Aristotle is a decisive opponent of that view of the world which wants to trace everything back to an abstract unity, as for instance feelings of the higher senses just to refined feelings of touch at a higher stage of development. Aristotle already recognized that a thing cannot be explained by removing what is particular or special to it and only stressing what it has in common with others. From the latter tendency

> derive those scientific theories wanting to trace all natural phenomena back to nebulous and abstract unified processes (e.g. material radiation, wave motions). One takes hold of a phenomenon precisely by seeking what differentiates it from others and makes it into a quite definite and special one.
>
> Aristotle thus sees in light a particular being, different from warmth and other phenomena of reality. When this being appears for itself, pure, it is then a self-activating product set into the world through transparency. Transparency is as it were the body of light, the latter the force penetrating transparency.
>
> When transparency goes over into activity, there arises light. This activity is not always one and the same; it specializes, individualizes itself, appearing in the most manifold forms. Different kinds of transparency and of its active product dependent upon it can therefore be found. The specific, quite definite 'thus' of the *actus* achieved by transparency is colour.

A further extensive section comprised a translation by Goethe into German of the entire book of 'Theophrastus or rather Aristotle on Colours'.

An Overview of the Whole

The second part in the history of the doctrine of colours was on 'Romans'. It opened with a lengthy quotation from Lucretius as translated into German verse by Knebel.

After a brief section on Pliny, Goethe then incorporated into his text a 'Hypothetical History of Coloration, Especially of Greek Painters' composed by another friend, Heinrich Meyer. This took the account right up to the eighth century.

★

The next section was headed 'Observations about the Doctrine of Colours and Treatment of Colours of the Ancients'. It began:

> How any person thinks about a particular case will only be perceived rightly if one knows how he is in general disposed. This holds good if we actually want to know the opinions, whether of single human beings or of schools and centuries, about scientific topics. The history of sciences is thus most intimately bound up with the history of philosophy, but equally too with the history of the life and character of individuals, as of peoples.

Rudolf Steiner added a footnote:

> Here lies a pointer to Goethe's whole scientific orientation. Research into the particular is only possible if one has a free and open eye for the whole. Since modern science becomes ever more lost in the particular, it is deprived of understanding for the *essence* of things. The particular as such can be *seen*, but not *understood*. For the latter we need to bring along in our observations the idea, which is only granted to us through a view of the whole.

> Goethe continued:

> So too the history of the doctrine of colour is only grasped in consequence of the history of all the sciences. For in order to gain insight into the slightest part there is needed an overview of the whole. Admittedly we can only point towards such a treatment. However, if among our materials we introduce much which does not seem to belong directly to the purpose, a place is actually granted to it only in order to recall general relations. In the history of the doctrine of colour this is all the more necessary, since it has had its own destiny and on the sea of knowledge now emerges for only a brief time, now sinks down again for longer and disappears . . .

★

The third part, 'Intermediate Time', opened with a section headed simply 'Gap'. It began:

> Those early geographers producing the map of Africa were accustomed, wherever there was a lack of mountains, rivers or towns, to draw if necessary an elephant, lion or other monster of the desert, without being thereby reprimanded. We too will thus perhaps not be blamed for inserting into the great gap where gladsome, living, progressive science abandons us some observations to which we can in future again refer.

Steiner added a footnote:

> Goethe had a need to express the ripest fruits of his cognition in the form of aphorisms. This is a form often chosen on the highest peak of knowledge. One may think of Leibniz's monadology and of the aphoristic form of Indian wisdom-teachings.

Goethe's aphorisms varied in length from single sentences to paragraphs or even sequences of paragraphs. Here is one of the latter:

> There are two moments in world history which now follow one another, now show themselves simultaneously in individuals and peoples, in part singly and separate, in part highly entwined.
>
> The first is that where single persons freely develop alongside each other. This is an epoch of emergence, of peace, of nourishment, of arts, of sciences, of good-naturedness, of reason. Here everything works inward, and at the

best of times strives towards a happy, domestic edification. But in the end this state dissolves into partisanship and anarchy.

The second epoch is that of usage, of war, of consumption, of technology, of knowledge, of understanding. Effects are directed outward; in the finest and highest sense this point of time grants duration and enjoyment, under certain conditions. Yet such a state easily turns into selfishness and tyranny, where however the tyrant does not need at all to be thought of as a single person. There is a tyranny of whole masses, which is highly violent and irresistible.

Steiner added a footnote:

> Actual production only takes place in times of the first kind. In them the disposition slumbering within a people comes out and to the surface. The other times are directed to what is personal, egoistic. They bring forth nothing, are sterile, could be struck out from history, if one wanted only to record in it what really helps mankind further and incorporates positive elements into its development.

⋆

Goethe's following sections were on 'Tradition' and 'Authority'. The latter ended:

> One who had enough perseverance, desire and self-denial to make himself fully acquainted with tradition, and at the same time retained enough strength and courage to develop independently his original being and in his manner work over and enliven what had often been accepted, would be held if not as the most excellent person yet as the most gifted and most fortunate. So how pleasant must it not be when, however seldom, we really encounter men of this kind in the history of science. Such is the one to whom we now turn. Ahead of many other splendid men from an admittedly lively but yet still bleak period, he steps vividly and gladsomely towards us.

Mathematics

Goethe's next section was entitled 'Roger Bacon 1216–1294'. Rudolf Steiner added a footnote:

> Roger Bacon was born in the year 1214 at Ilchester in Somerset as a member of a noble family. See below.

Goethe's text began:

> The culture effected in Britain by Roman rule, a culture introduced early enough through Christianity, was lost only too soon, destroyed by pressure

from wild insular neighbours and piratical throngs. With the return of an admittedly often disturbed peacefulness, religion too was rediscovered and worked for good in an excellent way. Splendid men were trained to become apostles for their own fatherland, indeed for foreign lands as well. Monasteries were founded, schools established and every kind of better education seemed to take refuge in these isolated lands, there to be maintained and intensified.

Roger Bacon was born in an epoch which we called the epoch of emergence, of free development of single persons alongside each other, a most fortunate epoch for a mind like his . . .

After discussing for a couple of paragraphs Magna Carta and other items in the political scenery of thirteenth-century England, Goethe then continued:

Although Roger was only a friar who wanted to remain within the sphere of his cloister, the breath of such surrounding events penetrates through every wall, and he certainly owes it to memorable national aptitudes that his mind could rise above the cheerless prejudices of his time and hasten forward into the future. He was gifted by nature with a well-ordered character, one which wants, seeks and finds certainty both for himself and for others. His writings give evidence of great calmness, level-headedness and clarity. He esteems authority, but does not deny the confusedness and uncertainty of tradition. He is convinced that insight can be obtained into the sensory and the supersensory, the worldly and the divine.

Steiner added a footnote:

Bacon studied first at Oxford, but from there went to Paris, hoping to discover richer literary aids for his further studies. Here he obtained the title of *doctor theologiae* and returned to England, entering the Franciscan Order, so that he could live totally for the sciences. His brothers in the Order, envying him on account of his mental superiority, suspected him of being devoted to magic and had him imprisoned. When in the year 1264 Bacon's patron Clement VI rose onto the papal chair, better times also arrived for the former. He could even send his works *Opus majus*, *Opus minus*, *Opus tertium* to the Pope. But after Clement's death Bacon was again condemned by Jerome of Escoli, legate of Pope Nicholas III, to ten-year imprisonment. The long confinement threw a dark shadow also onto his old age. He died in bitterness in 1294. More detailed biographical information about him is found in the foreword to Jebb's edition of the *Opus maius*, appearing in London in 1723. The reason for the many prosecutions of Bacon was probably not given by his scientific trend, which merely provided a pretext. For his professional colleagues the main offence was formed by the sharp condemnation he made of the clergy of his time.

Roger Bacon with a pupil, depicted in an illuminated manuscript of the fifteenth century

Goethe went on:

> First and foremost he knows how proper it is to acknowledge the testimony of the senses; yet he does not remain unaware that nature conceals much from a merely sensory human being. He therefore wishes to penetrate more deeply and realizes that he has to seek for appropriate powers and methods within his own spirit. Here his childlike mind encounters mathematics as a simple, inborn tool springing out from himself. He seizes it all the more since people had already for so long neglected everything of their own, heaped traditions together in a peculiar way and thus destroyed them as it were within themselves.

Steiner added a footnote:

> Bacon assumes three ways of cognizing, namely: by *sense* (representation), by comparison of representations (understanding) and by immediate grasping of a thing (intuition). He found this assumption in Alhazen. According to the three ways of cognizing, three sources are also named for knowledge: experience, authority and reason.

Goethe continued:

> From now onwards he uses his own organ in order to judge his predecessors and to feel Nature . . .

Steiner added a footnote:

> Nature is for Bacon 'the instrument of divine activity'.

Goethe's text went on:

> . . . Satisfied with the way he succeeds in many things, he proclaims mathematics to be the principal key of all hidden scientific matters.
>
> According to how objects are with which he concerns himself, so too is his success. In the simplest of physical cases a formula solves the problem. In more complicated ones it is certainly helpful, points out the way, brings us closer, but no longer penetrates to the foundation. In higher cases, and altogether in organic and moral ones, it remains a mere symbol.
>
> Although the matter he treats is very full in content, and also lacks nothing to interest a musing person, and although he approaches with great reverence the lofty objects of the universe, in order to substantiate his thesis he yet must do injustice to separate parts of what is knowable and feasible, to certain sciences and arts . . .

Steiner added a footnote:

> There was something uncertain in Bacon's views. On the one hand he says that Aristotle were best burned and the whole basis of science laid anew, for study of the Stagirite led only to the most fatal mistakes. On the other hand he ascribes all these mistakes merely to bad translations, and demands the most far-reaching process of perfecting one's linguistic knowledge in order to render transcriptions correct. He himself mastered the Latin, Hebrew, Greek and Arabic languages.

Goethe's text continued:

> . . . The elements in them which are peculiar, fundamental and elementary he does not recognize; he merely observes the side they present to mathematics. So he resolves grammar into rhythm and logic into music, and declares mathematics to be a better logic due to the certainty of its demonstrations.

Steiner added a footnote:

> Bacon regards mathematics as the most important of all sciences for two reasons: 1. Because it is inherent in the soul and does not derive from the outer world. 2. Because the virtues (essences) implanted into things are stamped onto matter through mathematical relationships. He therefore

> investigates the arrangement of primal forces according to lines, angles and figures.

Goethe went on:

> Since he is indeed partisan but in no way pedantic, he very soon senses where the fundamental maxims (*canones*) with which he wants to organize everything do not apply. Even to himself it does not appear really serious when he wants to adapt his mathematico-physical standard to spiritual and divine things, relating through a funny play of images matters which do not reach into each other.
>
> Nonetheless his great need for certainty makes him take steps which are thoroughly firm and decisive. What the ancients experienced and thought, what he himself has discovered and devised—all this he brings before our soul and feeling, not strictly methodically, but yet in a very understandable, naive presentation . . .

Steiner added a footnote:

> Bacon had an exact knowledge of his predecessors. Aristotle, Euclid, Ptolemy, Alhazen, Avicenna, Averroes, Pliny and others are diligently quoted.

Goethe's text went on:

> . . . Everything is related, everything has the most beautiful result, and since the known lies clearly before him, even the unknown is also not foreign to him.

Steiner added a footnote:

> Bacon mastered in a universal way all the sciences of his time and in each of them was also literarily active. His numerous works deal with grammar, geography, theology, philosophy, mathematics, physics, astronomy, alchemy and medicine.

At this point Goethe quoted a couple of substantial passages from the *Opus majus*—Steiner giving textual references in a footnote—and discussed in some detail Bacon's doctrine of light and colour.

Technology

Goethe then continued:

> Bacon's writings testify to a great calmness and level-headedness. He felt very deeply the struggle he has to conduct with Nature and with tradition. He realizes that he must seek for appropriate powers and methods within

himself. Here he finds mathematics as a sure instrument, springing out from his inner being. He operates with it against Nature and against his predecessors. His undertaking brings him success and convinces him that mathematics forms the basis for everything scientific.

Rudolf Steiner added a footnote:

Bacon is always thrown to and fro between idle speculation, as seems explicable from the scholastic position prevalent at his time towards Aristotle, and an exact scientific way of thought based on experience and mathematics.

Goethe went on:

Even if this organ did him proper service for everything measurable, in his tender feelings he nonetheless soon finds that there are regions to which it does not reach. He expresses very clearly that in such cases it is to be used as a kind of symbolism. But even in the performance he mingles the real service it gives him with the symbolical. At least he joins both kinds so exactly together as to ascribe to both of them the same degree of conviction, though his symbolizing sometimes amounts merely to a playful joke. In this little matter are contained all his virtues and all his faults.

Any person who holds fast to this view will become convinced that there is a false application of pure mathematics as well as a false application of applied mathematics. Evidently astrology has arisen from astronomy through the mistake here reprimanded: from the effects of known forces conclusions were drawn about the effects of unknown forces, and both of these treated as equally valid.

It may be seen that Bacon wants to bring mathematics closer to spiritual and clerical things through a charming and funny numerical game.

A large part of what is commonly called superstition has arisen from a false application of mathematics; even a mathematician's name was therefore equivalent to that of a trickster and astrologer. One may recall the signature of things, chiromancy, the art of pointing, even the compulsion of hell . . .

Steiner added a footnote:

Under 'signature' alchemists understood the deeper essence of things, which they then in their way described. Cf. Jac. Böhme; *De signatura rerum*, 1730. 'Chiromancy', the art of foretelling from lines of the hand. 'The art of pointing', foretelling from randomly designed points joined into figures according to particular rules.

Goethe's text continued:

. . . All of this non-being takes its bleak appearance from the clearest of all sciences, its confusedness from the most exact. One may therefore hold

> nothing more pernicious than when—as is happening again in recent times—mathematics is drawn over from the region of reason and understanding, where it has its seat, into the region of fantasy and sensoriality.

Steiner added a footnote:

> So much misuse is made of the mathematical element because a great number of human beings are unable to perceive that the qualitative absolutely cannot be attained through mathematics. Geometrical and mathematical formulae which physicists have put forward in order to present the life of man, his relation to God and the world; Herbart's unsuccessful mathematical laws in psychology; the claim of modern natural scientists that all quality must be derivable from quantity and thus susceptible to mathematical treatment, all derive from the same mistake. Mathematics is only in its place where quantity is also present.

After several further paragraphs (in course of which Goethe stated that 'the writings of Luther contain, if one wishes, much more superstition than those of our English friar'), the text went on:

> Roger Bacon's tendency to resolve the unknown through the known and master the distant by the close is what justifies his excellent mind. It is joined to a characteristic which deserves precise examination, having already before aroused historical doubt. From certain qualities of bodies known to him, from certain effects anticipated from their combination or from a certain particular form, he draws conclusions so correctly as to go far beyond what was achieved in his time, and talks about things as though they were already accomplished. He deals with gunpowder and in particular with the telescope so exactly as to make us convinced he had them before him, especially since he did already have segmented cubes and sections of cubes in glass.
>
> But anyone who knows how the human mind can hurry forwards before technology follows on will find nothing incredible here either.
>
> And so we dare to claim that with him these were only conclusions. Here too it goes with him in applied mathematics as in pure. Just as he applied the former where it did not belong, so he entrusted to the latter what it cannot accomplish.
>
> Through the described glasses one should not just perceive with one's own eye the most distant objects quite close up, and the smallest enormously large; but if these and other pictures are also projected outward upon the air, upon the atmosphere, they should bring to manifestation a whole crowd. So too many natural appearances dependent on refraction and reflection, the much later invented *camera obscura*, the magic lantern, the solar microscope and their various applications have made his prophecies literally true, because he foresaw all these consequences. But the way he expresses himself about these things shows that his apparatus

only worked within his mind, and there may thus have arisen some imaginary results.

Steiner added a footnote:

> Through the precision of his knowledge Bacon was able to form concepts of instruments for which a technical method of assemblage was only discovered much later. However, not knowing the boundaries consequent on technology, he often overestimated the action of the devised instruments. Among instruments foretold by him belong the telescope and spectacles.

Goethe continued:

> We notice first that like all inventors, far-seeing persons working with vigorous minds, he was approached by his contemporaries to do something directly for their benefit. Man is a being in such need of pleasure and assistance that it cannot be held against him if he looks around everywhere to find some fun in good fortune and some support in dire straits.
>
> Heroes of war have always been on the track of mathematicians, because one wants to increase one's own power mechanically, and with small forces oppose great effects against any superpower. Thus in Bacon is found the reiteration of ancient and the assurance of novel aids of this kind. Burning-mirrors to concentrate solar rays into the distance, copying mirrors whereby a few troops appear to the enemy as a great number, and other such things turn up in his writings. They look marvellous enough, and yet have been rendered at least partly feasible by enhanced technology, by the most practised arts of conjuring and in other ways.
>
> Being prosecuted for mistaken teaching is the destiny he has in common with all those who run ahead of their age. Being accused of magic was at the time quite natural. But his age was not alone in committing this haste of regarding what can be done by profound, unknown, firmly established, consequential and everlasting natural forces as subjected to will and whim, occasioned accidentally, in contest with God and Nature.
>
> Here too man must neither be scolded nor pitied; for he will not be rid of this kind of superstition as long as mankind exists. Such a superstition is always reappearing, just under another form. Man sees only effects. Causes, even the nearest, are unknown to him. Only very few persons, more deeply penetrating, experienced and attentive will realize—if need be—from where an effect may derive . . .

Boundless Empiricism

The fourth part in Goethe's history of the doctrine of colour was entitled 'Sixteenth Century'. It presented firstly sections on Thylesius, Portius, Scaliger, Paracelsus, and 'Alchemists'.

A section headed 'Intermediate Observation' then stated:

> We are now at a point where the division between the old and new time becomes ever more important. A certain reference to antiquity still continues in an unbroken and forceful way; yet from now on we find more human beings who depend on their own powers...

Further sections followed on Telesius, Cardano and Porta. The latter examined in particular Porta's work *De Magia naturali.*

★

Then came the final section in this part, headed 'Bacon of Verulam'. At the very start Rudolf Steiner inserted the following footnote:

> Francis Bacon, Baron Verulam, Viscount St. Albans, was born in 1561, studied at Cambridge, occupied high posts of state under Queen Elizabeth and under James I and made it to Lord Chancellor. In this post he was accused in open parliamentary session of bribery, a charge which he could not counter. He was deposed and died in 1626. Bacon set himself the task of reforming science from the ground up. In his opinion the latter had estranged itself from the direct present by holding onto principles belonging to a long past time which could only have validity and value for that time. Bacon proposes a method of observation and experiment not in his view susceptible to mistakes. Only *experience* should be the source of all knowledge. But Bacon's view suffers from a one-sided overestimation of experience. He knows nothing about the expression—at certain places within experience—of something higher which a spirit standing above experience may see and cognize. Since in the introduction we deal extensively with the relation between the Baconian and Goethean doctrine of experience, reference may here be made thereto.

Francis Bacon

In his introduction Steiner had not mentioned Bacon at all. But he had contrasted Goethe's doctrine with views held by nineteenth-century scientists like Helmholtz, Du Bois-Reymond and others in effect working out of the Baconian doctrine. The first part of his introduction, printed under the headline 'Inadequate modern concepts', had begun:

> There is much talk today about the fruitful development of the sciences in the nineteenth century. I believe one can only rightly speak about important scientific experiences which have been made, and about a change in practical conditions of life through these experiences. But as for the basic notions by which the modern view of Nature seeks to *grasp* the experiential world, I hold these as unhealthy and in regard to energetic thinking inadequate . . .

★

Goethe opened his section on Francis Bacon as follows:

> Usually we only take account of a significant man's writings in so far as they have affected us, have either promoted our education or conflicted with the same. It is according to such experiences undergone by ourselves that we judge our predecessors. As the sixteenth century closes and the seventeenth begins, what we venture to say about an admirable mind may also certainly be regarded from this point of view.
>
> What Bacon of Verulam bequeathed to us may be divided into two parts. The first is the historical part, mostly disapproving, exposing previous deficiencies, pointing out gaps, chiding the behaviour of predecessors. The second we would name the instructive part, didactically dogmatic, calling for new works of the day, stimulating, promising.
>
> Both parts have for us something pleasant and something unpleasant, which we indicate more closely in the following way. Pleasant in the historical part is his insight into what has already existed and occurred, but especially the great clarity with which he presents scientific interruptions and retardations; pleasant is his knowledge of those prejudices which prevent human beings both in particular and as a whole from progressing onwards. Highly unpleasant by contrast is his insensibility towards the merits of predecessors, towards the value of antiquity. For how can one calmly listen when he compares the works of Aristotle and Plato to slight tablets which simply because they consist of no effective content-filled mass might have been washed over to us on the flood of the time? Unpleasant in the second part are his demands, all going merely into the expanse, and his method, which is not constructive, not in itself conclusive, and does not even indicate a purpose but gives occasion for singularizing. Highly pleasant by comparison is his ability to excite, stimulate and promise.
>
> His reputation has arisen from the pleasantness. For who does not enjoy having the deficiencies of past times narrated to him? Who does not have confidence in himself, and who does not set hope on posterity? The

unpleasantness by contrast is indeed noticed by the perceptive, but as if cheaply tolerated and forgiven.

From this observation we venture to solve the riddle that Bacon could make himself so much talked about, without effect, indeed that his effect has been more harmful than useful. For since his method, in so far as one can be ascribed to him, is highly awkward, no school arose either around him or around his estate. It was therefore necessary and possible for outstanding men once again to appear, raising their age to more consequential views about Nature and gathering around themselves all who enjoy knowledge and understanding.

Since by the way he referred human beings to experience, they were left to themselves and fell into the expanse, into a boundless empiricism. At the same time they felt so shy towards method that they viewed disorder and waste as the true element in which alone knowledge can thrive. We may be allowed to repeat these statements according to our manner in a parable.

Bacon is like a man who perceives very well the irregularity, inadequacy and dilapidation of an old building, and knows how to make such aspects clear to its inhabitants. He advises them to abandon it outright, to spurn the foundation and the land, the materials and all the attachments, to search for another building plot and erect a new building. He is an excellent talker and persuader. He shakes some of the walls; they collapse, and the inhabitants are partly obliged to move out. He points towards new plots of land. People start to smooth the ground, and yet it is everywhere too narrow. He presents new sketch plans, but they are not clear, not inviting. But principally he speaks about new materials, and the world is now served. The crowd diperses in all directions and brings back endless single items. At home meanwhile new plans, new activities and settlements are occupying the citizens and engrossing their attention.

With all this and through all this the Baconian writings remain a great treasure for posterity, especially if the man no longer works upon us directly but historically. This should now really be possible, since between him and ourselves several centuries are already interposed.

Protest

Goethe went on:

It may be thought that these attitudes of Bacon, storming against tradition and authority, already in his time found opposition. There is also extant a protest registered in the name of antiquity and previous culture by a splendid learned man. Both by reason of its moderation and by reason of its toughness we partly translate and include it.

Sir Thomas Bodley

The knight Bodley, having spent part of his life in diplomatic business, then retired and devoted himself to the sciences, while assembling a large library which is still now preserved at Oxford. He was a friend of Bacon and received from him the treatise *Cogitata et visa.* For a scholar and researcher into antiquity this could not have been in any way pleasant. There has survived for us a letter of Bodley's written on this occasion, from which the following passages may here find place.

These passages, extracted (with a few omissions) from the letter written by Sir Thomas Bodley to Sir Francis Bacon on 19 February 1608, read in the original:

'I must deliuer vnto you for my priuate opynion, that I am one of that crew that saye there is and we possess a farr greater holdfast of Certaintie in your Sciences, than you by your discourse will seeme to acknowledge.'

'Nowe in case we should concurr to doe as you aduise, which is, to renounce our common notions, and cancell all our Theorems, axiomes, rules and Tenents, and soe to come babes Ad regnum naturæ, as we are willed by Scriptures to come Ad regnum cœlorum, there is nothing more certaine in my understanding, then that it would instantlye bringe vs to barbarisme, and after manye thousand yeeres, leaue vs more vnprouided of Theoricall furniture then we are at this present, ffor that were indeed to become verye Babes, or Tabula rasa when we shall leaue noe impression of anye former principles, but be driuen to begin the world againe, and to travell by tryalls of Action and sence (which are your prooffes by particulers) what to place in intellectum, for our generall conceptions, it being a maxim of all mens approuing in intellectum nihil esse quod non prius fuit in sensu. And so in appearance it would befall vs, that till Platoes yeere be come about our insight in learning would be of lesse reckoning then nowe it is accounted; as for that which you inculcate of a knowledge more excellent then nowe is among vs, which experience might produce, yf wee would but assaye to extract it out of nature by particuler approbacions, it is noe more vpon the matter, but to incite vs vnto that which without instigation, by a naturall instinct men will practise of themselues, for it cannot in reason be otherwise thought but that there are infinite numbers in all parts of the world, for wee maye not in this case confine our cogitacions within the bounds of Europe, which imbrace the course which you purpose, with all the deligence and care that anye Abillitye can performe: for euery man is borne with an Appetite of knowledge wherewith they cannot be so glutted, but still, as in dropsyes, they thirst after more.'

———

'I do not hold it an erronious conceipt to think of euery science, that as now they are professed, ffor they haue beene in all precedent Ages before, thoughe not alike in all places, nor at all tymes alike, in one and the same: but according to the changeings & turnings of tymes, with a more exact and plaine, as with a more rude and obscure kinde of teaching.'

———

'I must for finall Conclution inferre, Seeing all the endeauors, Studye and Knowledge of Mandkinde in whatsoeuer Art, or Science, haue euer bine the same as they are at this present, though full of mutabillities, accordinge to the changes and accidentall occasions of ages, and Countryes, & Clarkes disposition which can neuer be but subiect to intention and remission both in their deuices and in their practises of their knowledge.—If now we should accord in opinion with you, ffirst to condemne our present knowledge of doubts & incertitude (which you conferme but by auerment, without other source of Argument) And then to disclaime all our Axiomes, and maximes, and generall assertions that are left by tradition from our Elders to vs, which (for soe it is to be intended) haue passed all probations of the sharpest witts that euer were, & lastlye to deuise (being become nowe againe as it were Abecedarii) by the frequent spelling of particulers, to come to the notice of the newe generalls, & soe afresh to create new principles of Sciences, the end of all would be, that when wee shall bee dispossessed of the learning which wee haue, all our Consequent trauell will but helpe as in a circle to conduct vs to the place from whence wee sett forward and bringe vs to that happines to be restored in Integrum, which will require as manye ages as haue marched before vs to be perfectly atchieued. And this I writt with noe dislike of increasing our knowledge with new found deuices (which is vndoubtedly a practise of highe Comendacion, in regard of the benefitt they will yeeld for the present), that the world hath euer bene & will assuredly continue very full of such devisors whose industery that way hath bine verye obstinate and preeminent, & hath produced strange effects aboue the reach & the hope of mens common Capacities: And yet our notions and

Theormes hath allwayes kepte in grace both with them & with the rarest that euer were named anong the learned.'

It is not easy for opinions to be opposed so directly to each other as are here the Baconian and Bodleian ones, and we do not wish to confess ourselves exclusively to either of them. If the former leads us into an unforeseeable expanse, the latter wants to limit us too much. For as on one side experience is limitless because something new can still always be discovered, so too are the maxims, in that they must not rigidify, not lose the capacity to be themselves extended in order to encompass more, indeed to be consumed and lost into a higher view.

For Bodley probably understands here not subjective axioms, which suffer less change from a progressive time, than those which arise from observation of Nature and have reference to Nature. It may not be denied that for progress in true views of Nature such principles of older schools, especially if joined to religious convictions, stood very uncomfortably in the way. It is also interesting to observe what actually seemed so particularly restricting to a man like Bacon—himself certainly educated, trained and civilized according to ancient convention—that he felt obliged to behave in such a destructive way and as the proverb says to throw out the baby with the bathwater. Revolutionary attitudes are engendered in particular human beings more through particular causes than through general conditions, and in Bacon's writings we have met some axioms of this kind which he repeatedly pursues and persecutes with especial frustration; e.g. the doctrine of final causes, which to him is highly detestable.

In Bacon's way of thought, incidentally, much may be found indicating a man of the world. The very demand for limitless experience, the disregard, indeed denial of present services, the insistence on working activity are matters which he has in common with those who spend life working upon a large crowd and mastering and using its reaction.

If Bacon was unjust towards the past, his ever forward-pressing mind also did not allow him a calm appreciation of the world around. We want here to mention only Gilbert, whose endeavours regarding the magnet could have been and were known to Chancellor Bacon: for in his writings he mentions Gilbert, even with praise. But Bacon, to whom everything was equal in the expanse of phenomena, seems not to have grasped how important the subjects of magnetism and electricity are. For though he himself always indicates that one should only gather particulars in order to select from them, order them and finally reach universals, yet with him individual cases retain too many rights, and before simplification and finality can be achieved through induction—even that which he extols—life is spent and forces are worn out. A person who cannot become aware that one

William Gilbert

> case is often worth a thousand, and contains them all within itself, or who is not in a position to grasp and honour what we have called a primal phenomenon, will never be able to promote anything for the pleasure and use of either himself or others. Look at the questions Bacon throws up and the detailed investigations he suggests. Consider in this sense his tractate on the winds, and ask yourself whether in that way one can hope to achieve any purpose.

The reference is to Bacon's *Historia Ventorum*, published in 1622. After some further paragraphs, Goethe even added:

> . . . Bacon as an islander surrounded by the sea, member of a nation regarding itself as connected to the entire world, is moved by outer conditions to go into the expanse and the endless, and take as chief object of attention the most uncertain of all natural phenomena, the winds, since winds are of such great importance to those travelling on ships.

⋆

After some more general observations, Goethe ended this whole part as follows:

Were we now to glance back again at the sixteenth century, we would find its two halves clearly divided from each other. The first manifests a lofty culture, arising from thoroughness, conscientiousness, restrictedness and seriousness. It reposes on the second half of the fifteenth century. What was born and brought up in the latter shines henceforth in its complete value, in its full dignity, and the whole world will not easily experience such a phenomenon again. There appears indeed a conflict between authority and one's own activity, but still with a certain moderation. The two are not yet divided from each other, they work onto each other, are carried and uplifted.

In the second half, the striving of individuals towards freedom already becomes much stronger. For everyone it is already convenient to develop from what has emerged, to enjoy what has been gained, to walk through the freed-up space. Aversion towards authority becomes ever stronger, and as protest was once made in religion, so protest is made thoroughly even in the sciences, so that Bacon of Verulam finally ventures to run a sponge over everything previously drawn on the tablet of humanity.

Transition

The fifth part in Goethe's history of the doctrine of colour was headed 'Seventeenth Century'. It began:

> We spoke at the end of the previous century about Bacon of Verulam, whose life still continues into the fourth part of the present, and whose actual scientific efforts fall at the end of his career...

The statement that Bacon's life continued into the 'fourth part' of the seventeenth century presumably meant continuance into the fourth decade, which was a slip. Bacon—as correctly stated in Rudolf Steiner's footnote—died in 1626.

> ... Yet the protesting, revolutionary spirit preserved in his writings, striving against authority, was already developed in the previous century and in Bacon only appears, as regards natural sciences, in its highest energy.
>
> The task before us is to show how these very sciences take henceforward an opposite direction...

*

After some more 'General Observations' came a section on 'Galleo Galilei'. It included the following paragraph:

> If science appeared to be split forever through the Verulamian method of diffusion, it was at the same time gathered together again by Galilei; he led

the doctrine of Nature back again into man, showing already in his early youth that to a genius one case is valid for a thousand by developing from swinging church lamps the doctrine of the pendulum and of the fall of bodies. In science everything depends on what is called an *aperçu*, on becoming aware of what actually lies at the base of phenomena. And this becoming aware is endlessly fruitful.

Steiner added a footnote:

Cf. our introduction.

The section on Galilei was followed by further ones on Kepler, Snellius, de Dominis, Aguilonius, 'Intentional Colours', Descartes, Kircher, Marci and de la Chambre.

*

Then came a section headed 'Isaac Vossius'. Steiner provided an initial footnote:

Vossius, Latinized name from Voss. Vossius was born in Leyden in 1618 and died as a canon in Windsor in 1689.

Goethe began:

Vossius was a son and brother of outstanding scholars, and an active man for the sciences. He was educated early on in ancient languages and associated knowledge. There develops within him a passionate affection for manuscripts. He sets up as an editor of ancient authors, and chiefly occupies himself with geographical and astronomical works. Here he may have felt how factual knowledge for dealing with them is necessarily required; and so he approaches physics and mathematics. Widespread travels promote his conception of Nature.

Steiner added a footnote:

His travels went through England, France, Italy. In the year 1648 he followed a call from Queen Christine to Sweden, and in 1673 moved over to permanent residence in England.

After further discussion Goethe went on to quote several whole chapters from Vossius's *de Lucis natura et proprietate*. He then concluded:

... In the sequel we shall have occasion to indicate everything else preceding which paved the way for Newton's doctrine; but we cannot here leave unmentioned that Mathhäus Pankl in his *Compendium Institutionum physicarum*, Posoniae 1793, declares our Isaac Vossius a forerunner of Newton, by saying: 'To the ancients light was the simplest and most homogeneous essence. Isaac Vossius first suspected that the manifoldness of colours which we perceive upon bodies does not derive from the bodies but from parts of the light.'

Steiner added a footnote:

> Vossius is the man who forms a transition from the alchemistic trend of medieval philosophy to modern atomism, which originates from Newton's physical doctrines. In Vossius there is as yet no talk of an atomistic interpretation of the world of colours, but there is indeed of a view of phenomena on the basis of which such an interpretation must be reached.
>
> The section on Vossius was followed by one on Grimaldi.

The Mechanical Way of Conceiving

Goethe then went on to 'Robert Boyle. b. 1627, d. 1691.' Rudolf Steiner provided an initial footnote:

> Robert Boyle was the son of Richard Boyle, Baron of Cork. In his youth he went on a journey through Germany, Switzerland and Italy. Here (in Florence) he became acquainted with the writings of Galilei. From 1644

Robert Boyle

onwards he lived in his homeland, continuousy occupied with physical and chemical experiments and their scientific recording.

Goethe's text began:

> The division between spirit and corporeality, soul and body, God and the world had come about. Ethics and religion found here their advantage: for if man wants to claim his freedom, he must oppose Nature; if he strives to rise up towards God he must leave her behind him. In both cases it cannot be held against him that he ascribes as little as possible to her, indeed that he sees her as something inimical and annoying. Such men as thought about reuniting the separate matters were therefore persecuted. When the teleological way of explanation was banned, understanding was taken away from Nature; there was not the courage to ascribe reason to her, and she finally remained lying spiritless. What was required from her were technical, mechanical services, and finally it was also found that only in this sense could she be grasped and conceived.

Steiner added a footnote:

> In order to appraise these lines in the proper way, it should be considered that Boyle was a contemporary of Descartes and Spinoza, who divided the whole world in the strictest manner into thinking and being, spirit and matter, and thus founded the dualism of matterless spirit and spiritless matter. But thereby all explanation of natural phenomena which ascribed to any kind of spiritual beings a part in the production of the phenomena was ruled out. Previously individual occurrences in Nature had simply been explained by presenting Nature after the fashion of man as a being acting with understanding. When one perceived a phenomenon, one asked: what does Nature thereby intend, what does she want? Goethe names this kind of explanation that of the understanding (p. 226, 9). The right one is by contrast that which posits in Nature a series of formative principles and then for a certain phenomenon asks: why under the given conditions must the underlying principle develop in just this way? Since we accept these formative principles into our reason in the shape of ideas, Goethe names this kind of explanation the reasoning one (p. 226, 9). But it was not immediately attained at the time when the understanding one was discarded. So there was then nothing but Nature devoid of ideas, where everything was explained in a mechanical way. It was believed that spirit could only be retained in its purity by strictly differentiating it from Nature, and this in turn were best achieved by thinking of Nature as without spirit. By spiritualizing Nature it was feared to naturalize the spirit. This is how from the 17th century onwards the mechanical way of conceiving became increasingly widespread for explaining Nature.

Goethe continued:

> In this way it may be seen that a Robert Boyle with his tender, devout feeling could acquire an interest in Nature . . .

Steiner added a footnote:

> Boyle had a deeply religious character. Besides his numerous scientific treatises, he composed—if with little success—theological ones, learnt oriental languages to understand the Bible in the original text, furthered its translation into numerous languages and made an endowment for lectures which should promote the truth of Christianity as against other doctrines of belief.

Goethe's text went on:

> . . . Throughout his life he could occupy himself with Nature and yet gain from her nothing further than that she was a being who lets herself be extended and contracted, mixed and separated; and whose parts, working against each other by pressure and impact and turning into the most different states, also produce different effects on our senses.

Steiner added a footnote:

> It is easy to see that Boyle simply had that view about Nature which necessarily developed in the age of Descartes and Spinoza.
>
> Goethe continued:
>
> He had entered the doctrine of colour from the chemical side . . .

Steiner added a footnote:

> In his time Boyle was considered as a chemist of the first rank. He not only established important matters in the domain of factuality, as e.g. the saline composition of the sea, but was also the first to direct chemistry onto a new path by grasping the concept of an element differently from how this was customary at that time and ever since Aristotle. By element he understood a material which is no longer further divisible, and considerably more elements had to be recognized under this supposition than the four of Aristotle. The English call Boyle the 'great experimenter'.

Goethe's text went on:

> . . . He is the first since Theophrastus who takes measures to set up a collection of phenomena and to give an overview. He deals with the business only occasionally and hesitates to conclude his work; finally, when hindered by ocular illness, he brings together his experiments, as good as they go, in such form as if he were handing on an incompleted work to a younger friend for further treatment. On the one hand he certainly desires to look as though he were only assembling experiments, without thereby wanting to

> establish a hypothesis; on the other hand he is honest enough to admit that he tends towards the corpuscular, mechanical kind of explanation and believes that it can reach furthest . . .

Steiner added a footnote:

> Boyle was an adherent of the atomic theory. Atoms are differentiated by shape and size, and in relation to their own size have between themselves very considerable intermediate spaces.

Goethe continued:

> . . . He therefore deals most extensively with white and black, because with these a certain mechanism may at first admittedly become plausible. However, in regard to the actual colour phenomena of bodies and to apparent colours, he goes to work less methodically; but he puts together a mass of experiments which are interesting enough and after him are repeatedly brought up. We too, as far as we regard it necessary, have presented them in our sketch according to our manner and conviction.

Steiner added a footnote:

> Of the experiments which he assembles, important ones in this connection are: phenomena of fluorescence and phosphorescence, colours on thin sheets, colours on the surface of bodies, etc.

Goethe then quoted several passages from Boyle's *Experiments and Observations upon Colours.*

★

The next section was headed 'Hooke. b. 1635, d. 1703'. Steiner provided an initial footnote:

> Robert Hooke was assistant to Boyle, from 1662 Curator of Experiments to the Royal Society, from 1664 Professor of Geometry at Gresham College in London. From 1678 he was also Secretary of the Royal Society.

Goethe's text began:

> He is more of a bustling than an industrious observer and experimenter. He glances everywhere around and his restless activity spreads over the whole doctrine of Nature. It must be granted that he made good inventions, and treated happily what he had invented. Yet he is no theoretical mind, not even a methodical one.

Steiner added a footnote:

> Hooke is the inventor of a large number of physical instruments (helix spring of watches, alcohol spirit level, vernier, crosshair in telescopes, wheel

Robert Hooke

barometer, rain gauge) and discoverer of interesting facts (constancy of melting and boiling point in water). Together with Boyle he constructed the two-handled air pump. He was an unusually industrious worker, but less successful in theoretical exploitation of his discoveries than many of his contemporaries, who brought into currency more effectively—if also often somewhat later—various views which he also held. He therefore found himself in arguments with many scholars of the time about priority. For instance, he had unquestionably discovered the mechanics of gravitation before Newton; the latter just represented it more skilfully.

Goethe went on:

The doctrine of light and colour owes him a great deal...

Steiner added a footnote:

Colours of thin surfaces, those of soap-bubbles, were observed firstly by him, then by Boyle. The emergence of light also forms the subject of his experiments. When making remarks on this matter to the Royal Society in 1675, he was already putting forward the theory of transversal oscillations of light taken up again in our century by Fresnel.

Goethe's text continued:

> ...He observes the breaking force of ice, notices with Grimaldi the deviation of light and makes suggestions as to how one might look at the Sun without being blinded; arranges a portable *camera obscura* for more convenient demonstration and occupies himself with the reflecting telescope.

Steiner added a footnote:

> In a session of the Royal Society on the 5th of February 1674 Hooke presented a mirroring telescope.

Goethe then discussed Hooke's doctrine of colour.

There followed further sections on Malebranche, Sturm, Funccius, Nuguet and other seventeenth-century scientists.

Relevant Particulars

The next section was headed 'Transition to the History of Colouring'. Goethe began:

> After previously having seen ourselves thrown in theory as if upon waves from one side to another, it is to be expected that in practice no perfect certainty will meet us either. For although a practitioner, especially if compared to a theorist, acts as a whole man, and in a deed is always more compelled onto the right path by outer conditions, there thus occurs just as much restriction as benefit. And even if anyone achieves something exceptional through genius, talent or taste, the reason cannot be so easily transmitted either as a maxim or as a thing graspable in the hand.
>
> In the eighteenth century painters and colourists are definitely far in advance of philosophers and natural scientists as regards the doctrine of colour. They were however unable to be helped out of the confusion and inconsequence. The history of colouring since the restoration of art, which we insert at this point, will render visible relevant particulars. In order not to interrupt the discourse, this history is taken up to the present day. But it has to be foreseen that the dominant theory could not give the artist any help; it had banned from the doctrine of colour demarcation and shadows, which to a painter are such necessary conditions for contrasting with light.

Rudolf Steiner added a footnote:

> In the theoretical a one-sided view can very well last some time and carry on its mischief, but not in the practical, where the desired effects are simply not thereby achieved. For a theorist remains standing inside the world of thoughts. Therefore he often does not notice that he is grasping only one

side of an object and not its totality, the sum of natural conditions through which it arises. But a practitioner must introduce the natural process itself, must fulfil all the conditions Nature prescribes. If he overlooks one of them, it is then also lacking in what he should be producing, and the latter does not come about. However, without a good theoretical basis praxis will not be understood, for in the last resort all natural processes are conditioned by laws which are only penetrable conceptually, thus theoretically. If according to the model of such natural processes a practitioner wants to create something artistically, *he* admittedly need not hold to those laws. But they certainly cannot be understood in their deeper essence by someone who lacks that theoretical basis.

★

Then came a section on the 'History of Colouring since the Restoration of Art'. Steiner added a footnote:

> Until the 13th century Italian painting was completely without significance. Only from then onwards does it start to become important, thus generally introducing a new epoch of art.

Goethe then discussed from the aspect of colouring the work of a large number of painters, with Steiner adding informative footnotes such as these:

> Angioletto Bondone Giotto (1276–1336) lived in Florence as a sculptor, painter and architect.
>
> Leonardo da Vinci, b. 1452 in Vinci near Florence, lived in Milan 1452–1499, where he followed a call from Ludovico Maria Sforza, and founded there an artistic academy. In 1516 he became the court painter of Francis I of France. He died in 1519 at Amboise. Leonardo was a universal genius in the best sense of the word. He was an architect, sculptor, painter, musician and mechanic, and mastered the whole range of sciences of the time. His scientific writings are numerous and filled with original inventions and ideas. He also wrote a treatise on 'Light and Shadow'. His most important work is a fresco painting in Milan: *The Last Supper*. The superb effect of his pictures is founded on the sharp expression of form, towards which everything he does is aimed.
>
> Raphael Santi (Sanzio), b. 28th March 1483 at Urbino, d. 6th April 1520. Lived from 1508 in Rome. To his principal works belong: the *Spozalizio*, the *Entombment*, the frescoes of the *Camera della Segnatura*, a coloured painting of the *Four Sybils*, the *Sistine Madonna* and the *Transfiguration*.
>
> Hans Holbein (the elder), b. 1460 in Augsburg, d. there 1524. He painted a number of altar pictures. His son, Hans Holbein the younger, was born in

> 1497 and from 1526 was court painter to the King of England; he died in London in 1543. His madonnas are famous.

About a third of the way through this section, Goethe stated:

> Until now one quality of that part of painting whose history we have here undertaken to treat has not yet been touched on; we mean colour harmony. Usually indeed this is included under the general concept of colouring, but can also be thought of as separate. Harmony regarded by itself consists in skilful, purposeful juxtaposition and opposition of colours; colouring by contrast, in the strict and limited sense, means only their artistic mixture and the faithful depiction of Nature.

Steiner added a footnote:

> 'Colouring' is then the art of so mixing colours that an object treated by a painter makes an impression of naturalness; 'harmony' the art of so juxtaposing colours that through combination and contrast this juxtaposing makes an impression of beauty and calls forth aesthetic pleasure in the beholder. Colouring aims for truth, harmony for beauty.

Here are some more of Steiner's footnotes in this section:

> Peter Paul Rubens, b. 1577 in Singen, d. 1640 at Antwerp. He spent the time from his 23rd to 27th year in Italy, where he was especially concerned with studying the Venetian masters. Later he made journeys to England and Spain. His most famous works are: the altarpiece representing the *H. Family* in Antwerp, the *H. Anna*, the *Virgin Mary, St. Francis of Assisi*, the *Raising of the Cross*, the *Deposition*, all in Antwerp.
>
> Rembrand von Ryn (1607–1669), one of the most subjective painters of all time. With him conception is always placed above formal beauty. His pictures are outstanding through masterly treatment of light and dark.
>
> Claude Gelée, named Lorrain after his birthplace (1600–1682), obtained his artistic training in Rome. It was said of his paintings that they present earthly forms in truly heavenly clothing.[18]
>
> Don Diego Velasquez de Silva (1599–1660), was court painter to Philip IV. He lived in friendly relation to Rubens; made journeys to Italy. He was a naturalist, who gradually worked through to artistic conception.
>
> Antoine Watteau (1684–1743) painted with gracious finesse Italian masks and theatrical scenes. In his pictures he could reproduce charmingly the particularities of high society.
>
> Sir Joshua Reynolds (1728–1792), founder of the specifically English manner of painting, which is distinguished from others by depth of tone and lushness of colour.

Benjamin West (1738–1820), more splendid than Reynolds in conception, but less significant in colour. Most famous works: *Moses with the Rod of Iron*, *Paul on Melitta* (altar picture in the church at Greenwich Hospital) and several fighting pieces (*Death of General Wolfe*).

Heinrich Fuessli (by the English written Fuseli) lived 1741–1825. He unites noble drawing with a fantasy tending to extremes, which enjoys portraying the horrible.

Goethe ended this section as follows:

> . . . And so it may be hoped that artists return to a colouring which does not intend to affect violently by contrasts, but to intensify through pleasant charm on its part the grace of beautiful forms and tender shapes. They will soon also feel a need for harmonious juxtaposition of colours and will properly cultivate the study of this part of art.

Steiner added a footnote:

> Here lies at the same time a common artistic fundamental law, which Goethe wanted to have observed in all art. A work of art must make an effect not only through *outer truth*, which lies in faithful reproduction of the natural, but rather through a certain *inner truth*, which lies in all details being in truly harmonious agreement. The colouring in a work of art must not just give the colours of Nature. A certain necessity must at the same time be recognizable to the onlooker, as to why single colours are juxtaposed, why this one is more dominant, that one more subdued, etc.

Origin and growth of the London Academy

The sixth part in Goethe's history of the doctrine of colour was headed 'Eighteenth Century'. This part was divided into two 'epochs', the first being 'From Newton to Dollond'. Rudolf Steiner inserted a footnote:

> That is from 1670, the year when Newton first presented at Cambridge University his views on the doctrine of light, to the discovery of the achromatic telescope by Dollond. This period is one in which optics was totally dominated by the mathematic and mechanistic conceptions introduced into it by Newton.

Goethe's text opened:

> Hitherto members of several nations were concerned with the doctrine of colour: Italians, French, Germans and English. We must now turn our gaze principally onto this last nation, for an exclusive theory spreads out from England across the world.

Steiner added a footnote:

> The influence on physics of the Italians derives especially from Galilei and his student Toricelli, inventor of the barometer. On the 19th of June 1657 was founded in Florence the Accademia del Cimento (Academy of Experiment), which mainly had the purpose, by setting up experiments, of elaborating and confirming the great thoughts of Galilei and Toricelli. Its members were: Giovanni Alfonso Borelli, Vincenzo Viviani, Lorenzo Magallotti, Carlo Renaldini, Francesco Redi, Candido del Buono, Paolo del Buono, Alessandro Marsili, Antonio Oliva. What the French and the Germans achieved in physics we saw with Descartes and Nuguet, and respectively with Kepler, Athanasius Kircher, Markus Marci; the contribution of the English was supplied by Boyle and others. But with Newton and his time begins the exclusive influence of the English on the sciences and thus also of that tendency which treats science wholly without reference to a total conception of things, that tendency by which natural doctrine and religious need run beside each other without connection and which seeks no balance of the two. This very reason makes it possible that ecclesiastical orthodoxy could remain beside a wholly materialistic view of Nature.

★

Goethe's first section was headed 'London Society'. It read:

> If we want to visualize the state of the sciences in England during the second half of the seventeenth century, it is enough for our purposes to present with a fleeting pen the origin and growth of the London Academy. Sprat, Birch and the Philosophical Transactions give us here sufficient help. Afterwards we provide a sketch of the Society's history until the royal confirmation, and the outline of a history of the sciences in England, earlier times.

Steiner added a footnote:

> 'Royal confirmation': i.e. confirmation of the Academy's statutes by King Charles II in 1662.

★

The next section was headed 'Thomas Sprat. b. 1634, d. 1713.' Steiner provided an initial footnote:

> Thomas Sprat was born in Devon. He was a protégé of King James II and raised by the latter to various posts, finally to Bishop of Rochester.
>
> Goethe began:
>
> *History of the Royal Society of London*. The 1702 edition used by us seems not to be the first. The book was written for the moment, and certainly

printed at once. Already in 1669 a French translation too came out in Geneva.

Thomas Sprat, subsequently bishop, was early on a good chap, a talented, cheerful, passionate rake. As a young man with many hopes he had the fortune to attend the Society's earlier meetings in Oxford, thus learning of its origin and growth. When later a desire arose to bring something of the Society before the public, he was elected Speaker and provided with news and arguments, probably by Oldenburg, who held the post of Secretary . . .

Steiner added a footnote:

Oldenburg was the Society's second Secretary. He held this post together with Wilkens. The first Secretary was William Crown, the third Robert Hooke.

Goethe's text continued:

. . . So he wrote its history up to the royal confirmation and somewhat further, with much spirit, good temper and vigour.

Regarded as a writer, we find him more suited for courageously championing party affairs in brochures—as in a single little volume he sought with great vehemence to defend his fatherland against the intrusions of a French traveller, Desorbieres—than able to write a book which might be described as a deliberate work of art. Whoever makes such demands on him will judge him unreasonably, as has been done by Montucla (*Histoire des Mathématiques*. Paris 1758. Part IV. Liv. 8 p. 486. Note a.).

In any case, the first half of the book is more carefully written and methodically ordered than the second: for his work is unfortunately interrupted by the great double misfortune of the plague and the fire of London . . .

Steiner added a footnote:

In the year 1665 London was afflicted by a great plague, in 1666 by a fire.

Goethe's text went on:

. . . From then onwards the book seems to be written more off-the-cuff and really resembles a compilation. Yet he did great service for his time, as for posterity.

For he seeks to make clear and remove all the hindrances standing in the Society's way; and he certainly contributed to the enhancing of many an inclination and to the extinguishing of many a prejudice. Regarding what concerns ourselves, we come to know very well the course of the Society,

> its situation, its principles, its spirit and purpose. Its internal manner of behaviour, its relations to the outside, the idea the public had of its members, what was set up to oppose it, what it had to carry out for itself—all this lies in the work, in part expressed clearly and unadmiringly, in part indicated and concealed with rhetorical artistry . . .

The section on Sprat was followed by others on Thomas Birch and on the *Philosophical Transactions*.

★

Then came a section on 'The Society's Uncertain Beginning'. Goethe opened:

> The origin of important matters and products often goes back into an impenetrable mythological night. Beginnings are uncertain and unnoticed, and remain hidden to future researchers.
>
> Patriotic Englishmen would put the Society's origin early, from envy of certain Frenchmen, who were simultaneously meeting for such purposes in Paris. Patriotic Londoners will not award Oxford University the honour of becoming famous as the cradle of such a remarkable institute.
>
> Its earliest beginnings are therefore set around the year 1645 in London, where renowned friends of Nature were meeting once a week to discuss natural things. All questions of state and religion—of passionate concern to the country at the unfortunate time of the Civil War—were excluded. Boyle will recall these gatherings in his letters, under the name of the invisible or philosophical college.

Steiner added a footnote:

> In the year 1645 there came together in London a circle of scholars who formed the so-called invisible college. Until 1648 the college remained in that city.

Goethe continued:

> In the years 1648 and 49 there arose a similar circle at Oxford, either arranged or expanded by members of that first Society transferred there from London. Here too persons met in order through observation of eternally law-abiding Nature to be comforted about or upraised above the lawless motions of human beings.

Steiner added a footnote:

> In the year 1648 part of the members of the invisible college moved to Oxford. They reunited in Oxford and held their gatherings at the house of the apothecary Cross, where dwelled Robert Boyle. The latter now became a member and also induced his friend Robert Hooke to join.

Goethe went on:

> The universities of Oxford and Cambridge, as relatives of the Episcopal Church, had remained faithful to the King and thus suffered much from Cromwell and the republican party. After the King's execution in 1649 and the complete victory of the opposing party, the scholars who were gathered at both academies had every reason for staying quiet...

Steiner added a footnote:

> The reference is to King Charles I. Through fear of Cromwell's republican party the Society's members held their gatherings in secret, and precisely from this derives the name 'invisible college'.

Goethe's text continued:

> ... They held fast to innocent Nature, all the more earnestly banning from their gatherings all quarrels over political and religious matters; with their pure love for truth they harboured in complete quiet that aversion towards effusiveness, religious fantasy, resultant prophecy, and other monstrosities of the day.

Steiner added a footnote:

> The Society had indeed arisen in 1645 amid political confusions, and members had strictly set themselves the aim of keeping a distance from all political parties.

Goethe went on:

> So for ten years they lived alongside one another, at first coming together often, but later more seldom, each person faithfully telling the others about whatever especially interested him, what he had directly come across in his studies, without any resultant thought of an outer form or an inner order.
>
> In 1659 the largest part of members of this Oxonian society moved back to various posts in London. They still held to each other in traditionally intimate custom, meeting regularly every Thursday at Gresham College. It was not long before they were joined by many London scientists, among them several from the higher and lower nobility.

Steiner added a footnote:

> The nobles entering the Society were for the most part Tories and thus belonged to the Stuart party.

Goethe continued:

> Both classes of English nobility were richly blessed with temporal goods. The higher nobility possessed from long ago large properties and comforts, which it was always in process of increasing. The lower nobility was for a

long time obliged to economize and to improve its state of fortune, since two Kings, James and Charles, had encouraged it to dwell on its properties and to avoid life in town and court. Many among them were stimulated to scientific research and could join with honour the newly assembled scholars.

The growth and communications of this Society were disturbed only for a short time, since during the unrest arising after the abdication of Cromwell's son their place of assembly was changed into soldiers' quarters. Yet in 1660 they immediately came together again, and their number increased.

The 18th of November of that year marks the first session founding this great institution. About fifteen persons were present; they decided on the time of their meeting, entrance monies and weekly contributions, and elected a president, treasurer and secretary; twenty persons were proposed for admission. As men who had had enough opportunity to reflect about constitutions, they then soon ordered in an excellent and purposeful way other arrangements pertaining to outer form.

Scarcely had Charles II learnt that a meeting of such men as had always been attached to him had constituted itself into a Society than he offered them recognition, protection and every encouragement, and in 1662 confirmed all their statutes in the most honourable manner.

A Fleeting Overview

Goethe's next section was on 'Sciences in England'. It began:

> The King's involvement in natural sciences came just at the right time: for Bishop Sprat will give us a fleeting overview of how in part sciences as such and in part natural ones had previously been delayed.
>
> 'Till the union of the two houses of *York* and *Lancaster*, the whole force of our *Country* was ingag'd in Domestick Wars between the *King* and the *Nobility*, or in the furious contentions between the divided Families: unless sometimes some magnanimous *Prince* was able to turn their strength to forreign conquests. In King *Henry the Seventh*, the two *Roses* were joyn'd . . .'

Rudolf Steiner added a footnote:

> The union of both houses was accomplished by the accession of Henry VII in 1485. He banished Richard III, ended the war between the White and Red Roses and asserted himself against two pretenders to the crown.

Sprat's text went on:

> '. . . His Government was like his own temper, *close*, *severe*, *jealous*, *avaricious*, and withall *victorious*, and *prudent:* but how unprepar'd his time was for new discoveries, is evident by the slender account that he made of the proposition of *Columbus* . . .'

Steiner added a footnote:

> Columbus had turned in vain to Henry VII for support for his sea journeys.

Sprat's text continued:

> '... The Reign of King *Henry the Eighth* was *vigorous, haughty, magnificent, expensive, learned.* But then the alteration of *Religion* began, and that alone was then sufficient to possess the minds of men.'

Steiner added a footnote:

> Henry VIII at first set up as defender of the pope, but then had himself declared head of the English Church and treated most cruelly everyone who did not in that regard comply with him.

Sprat went on:

> 'The *Government* of King *Edward the Sixth* was contentious, by reason of the factions of those who manag'd his childhood: and the shortness of his life depriv'd us of the fruits that might have been expected from the prodigious beginnings of the *King* himself...'

Steiner added a footnote:

> Edward VI was the son of Henry VIII. He only reigned from 1547 to 1553.

Sprat's text continued:

> '... That of *Queen Mary* was *weak, melancholy, bloody* against the Protestants, obscured by a forreign Marriage, and unfortunate by the loss of *Calais*...'

Steiner added a footnote:

> Bloody Mary, daughter of Henry VIII, reigned 1553–1558. She executed the Duke of Northumberland, her opponent, as well as Jane Grey, who had been acclaimed counterqueen. Under her rule Catholicism was reintroduced and Protestants persecuted in the cruellest manner. In 1554 she married Philip II of Spain.

Sprat's text went on:

> '... That of *Queen Elizabeth* was *long, triumphant, peaceable* at home, and *glorious* abroad. Then it was shewn to what height the *English* may rise, when they are commanded by a *Prince* who knows how to govern their hearts, as well as hands...'

Steiner added a footnote:

> Elizabeth reigned from 1558 to 1603. She reintroduced Protestantism, ended the war with France in 1559, that with Spain in 1588 and thenceforth headed a government of peace.

Sprat continued:

> '... In her days the *Reformation* was setled, commerce was establish'd, and *Navigation* advanc'd. But though knowledge began abundantly to spring forth, yet it was not then seasonable for *Experiments* to receive a *publick incouragement:* while the writings of antiquity, and the controversies between us and the Church of *Rome* were not fully studied and dispatch'd.
>
> The *Reign* of *King James* was happy in all the benefits of *Peace*, and plentifully furnish'd with men of profound *Learning*...'

Steiner added a footnote:

> James I reigned 1603–1625.

Sprat's text went on:

> '... But in imitation of the *King*, they chiefly regarded the matters of *Religion*, and *Disputation:*...'

Steiner added a footnote:

> James favoured Episcopalians and persecuted Catholics.

Sprat's text continued:

> '... so that even my Lord *Bacon*, with all his authority in the State, could never raise any *Colledge of Salomon*, but in a *Romance*...'

Steiner added a footnote:

> 'College of Solomon': Bacon composed a book on the best form of state, which is a utopia; at its head were to stand the wisest in the country, the college of Solomon.

Sprat's text went on:

> '... That of *King Charles the First* began indeed to be ripe for such undertakings, by reason of the plenty and felicity of the first years of his *Government*, and the abilities of the *King* himself: who was not only an inimitable *Master*, in *reason* and *eloquence*, but excell'd in very many practical *Arts*, beyond the usual custome of *Kings*, nay even beyond the skill of the best *Artists* themselves...'

Steiner added a footnote:

> Charles I reigned 1625–1649.

Sprat's text continued:

> '... But he alas! was call'd away from the studies of *quiet*, and *peace*, to a more dangerous, and a more honourable reputation. The chief Triumphs that

> Heaven reserv'd for him, were to be gather'd from his suffering virtues, in them he was only exceeded, by his Divine Example of our *Saviour:* in imitation of whose Passion, those afflictions, and those thorns which the rude Souldiers design'd for his *disgrace*, and *torment*, became his *glory*, and his *Crown.*'

Steiner added a footnote:

> At Cromwell's instigation he was executed in 1649.

Sprat went on:

> 'The late times of *Civil War*, and *confusion*, to make recompense for their infinite calamities, brought this advantage with them, that they stirr'd up mens minds from *long ease*, and a *lazy rest*, and made them *active*, *industrious* and *inquisitive*... But now since the *Kings* return, the blindness of the former *Ages*, and the miseries of this last, are vanished away...'

Steiner added a footnote:

> Charles II, son of Charles I, who in 1660 was recalled through Parliament onto the English throne.

Sprat's text continued:

> '... now men are generally weary of the *Relicks* of *Antiquity*, and satiated with *Religious Disputes:* now not only the *eyes* of men, but their *hands* are open, and prepar'd to *labour:* Now there is a universal *desire*, and *appetite* after *knowledge*, after the peaceable, the fruitful, the nourishing *Knowledge:* and not after that of antient Sects, which only yielded hard indigestible *arguments*, or sharp *Contentions* instead of *Food*; which when the Minds of Men requir'd *Bread*, gave them only a *Stone*, and for a *Fish* a *Serpent.*'

Without Plan or Rule

Goethe's following section was on 'The Society's Outer Advantages':

> The involvement of the King was followed at once by that of princes and wealthy barons. Not only scholars and researchers, but also practitioners and technicians had to make efforts for such an institute. Commerce was widespread; becoming closer acquainted with its objects, bringing new products from foreign regions into circulation was advantageous for all the merchants. Travellers eager for knowledge were given long registers of questions; precisely those kind of things were sent to English residents in the most distant settlements.
>
> It was remarkable what henceforward soon came pressing in on all sides. Through the answering of those questions, through the submission of

instruments, books and other rarities the Society became every day wealthier and its influence more significant.

★

The next section was on 'The Society's Inner Deficiency'. Goethe began:

> For all these great outer advantages, there was also much opposing it. Fear of every kind of authority harmed it most. It could therefore attain no inner form, no purposeful treatment of what it possessed and what it had taken on.
>
> By reason of and through stimulus from Bacon the sense of the time had been directed onto the real and actual. This extraordinary man had the great merit of having fixed attention onto the whole expanse of natural science. For particular experiments he imposed a precise observing of conditions and an assessment of all accompanying circumstances. A view was opened into Nature's endlessness, and this by a nation which could most vigorously turn the view around both inwardly and outwardly. Very many persons found passionate enjoyment in such experiments, which repeated and assured their experiences and rendered them more manifold. Others by contrast were delighted in the immediate prospect of application and usage.
>
> But as work cannot easily be done in the scientific world without division, so here too a decisive split is found between theory and practice. Memory was still fresh of how retreating scholasticism had at once been replaced by a peculiar philosophy, by Cartesianism. Here again one saw an example of what a single excellent brain is able to produce on others, how it can form them according to its purpose. How far the Society was from allowing validity to the views of a single person was expressed under its coat of arms by the motto 'Nullius in Verba'; so that one would indeed be safe from everything general, from everything which a theory seemed if only from afar to indicate. An intention was definitely stated of observing phenomena as well as experiments in and for themselves, and of letting them stand singly, beside each other, without any artificial-looking connection.

Rudolf Steiner added a footnote:

> Turning away from the philosophy of Aristotle was for minds of that time unfortunately not enough. They mistook a certain theoretical and admittedly—in the form then prevalent in Europe—antiquated view for a theory of natural things in general. Added to which, however, Cartesianism was soon fostered at English universities in an equally spiritless and formalistic way as Aristotelianism had been before. The consequence of this was that members of the Royal Society fostered nothing but accumulation of endless experimental material, and did not concern themselves with guiding principles.

Goethe continued:

> Such clever people did not perceive the impossibility of carrying out this intention. They did not notice that questions very soon arose about causes, that the King himself in donating natural bodies to the Society enquired into the 'how' of effects. They could not avoid giving some account, as good and bad as it went. Partial hypotheses now arose, with the mechanical and machine-like way of conceiving gaining the upper hand; and it was still believed that when one had stated a conclusion one stated the object, the phenomenon.

Steiner added a footnote:

> The principle 'nullius in verba' was indeed very soon misunderstood in that ideas were taken as *verba* and with *verbis* ideas too disappeared. So all basis of thought for an edifice of Nature was lost, and only the world of sensory perception retained. Since this was held to be the only definite and certain one, perceptible processes in the sense-world were soon traced back to others, no longer perceptible but imagined completely on the analogy of sensorially perceptible ones. Thus arose the mechanistic theories.

Goethe went on:

> But while members declared themselves fearful of and averse to every theoretical treatment, they retained great trust in mathematics, whose methodical certainty in treating bodily things seemed to give it some reality even in the eyes of the greatest doubters. They could not deny its pre-eminent usefulness, especially when applied to technical problems. So they respectfully allowed its validity, not imagining that while trying to guard themselves against ideals they had admitted and retained what was most ideal of all.

Steiner added a footnote:

> This passage is a proof of the deep understanding Goethe had for mathematics. He recognized its value for determining the quantitative relations of the universe. But he also knew that within the quantitative there works a qualitative, not measurable and not weighable. He also knew that the mathematical itself is something completely ideal, and that the ideality of the universe is proven just because the results of mathematics, which are gained—without help from experience—purely ideally, may be applied to the real.

Goethe continued:

> Just as what method actually may be was almost entirely hidden to the Fellows' eyes, so too did they have an assured aversion towards a method for experiment. The Society's conversation in its earliest times had always been fortuitous. Each person brought forward studies of concern to some, or

novelties of interest to others, without being asked and as he pleased. Thus they abode by the anyway very formally drawn up constitution. Everyone communicates what just happens to be ready. Phenomena from the doctrine of Nature, bodies from natural history, operations of technology are all demonstrated in a muddled confusion. Many matters of unimportance, others of interest through a wonderful semblance, and still other merely curious ones find place and admission. Indeed experiments are even related whose closer circumstances are kept secret. One sees a Society of earnest and worthy men undertaking raids in all directions through the field of natural science, and because they recognize its immeasurability, roaming around inside it without plan or rule. Their sessions are often quodlibets, about which one cannot refrain from smiling, indeed even from laughing.

Steiner added a footnote:

This lack of rule and system in research has become in a bad sense exemplary for all recent natural science. Indeed today it has already been transferred onto spiritual sciences as well (science of language, history, history of literature). Everywhere one sees how scholars throw themselves onto some particular domain of science, and there gather as much material as they can with their respective means select. No one thinks of structuring the experiential material and of working in relation according to certain viewpoints.

Goethe went on:

The Society's fear of any rational treatment was so great that no one dared bring into the business even an empirical division and order. They could only separate different classes of objects from each other—physics, natural history and technology—and within these make the most necessary subdivisions. They then came to an arrangement that within each session only one subject should be worked upon. This was of great help to the matter.

Already a hundred years before, Porta had presented physical phenomena in categories. This book could be conveniently taken as a basis, ancient marvels little by little examined and erased, what had been discovered in the interim appended, and what arose every time in the Society then registered on the spot from the protocols. At least the greatest confusion was thus avoided and it was certain that nothing had been hidden or lost, as happened e.g. with Mayow's experiments. The Society had notice of them, but neglected them; naturally it did not learn further details because it did not admit Mayow, who was suggested for membership by Hooke.

In his New Atlantis Bacon had erected for the scientifically researching Solomonic college an immense romantic palace with many wings and pavilions, in which was also found many an extremely fantastic room. These indications could not of course afford much benefit to a Society arising in

> real life; but at the end of that novel he had expressed firmly enough a need to divide the different functions of such an undertaking among several persons, or if one will, to regard these functions as separate from one another, yet always progressing in equal value beside each other.

Steiner added a footnote:

> Bacon's *Nova Atlantis* is a writing which depicts in a utopian way the future form of human society, where Nature will be completely conquered by man, and the human mind alone will prevail. All natural laws will be discovered; man will know all working methods. All forces will therefore also be subject to him and at his service. How he imagines scientific business within this future state is shown in the text.

Goethe quoted:

> '*For the several* Employments *and* Offices *of our* Fellows, *we have Twelve that Saile into* Foreign Countries, *under the* Names *of other* Nations, (for our own we conceale,) *Who bring us the* Books, *and* Abstracts, *and* Patterns *of* Experiments *of all other* Parts. *These we call* Merchants *of* Light.
>
> *We have Three that collect the* Experiments *which are in all* Books. *These we call* Depredators.
>
> *We have Three that* Collect *the* Experiments *of all* Mechanical Arts; *And also of* Liberal Sciences; *And also of practices which are not brought into* Arts. *These we call* Mystery-men.
>
> *We have three that try new experiments, Such as themselves think good.* These *we call* Pioneers *or* Miners.
>
> *We have* Three *that draw the* Experiments *of the* Former Four *into* Titles *and* Tables, *to give the better light for the drawing of* Observations *and* Axiomes *out of them. These we call* Compilers.
>
> *We have three that bend themselves, looking into the* Experiments *of their* Fellows, *and cast about how to draw out of them* Things *of* Use, *and* Practice *for* Man's life, *and* Knowledge, *as well for* Works *as for* Plain Demonstration *of* Causes, Means *of* Natural Divinations, *and the easy and clear* Discovery *of the* Vertues *and* Parts *of* Bodies. *These we call* Dowry-men *or* Benefactors.
>
> *Then after divers* Meetings *and* Consults *of our whole number, to consider of the former* Labours *and* Collections, *we have three that take care, out of them, to direct New Experiments, of a* Higher Light, *more* Penetrating *into* Nature *then the* Former. *These we call* Lamps.
>
> *We have* Three *others that do execute the* Experiments, *so* Directed, *and* Report *them. These we call* Inoculators.
>
> *Lastly, we have three that raise the former* Discoveries *by* Experiments *into* Greater Observations, Axiomes, *and* Aphorismes. *These we call Interpreters of* Nature.'

> Of this happy division and arrangement there is no trace in the Society's procedure, and the same also goes for its slowly accumulating possessions. As the Society had declared every friend of Nature, without difference of rank and position, to be capable of joining, so too was it just as well known that the Society wanted to accept and preserve for itself everything relating even to some extent to Nature. In the general participation which it aroused, there arrived a great influx, as is accustomed to happen with all empirical accumulations and collections. The King, the nobility, scholars, economists, travellers, merchants, craftsmen, all pressed forward with gifts and curiosities. But here too there seems to have been a shyness about any order; at least one sees in the earlier time no institution for arranging its stores, making catalogues about them and thus indicating completeness if only from afar. Should one want to excuse the Society through the limitation and uncertainty of its venue, we allow only in part the validity of this objection; for with a true spirit of order these hindrances could probably have been overcome.
>
> Any one-sided maxim, even if it is found suitable for certain purposes, will be shown at others to be inadequate, indeed harmful. Sprat may praise and defend with however much eloquence the Society's intention not to theorize, not to methodize, not to order...

Steiner added a footnote referring to the passage in the previous section on Sprat about his *History of the Royal Society*.

Goethe continued:

> ...Behind his many arguments one believes one discovers only his bad conscience. Just by following the course of the Society's business in the protocols of some years, one sees that it quite certainly notices little by little the deficiencies arising from its maxim, and makes arrangements to counter them, but unfortunately inadequate ones.
>
> Experiments should not be presented off the cuff, but announced in the preceding session; tests are ordered in certain sequences. Committees are set up, which—be it said in passing—may be good in political and practical cases, but are of no use at all in scientific matters. Like or dislike, preconceived opinion in the commissioners are in the latter instances not so easy to control as in the former. Demands are further made for expert witnesses, overall views; but since nothing hangs together, one of them is forgotten for another. What had been put forward seldom happens, and if it does happen, it is for the most part insufficient or inadequate. And according to what standard should it be measured? By whom should it be judged?
>
> Perhaps it is also the fault of the initial monthly change of President. So too the uncertainty and inadequacy of the venue, the lack of a laboratory and other hindrances arising therefrom can also be brought forward in excuse.

There followed a section on 'Deficiencies Lying in the Surroundings and in the Time', and then in precisely this regard a further section on Robert Hooke.

All the Skill of his Mind

Then came the section headed 'Isaac Newton. b. 1642, d. 1727'. Goethe began:

> Among those working on natural sciences, two kinds of human beings may principally be observed.
>
> The first, genial, productive and forceful, bring forth from themselves a world, without much asking whether it will agree with the real one. If what develops within them succeeds in coinciding with the ideas of the cosmic spirit, truths will then be known before which men are astonished, and for which they have reason to be thankful for centuries. But should there arise in a capable, genial nature of this kind a delusion which finds no counter-picture in the common world, such a mistake can spread around no less forcibly, carrying human beings away and cheating them for centuries.
>
> Those of the second kind, ingenious, astute, wary, show themselves to be good observers, careful experimenters, cautious gatherers of experiences. But the truths they promote, like the mistakes they make, are small. Their truths are often set unnoticed beside what is recognized as correct, or get lost. Their errors are not accepted, or even if they are, they easily fade away.

Rudolf Steiner added a footnote:

> Goethe characterizes here those two categories of human beings who always stand opposite each other in the evolution of spiritual life, influencing it in an opposite way and giving it a quite different stamp according to whether the one or the other becomes dominant. Truth, knowledge, cannot be sought in the world of things, but must be produced in the mind. Men of the first kind are called on to fulfil the task here described. They go into the depths. They bring new truths to light. The second kind systematizes and schematizes. Its accomplishments are not new truths, or at most subordinate ones, lying on the surface of things. Such men go into the widths. Where the first are dominant, knowledge is really brought forward; new spiritual forms are placed into cultural life. Where the second are dominant, facts are worked over, registered and combined. Endless material is heaped up, its spiritual unity forgotten. Human beings of the first kind can make tremendous mistakes; they have nothing in directly tangible experience by which to assess their claims. Those of the second kind, naturally, are much less subject to error. They only note what they see and hear. All the busier are they in historically

> processing what has once been discovered. But their spiritual fruitlessness prevents them from making criticism. It suffices them to have something by which to show off their contentually deficient, merely formal scholarliness. Woe betide anyone who touches what has been historically handed down to them. It is they who always get in the way when someone arises to oppose an old mistake by a new conception.

Goethe continued:

> Newton belongs to the first of these classes, the better of his opponents to the second. He makes an error, and in a most decisive way. First he finds his theory plausible; then he hastily convinces himself, before he can become clear what arduous concepts would be needed to carry through by experience the application of his hypothetical *aperçu*. But he has already expressed it publicly, and now does not fail to muster all the skill of his mind to assert his thesis; thus maintaining with incredible boldness a complete absurdity as a proven truth—in the face of the world.
>
> In the more recent history of sciences we have a similar case in Tycho de Brahe. He too made a mistake, by setting into his world-system the derived as the original, the subordinate as the dominant. He also came out too fast with this untenable fad. In their confidential letters his friends and con-

Newton in 1689, aged 46

temporary admirers write about it quite irreverently, stating clearly that Tycho, had he not already published and for a length of time asserted his system, would probably accept the Copernican one and thus do science a great service; henceforward it is on the contrary to be feared that he will often pull and bend the sky according to his teaching.

Already Tycho's contemporaries and co-workers freed themselves from his fearsomely confusing opinion. But Newton imparted to his pupils his conviction, as also his obstinacy, and anyone acquainted with party spirit will not be surprised that they no longer have eyes and ears, but continually repeat the old creed as the master had taught it to them.

The character, abilities, behaviour and destinies of his opponents can only be presented one at a time. In part they did not grasp what the issue was; in part they perceived the mistake, but had neither strength nor fortune nor opportunity to destroy it.

We find Newton in 1666 studying at Cambridge, occupied with improving the telescope and with prismatic experiments to that end, setting down for himself his theory of colour. We have three works of his on the subject, from which we can oversee his manner of thought and follow the way he took.

There followed a section on the *Lectiones Opticae*:

After becoming a Master in 1667, and in 1669 Professor of Mathematics in place of Barrow, he holds lectures in this year and in the two following ones as a studious young man. In the lectures he tries by mathematical treatment to bring the physicality of colour phenomena as much as possible towards what is expected from him in his post. Afterwards he elaborates this work ever further, but leaves it aside, so that it is only printed after his death in 1729.

Steiner added a footnote:

'Mathematical treatment of colour phenomena'. There is something captivating about mathematical treatment of natural apparitions. Mathematical truths are gained by the human mind in an almost completely mechanical way. Methods press forward with irreversible force in the lines of argument. With every new step the mind does not need to apply anew its original power. But the more the mind is obliged to do out of its own initiative in bringing about one of its products, the greater does doubt in its work become. Thus the temptation for scientists to resolve the whole world into an event governed by mathematical laws. We then only have to find a *basic formula* from which everything arises with mathematical necessity, without the mind repeatedly needing to engage anew, thus also repeatedly being able to make new mistakes.

Goethe continued with a section on Newton's 'Letter to the Secretary of the London Society':

> In the year 1671 he becomes a member of the London Society, presenting to it his new katoptric telescope and at the same time his theory of colour, from which can be concluded that dioptric telescopes cannot be bettered.
>
> This letter actually concerns us here, because in it Newton relates at length the course he had taken in becoming convinced of his theory. It would anyway also be sufficient to give us a complete conception of the Newtonian doctrine.
>
> Linked to this letter are also the first objections to the Newtonian doctrine, which along with the author's replies continue until 1676.

An Eternal Back-to-front

There followed a section on the *Opticks,* beginning:

> After that year Newton enters into no further controversy, but writes the *Opticks*—coming out in 1705—since his authority had risen to the highest degree and he had been nominated President of the Society. In this work

Newton in 1702, aged 59

> the experiments and tests are presented in such a way as is meant to defy all objections.

Over several pages Goethe then presented in detail the six previously known conditions of the prismatic experiment which Newton attempted to eliminate. He then continued:

> Since Newton believes he has fully removed these six external conditions, he proceeds directly to the conclusion not only that colour is innate to light, but that colours in their specific states are contained in light as original illuminations, which were just manifested through refraction and other outer conditions, produced out of light and thenceforward presented in their primal originality and immutability.
>
> Through the *Experimentum Crucis* he attempts to convince himself and others that in these illuminations, developed and invented in such a way, no further change takes place. In thirteen propositions he thereupon brings forward his doctrine with all its clauses and provisos, just as it afterwards remained at its total standstill. Having first developed colours out of white light, he finally sees himself obliged to put white light together again out of them.
>
> He believes he accomplishes this by means of the lens, which he introduces without further preparation, and considers himself entirely satisfied if he can pass off a coloured image kept in focus as being reassembled, reunited and mixed.

Rudolf Steiner added a footnote:

> Through the *Experimentum Crucis* the different colours are supposed in the sense of the Newtonian doctrine to be reunited into white light. The coloured light-space is concentrated through a convergent lens onto a small circle, which appears white. In the sense of the Goethean view there has not here taken place a union of different illuminations, but rather the conditions producing light in other spatial areas are removed from the place where the white circle appears; therefore light has here its original clarity.

Goethe continued his account of Newton:

> Then the conclusion he draws from all of this is that it would be useless to bother with improving the dioptric telescope, and people must rather keep just to the katoptric one, for which he has thought out a new arrangement.
>
> These first confessions and claims by Newton were brought to the Royal Society in that letter we reported, and became publicly known through the *Transactions*. They are the first item in Newton's doctrine to appear in public, and for us are in various ways remarkable, especially too because his opponents' first objections are chiefly directed against this letter.
>
> Now we have seen that his principal mistake consisted in having too fast

and overhastily eliminated and denied those questions chiefly concerned with whether outer conditions affect the appearance of colour; he did this without looking more exactly at the closer circumstances. We were therefore obliged and able in some points fully to contradict him, in others partly, and yet again in others not at all; and we sought to make clear what points, and how far they are tenable or not. If one of his first opponents mistakenly strives against the tenable points, he must lose the controversy, and there arises a good prejudice regarding the whole. If an opponent strives against the untenable points, but not strongly enough and in an improper way, he must again lose, and falsity obtains the sanction of truth.

Already in this letter, as in all the replies he addresses to his first opponents, one finds that manner of treating his object which we show in polemics, and which he reproduced in his pupils. It is a continuous placing and lifting, an unconditional stating and momentary limiting, so that everything and at the same time nothing is true.

This manner, which is actually just dialectic and appropriate to a sophist who wanted to make best use of people, is found again in Newton, as far as I am aware, for the first time since the scholastic age. His predecessors from the revival of sciences onwards, if often limited, were yet always faithfully dogmatic; if inadequate, yet eloquently didactic. By contrast, Newton's

Newton c. 1706, aged about 63

exposition consists of an eternal back-to-front, of the craziest transpositions, repetitions and envelopments, of dogmatized and didacticized contradictions, which one tries in vain to grasp. Finally however one learns them by heart and thus believes oneself to have really obtained something.

Steiner added a footnote:

All explanatory methods must fall into this mistake if they do not go along a path in conformity to Nature through laying at their basis a simple, irreducible phenomenon, in order by adding ever new conditions to step forward towards what has been assembled; not by making interpretations around a finished and assembled phenomenon, in order cleverly to think up the reasons why it arises. One does not explain the world by interpreting its phenomena, but only by reproducing its working methods in thoughtful observation of what happens, or repeating the same in an experiment.

Goethe concluded:

And do we not notice in life, in many other cases, that if we vigorously grasp a false *aperçu*, be it our own or a foreign one, it can little by little become a fixed idea, and finally degenerate into a totally partial madness? This is chiefly manifested when one not only holds passionately fast to everything which favours such a conceptional method, and eliminates without further ado everything gently contradicting it, but also interprets what is strikingly opposed in its favour.

Scientific Superficiality

Then came a section on 'Newton's relation to the Society'. Goethe began:

Newton's merits, already as a young man providing him with an important teaching position, were indeed highly regarded. He was formed in stillness and lived mostly with himself and his mind: a type of existence which he also continued into later times. He had a very good relation to several members of the Royal Society who were about the same age as him, but especially with Oldenburg.

Oldenburg, born in Bremen, and consul of Bremen in London during the Long Parliament, left his public post and became a tutor to young nobles. While staying in Oxford he became acquainted with and a friend of the most outstanding men, and when the Academy was formed, Secretary of the same, or actually of its external affairs, when internal ones were entrusted to Hooke.

As a man of the world and a businessman, his activity and love of order was fully developed. He had very extensive contacts, corresponding with attentiveness and continuity. Through clever, consequential striving he was foremost in promoting the Royal Society's influence and reputation, especially abroad.

Hardly had the Society come into existence when Newton was admitted into it, in his thirtieth year. How he introduced his theory into a circle where all theories were decisively abhorred is for a historical researcher certainly worth investigating.

A thinker's own property consists of thoughts arising from himself. As each *aperçu* belonging to us spreads a particular well-being into our nature, so too the wish is quite natural that others recognize it as ours, since only thereby do we seem to become something. Arguments over a discovery's priority therefore become so vigorous. Considered really precisely, these are arguments about existence itself.

Already in earlier times everyone felt the importance of this point. Sciences could not be fostered without communicating with more people, and yet these more people were seldom great enough to recognize what they had received as having been received. They took the credit to themselves, and there are found quite many arguments over such pre-occupations. Galilei, to protect himself, put down his discoveries for his friends in dated anagrams, thus assuring himself the honour of ownership.

As soon as academies and societies were formed, they became the actual courts of law which had to accept and protect such things. A person reported his invention; it was taken up into protocol, preserved in the acts, and one's claims could thereby be validated. Later on, there arose from this in England the patent decrees, whereby an inventor was assured not only of his mental worth by science, but also of his economic value by the state.

In the Royal Society Newton actually brings forward for discussion only his newly invented katoptric telescope. He sets it before the Society and asks for his rights in it to be guarded. His theory he only brings by the way and in the sense that he wants thereby to establish even more his telescopic invention, because through the theory the impossibility of improving dioptric telescopes is to be set beyond all doubt.

This at once endangers the Society's false maxim of concerning itself with nothing theoretical. The Newtonian submission is received with good will and attentiveness, though no closer examination is undertaken. Hooke however immediately opposes it, claiming that one is just as well off, indeed better off, with his doctrine of vibrations. He also promises to bring forward new phenomena and other important things. It does not however occur to him to develop Newton's experiments. The manifestations put forward he also lets pass as facts, by which Newton quietly gains a great deal, though Hooke finally practises malice and carefully brings about the first reflecting telescope after a previous suggestion by Gregory, in order somewhat to minimize the value of the Newtonian invention.

Rudolf Steiner added a footnote:

> Here probably lies the reason for the historical importance which Newton's view has gained. The Society was only interested in the telescope. A desire for knowledge—itself necessary for investigating the theory of colours—was lacking. The theory was adopted because it originated from a man who had constructed a good instrument. The reason for adoption of Newton's colour theory was scientific superficiality; no further person then had the courage energetically to contest the matter.

Goethe continued:

> Boyle, working along in the Society in his quiet tender manner and in the monthly changes of President certainly once taking the chair, seems not to take the slightest notice of the Newtonian doctrine of colour.
>
> This is how things look inside the Royal Society, while now foreigners too, by that letter of Newton's instructed in his theory and stimulated thereby, have various objections both against the experiments and against the opinion. It is highly necessary to examine also the detail of this, because the opponents' rights and wrongs rest on very tender points. For many years the latter have no longer been considered, but rather everything taken lock, stock and barrel only in favour of the Newtonian doctrine.

A Favourable Prejudice

There followed a section on 'Newton's First Opponents, to whom he Replied Himself'. Goethe began:

> If we want to form a proper conception of past things, we must consider the time when something happened, and not for instance set our own, when we experience the matter, in its place. Natural though this requirement appears, imagining circumstances which accompanied distant actions remains more difficult than is usually thought. Fair judgement about individual credit and discredit is therefore so rare. Results of entire mass movements are spoken about more easily.
>
> We have already mentioned the bad condition of physical instruments generally in the second half of the seventeenth century, as well as the inadequacy of the Newtonian arrangements. He was using a considered, chosen, fixed apparatus; therefore in the *Opticks* with almost every test he must begin at the start laboriously to describe his arrangements. What lies just accidentally to hand is at once made use of and applied; his tests are thus full of needless subsidiary conditions which only confuse the chief interest. Sufficient proofs for this claim are found in the polemical part, and if Newton proceeded like that, how may it have looked with others!

Rudolf Steiner added a footnote:

> Here Goethe criticizes in Newton the circumstance that he did not especially construct his instruments for the purpose of solving the problem he was investigating, but rather approached the matter with accidental apparatus, which was thus not arranged precisely in order to bring clarity into this particular matter.

Goethe continued:

> If we turn from technical matters to interior and spiritual ones, we are met by the following observations. When on regeneration of the sciences people looked around for experiences and tried to repeat them through tests, the latter were being used for quite different purposes.
>
> The finest purpose was and always remains that of knowing in its whole totality a natural phenomenon presenting us with different sides...

Steiner added a footnote:

> Herewith is meant that we resolve the natural phenomenon presenting us with different sides into these very sides. We repeat the phenomenon artificially, either just through observation, by turning our perception of one side towards the other, in order thus also in our mind to assemble into a totality what appears as such in Nature immediately, or artificially, by setting up such conditions in an experiment that the phenomenon is revealed to us only from one side. When we have then come to know all sides of the phenomenon following after one another, what appears to us in Nature readily assembled we can ourselves assemble artificially. Compared with this sole generally applicable procedure, the above-mentioned one of Descartes, like that of Boyle and Grimaldi, appears one-sided.

This last reference was to the continuation of Goethe's text:

> ... Gilbert brought in this way the doctrine of the magnet far enough, just as people went consequentially to work in order to come to know the elasticity of the air and others of its physical qualities. Various natural scientists by contrast did not work in that spirit; they sought to explain phenomena from the most general theories, as Descartes applied the little globes of his matter, and Boyle his bodily facets, to explain colours. Others again wanted to confirm a general principle through phenomena, as Grimaldi through innumerable tests only ever indicated that light probably wanted to be a substance.
>
> Newton's procedure by contrast was quite peculiar, indeed unheard-of. To bring to light a deeply hidden attribute of Nature he makes use of not more than three tests, which presented in no way primal phenomena, but rather highly derivatory ones. His whole manoeuvre against the first opponents consists in recommending exclusively these three tests lying at the basis of his letter to the Society, that with the spectrum through the

simple prism, that with two prisms—*Experimentum Crucis*—and that with the lens, and in dismissing everything else.

Steiner added a footnote:

The unmethodical nature of Newton's kind of procedure has already been set out on p. 299, 7–24 note.

The reference was to the last footnote in the section on the *Opticks*, 'All explanatory methods must fall into this mistake . . .'

Goethe went on:

We note here that that letter to the Society summarized above was actually the first document through which the world came to know Newton's doctrine. Since his *Lectiones Opticae* and his *Opticks* henceforth lie before us, and the matter has been a thousand times spoken through and fought over, we can form no concept of how abrupt and abstruse the Newtonian kind of perception must have appeared in the scientific world.

Nor can scholars find their way into the matter. Nobody in practice wants to take it into their mind that the dioptric telescopes, to which so much is owed and on which so much trouble has been spent, should be completely rejected. In theory people hang onto general kinds of perception which they oppose to Newton; or they make particular objections. They can either not cope with his tests, or they suggest others, of which the fewest lead towards the aim, or to any decision.

We now briefly set out in extracts what has come down to us of Newton's controversy with his first opponents, in so far as it can be significant, letting everything pass which would only confuse the view and make necessary a much more extensive treatise . . .

Over several pages Goethe then examined in detail Newton's controversies with his first opponents. He ended:

We have translated the important passage with which this controversy terminates. Newton does not again appear polemical, except in so far as the *Opticks* is of polemical nature. But his pupils and successors continually repeat these words of their master. They first fix what is favourable to the doctrine *sub-* and *obrepticie*, and then proceed exclusively against Nature, sense and human understanding. It pleases first single people and then the crowd. Newton's other great services arouse a favourable prejudice towards his theory of colour. His reputation, his influence rises ever higher; he becomes President of the Society. He publishes his artificially assembled *Opticks*; through Clarke's Latin translation this latter too is spread into the world and gradually introduced into schools. Experimenting technicians go over to his side and so this narrowly conceived and in itself rigid doctrine becomes a kind of Ark of the Lord, the touch of which brings immediate death.

Newton in 1710, aged 67

So too does Desaguiliers, partly during Newton's life, partly after his death, proceed against everything venturing to contest the doctrine; as will henceforth be further elaborated by the historical presentation in which we further continue.

Copying Newtonian Experiments

After a section on 'Edme (Peter) Mariotte', there then came a section headed 'Jean Théophile Desaguiliers. Born 1683'.

Goethe began:

> Philosophers of antiquity, who were more interested in human beings than in the rest of Nature, observed the latter only in passing and theorized only occasionally about her. Experiences increased, observations became more exact and theory more penetrating; yet they did not come to repeat their experience, to experiment.

Rudolf Steiner added a footnote:

> Here one may think about the schools of the Stoics and Epicureans, to whom moral perfection was the only matter coming into account; they

practised theoretical sciences only in so far as a happy or virtuous life is thereby promoted.

Goethe continued:

> In the sixteenth century, after a fresh regeneration of the sciences, the important workings of Nature still appeared under the form of magic; they were surrounded by much superstition, into which they had sunk at the time of barbarism. In the seventeenth century people wanted if not to be astonished yet still to wonder, and arranged experiments became lost in strange affectations.

Steiner added a footnote:

> Basically there still lies here the tendency to practise sciences for the sake of the importance they have in perfecting moral life. Only slowly do they liberate themselves from such views, and the pure urge towards knowledge, for its own sake, becomes visible.

Goethe went on:

> And yet the matter had become ever more serious. Anyone thinking about Nature also wanted to behold her. Every thinker made henceforth experiments, but also still in passing. Towards the end of this time ever more men appeared who occupied themselves with particular parts of natural science, chiefly seeking to establish these by experiments.
>
> Through this lively connection of experimenting and theorizing arose now those persons who were called, especially in England, natural and experimental philosophers, just as there was also an experimental philosophy. Everyone treating objects of Nature not straight from hand to mouth like for instance a cook, everyone just somewhat consequentially attentive to phenomena had already a certain right to that honourable name, which of course might in that sense be attributed to many. Every general reasoning, deep or shallow, tender or crude, connected or disjointed, brought forward about natural objects was called philosophy. Without knowing this misuse of the word, it would remain inconceivable how the London Society had been able to choose the title *Philosophical Transactions* for the most unphilosophical of all collections.
>
> The chief deficiency of such inadequate treatment thus always remained that the theoretical views of so many single persons prevailed, and what was supposed to be seen did not appear to everyone similar. How Boyle, Hooke and Newton behaved is known to us.
>
> Through the endeavours of such men, but especially of the London Society, interest meanwhile became ever more general. The public too now wanted to see and to be instructed. Tests had to be presented again at any time on any demand, and one now found that experimenting had to become a profession.

> It first became such through Hawksbee . . .

Steiner added a footnote:

> Francis Hawksbee was Curator of Experiments in the Royal Society.

Goethe's text continued:

> . . . He made public tests of electricity, hydrostatics and pneumatics, and kept himself perhaps most clear from everything theoretical . . .

Steiner added a footnote:

> Hawksbee died already in 1705.

Goethe's text went on:

> . . . Keill became his pupil and successor. But the latter already declared himself for Newton's theory. Had he treated the doctrine of colour as Hawksbee the doctrine of electricity, everything would have taken on a different look. He worked in Oxford until 1710.
>
> Keill was followed by Desaguiliers, who had inherited from him, his master, a skill in copying Newtonian experiments according to the recipe, as well as an inclination towards this theory. His artistic skill was called upon when people wanted to examine tests, or prove something through the tests.

Steiner added a footnote:

> Jean Théophile Desaguiliers was born at La Rochelle and died in 1744 in London. He was at first a clergyman in his fatherland; but the repeal of the Edict of Nantes forced him to go to England. He became Professor of Physics at Oxford University. His physical lectures were brought out in London in 1734 under the title *A Course of Experimental Philosophy*. He was productive in the most various domains of physics.

Goethe continued:

> Desaguiliers became famous through his skill in experimenting. S'Gravesande says of him: 'cujus peritia in instituendis experimentis nota est.'

Steiner added a footnote:

> Storm van s'Gravesande (1688–1742), Prof. of Mathematics at Leyden.

Goethe's discussion of Desaguiliers ended:

> . . . He had adequate mathematical knowledge, as well as sufficient insight into what was then called natural philosophy.

There followed further sections on 'Desaguiliers against Mariotte', 'Giovanni Rizzetti', 'Desaguiliers against Rizzetti' and 'Gauger'.

One-sided Mathematical Development

The last section in this fourth volume of the scientific writings was entitled 'Newton's Personality'. Goethe opened:

> The purpose of what we intend under this heading to state is actually that of laying aside for a time that role of adversary and opponent which we have so long held and must also in future hold, so as to be as fair as possible, to investigate how such strange contradictions hang together in him and thus to compensate for our now and then as it were hefty polemics against him. It will perhaps be admitted that many a scientific riddle can only be grasped through an ethical solution, and we wish to try out whatever we may in the present case accomplish.

Steiner added a footnote:

> These words arise from Goethe's view, emphasized ever and ever again, that a man's conceptions want to be grasped out of his whole personality, out of the individuality of his being.

Goethe continued:

> Something has already been mentioned under Roger Bacon and Bacon of Verulam about the English nation and its circumstances, and Sprat's cursory essay also gives us a compressed historical picture. Without here going into the matter further, we just observe that what is particularly important and estimable about the English is the formation of so many tough and competent individuals, each according to their kind, and also contrary to the public or common being: an asset which perhaps no other nation shares, at any rate not to the same extent.
>
> The time into which Newton was born is one of the most pregnant of English, indeed of world history. He was four years old when Charles I was executed, and experienced the accession of George I. Tremendous conflicts were stirring Church and State, each for itself and both against each other, in the most manifold and alternating way. A king was executed. Opposing national and military parties stormed against one another; changes of government, changes of ministries and parliaments came packed in sequence. A restored royalty upborne in splendour was yet again shaken; a king expelled, the throne taken into possession by a stranger, and yet again not bequeathed, but transferred to a stranger.
>
> In such a time must not everyone have felt stimulated and challenged? But what a unique man must that be who is entitled by birth and abilities to a number of claims, and who rejects everything and calmly follows his researching vocation implanted by Nature!
>
> Newton was a well-organized, healthy, well-tempered man, without passion or desires. His spirit was of a constructive nature, and in the most

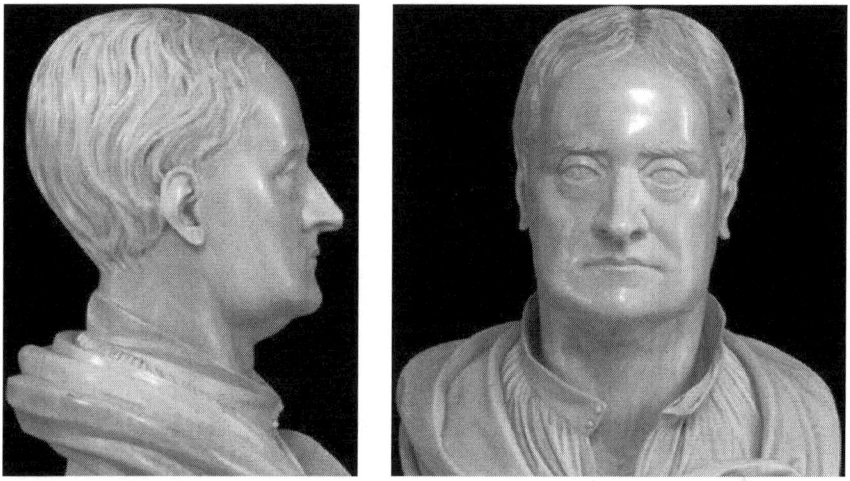

Bust of Isaac Newton in 1718, aged 75

> abstract sense. Higher mathematics was therefore given to him as the actual organ through which he sought to erect his inner world and to deal with the outer one. We make no judgement about this his chief merit, and readily admit that his actual talent lies outside our circle of vision. But we can state from our own conviction that he easily grasped what his forebears had achieved and brought it amazingly further. Average minds of his time honoured and revered him; the best recognized him as their equal, or even fell into contest with him over important inventions and discoveries. So with the rest of the world we should certainly proclaim him, without further evidence, to be an extraordinary man.

Steiner added a footnote:

> The development of our mind on the side of mathematical sciences is of great advantage, if balanced by a corresponding cultivation of spiritual sciences. Mathematics is a formative symbolic science. Whoever wanted to pursue it in such a way as only to analyse given experiential material would be unable to bring this to anything for that science. No one can prove through experience a mathematical theorem, or find in experience a mathematical fact. Through mathematics one may learn how science in truth relates to experience; by its method one may appreciate what is productive, formative and inventive in true knowledge. Minds with some mathematical cultivation will never be able to regard a merely analysing, unfruitful science as justified. One-sided mathematical development produces an underestimation of the individual and the ideal in the operation of the world.

Goethe's discussion of Newton went on:

> On the practical and experiential side, by contrast, he already comes closer to us. Here he enters into a world with which we too are acquainted, where we can judge his way of procedure and his success. We may do this all the more as it is an absolutely uncontested truth that however purely and surely mathematics in itself may be treated, with every step on the ground of experience it immediately goes tripping around. It can lead towards error just as well as any other maxim put into practice, indeed can make the error enormous and prepare itself for future embarrassments.

Steiner added a footnote:

> Mathematical judgements, like all others, are results of certain premises which must be accepted. Only if these premises are applied to experience in the right way must the latter also correspond to the conclusions. But the reverse may not be concluded. A fact of experience can agree quite well with mathematical conclusions one has formed, and yet other premises can exist in reality than are made by mathematical research into Nature. If e.g. the light phenomena of interference and diffraction agree with conclusions of the theory of undulation, the latter does not yet therefore need to be right at all. It is actually a quite false premise that a hypothesis must be right if facts of experience can be explained by it. The same effects may also derive from different causes, and justification of assumed premises needs to be proved *directly*, not indirectly through confirmation by means of results.

Goethe continued:

> We have laboriously set out above how Newton arrived at his doctrine, how he rushed into its first test. He then erects consequentially his theory, indeed seeks to validate as fact his way of explanation. He removes everything damaging and ignores it when he cannot deny it. Actually he does not enter into controversy, but is always repeating to his opponents: 'Grasp the matter like me; go on my paths; arrange everything how I arranged it. See like me, conclude like me, and then you will find what I found. Everything else is bad. What point is there in a hundred experiments when two or three establish my theory best?'
>
> The doctrine's whole success is actually due to this way of treatment, to this inflexible character. As the word 'character' has been expressed, may place be granted here to some compelling observations.
>
> Every being which feels itself to be a unity wants to maintain itself in its own condition undivided and unshaken. This is an eternal, necessary gift of Nature. So one can say that every single being has character, down to a worm which writhes when trodden on. In this sense we may ascribe character to the weak, indeed even to a coward; for he gives up what other human beings esteem above all, but which does not belong to his nature—honour, glory—just to retain his personality. Yet the word 'character' is normally used in a

higher sense: namely when a person of significant qualities adheres to his method and does not allow anything to turn him away from it.

A character is called strong when it powerfully opposes all outer hindrances and seeks to carry through its peculiarity, even with the danger of losing its personality. A character is called great when its strength is also joined to great unending qualities, faculties not to be overlooked; through it there appear wholly original, unexpected intentions, plans and deeds.

Now even though everyone well perceives that actually here exuberance, as in general, makes for greatness, one must yet not go wrong by for instance believing that one is talking about a moral person. The main foundation of morality is good will, which according to its nature can only be directed towards what is right; the main foundation of character is decisive willing, without regard for right and wrong, good and bad, truth and error. It is what every party esteems so highly in its own adherents. Will belongs to freedom, relates to the inner man, to an aim; will belongs to Nature and relates to the outer world, to a deed; and because earthly willing can only ever be limited, it may almost be presupposed that in practice higher rights can never or only by chance be willed.

Not nearly enough epithets, in our opinion, have been sought after for expressing dissimilarity of characters. As a trial, we want to use—in the manner of a simile—differences occurring in the physical doctrine of cohesion; so there would be strong, firm, thick, elastic, pliable, malleable, flexible, rigid, tenacious, fluid, and goodness knows what other characters. Newton's character we would count among the rigid ones, just as his theory of colours may be regarded as a fixed *aperçu*.

Newton in 1726, aged 83

Steiner added a footnote:

> By 'character' Goethe understands here the way a man lives out in the world the totality of his being, how he brings to manifestation what is fermenting and cooking inside him. A man of marked peculiarity does not ask, when intending to accomplish something, how it relates to the continued existence of already available knowledge; he rather wants a particular something because he is interested in it, because he follows an impulse inside him which strives to create existence for the willed object. Regarding this interest the question of true and false, right and wrong, good and bad does not at first arise. All true content-filled progress in the world's evolution reposes upon this being so. If with respect to original willing one were always to ask how what is already available stands towards it, the future could never bring anything truly new compared to the past, but always only consequences, results of the already existent. This applies equally to scientific as to technical and moral development.

Goethe went on:

> Regarding our present concern, we are actually touching only on the relation of character to truth and error. Character remains the same, whether devoted to the one or to the other. So it does not diminish in the slightest the great admiration we harbour for Newton if we state that as a human being, as an observer, he fell into error and as a man of character, as a rare mind, activated his insistence most strongly just by firmly declaring this mistake to its very end, despite all outer and inner warnings. Indeed he increasingly laboured upon it and attempted to disseminate it, to reinforce it and protect it from all attacks.

A Principal Ethical Problem

Goethe then continued:

> And here now occurs a principal ethical problem, one however which does not remain insoluble for anyone daring to look into the abysses of human nature. In the ferocity of polemics we have even accused Newton of some dishonesty; we are currently speaking again about disregarded inner warnings. How were this to be conjoined with the otherwise recognized morality of such a man?

Rudolf Steiner added a footnote:

> The dishonesty of which Goethe accuses Newton is one not to be measured at all by a moral standard. The term 'dishonest' is used to indicate a kind of scientific behaviour, without a feeling of moral censure being joined

> thereto. An expression is drawn from ethics without retaining the admixture of feeling it has within the latter.

Goethe went on:

> A human being is subject to error, and as he errs in a sequence, as he does so continuously, he becomes at once false to himself and to others; this error may consist in opinions or in inclinations. It becomes clearer to us from inclinations, because someone will not easily be found who has not undergone this experience in himself. By devoting more love, more respect to a person than they deserve, one must become at once false to oneself and to others; one is obliged to regard noticeable deficiencies as merits, and to validate them as such in oneself as in others.
>
> Reason and conscience do not by contrast allow their rights to be taken. One can lie to them, but not deceive them. Indeed we are not doing too much by saying that the more moral, the more reasonable a man is, the more lying he becomes as soon as he errs, the more enormous must the error become, as soon as he adheres to it; and the weaker the reason, the duller the conscience, the more is error proper to man, because he is not warned. Erring becomes merely regrettable, indeed it can appear endearing.

Steiner added a footnote:

> The more reasonable a human being is, the more means he has of defending a mistake, the more weighty and dangerous become his items of evidence, which give to the mistake a deceitful appearance of truth.

Goethe continued:

> But it is worrying to see when a strong character, in order to remain loyal to himself, becomes disloyal towards the world, and in order to be inwardly true, explains what is real to be a lie and thus shows himself quite indifferent if he be held to be hard-necked, obstinate, stubborn or laughable. Nonetheless, character always remains character, whether it wills and eagerly labours for the right or the wrong, the true or the false.
>
> With this, however, the whole riddle is not yet solved; something still more mysterious lies behind. For there can be found in man a higher consciousness, so that he gains a certain overview of the nature necessarily inhabiting him, in which through all freedom he can change nothing. To become wholly clear about this is almost impossible. Chiding oneself in particular moments will certainly do, but censuring oneself continually is given to nobody. Unless one has recourse to the common method of blaming one's defects onto circumstances or other human beings, there rises at last from the conflict of a reasonably judging consciousness with the admittedly modifiable but yet unchangeable nature a kind of irony in and with ourselves, so that we playfully treat our mistakes and errors like

naughty children, which perhaps would not be so dear to us if they were not afflicted with just such bad habits.

This irony, this awareness with which one watches one's defects, jests with one's errors and gives them so much the more space and course, because one believes or hopes that one can finally master them, can be found in manifold subjects by stages from the clearest madness to the dullest suspicion, and we would certainly venture to set up such a gallery of characters according to living and departed models, if it were not all too insidious. Were the matter then fully explained through examples, no one would hold it against us if he also found Newton in the series, who certainly felt a dim suspicion of his error.

Steiner added a footnote:

> The highest stage of development which man can attain is to judge his own activity, his being, his whole personality just as objectively as all the rest of the world. Such a man will censure the badness in his person, and laugh at what is risible, with complete objectivity, as he will recognize the good. Admittedly only few men can attain this proper self-assessment.

Goethe went on:

> For how might it be possible to one of the foremost mathematicians to use such lack of method that already in the optical lectures, by wanting to establish diverse refrangibility, he brings right at the end the experiment with parallel means, which belongs at the very start, because colour appearance first develops there? How could one who was concerned to acquaint his pupils with a phenomenon in its whole extent, so as to build thereon a tenable theory, also treat the subjective phenomena only towards the end and not at all in a certain parallelism with the objective ones? How could he declare them to be awkward—as they are without any question the easier—had he not wanted to evade Nature and establish before her his preconceived opinion? Nature expresses nothing which would be hard to herself; so much the worse when she becomes awkward to a theoretician.

Steiner added a footnote:

> This sentence expresses Goethe's conviction that Nature always strives towards her purposes on *straight* and *short* paths.

Goethe continued:

> After all this, since ethical problems can be solved in manifold ways, we wish to bring forward the supposition that perhaps Newton found so much pleasure in his theory because at every experiential step it presented him with new difficulties. One mathematician says himself: 'C'est la coutume des Géomètres de s'élever de difficultés en difficultés, et même de s'en former sans cesse de nouvelles, pour avoir le plaisir de les surmonter.'

But if in this way too one wanted to hold the excellent man not enough excused, let a glance be cast at the science of his times, at the philosophizing about Nature, as had become usual in part from Descartes, in part through other outstanding men, and from these circumstances one will sooner be able to realize Newton's own mental condition.

Steiner added a footnote:

From this side the mistake was made of wanting to explain Nature through arbitrary or symbolic representational formulae. Newton wanted to counter such bustle through experience and experiment. But instead of explaining a fact through facts, more complex phenomena through simpler ones, he sought to deal with manifestations by speculating about them.

Goethe ended:

In this and still many other ways we wish to make an adequate apology to the *Manes* of Newton, in so far as we might have offended it. Every error springing directly from a human being and the conditions surrounding him is forgivable, often venerable; but all successors in error cannot be treated so cheaply. A truth repeated already loses its grace; an untruth repeated appears fatuous and risible. Freeing oneself from one's own error is hard, for a great

Death mask of Isacc Newton, 1727

> mind and great talents often impossible; but anyone who takes up a foreign error and obstinately adheres to it demonstrates little ability indeed. The stubbornness of an original but erroneous person can incense us; the obstinacy of error-copyists makes us morose and annoyed. If in the battle against the Newtonian doctrine we have sometimes stepped beyond the boundaries of composure, we put all the blame onto the school whose incompetence and conceit, laziness and self-sufficiency, wrath and craving to persecute stand absolutely in proportion and balance with one another.

Steiner added a footnote:

> In the first representative of an error there comes into account precisely the enthusiasm for the matter which has awoken in the foundations of his soul. This enthusiasm restricts objectivity. A man has firstly a need to live himself out; a successor does not have this reason for retaining an error. In him, ease steps into its place; one who has become used to regarding a definite manifestational domain under a certain angle of vision finds it hard to rethink his views about it. Only interest in the truth can overcome this tendency. Human beings who occupy themselves with matters of science without a powerful urge towards truth are therefore the worst enemies of all new achievements.

Deserving of Note

The fifth volume continued the history of the doctrine of colour by opening with a section on 'Newton's First Pupils and Confessors':

Goethe began:

> Besides the previously mentioned experimentors Keill and Desaguiliers, the following men are to us deserving of note:
>
> Samuel Clarke, b. 1675, d. 1735, contributes most among all to disseminating the Newtonian doctrine. Destined to a clerical position, he shows in youth great talent for mathematics and physics, penetrates before others into the Newtonian views and becomes convinced by them.

Rudolf Steiner added a footnote:

> Samuel Clarke was one of the most famous English theologians of his time and furthermore an important mathematician, physicist and philosopher.

Goethe continued:

> He translates into Latin Rohault's physics, written according to Cartesian principles and used in schools. In his notes the translator presents the Newtonian doctrine, of which is then said, by occasion of colours: 'Experientia compertum est' etc. The first edition is from 1697. In this way

the Newtonian doctrine, alongside that of Descartes, was introduced into teaching and little by little drove the latter out.

Steiner added a footnote:

This translation was intended to set Newton's optics by a ruse into the place of the Cartesian. The notes in their totality brought an outline of Newtonian doctrine so coloured that a student was to be won over not to the Cartesian text but rather to the notes written according to Newtonian physics, which contradicted the text.

Goethe went on:

And yet the greatest service Clarke showed to Newton was the translation of his *Opticks* into Latin, which came out in 1706. Newton had himself revised it, and Englishmen state it to be more comprehensible than the original itself. But we cannot in any way accept this. The original is very clear, written with naive seriousness; the translation often has to make circumlocutions and phrases for the sake of Latin linguistic usage. But these very phrases perhaps sounded best in the ears of gentlemen who did not wish to think further about it.

The two men, incidentally, had a moral and indeed religious connection to each other, in being both inclined towards Arianism: a moderate doctrine, pleasing to many reasonable people of that time and preparing for the Deism of the following time.

Wilhelm Molyneux, one of the first Newtonian confessors . . .

Steiner added a footnote:

William Molyneux, b. in Dublin 17th of April 1656, died 1698, lived as a private person in Dublin and founded there an academy after the model of the Royal Society.

Goethe continued:

. . . He published a *Dioptrica nova*, London 1692, where he says on the fourth page: 'But the same Mr. Newton in his Dissertations concerning Colours and Light, publish'd in the *Philosophical Transactions*, has at large demonstrated, that the Rays of Light are not all Homogeneous, or of the same sort, but of different Forms and Figures, so that some are more refracted than others, tho they have the same or equal Inclinations on the Glass.'

No one will here fail to notice that, despite all faith in his lord and master, the doctrine is already quite on the way to becoming altered and distorted.

Steiner added a footnote:

A distortion of Newton's teaching took place in so far as symbols he made use of—rays, figures, etc.—were ever more interpreted in the sense of a grossly materialistic conception.

Goethe went on:

> Regnault: *Entretiens physiques* Tom. 2. Entret. 23. p. 395 ff. and Entret. 22. p. 379 ff. briefly presents the Newtonian doctrine.

Steiner added a footnote:

> Noel Regnault (1683–1762) was a Jesuit and Professor at the Collège Louis le Grand in Paris.

Goethe continued:

> Maclaurin: *Expositions des découvertes philosophiques de Mr. Newton.*

Steiner added a footnote:

> Colin Maclaurin (1698–1746) was a professor at Edinburgh University.

Goethe went on:

> Pemberton, *A view of Sir Isaac Newton's philosophy*, London 1728.

Steiner added a footnote:

> Henry Pemberton (1694–1771) was a doctor and Professor of Medicine at Gresham College in London. Newton also commissioned P. to supervise the publishing of the 3rd edition of his *Principia philosophiae naturalia.*

Goethe continued:

> William Whiston: *Praelectiones mathematicae.*
> Dunch: *Philosophia mathematica Newtoniana.*

Steiner added a footnote:

> William Whiston (1667–1752), clergyman, held at first various clerical posts and in 1703, when Newton resigned his professorship, became his successor. In the year 1710 he lost this post as a result of a work written against the doctrine of the Trinity. When in 1720 he was to be admitted into the Royal Society, Newton was opposed to it.

Goethe concluded:

> How far they were concerned with the doctrine of colour, and presented it more or less according to the letter, we do not here intend to investigate; it suffices for them to belong among those named in history as Newton's first supporters and confessors.
>
> Of foreign supporters we name first s'Gravesand and Muschenbroek.

Further sections followed on these two Dutch scholars.

What All Human Beings Desire

Then came a section on French Academicians and a further one on Mariotte. This was followed by sections on de la Hire, Conradi, Malebranche, Fontenelle, de Mairan and Polignac.

After that came a section headed 'Voltaire b. 1694, d. 1778'. It began:

> At the best time of this extraordinary man there had arisen the highest need to bring what was divine and human, heavenly and earthly before the public at large, especially before good society, to entertain, instruct, stimulate and upset it. Feelings, deeds, the present, the past, the near and the distant, phenomena of the ethical and of the physical world: all had to be drawn upon. Everything, even the inexhaustible, had to be superficially tasted.
>
> Voltaire's great talent for communicating himself in any way and in every form made him for a certain time his nation's absolute spiritual lord. What he offered to it had to be accepted. No opposition was of any use; he knew how to push his adversaries with every artistic power aside, and what he could not force onto the public, he could flatter it into acquiring through custom.
>
> As a refugee he found in England the best reception and every kind of support. On returning from there he made it his duty to spread even further the Newtonian gospel, which had anyway gained general favour, and in particular to inculcate the doctrine of colour . . .

The next section was headed 'Examples of Voltaire's Prejudices for Newton'. It began by quoting from a 'Letter to Monsieur Thiriot on the 7th of August 1738':

> 'Whoever accuses Signor Algarotti of an assertive tone has not read him. Rather could one accuse him of not having asserted enough, I mean of not having said enough things and of having spoken too much. Besides, if the book is translated on merit, it must make a fortune.'
>
> 'As for what concerns my book (*Elémens de la philosophie de Newton*), it is until now the first one in Europe to have called *parvulos ad regnum coelorum*. For *regnum coelorum* is Newton; the French are in general sufficiently *parvuli* . . .'

A further section on Algarotti was followed by one on 'Anglomania'. Here Goethe stated:

> The English are perhaps suited before other nations to impose foreigners. Their personal calmness, sureness, activity, obstinacy and affluence give an almost unattainable model of what all human beings desire. Without here going into generality, we only observe that complaint about Anglomania appears in French literature from the earliest times to the most recent. This enthusiasm of the French nation for the English is in particular most vividly

> expressed straight after concluding a peace. It may well arise through restored communication between both countries, because the wealth and comforts of the English must then shine out very desirably for the at least in earlier times monetarily poor and modest French.
>
> This preference for a foreign people and neglect of one's own can probably not be taken higher than we find above with Voltaire, who makes the Newtonian doctrine into the *regnum coelorum* and the French into the *parvulis*. But he certainly would not have done so, had prejudice in his nation not already been common. For all his boldness, he guards against putting something forward which he knows the general mood is against. And we despise him for expressing his deism everywhere and so decisively, merely to cleanse himself from the contempt of atheism: a manner of thought which at any time must befit only few people and be abhorrent to the remainder.

Steiner added a footnote:

> Voltaire also brought from England the shallow Lockean doctrine, out of which were developed in France materialism and shallow enlightenment.

★

The second 'epoch' in the part on the eighteenth century, 'From Dollond to Our Time', included *inter alia* sections on Joseph Priestley, Robert Waring Darwin—father of Charles Darwin—Edward Hussey Delaval and finally Robert Blair.

Fine Art

At the end came the autobiographical 'Author's Confession'. Goethe began:

> When we take part in any happening, nothing can be more welcome to us than that persons who have been involved may reveal to us the special circumstances by which this or that event had its origin. This applies to political as much as to scientific history; in both of which nothing may be regarded as so small that it might not once be important to some successor. So after having followed the course of life of many other persons, I did not want to omit also a portrayal of how I came to these physical and especially chromatic investigations. This may be all the more awaited because such an occupation has appeared to many as foreign to the rest of the course of my life.
>
> The crowd may well ascribe to someone a talent in which he has proved active and by which luck has not shown itself averse to him. But if he wants to transfer to another subject and duplicate his arts, it seems as though he

injures the rights he once acquired for himself from public opinion, and therefore his endeavours in a new region are seldom received with friendliness and pleasure.

Here the crowd can probably be right to some extent. For every single beginning has so many difficulties that it would need a whole man, indeed several together to attain to a desired end. Against this one must only consider that activities, in a higher sense, are not to be looked at as isolated, but rather come to help each other in turn; and a human being has often to step into an alliance, as with others so too with himself, and thus share in several abilities and practice several virtues.

How I fared in this as a whole could only be told by an elaborate narrative; so may the present one be considered as a single chapter of that greater confession which I will still perhaps have time and courage to set down.

Rudolf Steiner added a footnote:

This greater confession did not come to pass.

Goethe continued:

On the first appearance of my poetical endeavours, my contemporaries showed themselves friendly enough towards me, and if at the same time finding fault with much, at least ascribed to me with favour a poetic talent. I had myself my own wonderful relation to the art of poetry, which was just practical. I would carry and foster so long in my inner mind an object which took hold of me, a model which aroused me, a predecessor who attracted me, until something had arisen from it which wanted to be considered mine. After having developed it in stillness for years, I would finally fix it onto paper in one go, as it were off the cuff and to some extent instinctively. From this may be derived the vigour and effect of my productions.

However, both in regard to conception of a worthy object as to composition and development of individual parts, as well as what affected the technique of rhythmical and poetical style, nothing usable came towards me, either from academic chairs or from books. I knew various falsities to be detestable, but did not know how to recognize what was right and therefore even fell again into false tracks. I sought outside the art of poetry for a place upon which I could reach some comparison, and overview and assess from a certain distance what was confusing me nearby.

In order to attain this end, I could turn nowhere better than to fine art . . .

Steiner added a footnote:

The highest principles of art could only become an object of contemplation for German science when the impulse for it was given through our classic writers, especially through Goethe and Schiller. What the latter themselves found available in aesthetic science was scarcely more than some incidental empirical rules. German aesthetics was founded by the philosopher Baumgarten, whose presentations are however wholly entangled in abstract stereotyped concepts of Wolffian philosophy. Kant's *Kritik der Urteilskraft* (1790) first created general aesthetic principles. On it Schiller built his profound expositions in the *Briefe über ästhetische Erziehung des Menschengeschlechts*. Schelling and Hegel first penetrated from a philosophical standpoint into the being of art and of creative fantasy. In this respect philosophers were stimulated by the views of classic writers about art. In the eighties, when Goethe's reflection on the essence of coloration in painting was seeking for a certain direction, he could experience no support from aesthetic science. The laws disclosing the kinship of the arts were only discovered later by advanced philosophy. In seeking this kinship Goethe, and philosophers after him, related chiefly to fine art, because in it can be studied the one moment of a work of art, the outer, sensorially perceptible appearance; this is not possible e.g. in poetry, which moves in inner conceptual life.

Something Satisfying

Goethe's text continued:

> . . . I had several reasons for doing this, having so often heard about the kinship of the arts, which were also beginning to be treated in a certain combination. In lonely hours of an earlier time, I had become attentive to Nature as shown in landscape, and going from childhood onwards in and out of painters' studios, had made attempts to change into a picture, as good as it would go, what appeared to me in reality. Indeed I felt a much greater drive towards this, for which I actually had no aptitude, than towards what was for me easy and convenient by nature. So certain is it that false tendencies often inflame a man with greater passion than true ones; he strives much more eagerly after what he must fail in than after what might succeed.
>
> The less my natural aptitude was for fine art, the more did I look around for laws and rules. Indeed I paid much more heed to technicalities in painting than to technicalities in the art of poetry, as one tries to fill out through understanding and insight the gaps which Nature has left in us.
>
> The more I now as it were increased in insight through viewing works of art—in so far as they came before my eyes in north Germany—through conversation with the knowledgeable and with travellers, and through reading such works as promised to raise up to spiritual vision a long and pedantically buried antiquity, the more did I feel the lack of foundation to my knowledge, and perceived ever more that only from a journey to Italy might something satisfying be hoped.
>
> Having at last, after much hestitation, crossed over the Alps, I quite soon

felt, with the onrush of so many endless objects, that I had not come in order to fill out gaps and enrich myself, but had to start discarding entirely everything to which I had hitherto been accustomed, and seeking for what was true in its simplest elements. Fortunately I could hold fast to some maxims brought over from poetry, proven to me through inner feeling and long use. So through unbroken viewing of Nature and art, through vividly effective speech with more or less understanding cognoscenti, through continual life with more or less practical or thinking artists, it was indeed hard but not impossible for me little by little to divide art for myself without mutilating it, and to become aware of its different livingly interlocking elements.

Becoming aware of and holding fast to its thousand applications and ramifications had admittedly to be left to a future time in life. It also fared with me as with every person who in travelling or living acts with seriousness, that only at the moment of departure did I feel myself to some extent worthy of entering. I was comforted by the manifold and undeveloped treasures I had gathered; I rejoiced in the way by which I saw that poetry and fine art could mutually affect each other. Many things were plain to me in detail, many clear in their whole relationship. On one point I could not render myself the least account: it was colouring.

Rudolf Steiner added a footnote:

This is because the Newtonian theory of colour can never provide a basis for an 'aesthetics of colours'. Newton regards colours as something material, which arises purely according to mechanical and physical laws attached to matter. The non-material (ideal) references of colours do not here come into account. Newton's natural laws on colour appearances are erected as though such ideal references did not exist. On the basis of these natural laws Goethe could thus gain nothing which was suitable for giving information about how single colours relate to one another, and what their connection is to light and dark within the fine arts. He was first looking for a physical and physiological explanation of the aesthetic effect of colours.

Over several further pages Goethe indeed related how he had originally grown up with Newton's theory, but on coming later to examine it experimentally found it quite inadequate. In consequence he was led to develop his own ideas about light and colour.

Very Great Difficulties

In Chapter XXIII of his autobiography Rudolf Steiner recorded:

Once during the nineties, I spoke in Frankfurt-on-Main about Goethe's view of Nature. In the introduction I said I wanted to speak only about

Goethe's views of life; for his ideas about light and colour were such that no possibility existed in the physics of the present to build a bridge to these ideas.—But in this impossibility I myself was obliged to see a most significant symptom for the spiritual trend of the time.

The Frankfurt lecture was held on 27 August 1893. On the next day, Steiner wrote to Anna Eunicke:

Frankfurt,
On Goethe's birthday 1893

My dear Anna,

Yesterday I'd like to have written you a word. But I was together with the Foundation man the whole day long. The festivity matters went really well. Today I'm going in the morning into Goethe's house and in the afternoon would like to see something else of Frankfurt, which till this moment wasn't yet possible. It would be beautiful, my good Anna, if you could be here too. I would most like to take you along everywhere.

See you again tomorrow,

Yours,

Rudolf

★

A week later, Steiner wrote again to Joseph Kürschner:

Weimar, 4th of September 1893

Highly esteemed Herr Professor,

At last I am in a position to send you the manuscript. You will see from the same that editing precisely this chapter of Goethe's scientific writings was accompanied by very great difficulties. The matter made rather longer notes absolutely necessary; but these indeed we have had at other places of the scientific writings as well. I now only have to supply you with a few small appendices and the introduction to the two half-volumes, which will make no further difficulties and which you will quite certainly be receiving this week. You can certainly count upon it that I shall not be further delaying the printing. And now about your question concerning the proof-reading of the Goethe volumes and of the index. Both of these I am very willing to take on. I can definitely promise you that I shall carry out the matter fast. I have already made arrangements to do so and can begin with the work at once. I only request you to have a copy of the edition sent to me very soon, and to kindly let me know of particular wishes you have in the matter.

At the same time I permit myself to answer the question about the quarto lexicon. I have made notes about appendices. They must now be examined.

I shall send them to you as soon as possible. In the next few days I shall also be sending you the biographical notes you desire from me.

Hoping for an early reply,

Your most gratefully devoted

Rudolf Steiner

This further manuscript contained Goethe's work on *Entoptische Farben*, and then presented various *Paralipomena zur Chromatik*.

Appeal to Posterity

The *Paralipomena* included Goethe's 'Older Introduction', which began:

> The author of a sketch of the doctrine of colour has often been asked why he does not reply to his opponents, who with such great vigour deny any credit to his efforts, decrying his account as inadequate, his way of conceiving as inadmissible, his assertions as untenable and his reasons as unconvincing. His answer to particular friends was that he had always had little faith in any controversy. Thus he also never prefaced his earlier works, because behind a preface is usually concealed disagreement with the reader...

Steiner added a footnote:

> But nonetheless the 1810 *Doctrine of Colour* does have a preface. Cf. Vol. 3 of the *Naturwissenschaftlichen Schriften* p. 77 f.

Goethe continued:

> ...All the public and secret attacks on his doings and endeavours he also opposed by nothing except continuous activity; he decided to maintain this only by avoiding all argument, which usually diverts both author and public from the main point. I have never, he said, had opponents, but many adversaries.

Steiner added a footnote:

> *Opponents* in the above sense are only those who prove *factually* the contradictions in another's arguments, his faults and mistakes; *adversaries*, those who damn another's arguments, because they do not agree with their own. Adversaries condemn without examining. They only put forward in opposition the doctrine they had once received. Goethe had no such doctrine established beforehand. He first sought in Newton a solution to the riddle of colour. Only when not finding it here did he endeavour to find his own basis for a doctrine of colour. He was an *opponent*, not an *adversary* of Newton. The physicists of his time were merely his adversaries. Cf. Vol. 2 of the scientific writings p. 32, ll. 20–27.

The reference was to this passage in Goethe's article 'Significant Help from a Single Stimulating Word':

> Adversaries do not come into account; for my existence is hated by them, they reject the purposes towards which my doings are directed, and the relevant means they regard as just so much false endeavour. I therefore dismiss and ignore them, for they cannot help me, and that is what everything in life depends upon. But from friends I let myself be just as willingly conditioned as referred into infinity; I always attend to them with pure trust, for true edification.

The 'Older Introduction' continued:

> An author who appears with something unusual has the right to appeal to posterity, because a tribunal must first be built before which the unfamiliar can be judged. Such a court of law can only be established by a time which removes the foreigness from the peculiarity and sets it before us as something known. When comparing reviews of our day on the subject of aesthetics with those of thirty years ago, even if not always agreeing, one will yet be astonished at how high the judgement of Germans has risen, since they have been able to exercise it for so long on the productions of native writers. For no one judges what is foreign before understanding his own home.
>
> All this may equally be applied to scientific things. Many years ago the author brought out the little treatise on metamorphosis of plants...

Steiner added a footnote:

> *The Metamorphosis of Plants* appeared in 1890 (1st part) and 1891 (2nd part).

Goethe's text went on:

> ...People did not really know what to make of it. Botanists received it, if not unfriendlily, yet coldly. What it stated was let pass as at the most an ingenious notion, and the author was recognized to have some astuteness...

Steiner added a footnote referring to the article 'Destiny of the Printed Writing' as reproduced in the first volume.

Goethe's text continued:

> ...He quietly continued his observations, extending them over higher organisms, treated the transformation of insects—which no one denies—and worked energetically at comparative osteology. When hesitating to report something of this publicly, he was pleased to see that the same ideas were also developed in the public by natural mental progress...

Steiner added a footnote:

On the way in which views about the spinal nature of the skull permeated the public, cf. p. 322, 9–15 of the 1st volume of the scientific writings. Comparative anatomy forms an important part of natural science of the 19th century.

Goethe's text continued:

> ...The same concepts separated out and the same convictions formed, though under pressure from the dominant way of conceiving...

Steiner added a footnote:

> Pressure from the *dominant way of conceiving* refers to the manner of perception of Oken and his philosophical colleagues who, Goethe was convinced, distorted the truth through their fantastic hyperspeculative way of conceiving.

Goethe's text went on:

> ...No researcher any longer denies normal and abnormal changes of organic beings. Natural history thus receives new enlightenment, medical treatment a rational course. Admittedly here too can be noted several misconceptions and much hastiness, but from which science, progressing in purity, will soon recover. People rightly criticize that the word 'metamorphosis', whose meaning no one twenty years ago wished to know anything about, has already become an empty phrase. But they may always be satisfied that through this concept having been proposed and taken up so much good and healthiness has come to clarity.
>
> So must it also be with the doctrine of colour. Perhaps it will still take twenty years for a tribunal to be erected before which the matter can be ventilated and decided with proper insight. But in this subject no purely experiential doctrine can be set up without clearing away the impure, hypothetical, false Newtonian doctrine, or rather its remnants...

Within the City of God and Nature

Then came Goethe's 'Recent Introduction', which began:

> After this completed entoptic work, which we were occupied for several years in composing, and after fresh proof that every new discovery unites with our doctrine of colour in a friendly way, links into the whole and needs no particular theoretical explanation, we find it advisable also here to present and entwine into that unity various single things previously assembled. We therefore repeat the main point of our whole intention, because most of what has till now been publicly stated about colour shows

in the clearest way that people either do not know my endeavours or ignore them, do not understand them or do not desire to.

So it will not be too far-fetched if we say that our oldest ancestors, in looking at Nature, were content with the phenomenon. They certainly strove to know it, but without thinking of experiments to repeat it and make evident its generality. They contemplated Nature, visiting craftsmen and manufacturers, being instructed without becoming enlightened. People acted like this for a very long time. For how childish still was the type of experiment of, as it were, boiling iron filings in an iron pot through a magnet held underneath!

Rudolf Steiner added a footnote referring to the section on 'System of Science' in his introduction to the second volume, in the part on 'Knowledge and Action in the Light of Goethe's Way of Thinking'.

Goethe's text continued:

We do not want to tarry in the intermediate time, and only recall how in the 15th and 16th century the most endless mass of single experiences was pressing in upon the human being. Porta assembled knowledge and skills for many years throughout the whole world, and Gilbert showed with regard to the magnet that even a single phenomenon might be contained in itself.

Steiner added a footnote referring to the section on Porta in the *Geschichte der Farbenlehre*, and then stating:

Gilbert (1540–1603), since 1573 doctor in London and personal physician to Queen Elizabeth. At first he divided strictly between electrical and magnetic phenomena. In his work *De magnete, magneticisque corporibus et de magno magnete tellure Physiologia nova*, Londoni 1600, he even sought to establish distinctions between magnetic and electrical appearances. Thus too he first brought the magnetic effects of the Earth into a particular formula, by introducing the notion: the Earth is itself a great magnet.

Goethe went on:

At the same period of time Bacon pointed most vigorously towards experience, and stimulated a desire to pursue innumerable details which could not be overviewed . . .

Steiner added a footnote which again referred to the section on Bacon in the *Geschichte der Farbenlehre*.

Goethe's text continued:

. . . People observed ever more and more, making trials, tests, repetitions. They thought things over and considered them. So knowledge appeared of which there had previously been no concept. This however was not meant to pass by; what had once been discovered was rather to be held onto and

> repeatedly presented. So already in the second half of the 17th century effort was expended on somewhat improved instruments, and persons were found making a kind of trade from handling them. That was all good and praiseworthy; but the wish to theorize, against which Bacon had so violently expressed himself, cannot and ought not forsake a human being. So great is the might of thought, whether it be true or false, that it carries experience away with it; therefore even intensified and intricate machines must be of service to theory, and serve to confirm and establish the true as well as the false. Nowhere was this reversed process sadder than in the doctrine of colour. Here a quite false doctrine, founded on a false experiment, was made inaccessible through new and more intricate trials which were always concealing untruth and ever increasing the confusion. The doctrine became murkily veiled to pure common sense.
>
> I came into natural science as a volunteer, without prospect and intention of a university chair. Anyone sitting in such a chair must always be prepared to lecture just as much on what he does not know as on what he does know, for the sake of dear completeness. I by contrast was able to think of another completeness, returning along the Baconian path and assembling all the phenomena, as far as I could be aware of them. This is impossible for a thinking mind without a certain order, without placing them beside, above and among each other.

Steiner added a footnote once more referring to the section on 'System of Science' in his introduction to the second volume.

Goethe went on:

> How I acted in the doctrine of colour lies open to the gaze of anyone who wants to examine it. I would not know even now how to change the specialist work I have loved. Even now it gives me opportunity to join kindred things with kindred things. Witness the newly discovered entoptic colours, which let themselves be included into the rest of my exposition, just as if they had also been taken into account at the start. I thus find myself justified, indeed obliged to present in the same order what I have to bring afterwards. For it is not here a matter of dislocating the phenomena by a hypothesis, but rather of recognizing the clear, natural rights of each one and assigning it a place within the City of God and Nature, where it may then like to be put, indeed to settle down. And how should one give up such an advantage, largely achieved and tested? Anyone inventing an instrument which provides him in practice with special convenience but is unknown to others attempts to make such known, either to his own honour or—if he has the fortune to be an Englishman—to his temporal gain after lodging a patent . . .

9
THE DARWINIAN DIMENSIONS

Evolutionary Doctrine Carried Over Into Moral Life

In the autumn of 1893 Rudolf Steiner sent to the Berlin publisher Emil Felber the completed manuscript of his book *Die Philosophie der Freiheit.*

★

The work included certain British elements, if such they may be called. These were of two quite different kinds.

One kind comprised references made in course of the first part, 'Knowledge of Freedom', to two English-speaking philosophers. In the second (in 1918 renumbered as the first) chapter, 'Conscious Human Action', and also in the fifth (fourth), 'The World as Percept', quotations were adduced from works by the then 73-year-old Herbert Spencer, 'whose views are becoming every day more widespread'. In both cases, however, the relevant quotations were only included in order to be subsequently refuted. Much the same may be said regarding a further quotation adduced later in the fifth chapter, from a work by the eighteenth-century Bishop of Cloyne, George Berkeley.

★

It must also be added that Steiner's refutation of Berkeley's philosophy had been anticipated a couple of centuries previously in a briefer, more effective and down-to-earth manner by the great lexicographer Samuel Johnson. This well-known episode, recorded in *The Life of Samuel Johnson* (1791) by James Boswell, took place on Saturday, 7 August 1763—just ten years after Berkeley's death.

Boswell was travelling to Holland, and Johnson accompanied him as far as Harwich, where they visited the church:

> We went and looked at the church, and having gone into it and walked up to the altar, Johnson, whose piety was constant and fervent, sent me to my knees, saying, 'Now that you are going to leave your native country, recommend yourself to the protection of your CREATOR and REDEEMER.'
>
> After we came out of the church, we stood talking for some time together of Bishop Berkeley's ingenious sophistry to prove the non-existence of matter, and that everything in the universe is merely ideal. I

> observed that though we are satisfied his doctrine is not true, it is impossible to refute it. I shall never forget the alacrity with which Johnson answered, striking his foot with mighty force against a large stone, till he rebounded from it: 'I refute it *thus*.'

★

The other kind of British element in *Die Philosophie der Freiheit* appeared in the book's second part, 'The Reality of Freedom'. Here it was that famous scientist Charles Darwin to whom Steiner gave the unparalleled honour of having his name—or at any rate the theory deriving from his name—incorporated into the subtitle of the thirteenth (twelfth) chapter: 'Moral Fantasy (Darwinism and Morality)'.

At the centre of the chapter stood the following paragraphs. (Words or brief phrases added or substituted in the 1918 edition are placed in square brackets. More complex changes are given in full.)

> The same ethical individualism which I have developed on the basis of views already given could also be derived from the theory of evolution. The final conviction would be the same; only the path by which it was reached would be different.
>
> For evolutionary theory the appearance of completely new moral ideas through moral imagination is no more miraculous than the development of a new animal species out of an old one. Only, as a Monistic view of the world, this theory must reject, in morality as in science, every transcendental (metaphysical) influence [which is merely inferred and cannot be experienced ideally]. In doing so, the theory follows the same principle which guides it when seeking causes of new organic forms in already existing ones, not in the interference of an extra-mundane God...

In 1918 Steiner changed this to:

> ...when seeking causes of new organic forms without invoking the interference of an extra-mundane being...

The text continued:

> ...who produces every new species by supernatural influence, in accordance with a new creative thought. Just as Monism has no use for supernatural creative thoughts in explaining living organisms, so it is equally impossible for it to derive the moral world order from causes which do not lie within the [experienceable] world. It cannot admit either a continued supernatural influence on moral life (divine government of the world from outside) or a temporal one through a particular revelation (giving of the Ten Commandments) or through the appearance of God on Earth (divinity of Christ). For Monism, moral processes are products of Nature like every-

> thing else which exists, and their causes must be sought *in* Nature, since man is the bearer of morality.

In 1918 Steiner altered and expanded the last two sentences to:

> ... It cannot admit that the moral nature of will is accounted for by being traced back to continued supernatural influence on moral life (divine government of the world from outside), or a particular temporal revelation (giving of the Ten Commandments), or the appearance of God (of Christ) on Earth. What happens through all this to man, and in man, becomes a moral element only when, in human experience, it becomes an individual's own. For Monism, moral processes are products of the world like everything else which exists, and their causes must be sought *in* the world, that is in man, since man is the bearer of morality.

The text continued:

> Ethical individualism is then the crowning feature of the edifice which Darwin and Haeckel have erected [striven after] for natural science. It is [spiritualized] evolutionary doctrine carried over into moral life.

Slide Into the Abyss

Die Philosophie der Freiheit actually came out on 15 November 1893. In his autobiography Rudolf Steiner recalled:

> As soon as my *Philosophie der Freiheit* was printed I sent it to Eduard von Hartmann. He read through it with great attention, for I soon received his copy of the book with extensive marginal comments from start to finish ...

The copy was accompanied by a letter dated 21 November and opening as follows:

> Sir,
>
> I have now read through your book. With what vivid interest I have done this you may infer from how much I have noted down. I permit myself to send you the marginal notes in the original, requesting their kind return. Copying would have taken too long. This glossing of the text seems to me to come closest to the vividness of oral discussion ...

Steiner's account continued:

> ... Among other things he wrote to me that the book should have the title 'Epistemological Phenomenalism and Ethical Individualism'...

What Hartmann actually noted on the title-page was:

> The title should read 'Epistemological Monism and Ethical Individualism'. The discussion of freedom 1.) has no considerable place in the book, 2.) offers nothing new and particular, and 3.) by presupposing freedom in the title misleads a reader, as though it were dealing with an indeterministic freedom, since there is no reason whatever for stressing in this way a deterministic form of freedom through the title. That it is here a question only of one of the deterministic forms of freedom (logical self-regulation of will-content through intuitive thinking) should at least be placed in the foreword or at the start of the book at the top, to protect a reader from the misunderstanding caused by the title.

Steiner's account went on:

> ...He had completely misunderstood the source of the ideas and my purposes. He thought about the sensory world in a Kantian way, albeit modified. He considered this world as the effect of essentiality on the human soul through the senses. According to his opinion this essentiality can never enter the field of vision which the human soul grasps with consciousness. It remains beyond consciousness. Only through logical conclusions can hypothetical notions be formed about it. The sensory world does not therefore present something existing objectively in itself, but a subjective appearance which only exists in the human soul as long as the latter grasps it with consciousness.
>
> In my book I tried to explain that there is *no* unknown lying *behind* the sense-world, but the spiritual world *within* it. And I tried to show that the world of human ideas has its existence in this spiritual world. The essence of the sense-world is therefore only hidden to human consciousness *as long as* the soul *only* perceives through the senses. If ideas are experienced as well as sense-perceptions, the sensory world is experienced by consciousness in its objective essentiality. Cognition is not the human soul copying an entity, but entering livingly into that entity. *Within* consciousness a step is taken from the still inessential sensory world towards its essence. So the sensory world is only appearance (phenomenon) as long as it is not yet fully penetrated by consciousness.
>
> Therefore the sense-world is in truth also a spiritual world; and the soul lives together with this recognized spiritual world by extending consciousness over it. The aim of the cognitional process is a conscious *experience* of the spiritual world, before whose vision everything resolves into spirit.
>
> Against phenomenalism I set the world of spiritual reality. Eduard von Hartmann thought I wanted to remain within the phenomena and merely forego drawing conclusions from them in regard to any objective reality. So to him it seemed that my way of thinking was condemning human cognition not to approach reality at all, but to have to move within a world of semblance which only exists in mental pictures (as phenomena).

On the final page of his copy Hartmann noted down his thoughts as follows:

> In this book neither is Hume's in itself absolute phenomenalism reconciled with Berkeley's phenomenalism supported on God, nor this immanent or subjective phenomenalism with Hegel's transcendent panlogism at all, nor Hegelian panlogism with Goethean individualism either. Between any two of these components there yawns an unbridged gulf. But what has been overlooked above all is that phenomenalism leads with inevitable consequence towards solipsism, absolute illusionism and agnosticism, and nothing has been done to avoid this slide into the abyss of unphilosophy, because the danger is not recognized at all.

★

A month later, on 28 and 29 December, the book was competently though also not uncritically reviewed in the author's Austrian homeland, in two successive numbers of the *Wiener Zeitung*. The reviewer was the postal official and feature-writer Friedrich Beck, Steiner's junior by some three years, whom he had known during his time in Vienna.

The last two paragraphs of Beck's extensive review read:

> The ethical individualism supposed to crown the edifice of Darwin and Haeckel forgets that evolutionary doctrine does not regard the world as unchangeable, but as having become and in process of becoming. This doctrine is not content to establish regularity in phenomena, but also wants to gain insight into causal relationships. If a contrary assurance is made that 'things in and of themselves demand no explanation, and knowledge is thus no concern of the world but rather a business man must settle with himself', it must be most emphatically recalled that for Monism no contrast exists between the cosmos and a being seeking knowledge, and that every need stirring in the human mind is at the same time a general prerequisite for the world.
>
> Whether gratification of individual desire really affords a perfectly developed man the strongest sensation of pleasure, or whether the opposite view, which with Thomas Carlyle considers happiness within individual endeavour to be absolutely unattainable, boasts of truth with better right may here remain quite undiscussed. The question of morality is not affected by the extent of pleasure life is able to provide. At no time indeed have attempts been lacking to identify the pleasant with the good, and the unfavourable with the bad, and from the tendency towards pleasure to infer inborn moral ideals. The ethics of Socrates and his immortal disciple already rest on a similar thought-operation. Plato presupposes man's natural moral disposition, and the theory of concepts arriving into consciousness intuitively by perception recalls his theory of ideas. However, he distinguished

very well between natural and moral action, and made insight an adviser for urges and instincts, to draw caprice up to the domain of morality. To start with, Rudolf Steiner too holds fast to reasonable insight as a guide in life; but later on he begins speaking out in favour of 'strong will according to intuitions of the free personality'. What he does not consider is that a deed deriving 'from a being's pleasure', however high a potency be therein expressed, is lacking in insight as a product of moral or intellectual impulses. Regardless of the effect it produces, it appears tainted with a stigma of unfreedom and moral indifference. So long as man arranges his life only according to the wishes of his individual disposition—even be it the most perfect conceivable—he remains on the unfree level of a natural being. As such he stands like Friedrich Nietzsche, the most ingenious and peculiar advocate of 'master morality', beyond good and evil. In the relation of a single person to himself there are no moral aims; the only law here is the pleasure which deeds blindly produce. Only social connections of human beings create morality; they teach the valuer of his own self to subject desires to consideration, and to replace intuitions by willing according to plan. 'Ethical individualism' mistakes the will-expressions of an inborn attitude for moral freedom. It will have to recognize that this latter is attained not in the single subject but only within a totality, and that the leadership of the human race belongs to morality liberated from the yoke of self-will. On the analogy of 'ethical individualism' this might be called 'ethical socialism'.

A Monument Suggested

Over in Britain at this time, *The Shrewsbury Chronicle* published on Friday, 5 January 1894 an article on 'Charles Darwin: a Monument Suggested':

> Mr. Edwin Powell, of Rowton Lodge, has laid before us a letter from a personal friend of his, on the subject of Shrewsbury's neglect of her famous son, Charles Darwin. We have read the letter and, being pleased with its contents, publish it *in extenso*:—
>
> Rhodyate House,
Congresbury,
Dec. 30, 1893.
>
> Dear Powell,
>
> As we walked into Shrewsbury from your place the last time I was there, your son Edwin called my attention to a large red-bricked house standing back from the road and said 'That's the Mount'. I carelessly replied, 'Well I suppose it is. What of that?' 'Oh,' he said, 'That's where Charles Darwin was born.' I immediately took off my hat, and inaudibly apologized to that establishment for never having acknowledged it before (as I must have

passed it many times going to and from Rowton Lodge). Strange to say, 'The Mount' did not look at all offended by my neglect; on the contrary, it maintained its calm serenity, as if still influenced by the 'touch of a vanished hand'. I always feel that there is a good deal of individuality about country houses. Some certainly look more inviting and 'chummy' than others, as if one could have 'a good old time' in them, and be well supplied with port wine and ghosts *ad. lib.* (They go well together, and both improve with age. I don't know which is the more objectionable—new wine or new ghosts.) Whilst others seem to suggest weak tea in the parlour, and beetles in the kitchen. Please don't imagine 'The Mount' suggested either, or any of these things; it simply brought me up with a jerk. Well, soon after I said 'Goodbye', and did what I usually do when there—a prowl round the Quarry. And what a grand old place it is for a prowl! I remember going round there one evening with a big cigar (a very big cigar; it lasted a good hour), and walking up and down. I had it all to myself—the Quarry—as well as my cigar; excepting that every now and again I heard a fish jump in the river. I also heard that peculiar chirp of insects which is always, I am told, audible on warm summer nights (although I never heard it before). As I stood still to listen to these other evidences of life, I looked up (it was a bright moonlit night), and saw that very old statue of Hercules (if it is Hercules!) and wondered what on earth *he* had to do with Shrewsbury and the Quarry, or if there were any Augean Stables in the neighbourhood, or whether he had a hand in excavating the place, or why this mythical giant was placed in such a grand site. Of course, in bygone days there may have been a good and sufficient reason for the honour done to this muscular god; but now that you good people of Shrewsbury have been fortunate enough to give birth to a real giant, a giant beside whom our old friend Hercules dwindles down to a mere pigmy, has it not struck you as being strange, not to say unnatural, for a town the mother of such a one as Charles Darwin, not to have raised a statue to him? If in recognition of man's abilities it is the custom as a mark of respect in all civilized centres to put up monuments to their great men, surely—surely Darwin should have one erected in his birthplace, for certainly no greater man has died this century, and perhaps in no other; a man who makes an epoch in science &c. as great as Copernicus, Newton, Shakespeare and Harvey did in their times. Well, Darwin has been dead about ten years, and all that Shrewsbury has done for him is, I believe, to give his name to a street. Certainly it is a recognition, but a strangely inconsistent one. Of course I know there is a splendid statue of him in the Natural History Museum at Kensington, which was subscribed to by every country in Europe, America and the Colonies, Sweden alone sending 2,296 subscriptions. This only makes it the more marvellous that your ancient town has neglected the opportunity, an opportunity that every country in the world would jump at, if *they* could only truthfully say 'Darwin was born here, and *that* is his statue'! Talk about a prophet not being appreciated in his own country! Is it not true? For if ever there was a site suitable for a man, or a man for the site, it is the Quarry, and Darwin is the man, universally acknowledged as the master-mind on all subjects he touched. He seemed to have the extraordinary faculty of gathering together all the old, dried, tangled ideas of entomologists, biologists, naturalists, horticulturalists, and many other branches of kindred societies, sorting them out, rearranging, controlling and eventually starting them all afresh on the right line—a line which, if ever we are to know the genesis of life, seems to be that grand trunk line of evolution laid down by Darwin, along which modern thought must travel, and is travelling, the terminus of which is the *Origin of Species*.

Don't you think it is about time you woke up to the fact that you have no statue in Shrewsbury to this genius? Do you realize what manner of man he was? One would as soon expect to find no statue to Shakespeare at Stratford, to Burns in Scotland, to Bunyan at Bedford, or to Newton in Westminster Abbey, as none to Darwin in Shrewsbury. Not being a Salopian, I suppose I should not be allowed to contribute my mite towards a fund for the purpose; but if I were I should be proud to do so, and if you can get a hundred others to do the same I shall be pleased to send you a cheque for five guineas, and you really should not let 1894 go by without at any rate making an effort to do honour in this way to one of England's greatest men.

You I consider a very proper person to move in this matter, because have you not for years been practising what Darwin preached—*in re* your dogs and horses, selecting and breeding from the fittest? Pure evolution—'survival of the fittest', etc.—

Yours very sincerely,

Fred. P. Martin

The Desired Response

In the following week's issue, on 12 January, *The Shrewsbury Chronicle* carried among various 'Letters to the Editor' a couple on 'The Proposed Darwin Memorial':

Sir,—

The suggestion that a suitable memorial be erected in perpetuation of the memory of Charles Darwin—one of Salop's greatest sons—should, I think, be warmly taken up. It has frequently been remarked by visitors to our interesting old town that Salopians did not seem to make much of the honour of having given birth and education to one who stands forth so prominently among the great men of the century. It does seem blameworthy that nothing has been done to give public honour to one to whom honour is so pre-eminently due. Would it not be well, ere the century closes, to try to do something to remedy the neglect, and to show to the world that his native place is not insensible to the high distinction of having a name so great to enrol among her native sons—sons of note—whose memories the world will not willingly let die? As regards the site for memorial, I should suggest the open space in front of the Free Library as more suitable than the Quarry, being more prominent and closely associated with the great school where he first imbibed that knowledge of which he made so good use in his after years. I feel convinced it only requires a start to be made to make the 'Darwin Memorial Fund' a great success. Trusting you may give the subject your valuable advocacy,

J. Laing

*

Sir,—

The letter of Mr. Powell's friend, printed in last week's issue, touches a point which, although it has more than once been brought before the public, has never yet been taken up with the energy it deserves. The question is the non-recognition of Charles Darwin's greatness by his fellow townsmen in any tangible manner. 'No greater man has all this realm of England produced in this 19th century.' These words of one of your contemporaries are known to be true by everyone who has watched the development of science during the last 60 or 70 years. He was head and shoulders above the majority of his fellows, if not indeed superior to them all. It is equally true that his merits have met with no recognition of the kind generally granted to men of his calibre. But it is not too late. The nineteenth century is not yet expired, and something yet might be done. Might not our worthy Mayor be requested to call a public meeting to consider the question? I feel sure that he would do so, and if he will take this letter, hurriedly written by one who distinctly recollects the residence of the old doctor and his family at the Mount, some fifty years ago, as a sufficient inducement to make him do so, I shall not regret having written it. I have before me now an autograph letter, dated May 24, 1877, in which Charles Darwin wishes me success in an undertaking afterwards fully carried out, and encloses a substantial contribution. He writes in a kindly spirit, displaying his interest in the welfare of a district, now a parish, in which his boyhood was spent. It must not be said by posterity that our enthusiasm for his fame and memory resulted in merely giving his name to a second-class street near his paternal home. I should like to see a table on the wall of St. George's Church, where the family had a pew from the day of opening, recording the fact that in this building they worshipped God in sincerity and truth.

C.H. Drinkwater

St. George's Vicarage,
Shrewsbury, Jan. 11th 1894

★

The editorial column also now carried an article on 'The Suggested Darwin Memorial':

> It is with pleasure we record that the suggestion made in the *Shrewsbury Chronicle* last week in favour of a Darwin Memorial is meeting with the desired response. In another column will be found letters from gentlemen who have a right to be heard on a subject of such importance to the people of Shrewsbury. One of the writers—the Rev. C.H. Drinkwater, vicar of St. George's (where the Darwins 'worshipped God in sincerity and truth')—shows that what we have to complain of is 'the non-recognition of Charles Darwin's greatness by his fellow-townsmen in any tangible manner'. Competent authorities are agreed that so far as the Empire is concerned, Darwin's is the greatest and most conspicuous figure of the century. 'He was,' to again quote Mr. Drinkwater, 'head and shoulders above the majority of his fellows, if not indeed superior to them all.' Mr. J. Laing suggests that a monument should be erected not in the Quarry, but in the open space opposite the Free Library, which is 'more closely associated with the great school' where Darwin 'first imbibed that knowledge' of which in after years 'he made such good use'. The great naturalist was not only born in this borough; he was baptized at St. Chad's Church, and he resided here with his family for many years. It has been asserted, and with much truth, that monuments are often erected to men who would otherwise be forgotten; but the memory of Charles Darwin will be revered, as his work will endure, while his nation lasts. In truth, he needs no effigy. If any of our great ones can dispense with such 'honours', he can. But we in the locality from which he sprang will do well to view the matter from an altogether different standpoint. It is not seemly that we should ignore the ancient and beautiful custom of erecting memorials to the great. Our reputation as a community is at stake in this matter, and for that reason we hasten to give publicity to the news that a meeting, over which his Worship the Mayor of Shrewsbury has consented to preside, will shortly be held to take steps for raising a 'Darwin Memorial Fund'. In wishing the movement success, we promise it all the assistance we can render, so that the stigma of neglecting her greatest son, under which Shrewsbury has so long rested, may be removed without further delay.

Views on the Origin of Man

The next week's issue of *The Shrewsbury Chronicle*, on 19 January, included among its 'public notices' printed on the very front page one entitled 'Borough of Shrewsbury: the Late Charles Darwin':

To his Worship the Mayor of Shrewsbury

We, the undersigned, being ratepayers, humbly request that you will call a public meeting to take such steps as shall appear desirable to recognize in a public way the merits of the late Charles Darwin, one of the most eminent men of science which modern times have seen, who was a native of this town, and partly educated at the Free Grammar Schools. We leave the time and place of such meeting to your Worship's wise discretion.

January 12th, 1894

I.T. Shrewsbury, Vicar of St. Chad's,

J. Spencer Phillips, Thos. Maynard How, Thos. Southam, George Burr, John Parson Smith, T. Middleton Howells, C.H. Drinkwater, William Phillips, S. Meeson Morris, W. Gowen Cross, Geo. Evans, E. Cresswell Peele, John R. Carless, Charles Parker, G. Sandford Corser, Saml. Ebrall, J. Gray, Thomas Corbett, L. Burd, Henry H. Hughes, Admitt and Naunton, William Adams, Alf. Attfield, John D. Harries, R.G. Harrison, Henry E. Rogers, G. Williams-Freeman, Henry Wells, Geo. Baker, T.W. Hayes (*Shrewsbury Chronicle*), D.H. Owen, Arthur Gill, Edward Corbett, junior, W. John Wyley, Henry J. Hearn, Chas S. Thomas, Thos. T. Whitehurst, C.J.S. Churchill, F.E. Bennett, E. Calvert, J.D. Southam, W. Patchett, Geo. J. Holt, J. Laing, H. Edward Forrest, W.E. Harding, John Barker, George Mitchell, J.E. Adams, J.E. Parson Smith, Donald Grant, John M. Harding, Edward Burd, F.W. Wateridge, W.B. Walker, W.E. Litt, Samuel Heighway, Thomas Richards, F.J. Lowe, T. Slaney Eyton, A.T. Davis, C.J. Groves, Edwin Powell, Edwin Powell, jun., John Watton, Robert Watkins

In accordance with the above requisition, I hereby convene a public meeting of the inhabitants of the borough of Shrewsbury, to be held at the Guildhall, in the said borough, on Tuesday the 30th day of January 1894, at three o'clock in the afternoon.

Wm. Lyon Browne, Mayor.

Guildhall, 18th January 1894

★

An editorial on another page commented:

We are delighted to find that the movement started by Mr. Edwin Powell for raising a memorial to Darwin (it were a waste of words to refer to the great naturalist as 'Charles Robert Darwin') is meeting with the support of nearly every enlightened man in the borough. It is not necessary at this stage to dwell upon the wisdom of the proposal before us. Two or three gentlemen have, we were surprised to hear, held back their names from the requisition sent to the Mayor, and which appears at full length in our advertising columns. Their reason for this is Darwin's views on the origin of man, but the fact remains that Darwin was not only a scientist of the very first rank, if not the greatest of this or any age, he was a friend of the Christian religion. He gave time, money and personal help to further the work of the parish in which he resided; and his pure life, noble example, and transcendent genius have received no finer tribute than that paid by the Vicar of Down, where he resided during the closing years of a long and remarkable life. We trust that we are not blind to the claims of religion in asserting that men and women of every creed, as of every party, may join in supporting a proposal for the consideration of which his Worship the Mayor has consented to preside over a meeting to be held at the Guildhall, Shrewsbury, on Tuesday the 30th inst. If we were at all dubious as to the propriety of erecting in Shrewsbury a memorial to our famous townsman, our doubts would at once vanish in view of the names placed at the foot of the requisition. The Bishop of Shrewsbury, setting an example which some younger and less courageous clergymen have hesitated to follow, takes a very prominent place, and Mr. W.L. Browne, with many others of 'light and leading' in local circles, make it no secret that they approve of the step. After all, however, the memorial, whatever shape it assume, is not to Darwin, but to ourselves—his successors in the borough which is honoured by being able to claim him as its own. The memorial, more than anything else, will point to the fact Darwin is appreciated even in 'his own country'. It will inform future generations that we of the last decade of the nineteenth century were, in part at any rate, able to perceive the merits of a great one born in our midst, and whose ashes repose in the Abbey of Westminster. It has taken eleven years to accomplish in us this creditable awakening; but 'better late than never'.

*

The following week's issue, on 26 January, included among various 'Letters to the Editor' one on 'Charles Darwin':

Sir,—

The following which appeared in the *Birmingham Post* on the occasion of Darwin's 70th birthday will be of interest at this juncture:—

'It is too much the fashion in England to allow our great men to die before public recognition is made of the services they have rendered. This may or may not be a wholesome practice, but it stands out in striking contrast with that of other nations, when we find that not only do they honour their own great men while alive, but that they give tribute to those of foreign countries. This was the case last year, when, on the seventieth birthday of Charles Darwin, the whole of scientific Germany united to pay a mark of respect to the man who has exercised a wider and deeper influence on human thought than anyone who has lived during this century. The day was celebrated by congratulatory addresses to Mr. Darwin, by the presentation to him of an album containing photographs of nearly all the eminent men of science in Germany, and the publication of a 'Gratulationsheft zum 70 Geburtstage Ch. Darwin' of *Kosmos*; but so far as we know, not the slightest notice of the event was taken in England. Today being the seventy-first birthday of the great veteran of biological science, it is proposed to remedy the omission, as far as can be, in this town, the centre of the district with which his family has been so long associated. When we remind our readers that Dr. Erasmus Darwin, the great foreshadower of his grandson, was the consulting physician for this district for a period of nearly thirty years, and that when any of our notables were ill he was sent for from Lichfield to Birmingham as is narrated by Mrs. Shimmelpenninck, that Charles Darwin is also the grandson of Josiah Wedgwood and a cousin of the Galtons, and that he was born and brought up at Shrewsbury, we give sufficient reason for our taking a more than ordinary interest in this eminent biologist. But to every Englishman the great men of his country must be dear, and especially so must be one who is universally allowed to have revolutionized every department of national science, and to have founded a system of philosophy which has influenced every phase of human thought. That this philosophy has upset many cherished traditions is undisputed; but as Mr. Darwin himself points out, 'we are not concerned with hopes and fears, but only with the truth as far as our reason will allow us to discover it'. And then he sums up his conclusions on the origin of species in the forcible and memorable words: 'There is grandeur in this view of life, with its several powers having been breathed by the Creator into a few forms or into one; and that, whilst this planet has gone cycling on, according to the fixed laws of gravity, from so simple a beginning, endless forms most beautiful and most wonderful have been and are being evolved.' Though the scientific world has now generally adopted the conclusions of the *Origin of Species*, they continue to be popularly misrepresented and disliked. But whatever be the time at which they may become part of popular education and belief, or if they never should be—indeed, had the book in question never been written—Charles Darwin would remain one of the greatest men of science this country has ever produced, the most indefatigable worker alive and the most original, and to those who have been favoured to see and know him in his quiet home in Kent, he will ever be one of the most gentle and lovable of natures. The Birmingham Natural History Society have already marked their sense of appreciation of Mr. Darwin's worth by electing him their Honorary Vice-President; and tonight it will be proposed in the Philosophical Society to confer upon him the first honorary membership of that society, and to present him a birthday address.'

E. Powell

Royton Lodge, January 23, 1894

A Numerously Attended Meeting

The next week's issue of *The Shrewsbury Chronicle*, on Friday, 2 February, included in its column on 'Local and District Intelligence' an article headed

'Proposed Memorial to the late Charles Darwin: Public Meeting in Shrewsbury':

> On Tuesday afternoon a numerously attended meeting of the inhabitants of Shrewsbury was held in the Guildhall to consider what steps should be taken to recognize in a public way the merits of the eminent scientist, Charles Darwin, who was a native of the town, and partly educated at Shrewsbury School. His Worship the Mayor (W.L. Browne, Esq.) presided, and the attendance was fully representative of all sections in the town.
>
> Prior to the commencement of proceedings the Town Clerk read a number of letters from gentlemen unable to be present. The Bishop of Shrewsbury wrote:
>
> Quarry House, Shrewsbury,
> 29th January, 1894.
>
> My dear Mr. Mayor,—
>
> I am full of regret that I am called away tomorrow very early, first to attend the funeral of an old friend in Staffordshire, and then to proceed to London for the Session of Convocation. I shall therefore be unable to take part in the meeting which you have summoned to consider in what way Shrewsbury can do honour to and perpetuate the memory of one of her most remarkable sons; if he does not deserve the very highest place among them. For as a patient investigator of natural science, and a diligent seeker after truth, and one fearless to proclaim the results at which he had arrived, Charles Darwin will always stand forth conspicuous in his generation. His conclusions startled and alarmed pious minds at first, as though they were subversive of the truth of revelation. But the panic has subsided, and it is recognized that the admission of Darwin's theories does not necessarily involve any contradiction of the inspired story of Creation, though it may require modification of the interpretation most commonly affixed to it. The more firmly we believe that it is one and the same Almighty Being who made the Universe, and gave us the Bible, the less we shall fear, and the more we shall be grateful to those who, like Darwin, are honestly and patiently seeking to penetrate the secrets which it is the object of natural science to bring to light. I trust your meeting may be a harmonious one, and encourage you to go forward.—
>
> Believe me
>
> Yours very sincerely,
>
> I.T. Shrewsbury
>
> I would add, by way of postscript, that I shall be glad to subscribe to any memorial to be erected in Shrewsbury; but the modest sum which I can afford (£5) had better wait its turn until larger sums have been announced.
>
> The following letter was read from Mr. H.D. Greene, Q.C., M.P.:—
>
> 4, Brick Court, Temple, E.C., 22nd Jan., 1894.
>
> Dear Sir, Your note of 20th inst. has reached me this morning. I had received no communication before with reference to the movement to get

up a memorial to Darwin. I entirely concur in the efforts that are being made, but I deeply regret to say that I cannot be in Shrewsbury on the 30th inst. at three o'clock, and shall therefore be unable to attend the meeting. I have to discharge on that day an official duty which will prevent my being with you. You have my best wishes, and I assure you I regret very much my inability to be with you.

Mr. S.K. Mainwaring (Chairman, Salop County Council) wrote:—

I can only hope that as a result of your meeting, something worthy of the object of it, 'the memory of the late Charles Darwin', may be settled upon that will be of advantage to present and future generations of his town and county, and so keep his memory before them in perpetuity.

The Ven. Archdeacon Lloyd wrote:—

Dear Mr. Mayor, I am sorry that two engagements tomorrow will prevent my presence at the meeting in promotion of a Darwin memorial, but I shall be glad to do anything I can in support of the movement. I presume that a committee will be formed to endeavour to interest a wider area of English society, and especially of scientific clubs and individuals, in doing honour to Darwin's works. We should not be content with less than a bronze statue in front of the old Schools.

Mr. J. Watson, Berwick, wrote:—

I shall have pleasure in adding my name to the list of subscribers to the fund. I regret that an engagement in Lancaster will prevent my attendance at the meeting.

Mr. W.E. Garnett-Botfield (President of the Caradoc and Severn Valley Field Club) wrote:—

I shall only be too pleased to help in any way I can. I hope the whole country will join in showing honour to the memory of Charles Darwin.

Dr. Callaway, Wellington, wrote:—

Dear Mr. Mayor, I should have been very glad to accept your polite invitation to the town's meeting on Tuesday next, but unfortunately I have an important engagement elsewhere. I have for many years thought and said that Shrewsbury ought to do something in honour of the greatest Englishman of the age, who was also one of the greatest thinkers of all time. Darwin himself would, I think, have preferred that any memorial to him should take the form of a scholarship or some other method of advancing scientific knowledge, but as the County Council has established scholarships in science, it would perhaps be well if the genius of your fellow townsman was commemorated in a more conspicuous way. I should be disposed to support the idea of a statue to be placed on the open space in front of the Free Library and Museum.

Letters were also read from Mr. Stanley Leighton, M.P., the Dean of Christ Church, Oxford, Mr. J. Spencer Phillips, Mr. G.J. Holt, Captain Williams-Freeman, Rev. G.T. Hall, and Mr. T. Corbett.

The Mayor said it had afforded him very great pleasure to call that meeting in obedience to the numerously and influentially signed memorial presented to him, for the object of it was to do honour to the memory of a man who had conferred very great honour and distinction upon them. (Applause.) It was true that during his lifetime Darwin immortalized himself by his works, and shed a lustre on his native town, which was their town, and probably some might think that whatever course they took, that would not perpetuate his memory, for that would live for many generations without any effort on their part. But still it was due to him as well as to them, that they should try to do honour to one of the greatest men who ever lived. (Applause.) Many suggestions had been made as to the form which the memorial should take, but that was a matter which would probably be left to a committee to decide exactly what should be done. It might be for the convenience of the meeting, however, if he sketched out one or two suggestions that had been made to him in conversation with gentlemen interested in the matter. It had been suggested that the memorial should take the form of a bronze statue, to be erected in front of the old school wherein Darwin studied. (Applause.) Another suggestion was that the memorial should not only take the form of a statue, but if sufficient money could possibly be raised, to combine with it a scholarship at Shrewsbury School. (Applause.) And a third suggestion, which perhaps was the largest, and one that had received the greatest amount of support from those with whom he had spoken, was to make it a national memorial. (Loud applause.) The idea was not to confine it to the town and county alone, but to seek assistance from all parts of the globe, and it was also thought that the memorial should take the shape of a hall of science for technical and scientific teaching to be erected in Shrewsbury, and endowed in a manner that would secure its continuance for the benefit not only of this generation, but generations to come. (Applause.) But this was a matter which the committee to be hereafter appointed would have to go into and decide in accordance with the funds at their disposal. (Hear, hear.) He thought it would be satisfactory to those gentlemen who had taken so much interest in this matter to find that there was such a large attendance that day. It showed that a genuine feeling had been aroused, and he hoped that the enthusiasm thus created would culminate in a still wider interest throughout the whole of the land. (Applause.)

The Rev. H.W. Moss (Headmaster of Shrewsbury School) moved the first resolution, as follows:— 'It is the unanimous opinion of this meeting that Shrewsbury, the birthplace of Charles Darwin, should possess an appropriate national memorial of him, and that a subscription list be at once opened for this purpose.' He said he felt it a great honour to have this duty entrusted to him. He could only express his surprise—a surprise which he thought many around him would share—that no steps had hitherto been taken in that borough to identify and associate itself with the reputation of that great man, Charles Darwin. (Applause.) Nearly 12 years had elapsed since his remains were interred in Westminster Abbey with all the solemn ceremonial of a nation's mourning. England then gave proof that he was a man to be regarded with the highest honour. (Hear, hear.) Men of affairs were common enough in this country. They contributed much to the comfort and happiness of those among whom their lot was cast, and they might be counted by tens of thousands, not only in their own country, but throughout the civilized world. Great commanders might rescue nations from ruin or even change the map of the world; statesmen made their way into eminence, some by their almost prophetic power, some by their indomitable will; but it might be doubted whether men of affairs, or generals, or inventors, or statesmen contributed as much to the great results of time as the class of men to which Charles Darwin belonged. (Applause.) They scattered ideas in the world which germinated into unexpected developments of usefulness. (Hear, hear.) Charles Darwin originated theories which might in some instances have been applied in regions where they were inapplicable. But time would correct all that, and time would show what part of Darwin's great thoughts was to remain a permanent inheritance of mankind, and what part was destined to perish. (Applause.) They, at any rate, the inhabitants of this town, where his early years were spent, would, he thought, be doing an injustice to Darwin and to themselves if they did not endeavour to commemorate that great man, and commemorate him in a suitable way. (Applause.) He entirely agreed with the view expressed by some of those with whom the Mayor had communicated that the memorial which they were about to erect should be regarded not as a local but as a national one. (Applause.) It was his privilege nearly twelve years ago, as Headmaster of Shrewsbury School, to attend the funeral of Charles Darwin at Westminster Abbey, and he was then greatly impressed with the eminence of the men who followed him to his grave. Some of those men were still living, and surely many of them would be only too glad to help them in Shrewsbury in what they were about to do. (Applause.) He trusted, therefore, that they would look at this memorial as a national one, would not limit its boundaries, but would endeavour to get all the help from outside the borough which they could. For indeed Charles Darwin was not only or mainly a local worthy—his fame had extended into every region of the civilized world (applause)—and in his judgement his name would be one of the three or four names which would illustrate in a special manner the annals of the century, and in time to come be regarded as peculiarly emblematic of the spirit of the present age. (Loud applause.)

Mr Butler Lloyd said he attended the meeting in anticipation of listening to some interesting speeches, and he certainly had heard two most interesting ones. (Hear, hear.) He had very little to add on this important subject.

The only wonder was that Shrewsbury had not done something in this direction sooner, but 'better late than never.' (Hear, hear.) He certainly agreed with what Mr. Moss had said that they should unanimously agree upon doing something to perpetuate the memory of Charles Darwin, one of the greatest men not only in Shrewsbury or Shropshire but, he might say, in England, and one for whom he personally had the greatest admiration. (Applause.) He quite agreed with the idea that they should try to make this a national movement. It was perfectly true, and they were proud of the fact, that Charles Darwin was born and bred in Shrewsbury and educated in Shrewsbury under Dr. Butler, and he thought it was only right for Shrewsbury to make a start in the matter, and then apply to all the learned societies and the learned men of the day—of whom there were a great many—to help them in erecting a national memorial in Darwin's native town. (Applause.) He agreed with the resolution proposed by Mr. Moss, but thought the latter part which referred to the opening of a subscription list might very well be left out as the time had not quite come when they should be asked to put their names down for certain sums. (Hear, hear.) If the movement became a national one they would feel much more inclined to give liberally than if it were only taken up locally. At present they did not know what they were going to subscribe to—whether to a bronze statue, or a statue and a scholarship, or a hall of science. If Mr. Moss would agree to omit the latter part of the resolution he should be happy to second it. (Applause.)

Mr. Moss said he should be only too glad to fall in with the suggestion.

Mr. William Phillips moved the following resolution:—'That at an early date a public meeting be convened and held in Shrewsbury for the purpose of considering the best measures for carrying out the project of the previous resolution.' He said it could not for one moment be concealed from them that they were doing themselves great honour in the steps they were taking. They were not merely honouring a great and excellent man, but they were really admitting that they had hitherto neglected his merits. However, it could not be said that absolutely nothing had been done, for the first step the Shrewsbury Free Library Committee took was to obtain as good a portrait as they could of Charles Darwin, and hang it in a prominent place at the Library. (Hear, hear.) Then came the subscription list for a memorial of Darwin, which took the form of a statue in the South Kensington Museum. That movement being before the world, many local people thought at the time it would not be wise to take any action locally, but he was glad to say that now the time had arrived when they could do something and appeal, not only to the town and county, but to the whole world, with the confident hope that they would be amply assisted, and the result would be most gratifying. (Applause.) He expressed a doubt as to whether that was the proper time to lay down the exact line they should take, although there could be no question that the three schemes mentioned were each excellent. However, he should like to see some material memorial of Darwin, whatever that might be, in the town, because although a scholarship was quite in harmony with Darwin's character, and would be a worthy memorial to him, still he thought a visible monument in some shape or other should be erected. (Applause.) He thought they should aim at providing a statue and a scholarship, for he doubted whether they would ever receive—he did not wish to throw cold water on the suggestion—money enough to establish a Technical College, because it meant raising a large sum of money. But it was time enough when they had caught the hare to cook it. (Laughter and applause.)

The Rev. E. Myers, in seconding the resolution, said he felt perfectly sure that not only the inhabitants of the town would rejoice with great joy, but the inhabitants of the county would be exceeding glad to know that steps are at last being taken to honour—he should say not one of the greatest, but absolutely the greatest scientist, not only of this country, but the greatest scientist the world has ever seen, not only in this age but in any age of civilization. (Applause.) He rejoiced to think that Shrewsbury had at last awakened to the fact that long ago some action in respect to that matter was expected of its people. They knew that long before Darwin died the German people erected a statue to his memory. They knew, as far as national feeling was concerned, there was a statue, erected as a national statue, in the South Kensington Museum. Still, he agreed with Mr. Phillips in thinking that not only should that effort be a town, county or country effort, but an imperial effort, in order that the world-wide known man should receive in the town of his nativity some satisfactory recognition and satisfactory memorial of his wonderful and marvellous genius and life. (Applause.) Darwin was a townsman of theirs, and though he (the speaker) was only an importation, still he was glad to be imported into the town in which such a distinguished man lived. (Applause.) Therefore they should do their best to make any memorial of him as great and as grand as possible. He hoped the time would come when in every English town or village which had the honour of being the birthplace of some great man—whether a scientist, a politician, a distinguished soldier or sailor—there would be some memorial of such men, so that the children of coming generations when asking for information might be told by their parents who the man was who was honoured and revered, and what noble works he had performed in his day. (Hear, hear.) He had received several letters from friends outside the town asking if they might attend the meeting that day, but he could only send them a copy of the notice convening a meeting of the inhabitants of Shrewsbury. He thought they might indeed make that a world-wide movement, and he felt sure a properly representative committee, if elected, would have a ready response to any appeal sent out with the object of raising a memorial to the memory of that great man whom they honoured themselves in honouring. (Applause.)

Alderman E.C. Peele moved that a committee be appointed to make arrangements for a public meeting, and take such steps as may be deemed necessary, with power to add to their number.

The Rev. W.H. Draper seconded the resolution, and in doing so said it was unquestionably true that Charles Darwin was a conspicuous example of the way in which the second book of God—the book of Nature—ought to be studied, not only by men of science who were followers in the footsteps of Charles Darwin, but by all, and then there certainly would not be one half the mistrust in the world on the part of those people who love truth most sincerely from whatever quarter it comes. Therefore he was proud to take any part in forwarding a movement to perpetuate the memory of that great man who did his work in so truly a religious spirit. (Applause.)

The resolution was carried by acclamation, and the following were appointed as the committee:—The Bishop of Shrewsbury, Rev. H.W. Moss, Rev. C.H. Drinkwater, Rev. E. Myers, Major General the Hon. W.H. Herbert, Dr. Burd, Mr. Edwin Powell, Mr. W. Phillips, Mr. E.C. Peele, Rev. Charles Parker, Mr. T.P. Blunt, Mr. T.S. Eyton, Mr. Clement Southam, and Mr. W.H. Wood (one of Darwin's schoolfellows).

On the motion of Dr. Burd, seconded by Mr. D.H. Owen, a vote of thanks was accorded to the Mayor for presiding, and the proceedings terminated.

A God-dishonouring Transaction

The next week's issue of *The Shrewsbury Chronicle*, on 9 February, included among various 'Letters to the Editor' one on 'Charles Darwin (from a Lady's Point of View)'.

Dear Sir,—

After reading the eulogy on Charles Darwin in your last week's issue, permit me a small space in your columns to protest, as a Christian, against the dishonour contemplated to the Creator and Sovereign of the Universe by the proposed memorial to Charles Darwin, about to be raised in Shrewsbury. Here we have a man who by his science, falsely so called (1 Tim. 6:20) has done more to propagate that infidelity which is now rampant throughout the world than any other man of this century; a man who, whatever his private virtues may have been, has denied, and taught others to deny, the inspired Scriptures, and consequently, Him who is the Author of them; a man who has set up his own thoughts and theories in contradiction to the Word of the Living God—that Word which will judge *all men* who reject it in the last day (John 12:48); that word, *the whole* of which from Genesis to Revelations stands or falls together as the inspired Word of God to man, and the whole of which is God-breathed (2 Tim. 3:16).

And are Christians to be called upon to support such a God-dishonouring transaction? To honour the memory of a man who spent the greater part of his life in trying to prove 'God a liar' (1 John 5:10), for God says: 'He created man in His own image'; Darwin says: 'Facts leave nothing to be believed but that man gradually evolved out of nothing.' God says man is lost and irretrievably ruined, and needs a Saviour, without whom he will grow more and more lawless and wicked, until that awful day arrives when the Man of Sin shall be worshipped as God (2 Epis. Thess. 2:3–12); but Darwin's works teach the opposite to this. Now, which are we to believe—the Living and True God, or Charles Darwin? Are we in Shrewsbury to follow the example of infidel Germany?

Let us heed that solemn warning from the lips of Our Lord Himself in St. Luke 16:15, 'That which is highly esteemed among men is abomination in the sight of God'; and let Christians in Shrewsbury be at least as faithful as the three Hebrew captives in Babylon who chose the fiery furnace rather than dethrone God from His sovereignty. Will any who name the name of Christ join with unbelievers in thus dishonouring Him and denying their Sovereign, Lord and Master, which doing honour to one who has by his writings endeavoured to dethrone Him from His rightful place as Sovereign and Creator of His own Universe practically is?

True science supports and upholds the inspired Word of God. Not so 'oppositions of science falsely so called' (1 Timothy 6:20) and which in a few years' time may all be exploded when new theories arise; but the Word of the Lord endureth for ever. A Frenchman lately traced all the anarchy and lawlessness abroad in the present day to the teaching of those men who have taken away the foundations of religion and destroyed man's faith in God. And will Christians in Shrewsbury join in such work? God forbid. Honour to whom honour is due. But is honour due from Christians to the memory of one whose glory was attempting to destroy the foundation truths of God's Word?

A Believer

Shrewsbury, Jan. 31.

★

The next week's issue, on 16 February, published several letters in reply. One was headed 'Darwin—the Laughing-Stock of Fools'.

Sir,—

It was somewhat of a treat to read the epistle of 'Believer' in your last week's issue. Verily and indeed, as the wise king hath it, 'there is nothing new under the Sun'. Methinks the *anathema maranatha* pronounced against Darwin for his work in the laboratory of Nature was something akin to that excommunication which placed Galileo in the dungeon for saying the world was round, in contradiction to the 'divine' idea of David, who thought in his day that it was a great flat plain, with the heavens spread above it 'like a tent'; something related also to the bigotry which would fain have wrought the ruin of Columbus because he dared to say there was a world beyond the sea, of which the 'inspired' writers never guessed or spoke.

But softly! 'Believer' claims, or confesses, to be a lady. Therefore one must speak at least in charity. But, in sooth, it is rather too bad to pile up all the adjectives and texts upon the head of Darwin. If 'infidelity is rampant'—whatever 'rampant' may mean in this connection—what has that to do with the gentle naturalist? And how is the erecting of a memorial to so great a lover and seeker of truth going to 'dethrone God from His rightful place as Sovereign and Creator of His own Universe'? Surely the authority of the Omnipotent must be in a parlous state when the raising of a few feet of marble can make an end of it! I guess not the most 'rampant' of infidels has yet ventured to think so lightly of the strength still left in the religious instinct.

'Facts leave nothing to be believed but that man gradually evolved out of nothing.' So says Darwin; or so at least quotes our good lady friend. Where is the blasphemy, where the iniquity, seeing that Moses also in his day with his limited means of information—wrapt up as he and all men then were in hide-bound superstition—when Moses, even in his philosophy, such as it was, would have us believe that in the beginning things were created, that is 'evolved out of nothing'?

Verily, if one more proof be needed of the truth of evolution, it should be seen in the presence among us at this latter day of such an antediluvian state of mind as that shown forth by 'Believer's' letter. One might almost be reading the early days of Jane Austen, or penetrating into the theological views of the late lamented Mr. Stiggins. 'Believer's' epistle to the Darwinians breathes a fine old flavour of the high and dry Calvinistic doctrine which, in its day, has brought despair and darkness enough into the world. If any more such as 'Believer' remain as fossil types in this more generous age, let them at least nurse their gloomy creed in silence and not drag it out from the fustiness of oblivion into the light of modern day.

No, no, my good friend! We are not all 'lost and irretrievably ruined'. The human race has not left its palmiest stage behind, with only destruction and decay before it. We have buried that idea with the fogies who made it a crime to whistle on a Sunday and taught that happiness in 'unregenerate man' is sin. We are standing now on the upward not the downward plane. Whether Moses or Darwin be true (I do believe both were, as far as their light went), this one thing we know: that humanity through countless centuries of toil and suffering has ever been working out its ultimate salvation, it may be blindly, it may be under the direction of some unseen controlling force, yet ever ascending and ever straining to a still higher level. The millennium is not yet. But we are nearer to it than our fathers were, and we, without troubling ourselves overmuch as to beliefs and creeds, can each do something to help forward the day of universal truth.

Such, in its way, was the end of Darwin's labour. Through all his work he steadily plodded on in face of inattention and opposition, making himself (as every wise man yet) the laughing-stock of fools. And still he toiled along, as seemed to him his duty, following step by step the search for truth until at last the glimmer of his lantern woke the world, and today all who seek the truth whether in science or religion can recognize in Charles Darwin one of those great master-minds who have left the world wiser than they found it.

Go on, Mr. Editor, in your support of the proposed memorial. Already the project is attracting the attention and sympathy of the press throughout the country. Let us all delight to honour him, and let those of us who are proud Salopians be doubly proud that the old town can never be the least among the cities of the world since it hath given to the nineteenth century its greatest scientist.

H.

Manchester, Feb. 14, 1894.

There followed an editorial note on 'The Darwin Correspondence':

A number of letters reached us this week too late for inclusion in the present issue. One of them is a second volley from 'A Believer', who soundly rates us for having dared to alter a word or two in her initial epistle. The whole of the belated correspondence shall appear in our next.—Ed., *S.C.*

Serious Damage in Shrewsbury

Now the very same page of the issue of *The Shrewsbury Chronicle* on Friday, 16 February 1894 which included these letters also contained a lengthy article entitled 'The Terrific Gale: Serious Damage in Shrewsbury'.

One of the most disastrous gales which has been experienced for very many years past swept over the kingdom on Sunday, and was attended by most serious, not to say calamitous consequences. The gale was doubtless the outcome of cyclonic disturbances wired from North America some days previously, the effects of which were expected to be felt in this country somewhat earlier. Unfortunately, however, the delay in the arrival of the gale did not lessen its fury, and it pursued its way across the country with devastating effect, wrecking houses and buildings, blowing down church steeples, and inflicting in many instances serious and fatal injuries. Shrewsbury had its full share of everything that happened save in one particular—no fatalities of any kind occurred; indeed, as far as we can learn, not a single personal accident has been recorded, which is nothing short of marvellous, considering the highly dangerous state of things that existed throughout Sunday.

Commencing on Saturday, the weather, for the second time during the past ten days, was extremely squally, and remained so on Sunday morning, but proved nothing exceptionally severe until midday had passed, when the wind gradually increased in strength, and gusts were howling through the street with terrific force. Matters went from bad to worse. By nightfall the boisterous wind had become a gale, which then burst forth in all its fury, creating general terror and alarm. Many people were afraid to venture out of doors, and those who did so had an experience the like of which they had never gone through before. It was almost impossible to walk along the streets, so exceedingly rough was the wind; it was very dangerous, too, for bricks, slates and tiles were being dashed from the housetops in all directions. From one house alone six large slates and a chimney-pot fell in less than five minutes, and some schoolchildren narrowly escaped being injured by them. But this experience soon became general throughout the town, causing the utmost consternation. Scores of chimney-pots were blown from their positions, falling onto roofs, breaking the slates, and leaving holes for the wind to enter and speedily unroof half the buildings. One of the earliest incidents happened in Chester Street, where the storm lifted a roof of galvanised iron, weighing about five cwt., off the premises of Mr. Ince, tinsmith, and blew it over the houses into Castle Foregate just above the railway bridge, where after striking the station buildings it fell to the ground with an alarming crash. A large haystack was blown over in Corporation Lane, and the hay was speedily scattered to the winds; and shortly after noon a chimney fell in Longden Coleham, scattering bricks and masonry all over the street. But as we have stated, the awful effect of the gale was not felt to any degree until after dark, when the work of devastation went on uninterruptedly for many hours. Persons who ventured out to church or chapel were more or less terrified by the wind which, driven against the windows with terrific dash, threatened to force them in. Fortunately, however, nothing serious took place; but there was a general feeling of disquietude that, should the tempest continue in its wild course, it would leave behind it consequences too serious to contemplate.

Shortly before half past nine, while the wind was roaring with a noise that resembled the roaring of the sea when in its most furious state, many of the residents of Castle Street, St. Mary's Street and the immediate locality were suddenly startled by a tremendous crash, which rose clearly above the noise of the gale raging without, and filled not a few with fear and trembling. No-one for a moment thought of what had really happened. It was a sort of noise resembling the discharge of cannon in rapid succession, followed immediately by a crackling sound which might be produced by timbers being suddenly snapped in two. Then came a heavy thud, and the disturbance apparently ceased. Many persons rushed into the street to ascertain the cause, when it was seen that a considerable portion of the steeple of St. Mary's Church had been blown down onto the roof of the building. The situation at that time was too pregnant with danger to allow of any close inspection into what had actually happened, but sufficient was seen to show that one of the most beautiful churches in the town had suffered very considerable damage. The news of the catastrophe spread like wildfire throughout the town, and many persons braved the elements and hurried to the spot, but the intelligence was not generally known until Monday morning, when on all sides there were heard expressions of profound regret. Throughout the day crowds of persons visited the scene in order to ascertain what had actually occurred, but the exterior view, bad as it was, was nothing to be compared with the scene of desolation which the interior presented. It was seen that about 40 feet of the heavy stonework forming the steeple had been blown down onto the nave of the church, carrying with it the whole of that portion of the building, which fell into the sacred edifice beneath. Some idea may be formed of the violent character of the crash, when we state that the height of the tower and steeple is 233 feet. The steeple has been under repair for some time, and several feet of new stone had been placed on the top—a work which, of course, necessitated the erection of a great deal of scaffolding; and it is thought that this had a great deal to do with the serious disaster which occurred, the planks and other material acting as a sort of lever for the wind. It is a remarkable fact, however, that the steeple was not blown off at the point where the new work commenced, but many feet below, and, looking at the structure from the street, it appeared as if it had been abruptly snapped apart. The entire floor of the nave was filled up with wreckage, and was generally in a sad state, masonry and woodwork being all jammed together in a heap. Of course every seat between the pillars of the nave for its entire length was smashed to pieces, and in the roof above there was a long wide gap, through which could be seen the whole of the remaining portion of the steeple, the top of which appeared to be in a very unsafe condition. The scene was a sad and extremely piteous one. The remains of the most beautiful ceiling, with tons upon tons of masonry, plaster, carved oak, &c., were piled up between the pillars supporting the aisles to a height of several feet and covering the entire area of the floor. The font had escaped destruction, as had also the pulpit, but the fine brass lectern was caught by the falling debris and was knocked back against the choir stalls. The damage done amounts to several thousand pounds.

> The accident happened, as we have previously stated, at half past nine, when the church was empty, but had it occurred a little more than an hour earlier the consequences would have been most appalling. Sunday was the day fixed for making the collections on behalf of the Shrewsbury hospitals, and at the evening service there was a very large congregation, and it is not difficult to forecast what must have been the fate of these people had the roof given way while they were inside. It seems that a few days previously one of the planks forming the scaffolding at the top of the steeple was blown onto the roof of the church while service was going on, causing considerable alarm; and on Sunday morning it was announced from the pulpit that there was no need for further alarm, as the scaffolding had been made secure. At that time no-one, of course, contemplated how soon scaffolding and steeple would find its way into the body of the church.
>
> On Monday afternoon a meeting of the authorities of St. Mary's was held, when it was decided to proceed with the work of restoration immediately. An appeal for subscriptions has been issued by the Rev. N. Poyntz, vicar. As soon as possible a number of workmen commenced operations with a view to clearing out the debris, and work is proceeding rapidly. Many hundreds of persons have passed through the church for the purpose of witnessing the wreckage. A box for donations in aid of the restoration fund has been placed at the door of exit, and the most practical sympathy has been shown with the movement. It is contemplated to hold services in the chancel and the adjoining chapel as soon as the screening required between the two portions of the building can be erected. We are also informed that it has been decided to hold a thanksgiving service in St. Chad's Church.

On another page was an editorial headed 'A Disastrous Gale':

> The fearful south-westerly gale which blew over the British Isles on Sunday last, and which did serious damage in all parts, seems to have concentrated itself for a special effort in this locality. But awful as some of its effects were, there was happily little loss of life, for which under all the circumstances Salopians have perhaps more reason to be grateful than residents of any other county. St. Mary's Church, so long the pride and boast of Shrewsbury, has suffered terribly. Its noble spire, one of the highest and most conspicuous in the land, was being repaired, and the workmen, just on the point of completing their perilous task, had left scaffolding at the summit in the expectation of being able to return to the work on Monday. But on Sunday night the wind became so violent that between forty and fifty feet of the steeple was toppled over and, falling towards the east, dropped right into the centre of the nave, destroying the roof and an exceptionally fine ceiling, together with the seats and much of the flooring. The Rev. Newdigate Poyntz, the vicar, writing on the subject on Monday, said St. Mary's 'stands

on the site of a previous Saxon church, and has a Norman tower on which a very lofty spire, reaching to a total height of 222 ft. was placed about A.D 1440; the nave arcade is very Early English, and until last night there was a very fine oak ceiling of the Perpendicular period; the tower and spire had shown signs of weakness, and workmen were engaged in replacing some of the top of the spire, which was badly cracked, when last night, about 9.30, the town was visited with a terrific gale, during which a large portion of the spire fell in upon the nave. The destruction wrought is indescribable, nearly the whole of the old oak ceiling is destroyed, and all that can now be seen in the nave is a heap of ruins 5ft. or 6 ft. high. I was endeavouring to raise funds to make the tower and spire safe, and am quite heartbroken at this terrible catastrophe, although there is much to be thankful for, as the church was filled an hour sooner with a large congregation, and had the fall occurred then 300 at least would have lost their lives. May I appeal most beseechingly to your readers for help to restore our ruin as far as it is possible?' In a circular signed by the Vicar and Churchwardens of St. Mary's, dated February 12, we find that the estimated cost of restoring the nave, tower and spire will be not less than £6,000, and towards this sum £500 of the donations already promised for the repair of the tower and spire will be available, leaving £5,500 to be raised. Thus the position is serious, but it might have been worse. The truth is, the borough has been saved, as by a miracle, from one of the most appalling calamities. But for this good fortune, hundreds of our friends and neighbours would have lost their lives—the whole town would have been turned into a place of mourning. We most sincerely sympathize with the Vicar and congregation of St. Mary's in the loss they have sustained. Heartily endorsing the appeal for financial aid, we are sure the response will be ready and generous, so that this old, historic pile may be at once restored to something of its former magnificence.

Religious Politics

The next issue of *The Shrewsbury Chronicle*, on Friday, 23 February, carried *inter alia* reports from other papers. One was headed: 'Musings of an Agricultural Philosopher'.

A most terrific storm swept across our county last Sunday week; even our towns had to feel its destructive effects. The spire of St. Mary's Church, which I believe stood highest and loftiest in Shrewsbury, and had just been repaired at a cost of over £1,000, was blown down into the church soon after the congregation had dispersed, causing a fresh damage that will take six or seven thousand to repair. Why spend so much on ornamental work, while thousands are perishing for want of knowledge at home and in foreign lands? In the country stacks are blown over, roofs are stripped, trees falling

> across one another in heaps, large boughs torn asunder—they help the firewood now coal is so dear. But the storm, like the deluge, purified the earth. Since then the temperature is milder, the air is calmer, the fields look greener, and the birds sing sweeter...
>
> G. Wright, Bellaport, Market Drayton (Feb. 16), in the *Mark-lane Express*

Another titbit of news in the same issue of *The Shrewsbury Chronicle* was headed 'Darwinism':

> The Duke of Saxe-Meiningen, Prince Bismarck and many other distinguished admirers of Professor Häckel, of Jena, the most eminent of the German Darwinites, sent him congratulatory telegrams on his sixtieth birthday on the 16th inst.

★

In Chapter XXV of his autobiography, Rudolf Steiner continued his discussion of Ernst Haeckel:

> At first I felt no need to meet Haeckel personally, though I was forced to think a great deal about him. His sixtieth birthday then arrived. I was induced to take part in a magnificent celebration arranged at the time in Jena...

The celebration took place on the next day, 17 February.

> ... The human aspect of this festivity attracted me. During the festive meal Haeckel's son, whom I had come to know in Weimar where he attended the art school, came up to me saying his father wanted to have me introduced to him, which the son then did.
>
> Thus I came to know Haeckel in person. He was an enchanting personality. A set of eyes looking naively into the world, so mildly that one felt his glance would shatter if penetrated by sharp thinking. It could only endure sense-impressions, not the thoughts manifested by things and processes. Every movement of Haeckel's was designed to give free play to what the senses express, not letting thoughts dominant in the movement be revealed. I understood why Haeckel was so fond of painting. He was absorbed in sense-perceptions. Where he had to start thinking, he ceased developing mental activity, preferring to capture what he had seen with his brush. This was the actual being of Haeckel. Had he developed only this, it would have revealed something unusually charming and human.
>
> But in a corner of his soul there was rummaging something which obstinately desired to assert itself as a particular thought-content. Something originating from quite different sources in the world than his sense for Nature. The trend of a previous earthly life, with a hint of fanaticism directed not towards Nature but towards quite other things, wanted to have

its fling. From subconscious regions of his soul, religious politics rose into life, using ideas of Nature in order to come to expression.[19]

Inside Haeckel were living two beings in this contradictory way. A human being with a mild, love-filled sense for Nature, behind whom was something like a shadow-being, with ideas incompletely thought-out, narrowly restricted and breathing of fanaticism. When Haeckel spoke, his mildness would hardly allow the fanaticism to pour into his words: it was as though a hidden demonic element was dulled down in his speech by a naturally willed gentleness. A human riddle, which when seeing it one could only love. When it gave judgement, one might often fall into anger. This was how I saw Haeckel, in the nineties of the last century, while he was preparing what then led to the wild spiritual battle which raged at the turn of the century on account of his trend of thought.

Sufficient Funds

With reference to religious politics, *The Shrewsbury Chronicle* of 23 February 1894 also carried in its column on 'Local and District Intelligence' an article headed 'Darwin, Providence, and the Steeple: A Funny Suggestion':

> The serious accident to St. Mary's Church during the gale on Sunday week was very naturally the topic of observations by most of the preachers on Sunday.
>
> The Bishop of Shrewsbury touched lightly upon the subject, and other congregations were reminded of the visitation and the marvellous escape from personal injury.
>
> The Vicar of St. Mary's (Rev. N. Poyntz), preaching within the damaged church itself, naturally could not pass it over without comment. Taking his text from 1 Chronicles 19:12 and 13, he said he desired to express great gratitude to the many friends of St. Mary's in Shrewsbury and elsewhere for the great sympathy and kindness they had shown in the great trial which had befallen them, and without which it would have been very hard indeed to bear. The circumstances under which they were assembled at that moment preached more eloquently than any human voice could possibly do. Could anyone (he asked) in the future doubt the providence of God? Not one soul was lost. Could they therefore doubt that God's hand was present throughout all, and that He was guiding, and ruling all? The fall of the spire should stop forever, in their mouths at least, the jargon about natural laws, natural forces and the like so common in the present day. Proceeding, the Vicar said he would make in a vague, indefinite way the following remarks:—One day this month—*this* month—a certain event occurred in Shrewsbury, and a few days after the spire was blown down by the act of God. Was there any connection between the two events? He thought it

likely, on account of a certain similarity of subject-matter between the two. If he (Mr. Poyntz) was right, it was at least possible that many had received a warning. Let them act upon it. If they pondered well over his remarks and digested them, they ought to bring in during the week sufficient funds to restore the church twice over. His last remark was a very brief one. Although the disaster was lamentable, still he could say—thank God it is as it is.

With regard to the 'event' above referred to, it is generally understood that Mr. Poyntz was alluding to the recent Darwin memorial meeting.

★

On another page in this same issue of *The Shrewsbury Chronicle* was printed 'The Disaster at St. Mary's, Shrewsbury: First List of Subscribers to Restoration'.

	£	s.	d.
Memor, J.G.W.	10	10	0
Bather, Ven. Archdeacon	10	0	0
Meakin, Mrs.	5	0	0
Butler, S.	10	0	0
Mears, Rev. H.G.	1	0	0
Brown, Rev. E.	1	1	0
Johnson, Rev. H.	15	0	0
Jelf, A.R., Q.C.	10	0	0
Burd, Miss, The Dana	5	0	0
Paget, Stephen	3	0	0
Working Man, eight half-crowns	1	0	0
*Shrewsbury, Lord Bishop of, and Lady Stamer	50	0	0
Hammonds, T.	2	2	0
Burd, Dr. C'warden	150	0	0
Atkinson, Mrs.	2	0	0
Bridges, Miss	10	0	0
Butler, Miss	5	0	0
Stanton, Geo.	500	0	0
Burd, Dr. and Mrs. Lycett	7	7	0
Bennett	0	10	0
Whitwell, Miss C.A.	1	1	0
R.A.L., Worcester	2	0	0
Thackeray, Mrs. M.T.	1	1	0
Smith, Miss Bryan	25	0	0
Genge, Rev. R.S.	1	1	0

	£	s.	d.
Simpson, Miss	2	5	0
Old Salopian (G.C.)	1	1	0
Allen, Prebendary	2	2	0
R.P.	10	0	0
Piper, E.J.	2	2	0
Wells, H.	50	0	0
Cuthbert, Rev. G.S.	1	1	0
*Steward, H.	20	0	0
Lovell, Mrs. Palmer	2	0	0
*Poyntz, Rev. Newdigate and Mrs., a thank-offering	450	0	0
A Widow's Mite	0	10	0
Osborne, Mrs.	1	1	0
Lawson, A.G.	8	3	0
Barker, S. (London)	2	0	0
Jenkins, E.F. (London)	5	5	0
Sale, Rev. C.J.	20	0	0
Haycock, Miss	1	1	0
Haycock, Miss M.	1	1	0
Sweeting, A.	0	10	0
Heber-Percy, Mrs.	1	0	0
Old Salopian	1	1	0
*Rope, H.J.	110	0	0
*Hawkins, Misses	110	0	0
Chance, A.F.	20	0	0
*Gough, W. and Mrs.	5	0	0

Name	£	s.	d.
Williams, Rev. J.E.	5	0	0
Salt, Miss	5	0	0
*Salt, Miss A.	20	0	0
Downward, Misses	35	0	0
Lloyd, Ven. Arch.	550	0	0
Phillips, Spencer	100	0	0
How, T.M.	50	0	0
Herbert, Major-Gen The Hon. W.H.	40	0	0
Bradford, Right Hon. The Earl of, Lord Lieutenant	100	0	0
Fenton, H.	150	0	0
Allcroft, H.J., High Sheriff	60	10	0
Ledger, E.H.	20	0	0
Graham, A. and Mrs.	10	5	0
Crump, V.	15	0	0
Parker, Rev. C.	25	0	0
Parker, Mrs. F.	10	10	0
Pavin, Miss	1	0	0
Thiselton, Rev. A.C.	1	1	0
Bell, Raisbeck	0	5	0
Saxton, Mrs.	50	0	0
Williams, W.M.	4	4	0
Lichfield	1	10	0
Bourne, W.	5	0	0
Bourne, R.H.	5	0	0
Two Ladies	0	10	0
Scarth, Miss	1	1	0
Arrowsmith, Miss	1	1	0
Arrowsmith, Miss E.	1	1	0
National and Provincial Bank	5	5	0
Graham, Miss	2	2	0
Poyntz, Rev. Nath.	5	0	0
Brett, Capt. R.N.	5	0	0
Brett, Mrs.	5	0	0
Bilton Club	10	0	0
Craig, W.W.	5	0	0
Stokes, Rev. H. and Mrs.	5	5	0
*Morris, W.B.	20	0	0
*Corbet, Lady	40	0	0
Robinson, Mrs. H.	2	2	0
Allen, Rev. E.E.	2	2	0
Hall, Rev. G.	10	0	0
Anstice, R.E.	5	0	0
Wakefield, Right Rev. Lord Bishop of	10	0	0
Anstice, Mrs. S.	10	0	0
Vane, Rev. Hon. H.T.	3	3	0
Mytton, B.A.	5	0	0
Scott, Mrs. W.	5	0	0
Moser, Miss	50	0	0
Wilding, Miss	2	2	0
Symes, Rev. J.E.	1	1	0
Carpenter, Rev. E.S.	2	2	0
Auden, Rev. T.	10	10	0
Salwey, A.	1	1	0
Corbet, Miss I.A.	10	0	0
Corbet, Miss G.U.	10	0	0
*Price, Thomas, and daughter	8	0	0
Brandon, Gustavus	10	10	0
*Eyton, Mrs. R.M.	5	0	0
Heitland, Mrs.	1	1	0
Moser, E.B.	100	0	0
Patchett, Major	10	10	0
Cope, Miss H.	1	1	0
Atkinson, A. (Dover)	1	0	0
Gavin, Miss	4	0	0
Howells, T.M.	50	0	0
Tipton, Miss	10	0	0
Blunt, W.E. (London)	5	0	0
Baker, G.	1	1	0
*Brace, Mr.	20	0	0
*MacCleod, H. and Mrs.	4	4	0
*Poole and Son	20	0	0
*Hay, W.R.	20	0	0
Webster, J.B. and Mrs.	3	3	0
Jackson, Mrs.	0	5	0
Panting, Miss	10	0	0
Edwards, T.	1	0	0
Colvill, J.C.	5	0	0
Burd, Miss M.	2	0	0
Calvert, E., LL.D.	5	0	0

	£	s	d
*Williams, Mr. and Mrs., Hotspur St.	10	10	0
Juson, Mrs.	5	5	0
Morgan, Mrs. and the Misses	5	0	0
Meyrick, Colonel Sir T.C., Bart	5	5	0
Hawkins, W. (Manchester)	20	0	0
Taylor, R.	10	0	0
Pickering, J.E.	5	5	0
Juckes, the Misses	1	10	0
Humphreys, Mrs.	50	0	0
Humphreys, Miss R.	10	0	0
Humphreys, W.W.	50	0	0
Sprott, Mrs.	5	0	0
Lock, G.H.	10	0	0
James, E.	2	2	0
Hancocks, M.W.	1	1	0
Gottlieb, A.W.	1	1	0
Bather, Miss E.L.	1	1	0
Heitland, W.E.	1	1	0
Hutchison, Rev. E.A.	1	1	0
Corser, Mr. and Mrs., The Crescent	20	0	0
Anon.	1	0	0
Salt, Mrs. W.	5	0	0
How, W.M.	21	0	0
Saunders, Rev. A. and Mrs.	5	0	0
Wrangham, F. (Camb.)	1	1	0
Toye, W.	2	2	0
Carr, Mrs.	1	1	0
Fisher, E. (Newton Abbot)	5	0	0
M.B. (Kennington)	15	0	0
T.R.	1	0	0
Gethin, J.	5	0	0
Pigg, Mrs.	1	1	0
Cureton, E., M.D.	15	0	0
Higgin, Mrs. (Oban)	1	0	0
E.C.A.	2	2	0
Rope, Monica, a new half-crown	0	2	6
Do., (collected by)	1	1	0
Watson, J.	100	0	0
Southam, T.	25	0	0
Barker, J.	7	2	0
Billson, J.W.	0	5	0
E.C.A.	2	2	0
Giovanetti	1	0	0
Corrie, Mrs.	2	2	0
Adams, Mrs., Newport	5	0	0
Mainwaring, Mrs. A.M.	5	0	0
Twentyman, H.	1	0	0
Anderson, Mrs. R.	1	1	0
Forrest and Son	5	0	0
Davies, H.W.	2	2	0
Williams, Miss H.	1	1	0
Gwynne, T.	1	0	0
Mole, J.H.	2	2	0
Manton and Mole	2	2	0
Withers, R.W.O., M.D.	35	0	0
Heighway, Mr. and Mrs.	5	0	0
Adams, F.E.	2	2	0
Salusbury, Rev. A.P.	2	0	0
Mordaunt, Rev. O.	1	0	0
Hunt, Rev. H.B.	1	0	0
Haslehurst, Rev. W.G.	1	0	0
Pardoe, Mrs.	5	0	0
Hallam, G.H.	5	0	0
Moss, Rev. Preben.	200	0	0
Middleton, R.	5	0	0
Acton, E.W.T., Captain	5	0	0
Beck, P.A., J.P.	5	0	0
Chandless, W.	10	10	0
Parson-Smith, J., J.P.	10	10	0
Marten, H.	2	0	0
Maddock, H.F.	2	0	0
Laing, J. (sale of photos)	5	0	0
Thankful for mercies	5	0	0
Selwyn, Rev. W.	5	0	0
Oxley, Mr. and Mrs.	10	0	0
Halke, Rev. J.	5	0	0
Bather, Mrs. E.	5	0	0
Guise, Miss	10	10	0
Blunt, T.P.	2	2	0

Name	£	s.	d.
Parrock, R.	0	10	0
Corbet, Rev. A., R.D.	5	0	0
Burd, Rev. Preben.	5	0	0
Bennett (Castle Gates)	3	3	0
Townsend, Mr. and Mrs. (Castle St.)	5	0	0
Williams, Miss (Princess Street)	2	0	0
Craig, Mrs. (Crescent)	5	0	0
Levett, Captain	1	0	0
Wakeman, Sir Offley, Bart.	52	2	0
Herbert, Hon. R.C.	5	0	0
Harries, H.	1	1	0
Buddicom, Rev. R.J. and Mrs.	1	10	0
Corbet, Prebendary Rev. G.W., R.D.	50	0	0
Horner, Mrs. E.	3	3	0
*Charlewood, Rev. G.S. and Mrs.	3	0	0
Charlewood, Mrs. T.	1	0	0
Hopkins, Miss H.	10	0	0
Williams, P. (Hinstock Hall)	50	0	0
Griffithes, F.K.	1	1	0
Whately, Mrs. W. (Hull)	5	0	0
Harding, W.E.	10	0	0
Penn, C.	5	5	0
Warwick, Geo.	5	5	0
Trouncer, Mr. and Mrs.	40	0	0
Honyman, Sir W. and Lady	20	0	0
Churchill, Rev. C.J.	10	0	0
All Saints, Shrewsbury	2	14	4
Cree, Rev. J.A. and Mrs., Sunningdale	10	0	0
Wenlock, Dowager Lady	5	0	0
Hasker, Miss	5	5	0
Dales and Son, Wyle Cop.	12	12	0
Evans, Miss, Severn House	5	5	0
Pearce, Mrs. E.	1	0	0
Bennett, F.E., The Schools	5	5	0
Brooke, Rev. C.E.	1	1	0
Waxworks Museum (Mr. Rowley), a day's receipts	2	13	4
Byolin, H.	10	0	0
Hamlin, Rugely	1	0	0
Naylor, Mrs.	5	0	0

*These payable in four years

The following subscriptions had been made to the former Fund for the Repair of the Tower and Spire, and still stand good:—

Name	£	s.	d.
Greene, H.D., Q.C., M.P.	25	0	0
Field, Colonel	25	0	0
Barnard, Right Hon. Lord	20	0	0
Lloyd, G.B.	5	0	0
The Mayor (W.L. Browne)	10	0	0
Eddowes, W.	5	0	0
Kenyon, Rt. Hon. Lord	5	0	0
Taylor, R. (Stroud)	5	0	0
Stone, S., 1st don.	10	0	0
Wilding, L.	5	0	0
Evans, Geo.	10	0	0
Williams, W.T.	3	3	0
Goodwin, J.	5	0	0
Goodwin, R.	5	0	0
Woodhouse, W.	5	0	0
Scull, Messrs.	5	0	0
Sandford, H.	5	0	0
Lowndes, W.L.	1	0	0
Oakley, Mrs. (Shelton)	5	0	0

A total sum of not less than £6,000 will be required to restore the nave and spire and make the tower safe. Towards this contributions, which may be paid in four yearly instalments, are most earnestly asked, and may be paid to the Vicar, the Rev. Newdigate Poyntz.

Further list next week.

The Cause of the Downfall

In this same issue of *The Shrewsbury Chronicle* on 23 February the 'Letters to the Editor' opened with one entitled 'A "Judgement" on Shrewsbury':

Sir,—

On Sunday last I attended the evening service at St. Mary's Church. Our worthy Vicar in the course of his sermon stated that the disaster which occurred on the previous Sabbath was a judgement on the town for wishing to promote a memorial to Charles Darwin. Would it not be nearer the mark that it was the displeasure of the Almighty at the Vicar's allowing the mountebank performance called 'High Ritual' to be carried on to the great extent that it is, to the detriment of pure Protestantism?

Parishioner.

February 21st, 1894

A further series of letters was headed 'Charles Darwin':

Dear Sir,–

When I sent my letter for publication last week, I was not aware that you reserved to yourself the right to add to letters sent to you for publication, or to keep back certain portions of them. I understood they were published as sent, for only thus do they correctly represent the views of the writers. But I find in the case of the one I sent to you, on the Darwin memorial, you have added an unauthorized heading, viz., '(From a Lady's Point of View)'. You have left out the last paragraph, which runs thus: 'But the foundation cannot be destroyed; it is a sure foundation. (Isa. 23:16).' Also the closing words, 'Leaving this with your Christian readers,' are omitted; and the signature is altered from 'A Believer in the Inspired Word of God' to simply 'A Believer'. Is this fair? And what can be the object of these alterations, omissions and additions? I beg to return to you, with the writer's permission to publish them, two letters, received through you and forwarded on to me. They will show that there are others who, like myself, sigh and cry for the abominations about to be done in our midst (Ezek. 9:4 and 8:11–12) and that it is not only 'from a lady's point of view' that the Darwin memorial is thus regarded. Kindly print them in full, and oblige

Yours as previously,

A Believer in the Inspired Word of God

(Copies)

Ley Grange, near Shrewsbury, Feb 9th, 1894.

Dear Anonymous Lady,—

I have today read, and rejoice over, your most excellent letter in the *Shrewsbury Chronicle*. I now beg leave to present, and trust you will accept, my most grateful thanks. Oh that other Christians and Ministers of the Word 'were not dumb dogs, lying down, loving to slumber', but spoke as loudly, plainly and honestly as you have done, for the truth, the honour, and the glory of God! I had myself written a few lines for the *Chronicle* this week; but did not send it, as I felt it would be tedious to an octogenarian to probably enter into controversy and letter warfare with a host of infidels, and that I had better adopt instead the prayer of the Psalmist:—'Set a watch, O Lord, before my mouth, and keep the door of my lips.' (Ps.1:30.) I have asked the Editor of the *Chronicle* to direct this for me, as I know not your honoured address; and with renewed thanks, believe me

Your obliged and faithful

Robert Dayrell (Clerk, M.A.).

P.S.—I will add overleaf what I wrote myself—not half so good as yours.

(What I wrote but did not send to Editor of *Chronicle*):

'I see in *Shrewsbury Chronicle* it is proposed to raise a subscription or memorial to the late Charles Darwin. I am at a loss to know what real benefit or real advantage the inhabitants of Shrewsbury have received, or are receiving, from the late Charles Darwin. I feel almost sure he was a contemporary with me at Shrewsbury School, and remember him being at Christ College, Cambridge, and one day an acquaintance of his said: "Look, here goes Darwin, he's off to examine a dead hare he knows of, and expects to find a particular beetle, as the hare will be ripe enough to hold one today." If I am told the subscription is for the benefit the inhabitants of Shrewsbury have received from his book on the *Origin of Species*, the first question I ask is: have they read this book, or have they not? If they have, let them tell me what benefit they have derived from it! And if they have not, what good has this book been to them?

I, for one, have not read it, being perfectly satisfied upon the "origin of species" as told me long before Darwin was born. Thus: "My bones are not hid from thee. Though I be made secretly and fashioned beneath in the earth, Thine eyes did see my substance, yet being imperfect, and in Thy Book were all my members written, which day by day were fashioned when as yet there were none of them." Instead of this memorial let Protestants (alas how few) propose one to the noble army of English martyrs—Rogers, Ridley, Latimer, Cranmer, etc. I will gladly subscribe thereto. Isa. 55, 2 v.: "Wherefore do ye spend money for that which is not bread and your gains for that which satisfieth not?" '

Ley Grange, near Shrewsbury, Feb. 13, 1894.

Dear and Respected Anonymous Lady,—

Allow me again to present through the Editor of the *Chronicle* my grateful thanks for your condescension and Christian kindness in writing to me, and also for your two very acceptable hymns. I thank God that I find there are still those within reach of me who fear, love and honour God their Creator and Jesus Christ their Redeemer, and are ready if need be to suffer for the Christian religion. Therefore let us put on the noble armour of God, that we may be able to stand against the wiles of the devil. For we wrestle not only against flesh and blood, but against principalities, against powers, against the rulers of the darkness of this world, against spiritual wickedness in high places. If you elect to publish my two previous letters on this, in reply to yours in last week's *Chronicle*, pray do so with or without my signature, as I am not ashamed of the Gospel of Christ. Again and again, dear anonymous lady, accept my humble thanks, and believe me

Your obliged and faithful servant,

Robt. Dayrell (Clerk, M.A.)

Another letter was headed 'Why Did the Steeple Fall? The Question Answered':

Sir,—

In view of the recent calamity which has befallen the finest of Shrewsbury churches, I cannot but recall to mind a conversation I had many years ago with the late Mr. S. Pountney Smith. When entrusted with the repair of the spire of St. Mary's Church, in or about the year 1850, he surrounded the whole of the tower and spire, from top to bottom, with a carefully constructed and securely bolted scaffolding, the admiration of all who beheld it for its simplicity of design, its strength and stability. On the occasion to which I refer he was showing me a sketch of this scaffolding, of which he was justly proud, when I asked him why he considered it necessary to surround the *whole* structure, rather than those particular portions only which needed repair. His reply I well remember: 'If I had placed inadequately supported scaffolding halfway up that spire or near the top of it, the first gale of wind would probably have brought the entire steeple down with a crash.' His words, alas, have proved prophetic.

A London Vicar

Feb. 20, 1894

Yet another letter was headed 'An Extraordinary Suggestion':

Sir,—

In a sermon preached by the Vicar at St. Mary's, upon the sad calamity which occurred a week or so ago, I notice that Mr. Poyntz infers that possibly the cause of the fall was due not to what everybody else believed, viz. the terrific gale aided by the fact of certain scaffolding attached to the spire, but from the fact that a certain meeting was held in Shrewsbury a few weeks ago!! Well, this is enough to stagger anyone, but it yet remains to be told what the supposed meeting was; and now, by looking further down, I see it is generally understood that Mr. Poyntz was alluding to the recent Darwin Memorial Meeting!!! Is this so, Mr. Poyntz? If so, I can only say, good gracious, are we living in the 19th century or not? If I remember rightly, when the aforesaid meeting, a most influential one, was held, the following were some of the strongest supporters of the proposed Darwin Memorial Fund:—The Bishop of Shrewsbury, Archdeacon Lloyd, Rev. H.W. Moss, Rev. Myers and Rev. Draper; and now we are told, indirectly perhaps, that the fact of this meeting being held was the cause of the downfall of St. Mary's spire!!! Well, I've no wish to attempt to eulogize upon the memory of the noble man Darwin, for that is unnecessary; but I would respectfully suggest that the Vicar of St. Mary's should think a little more deeply before he speaks, and I can hardly realize that the clergyman of such an important church as St. Mary's, Shrewsbury, should endeavour to implant upon his followers such an extraordinary suggestion, and I think the Rev. Poyntz will on reflection consider he has somewhat overstepped his mark, i.e., if he is a co-worker in the Church with the respected clergymen whose names I have mentioned as staunch supporters of the Darwin Memorial.

Salopian

21st Feb., 1894

★

This same issue of *The Shrewsbury Chronicle* also carried an editorial on 'St. Mary's Steeple':

> The disaster which has befallen the most beautiful, if not the most ancient, of our Shrewsbury churches naturally has called forth expressions of regret from every part of the kingdom, and we are glad to say that subscriptions towards the immediate restoration of the stately edifice are being sent in so freely that there is little if any danger that the Vicar will be embarrassed through want of funds. This is as it should be. It is only right that we vie with one another in supporting appeals of this description. Everybody admits that the social and material well-being of the country depends in no small measure on the splendid work which the Christian Church is performing, and when unruly elements overturn a steeple, or some other kind of misfortune overtakes a congregation, men of all sorts and conditions will at once step forward to assist in repairing the loss. It is very gratifying to us to perceive that there is in this matter so much unanimity in Shrewsbury. With scarcely an exception, the Churches of all denominations have made special pulpit reference to the disaster, and there is no doubt that in most of them

there will be collections to aid in raising the £6,000 necessary to restore St. Mary's to something like its former condition. Even the Romanists who boast of a 'Cathedral' in Shrewsbury have made the occasion one for showing that, in essentials at any rate, they are in full sympathy with the rest of the Christian Church. We learn that their evening service on Sunday last week was one of thanksgiving 'for the preservation of the lives of so many of their fellow townspeople'. As might have been expected at such a time, there has been no lack of explanations why so prominent a landmark as St. Mary's succumbed before the gale of the 11th. The following day was the anniversary of the birth of Charles Darwin, and one gentleman (or was it a lady who wrote to us on the subject?) says it is clear that the Creator overturned the spire to evince His displeasure at the proposal to erect a memorial of the famous scientist! The Vicar of St. Mary's, preaching in the wrecked sanctuary on Sunday evening, and surrounded by countless signs of the fearful havoc wrought by the storm, took up the same parable, and made pointed reference to the recent meeting held in the Guildhall: 'Could anyone,' said Mr. Poyntz, 'in the future doubt the providence of God? Not one soul was lost. Could they therefore doubt that God's hand was present throughout all, and that He was guiding and ruling all? The fall of the spire should stop forever, in their mouths at least, the jargon about natural laws, natural forces and the like, so common in the present day . . . One day this month—*this* month—a certain event occurred in Shrewsbury, and a few days afterwards the spire was blown down by the act of God. Was there any connection between the two events? He thought it likely, on account of a certain similarity of subject-matter between the two. If he was right, it was at least possible that many had received a warning. Let them act upon it. If they pondered well over his remarks, and digested them, they ought to bring in during the week sufficient funds to restore the church twice over.' Thus the Vicar of St. Mary's identifies himself with the belief that God, disapproving of the erection of a Darwin memorial in Shrewsbury, shattered the spire as a solemn warning to us not to proceed further in that project. The builders of Shrewsbury have also entered the field with a theory as to the cause of the misfortune, and in our 'Letters to the Editor' still further explanations will be found, including the suggestion of a London Vicar, a native of Shrewsbury, who seems to corroborate that of our local experts. Where so many valuable opinions have been expressed, it is not for us to say who are right; nor are we sufficiently concerned to venture on the assertion that any particular opinion is erroneous. What we are anxious about is not the cause of the disaster to our magnificent old church, the finest and most beautiful that we possessed, but the restoration of the structure. Instead of theory let us have practice. Now is the time, not for talk, but for benevolence; and there is no higher kind of benevolence than that which upholds the Christian religion.

This Generous Spirit

In the next issue of *The Shrewsbury Chronicle*, on 2 March,[20] the 'Letters to the Editor' opened with one headed 'Wind':

Sir,—

The gale which destroyed part of St. Mary's spire seems to have brought with it threatenings to a structure yet unbuilt, the 'Darwin Memorial'.

There is, however, no real cause for fear. It is only a little wind from *certain points*, and not dangerous.

Œolus.

Feb 24th, 1894.

There was also a series entitled 'The Fallen Spire':

Sir,—

If the catastrophe which befel St. Mary's spire on the night of the 11th February was the work of the 'hand of God', and a warning to us not to proceed further in the matter of the Darwin memorial, it is curious that St. Chad's, whose Vicar (the Bishop) is known to be highly in favour of the movement, came out of the gale 'scot free'. The dome was not doomed. One would have thought that the spire of St. Mary's would have escaped, since Mr. Poyntz was the only clergyman who refused to sign or countenance the requisition appealing to the Mayor to convene the Darwin meeting. Is it possible, Mr. Editor, that this refusal to sign was the cause of God's anger and of the overthrow of the steeple?

O.E.H.

February 27th, 1894.

Sir,—

More than four decades since, when Mr. S. Pountney Smith's admirable scaffolding surrounded St. Mary's spire, a shrewd Salopian lawyer and I met in full view of the work going on. The gentleman remarked: 'I do admire Pountney Smith. He has taken that mass of stone in his arms as safely as a loving mother holds her infant.' I could but approve of the apt illustration, for truly Mr. Smith had combined science, common sense, mathematics and geometry together. One structure of wood and iron enabled him to smile at the gale, and the pile was kept in safety.

A friend of S.P.S.

Feb. 24, 1894.

P.S.—I have received the following from a friend in the town:—

(Copy.)

'I am glad you take the view you do about Darwin, and heartily approve of your letter thereon. I presume that neither you nor I could endorse

Darwin's general views on theology; but that should not for a moment interfere with our approval of him (and admiration too) as a great interpreter of God's Word in Nature. What does the first chapter of Genesis teach but gradual development, the time "day" being taken in its common-sense meaning of "period"? It is always "first the blade, then the ear, then the full corn in the ear."'

Yours very truly,

'W.T.'

Feb. 20, 1894.

Sir,—

I have read the correspondence in your valuable *Shrewsbury Chronicle* in reference to the Darwin Memorial, and the opposition of the 'Believer' or 'Believers' (for I see there are two of them) to any such object. I can quite entertain the idea of opposition from some over-zealous Christian to the memorial, but it caps all I ever expected at this advanced and enlightened period to find a gentleman (Rev. Poyntz) intimating to his flock that natural laws and forces had nothing at all to do with the fall of St. Mary's spire, but that it was the act of God as a punishment for holding a meeting to commemorate Charles Darwin. I will for a moment suppose, or try to suppose, that it was the act of God to show His displeasure to those who were the prime movers in the Darwin Memorial meeting. Such being the case, can I solicit money to rebuild what God in His anger has cursed? If it were the act of God, why is the contractor changed? Somebody must think that he is to blame, and if all I hear be true, there were some very good natural causes assisting the wind to blow down this identical spire. I am glad to see that money (nearly enough) is already obtained to rebuild the spire and restore the church; and I have no doubt as to the funds for the Darwin Memorial being provided at an early date, notwithstanding the opposition of even three 'Believers', for I will put the minister down for one. I am pleased to find that our worthy Mayor (although a sympathizer and subscriber to the restoration fund) has got pluck enough left to carry on the Darwin Memorial efforts to a successful termination.

I have before me an old Directory of Shropshire, which, speaking of the building of our two toll-free bridges at a cost of £30,000, the writer says: 'Thus while in cities of greater commercial importance no public works of great extent have been carried on without the exaction of tolls and contributions, the inhabitants of this town and county, to their immortal honour, erected two noble bridges by which the trade of the adjacent districts was freed from the burden of a vexatious tax, and the whole of the money was raised by voluntary subscriptions. This is one of the numerous instances of that public spirit which has often been remarked as a leading characteristic of the Salopians.' Hoping that the Darwin Memorial Fund will give undoubted evidence that this generous spirit still exists (and the response to the church restoration shows that it certainly does), I will say no more.

William Leah

St. Alkmond's Place, Feb 27, 1894.

Subscribers to Restoration

On another page in this issue of 2 March was printed 'The Disaster at St. Mary's, Shrewsbury: Second List of Subscribers to Restoration':

	£	s.	d.
Taylor, Edmund, Oxton	100	0	0
Mostyn Owen, C.R.	2	2	0
Jones, Rev. W.L.	1	1	0
Beach, F. Stone	2	2	0
Thacker, G., Huddersfield	2	2	0
R.E.W., London	50	0	0
Jurgens, Ant, Holland (per Mr. Steward, Pride Hill)	5	0	0
Edgell, Col., the family of	3	0	0
Pitman, W.M., London	1	1	0
Wright, A.	1	1	0
*Adnitt, H.W.	5	0	0
Mathias, J.P., Chester Street	2	2	0
Wood, Miss, Belle Vue	3	3	0
Meire, R.A.	10	10	0
Edgell, R.A.	1	1	0
Ingram, Rev. H.S., The Schools	5	5	0
McCorquodale, A.C.	5	0	0
Thanksgiving Service at St. Chad's	28	6	0
Bryce Smith	1	1	0
Cassels, H.W., Pride Hill	1	1	0
Greene, H.D., Q.C., M.P.	300	0	0
Betham, Mrs.	1	0	0
Woodward, Rev. H.H.	2	0	0
Corser, E.G.S.	5	0	0
Rouse Boughton, The Misses	2	0	0
Johnstone, Rev. R.	2	2	0
Holt, G.J.	10	0	0
Ralph, Mrs.	1	1	0
Eddowes, W. and Mrs.	10	0	0
Old Salopian	2	2	0
Pitt, Rev. K.M.	0	10	0
*Sheringham, Rev. W.A., R.D.	5	0	0
Wood, W.H.	2	0	0
Price, Mrs. T.S.	2	2	0
*Glennie, Rev. H.J.	2	0	0
Burd, Rev. F.	1	0	0
Buchanan, Phillips	5	0	0
Salter, Mrs. J.	1	1	0
Green-Price, Sir R., Bart	5	0	0
*Elsmere, W.	10	0	0
Lichfield, Lord Bishop of	10	0	0
Cooper, Miss	50	0	0
Wakeman, H.O., Oxford	5	0	0
Juson, Mrs.	25	0	0
Burr, G.	10	10	0
Alcock, R.W.	1	1	0
Nicholls, The Misses	5	0	0
E.H.	0	5	0
Corbet, Miss S.R.	10	0	0
Corbet, Miss S.H.	10	0	0
Southam, W.T. and Mrs.	4	4	0
Deedes, Whyndam	5	0	0
Warter, Mrs. T.	2	0	0
Mainwaring, R.K.	5	5	0
Letts, Rev. J.D., Stamford Hill	2	2	0

Name	£	s	d	Name	£	s	d
Harwood, Rev. T.E.	0	10	6	Russell, Henry	2	2	0
Jones, Rev. J.R.	1	1	0	Plimmer, T.	2	2	0
Hughes, H.H.	2	2	0	*Cartwright, J.J.	2	2	0
Rowland, A.C.	1	1	0	Hasler, Mrs.	1	1	0
Evans, S., Belle Vue	1	0	0	Bridgeman, Mrs. H.	2	0	0
Edwards, Mr. and Mrs., Coton Hill	0	10	6	Isham, Sir Charles, Bart.	5	0	0
S.E.J., in memory of	100	0	0	Sladen, F.St. B.	2	2	0
Cooper, Rev. N., R.D.	25	0	0	Millbank, Mrs., Bicton	10	0	0
Billings, Rev. E.T., R.D.	10	10	0	Venables, Mrs.	2	2	0
Blower, B.	10	0	0	Burd, Mrs. and Misses, Edgmond	1	1	0
Hughes, Mrs., Coatham	1	1	0	Rabone, Rev. T.H.	1	1	0
Eyton, Miss A.M., Hants.	1	1	0	Druce, Miss F., London	5	0	0
Ramsbotham, Mrs.	5	0	0	Spearman, R.H., & Mrs.	1	0	0
Peele, E. Cresswell	100	0	0	Bullock, E., Milk Street	2	2	0
Oxley, Mrs. R.	5	0	0	Jackson, A.	10	10	0
Randles, E.	2	2	0	Jackson, Conway, a new crown	0	5	0
Broadbent, H.	5	0	0	Norton, G.	5	5	0
Salter, Benj.	5	5	0	Lang, 2nd don. from sale of photos	5	0	0
Kitson, W. and Mrs. Shiphay	10	0	0	Southam, S. Clement	5	0	0
Haydon, W.D., The Schools	10	10	0	Southam, J. Downes	5	0	0
Foster, W.O.	100	0	0	Blunt, Miss A., sale of pictures	1	0	0
Thomason, Miss	1	1	0	Blunt, Miss E.M., sale of verses	2	10	0
Norris, Mr. and Mrs., Tenbury	3	0	0	Oakley, Mrs., Shelton	25	0	0
Scott, W.E., Monkmoor.	5	0	0	Ditto, collected by	15	6	0
Johnson, Rev. J.E., Loudon	0	14	0	Sandford, Mrs., Sandford	25	0	0
Windsor-Clive, Lt.-Col.	20	0	0	Chance, G., London	10	0	0
Turnbull, Mrs. Cheswardine	0	10	0	Annand, Rev. A.W.	2	2	0
Lonsdale, Miss, Herts.	5	0	0	Corser, G.W.S., Clevedon	1	1	0
Gardner, H.W., Swan Hill	4	4	0	Hamilton, W.P.	2	2	0
France, John	3	3	0	Little and Cooper	1	1	0
Meyricke, T.C.	0	10	6	S.S.	1	1	0
Whitfield, Mrs.	2	2	0	W. (Anon.)	0	10	0
Fox, G.J.	5	5	0	Gouldborne, W., Pride Hill	1	1	0
Armytage, F.R.	5	5	0	Thrutchley Bros., L. per J. Breeze	5	5	0
Purslow, H.T., 2 Pride Hill	3	3	0	Pigott, Dr. and Mrs.	5	0	0
				Watkins, Robert	1	0	0

*These payable in four years

Errata last week corrected.

Hay, W.R.	5 0 0	Cureton, E., M.D., and Mrs.	5 5 0
Colvill, J.C.	10 0 0	Juson, Miss	5 5 0

Further contributions, which may be paid in four yearly instalments, will be gratefully received, and may be made to the Rev. Newdigate Poyntz, Vicar; or to either of the Churchwardens, or at any Bank in the town.

Of the Highest Service to the World

The next issue of *The Shrewsbury Chronicle*, on 9 March, contained under the title 'The Fall of the Steeple' a note:

The correspondence on this subject must now cease.—Ed, *S.C.*

This note was immediately followed by a letter headed 'Darwin Memorial: Another Lady's View':

Sir,—

Ladies have figured prominently in the correspondence evoked by the Darwin Memorial Scheme. Will you allow another lady to submit a point of thought, viz: how by the results of such work as Darwin's, one can be led more and more 'through Nature up to Nature's God'—how those who in the secrets of Nature love to read the wisdom of God can gain a more cultured piety, a deepened intellectual faith. Most among the Church's gifts to me, I love and revere the inspired Word of God, but I love and revere too that second and supplementary Word of God in His Book of Nature. Between the two books I know there can be no irreconcileableness or disharmony except in seeming, and that by reason of our clouded vision, defective knowledge and imperfect powers. And one is grateful to the apostles of that second and supplementary revelation, whose trained genius, invincible ardour and patient self-devotion have disclosed to us more of its veiled mysteries and hidden love.

A Salopian Lady

Gloucester, Mar. 3, 1894.

★

The correspondence columns in the next issue, that of 16 March, published further letters on the subject. The first was headed 'Darwin and Revelation':

Sir,—

It is proposed to institute some memorial in honour of the late Professor Darwin as one illustrious as a man of science, especially in the domain of

Nature, and in this as a maintainer of what is understood by the word 'Evolution', as shown in his works such as the *Origin of Species* and the *Descent of Man*. This leads me to ask whether the Professor believed mankind to be the descendants of lower grades of animal creation. If so, and if he thus disbelieved the scriptural declaration that man was made, in his perfect character, directly from the dust of the earth, how can those who believe that Scripture to be a divine revelation consistently honour—as it is proposed to do—one who did not so believe it?

Suum cuique

March 13, 1894.

The second was headed 'Darwin and his Work':

Sir,—

Had St. Mary's steeple top gone up instead of coming down when dislodged by the force of the wind, we might with some show of reason have regarded it as a sign that heaven was displeased by the late discussion on the subject of a memorial to Darwin as a student of natural law. As it was, the never-ceasing forces of natural law were seen in its fall before the gale, and the lesson taught us was that we ought more carefully to study those laws and attend to their requirements. I refer to the laws of gravitation and exact science, of course, for it is on their power being rightly made use of and obeyed that the safety of steeples depends.

Men of science teach us something of the many laws by which, as we learn from Scripture, God as the centre of all life and power rules the material world. From the beginning, says the Scripture, the things that are made show forth His power and divinity. Newton was the great founder of the study of exact science. Darwin pursued his investigations chiefly on the laws of growth. He, as other students do on their special lines of work, propounded theories. Such theories are mostly regarded by the men who suggest them merely as tentative. They are almost necessary to them for the purposes of investigation; and as experiment and further observation prove them more or less false they are qualified or entirely discarded by men of science themselves who, while many of their theories seem to militate against Scripture-witness, by their discoveries are proving more clearly the wisdom with which truth has for ages been enshrined amidst the beautiful figures of Scripture. By their studies many superstitious falsehoods have been dissolved, and our fixed and very limited interpretations of Scripture often broken, though only to allow the testimony there given to rise higher on its own great and central line in harmony with the rising standards of science, so far as they are held only on behalf of ascertained truth in regard to the material world.

Students of science, merely as such, are often—as in the case of Darwin—less than no guide to the knowledge of theology to which one of your correspondents refers. He remarks we may value Darwin's researches for what they are worth without adopting the theological views. I should think so; but it is very doubtful if he had any such views. He was contented to spend his life in the study of the laws of growth, as Newton in the studies of other laws. Whatever value such studies have in relation to the material world, they open not to man the mysteries of the spiritual world. From Scripture we learn that the things of that kingdom the natural man seeth not, neither can he know them. Even St. Mary's steeple belongs not to that kingdom, for we all can see it plainly enough. It belongs to the material world, and upon the laws of God that rule that world its safety depends. Let us hope we soon shall see its sharp-cut top rebuilt with due regard to the action of those laws, so that it will stand. Certainly as a thing of beauty, and for long as a reminder, calling to thankfulness that the church services were over before it fell before the conflicting forces that raised that wind. With great esteem for natural law, and for the revelation of Scripture,

I am

Common Sense

Wonderful Sympathy and Generosity

The next week's issue of *The Shrewsbury Chronicle*, on 23 March, carried *inter alia* the following advertisement:

MUSIC HALL, SHREWSBURY
an
EVENING CONCERT
will be given in the above Hall
ON THURSDAY MARCH 29TH
by the
MEMBERS OF MISS RACHEL GRAY'S SINGING CLASS,
in aid of
ST. MARY'S RESTORATION FUND

Two Cantatas will be performed for the first time in Shrewsbury:
'THE REVENGE' Villiers Stanford
'THE SUN WORSHIPPERS' Goring Thomas

Vocalists: Miss Annie Swinfen, Mr. Charles Chilley.
Solo Violin: Mr. Hubert Salt
Solo Violoncello: Mr. A.J. Priestley
Solo Pianoforte: Miss M. Holloway
Piano: Mr. H. Byolin
Organ: Mr. J.T. Rawlings

Admission: One Shilling
Reserved Seats, 4s. Second Seats, 2s.
To be obtained at Messrs Forrests', Castle Street, where a plan of the Hall may be seen and seats secured; also of any member of the Class.
Doors open 7.30; Concert 8; Carriages 10.15 p.m.

★

Eight days after the performance of this concert, the issue of *The Shrewsbury Chronicle* for 6 April carried an article on 'St. Mary's Steeple':

> Our readers, to whatever religious denomination they may belong, will be glad to hear that the appeal of the Vicar of St. Mary's, Shrewsbury, for funds with which to repair the damage caused by the fall of the steeple has met with so ready and generous a response that the sum required—£6,000—has already been exceeded by more than £1,000. The Rev. Newdigate Poyntz, calling attention to this very gratifying testimony to the popularity of the Church in the capital of 'proud Salopia', writes:—'You were kind enough on February 16th to insert a letter from me giving an account of the disaster which befel St. Mary's Church in the great gale of February 11th. I shall now be greatly obliged if you will allow me space to put on record the wonderful sympathy and generosity which the disaster has evoked, not only throughout Shropshire, but throughout England. I sent out, in conjunction with the churchwardens, an appeal for help far and near, and so prompt and generous was the response that within a fortnight I had received, in promises and payment, £6,000, which was at first sight what we thought would be sufficient. I have since received about another £1,000, so that within six weeks £7,000 has been subscribed, and this in the face of "hard times" for very many. We should be glad to raise another £1,000 to spend on other parts of the exterior, and I think that then the building would stand for many generations.'

The Darwin Memorial Fund

Just over a month later, on Friday, 18 May, *The Shrewsbury Chronicle* carried an article headed 'The Proposed Memorial to Charles Darwin: Public Meeting in Shrewsbury':

> On Wednesday afternoon a well-attended meeting was held at the Shire-hall, Shrewsbury, in furtherance of the movement for erecting a memorial to the late Charles Darwin. The Mayor (Mr. W.L. Browne) presided, and among those present were—Mr. H.D. Greene, Q.C., M.P., Mr. Alfred Cock, Q.C., the Ven. Archdeacon Lloyd, the Rev. Prebendary Moss, the Hon. W.H. Herbert, Mr. Butler Lloyd, Mr. W.G. Cross, Mr. W. Phillips,

Rev. C.H. Drinkwater, Mr. E. Powell, Mr. T.P. Blunt, Mr. E. Powell, jun., Mr. Lloyd, Mr. James Cock, Mr. S. Heighway, Rev. E. Myers, Mr. H.E. Rogers, Captain Williams-Freeman, Mr. R.B. Benson, Mr. W.H. Whitaker, Mr. W.E. Litt, Rev. W.H. Draper, Mr T. Corbett, Mr. A. Mansell, Dr. Burd, Mr. D.H. Owen, Mr. G.J. Holt, Dr. Gray, Mr. A. Gill, Dr. Gardner, Mr. R. Taylor, Major S.C. Southam, Mr. W.M. How, Mr. Armytage, Mr. J. Woodhouse, &c.

The Mayor, in opening the meeting, said they had met that day to confirm what was done on the 30th January, when the first meeting in connection with this movement was held. Some delay had taken place, and he thought it right to refer to it, because many gentlemen had written and spoken to him, asking why they had not moved in the matter before; but the committee desired to express its sympathy with a certain section of the community in their endeavours to raise funds for the restoration of one of our most beautiful churches, and any further step was postponed until sufficient money had been raised. (Hear, hear.) The committee now felt that the ground was pretty free for them to work upon, and wished to go forth to the world with the project which they had before them. Unfortunately, although they took every care, as far as they could do so, the day happened after all to be inconvenient to many learned gentlemen who presided over colleges, or were connected with the universities. The many letters of apology for non-attendance clearly showed that the day was not a suitable one, but they also showed that sympathy with the movement had been created throughout the country, and no doubt when the committee were in a position to ask for subscriptions, they would receive a very general amount of support. (Applause.) His Worship then went through the letters of apology, some of which we append.

Sir Robert S. Ball, writing from the Observatory, Cambridge, said: 'I sympathize heartlily with the proposal to do honour to the birthplace of Darwin. With Shakespeare and Newton his name must be forever associated. I shall be glad to subscribe to the scheme.' Mr. W.E. Garnett-Botfield (President of the Caradoc and Severn Valley Field Clubs) wrote: 'I do not know what you propose to do, but if a national subscription is started, I suppose a statue will be erected. In addition to this, I should like to see something of scientific value to Shropshire undertaken. The various scientific societies in the county would be greatly helped if there was in the county town a building where they could meet for lectures, conversation, &c. I don't think Shropshire people quite realize how extremely interesting the county is from a scientific point of view. A Darwin Memorial Hall would be a standing reminder that there were societies formed for the study of and instruction given in those branches of science which are so interesting in Shropshire. I presume that the various scientific bodies on the Continent and in America will be invited to assist us. I can see no reason why the subscription should be confined to the United Kingdom. Darwin's work was world-wide, and I think his many foreign admirers would be only too glad to help. If we had a fitting memorial to Darwin, Shrewsbury ought to become to men of science what Stratford is to the admirers of Shakespeare.' Apologies were received from the Lord Chancellor, Dr. Lawson Tait, Mr. S.K. Mainwaring; Rev. W.H. Brown, Head Master, Charterhouse; Dr. H.M. Butler, Trinity Lodge, Cambridge; Mr. A.H. Brown, M.P., the Rev. J.R.O. Bridgeman, Weston; Mr. Joseph Beckitt, Whitchurch; Professor Cunningham, Queen's College, Belfast; the Marquis of Dufferin; Lord Dillon, Ditchley; the Master of University College, Durham; Mr. R.J. Duncan, Shrewsbury School; the President of the University College of London; Rev. P.A.E. Emson, Shrewsbury; Mr. A.W. Franks, President, Society of Antiquarians; the Vice-Chancellor of University of Aberdeen; Professor Green, Oxford; the Head Master of Dulwich College; Professor Huxley; the Provost of Eton; the Head Master of Sedbergh; Mr. W.M. Hulton-Harrop, Lythwood; Mr. T.M. How; Mr. James Hamilton, Shrewsbury School; Rev. S.J. Hawkes, Pontesbury; Mr. H.H. France-Hayhurst, Wellington; the Provost of Worcester College, Oxford; the Principal, University College of South Wales; Mr. J.P.B. Johnston, Leanox Gardens, S.W.; Mr. Daniel Jones, Kilsall Hall, Shifnal; Mr. R. Ll Kenyon, Pradoe; Rev. W.C.E. Kynaston, Hardwick; Mr. E.C. Kelly, Shrewsbury; the Vice-Chancellor, King's College, Cambridge; Sir John Lubbock; Mr. A.H.O. Lloyd, Park Lane, W; the Principal, University College, Bristol; the President, Queen's College, Galway; Mr. H.W.M'Kenzie, Lancing College, Shoreham; Mr. F. Mainwaring, Aldershot; Mr. E.B. Moser, Shrewsbury; Professor A. Newton, Magdalene College, Cambridge; the Vice-Chancellor, University of Oxford; the Principal, Owens College, Manchester; Lord Powis; Mr. J. Owen, Shrewsbury; Mr. Rice-Oxley, Shrewsbury; Sir James Paget, Bart.; Professor B. Price, Pembroke College, Oxford; the Head Master of Rugby School; the Head Master, School House, Bedford; Mr. E.B. Poulton, Oxford; Mr. R. Pollock, Wellington College; R.B. Poole, D.D., Bedford; Mr. T.E. Pickering, Shrewsbury School; Lord Reay; the President of the Royal Geographical Society; Principal Rendall, University College, Liverpool; the Principal, University College of North Wales; Lord Selborne; Prof. Sedgwick, Cambridge; the Head Master of Uppingham School; the Head Master of Sherborne School; Colonel Kenyon-Slaney, M.P.; Sir F. Smythe, Bart.; the Warden of Radley College, Abingdon; Professor Vines, Oxford; Lord Walsingham; the Head Master of Harrow School; the Principal of Owen's College, Manchester; Mr. James Watson, Berwick; &c. The Bishop of Shrewsbury wrote: 'My dear Mr. Mayor, I think I told you how much I regretted that an engagement calling me into Staffordshire tomorrow would prevent me from attending the Charles Darwin meeting. I hope you will be well supported, and that our proposal to erect a memorial in Shrewsbury will take definite shape. The great thing will be not to aim at too much; and a statue in some public place, as the front of the Old Schools, will do honour to our man, while we are saved from the imputation that we are making this distinguished townsman's name a cat's paw for getting something to benefit ourselves.' Mr. A. Sparrow (Preen Manor) wrote:—'As I fear that I may be unable to attend the meeting on Wednesday next, I write a line to say how glad I shall be to join in any movement that may be initiated to perpetuate the memory of Charles Darwin, one of the most remarkable men not only of this but of any age—a man who may be said to have revolutionized science.' The following was read from Mr. Philip Williams (Hinstock Hall):—'Dear Sir, It is certainly most fitting that Shrewsbury should raise a memorial to that most eminent man, the late Charles Darwin—in fact, she could not do less, and though I shall be unable to attend the meeting, I herein enclose cheque for £10 and wish all success to the movement.' Mr. C.C. Walker (Lilleshall) wrote:—'Shrewsbury should possess a memorial to Darwin, whom the most competent to judge in all nations consider not only one of the foremost men of this generation, but one who has more advanced the knowledge of the operations of Nature than any man since our own pre-eminent Sir Isaac Newton, without doubt the greatest mind in the world's history. Every civilized people would be glad to claim Darwin as their countryman, and it would seem that, if Shropshire and Shrewsbury did not, they would be open to the reproach that "a prophet is honoured, but not in his own country and his own house." Shrewsbury, therefore, should shew their admiration by a suitable memorial, and be always able to point to the house that gave him birth and say "He was born there!" I regret I am unable to take an active part in it, but will be glad to contribute to something worthy of such a great Shropshire man.'

The Rev. Prebendary Moss, who was received with hearty applause, said if anything were needed to justify the decision which was arrived at when they met together in that place a few months ago, it was the voluminous testimony which the Mayor had just read to them of the esteem in which Darwin's genius was held by some of the most distinguished scientific men of the day. (Applause.) He felt in standing before them that afternoon that he was speaking in a twofold capacity. First, in common with his fellow townsmen, he was proud to reside in the place where so great a man as Charles Darwin was born and had spent the early years of his life; and again, as headmaster of the school at which Darwin received a substantial part of his education, he was proud to recognize his name as amongst their chiefest glories. (Hear, hear.) At the same time, in the latter capacity, he could not but feel that he was addressing the meeting to a certain extent under false pretences. It might well be that Charles Darwin benefited more than he supposed by the strict grammatical methods and the rigorous classical curriculum which were then in vogue at Shrewsbury School, and he was not at all inclined to depreciate the merits of the educational system which then prevailed. To the studies which were established at Shrewsbury by his (Mr. Moss's) great predecessor, Dr. Butler, was undoubtedly due that eminence to which some of our most distinguished men in Church and State had attained. (Applause). Still, he feared that for a man of exceptional genius like Charles Darwin those studies were ill-adapted. They did not make sufficient allowance for the eccentricities of genius. If Darwin could come to life again and inspect their well-appointed laboratory and lecture-rooms—if he could witness the interest which so many of the boys took in scientific study, he (Mr. Moss) thought he would almost wish to live his boyhood over again. (Applause.) It was not for him to estimate Charles Darwin's place in the list of scientific worthies—that was a matter for experts; but they could form some opinion from the testimony which the Mayor had read to them of the high place assigned to him by those most competent to judge. (Applause.) Sir Robert Ball, than whose verdict no better could be obtained, placed Darwin in the same rank with Shakespeare and Newton. (Hear, hear.) But it was a matter of common knowledge that Charles Darwin was recognized throughout the civilized world as one of the greatest men England had ever produced. (Applause.) He was one of those originators of new ideas whose theories had developed, and were likely to still develop, into many ramifications of useful consequence. (Applause.) The Mayor had referred to some delay taking place in this matter, but delays were often of value. At the last meeting, regret was expressed more than once that no step had been taken for more than twelve years to bring about this memorial; but he was not so sure that the lapse of these twelve years had not been an advantage. It often happened that men who stood high in the opinion of their contemporaries were allowed to sink into a kind of insignificance as years went on. Charles Darwin was fortunate in that contemporaries recognized his merits. He attained to the highest distinction, and when he died England recognized his greatness by according to him a national funeral. (Applause.) The lapse of 12 years had not detracted from Charles Darwin's fame, but had rather made that fame more conspicuous and more universally acknowledged. They could anticipate now to some extent the value of such a life in the judgement of posterity. They could see clearly, what they could not see so clearly twelve years ago, that Charles Darwin's name would rank among the greatest names that belonged to the human race (Loud applause.) No doubt Darwin made his mistakes. No doubt some of his theories would not bear the strain of close critical examination, and probably later researches might throw some of them into the background; but in saying this of Charles Darwin he was saying what was true of every original genius. But at the same time they recognized with pride and with gratitude the light which he had thrown on the laws of Nature—(applause)—and they recognized with gratitude the light he had thrown on the workings of the Divine Mind—(applause)—and they were anxious to do what they could to commemorate a man for whom their admiration was so great. (Applause.) He had much pleasure in moving the following resolution:—'It is the unanimous opinion of this meeting that the resolution passed at the town's meeting on the 30th of January 1894 be and is hereby confirmed.'

The Ven. Archdeacon Lloyd said he had been asked to second the resolution, and he was glad to have an opportunity of doing so on two or three grounds. First, because he was not able to be present at the last meeting, which he would gladly have been had his engagements permitted; and secondly, because during the last three or four months he had been about a good deal among the clergy, and he felt—though he had no actual commission to say so—that he was expressing their opinion when he said they thought that this memorial ought to be raised, and they had no hesitation, as far as their needs permitted, in taking part in the movement. (Applause.) The clergy did not find in reading Darwin what they did occasionally find in works of other scientific writers—they did not find any sneer at Scripture—(applause)—for Darwin carefully abstained from stepping at all out of the course he laid down for himself. There was nothing which most of them thought could not be very well reconciled with the letter of Scripture. (Hear, hear.) He wished to say that he was present as a representative of the Governing Body of Shrewsbury School. They would feel an interest in this matter, as being connected with the past history of the school which they now governed in their turn, and in which Darwin received his education. He had been looking at the record of Darwin's career at the school, and found that he spent the whole of his school time there; he began at the very bottom, and received the mark 'improving', 'improving', 'improving', right down to the time when he left to go to Edinburgh University. It might be that the studies then given at the school were not adapted to his peculiar genius, but he felt as regards the classical studies that they were eminently qualified to turn out a very good tool for any class of life, and he thought Darwin's perception and imagination were very much developed by what he learned at school. (Hear, hear.) The Mayor had alluded to the reasons for the delay which had taken place. It was a very grateful act on the part of His Worship to wait until sufficient funds had been raised to restore St. Mary's Church, and he was fully satisfied that the effort now put forth to erect a memorial would not suffer on that account. (Hear, hear.) Seeing the wide area they would cover, they would not require large subscriptions. (Hear, hear.) For his own part, he thought it would be better to rest content with a statue in Shrewsbury, leaving other places where Darwin spent the latter years of his life to do something of a different character. (Hear, hear.)

The resolution was then put and carried unanimously.

Mr. H.D. Greene, Q.C., M.P., said it was as a resident and not in any representative capacity that he enjoyed the privilege of proposing the next resolution. The motion that was arrived at on the 30th of January, by no means hastily, had been confirmed after due deliberation of three months, and they therefore had arrived most solemnly at the decision of the town, of the county, and of the public at large that something should be done to perpetuate the memory of their illustrious fellow-townsman. (Applause.) That being so, the proposal would be rendered ineffective unless its business aspect were presented to the meeting, and he therefore begged to move—'That a subscription list be opened, to be called "The Darwin Memorial Fund", that subscriptions be invited, and that the banks in the town be asked to receive the same.' He believed a further resolution would be submitted dealing with the formation of a committee, and he would express a hope that this committee would see its way to establish in the town some permanent mark, such as a statue or building, which should appeal to the eye. They already had a statue of Lord Hill, one of Lord Clive, and then there was the Clement Memorial, and he should be extremely pleased if they could add another feature of beauty to the town. The arrangements must, of course, be left to those gentlemen who were able to supply their time in carrying out the wishes of the meeting. (Hear, hear.) With regard to the subscriptions, he hoped that in some way the subscription lists would be brought before the public not only in this county but in the university towns, and that application would be made to the learned societies. (Applause.) He had heard many people express a willingness to join in the movement, and after the enormous testimony they had had that afternoon in the letters read by the Mayor, he thought that many of the writers of those letters would be glad of an opportunity to subscribe. (Hear, hear.)

The Hon. W.H. Herbert, in seconding the motion, said he felt strongly that Charles Darwin was one of the most illustrious sons Shrewsbury had ever produced, and they certainly ought to have a memorial of him in their midst, not only to show their appreciation of his genius, but also as a means of encouraging those of the present day and coming generations to emulate him in the work which he carried out, not only for the goal of one class but for the good of mankind generally. (Applause.) He wished the movement every success.

The resolution was carried *nem. con.*

Mr. Alfred Cock, Q.C., said it was with very great pleasure that he availed himself of this opportunity of expressing the sentiments which those who were connected with the town of Shrewsbury, but were not living here, viewed the form which the townspeople had taken to commemorate the memory of her greatest son. There had been some delay in calling the meeting, for reasons which they all deeply regretted, but, speaking for himself, he could only congratulate himself that the delay had given him an opportunity of adding his feeble voice of gratitude and reverence to the memory of the great man whom they were trying to honour that day. (Applause.) He did not know whether all had had quite the same opportunities of appreciating the connection that existed between the name of Darwin and the town of Shrewsbury. It had twice been his fortune, in different parts of the continent, to be at assemblies when the name of Shrewsbury had been referred to. Once in Paris, a few months ago, and once in Berlin. On these occasions something turned up, and he mentioned the name of Shrewsbury, and each time two persons said: 'Why, that's the birthplace of Darwin!' (Applause.) He felt rather ashamed, at hearing that remark, that in this his town there was no sort of memorial raised by his fellow-townsmen to show the world at large how much they thought of him. But if anything of the kind occurred again he hoped he should be able to say that not only were they proud of the connection of Shrewsbury with Darwin, but that Shrewsbury herself had shown that she was proud of it too. (Applause.) There were many reasons why they should reverence the name of that illustrious man. Apart from his scientific distinction, he (Mr. Cock) would like to say one word as to the great and able moral qualities which he had outside the great distinction of intellect, and which they all reverenced so much. (Applause.) He doubted whether it would be possible in the history of the country—he was going to say in the history of humanity—to find a man with more devotion to that which he considered his career in life (applause), with a greater simplicity, an utter disregard of self-appreciation, with more toleration for the criticisms of others. (Applause.) There never was a scientific or literary man who accepted with more consideration the criticism which the most virulent of critics heaped upon him, if there was anything behind it. (Hear, hear.) He took no part in controversy, and hated the fighting part of a man of science or letters; but where his contemporaries gave him the opportunity of reconsidering any of his data, there never was a man more ready to accept it or more sincerely desirous of seeing how far their views were in accord with his own. (Hear, hear.) These were very great qualities in a man whose name had been the sign almost of the progress of science in the 19th century. (Applause.) They had the great advantage of having had Darwin for a fellow-townsman, and he was always more or less before their eyes; but it was to be hoped that they would have a fitting and suitable memorial to his great name. (Hear, hear.) What form the memorial would take must depend on various considerations. It must depend upon the way in which the resolution was responded to; but there were some things about which they were all agreed. They were certainly agreed, as far as he could judge, that there should be a statue. (Hear, hear.) He then moved—'That a committee be appointed to consider what form the proposed memorial shall take, and generally to further the project in view.' (Applause.)

The Rev. E. Myers had much pleasure in seconding the resolution, which had been so ably and so eloquently proposed by Mr. Cock. He thought, after the splendid list of brilliant names which the Mayor read at the opening of the meeting, there was little doubt that this movement in Shrewsbury would be a great success, and that it would extend not only throughout this county but throughout Great Britain—(hear, hear)—and he really hoped it would extend, as Archdeacon Lloyd had said, to the whole world. (Applause.) Charles Darwin's name had taken a central position, as regarded science, that was looked at mentally, from every point of the civilized world. (Hear, hear.) But Darwin was not only the greatest (as he thought) scientific man of this or any age: he was more than that. He was a thoroughly good man. (Applause.) In the letters which the Mayor read just now, he (Mr. Myers) noticed that one of the correspondents said that Darwin was a very great and good man. He was a great man unquestionably as a scientist, but he was more than that. As a moralist, as a moral man, as a true Christian, a man full of deep piety, with largeness of soul, he had a love generally for everything that was good, everything that was elevating, everything that was true. (Applause.) To him (the speaker) Charles Darwin represented all the splendid qualities of the moral, intellectual and religious nature. He was a man who he (Mr. Myers) thought rose far above the smaller views of other men in respect to religious matters. (Hear, hear.) He thought they had reason to believe from the list of names read out that not only would that appeal be approved of and answered by scientific men, but that there was a large number of men who occupied a different position in the world—dignitaries in the Church of England—who would respond. (Hear, hear.) He was rejoiced to find from what Archdeacon Lloyd had said that there was a feeling among the clergy in favour of the movement. He was glad to hear this, and hoped the committee would receive a general response from all classes of society, from all churches and from all denominations, toward the proper recognition of him whom he regarded as one of the grandest men of science, one of the truest, one of the humblest, one of the meekest followers of the great Father and of the great Master. (Applause.)

The motion was then put, and carried unanimously.

Mr. Butler Lloyd then moved 'That the following gentlemen form the committee:—The Mayor, the Bishop of Shrewsbury, Mr. S.K. Mainwaring, Rev. H.W. Moss, Mr. H.D. Greene, Q.C., M.P., the Rev. Charles Parker, the Rev. C.H. Drinkwater, Rev. E. Myers, Dr. Calvert, Dr. Burd, the Hon. W.H. Herbert, Mr. T. Slaney Eyton, Mr. W. Phillips, Mr. T.P. Blunt, Mr. E.C. Peele, Mr. E. Powell, Major S.C. Southam, Mr. F.R. Armytage, Mr. W.H. Wood, Mr. S.M. Morris, Mr. G.J. Holt, Mr. James Cock, Captain Cholmondeley and Mr. Alfred Cock, Q.C., with power to add to their number.

Captain Williams-Freeman, in seconding the motion, suggested that those gentlemen who had written to the Mayor from other towns be asked to form small committees among themselves in furtherance of the movement. (Applause.)

The resolution was carried.

The Rev. W.H. Draper proposed that the Mayor be chairman of the committee and treasurer of the fund, and the Town Clerk be the honorary secretary.

This was seconded by Mr. E. Powell and carried.

A vote of thanks to the Mayor for presiding terminated the proceedings.

A subscription list was opened in the room, and over £100 was subscribed by those present.

10
THE GOETHEAN ASSERTIONS

A Historical Failure

In the present context there is no need to go in a similar way into every detail of the further story of the Goethe Memorial in Vienna as recounted in Walter Beck's biography of Karl Julius Schröer. Suffice to say that by this time the whole matter had become complicated, protracted and emotional. Schröer's own view that Victor Tilgner would be the ideal sculptor to undertake the commission was not shared by all members of the Viennese Goethe Society. On this point Beck indeed states that within the Society 'there built up an opposition to Schröer'.

The term 'opposition' is of interest since it was also used by Rudolf Steiner when describing some of his own feelings towards Schröer in his karma lecture at Dornach on 24 September 1924:

> ... Again and again there mingled into the striving of my soul a certain opposition against Schröer.

Other formulae might also be found appropriate. In the terminology of *Die Philosophie der Freiheit*, for instance, it might be said that every individual member of the Goethe Society was free to form their own moral intuitions about the Goethe Memorial. And according to some of these intuitions the right man to undertake the commission was Edmund Hellmer.

In the end the committee appointed to settle the matter decided that the statue—which Schröer wanted to have in marble and representing Goethe in his thirties—should be in bronze and represent Goethe at the age of 50. It also gave the commission to Hellmer.

The disappointed Schröer instigated the calling of an Extraordinary General Meeting of the whole Society in order to assess the committee's decisions. This meeting took place on 13 June 1894. During the proceedings it became quite apparent that not everyone agreed with the views of Schröer, and after extensive debate the motions brought forward by him and his supporters that the whole matter be given further consideration were overruled.

Beck's account continues:

> On 19 June, six days after the meeting, when all attempts to change the committee's decision had failed, Schröer announced his withdrawal from the Goethe Society and his resignation as editor of the *Chronik*.

Marianne Hainisch published Schröer's letter, which subsequently also appeared in daily newspapers. He wrote to President Stremayr:

'I must this time request your Excellency to be permitted most devotedly to set down into your hands my withdrawal from the Goethe Society. The path which the Memorial Committee seems to have definitely taken cannot be mine. It is not a matter of Tilgner or Hellmer, but of an ideal work of art to set before our eyes the spirit of Goethe in an uplifting way. Our committee now means to award the prize to a work of which it has had no sight whatever! Although so close to the thought of a Goethe Memorial in Vienna, which I have at heart, I am unable to proceed along this path.

I request you most kindly to accept notification of this my definite decision . . .'

Stremayr replied on the same day:

Vienna, 19th June 1894

Highly revered Herr Professor,
Dear friend and colleague in Goethe,

During the agonizing days of my illness I have felt no pain so deep as is caused to me by the content of your precious communication.

No, my dear friend, I am unable to accept and transmit your withdrawal from our Society, which you founded, and of which you have been and are the firmest pillar . . . Hold out then, most venerated Sir, until my illness departs, and let us decide on further measures. At the moment I do not take your resignation as having happened, and beg and entreat you to hold out still further.

In sincere and high estimation,

Your wholly devoted

Stremayr

Schröer, in deep depression, had declared his withdrawal from the Goethe Society, feeling himself alone and 'attacked by brutality and roughness', and Stremayr's words seemed like a 'blessing from heaven'. But nonetheless he did not retract his withdrawal.

He not only felt the departure from his intentions in the Goethe Society as a personal renunciation, but also saw in this process a historical failure.

With the Deepest Interest

In Chapter XV of his autobiography Rudolf Steiner described his connection to the writer and publisher Ludwig Laistner:

> Ludwig Laistner at that time was responsible for producing in the 'Cotta Library of World Literature' a complete Schopenhauer edition and an edition of selected works by Jean Paul. He passed both of these on to me.

And so I had to include among the tasks I then had at Weimar a proper study of the pessimistic philosopher and of the genially paradoxical Jean Paul. Both works I took on with deepest interest, because I loved putting myself into states of mind strongly opposed to my own. Ludwig Laistner had no outer motives for making me editor of Schopenhauer and Jean Paul. The commission arose entirely from talks we held about these two personalities. Indeed, the thought of passing these tasks on to me came to him in the middle of a talk.

The first three volumes of the Schopenhauer edition came out in 1894. Steiner's general introduction included a biographical sketch, describing *inter alia* the extensive European journey undertaken by the future German philosopher as a 15-year-old youth:

> ... In the spring of 1803 Arthur Schopenhauer left Hamburg with his parents. Their next destination was Holland, where the journey then continued to England. After six weeks' stay in London Arthur was left behind for three months in Wimbledon, to learn the English language properly at Mr. Lancaster's. During this time the parents travelled through England and Scotland. His stay in England engendered in Schopenhauer a hatred of English bigotry which remained with the philosopher for the rest of his life, but also laid a basis for that thorough mastery of the English language which in later conversations with Englishmen made him appear as one himself. For Schopenhauer, life in Lancaster's guesthouse held little appeal. In letters to his parents he complained of boredom and the stiff ceremonial being of Englishmen. He was seized by a general disgruntlement which, it seems, could only be driven away by immersion in fine literature, especially the works of Schiller. From her letters we see his mother's concern that predilection for reading poetry might blunt her son for the serious things in life. 'Believe me,' she writes to him on the 19th of July 1803, 'if Schiller in his youth had only read poets, he would never have been what he is'...

★

Meanwhile, during the summer of 1894 some continental philosophical works received fleeting notice in a British publication. On 7 July, *The Athenaeum,* a 'Journal of English and Foreign Literature, Science, the Fine Arts, Music and the Drama', published an article by the now septuagenarian Robert Zimmerman, Professor of Philosophy in the University of Vienna—whose lectures Steiner had been attending in the early 1880s.

The article, which gave English readers a quick survey of the latest in contemporary German culture, included these sentences:

> ... The tendency of the day is to run into extremes. For example, Rudolf Steiner in his book entitled *Philosophie der Freiheit* and Bruno Wille in his

> *Philosophie der Befreiung* start from Nietzsche's standpoint, but go far beyond him and end in a theoretical anarchy which, even in the domain of practice, allows of no moral prescriptions . . .

Steiner himself evidently learnt of this remark, for many years later he referred to it in a lecture given at Stuttgart on 13 June 1921.

Quick-witted English Feature-writers

In his biography of Karl Julis Schröer, Walter Beck continues:

> After finishing the correspondence with Stremayr, Schröer and Hermine went to Freiburg, in order to visit their son Arnold and family . . .

Arnold, Schröer's elder surviving son, had progressed from a teacher of languages at a Viennese school to an academic post at Freiburg University. Beck continues:

> . . . Production of the *Chronik* was interrupted. After the May number, the next and last issue of the year 1894 appeared only in October, reporting the meeting of 13 June and publishing an extensive final article by Schröer, 'Farewell Words from the Editor'.
>
> In these parting words Schröer put forward general principles, saying nothing about the reasons for his resignation. He composed the farewell words in Freiburg, starting with drafts in a notebook referring briefly to past events, mainly the written correspondence. Not all notes in the little book are by him, a series of entries being made by his youngest son Rudolf.

It is of interest that Rudolf Schröer was by profession a sculptor.

> The book begins with a brief note from Freiburg on 11 September 1894, with which Schröer obviously wanted to distance himself from past events. The same is evident in farewell words intended for the *Chronik*. The introduction to these farewell words reads in Schröer's own handwriting:
>
> 'The importance of erecting a Goethe Memorial in Vienna is generally felt, even if not recognized everywhere in its entire scope. It should also be given expression, as witnessing the attitude of Vienna, from which grew the thought of this undertaking.
>
> We know quite well that ardent youth, always desiring novelties, often strives towards aims different from our ideals, e.g. so-called naturalism in art. The world thus forgets what is signified by the emergence of Goethe! The validity of the customary saying that works by our classic writers are for eternity is calmly accepted. But youth's yearning for progress does not prevent it from finding old-fashioned the work of Goethe and Schiller—which we have not yet caught up with! Merely for our taste, the views of

Germany's greatest thinkers must be our guideline; but they seem forgotten. In quick-witted English feature-writers we sometimes meet the ideas of our philosophers, and hear admiration expressed through English perceptiveness for these ideas originating from Germany. The bent towards England, which we encounter in Germany, brings these ideas to prevalence as a novelty.'

Here the question inevitably arises: how did Schröer know what was being written at that time by 'quick-witted English feature-writers'?

The answer is not hard to guess. For the academic position gained by his son Arnold at Freiburg University was that of Professor of English Philology. Arnold Schröer had already begun to produce an extensive output of books for German readers on a wide variety of subjects in the field of English language and literature.

The Way Goethe is Currently Regarded

Later in the year, Rudolf Steiner wrote to Karl Julius Schröer:

Weimar, 3rd of November 1894

Highly esteemed Herr Professor,

Through my silence towards you for months on end, most revered Herr Professor, I have loaded myself with a heavy debt. I am now asking you not to interpret this silence as if it could even just in the remotest way indicate a cooling of my heartfelt affection and gratitude. These latter are firmly rooted in me and will always remain so in undiminished strength. With my letter I wanted also to submit to you an article setting the manner of your Goethean research into the right light and showing that you are the only person who understands how to appreciate Goethe's relation to German philosophy (with its idealism). In your last letter you told me yourself that such an article would be welcome to you. But you cannot believe how hard it is today to undertake Goethean studies conducted in this sense of genuine idealism. With my article I have not until now been able to get anywhere. But the hope of submitting the article to you along with this letter also delayed the letter itself in—as I readily admit—an irresponsible manner on my part. I do beg you however not to account to my loyalty what has its reason only in my dilatoriness!

The article, 'Goethe's View of Nature according to the latest Publications of the Goethe Archive', reproduced Steiner's Frankfurt lecture from the previous year. It appeared in 1894 in the *Berichte des Freien Deutschen Hochstiftes zu Frankfurt am Main*.

I hear with greatest pleasure from Wahle that your Faust (2nd part) is now also to appear in a third edition . . .

Julius Wahle worked at the Archives as editor of Goethe's diaries.

> ... Friends gained by this edition cannot be removed from it through idle prattle of mindless critics (of whom one is that in 'Euphorion'). In Goethean meetings here there is sufficient opportunity to come to know the sort of philologists now spreading around in literary science. These people are armed with blinkers against everything called 'idea'; they see only letters, spirit-denuded letters, which they call 'reading', 'variant' and the like, and from which they promise themselves more than from any reflection which enters into Goethe's spirit. One can experience wonders in observing how today any word spoken against Goethe is greedily snapped up. I had opportunity to do so in this year's Goethean meeting.
>
> The behaviour towards you of the Viennese Goethe Society has pained me. Considering the way Goethe is currently regarded in Germany, one thinks it might perhaps be possible for the true reverence of Goethe to flee to Germans outside the realm. But what should become of this comforting hope when such a position is taken up in Austria against a memorial worthy of Goethe?
>
> How distressing to hear that the Viennese Goethe Society has not even an inkling of how a statue worthy of Goethe must look. So nothing is felt there of a necessity lying in the matter, which should not be argued against in the least.
>
> You will have heard that Dr. Eduard von der Hellen has left the Association for the Goethe Archive ...

Hellen had been editing Goethe's letters.

> ... He is now editing Nietzsche with the same inner engagement, namely none, with which he was editing Goethe up to the 1st of October of this year. It does not of course occur to me to hold the Nietzsche editing against Hellen. As you have known for a long time, I am far removed from underestimating Nietzsche. Why not appreciate greatness when it exists, even if appearing in the Nietzschean form? But Hellen knows Nietzsche as little as he knows Goethe. I cannot stand this outer relation to an object, which clings onto present philology, this loveless grinding-out of every author—now called an objective way of observing. I do not like such objectivity at all.
>
> For the second part of Faust I have made various notes. I shall let you have them in the next few days.
>
> As you will have seen from the edition, my work has progressed to the 12th volume of the scientific writings. That is the last. It lies in the nature of the relationships that I have nothing further to hope for from Weimar. Nor was I ever striving after anything here ...

The relationships referred to were chiefly the complex and problematic ones with the Director of the Goethe Archives, Bernard Suphan, who by writing Steiner a bad reference had dashed his hopes of an academic career elsewhere.

> . . . Of course, the reaction flooding the whole of central and western Germany may also be noticed in Thuringia. A wind is blowing which in the next few years will hardly allow open ears to develop for free science. There are not a few who want to reinterpret Goethe's elevated views into an orthodox Lutheranism. It seems no longer paradoxical to say that by certain people Goethe is let pass only in so far as he can be placed—naturally with complete misunderstanding of his views—into the service of a mendacious servility. I am not saying such things out of the blue, but with regard to quite particular experiences of the most recent time, which I have undergone here in Weimar in my own person.
>
> With that I want to close for today. I request you to send my best recommendations to your wife, and ask you to forgive much to your
>
> ever the same thankfully revering you
>
> Rudolf Steiner
>
> Most revered Herr Professor, have you then not received my 'Philosophie der Freiheit', which came out a few months ago?

This Millenium Stage

In January 1895 the last-mentioned book was given an unsigned review in the pages of *Mind*, a British quarterly of psychology and philosophy.

> *Die Philosophie der Freiheit.* Grundzüge einer modernen Weltanschauung. Von Dr. Rudolf Steiner. Berlin. Verlag von Emil Felber. 1894. London. Williams and Norgate. Pp. 229.
>
> Dr. Steiner believes that in spite of an apparent tendency to superficial socialism prevalent in the present age, there is in human nature an abiding and resistless individualism—a love of freedom—an independence. The justification of this opinion is the *raison d'être* of the essay before us. On p. 8 Dr. Steiner asks: what is the relation of philosophy to the idea of freedom, and how far can freedom be realized by the individual agent? The answers to these two questions form the content of the two main divisions of the work, entitled respectively 'The Science of Freedom' and 'The Reality of Freedom'. Dr. Steiner devotes the first part to a psychological analysis of the processes subordinate and co-ordinate to the act of willing. Knowing and willing are, he thinks, inseparable functions. Hence there is both a cognitive and a motive factor in all human states. The opinions of Dr Steiner most relevant to the topics under discussion are to be found in sub-Section VII, p. 100, entitled 'Human Individuality'—'*Die menschliche Individualität*'. The

author here follows the usual lines of modern psychologists, comparing and connecting the percept, the image, and the concept.

We apprehend objective reality by means of perception and conception, while through the mental individual image, '*Vorstellung*', we have the subjective representation of reality (p. 105). Th act of subjectivizing through a particular image gives us the apprehension of individuality, makes us conscious, as it were, that the tree we are imagining is a tree we have ourselves seen in the concrete, and not a mere group of abstract attributes. The subjective is the apprehension of individuality, as contrasted with the objective, which is the apprehension of generality.

With the image of the concrete is associated a feeling of pleasure or pain—desire or aversion. This feeling is purely subjective and clings to the mental image, '*Vorstellung*', while it is totally absent from the objective concept, '*Begriff*'. Human desire has for its goal the satisfaction of the individual, while it is quite uninterested in the abstract and general.

In Part II, Section XI. p. 168, we are first introduced to Dr. Steiner's distinct enunciation of the philosophy of freedom, which he calls Monism, but which some would designate Anarchism pure and simple. Our author has, however, prepared us for his doctrine at the outset by accepting in Part I Spinoza's position that freedom means a free necessity, but not a free choice (p. 12). Hence each man is called upon to develop his own potentiality, as a rosebud is bound to become a rose. The principle of growth is entirely from within; there shall be no external stress, no authority, no subordination, nothing but the unhampered development of infinite potentiality.

The only concession that Dr. Steiner will make to popular prejudice in favour of established law, order and government is the reluctant admission that this complete state of freedom is not attainable at one stride. The human race must be habituated and educated up to the point of development at which it is capable of enjoying perfect freedom, and we need hardly say that this millennium stage has not yet been reached.

On this latter point, one may also compare the two final paragraphs of another review of *Die Philosophie der Freiheit* by the Catholic theologian Dr Konstantin Gutberlet, appearing that same year in the *Philosophisches Jahrbuch*:

The free moral beings presupposed by the author are a utopia, and when he speaks about them as real, indeed as actual men, he presupposes quite thoughtless readers or such as may however exist among atheists, to whom moral life is a fully unknown domain. Perhaps his philosophy of freedom could according to his own statements be called 'philosophy of the future' or astral ethics. For the beings he has in mind have not yet been born. Perhaps the breeding process has already brought them to realization on other heavenly bodies, on the Moon or on Mars, by culling the adherents of slave morality. Indeed the author expressly describes his ethics as crowning the edifice erected by Darwin and Haeckel. But the spiritist and Darwinist du Prel shows with decisive evidence that with our present normal human beings the edifice of evolutionary theory is not yet completed; further development of men to 'spirits' must therefore be supposed, and what appears with us only sporadically must already be a normal phenomenon on other heavenly bodies. The ethics of freedom are evidently intended for these future astral men, and our author's thoughts curiously co-incide here with those of another even more famous Darwinistic and monistic moralist, Herbert Spencer. According to him in a distant future all moral actions will be carried out by breeding, with as much of the purest enjoyment as heretofore only the activities of nutrition and reproduction. So pleasure and morality, conscience and fantasy, virtue and poetry, free morality and free love will fall together into one. For as noticed, our author expressly declares that if the question of women has till now been solved so unsatisfactorily, this derives from woman having been conceived too much according to species rather than according to individuality.

The morality of the future curiously co-incides here with the ideals of the future state of the Social Democrats, whose 'moral fantasy' and 'intuition' show free love alongside other 'freedoms' in the most enchanting colours. Yet such a co-incidence is again quite natural, since the point of departure is the same, namely Monism, i.e. atheism.

The Highest Peaks of the Human Spirit

In his biography of Karl Julius Schröer, Walter Beck describes a memorable occasion:

> On 11 January 1895 Schröer celebrated his seventieth birthday. For the wide circle of his friends it was a specially festive day. A notebook names a hundred and fifty people who congratulated him, some coming themselves, some sending letters, some bringing flowers . . .
>
> For previous attenders at Schröer's lectures, this birthday gave occasion to arrange various festivities . . .

The festivities took place on the 20th of the month.

> A printed address was distributed by H. Rosche. Rosche thanked Schröer for having provided humanistic training even at the Technical College, and presented him with a declaration of gratitude on his seventieth birthday as 'a mark of love from his pupils'. In his address Rosche said:
>
> '. . . In your lectures you led your listeners up to the highest peaks of the human spirit and of poetic fantasy.

You explained the tremendous world of Shakespeare, the ideal figures of Schiller, the fine humanity and all-embracing genius of Goethe in a way which awakened enthusiasm, with a lofty understanding...'

During the days after the festival there followed thank-yous to those who had congratulated him, among them Professors Toula and Bayer from the Technical College, the Arnthaler family with whom Lili had often stayed as a young girl, E. Glatz in Budapest, Erhardt Dieffenbach, Egger von Möllwald, Rosegger, Victor Capesius, Marianne Hainisch, Melanie Lefevre, Professor Minor, Professor Suess, Emil Schönaich in Troppau and Rudolf Steiner.

On 13 February Rudolf Steiner forwarded such volumes of Goethe's scientific writings as had since appeared in the Sophie edition...

During that summer Schröer composed as his last work an extensive foreword to his third edition of Part 2 of Goethe's *Faust*. And at the end of the year, in December, he finally retired from his Professorship at the Technical College in Vienna, after 35 years in the post.

Not in Agreement

In the following month in England, on Friday, 31 January 1896, *The Shrewsbury Chronicle* published a notice on 'Darwin's Statue':

> During the Mayoralty of Mr. W.L. Browne a public meeting was called for the purpose of considering what steps should be taken by the town with a view to erecting some public memorial to the great Salopian naturalist. The committee have now decided upon the form which the memorial shall take, viz., a statue outside the present Free Library buildings—the old Shrewsbury School, in which Charles Darwin received an important part of his early education.

The same issue also carried an editorial on 'The Darwin Memorial':

> The movement set afoot some time ago to raise a fitting memorial to the world-renowned philosopher and savant, Charles Darwin, in his native town hangs unaccountably laggard. The subscription list lies before us. Its grand total stands still at less than £400. It ought ere this to have reached as many thousands. In saying this we would not of course have it understood that we cast any reproach upon Salopians, and still less upon those whose names we note as creditably included in the list up to date; but remembering the vastly wider range of the noble service rendered by Darwin to the cause of humanity and truth, of scientific investigation and independence of thought, we would earnestly put it to our countrymen at large—indeed, to Britons everywhere—whether as yet they have in this matter done all that

the occasion demands? Surely we need not, at this late day, urge a single word in vindication of the work achieved by Charles Darwin, or in support of the proposal locally to set up a lasting memorial in his honour. He has laid the world under a debt the magnitude and preciousness whereof will grow with the centuries, and bulk ever larger and larger in the wonder of succeeding generations. At first sight and superficially, no doubt his novel theories of evolution, as revolutionizing modern thought on questions of the deepest moment, did startle orthodoxy from its ancient propriety, and provoke a tempest of conflicting opinion; but inasmuch as all truths, however seemingly variant and contradictory, must finally harmonize, even they whose alarm and rage was once fiercest are beginning calmly and reasonably to realize that, after all, truth can have really nothing to fear from so fearless a lover and pursuer of the truth as was Charles Darwin. Theologians have raved and railed, but there is an ever-enlarging majority who value truth higher than theology, and with these—his enduring inheritors—the work and fame of our great Salopian naturalist and philosopher are for ever secure. It is not alone with the view of honouring Darwin, but rather of giving Shrewsbury and Shropshire, and England also, opportunity of honouring themselves that we now renew our appeal for an addition to the subscription list more adequately worthy both of its object and its promoters. The memorial should be more than local; it should be national. And what more appropriate site could be found for it than in the town of his birth, and in front of the grand old building wherein he learned his earliest lessons as a schoolboy? We have in our town already fine statues of Clive, the Salopian conqueror of India, and of Hill, the Salopian hero of the wars of the Peninsula. It were indeed a reproach to our patriotism, as well as a reflection upon our ability to recognize true worth, if we now permit another Salopian hero no less remarkable than those two, though on other and peaceful fields, to remain unhonoured with a like memorial not less splendid.

★

A fortnight later, the issue on 14 February carried in its correspondence columns a letter on 'The Darwin Memorial':

Sir,—

The proposal to erect a memorial to the late Charles Darwin has been revived. Why has it not been effected before this? May I suggest a cause? Darwin is well known as a natural philosopher, whose studies led him to such conceptions as to natural objects as the 'Origin of Species', 'Evolution', 'Natural Selection', 'Survival of the Fittest', and also the 'Descent of Man', supposed, by certain resemblances, to be descended from the lower animal creatures. There is indeed an undeniable strong resemblance to man in many of those creatures as to not only his material, but also in some respects his intellectual nature; and so far the resemblance between them is of an exceedingly interesting character. Moreover, there are sufficient and most important reasons why there should have been a common character, so to speak, between them, which reasons however need not here be shown. But as to man's descent from the lower animals, that Divine Revelation which has been given to us shows that man was not so descended at all, but made on the same day with them directly from the dust of the earth, and at the same time in an infinitely superior character, as in the image of the Creator Himself. It can be no wonder, therefore, that such as receive the Bible as the Word of God should think it inconsistent, and therefore decline, to honour one whose views and statements were not in agreement with the same.

E.

Feb. 9, 1896.

The World's Eternal Ideals

In Austria, Karl Julius Schröer completed during February 1896 the corrections to the proofs of his revised edition of Goethe's *Faust*. The book came out in March, Schröer sending copies to various friends and to the libraries of both the Viennese Technical College and the Viennese Goethe Society. For despite his withdrawal from the latter, he had subsequently been made an Honorary Member.

In his biography of Schröer, Walter Beck continues:

> On 16 April 1896 his friend Victor Tilgner died in Vienna, an event which moved Schröer deeply; Tilgner was spared from seeing the completed Memorial by Hellmer.
>
> On 25 April there followed in the notebook a maxim by Schröer which shows fully his mental alertness, but at the same time (in the strokes of the letters) also his physical limitation. The handwriting had dwindled to a minimum.
>
> 'What a human being can strive towards above his earthly existence may surely be sought in the consonance with which he stands to the world's eternal ideals. 25th Apr. (1)896. K.J. Schröer.'

This final written statement—set down little more than a week after Tilgner's death—may well be considered in the context of Schröer's belief that the Goethe Memorial in Vienna should have presented, in the words of his 1894 letter to Stremayr, 'an ideal work of art placing before our eyes the spirit of Goethe in an uplifting way'.

★

Beck continues:

> For the summer months of 1896—now a period unaffected by college holidays—Karl Julius and Hermine, according to memories of their grandson Edgar von Mojsisovics, rented a dwelling in the manor house 'Hagmüllerdorf' in Maxglan, a suburb of Salzburg. Schröer was pushed in a wheelchair, his time of free mobility being past.
>
> Their granddaughter Elisabeth Palme-Schröer related that the Schröers—seemingly *after* the stay in Maxglan—rented a summer-house in Hinterbühl near Mödling, where they were often visited by friends. Here the granddaughter and grandson would play with a little squirrel tamed by their Schröer grandfather.

A Picture of Goethe's Personality

In Chapter XXII of his autobiography, Rudolf Steiner wrote:

> Towards the end of my Weimar period arose my book *Goethes Weltanschauung* and the introductions to the last volume I had to bring out for the edition in 'Kürschners Deutscher National-Literatur'. I recall in particular what I wrote to introduce my edition of Goethe's *Sprüche in Prosa* compared with how I formulated the content of the book *Goethes Weltanschauung*. If things are regarded only on the surface, this or that contradiction can be made out between the one and the other in my accounts, which arose almost at the same time. But if one looks below the surface at what is *living*, what wants to reveal itself as a *view* of the depths of life, soul and spirit within formulations merely shaping out at the surface, one will not find contradictions but rather in my works of that very time a *struggle* for expression. A struggle to bring into concepts for a view of the world what I have here described as the experience of knowledge, of the relation of man to the world, of the arising of riddles and solving of riddles inside a true reality.
>
> When about three and a half years later I wrote my book *Welt- und Lebensanschauungen im neunzehnten Jahrhundert*, much had gone through further development within me; and I was able to make the cognitional experience here described fruitful for depicting particular views of the world appearing in history.
>
> Anyone who wants to reject writings because in them soul-experience is *struggling* for knowledge, which in light of the account given here means that in them the world's life is further developing in *its struggles* on the stage of a human soul, will not succeed—in my opinion—in immersing himself with his cognizing soul in true reality. This is something which at that very time consolidated within me as a view, while it had already long been pulsating through my conceptual world.

Steiner completed his above-mentioned edition of Goethe's *Sprüche in Prosa* in the summer of 1896.

Exactly how or when he had been commissioned by Kürschner to edit this work, which does not as such form part of Goethe's scientific writings, is not recorded. Evidence given by numeration in an addendum notice shows that it was originally meant to stand as a quite separate volume in the Kürschner series, a volume which would have been a very attractive one in its own right. For unknown reasons, presumably of a publicational nature, it was in the event simply added to the end of the fifth volume of the scientific writings as an enormous 'appendix' of some 200 pages—a highly regrettable decision which had the effect of making this fifth volume both awkwardly bulky and thematically disjointed.

★

To students both of Goethe and of Steiner the work itself is however of great interest. The opening section of Steiner's introduction began:

> Man is not satisfied with what Nature willingly presents to his observing mind. He feels that in order to bring forth her manifold creations she needs driving forces which from an observer she at first conceals. Nature does not herself speak out her last word. Our experience shows us what Nature can create, but it does not tell us how this creation happens. In the human spirit itself lies the means to unveil Nature's driving forces. From the human mind there arise ideas which bring enlightenment on how Nature produces her creations. What is concealed by the phenomena of the outer world is revealed within man. What the human mind thinks up as laws of Nature is not invented onto Nature. It is Nature's actual being, and the mind is only the stage on which Nature allows the secrets of her activity to become visible. What we *observe* in things is only part of things. What wells up in our mind when facing things is the other part. It is the same things which speak to us from outside, and are speaking within us. Only by holding together the language of the outer world with that of our inner being do we have full reality. What did true philosophers of all times want? Nothing else than to proclaim the nature of things, which these themselves express when the mind is presented to them as an organ of speech.
>
> When man lets his inner being speak about Nature, he then recognizes that Nature remains behind what it might by virtue of its driving forces achieve. The mind sees what experience contains in a more perfected shape. It finds that Nature does not achieve her purposes with her creations. It feels itself called upon to present these purposes in a more completed form. It creates shapes in which it shows: 'This is what Nature wanted: but she could only accomplish it to a certain extent.' These shapes are works of art. In them man creates in a perfected manner what Nature shows as imperfect.

Philosopher and artist have the same purpose. They seek to give shape to the perfection their mind envisages if they let Nature work upon them. But various means are available to them for achieving this aim. In the philosopher there lights up a *thought*, an *idea*, when facing a natural process. This he expresses. In the artist there arises a *picture* of this process, which shows the latter more perfect than may be observed in the outer world. Philosopher and artist develop observation further in different ways. An artist does not need to know Nature's driving forces in the form in which they are disclosed to a philosopher. If he perceives a thing or a process, a picture arises directly in his mind onto which Nature's laws are stamped in a more perfect form than in a corresponding thing or process of the outer world. These laws do not need to enter his mind in form of thought. And yet knowledge and art are inwardly related. They demonstrate Nature's *tendencies*, which do not come to full development in mere outer Nature.

If now in the mind of a genuine artist, besides perfect pictures of things, Nature's driving forces are also expressed in form of thoughts, the common source of philosophy and art comes especially clearly before our eyes. Goethe is such an artist. He reveals to us the same secrets in form of his works of art and in form of thought. What he shapes in his poems he expresses in his scientific and artistic articles and in his *Sprüche in Prosa* in form of thought. The reason for the deep satisfaction emanating from these articles and sayings is that one sees a harmony of art and knowledge as realized in a personality. The feeling which appears with every Goethean thought has something uplifting: here speaks someone who can at the same time see in pictures the perfection he expresses in ideas. The power of such a thought is strengthened through this feeling. What derives from the highest needs of *one* personality must belong together. Goethe's wisdom-teachings answer the question: what kind of philosophy is appropriate to genuine art? . . .

Here is a further passage from a later section, 'On the Order of the *Sprüche in Prosa*' (not included in the set of reprinted introductions):

. . . To my feeling, an edition of the sayings must begin with those referring to human *knowledge*. Through them it becomes clear how Goethe thought about the possibility to understand the bustle of the world, and on the basis of this understanding to gain a position towards the world and its particular forms of manifestation. Afterwards I follow with aphorisms showing what form this knowledge takes in *science* in general, then in the separate sciences of *mathematics*, *natural science* and *psychology*. Next I put sayings which have as subject the relation of man to man (*ethics*, *sociology*, *history*) and to the highest things (*religion* and *art*). In the single parts I have endeavoured to assemble everything bearing on *one* thought. I hope through my edition to have supplied a *picture of Goethe's personality*, as far as it is presented in these sayings . . .

The picture of Goethe's personality was thus presented in *literary* form. This may of course be compared with the intended picture of Goethe presented in *sculptural* form which had so engaged the attention of Karl Julius Schröer.

Examples will now be given in separate sections from each part of Steiner's edition. Section titles are those heading the parts.

Knowledge

The first part opened with the following of Goethe's sayings:

> If I know my relationship to myself and to the outer world, I then call it truth. And so each person can have his own truth, and yet it is always the same one.

Steiner added a footnote:

> Truth is nothing of and for itself. It develops in man when the latter allows the world to influence his senses and his mind. According to his organization every human being has his own truth, which in its intimate features *only he* can understand. Anyone who demands a generally valid truth does not understand himself.

Goethe's sayings continued:

> It would not be worthwhile becoming seventy years old, if all the world's wisdom were foolishness before God.

Steiner added a footnote:

> Despite the individual character which human truth has, it accords with man's spiritual needs. If there were a wisdom of another (divine) being, it would for man have no significance. Human wisdom cannot therefore be brought at all into relation with divine, nor thus be called foolishness 'before God', as stated in 1 Corinthians 3:19. A man who does not know himself and his relation to the outer world falls into mistrust of his own mental powers and dreams of a 'higher, divine wisdom', compared with which his own is foolishness.

Goethe's sayings went on:

> Man is sufficiently provided for all earthly needs, if he trusts his senses and develops them in such a way that they remain trustworthy.

⋆

Here is another of Goethe's sayings:

> It is always only our eyes, our kinds of notions; Nature alone knows what she wants, what she has wanted.

Steiner added a footnote:

> Acknowledgement of this truth is necessary if one wants to understand one's relation to oneself and to the outer world. Just as it is correct that human truths suffice for human needs, so is it equally correct that human knowledge is determined by the human organization. There is therefore no sense in speaking about any other than a *human* truth.

Goethe's sayings continued:

'Give me somewhere to stand!'
Archimedes.
'Take yourself, where you are standing!'
Rose.
'Assert, where you stand!'
G.

Steiner added a footnote:

> The starting point for human truths cannot be sought outside, but only *inside* a human being. Goethe's maxim is to place oneself at the central point of the world and relate all things to oneself. Rose published in the year 1820 the work *Historische Symbole, die Basaltgenese betreffend.*

Goethe's sayings went on:

> Everything which is in the subject is in the object and still something more.
>
> Everything which is in the object is in the subject and still something more.
>
> We are lost and hidden in a double way. Conceding to the object its 'more' and renouncing our subjective 'more'. Upraising the subject with its 'more' and not recognizing that former 'more'.

Steiner added a footnote:

> It is one of Goethe's fundamental convictions that objective Nature and the human being's subjective personality correspond to one another. He thus stands on the ground of ancient Greek philosophy, that same can only be recognized by same. Cf. Vol. 35 p. 88: 'We here recall the ancient Ionic school, which repeated with such great significance that same is only recognized by same.' [Introduction to the *Doctrine of Colour.*] The 'more' of the subject over against the object as contrariwise the 'more' of the object over against the subject makes it necessary that a man be conscious of the subjective origin of his knowledge, that he know his relation to himself and to the outer world.

Goethe's sayings continued:

> In observing Nature as a whole as in detail, I have unceasingly asked the question: 'Is it the object here expressing itself, or is it you?' And in this sense I would also observe predecessors and co-workers.

Steiner added a footnote:

> In regard to the truth contained in 352, 10–15 [the previous saying] this question must be asked.

★

Here are more of Goethe's sayings:

> Every man looks on the finished and regulated, formed, perfected world only as an element from which he endeavours to create a special world appropriate for himself. Capable men grasp it without reflection, thus seeking to behave as things go; others hesitate about it; some even doubt its existence.
>
> Any person who felt rightly permeated by this fundamental truth would argue with no one, but just regard another's way of conceiving as a phenomenon, like his own. For we experience almost daily that one person may comfortably think of what is impossible for another to think about, and indeed not in the kind of things which might have some influence on weal and woe, but in things which are for us completely unimportant.
>
> ———
>
> One actually knows what one knows only for oneself. If I speak with another about what I believe I know, he immediately believes he knows it better, and I must ever again withdraw with my knowledge into myself.
>
> What I properly know, I know only for myself. Words spoken out seldom further anyone. They mostly arouse contradiction, stoppage and standstill.

Steiner added a footnote:

> The truths gained by a human being are so intimate and individual in their fine ramifications and in the nuances of feeling by which they are accompanied that they cannot, in their full content, be completely grasped by a second human being. Actually one can always properly understand only oneself. In a discussion the mental pictures connected by two persons to one and the same word never exactly correspond.

★

Here are still more of Goethe's sayings:

> Those who contradict and argue should now and again reflect that not every language is understandable to every person.
>
> ———
>
> For every person only hears what he understands.

★

Here is another of Goethe's sayings:

> Dialectics is the development of a spirit of contradiction, given to man so that he learns how to recognize the difference of things.

Steiner added a footnote:

> Dialectics is the art of setting into relation the concepts man makes about things. The relations and differences of things are thereby explained. In this sense Plato practised dialectics. Since a thing can be looked at from different viewpoints, different or indeed opposite concepts can be formed of one and the same thing. In juxtaposing such opposite concepts lies the possibility to grasp a thing, i.e. to differentiate it from others.

★

Here are yet more of Goethe's sayings:

> Anyone who contents himself with pure experience and acts accordingly has truth enough. A growing child is in this sense wise.
>
> ———
>
> Experience is first useful to science, then harmful, because experience makes one aware of law and exception. The average of both does not in any way give the truth.

Steiner added a footnote:

> These two sayings juxtapose the value and harmfulness of pure experience, and do so dialectically according to 356, 21–23 ['Dialectics is the development of a spirit of contradiction . . .']. The resolving of the contradiction lies in the following sentence 21f. Law should not be removed from experience, but rather must serve to divide the necessary within it from the accidental. To that extent it *cleanses* experience from accidental exceptions, which harm science if too much value is placed upon them.

The following sentence was:

> Theory in and by itself is of no use, except in so far as it makes us believe in the connection of phenomena.

Sciences in General and their History

The second part opened with the following of Goethe's sayings:

> Sciences always depart on the whole from life and return to it again only by a detour.

> For they are actually compendia of life; they bring outer and inner experiences into generality, into a relationship.
>
> Interest in them is basically aroused only in a particular world, in the scientific one. That the rest of the world is also summoned towards them and given notice about them, as happens in more recent times, is an abuse and brings more harm than benefit.

Rudolf Steiner added a footnote:

> By going into generality, sciences depart from life, which is always concerned only with particular things. A special interest in generality belongs to pursuit of the sciences. The presence of this interest characterizes scientific ability. If human beings who have no interest in generality concern themselves with sciences, this then harms science, for it is sullied by unscientific interests.

Goethe's sayings continued:

> Science helps us above all by somewhat lightening the wonder to which we are summoned by Nature, then however by awakening new skills for ever-increased life, to avoid the harmful and introduce the useful.
>
> ———
>
> Only through heightened practice should sciences affect the outer world; for actually they are all esoteric and can become exoteric only by improving some activity. All other participation leads to nothing.

Steiner added a footnote:

> By teaching one to know the law-abiding nature of the world, science leads by 'a detour' back again to life. It makes possible a rational treatment, not directed against natural laws, nor making senseless experiments, but placing natural laws in its service.

★

Here are more of Goethe's sayings:

> A great evil in sciences, indeed everywhere, arises when men who have no ideational capacity presume to theorize, because they do not grasp that even however much knowledge does not justify them in doing so. At the start they certainly go to work with a praiseworthy common sense, but this has its limits, and when stepping over them it comes into danger of becoming absurd. The domain and inheritance allocated to common sense is the realm of doing and acting. When active it will seldom go astray. Higher thought, conclusion and judgement is however not its business.
>
> ———
>
> What is not original does not matter. And what is original always bears the affliction of an individual.

Steiner added a footnote:

> The world's laws (ideas) can only be found by one who *produces* them in himself (in his mind). From observation alone the laws of the actual may not be inferred. Since production of ideas can only take place in an individual, ideas will always have an individual stamp.

★

Here are more of Goethe's sayings:

> *History of Sciences*
> The real part is the phenomena.
> The ideal the views of phenomena.
>
> ———
>
> The sciences as much as the arts consist of a transmittable (real), learnable part and of an untransmittable (ideal), unlearnable part.
>
> ———
>
> A common scientist holds everything to be transmittable, not sensing that the baseness of his views does not allow him to grasp even the actually transmittable.

Steiner added a footnote:

> The part of sciences resting on productive power by an individual (cf. 386, 1–2 and its note) ['A great evil in sciences . . .'] cannot be transmitted. In every individual it must be produced anew. Knowledge can be transmitted, but not ideas.

Goethe's sayings went on:

> In the history of sciences the ideal part has another relation to the real than in the rest of world history.

Steiner added a footnote:

> Ideas referring to what is practical, religious, etc. are handed down from one generation to another. They rest on needs generally disseminated in mankind. Scientific ideas rest on scientific interest, which is not general. (Cf. 384, 3–12 and its note.) [The part's opening saying]. They only arise in one who has an interest in the world's conformity to law, in generality. This arises in an individual when his ideational capacity is stirred. In ideally unproductive individuals it does not arise. For them the ideal part of the sciences remains without significance.

Goethe's sayings continued:

> What one invents, one does with love; what one has learnt, with certainty.

Steiner added a footnote:

> What one invents is part of one's own personality; what one has learnt is received from outside.

Goethe's sayings went on:

> Everything clever has already been thought. One must just try to think it again.
>
> ———
>
> The history of the sciences is a great fugue, in which the voices of the nations little by little come out.
>
> ———
>
> What was discovered long ago is buried once again. How Tycho exerted himself to make comets into regular bodies, which Seneca had long recognized them to be!
>
> ———
>
> How long did people argue this way and that about the antipodes!
>
> ———
>
> Every day there is reason to enlighten experience and to cleanse the mind.
>
> ———
>
> The most original authors of recent times are not so because they bring forward something new, but only because they are able to say such things as though they had never been said before.
>
> ———
>
> The finest sign of originality is therefore knowing how to develop fruitfully a received thought in such a way that no one would easily have found how much lies hidden within it.
>
> ———
>
> Many thoughts first arise out of general culture like blossoms from green twigs. In the rose season one sees roses blossoming everywhere.

Steiner added a footnote:

> On the repetition of truths in the course of history, cf. Vol. 36,1 p. 5 ff. of this edition.

The reference was to the introduction of the *Geschichte der Farbenlehre*. Goethe's sayings continued:

> Actually everything depends upon attitudes. Where these exist, thoughts also arise, and as they are, so too are the thoughts.

Steiner added a footnote:

> Truth is founded in the whole personality, receiving its character not only from understanding and reason but from character (attitude). If one wants to depict a scientific personality, it does not suffice merely to list the truths which have sprung from his mind. One needs to know the entire human

being, in order to grasp why ideas and concepts have in this case taken just this particular form. Goethe proceeded in the way here indicated in his *Geschichte der Farbenlehre.*

Goethe's sayings went on:

> The most foolish of all mistakes is when good young minds believe they are losing their originality by recognizing a truth which has already been recognized by others.

★

Here is another of Goethe's sayings:

> From Bacon of Verulam dates an epoch of experiential sciences. And yet its path has often been cut across and rendered impassable by theoretical tendencies. Precisely considered, from each day there can and should date a new epoch.

Steiner added a footnote referring first to the section on Bacon in the *Geschichte der Farbenlehre*, and then stating:

> The course of the sciences cannot be such that an outstanding mind at a certain point of time declares tendency and method once and for all. There are continually appearing productive personalities who have new ideas and set before them their particular aims.

★

Here are more of Goethe's sayings:

> Complaint is made of scientific academies, that they do not penetrate enough into life; the fault however is not theirs, but that of the way science is generally treated.
>
> ———
>
> The exceptional men of the 16th and 17th century were themselves academies, like Humboldt in our time. When knowledge became so tremendously rampant, private people came together to achieve in unison what was for an individual impossible. They held themselves at a distance from ministers, princes and kings. How the quiet French conventicle did not try to reject lordship by Richelieu! How the English union in Oxford and London hindered the influence of the favourites of Charles II!
>
> Since however it had once happened, and sciences were felt to be a member of state in the body politic, gaining rank at processions and other festivities, a higher purpose was soon lost to view. One showed off one's person, and the sciences too had a little cloak around and a little cap on. In my history of the doctrine of colour I referred extensively to this kind of thing. But what stands written is standing there for the purpose of being continually fulfilled.

Steiner added a footnote:

> Sciences can only penetrate into life when single *free* personalities take on to mediate them. Only scientific interest, the ideal world which such personalities ensoul can have a living result. Neither the state nor a society can regulate the progress of science, since it is effected only through the originality of single minds.

★

Here are still more of Goethe's sayings:

> Every scientist must absolutely regard himself as one summoned before a jury. He must only attend to how far his speech be complete and explained through clear instances. Afterwards he sums up his conviction and casts his vote, whether his opinion coincides with that of the expert or not.
>
> ———
>
> He thus remains equally calm when the majority agrees with him as when he finds himself in a minority. For he has done his bit, has expressed his conviction. He is not lord over minds or over feelings.

Steiner added a footnote:

> A single scientist does not give out anything of general validity, but rather the individual pictures arising in his mind. The more he surrenders himself to his individuality and allows it to work, the more peculiar his ideas will be. Others appear alongside or after him, having another peculiarity. From the combination of individualities arises the progressive development of the sciences.

★

Goethe's final sayings in this part were:

> The Germans—and not only them—have the gift of making sciences inaccessible.
>
> ———
>
> An Englishman is master at making immediate use of what has been invented, till it leads again to new inventions and fresh deeds. One may then ask: why are they everywhere ahead of us?

Mathematics

The third part opened with the following of Goethe's sayings:

> Mathematics, like dialectics, is an organ of the interior higher sense. In practice it is an art like eloquence. For both, nothing has value but the form; to the content they are indifferent. Whether mathematics reckon in pennies

or guineas, whether rhetoric defend the true or the false, is to both absolutely the same.

But here it depends on the nature of the man pursuing such a business, practising such an art. A drastic lawyer in a justified case, a penetrating mathematician before the starry sky, appear both equally godlike.

Rudolf Steiner added a footnote:

In these sentences the relation of mathematics to other sciences is exhaustively stated. Mathematics has of and for itself no *content*; its truths are empty husks, to which a content must arrive from outside. What it calculates, proves etc. is not true because it calculates, proves it etc. but because of the nature of the content, with which it fills its calculations and formulae.

*

Here are more of Goethe's sayings:

We remember quite well the years when no one dared to talk about secret machinations creeping around, at the very time when they were undermining the fatherland. We also know quite well who was practising this censorship and what advantages were gained thereby.

So has the physico-mathematical guild exercised already for twenty years its ban against my *Doctrine of Colour*; they shriek against such things in colleges and anywhere else. For thirty years now men have been telling me enough about it, and they are not mistaken. The possession in which they feel strong is threatened by my doctrine of colour, which can in this sense be called revolutionary. That aristocracy has every reason to guard itself against it.

Physics must be presented as separate from mathematics. The former must consist in a decisive independence, trying to penetrate with all its loving, reverent, devout powers into Nature and its sacred life, quite untroubled by what mathematics on its side is achieving and doing. The latter by contrast must declare itself independent from all externality, go on its own great spiritual course and develop more purely than can happen if it concerns itself as before with what is available and tries to gain something from this or fit something to it.

Steiner added a footnote:

Physics should focus independently from mathematics onto the forces of Nature and determine their working method. Mathematics should develop in itself its spatial views and numerical formulae. Only when these latter, after first having been developed in the domain of abstract thought, are applied to the qualitative part of Nature transmitted by the physicist is a complete result to be expected.

Goethe's sayings continued:

> It would be a great task to ban mathematico-philosophical theories from the parts of physics where instead of promoting knowledge they only prevent it, and where mathematical treatment has been so distortedly applied through one-sidedness in the development of recent scientific education.
>
> ———
>
> This would set forth what is the true path of natural science, how it reposes on the simplest progress in observing, how observation is intensified into experiment, and how the latter finally leads to a result.

Steiner added a footnote referring to Goethe's article 'Experiment as Mediator between Subject and Object', published in the second volume.

Goethe's sayings continued:

> If hopes be realized that human beings unite with all their forces, with heart and mind, understanding and love, and come to know each other, what no man can yet think of will then come about. Mathematicians will enjoy being received into this general moral union of the world as citizens of an important state, and little by little relinquish the conceit of ruling over everything as universal monarchs. They will no longer allow themselves to start declaring everything invalid, inexact and inadequate which is not subject to calculation.
>
> ———
>
> We must recognize and confess what mathematics is, how it could be of considerable service to natural science, where by contrast it does not belong, and into what wretched lapses science and art have fallen since their regeneration through applying it wrongly.
>
> ———
>
> Tycho de Brahe, a great mathematician, could only half break away from the old system, which at least accorded with the senses. But he wanted to replace it by a complicated clockwork, neither perceivable by the senses nor attainable by thoughts.
>
> ———
>
> Newton, as a mathematician, stands in such high reputation that the clumsiest mistake—namely that clear, pure, ever undimmed light is made up from dark luminations—has been retained to the present day. And is it not mathematicians who are still defending and straightaway repeating this absurdity to the commonest listener in words by which nothing can be thought?

Natural Science

The fourth part included the following of Goethe's sayings:

> In natural science a categorical imperative is needed as much as in moral

science; it must only be considered that one is not thereby at the end, but just at the beginning.

Rudolf Steiner added a footnote:

> A categorical imperative in morality consists in a demand that man arrange his actions according to his moral maxims. Anyone standing like Kant upon the standpoint that there are absolute, generally valid moral laws sees a categorical imperative in the demand that one absolutely has to subject oneself to these general moral laws. Goethe is not standing upon that standpoint. He recognizes that like all ideas moral ones too must be created by an individual out of his own productive spiritual power. Therefore a categorical imperative can for him consist only in the requirement for an individual to accord with his own moral views. Transferred into the domain of natural science this means: an individual should make clear to himself which maxims in natural science he can recognize, and then remain faithful in detail to these maxims, i.e. to himself.

★

Here is another of Goethe's sayings:

> Light and spirit, the former in physics, the latter in morals, are the highest thinkable indivisible energies.

Steiner added a footnote:

> Light is for Goethe a unity and indeed the highest unity existing in the physical world; all other physical qualities (warmth, tone) are of subordinate kind. So too is the spirit for Goethe a unity. The view of recent psychologists who hold the spirit as merely a conglomerate of particular feelings and notions is totally incompatible with Goethe's kind of mental picture.

Goethe's sayings continued:

> We ascribe our conditions now to God, now to the devil, and in both cases are wrong. The riddle lies in ourselves, being a monster of two worlds. Just the same goes for colour. People seek it now in the light, now outside in the cosmos, and cannot find it precisely where it is at home.

Steiner added a footnote:

> Anyone who wants to understand sensory phenomena cannot stop with things and processes lying outside man. He must investigate the counter-influences with which our sensory organs reply to influences of the outer world. In the doctrine of colour Goethe starts from the regular action of the eye.

Goethe's sayings went on:

And does not colour actually belong wholly to sight?

I have nothing against it, if people believe that colour can even be felt. Its own particularity would be thereby only still more confirmed.

It can also be tasted. Blue tastes alkaline, yellow-red sour. All manifestations of a being are related.

Those who put together the one fundamentally clear light out of coloured luminosities are the actual obscurantists.

★

Here are more of Goethe's sayings:

By looking through physics exactly, one will find that the phenomena, just like the experiments on which it is built, have a different value.

Everything depends on the primary, primal experiments, and the chapter built upon them stands sure and firm. But there are also secondary ones, tertiary ones, etc. If these latter be granted an equal right, they only confuse what was illumined by the first ones.

Steiner added a footnote:

Some present essential phenomena, others just accidental ones. What matter are the first, for only they lead into the necessary conformity of Nature to law.

★

Here are still more of Goethe's sayings:

There will come a time when a pathological experimental physics is presented and all those mirroring shams brought to light which circumvent understanding and—what is worst about it—hinder all practical progress. From the murky empiric-mechanic-dogmatic torture-chamber the phenomena must be brought out once and for all before the jury of common sense.

That Newton in his prismatic experiments made the opening as small as possible, so as to symbolize a line conveniently into a ray of light, has brought over the world an incurable confusion, from which maybe centuries will still be suffering.

Through this tiny hole Malus was driven to an adventurous theory, and had Seebeck not been so circumspect, he would have been prevented from discovering the primal cause of these phenomena: the entoptic figures and colours.

Rudolf Steiner added a footnote in respect to Malus and Seeback referring to the work on *Entoptische Farben*, and then stated:

> To Goethe an experimental physics seems pathological which does not attempt to deal with essential phenomena through experiments, but rather holds to intricate or inessential manifestations and sets up theories about them. Goethe calls healthy an experimental physics constructing assembled phenomena from simple ones; these let the essential be recognized.

Goethe's sayings continued:

> But what is most peculiar of all is that even if a human being uncovers the cause of the error, he will not thereby be freed from the the error itself. Several Englishmen, especially Dr. Reade, speak passionately against Newton: 'the prismatic image is in no way the image of the sun, but rather the image of the opening of our shuttered window, decorated with coloured edges; in the prismatic image there is no original green; this arises through blue and yellow merging over one another, so that a black band just as well as a white one can appear resolved into colours, if one wants to speak here of resolving.'[21] Enough. Everything we have been setting forth for years, this good observer likewise presents. But the fixed idea of a diverse refrangibility does not now let him go; he turns it around and is possibly even more prejudiced than his great master. Instead of tearing himself away from that chrysalis state enthused by this new view, he tries to bring the already grown and unfolded members once again into the old pupa skins.
>
> ---
>
> False idea: that a phenomenon could be dismissed and removed through calculation or through words.

Steiner added a footnote referring to the first saying in the part on 'Mathematics'.

Goethe's sayings went on:

> Copies, verbal description, measure, number and sign still do not present any phenomenon. The Newtonian doctrine was able to last for so long just because the mistake was embalmed for a couple of centuries into the quarto volume of the Latin translation.
>
> ---
>
> Let one enquire into a phenomenon, taking it as exactly as possible, and seeing how far one can come with it in insight and in practical application, while letting the problem quietly lie. Physicists act the other way round: they go straight into the problem, and on the way become entangled in so many difficulties that for them every prospect finally disappears.
>
> ---
>
> The Petersburg Academy has therefore received no answer to its prize question; even the extended deadline will not help. The Academy should

> now double the prize and promise it to the person who laid out clearly and plainly before the eyes *why no answer arrived, and why none could be forthcoming.* Anyone able to do this would well have deserved that prize.

Steiner added a footnote:

> Physicists should put together those experiments which shed light from all sides on an essential manifestation of Nature, and await the conceptual result arising for unbiased thinking from the nature of the phenomena. Instead of which, they approach the phenomenon with a specific intention of interpreting it *conceptually*. They do not let the phenomenon speak, but rather *think* their theories and views into the phenomenon.

Goethe's sayings continued:

> Since there have been for some time further enquiries about my *Doctrine of Colour*, the need arises for freshly illustrated plates. While attending to this small matter I have to smile at the unspeakable trouble which I took to render palpable the reasonable as well as the absurd. Little by little both will be grasped and recognized.

———

(3086)

about three foot radius (ſuppoſe a broad Object-glaſs of a three foot Teleſcope,) at the diſtance of about four or five foot from thence, through which all thoſe colours may at once be tranſmitted, and made by its Refraction to convene at a further diſtance of about ten or twelve feet. If at that diſtance you intercept this light with a ſheet of white paper, you will ſee the colours converted into whiteneſs again by being mingled. But it is requiſite, that the *Priſme* and *Lens* be placed ſteddy, and that the paper, on which the colours are caſt, be moved to and fro; for, by ſuch motion, you will not only find, at what diſtance the whiteneſs is moſt perfect, but alſo ſee, how the colours gradually convene, and vaniſh into whiteneſs, and afterwards having croſſed one another in that place where they compound Whiteneſs, are again diſſipated, and ſevered, and in an inverted order retain the ſame colours, which they had before they entered the compoſition. You may alſo ſee, that, if any of the Colours at the *Lens* be intercepted, the Whiteneſs will be changed into the other colours. And therefore, that the compoſition of whiteneſs be perfect, care muſt be taken, that none of the colours fall beſides the *Lens*.

In the annexed deſign of this Experiment, A B C expreſſeth the Priſm ſet endwiſe to ſight, cloſe by the hole F of the window

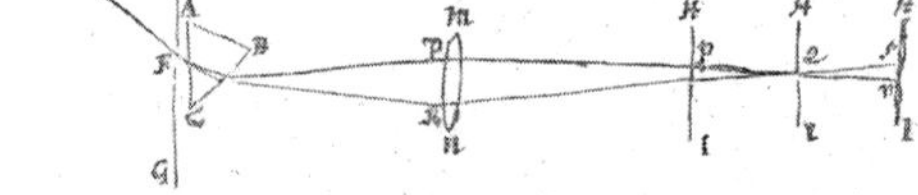

E G. Its vertical Angle A C B may conveniently be about 60 degrees: *M N* deſigneth the *Lens*. Its breadth $2\frac{1}{2}$ or 3 inches. S F one of the ſtreight lines, in which difform Rays may be conceived to flow ſucceſſively from the Sun. F P, and F R two of thoſe Rays unequally refracted, which the *Lens* makes to converge towards Q, and after decuſſation to diverge again. And H I the paper, at divers diſtances, on which the colours are projected: which in Q conſtitute *Whiteneſs*, but are *Red* and *Yellow* in R, r, and ρ, and *Blew* and *Purple* in P, p, and π.

If

Newton's account of the experimentum crucis

> The Newtonian mistake stands so nicely in the lexicon that one only has to learn by heart the octavo page to be rid of colour for the whole of life.
>
> ———
>
> The fight with Newton actually takes place in a lower region. One is contesting a badly seen, badly developed, badly applied, badly theorized phenomenon. One is accusing another person of rashness in experiment, intentionality in sequence, haste in theorizing, obstinacy in defence, in all a semi-conscious, semi-unconscious dishonesty.
>
> ———
>
> Completely vacuous words, like decomposition and polarization, must be removed from physics if something is to come out of it. Yet it would be possible, indeed it is probable, for these spectres to be still stalking right over into the second half of the century.
>
> ———
>
> Let this not be taken amiss! Precisely what no one admits, no one wants to hear, must be all the more often repeated.

Steiner added a footnote:

> 'Decomposition', i.e. breaking down of light, is for Goethe a vacuous word, because simple light cannot be broken down. 'Polarization' is a word for the quality ascribed to light of appearing different in different directions, if reflected or refracted. Light is supposed *thereby in itself* to suffer a change. Goethe takes the view that all phenomena described by the word polarization do not indicate a change *in* light, but are rather produced *onto* light through the reflecting and refracting body.

Goethe's sayings continued:

> The Newtonian experiment on which the conventional doctrine of colour reposes is of the most manifold complexity; it links together the following conditions.
>
> In order for the spectre to appear, there is needed:
>
> Firstly—a glass prism;
> Secondly—three-sided;
> Thirdly—small;
> Fourthly—a shuttered window
> Fifthly—an opening in it;
> Sixthly—the latter very small;
> Seventhly—sunlight falling in;
> Eighthly—from a certain distance;
> Ninthly—falling in a certain direction onto the prism;
> Tenthly—reproduced onto a plate;
> Eleventhly—which is placed at a certain distance behind the prism.
>
> Of these conditions, if three, six and eleven be taken away, the opening

be made large, a large prism be taken, and the plate be put nearby, the beloved spectre cannot and will not appear.

Steiner added a footnote:

The many conditions under which Newton presents the basic manifestation render the latter a complex one; Goethe wants to arrange basic manifestations under the simplest of conditions, and when he has observed their result, add further conditions, in order little by little to construct a complex phenomenon out of simple ones.

Goethe's sayings went on:

A hundred grey horses don't make a single white one.

Steiner added a footnote:

i.e. a hundred colours, which are as such darker than light, do not give the *white* light Newton wants to put together out of seven dark colours.

Psychological Observations

The fifth part included the following of Goethe's sayings:

I pity human beings who make much ado about the transitoriness of things and lose themselves in observation of earthly nullity. For we are indeed there to make the perishable imperishable. This can only happen if one knows how to appreciate both.

Life, however common it looks, however easily it seems to be content with the normal, the everyday, is yet always harbouring and fostering quietly certain higher demands, and looking for means of satisfying them.

It can well be that a human being is at times dreadfully broken through public and domestic fate. Ruthless destiny, however, on meeting bounteous sheaves, crumples up only the straw. But the grains feel nothing of this and now and again spring cheerfully onto the threshing floor, untroubled whether they wander to the mill or to the cornfield.

Steiner added a footnote:

What is truly valuable has in itself the power to develop. It works on, even when a human being does not particularly experience the value and therefore feels himself unlucky.

Goethe's sayings continued:

> Anyone who would always allow himself to regard the world as badly as adversaries depict to us must have become a miserable subject.

Steiner added a footnote:

> Such a one only shows that he is incapable of doing anything for perfecting the world. A worthy personality creates goodness out of himself and rejoices in the value, which only he can lend to the world.

Goethe's sayings went on:

> The longer I live the more morose I become when I see man—who is actually there on his highest place in order to have command over Nature, in order to liberate himself and his own from violent necessity—when I see how out of some preconceived false notion he does just the opposite of what he wants, and then, because aptitude as a whole is corrupted, bungles wretchedly in detail around.

Steiner added a footnote:

> A human being with productive ideational capacity will find in himself a drive towards action, towards intervening in the bustle of the world. If out of prejudice he does not entrust himself to his genius, he will be swept along by blind chance. His activity will then lack inner unity, and be pulled now here and now there.

Goethe's sayings continued:

> What one does not understand, one does not possess.

Steiner added a footnote:

> A thing only becomes valuable and useful for man if he knows its conformity to law, and understands how to value it in accordance with the latter.

Goethe's sayings went on:

> If you can read, then you should understand; if you can write, then you must know something; if you can believe, then you should conceptualize. If you desire, you will be obliged; if you demand, you will not attain; and if you are experienced, you should make use.

Steiner added a footnote:

> A merely passive relation to a thing does not suffice. One must relate to it actively, make it one's own. Anyone who reads, without making what is read come alive in himself, who writes, without setting his deepest inner being into the writing, who believes, without processing the belief in clear concepts, who desires, without progressing to energetic willing (obligation),

who gathers experiences, without making use of them for himself, is an imperfect human being. Anyone who demands, without getting down to a deed, attains nothing.

★

Here is another of Goethe's sayings:

> Genius practises a kind of ubiquity, in generality before, in particularity after experience.

Steiner added a footnote:

> Experience and knowledge of the world remain closed to an unproductive, ungenial human being. The power of a genius penetrates into all depths. He acquires omnipresence (ubiquity). He perceives, even before experience, in *generality* the world's conformity to law, and feels it in the particular when he has come to know the same.

Goethe's sayings continued:

> An active scepticism is one which ceaselessly endeavours to overcome itself and to attain through regulated experience a kind of conditional reliability.
>
> ——
>
> The generality of such a spirit is the tendency to enquire into whether some predicate really befits some object, even if this investigation happens for the purpose of being able to apply in practice, with sureness, what is found proven.

Steiner added a footnote:

> It will not occur to a mind endowed with active scepticism to hold as unconditionally profitable a notion with which it has become obsessed. It puts forward requirements on a trial basis, and tests their capacity for achievement by introducing them into practical life. From this interaction of idea and practice it forms sure tendencies for life.

★

Here are more of Goethe's sayings:

> I can promise to be honest, but not to be impartial.
>
> ——
>
> 'There is no such thing as an impartial representation. A looking-glass, one might be apt to imagine, was an exception to this proposition; and yet we never see our own faces justly in one. It gives us nothing but the translations of them. A mirror ever reverses our features, and presents our left hand for our right. This is an emblem of all personal reflections.'

Steiner added a footnote:

> This saying derives from Sterne's *Koran*, II, 6. It connects so perfectly to 450, 16–7 [the previous one] that I am not placing it with the remaining sayings drawn from Sterne, but here.

★

Here are yet more of Goethe's sayings:

> Everything of excellence momentarily limits us, by our not feeling equal to the same. Only in so far as we afterwards receive it into our culture, acquire it with our forces of mind and soul, does it become dear and valuable to us.
>
> ———
>
> No wonder that we all more or less delight in mediocrity, because it leaves us in peace. It gives a contented feeling, as if one were going around with one's equal.

Steiner added a footnote:

> Excellence has first an amazing effect, being directed against the habitual. Only when it is received into habits does it appear tolerable.
>
> Goethe's sayings went on:
>
> Lasciviousness is a game with the enjoyable and with the enjoyed.

Steiner added a footnote:

> Lasciviousness is desire which lacks seriousness. A lascivious person feels a kind of contentment, by *triflingly* surrendering with his feelings to the thought of pleasure. This living in a contented, easy game of mental pictures accompanies his enjoyment and his thoughts of what is enjoyed.

★

Here is another of Goethe's sayings:

> Every age of man answers to a certain philosophy. A child appears as a realist; for it finds itself as convinced of the being of pears and apples as of its own. A youth, stormed by inner passions, must look to himself, sound himself out; he changes into an idealist. A man has by contrast every reason to become a sceptic; he does well to doubt whether the means he has chosen for the end be also the right one. Before acting, in acting, he has every reason to keep understanding mobile, lest he afterwards have to grieve over a false choice. An old man however will always confess himself to mysticism. He sees that so much appears to depend on chance. The unreasonable succeeds, the reasonable goes awry, fortune and misfortune are unexpectedly placed onto the same level. So it is, so it was; and old age is comforted in Him who is, who was and who will be.

Steiner added a footnote:

> Life is for a human being a continual *process of liberation* from the outer world. A child lives in and with things. Its self is still inseparate from them. Only when it comes to consciousness of this self and *frees* itself from things does it become aware of the spiritual (ideal) in itself, which can only appear in man himself. A youth will first appreciate the value of the spiritual, but also *overestimate* it, for he produces ideas with fresh power from out of himself and loves them as *his own*. He has scant regard for the outer world, which he does not first need to produce, which comes towards him like a gift. A mature man finally becomes aware that real knowledge is only possible through inner fusion of idea and experience. He therefore becomes sceptical towards the intrinsic value of the ideal; he seeks to come to terms with reality. He will develop the active scepticism mentioned in 449, 1–3 ['one which ceaselessly endeavours to overcome itself...'], which tests ideals on the outer world before it makes them into tendencies for life. Whether an old man really becomes a mystic, I am unable to decide.

Ethics

The sixth part began with the following saying by Goethe:

> Every human being must think according to his manner. For he always finds on his way a truth, or a kind of truth, which helps him through life. But he may not let himself go. He must control himself. Mere naked instinct does not accord with man.

Rudolf Steiner added a footnote:

> Blind instinct, arising from unconscious soul-life, will not be a guideline for action to a more highly developed man, but ideas appearing on the scene of conscious soul-life. In my book *Philosophie der Freiheit* (Weimar, Emil Felber) I called the ability to produce ideas regarding ethics 'moral fantasy', and showed its effectiveness as well as its relation to the life of instinct.

Goethe's sayings continued:

> Lessing, who unwillingly felt various limitations, makes one of his persons say: 'No one must be obliged.' A perceptive, cheerful-minded man said: 'Whoever wills, is obliged.' A third, admittedly an educated one, added: 'Whoever recognizes, also wills.' And so the whole circle of knowing, willing and being obliged was believed to have been closed. But on average, man's knowledge—of whatever kind it be—determines his action and inaction. Therefore also nothing is more dreadful than to see ignorance acting.

There is nothing more dreadful than an active ignorance.

Duty, where one loves what one commands oneself.

Steiner added a footnote:

> Lessing makes Nathan say to the dervish: 'No one must be obliged, and a dervish must be?' Goethe rejects every norm of action imposed on man from outside. A free-minded human being produces his moral ideas out of himself and imposes these onto himself as duty. He *loves* this his own duty, because it is *his* child. And *because he loves it,* his will acts in accordance, without being forced. As soon as he has produced a moral idea and recognizes its usefulness, there is for him no reluctance.

★

Here are more of Goethe's sayings:

> From time to time I meet a youth in whom I would not wish anything changed or improved. What makes me uneasy is just that I see many perfectly suited to swimming onward in the stream of time. And it's this to which I continually want to draw attention: a rudder is given into man's hand in his fragile boat precisely so that he follow not the caprice of the waves, but the will of his insight.

> But how should a young man come by himself to regard as blameworthy and harmful what everyone does, approves and promotes? Why should he not let go of himself, and of his disposition too?

Steiner added a footnote:

> A young man, instead of raising himself to moral training, which enables him to act according to his moral insight, will easily be directed according to his lower disposition—his unconscious instincts.

Goethe's sayings went on:

> If we then take up the significant expression 'Know thyself', we must not interpret it in an ascetic sense. It does not in any way mean the heautognosis of our modern hypochondriacs, humorists and heautontimorumenists. Rather it means quite simply: 'Attend somewhat to yourself, take notice of yourself, so that you become aware how you come to stand to the likes of yourself and to the world.' This does not need any psychological torments. Every capable person knows and experiences what it should mean. It is good advice, redounding in practice to everyone's greatest advantage.

> How can one come to know oneself? Never through observing, but rather through acting. Try doing your duty, and you know at once what is in you.

Steiner added a footnote:

> Merely observing his own self gives no information about a human being's value. Man must produce ideas and allow these to penetrate into life; he will then become aware of what capability and worth he is. The content of a person is only shown in his *creativity*. Passive observation of one's own mind does not unleash creative forces.

★

Here are yet more of Goethe's sayings:

> It is not enough to know, one must also apply; it is not enough to will, one must also do.
>
> ———
>
> Blowing on a wind-instrument is not warbling. You must move the fingers.
>
> ———
>
> When a human being reflects on his physicality and morality, he usually finds himself ill.

Steiner added a footnote:

> The self-contemplation reprimanded in 461, 15–25 [in the saying 'If we then take up the significant expression "Know thyself"'...] leads to the belief that one who observes himself is ill, because through passive gazing into self it does not let the personality's active side come to development. Man then believes himself to be lacking in forces, while he is just suppressing them.

Goethe's sayings continued:

> The effects to which we must attend if we want to be furthered are:
> Preparing,
> Accompanying,
> Contributing,
> Supporting,
> Promoting,
> Strengthening,
> Hindering,
> Resulting.

Steiner added a footnote:

> We must consider these effects when it is a matter of translating an idea into reality.

★

Here are still more of Goethe's sayings:

> Character in great and small is that man gives a constant sequence to what he feels himself capable of.
>
> ———
>
> The happiest man is one who can set the end of his life into connection with the beginning.
>
> ———
>
> Men's prejudices rest every time on men's character; they are thus, closely united to the condition, quite insurmountable. Neither evidence nor understanding nor reason have the least influence upon them.

Steiner added a footnote:

> A man's character is expressed in the nature of the moral maxims he lays at the basis of his actions. This is a consequence of his aptitudes and abilities. A perfect character is one where this nature is harmonious in itself and throughout the whole of life has *one* essential trait. Character does not rest on understanding and reason, which serve insight, but rather on the whole psychological nature of a personality. It depends upon this what particular moral ideas in a human being come to the fore.

★

Here are Goethe's final sayings in this part:

> Devoutness is no end, but a means for attaining through the purest calm of mind to the highest culture.
>
> ———
>
> It may therefore be noticed that those who put up devoutness as end and purpose mostly become hypocrites.

Steiner added a footnote:

> Devoutness is a state of mind. Such a state cannot be an end in itself, since it presupposes something towards which one can come into a devout mood. A person is devout if he surrenders himself to an object he has recognized as absolutely valuable, merges into it; if he cannot think about it without sinking into an adoring reverence. The satisfaction produced by living into an object in this way brings about a calm of mind leading to the highest culture, i.e. to balance of spiritual powers.

Life-wisdom and Education

The seventh part included the following sayings by Goethe, some of which were set in quotation marks.

Those from whom we always learn we cheaply call our masters. Not everyone from whom we learn deserves this title.

A genuine pupil learns how to develop the unknown from the known, and approaches the master.

'But men are not easily able to develop the unknown from the known. For they do not know that their understanding pursues just such arts as Nature.'

For the gods teach us to copy their very own work. Yet we know only what we do, but do not recognize what we copy.

Everything is similar, everything dissimilar, everything useful and harmful, speaking and dumb, reasonable and unreasonable. And what one acknowledges about particular things is often contradicted.

For human beings imposed law onto themselves, without knowing what they were giving laws about. But all the gods ordered Nature.

Now what men have set up does not want to fit, be it right or wrong. But what the gods set up is always in its place, right or wrong.

But I want to show that the known arts of man are like natural events, which happen openly or in secret.

Of this kind is the art of prophecy. From the revealed it recognizes the hidden, from the present the future, from the dead the living, and the point of the pointless.

'So an instructed person always recognizes rightly the nature of a human being. And an uninstructed person sees it now thus, now thus, and each one copies it in his own way.'

'If a man encounters a woman and there arises a boy, something unknown comes out of something known. If by contrast the dark mind of a boy takes into itself clear things, he becomes a man and from the present learns to know the future.'

'An immortal may not be compared with a living mortal, and yet even the merely living is sensible. So the stomach knows quite well if it thirsts and hungers.'

'Thus does prophecy relate to human nature. And to those with insight both are always right; but to the limited they appear now thus, now thus.'

Rudolf Steiner added a footnote:

These sayings are taken from the work of Hippocrates *περι διαίτῆς το πρώτον* (About Life-wisdom).—God has placed into man the capacity so to act that his action proceeds in exactly the same way as events in Nature. Human action is an exact copy of natural occurrence. Man cannot comprehend Nature in her work; therefore he does not know that he is acting in the same sense as she. He believes he is giving himself laws which are common to him and to Nature, and so must derive from a source superordinate to both of them. Nature engenders from a man and a woman, thus from the known, the child, the unknown. The prophet produces from observations, thus the known, ideas about the unobservable primal foundation, thus about the unknown. The stomach knows about hunger and thirst, i.e. the mindless has knowledge just as has man himself. So Nature and the human mind are of like kind in their work. In these sayings may be recognized the influence upon Hippocrates of Heraclitus. Heraclitus taught that there is *one* reason in the universe guiding everything and that it is man's highest task to recognize this guiding wisdom, which is active as much in Nature as in the human being. Man must live according to this general wisdom, not in the sense of his particular laws. Heraclitus finds the highest insight in the knowledge that everything a human being does is a product of the highest wisdom. One should not believe at all that Goethe agreed with these appropriated sayings in every detail. But he found in them an echo of his own basic conviction that the world's conformity to law is a unified one, and that man is only a special member of the general cosmic process. He was however clear that this special member must also be specially regarded, and that the conformity of human action to law is not a mere parallel phenomenon to general laws of Nature, but rather presents a higher stage in relation to them. Nothing is gained by blurring the difference of degree between human and natural laws so as to let everything melt into the mist of the general laws of the world.

★

Here is another of Goethe's sayings:

What kind of education may be held as the best? Answer: that of the Hydriots. As islanders and seafarers they take their boys straight into a ship, letting them crawl into service. As they achieve something, they take part in the gains. So they are already occupied in commerce, exchange and booty, and become the most competent of coastal seafarers, the cleverest of mer-

> chants and the most daring of pirates. From such a crowd heroes can certainly come forth, clamping with their own hands a pernicious firebrand onto the admiral's ship of the enemy fleet.

Steiner added a footnote:

> Hydriots are inhabitants of the Greek island Hydria.

Goethe's sayings continued:

> Timon was asked by someone about teaching for his children. 'Let them,' he said, 'be taught what they will never grasp.'

Steiner added a footnote:

> What is conceptual, graspable in concepts, is only part of the world. Teaching must also extend to what is only accessible to more intimate soul-forces. The above saying expresses this thought in humorous form, while at the same time it suggests that the aims of teaching cannot be set high enough.

Goethe's sayings continued:

> One could be genuinely aesthetic and didactic if with one's pupils one passed over everything worth feeling, or brought it to them at the moment where it culminates and they are highly receptive. But since this requirement may not be fulfilled, the highest pride of an academic teacher must be to bring to life the concepts of so many manifestations in his pupils in such a way that they become receptive for everything good, beautiful, great and true, grasping it with joy when it meets them at the right time. Without their noticing and knowing it, the basic idea from which everything proceeds would thus have come alive in them.
>
> ———
>
> Certainly, competency, you can't *doceate*; it is—like preaching, given by our condition—truly useful, if conversation and catechization follow, as was also originally done. But you can and you will *teach*, that is: when deed helps judgement to life, and judgement deed.

Steiner added a footnote:

> A teacher should train his pupils individually; he should awaken not only thoughts, but also feelings. He can only do this by bringing forward suitable objects through which these feelings must arise. Doceating is teaching without entering into the pupil's particular individuality.

The last of Goethe's sayings in this part was:

> Textbooks should be attractive. They will only be so when they present the brightest, most accessible side of knowledge and of science.

Sociology

The eighth part included the following saying by Goethe:

> The understanding person does not rule, but Understanding; not the reasonable person, but rather Reason.

Rudolf Steiner added a footnote:

> From the sayings on p. 460, 1–16 [the first two in the part on 'Ethics'] it follows that Goethe is a representative of ethical individualism. He sees the source of activity in an individual, not in common ethical norms. Now it may be said: how is human community possible if every person only does what he commands himself? The question may be answered in the sense that human beings are by and large of *one* mind. A free person lives in the trust that another free person belongs with him to *one* spiritual world, and will meet him in his intentions. For in all men Understanding and Reason bear the same characteristic features. If then each single person only follows his particular ethical intentions, the activity of one will yet be accompanied by Understanding and Reason, which are of the same kind as Understanding and Reason in another. In the cooperation of human beings will thus be noticed the *one* primary trait of Understanding and Reason which is living in them *all*, i.e. although individuals act, Understanding and Reason rule.

Goethe's sayings continued:

> There occurs nothing unreasonable which Understanding or chance might not again straighten out; nothing reasonable which ignorance and chance were unable to misdirect.
>
> ———
>
> The reasonable world may be regarded as a great immortal Individual, which unceasingly brings about what is needed and thus even becomes master over the incidental.

Steiner added a footnote:

> From the cause given in l. 3 f. [the first saying in this part] human development bears in general a unified, reasonable character. Regarded as a whole, Reason in manifesting itself even works as if it were not countless individuals acting together, but rather a single Individual who had all the strings of reasonable events in hand.

Goethe's sayings went on:

> The world is a bell which has a crack. It rattles but doesn't sound.
>
> ———

> The empirical-moral world consists for the most part only of bad will and jealousy.

Steiner added a footnote:

> These sayings present the opposite side of what is contained in ll. 3–10 [the previous ones]. The differences may be united in that here the empirical-moral world is spoken about, i.e. the one presented to our observation when we do not penetrate deeper into the causes of events; there however a contemplation of the world is talked about which understands the deeper impulsive forces of all action, life's great relationships.

★

Here is another of Goethe's sayings:

> The present world is not worth our doing anything for it, as the existing one can in a moment pass away. We must work for the past one and the future one: for the former, that we recognize its merit, for the latter, that we seek to raise its value.

Steiner added a footnote:

> If a man by absorption of past culture joins himself to the previous world and so arranges his work that he hands on valuable cultural elements to those born after him, his being is ordered into the evolution of mankind. If he is wrapped up in the interests of the day, he remains standing between past and future as an isolated individual.

Goethe's sayings continued:

> Every person may ask himself with what organ he can and will if needs be have an effect on his time.
>
> ——
>
> Let no one think that he has been expected as the Messiah.
>
> ——
>
> What is absent works on us through tradition. The ordinary one may be called historical; a higher one, related to imaginative power, is mythical. If one seeks behind the latter for a third thing, some meaning, it changes into mysticism. It also easily becomes sentimental, so that we acquire only what is pleasant.

Steiner added a footnote:

> Tradition turns into mysticism if the feeling of darkness which is connected to the absent or unknown presses into the foreground and overcomes calm and reasonable consideration.

★

Here are more of Goethe's sayings:

> A historical feeling for human beings means one formed in such a way that in appreciating contemporary merits and commendabilities it also takes the past into account.
>
> ———
>
> 'Among all peoples the Greeks have dreamed most beautifully the dream of life.'

★

Here is yet another of Goethe's sayings:

> The sentimentality of the English is humorous and tender, of the French popular and lachrymose, of the Germans naive and realistic.

History

The ninth part was shorter than the others, and will here be reproduced in full. It opened with the following of Goethe's sayings:

> The best we have from history is the enthusiasm it awakens.

Rudolf Steiner added a footnote:

> The value of man lies in his *creativity*. Observation of the past cannot be an aim in itself. It only has value if it serves as a stimulus to present creativity.

Goethe's sayings continued:

> Writing history is a way of getting the past off one's neck.

Steiner added a footnote:

> We best protect ourselves against the pernicious influence of the past, living in us as an inheritance, if we understand it.

Goethe's sayings went on:

> The duty of a historian is to distinguish the true from the false, the certain from the uncertain, the dubious from the rejectable.
>
> ———
>
> A chronicle is only written by one to whom the present is important.
>
> ———
>
> No one can judge about history without having experienced history in himself. So it goes with whole nations. The Germans can only judge about literature since having a literature themselves.

Steiner added a footnote:

> History can actually only be written by one who searches in the historical persons and events for what is hidden behind the merely factual. To this end he must lead a powerful life of his own, for the driving forces of personal action can only be observed in oneself.

Here are the rest of Goethe's sayings:

> The question 'Who stands higher, a historian or a poet?' may not be raised at all. They do not compete with one another, as little as a runner and a boxer. Each deserves his own crown.
>
> ———
>
> The duty of a historian is twofold: firstly towards himself, then towards the reader. For himself he must precisely examine what might probably have happened, and for the sake of the reader he must establish what did happen. How he treats his own self he may arrange with his colleagues, but the public must not see into the secret of how little in history can be stated to be decisively settled.
>
> ———
>
> A historian cannot and need not lead everything into certainty. Mathematicians too do not know how to explain why the comet of 1770, which should have returned in five or eleven years, has not yet been seen again at the determined time.
>
> ———
>
> Against the particular wrongs of the day one should always set only great masses of world history.
>
> ———
>
> But since we are called to this general consultation of the world as assessors, though *sine voto*, and receive daily reports from newspaper-writers, it is good fortune also to find competent reporters from previous times. Most recently von Raumer and Wachler have become such for me.

Religion

The tenth part opened with the following of Goethe's sayings:

> Faith is a domestic, homely capital, just as there are public savings and relief banks, from which in days of necessity single persons are handed what they need. Here a believer quietly takes his interest himself.

Rudolf Steiner added a footnote:

> Faith serves as a support for a weak person and for times of need; a strong person is satisfied only by insight and his own strength. Faith gives an outer security where the inner is lacking.

Goethe's sayings continued:

> Faith, love and hope once felt in a calm sociable hour a plastic impulse in their nature. They made a great effort together and created a lovely shape, a Pandora in a higher sense, patience.

Steiner added a footnote:

> Patience springs from faith in divine wisdom, which teaches one to bear suffering, because a sufferer comforts himself that this wisdom will have its good purposes in suffering; it springs from love, because the latter suppresses selfishness and subdues any grumbling over one's own suffering; it springs from hope, because a sufferer hopes to be compensated for present pain by future pleasure.

Goethe's sayings went on:

> 'I believe in one God!' This is a fine, praiseworthy statement. But to recognize God where and as He may reveal Himself is actually blessedness on Earth.

Steiner added a footnote:

> In the statement 'I believe in one God' the nature of God remains indefinite; He is believed in as something unknown. The opposite of that is finding God in Nature and permeating oneself with a definite, cognizable, divine content.

Goethe's sayings continued:

> Kepler said: 'My highest wish is to become aware also internally, just as much inside myself, of the God whom outside I find everywhere.' The noble man felt, unconsciously to himself, that at this moment the divine in him was standing in a most precise connection to the divine in the universe.

Steiner added a footnote:

> The divine in the universe is only found by one who discovers it in himself. But what announces itself within as divinity is the same as outer divinity. When divinity dawns on someone, the difference ceases between inner and outer. One merges with the outer world and lives oneself into the *united* divinity.

Goethe's sayings went on:

> There are only two true religions: the one, which recognizes and worships the holiness dwelling in and around us, quite formlessly; the other, which does so in the most beautiful form. Everything lying between is idolatry.

Steiner added a footnote:

> The idea, as well as perfect beauty, is divine, everything thing else is undivine. But if it is revered as divine, man must then be arbitrarily ascribing to it divine qualities.

Goethe's sayings continued:

> The teleological proof of God's existence has been set aside by critical reason; this we put up with. But what does not pass as a proof should pass for us as a feeling, and we therefore summon again all devout endeavours of that kind from brontotheology to niphotheology. Should we not be allowed to sense in lightning, thunder and storm the proximity of a more than tremendous power, or in scent of blossom and mild whistling of air a lovingly approaching being?

Steiner added a footnote:

> What Goethe requires is a *devout mood*. Through our disgodding of Nature, i.e. recognizing that she is not the work of a personal god, we should not forget reverence and appreciation of what lives in Nature.

Art

The final eleventh part began with the following of Goethe's sayings:

> One to whom Nature begins to disclose her obvious secret feels an irresistible longing for her worthiest interpreter—art.
>
> ———
>
> The beautiful is a manifestation of secret laws of Nature, without whose appearance they would have remained forever concealed from us.

Rudolf Steiner added a footnote:

> Art and the beautiful are not brought forth by human beings arbitrarily. They are higher forms of the general world-process, which is announced just as much in artistic productions as in the fall of a stone. An artist supplies works which are in the highest sense works of Nature. He can only create something of value if secrets of Nature are disclosed to him. These he incorporates into his works.

Goethe's sayings continued:

> The secrets on life's path may not and cannot be revealed. There are stumbling-stones over which every wanderer must trip up. But a poet points to the spot.

★

Here are more of Goethe's sayings:

> With every work of art, large or small, even the smallest, everything depends on the *conception*.
>
> ———
>
> The *what* of a work of art interests human beings more than the *how*; the former they can singly apprehend, the latter they cannot grasp as a whole. Hence comes the emphasizing of passages, by which lastly—if one attends well—the effect of the totality is also not absent, but to every person unconsciously.
>
> ———
>
> The question: 'Where's the poet got it from?' is also only concerned with the *what*; no one experiences thereby anything of the *how*.

Steiner added a footnote:

> With a work of art what matters is whether an artist really perceives the deeper conformity to law which Nature herself does not perfectly realize in an object, and whether he fashions in sense of this conformity to law. The *what* is the directly given object in the realm of the factual; the *how* the conformity to law, which the artist grasps. He gives it a shape which it does not yet have in reality. An artist perfects the works of Nature. It does not matter what the objects are from which he starts out, but what shape he gives to them.

⋆

Here is another of Goethe's sayings:

> Rhythm has something magical; it even makes us believe that the sublime belongs to us.

Steiner added a footnote:

> Numerical relationships in objects of Nature are regular and at the same time irregular. Rhythm only takes up the regular. It offers mere regular relationships, thus something to which Nature is indeed disposed, but does not achieve.

Goethe's sayings went on:

> Imaginative power is only regulated through art, especially through poetry. There is nothing more dreadful than imaginative power without taste.

Steiner added a footnote:

> Imaginative power would create shapes into infinity unless regulated by poetic taste, which selects from the shapes what is artistically usable.

Goethe's sayings continued:

> The absurd presented with taste arouses disgust and admiration.

Steiner added a footnote:

> The absurd presented with taste arouses disgust by reason of its own nature, but admiration by reason of an artistic ability which even lends to what has no conformity to law the semblance of conforming to law.
>
> Goethe's sayings went on:
>
> The mannered is a failed ideality, a subjectivized ideality. Thus it does not easily lack ingenuity.

Steiner added a footnote:

> The mannered has its origin in a treatment of matter which is not culled from this matter, but rests on a peculiarity of the treating person and is inwardly foreign to the matter. If the person has ingenuity, it can be ingenious; it is not artistic in the sense brought forward above in 494, 15–19 [the part's opening sayings] and their note.

★

Here are more of Goethe's sayings:

> The romantic has already run into its abyss. The utter hideousness of recent productions can hardly be thought of as sinking any lower.
>
> ———
>
> Englishmen and Frenchmen have outdone us in finding uplift through corpses decomposing in bodily life and through detailed observation of their decay; dead persons, who remain alive to deprave others and nourish their death on the living—our producers have come to that.
>
> In antiquity phenomena of this kind only haunt around as rare cases of disease. In recent authors they have become endemic and epidemic.
>
> ———
>
> Literature becomes corrupted only in the measure that human beings become more depraved.
>
> ———
>
> What a time it is in which one must envy those who are buried!
>
> ———
>
> As soon as the same rights were lent to subjective or so-called sentimental poetry as to objective, presentational—as indeed could perhaps not have been otherwise, because one would have had to reject modern poetry completely—it could be foreseen that if truly poetic geniuses were also to be born they would present ever more the pleasantness of inner life than the generality of the great life in the world. This has now occurred to the extent that there is a poetry without tropes, to which by no means all approval can be denied.

Steiner added a footnote:

> Schiller gives (in his article 'On Naive and Sentimental Poetry') the following difference between sentimental and naive poetry. The naive has grown up in intimacy with natural law, with Nature's secrets, and embodies these directly in its products. The sentimental poet has become alienated from Nature, he *seeks* it; his creations express his longing for Nature. This alienation derives from the sentimental man being more occupied by what is inside him, the naive more by the external. It will be hard for a sentimental man to fashion the shapeless interior. This is easy for the naive, he lives in a shape, he imagines in pictures. His relation to Nature is such that he always clothes his conceptions in sensory garb. Tropes are nothing but the natural way in which his conceptions exist. The sentimental man must first seek pictures for his unpictorial conceptions.

Goethe's sayings continued:

> There is poetry without tropes, which is a particular trope.

Steiner added a footnote:

> Such poetry is a particular trope, because it gives a picture of the poet himself. It does not reproduce anything external, but does reproduce the yearning search of the poet.

Goethe's sayings went on:

> A poet relies on presentation. Its highest level is when competing with reality, i.e. when its depictions are in such a way alive through the spirit that they can count as present for anyone. On its highest peak, poetry appears quite outwardly; the more it withdraws inside, is it on the way to sinking.—That which only presents the inner, without embodying it through an outer, or without letting the outer be felt through the inner, are both final stages from out of which it enters into common life.

Steiner added a footnote:

> When a poet only any more presents his shapeless interior, he abandons the domain of art, which can only live in what is shaped. An artist does indeed present the spiritual, but he lends the spiritual a shape, a pictoriality. The peak of art is to present something sensory, or a sum of feelings and notions, in such a way that the presentation appears spiritualized, that it is upborne by an idea.

Goethe's sayings continued:

> The art of speaking relies on all the advantages of poetry, on all its rights. It takes hold of the same and misuses them, in order to attain certain outer—moral or immoral—momentary advantages in bourgeois life.

★

Here are still more of Goethe's sayings:

> Upon recitation reposes all declaiming and facial expressiveness. Now since when reading aloud the former quite alone is to be regarded and practised, it becomes obvious that *readings* must remain the school of the true and the natural, if men who take over such a business are permeated by the value, by the worth of their calling.
>
> ———
>
> Shakespeare and Calderón have granted a brilliant entry to such readings. Yet at the same time let one always consider whether precisely the imposing foreignness, the talent enhanced into untruthfulness, must not here become harmful to German education!
>
> ———
>
> Peculiarity of expression is the beginning and end of all art. But every nation has a special particularity deviating from the general peculiarity of mankind, one which indeed may to begin with oppose us, but in the end, if we were to let ourselves enjoy it, if we surrendered ourselves to it, would be able to overcome and suppress our own characteristic nature.
>
> ———
>
> May writers of a following age historically note how much falsity Shakespeare and especially Calderón have brought over us, how these two great lights of the poetic firmament have for us become will-o'the-wisps.

★

Here are yet more of Goethe's sayings:

> People have complained in an insistently kind and loving way that I prefer to communicate my thoughts about external literature than about our own. And yet it is quite natural. Foreigners either do not learn what I say about them, are not concerned with it, or are pleased by it. One is not impolite at a distance. Nearby, however, one should—as in good society—bring forward nothing insulting; and yet every disapproval is regarded as an insult.
>
> ———
>
> There is no patriotic art and no patriotic science. Both of them belong, like everything highly good, to the whole world, and can be promoted only through a general free interaction of all those alive at the same time, in continual regard for what is left and known to us from the past.

★

Here are further sayings by Goethe:

> Lord Byron is a talented person trained in natural truth and greatness, though wildly and uneasily, and thus scarcely another is comparable to him.
>
> ———

Shakespeare is dangerous for budding talents to read. He obliges them to reproduce him, and they imagine they are reproducing themselves.

Shakespeare is rich in wonderful tropes, which arise from personified concepts and would not clothe us at all, but with him are entirely in their place, because at his time all art was ruled by allegory.

He also finds similes where we would not adopt them, e.g. in the book. The art of printing had already been invented for over a hundred years. Nonetheless a book still seemed something holy, as we see from covers of the time, and so to the noble poet it was dear and worthy of honour. But we now bring out everything in paperback and do not easily have respect either for the cover or for its content.

Arden of Faversham, a work from Shakespeare's youth.[22] It is the wholly pure, faithful seriousness of conception and reproduction, without trace of regard for effect, fully dramatic, quite untheatrical.

Shakespeare's finest plays here and there lack facility. They are rather more than they should be, and for that very reason they indicate a great poet.

Henry IV, by Shakespeare. If everything were lost which had ever come down to us written in this way, poetry and rhetoric could be fully re-established from it.

★

Here are still further sayings by Goethe:

Laurence Sterne was born in 1713, died in 1768. In order to grasp him, one should not disregard the moral and and ecclesiastical formation of his time. In this respect one must consider well that he was a contemporary of Warburton.

A free soul like his comes into danger of growing impudent, unless a noble good will restores the moral balance.

With his capacity to be easily affected, everything for him developed from inside outwards. Through continual conflict he distinguished the true from the false, held fast to the former and acted ruthlessly towards the other.

Steiner added a footnote:

William Warburton was a theologian, actually a representative of the rationalist trend within his science. He practised sharp criticism towards ecclesiastical tradition. Goethe is of the view that at a time when religio-moral convictions encounter sharp opposition, a 'free soul' falls easily into

Laurence Sterne

> danger of intensifying its feelings and ideas into unrestrainedness, unless, as with Sterne, a noble cast of mind holds back from unrestrainedness. Liberation from traditional ideas leads to conflicts, unless a strong, healthy nature comes to help, knowing how to give itself once more the lost direction from out of its own self.

Goethe's sayings went on:

> He felt a decisive hatred towards seriousness, because it is didactic and dogmatic and quite easily becomes pedantic, for which he harboured the most extreme repugnance. Hence his distaste for terminology.
>
> ——
>
> In his most manifold studies and reading he discovered everywhere what was inadequate and ridiculous.
>
> ——
>
> The impossibility of thinking for two minutes about a serious subject he calls Shandeeism.

Steiner added a footnote:

> Shandism means a way of thought like that of his Tristram Shandy, hero of his novel.

Goethe's sayings continued:

> This rapid alternation of seriousness and fun, involvement and indifference, sorrow and joy, is supposed to lie in the Irish character.
>
> ———
>
> Sagacity and penetration are with him limitless.
>
> ———
>
> His cheerfulness, undemandingness, tolerance on a journey—where these qualities are most tested—do not easily find their equivalent.
>
> ———
>
> However enraptured we are by the sight of this kind of free soul, just so much are we in this very case reminded that we ought not take into ourselves anything from all that, or at least from most of what delights us.
>
> ———
>
> The element of lasciviousness, in which he behaves so daintily and aptly, would to many others be corrupting.

Steiner added a footnote:

> Cf. the psychological explanation of lasciviousness given in 451, 21–22 ['Lasciviousness is a game . . .'] and its note.

⋆

Here are more of Goethe's sayings:

> 'Pereant, qui ante nos nostra dixerunt!'
>
> Only one pretending to be an autochthon could speak so strangely. Whoever holds it an honour to descend from reasonable ancestors will grant them at least as much human sense as himself.

Steiner added a footnote:

> This quotation from Sterne stands in the introduction to his *Koran*, where he says: 'So that I am sure: I have reason to cry out with Donatus apud Jerom: Pereant . . .'

Goethe continued:

> Yorick Sterne was the most beautiful spirit who has ever been at work. Anyone reading him feels at once free and beautiful.[23] His humour is inimitable, and not every humour liberates the soul.

There followed a series of quotations, with Steiner adding a footnote:

> These sayings are from the anonymous work *The Koran: or Essays, Sentiments, Characters, and Callimachies of Tria Juncta in Uno* (1770, 3 Parts). This book is ascribed to Sterne.[24] A German translation was brought out in 1771 in Leipzig by Engelhart Benjamin Schwickert.

The series began:

> 'Spare diet and clear skies are Apollo and the Muses.'
>
> ———
>
> 'Sight is by much the noblest of the senses. We receive our notices from the other four, through the organs of sensation only. We hear, we feel, we smell, we taste, by touch. But sight rises infinitely higher. It is refined above matter, and equals the faculty of spirit.'

Steiner added a footnote:

> This saying must have affected Goethe sympathetically, for like his own expositions on the doctrine of colour it is directed against the gross idea which sees in light something material and believes seeing to rest on a mechanical effect upon the eye.

The sayings went on:

> 'To put ourselves in other persons' places would obviate a great deal of the jealousies and resentments we are too frequently sensible of towards them; and to put others into ours would considerably abate the pride and haughtiness of ourselves.'
>
> ———
>
> 'One of the fathers compares contemplation and action to Rachel and Leah. The first was fairest, but the latter more fruitful.'
>
> ———
>
> 'Nothing in this life, after health and virtue, is more estimable than knowledge—nor is there anything so easily attained, or so cheaply purchased—the labour only sitting still, and the expense but time, which, if we do not spend, we cannot save.'
>
> ———
>
> 'If time, like money, could be laid by, while one was not using it, there might be some excuse for the idleness of half the world—but yet not a full one; for even this would be such an œconomy as the living on a principal sum without making it purchase interest.'
>
> ———
>
> 'Modern poets put too much water into the ink.'
>
> ———
>
> 'Among the many curious impertinences of the schools, there is none that appears to me so truly ridiculous, as the strife about the authority of the works of the ancients. Is it the author or the writing we admire or criticise? But it is still the authors we have before us, no matter for their names, when we are commenting upon any work of genius.'
>
> ———
>
> 'I do not pretend to say that we have Virgil or Homer before us

when we read those words imputed to them. But we have certainly the writers of them—which is all we need contend for. And I really think that those scholars who affect a precision in this very immaterial matter are not a bit wiser than a very pretty woman, who asked me once, with the sweetest smile imaginable, "Who was the author of Shakespear's plays?"'

'It is better to do the idlest thing in the world, than to sit idle for half an hour.'

'Courage and modesty are the most unequivocal virtues—because they are such as hypocrisy cannot imitate—and they have this property in common also, that they are both expressed by the same colour.'

'Of all knaves, your fools are the worst—because they rob you both of your time and temper.'

'To have a respect for ourselves guides our morals; and to have a deference for others governs our manners.'

'Art and Science are words frequently made use of, but the precision of which is so rarely understood, that they are often mistaken for one another.

I don't like any of the definitions of the schools. I met with a distinction, somewhere once, comparing science to wit, and art to humour; but it has more of fancy than philosophy in it. It serves to give us, however, some idea of the difference between them, though no idea of either.

I think that science may be styled the knowledge of universals, or abstract wisdom; and art is science reduced to practice—or science is reason, and art the mechanism of it—and may be called practical science. Science, in fine, is the theorem, and art the problem.

I am aware that this objection will be made—that poetry is deemed an art, and yet it is not mechanical. But I deny it to be an art—neither is it a science. Arts and sciences may be taught—poetry cannot. But poetry is inspiration—it was breathed into the soul, when it first quickened, and should neither be styled art nor science, but genius.'

'One does not require nor think of a fire, often, in spring or autumn; yet I don't know how it is, but when we have happened by chance to pass near one, the sensation it communicates is so pleasant, that we feel ourselves rather inclined to indulge it.

This is analogous to temptation.'

'Marcus Aurelius says that he had learned from Apollinus, "not to be impatient when his arguments happen not to be apprehended".'

Even now at this moment every educated person should again take to hand the works of Sterne, so that the 19th century too might experience what we owe him, and perceive what we might come to owe him.

★

Here is another of Goethe's sayings:

Goethe on himself.

I troubled myself so long over generality, until I learnt to perceive what excellent men accomplish in particular.

★

And here is Goethe's last saying in this part—thereby the last in the whole collection:

'Panoramic ability' is ascribed to me by an English critic, for which I must express the very greatest thanks.

In a Sympathetic Spirit

In England, the minute-book of the Shropshire Horticultural Society records:

A General Committee meeting was held in the Society's Office on 16th of November 1896.

Present: Mr. Salt in the Chair.

Mr. Taylor	Mr. Morris	Mr. Greatorex	Mr. Blockley
" Bowyer	" Vine	" Cock	" Litt
" Peele	" Hollier	" Hearne	" Adams
" Clarke	" Southam	" Groves	" Mitchell
" Hawkesford	" H. Jones	" Pritchard	" Phillips
" Cross	" Blower	" Hughes	" Patchett
" D.H. Owen	" Fox	" Bremmel	" Kent

The minutes of the previous Committee Meeting were read and confirmed.

The Chairman proposed and Mr. Taylor seconded: That this meeting having considered the Mayor's letter of the 12th inst. suggesting a portion of the Society's funds be devoted to the purpose of erecting a statue to the memory of our eminent townsman the late Charles Darwin do hereby resolve to adopt such suggestion.

As an amendment Mr. Adams proposed and Mr. Mitchell seconded: That this Society subscribe a sum not exceeding £600 to the Fund which has already been promoted for the purpose.

The amendment having been put to the Meeting was lost, and the original proposition was afterwards carried unanimously.

It was then proposed by Mr. D.H. Owen and seconded by Major Patchett: That the following gentlemen be a Sub-Committee to ascertain the probable cost of a suitable statue with the view of perpetuating the memory of the greatest scientist in horticultural and other researches this nation has ever produced, and obtain such further information as they may deem necessary, that such Committee report the results of their investigations to a subsequent Meeting to be called for the purpose of considering and carrying out same.

Mr. Salt
Mr. Peele
Mr. Taylor
Mr. Phillips
Mr. W.L. Browne
Mr. Adams

Carried unanimously.
Geo. M Salt

⋆

A Meeting of the Sub-Committee appointed at the last Meeting was held on 23rd November 1896.

Present: Mr. Salt in the Chair.
Mr. Taylor
Mr. Peele
Mr. Phillips
Mr. Brown
Mr. Adams
Hon. Sec.

Letters were read from several applicants asking permission to prepare statue and among them one from Mr. H. Montford, 8 Winders Road, Battersea S.W., estimating cost of statue at about £800.

Testimonials of his ability were read from Hans Thornycroft R.A. & E. Onslow Ford R.A. which the Committee considered most satisfactory & eventually resolved to recommend the General Committee that he be employed to prepare the statue of the late Charles Darwin . . .

⋆

Darwin Memorial
Report of Sub-Committee

In compliance with the resolution passed on the 16th ulto. we beg to report as follows.

We have obtained from the former Committee, and carefully considered the testimonials and other documents in their hands, and have come to the conclusion that their selection of Mr. Horace Montford to carry out the work is fully justified for the following reasons:–

1. The satisfactory nature of the statuary work executed by him in (among other places) London and Liverpool and also of the models which he has now submitted to the Committee.
2. The exceptionally favourable testimonials which have been received from two eminent sculptors, both Royal Academicians, Mr. Hans Thornycroft and Mr. Onslow Ford.
3. The fact that he was selected by the President & Council of the Royal Academy to take charge of the newly formed School of Sculpture, and
4. That he is a native of Shrewsbury

On Saturday Mr. Montford inspected the proposed site for the Memorial in School Gardens and after satisfying himself of its eligibility, decided on what spot and position the statue should be erected in order to obtain the most effective result.—We subsequently had an interview with him when he replied to many questions and entered into many interesting details, and he left us with two papers explaining the proportions of the statue and its pedestal and stating the terms on which he would undertake the completion of the work.

We have unanimously come to the conclusion that we may safely and properly adopt the expressive terms made use of by Mr. Thornycroft and recommend to the Committee that

> 'The Society cannot do better than entrust the Memorial to Mr. Montford who will do the work in a sympathetic spirit and give us a fine portrait of the man of whom England is so proud.'

December 1st 1896—Signed by the Committee
Geo. M. Salt.

Othello

In Germany, Rudolf Steiner forwarded to the Cotta publishing firm in late 1896 an introduction to selected writings of Jean Paul. The opening read:

> There are works of the spirit which lead such an independent existence that one may surrender oneself to them without thinking for a moment about

their originators. The *Iliad*, *Hamlet* and *Othello*, *Iphigenie* can be followed from start to finish without one being reminded of the personality of Homer, Shakespeare or Goethe. These works stand before the observer like beings with a life entirely their own, mature people whom we accept for themselves without enquiring about their father. The works of Jean Paul are not of this kind...

The reference here to *Othello* was followed a couple of months later by another quite different one, in a letter Steiner wrote to Anna Eunike (who must have been absent from Weimar at the time, but evidently not far away).

2nd December 1896

My much loved Anna,

I'm expecting a letter from you any hour. I do ask you to write and tell me what you're doing, how you are and what mood you're in. When you were last here, my dear good Anna, I was thinking to myself that some disgruntlement which you believed you had noticed in me had put you out. But there's really no reason for it. If I was rather quiet and perhaps disgruntled, the reason is that the work I must now finish off in Weimar isn't proceeding as fast as I want. But in the next few days things will certainly improve, and I'm now hoping for sure to be finished in a week or two. And then, my much loved Anna, I'll summon up everything to gain a place in life satisfying to both of us. I'm aware that I have strength for this, and I'll succeed, if my good Anna holds her head up and doesn't allow herself to be tormented by worries.

Just after you left, Koegel joined me from the station and told me something about his engagement. His bride-to-be is a nineteen-year-old girl, daughter of Professor Gelzer in Jena. The whole story gives me a proper honest-German-bourgeois impression, and from what I hear about it I don't feel exactly blown upon by Nietzsche's 'free spirit'.

Böhler arrived the same Friday evening. He was passing through to the burial of his betrothed, who had died in Hildburghausen. As soon as he'd arrived, about 10 o'clock in the evening, he sent me to Crompton. We both went to the 'Russischer Hof', and tried to lighten his evening hours. The poor chap really is in a truly pitiable state.

On Sunday as *Othello* only finished at about 10.30 and I wasn't promising myself anything special, I didn't ask you to come over. I was right, because it really was as bad as I expected. Wüllner is to me an uninteresting actor. Monday by contrast was a really pleasant evening of songs, given by Gmur together with his wife in the 'Erholung'. When the concert had finished, Böhler too was back again, and the Cromptons, Fresenius, Franke and I spent the evening with him. He was also invited yesterday to a meal at the Cromptons.

Little Crompton is already in bed again. He's got a flushed neck, but no fever.

Otherwise I haven't much news. The end of my work is in sight, and I can let the discomforts of my present position pass me by. If only I were certain, my dear Anna, that you weren't worrying about me. I do ask you always to remember what I recently wrote to you. We want to keep firmly together.

I'll write again quite soon and we'll be seeing each other very shortly.

Yours truly

Rudolf

★

The widowed Paul Böhler edited the Weimar newspaper *Deutschland.* A few days later, this paper published an article by Steiner entitled 'Dr. Wüllner as Othello: a play in the Hoftheater, Weimar':[25]

Whoever first explained the greatness of Shakespeare's plays by the circumstance of their author being an actor had a happy and illuminating notion. It is less a matter of this poet having vocationally practised the art of acting than of his having been a natural actor through his basic disposition. A being of this nature can intrinsically immerse itself in foreign characters with complete denial of its own personality. An actor renounces being himself. He is given the possibility to speak out of foreign essences. And the suppler, the more capable of transformation he is, the more of an actor he will be. That we know as good as nothing about Shakespeare as a person has a deeply symbolic meaning. Does he as a person concern us? He does not speak to us as a person; he speaks to us in roles. He is the true chameleon. He speaks to us as Hamlet, Lear, Othello. Even when writing plays Shakespeare is play-acting. When creating the figures of his plays he no longer feels what is happening in his mind. Since Shakespeare was only an actor, it is only by true actors that his dramas can be played. If an actor's art breaks down in Shakespearean dramas it will always be a sign of his deficiency.

These were thoughts going through my head last Sunday after seeing Herr Wüllner's Othello. During the whole performance I could not rid myself of a certain impatience. I wanted to see Othello, and saw the whole evening only Herr Wüllner. I wanted to grasp how Othello can slowly get into this dreadful rage of jealousy, and only learnt about the feelings which overcome Herr Wüllner on contemplating Othello. Herr Wüllner does not have that ability to relinquish himself which makes a real actor. At every moment he lets one see the foundation of his own being.

One should not be unfair to Herr Wüllner. His art is not negligible. He has great control over his means of expression, and is a master of histrionic nuances. It would be tedious to go into details, though there is much to be praised. But it is annoying to see such art being applied when the principal thing is missing.

Herr Wüllner was formerly a learned philologist. I believe that in the actor too the scholar can be recognized. A scholar lacks ability to slip into what is foreign. He just contemplates it, mostly just broods over it. And Herr Wüllner did not play Othello, but played *about* Othello. What he played was what he had been brooding over about Othello. But what does it matter to a spectator what Herr Wüllner feels about Othello, vivid though his feelings may be? I would sooner see Herr Wüllner's feelings and thoughts about Othello's character set down in a literary work than acted on stage. I have no doubt that such a work would be interesting. But on stage I am not interested in any interesting doctrines. There they become uninteresting. So it was boring and tiresome to watch Herr Wüllner's Othello to the end. It seems Herr Wüllner cannot manage to present a character which stands as if cast from a mould, so that in every gesture, in every step a spectator feels that this is how it all must be. In every detail one had the feeling that it could also be done differently without anything in the world being changed. Herr Wüllner offered a mosaic of histrionic nuances, but no unified character. His art lacks style, and its effect is mannered. It presents the reverse of good acting. It denies everything which makes good actors great. Herr Wüllner cannot rid himself of the 'Doctor'.

A False View

In Chapter XVIII of his autobiography Rudolf Steiner stated:

> ... In the last part of my Weimar period Goethe once again placed himself dominantly before my gaze. I wanted to characterize the way taken by mankind's life in world-conceptions up to Goethe, in order then to present Goethe's kind of conceiving in its emergence from that life. This I attempted in the book *Goethes Weltanschauung*, which came out in 1897.

Steiner completed the manuscript in April, and the book appeared a couple of months later, around the end of June. (During that year the fourth and fifth volumes were also finally published—tardily but appropriately—of his edition of Goethe's scientific writings in the Kürschner series.)

Over two decades later, in 1918, Steiner brought out a new edition of *Goethes Weltanschauung*, the text of which has been republished ever since. It opens with a foreword stating *inter alia*:

> ... Only additions and expansions which seem to me important distinguish the new edition from the old one.

At the end of the new text there is also an afterword, including the differently worded comment:

> . . . Only in particular places have I made changes, which do not extend to the trend of thoughts, but merely to the stylization of particular remarks . . .

As however pointed out by David Hoffman in the latest *Gesamtausgabe* edition of 1990, two chapters in the opening part on 'Goethe's Place in the Development of Western Thought' were in 1918 decisively revised not only in style but also in content, namely those on 'The Platonic View of the World' and 'Consequences of the Platonic View of the World'.

Once again it is of interest to examine the revisions Steiner made in these chapters. Here for instance is a passage from the chapter on 'Consequences of the Platonic View of the World'. Words added or substituted in the 1918 edition are placed in square brackets.

> When a time began with Bacon of Verulam and Descartes in which there was asserted a will to seek for truth through the power inherent in human personality, habits of thought were so corrupted [had taken such directions] that all endeavour led to nothing else than setting up views which despite their apparent independence from the Platonic and Christian [from the preceding Western] conceptual world were indeed only new forms of it. Even Bacon and Descartes acquired, as heirloom of a degenerate philosophy [world of thought], a pernicious view of the relation between experience and idea. Bacon only had a sense and understanding for Nature's details. By assembling the same or similar elements running through spatial and temporal diversity, he believed he could come to general rules about natural events. Goethe aptly says of him: 'For though he himself always indicates that one should only gather particulars in order to select from them, order them and finally reach universals, *yet with him the individual cases retain too many rights*, and before simplification and finality can be achieved through induction—even that which he extols—life is spent and forces are worn out.'. . .

The quotation is taken from the section on Bacon in the *Geschichte der Farbenlehre*, with one phrase italicized.

> . . . For Bacon these general rules are a means which make it possible for reason to have a comfortable overview of the realm of details. But he does not believe these rules to be founded in the ideational content of things and to be really creative forces of Nature. Nor therefore does he seek an idea directly in the detail, but rather abstracts it from a multiplicity of details. A person who does not believe an idea to be living in a particular thing can also have no inclination to seek it there. He accepts the thing as it presents itself to mere outer perception. The significance of Bacon may be sought in

> the fact that he pointed to an outer mode of perception which had been disparaged by Plato and Christianity [by the one-sided Platonism characterized above]. He stressed that in it lies a source of truth. But he was in no position to help the ideal world establish its rights in the same way over against the perceptible world. He declared what is ideal to be a subjective element in the human mind. His manner of thinking is reversed Platonism. Plato sees reality only in the ideal world, Bacon only in the perceptual world devoid of ideas. In Bacon's conception lies the starting point for that cast of mind governing natural scientists right into the present time. It suffers from a false view about the ideal element of the experiential world. [It could not rightly cope with the view of the Middle Ages, which had arisen through a one-sided forming of a question, to the effect that ideas are just names, not realities lying in the things.]

After this chapter came another on 'Goethe and the Platonic View of the World'. It examined *inter alia* the differences between Goethe and Schiller, and ended by quoting from the 'higher contemplations of Nature' found in Goethe's 1784 essay 'Über dem Granit'.

Living in the Truth

The next chapter, 'Personality and View of the World', opened as follows:

> Man learns to know the outer side of Nature through perception; its deeper-lying driving forces are disclosed within his own inner being as subjective experiences. In philosophical contemplation of the world and in artistic feeling and production, subjective experiences permeate objective perceptions . . .

A further section continued:

> Subjective experiences of different human beings take different forms. For those who do not believe in the objective nature of the inner world, this is one more reason to deny man the ability to penetrate into the essence of things. For how can what appears to one person one way and to another person another way be the essence of things? For someone who perceives the true nature of the inner world, there follows from the differences of inner experiences only that Nature can express its abundant content in different ways. Truth appears to the single human being in an individual garb. It adapts itself to the particular nature of his personality. This is especially the case for the highest truths, those most important to man. In order to gain them, man carries over into the perceptible world his spiritual, most intimate experiences, and along with them what is most particular to his person. There are also generally valid truths which every human being

takes up without giving them an individual colouring. But these are the most superficial, most trivial ones. They correspond to the general character of men as a species, which is the same for all. Certain qualities which are the same in all human beings also produce the same judgements about things. The way people regard things according to measure and number is the same for all. Therefore everyone finds the same mathematical truths. But within the particular qualities in which a single personality raises himself from the general character of the species lies also the basis for individual forms of truth. It is not a matter of truth appearing in one human being differently from in another, but rather that all individual forms coming into view belong to a single whole, to the unified ideal world. Inside single people truth speaks different languages and dialects; in every great man it speaks a particular language which befits only this *one* personality. But it is always the one truth speaking there. 'If I know my relationship to myself and to the outer world, I then call it truth. And so each person can have his own truth, and yet it is always the same one.' That is Goethe's opinion. Truth is not a rigid, dead conceptual system, capable only of one single form; it is a living sea, in which lives the mind of man, and can show on its surface waves of the most different form. 'Theory in and of itself is of no use, except in so far as it makes us believe in the connection of phenomena,' says Goethe. He values no theory which claims completeness once and for all and is supposed to represent in this form an eternal truth. He wants living concepts through which the mind of a single person draws his perceptions together according to his individual particularity. *Knowing* the truth means for him *living in the truth*. And living in the truth, when observing every single thing, is nothing else than watching what inner experience occurs when one confronts this thing...

The final chapter of this part was on 'The Metamorphosis of World Phenomena'.

A Marvellous Show

The next part, headed 'Views on the Nature and Development of Living Beings', comprised only one chapter, the longest in the book, entitled 'The Doctrine of Metamorphosis'. Here is a section from this chapter:

In his studies of the plant and animal worlds Goethe strove to picture to himself the organism's germination, growth, transformation of organs, nourishment and propagation as a process both sense-perceptible and supersensible. He noticed that this sensible-supersensible process in its *idea* is the same in all plants, and that it takes on different forms only in outer *manifestation*. Goethe could establish the same thing for the animal world. If

> one has developed in oneself the idea of a sensible-supersensible archetypal plant, one will then find it again in all individual plant forms. Diversity arises through what is the same in idea being able to exist in different forms in the perceptual world. A particular organism consists of organs which can be traced back to one basic organ. The plant's basic organ is the leaf, with the node on which it develops. In its outer manifestation this organ assumes different forms: cotyledon, main leaf, sepal, corolla etc. 'Whether the plant be sprouting, blooming or bearing fruit, it is always only *the same organs* which, in manifold conditions and under often altered forms, are fulfilling the orders of Nature.'

Steiner was quoting from Goethe's prose treatise *The Metamorphosis of Plants*. He continued the next section as follows:

> In order to gain a complete picture of the archetypal plant, Goethe had generally to follow the forms which a basic organ goes through in the process of plant growth from germination to seed maturation. At the start of its development the whole plant form rests in the seed. In this latter the archetypal plant has taken on a shape through which as it were to conceal its ideal content in outer manifestation.

Steiner then quoted a passage from Goethe's poem 'Die Metamorphose der Pflanzen', even giving the relevant page number in the first volume of his Kürschner edition.

This poem had of course been included before in other editions, as for instance in the *English Hexameter Translations* of 1848, where the original German later quoted by Steiner was printed facing an English version made by William Whewell:

> Slept in the seed such power; an inborn type of the future
> Lay, wrapt fold within fold, deep in the heart of the mass—
> Leaves, and the root, and the bud, as yet unformed and uncoloured;
> So the dry kernel holds, stilly, the springs of a life.
> Then the young birth breaks forth, confides in the genial moisture,
> Gathers and lifts itself up, out of the chaos of night.

Steiner went on:

> Out of the seed the plant develops its first organs, the cotyledons, after leaving 'its husks more or less in the earth' and securing 'its roots in the ground'. And now shoot follows shoot in further course of growth; node after node towers one above the other, and at every node is found a leaf. The leaves appear in different shapes. Lower ones are still simple, upper ones variously serrated, notched, composed of several leaflets. At this stage of development the archetypal plant spreads out its sensible-supersensible content into space as an outer sense-perceptible phenomenon. Goethe imagines that leaves owe their

progressive development and refinement to light and air. 'If we find those cotyledons produced in the enclosed seed husks to be as it were only stuffed with raw sap, and almost not at all or only crudely organized and undeveloped, the leaves of plants growing under water appear to us more crudely organized than others exposed to the open air. Indeed, the same species of plant even develops smoother and less refined leaves when growing in low, moist places, while if transferred to higher regions, it brings forth rough leaves covered with hairs, and more finely developed.' (Kürschner, Volume 33, p. 25 f.) In the second period of growth the plant draws together again into a narrower space what it had previously spread out.

Steiner then quoted once more from 'Die Metamorphose der Pflanzen'. Here is the passage as translated by Whewell:

> But at this point arriv'd, the expanding urgency Nature
> Checks with her mighty hand—guides to a loftier plan—
> Tames the flow of the juices—contracts the vessels—and straightway
> Finer workmanship shows in the refinement of form.
> Back to the centre retreats the expanding thrust of the margin:
> Fuller the leafy rib gathers itself in the midst.
> Leafless and smooth, a more delicate stalk springs rapidly upwards,
> And a marvellous show meets the contemplative eye.
> Close ranged round the stalk—or fixed in number or boundless—
> Leaflets, each like each, gather themselves in a ring.
> Here, with protesting circle, the calyx girdles the axis,
> And in the fairest forms lovely-hued coronets wears.

Strict inductive method

At a later point in this same chapter on 'The Doctrine of Metamorphosis', Rudolf Steiner went on to state that Goethe

> ... was concerned to gain an idea about the fundamental laws of living things. In the process it became clear to him that living forms are not rigid and unchangeable but engaged in continual transformation. He lacked observations to establish in detail how this transformation occurs. The researches of Darwin and the inspired reflections of Haeckel first shed some light onto the actual conditions relating individual organic forms. From the standpoint of Goethe's view of the world one can only agree with the assertions of Darwinism in so far as they are concerned with the actual emergence of one organic species from another...

After subsequently quoting a passage from a book by the scientist Oscar Schmidt entitled *War Goethe Darwinianer?* (1871), Steiner went on some pages later to include a more specific reference to Darwin's researches, prompted by another writer. The context was Goethe's interest in the lectures published by Karl Friedrich Philipp von Martius on the 'Vertical and Spiral Tendency of Vegetation'.

> Martius thought the growth of plants to be governed by two tendencies, a striving in the vertical direction, which governs root and stem; and another, by which the organs of leaf, blossom, etc. are caused to be joined with the vertical organs according to the form of a spiral line. Goethe took up these ideas and brought them into connection with his mental picture of metamorphosis. He wrote a long article (Kürschner, Volume 33), where he brought together all his experiences relating to the plant-world which seemed to him to indicate the presence of the two tendencies. He believes these tendencies must be taken up into his idea of metamorphosis. 'We had to assume that in vegetation a general spiral tendency holds sway through which, in connection with vertical striving, all structure and every form of plants is accomplished according to the law of metamorphosis.' Goethe takes the presence of spiral vessels in individual plant organs as proof that a spiral tendency deeply governs the life of plants. 'Nothing is more in accord with Nature than that what she intends as a whole she puts into activity through the most detailed part.' 'Let one go in summertime to a stake driven into garden soil, on which a bindweed (convulvulus) rises from below, winding into the height, and follow its living growth with close attention. Let one now think of the convolvulus and the stake, both equally alive, rising up from one root, alternately bringing each other forth and in this way ceaselessly progressing. Anyone who can transform this sight into inner vision will have made the concept much easier for himself. The climbing plant seeks outside itself for what it should be giving to itself and cannot.' On the 15th of March 1832 Goethe uses the same comparison in a letter to Count Sternberg and adds the words: 'Admittedly the comparison does not entirely fit, for at the start the creeper would have had to wind around the rising stem in scarcely perceptible circles. But the closer it came to the upper end, the faster would the spiralling line have had to turn, in order finally (at the blossom) to gather together into a circle on a disc, as in a dance, where quite often in youth one saw oneself pressed even against one's own will, with the nicest children, breast to breast and heart to heart. Pardon these anthropomorphisms.' Ferdinand Cohn remarks at this point: 'If only Goethe had experienced Darwin! . . . How he would have rejoiced in this man who knew how to find by strict inductive method clear and convincing proofs for his ideas . . .' Darwin believes he can show with regard to almost all plant organs that during their growth period they have a tendency to spiral-like movements, which he calls circumnutation.

The Breslau botanist Ferdinand Cohn had published in 1885 a work entitled *Goethe als Botaniker*, from which Steiner's quotation was taken.

Five years before, the matter had been extensively examined by Darwin in a work brought out in 1880, *The Power of Movement in Plants*.

My View

Describing in Chapter XXII of his autobiography the period of this last year in Weimar, Rudolf Steiner wrote:

> My concern was to speak in such a way about knowledge that the spiritual be not merely *accepted* but also recognized *in such a way* that a human being could attain it with his vision. It seemed to me more important to establish that the 'primordial foundations' of existence are lying *within* what a man can attain in his whole experience than to acknowledge in thought an *unknown* spirituality in some realm 'beyond'.

All the italics are Steiner's. One may compare here the dominical statement: 'The kingdom of God is within you.'

> My view therefore rejected the way of thought which considers the content of sensations (colour, warmth, tone, etc.) as merely something which an unknown outer world calls up in man through sense-perceptions, while this outer world itself can only be conceived hypothetically. My experiential knowledge felt that the theoretical ideas lying at the basis of physical and physiological thinking according to that trend are particularly harmful. In the period of my life depicted here, this feeling was heightened to the greatest vividness. Everything described in physics and physiology as 'lying behind the subjective sensation' caused in me, if I may use the expression, cognitional discomfort.
>
> By contrast I saw in Lyell, Darwin and Haeckel a way of thinking which, even if appearing in an incomplete form, can be healthily developed.

Darwin and Haeckel, linked by Steiner both in *Die Philosophie der Freiheit* and in *Goethes Weltanschauung*, were now joined by Lyell, mentioned in this latter book in a chapter on 'Thoughts about the Developmental History of the Earth'. And indeed the illustrations of what Steiner meant by his last remark were taken not from Darwin at all, but only from Lyell and Haeckel:

> The principle of Lyell, that phenomena in the part of earthly evolution lying in prehistory and inaccessible to sensory observation are explainable by ideas given through observing current development, seemed fruitful to me when taken in the direction indicated. Seeking understanding of man's physical structure by deriving its forms from those of animals, as Haeckel does in a comprehensive way in his *Anthropogenie*, I considered a good basis for further development of knowledge.

I held that a person who sets up a limit of knowledge, beyond which 'things in themselves' are supposed to exist, bars himself thereby from entering the spiritual world. But if he relates to the sense-world in such a way that one thing inside it explains another (present processes in earthly development explaining geological prehistory, and forms of animal structures explaining human ones), he will then be prepared to extend *this explicability* of beings and processes into what is spiritual.

Regarding my feelings in this realm as well, I can say: 'This is something which at that very time consolidated within me as a view, while it had already long been pulsating through my conceptual world.'

11
THE *MAGAZIN* CONTRIBUTIONS

Quite Individual

In June 1897 Rudolf Steiner moved from Weimar to Berlin, having 'seized the chance'—as described in Chapter XXIV of his autobiography—to take over as editor of the *Magazin für Litteratur.* His editorship began on 1 July.

The journal came out every week. Issues ran on average to 12 sides, closely printed in double columns.

Besides publishing matter contributed by other writers, Steiner also regularly included in the journal articles of his own. He referred to these in a lecture given at Dornach on 27 October 1918 in the course on 'Historical Symptomatology':

> . . . In the background I always had the question: how could the time take up something like the ideas of the *Philosophie der Freiheit*? If one wants to, one will see the spirit of the *Philosophie der Freiheit* wafting through everything I wrote in the *Magazin für Litteratur* . . .

Within the context of the present book, it is of course impossible to examine everything Steiner wrote in that journal. But certain examples relevant in one or other way to the subject of this book may serve to illustrate the liveliness, the depth, and the variety of his contributions.

★

The first of Steiner's articles appeared in the issue for 10 July. It was on 'Modern Criticism'.

> Like so many others I too during my student time sought the model of all critical art in Lessing's *Hamburgischer Dramaturgie.* In single things, I told myself, we have learnt an endless amount about the essence of the arts; but his view of a critic's vocation I considered the only true and genuine one. The spirit permeating his critical achievements appeared to me decisive for all times. School tradition ensures that during our upbringing we are captivated by such views. But after immersing myself in modern psychological insights and working through to my own ideas on the nature of the human mind—the conviction of my youth seemed to me illusory. Lessing trustingly took on the spirit in which Aristotle wrote his *Poetics.* As a Christian stands to the Bible, so does Lessing stand to the Greek thinker's aesthetics. On reading the *Hamburgische Dramaturgie*, one senses that the reformer of

German criticism means to uplift Aristotle in aesthetics to the height from which he has long been toppled in science by Bacon and Descartes. The more often I took up this *Dramaturgie*, the stronger became my feeling that within it the spirit of scholasticism was once more coming to life. Scholastics had no vision of reality. A truly impartial observation of the world is not to be found in them. They immersed themselves instead in the writings of the Stagirite and believed that in these latter all wisdom was already contained. The authority of experience or observation was for them worth nothing; but all the more that of Aristotle. In Lessing's science of art, this scholastic spirit seemed to me again resurrected. He looks at the nature of artistic creativeness through the spectacles of ancient tradition, not with free naive sight. Whoever has developed within himself a modern scientific way of conception must turn away from the *Hamburgische Dramaturgie* just as he does from the philosophy of Thomas Aquinas. Aristotle speaks, and Lessing speaks as well, about eternal artistic laws revealed—from where I do not know—to the human mind. Basically the whole choir of aestheticians in the century just passing away also speak of such rules. All of them, from Kant to Carrière, Vischer and Lotze teach how a tragedy, a comedy or a ballad must be formed. They do not observe the real life of art like a botanist studying the life of a plant; rather they behave like a lawgiver, making the laws which reality should follow emanate from pure reason. Here in my mind arises the deterrent example of Vischer, who discovered from aesthetic science how Goethe should have composed his *Faust*. Not a trace of genuine psychology is living in this manner of aesthetic observation. It leads to the view that aesthetics like those of the nineteenth century are a—nonsense. There can be no aesthetics in the sense that there is botany and zoology. For plants and animals have something in common, living in all of them. Laws of Nature are the expression of this commonality. A plant is a plant by bearing within itself the generality of plant nature. But a work of art springs from human individuality. And the greatest value in a work of art, that by which it receives its highest perfection, derives from the artist's peculiarity, which is present in the world only once. A work of art is all the more significant, the more it bears in itself what is unrepeatable, what is present only in a single person. An individual plant cannot be original, for it lies in its being to express the species. A work of art of highest rank is always original, for the spirit it derives from is not found in the world a second time. One cock-chafer is organized like another; a genial individual is only present in one copy. There can be no general artistic laws, no general aesthetics. Every work of art demands its own aesthetics. All criticism founded on the superstition that aesthetics exists belongs for a scientifically thinking person to the scrap heap. Almost all our criticism is unfortunately still more or less dominated by this old superstition. Even those younger critics who have in theory overcome aesthetics mostly write in such a way as to show in every single line that in them there is yet slumbering unconsciously a belief in generally valid artistic laws.

No. Just as every true work of art is an individual, personal product of a single human being, so all criticism too can only be a quite individual reproduction of feelings and ideas arising in the mind of a single observing person while giving himself up to the enjoyment of a work of art. I can never say whether a poem is objectively good or bad, for there are no norms of good or bad. I can only depict the personal impression a work of art makes upon me. As a critic I can never demand from a reader that through my criticism he learn something about the 'objective value' of a work of art, but only that he be interested in the way it affects me and in the expression I can give to this effect. I simply report: this happened inside me while I was looking at the work. I depict a process of my inner life. Anyone interested in what is happening inside me while I listen to a tragedy or observe a landscape will read my criticism. A person indifferent to my feelings and mental pictures about a play or a picture will also not be persuaded that through my criticism he will learn anything of the significance of a work of art. All those who have set down their judgements in general aesthetics could also offer nothing else than their individual personal opinions on art. From Vischer's aesthetics no one can learn how a comedy should be made, but only what went on in Vischer's mind when he saw or read a comedy. Criticism is therefore all the more valuable the more significant the personality from whom it emanates. Just as the feelings a lyricist brings to expression in a poem are individual, so too the judgements are individual which are brought forward by a critic. We do not read a critique because we want to learn whether a work of art is as it should be, but rather because we are interested in what the criticizing person is inwardly living through when giving himself up to enjoyment of the work. Real modern criticism cannot recognize any aesthetics. For it, every work of art is a new revelation. In every critique, it judges according to new rules, how in every work a true genius creates according to new rules. Thus this criticism also makes no claim to say anything conclusive or generally correct about an artistic work, but only to express a personal opinion.

Always Flowing and Becoming

Three weeks later, at the end of July, Rudolf Steiner published in the *Magazin für Litteratur* an article entitled 'Wilhelm Preyer. Deceased on the 15th of July 1897'.

Wilhelm Preyer was a bold researcher full of stimulating ideas, a tireless seeker after new ways and goals in science and cultural life. At the centre of

> his creativity stood physiology. His comprehensive mind was at home in all domains of natural science. The thoughts and facts he worked out in the great edifice of ideas suspended before him as physiology, in the widest sense of the word, flowed from everywhere towards him. His writings open up broad and illuminating vistas. It was quite impossible for him to go down beaten tracks. Whatever he took up became through his work and thought something new. He had a free untroubled vision for everything significant appearing in recent decades in spiritual life. He always knew what had a future. Ernst Haeckel says in a foreword prefaced to Preyer's recently published biography of Darwin: 'You belong like me to the small number of those scientists who, straight after the appearance of Darwin's epoch-making work on the origin of species, were convinced of its tremendous importance and had the courage decisively to represent its fundamental views at a time when the great majority of specialist colleagues were still taking a disapproving or inimical stand.' . . .

Preyer's book *Darwin, sein Leben und Wirken* had come out in the previous year, 1896.

> . . . Preyer did not belong to those scholars and thinkers who are happily limited because they acquire a sum of beliefs handed down to them and then themselves take some steps in the direction thus pointed out. The notion of being upon a sure pathway makes such scholars unsuited to making big mistakes. They do not allow themselves any daring risks in science. Preyer risked a lot. Various of his ideas will be considered errors within the circle of his specialist colleagues. Much of what he presented as his view will in course of time be shown to be untenable. But as a person in error he was more stimulating than those others; they cannot go wrong because big mistakes cannot be made by trading with scientific small coin. Lombroso is said to be sympathetic to new things in spiritual life just because of their novelty. Something similar holds good for Preyer. He had a predilection for absorbing himself in younger domains of science. Hypnotism, graphology, the question whether Bacon is the author of Shakespeare's plays[26] occupied him and stimulated him to works and articles of value and originality, even when their content raises strong doubts. Preyer applied his work and thought to things which some find so absurd that they do not want seriously to discuss them. In his last period his favourite occupation was scientific study of handwriting. Finding in handwriting the soul, the being, the character of man, was for him the task of a scientific graphology. Scientific prejudices and a certain trend of scholarly education lead many to believe that becoming involved in certain things is unscientific. Most of our scientific contemporaries hold the opinion that such things as graphology are incapable of being dealt with scientifically. They reach this opinion through having formed quite definite conceptions as to what in Nature is possible and what is not. Whatever does not agree with

> these conceptions they simply reject. Minds like Preyer cannot be imprisoned by such conceptions. They know how unstable stand the 'truths' comprising the content of our sciences. They know how uncertain, how hypothetical much is which for most of the scientifically educated stands as absolutely definite. They are therefore convinced that even things appearing at first quite dubious may provide important knowledge and experience. Nothing in spiritual life stands so firmly that one can say: because we recognize these or those laws about one domain of Nature, anything else can only be classed among impossibilities. Everything must be tried, everything must be thought through: this was Preyer's leitmotif. It led him to his extremely interesting researches into the soul of a child. In a book he wrote on this subject, *Die Seele des Kindes,* stand a greater number and more important psychological experiences and ideas than in the works of precise and fashionable psychologists, who want to approach man's soul by experimenting in laboratories...

Die Seele des Kindes was published many years previously, in 1882.

> ...Preyer has a fine insight into the intimacies of a child's life, and an immense combinational gift. His observations join admirably together into a big scientific edifice. Preyer is both a master of detailed work and an ingenious discoverer of large connections. His biography of Darwin is a masterpiece in penetrating the matter with great effective ideas. In a few significant strokes Preyer sketches the part played by Darwinism in all domains of modern spiritual life.
>
> Never is Preyer just concerned with knowledge alone. What is acquired by scientific observation he wants to put into the service of life. His book *Die Seele des Kindes* does not just have the task of investigating man's soul-life, but also another one, of creating a solid psychological basis for pedagogy. 'The way is ever more paved towards knowledge that psychogenesis forms a necessary basis for pedagogy. Without studying the development of a small child's soul, education and the art of teaching cannot indeed be founded on firm ground... The art of *allowing* a small child *to become* is much harder than that of training it prematurely,' he says in a preface to this work. From the same source flow the views he expressed about the necessary reform of higher schools. Here Preyer is radical. He wants to have the classical *Gymnasium* training replaced by one held in the spirit of a modern scientific way of conception. The *Gymnasium* should transmit to a young person the knowledge stirring our time. One only need have the courage to think in the spirit of our time, and one *must* agree with Preyer's ideas. Only cowardly minds averse to any reform can here contradict. Such minds are afraid of any turnabout. They see how the old works; they cannot or do not wish to make any conception of how the new will work. They want the old because of its comfort. Lively minds like Preyer hate a standstill as such.

They will always consider reformatory ideas, because they want everything to be always flowing and becoming.

A Witness for All Time

In his biography of Karl Julius Schröer, Walter Beck states:

> Only few details have been transmitted about Schröer's following years. In the summer of 1897 Karl Julius and Hermine, together with their widowed younger daughter Ida Revi and her two small children, rented a dwelling in Baden, near Vienna. These two grandchildren—Heinrich, later a painter, and Richard, later an actor and producer—are said to have been very attached to their grandfather. The granddaughter Elisabeth also often visited her grandfather in Baden and reported on the many visitors. 'There was continually taking place a kind of pilgrimage to him.' Elisabeth listed the visits: Marianne Hainisch with her daughter Maria Fiktor, the Marx family from Baden, Hofrat Bernatziks, Leopoldine Winter, Jakob Minor, Dieffenbach, Demelius, Rollett, Ekhardt, Baron Torresani who had married a daughter of Hofrat Bernatziks, the English friend Mister Haswell and others. Here too, according to Elisabeth, there were stimulating discussions.

This list of visitors included at least four members of the Viennese Goethe Society: Marianne Hainisch was authoress of a brochure, *Der Wiener Goethe-Verein und seine Denkmal-Geschichte von 1878–1894* (1895) which in effect set out Schröer's views on the Goethe Memorial. Jakob Minor was Professor of Literature at Vienna University. Hermann Rollett, a doctor and poet—himself resident in Baden—was author of *Die Goethe-Bildnisse* (1881), a work with which Schröer had been closely associated and which had greatly furthered his interest in the erection of a Memorial representing Goethe in a suitably artistic way. Finally, James Haswell was an English pupil of Schröer's from the 1860s, who declaimed poetry.

One can hardly help wondering whether in the company of such visitors the 'stimulating discussions' mentioned by Schröer's granddaughter may perhaps have included some on the topic of the Goethe Memorial. For although the commission to erect this statue had been awarded to Edmund Hellmer, the design was still unaccomplished.

★

Over in England during that same summer, on Friday, 13 August *The Shrewsbury Chronicle* carried an article 'In Honour of Darwin—An Honour to Salop':

The present week has seen the accomplishment of a design long talked about in Shrewsbury—the erection of a statue to her greatest son, Charles Robert Darwin. That some memorial of the foremost scientist of the nineteenth century has not long since been erected in Shrewsbury is a matter of reproach to the town and to the county; but this reproach is now removed and atoned for by the generosity of the Shropshire Horticultural Society in devoting some £1,000 of its surplus money to the payment of a debt which ought to have been discharged years ago by the public at large. So little do we, in the midst of the struggle for daily bread or the pursuit of fleeting pleasure, notice the flight of time, that probably many will feel surprise on being reminded that it is over 15 years ago that Darwin died; to be literally exact, it was on April 19th, 1882—a year to the day from the date of the death of that other great man, the Earl of Beaconsfield—that the 'searcher after truth' ended his quest. Thus it was high time that in his native town something was done to outwardly perpetuate his memory. Far away Russia established scholarships in his honour very shortly after his death, and Sweden sent over two thousand subscriptions for the statue in the Natural History Museum in South Kensington, to which America and every country in Europe also contributed. These foreign recognitions of Darwin's work only served to emphasize the want of action at home; and it is with the greatest possible pleasure, therefore, that we can now announce the fulfilment of a too long neglected duty. Visitors to Shrewsbury need no longer look in vain for the Darwin memorial. It boldly stands, a splendid statue of the man himself, in front of the old Grammar School, a witness for all time that Shrewsbury gave to the world perhaps the greatest man of the century.

The circumstances leading up to the erection of the statue make quite a long, and in some respects not altogether satisfactory story. A Darwin memorial in Shrewsbury, we believe, was suggested a very long time ago; but it was not until Mr. Edwin Powell, of Rowton Lodge, interested himself in the matter in December 1893 that any definite steps were taken. In that month Mr. Powell sent a communication to the editor of the *Shrewsbury Chronicle*... The next step was the presentation of a requisition to the Mayor (Mr. W. Lyon Browne) to call a public meeting... The Mayor accordingly convened a public meeting, which was held on January 30th 1894... A resolution in favour of taking steps to secure a memorial was carried, and it was resolved to call another public meeting with the view of securing an even more representative attendance... The second public meeting was held on May 16th 1894... It was decided to open a subscription list, and a committee was formed, with Mr. H.C. Clarke as Hon. Sec. Several large sums were promised, but subscriptions did not come in quite so readily as was anticipated; and for various reasons the matter dragged on until January 1896. The committee then decided definitely in favour of the erection of a statue in front of the Free Library, and made a further appeal for subscriptions, the sum received up to that time being utterly inadequate. But to the shame of the town and county, and a little to the discredit of the country at large be it said, the second appeal had not the desired result, the subscriptions all told not amounting to (we believe) more than £400. The movement hung fire, as it were, and threatened to fizzle out altogether, or to be an unconscionably long time in coming to fruition. But just as the prospect of getting a statue of Darwin in Shrewsbury seemed to be hopeless, the Shropshire Horticultural Society came to the rescue. At intervals for many years this society has spent large sums of money for the benefit of the town, and now they resolved to add one more to the already large number of their benefactions by undertaking the entire responsibility of the Darwin Memorial. The committee of the Society met in November 1896, and resolved to bear the whole cost of a bronze statue, estimated at about £1,000, and commissioned Mr. Horace Montford, a clever London sculptor who is a native of Shrewsbury, to do the work. The Shrewsbury Town Council readily gave their permission for the statue to be erected in front of the Free Library, the exact spot selected being on the flags before the archway, a most commanding site, and Mr. Montford, who had prepared a sketch model for the original committee, which he somewhat modified afterwards, set about the modelling as rapidly as possible, having only seven months in which to do the work...

In the carrying out of the many arrangements necessary on the part of the Horticultural Society, both as regards the construction of the statue and its erection and unveiling, Messrs Adnitt and Naunton, of The Square, the Hon. Secretaries to the Society, have been most assiduous, and have in all matters displayed their accustomed courtesy. As has already been announced, the subscriptions collected for the original fund have been returned to their donors.

At High-Street Unitarian Church on Sunday evening the Rev. J.C. Street delivered a powerful sermon on Darwin, basing his discourse on strikingly appropriate 'readings' from the book of Ecclesiasticus and the Epistle to the Hebrews. He said he noticed that on the following Tuesday there was to be unveiled in Shrewsbury a statue of one of the most illustrious men of this century. He could have wished that the statue had been built by the men of Shrewsbury; that they by their own acts and benefactions had built a name for themselves in doing honour to their most illustrious townsman. He could have wished that the professional and the educated classes of that community—the clergy, and the lawyers, and the physicians, men who were supposed to have had something like a university training—had recognized what their fellow-townsman had done, and conferred not only honour upon that place, but honour upon the whole of the English-speaking race and the whole of humanity. And further, he could have wished that the lads on yon hill, who were the inheritors of the wonderful work he had done, had clubbed their shillings and their sovereigns together and helped to erect a monument to the name, and the fame, and the glory of Charles Darwin. But none of those things had been done. If, however, the statue had not been erected by any of those to whom he had referred, he would pay a tribute of honour and respect to the society which had so beneficently presented that statue to the town. He had had an extract from a Shrewsbury parish magazine placed in his hands, and therein was a statement to the effect that if a statue had been erected at the time of Darwin's death it would have been taken as a natural and common-place affair, but since his death his name had become so closely associated with the extreme theories of evolution that it would be exceedingly difficult to pay much honour to Darwin without accepting those theories. It was a subject, the writer further stated, on which it was no use to mince matters; men must make their choice between the faith of Jesus Christ and the conclusions of those who said that modern discoveries had shown that great faith to be untenable. The preacher said he had intended to refer to Charles Darwin and his work that night, and when he saw these statements he felt there were special reasons for doing so. He was present at the late Church Congress, and he heard distinguished men—leaders of the Church of England—emphatically express their approval of the working hypothesis of evolution, and about such wonderful results. What was that wonderful doctrine of evolution? It was that somewhere in the far-distant eternities the Spirit spoke and gave to the different species of creation powers to develop—age after age, generation after generation, and cycle after cycle, until there should blossom upon the world the humanity and the life of the present day. The old doctrine of creation—the doctrine that God specially created every special thing by a special act of creation, here a man, there a tiger, there an ant, there a star, there a planet—that God by successive acts of special creation brought these things into existence—might be brought into contrast with the doctrine which was involved in that mighty doctrine of evolution. Which was it that suffered by the comparison? Both referred creative acts to God, and both recognized his imminence and his constant power. Both these theories might be wrong, but he claimed for the one a majesty like the majesty of the laws which ruled the universe. There was a majesty in it which dwarfed all comprehension, and rendered a statement like that contained in the magazine he had referred to simply folly. Referring to Darwin's influence, the rev. gentleman said that his thinking had permeated the whole of the theological literature of the last 30 years; not a single book had been written by any theologian of note that had not paid heed to his thinking. They had other statues in the town—statues of warriors and statesmen—but the names of soldiers and statesmen would one by one disappear. The name of Charles Darwin, however, would stand out in the centuries to come as one of the mightiest names to conjure with. It marked one of the loftiest reaches of the human intellect, and his name was the high-water mark in the history of humanity. In conclusion Mr. Street said he paid his tribute of honour and respect to every patient enquirer and every patient student, but first and foremost on the list he paid honour to Charles Darwin.

Divergency of Opinion

The account continued:

The unveiling ceremony took place at 12.30 on Tuesday in beautiful weather, and in the presence of a large concourse of townspeople and others. The function was performed by Lord Kenyon (President of the Shropshire Horticultural Society), and among those present were:—the Mayor and Mayoress of Shrewsbury (Mr. and Mrs. Cresswell Peele), the Bishop of Shrewsbury, the Ven. Archdeacon Maude, the Rev. T.M. and Hon. Mrs. Bulkeley-Owen, Professor Sir J.D. Hooker, F.R.S., Lady Hooker, Professor G.H. Darwin, F.R.S., Mr. W.E. Darwin, Mr. Lawson Tait, Mr. Stanley Leighton, M.P., Rev. J.D. La Touche, Professor Wheeler (Calcutta), Mr. Horace Montford, Rev. Prebendary Moss, Miss Shaen (an old friend of Darwin's), Mr. T. Slaney Eyton, Rev. C.H. Drinkwater, Major C. Southam, Mr. E. Powell, Rev. W.H. Draper, Mr. W. Phillips, Colonel Prideaux, Mr. J. Cook, Major Patchett, Mr. G.M. Salt, Rev. T. Hosking, Mr. H.E. Rogers, Dr. Cureton, Rev. W.S. Burns, Rev. S.T. Richards, Dr. Gardner, Capt. Williams-Freeman, Mr. G. Butler-Lloyd, Mr. W. Eddowes, Mr. R. Ll. Kenyon, Rev. W. Hinton Jones, Major H.R.H. Southam, Rev. J. Mackay, Mr. G.J. Holt, Mr. W.E. Garnett-Botfield, Mr. R. Taylor, Mr. G. Mitchell, Mr. J. Evans Jones, Mr. A. Gill, Mr. J.P.G. Smith, Mr. F.E.R. Armytage, Mr. W. Beacall, Rev. F. Tinkler, Mr. W.L. Browne, Mr. H.W. Adnitt, Mr. W.W. Naunton, Mr. H.C. Clarke, Rev. W.G.D. Fletcher, Rev. J.C. Street, Mr. W. Thirne, Dr. N. Edwards, Captain Walcott, Mr. W.L. Southwell, Colnel Hore, Mr. Moser, Mr. A. Sparrow, Dr. Calvert, Messrs. W.E. Litt, R.G. Harrison, T.P. Deakin, F.W. Wateridge, R. Watkins, J. Woodhouse, W.F. Watkins, J. Oliver, S. Evans, W. Davies, E. Powell, junr., Scott, Harris (High-street), E. Williams, G.J. Groves, R.S. Hughes, P. Robbins, B. Blower, S. Ebrall, J. Williams, F. Blower, J. Lister, H. Forrest, E.J. Piper, H. Blackwell, J. Barker, Roff King, W.P. Hamilton, H.W. Hughes, H.F. Newman, T. Morris, and many others. There was also a large attendance of ladies.

Lord Kenyon, in addressing the company, said that in the town that saw his birth, under the shadow of the school wherein he studied, and at the hands of a society devoted to horticulture—a science which he loved—they raised the statue to the memory of Charles Darwin. (Applause.) To the

Mayor, as representing the citizens of Shrewsbury, they handed over the statue, hoping that His Worship would see that every care was taken of it, as he (Lord Kenyon) was confident would be done. (Applause.) He would now unveil the statue in order that those present might see what the Horticultural Society had offered to the town. His Lordship then removed the covering from the figure amid the heartiest applause.

The Mayor, who was warmly received, said that on behalf of the citizens of that ancient town he accepted with the greatest possible pleasure that noble gift of a society which had made in the past 22 years of its existence so many and so very valuable gifts to the town. (Applause.) He thought that in giving that exceedingly noble present the society had excelled themselves. (Hear, hear.) They had already done much to beautify one part of the town, and he was glad to think they had also assisted the charities of the town. (Hear, hear.) This was one of the objects which he hoped they would ever keep before them, and that they would continue to do in the fashion as they had done in the past, in spite of the handsome manner in which they had already acted. (Applause.) He thought that there was an appropriateness in the position and year in which they erected that statue. They had just been celebrating the Diamond Jubilee of Her Majesty the Queen, and in Shrewsbury they had erected that statue to one of the great men of her

The Darwin memorial in Shrewsbury

reign. (Applause.) It was most appropriate in its position, because it was erected on a site which the great man it represented must thousands of times have passed over. (Hear, hear, and applause.) In conclusion, he could only say on behalf of the town that he accepted the statue most gratefully, and he could assure them that it would be their constant charge in years to come to see that it was preserved and prevented from suffering any decay or injury. (Hear, hear.) He most cordially thanked the Horticultural Society for their most valuable gift and Lord Kenyon for his presence that day. (Loud applause.)

The first part of the proceedings then terminated.

A public luncheon afterwards took place at the Music Hall, and was largely attended. Lord Kenyon, who presided, was supported on the right by the Mayoress, Sir J.D. Hooker, Mrs. Bulkeley-Owen, Professor Darwin, Rev. Prebendary Moss, and Mr. Stanley Leighton, M.P.; and on the left by Lady Hooker, the Mayor, the Bishop of Shrewsbury, Mr. W.E. Darwin, Rev. J.D. La Touche, and Mr. Lawson Tait; while the general company included a large number of those present at the unveiling ceremony. Letters of apology for absence were received from Lord Salisbury, Sir John Lubbock, Bart., M.P., Mr. A.J. Balfour, M.P., Mr. Gladstone, Lord Kelvin, Mr. J. Chamberlain, M.P., the Earl of Powis, Mr. A.H. Brown, M.P., Mr. F. Darwin, Sir H.H. Howarth, Bart., M.P., Sir Trevor Lawrence, Bart., Mr. H. Darwin, Major L. Darwin, Professor Poulton, Professor C. Lloyd Morgan, Mr. F. Galton, Mr. T. Dyer, Sir George Stokes, Bart., Sir Offley Wakeman, Bart., Mr. Grant Allen, Mr. A.R. Wallace, Mr. Edward Clodd, Mr. Herbert Spencer, Sir Archibald Geikie, Bart., Sir H. E. Roscoe, Colonel W. Kenyon Slaney, M.P., Mr. H.D. Greene, Q.C., M.P., Mr. A.R. Jelf, Q.C., Mr. B.B. Woodward, the Archbishop of Canterbury, and the Bishops of Hereford, Lichfield and Wakefield. Mr. T. Plimmer, of the Castle Restaurant, carried out the catering most successfully, and music was supplied by Mr. Vine's string band.

The same issue of *The Shrewsbury Chronicle* carried an editorial on 'The Darwin Statue':

The erection of a statue representing and honouring Charles Darwin in his native town is an event of more than merely local interest, great as that interest undoubtedly is. That there should be some divergency of opinion in regard to the propriety of such a thing can hardly be a matter of surprise, remembering the storm of indignant dissent which the great natural philosopher's theories in connection with human evolution at first evoked and the bitter controversies to which those theories gave rise—controversies which, as broadly marshalled for 'science' on the one side and for 'religion' on the other, are a long way yet from being reconciled. When the suggestion of a statue to the author of *The Origin of Species* was originally mooted in our columns, the idea was variously greeted both locally and in circles farther afield, and many of the orthodox received it but coldly. The greatest philosopher of the century failed of recognition by the multitude, to whose intelligence he was only vaguely known as the man who had designated our common primordial progenitor as at the best but an ape! What! Raise a statue to the memory of one who could so belittle and depose mankind from their ancient pride of place, and who, worse even than that disloyalty, could discredit revelation and sap the very foundations of religious belief! The notion, in the estimation of some estimable persons, was not nice. And so the movement hung in the air. Local patriotism seemed chilled by some influence adverse to the proposal; and not even the local sentiment of pride and love for a most illustrious fellow-townsman—a Salopian born and bred—seemed proof against the benumbing negations of orthodox antagonism and ignorant indifference. But when all effort of its promoters seemed vain, and the Darwinian statue for Shrewsbury was on the brink of sinking beyond hope into the limbo of the things that might have been, rescue, ample and generous as unexpected and welcome, came from a quarter whence Salopians have long learned to look for the doing of good deeds. The Shropshire Horticultural Society handsomely contributed the amount required to accomplish the work. In this there was a special appropriateness. Not only is the Society the only public representative body locally whose funds are free to be so utilized, but it is the one organization that by its surpassingly prosperous encouragement of horticulture and floriculture has in a highly honourable way won for itself the proud right to honour itself and the town it benefits by helping to do honour to one of Shrewsbury's most famous sons, one of the most illustrious of 'Old Salopians', and one whose claim to fame largely rests upon the vast and valuable contributions he himself made to botanical science. And there are other aspects in which the event has a peculiar fitness. The memorial, which itself is the artistic creation of a Salopian sculptor, occupies a site in the open space fronting the Old School wherein, in the great days of the illustrious Dr. Butler, the future philosopher sat as a scholar. In all this there is, we think, a natural and harmonious fitness, and Shrewsbury has done well in thus rendering enduring honour to her most famous son. Charles Darwin, laborious and profound as a diligent investigator of scientific mysteries, sought truth only, and followed faithfully and fearlessly whithersoever it might lead. Scientific truth can never be antagonistic to religious truth, though it may appear so on an incomplete view of some of its hypotheses. Evolution is one or part of one of a vast number of truths or rival hypotheses, and inevitably so far as it is truth it will reconcile itself finally as consistent with all other truths. In this mingling of apparently paradoxical agreement and disagreement, harmony and discord, lies the explanation of the vehement opposition with which the evolution theory was at first met and the gradually greater tolerance, if not indeed greater measure of agreement, with which it is now received in quarters once implacable. Objectors, though an ever-lessening number, may still be troubled with misgiving as to whether Shrewsbury does right in conspicuously honouring one of the arch-promoters of 'philosophic doubt', but, confident that truth must prevail, we may leave them to their narrow view and narrower fear. It is by no means only upon his memorable achievement in propounding a new scientific theory, great as that theory was—'essentially a new creative thought', as Helmholtz has well said—that we would rest Charles Darwin's claim to honour in his native town. It rests firmly on the broad base of his splendid work in scientific and philosophic fields of remarkable range. He not only wrought as complete a revolution in biological science as the author of the *Principia* did in astronomy, but his contributions to the study of geology, zoology and botany were splendid as they are priceless. And last but not least we hold him in high honour for that he was ever a searcher after truth, a pursuer of the light, and as we have said, amid all difficulties, questionings and tribulations, faithful and fearless in the quest. No man's life-work ever more amply merited honourable recognition. This memorial to Charles Darwin is raised in testimony of pride in and gratitude for his surpassing scientific achievements, and as an incentive to Salopian youth of coming generations to emulate his passion for truth and his devotion to the task of making the bounds of human knowledge wider yet.

The correspondence columns of the same issue, however, also carried the following letter:

Sir,

The putting up of a statue to the memory of the late Charles Darwin in his native town is, I think, a fitting tribute to the memory of one who has achieved such distinction, and done so much in the interest of science; and is also a credit to those who first took the matter up and brought it to its present issue. At the same time I can fully sympathize with those who felt themselves unable to take any part in the proceedings connected with the memorial, owing to religious scruples.

In the course of the discussions on evolution which took place during the Church Congress last year, I believe most, if not all, of the speakers endeavoured to prove that there was no real inconsistency between the theory of evolution as propounded by the late Mr. Darwin and the creation of man as set forth in the Book of Genesis, but I have been told by several persons who attended those discussions that the speakers invariably stopped short of explaining (at any rate to their listeners' satisfaction) how the two aspects of the case could be reconciled and made to agree. If man has reached his present state of existence through a process of evolution reaching back to far distant ages, how are we to harmonize this with what

> we read in the Book of Genesis, viz., that God created man in His own image out of the dust of the earth, and gave to him what He gave to no other living creature, an immortal soul? This it is which separates man more than anything else, and makes him entirely distinct from the rest of creation. Every Christian believes that death is to them the end of all things, whereas with regard to man, this life is regarded merely as a period of probation before entering upon an endless futurity. But if the human race has been evolved out of some species of created living matter, whence comes this germ of immortality which man alone possesses?
>
> There is no trace whatever of the process of evolution to be found in the study of the Bible, except the moral one of Adam and Eve, brought about by a direct act of sin; and it is no wonder, therefore, that there are many persons, especially amongst the thoughtful portion of our clergy, who however much they may admire the man for his scientific attainments, view with repugnance the views which he set forth, and which they consider not to be in keeping with the doctrines of Christianity.
>
> H.

Darwinism and the Present

Towards the end of the month Rudolf Steiner composed for the *Magazin für Litteratur* an article relating to the subject, 'Darwinism and the Present'. It was published in the issue for 28 August—by a remarkable coincidence the hundred and forty-eighth anniversary of the birthday of Johann Wolfgang von Goethe!

> In these very days it has been reported in the newspapers that the Darwin enthusiasts, who three to four years ago set about instituting a collection towards a monument for the great natural scientist, have been badly treated by a certain incident. The memorial was to be erected in Shrewsbury, the town where Darwin was born. Hardly had arrangements for the collection been made when there arose a dreadful storm which threw down the tower of Shrewsbury church. To the devout this was a sign from God. It had been revealed to them that they should not contribute anything towards a memorial for the great heretic. By contrast, moneys have been pouring in to rebuild the church tower, which must have been an instrument for a higher will. I do not know whether the story is true. It interests me as a symptom of the stark contrast existing at present between two conceptions of the world: the Christian one, and the manner of thinking erected on a scientific foundation.

Steiner was indeed prudent not to commit himself regarding the veracity of the German newspaper accounts. The main lines of the story were indeed true, but in the process of its transmission from England to Germany the spire of St Mary's Church had turned into a whole 'church tower'! The moneys 'pouring in' to St Mary's Church Restoration Fund were not, as German newspapers appear to have been claiming, 'to rebuild the church tower', which had never fallen at all, but rather to rebuild the upper part of the spire and the nave onto which it had fallen, and to make the tower safe.

Steiner continued:

> The case of Bautz, and many other things, came again to my mind. Bautz is that Professor of Theology in Münster who both in oral speeches from his professorial chair and in his writings supports the view that Hell and Purgatory are situated in the interior of the Earth and are related to volcanoes and earthquakes. As soon as things of this kind become known through the press, calls of indignation may everywhere be heard from our freethinkers, progressives and others who 'keep up to date'. What they would most like to do is to call on the power of the state and have a man teaching things like that removed from his post.
>
> Whenever I become aware of the contrast between these two conceptions of the world, the question entering my mind is: what weapons are being used on this side and on that in the battle? The fighters in highest esteem are those who best sharpen their weapons. Just in regard to preparing their means of fighting, our 'moderns' could learn an endless amount from men like Bautz. What distinguishes Bautz is courage in thinking out to their end the thoughts which necessarily arise from his conception of the world. He expresses the final ideas to which he is obliged to come if he accepts the initial ones of his creed. His method is far more valuable than that of liberal theologians who dilute the content of Christian teaching so much that even modern Darwinism can if needs be form a component of the Christian creed. But however much trouble be taken, nobody will ever achieve harmony between the Christian conception of the world and the modern scientific one. Without a wise personal guidance of the world's destiny, announced in times of need by hints like the toppling of the tower at Shrewsbury, there is no Christianity. Without denying such guidance, and recognizing the truth that all causes of events lie in this world accessible to our senses, there is no modern way of thinking. Nothing supernatural ever interferes in Nature; all occurrences depend on elements which we attain with our senses and our thought. Only if this insight has penetrated not only into thought, but into the depths of feeling-life can one talk about a modern way of perception. But from this our 'modern minds' are very far removed. It is all right with thinking. The understanding of contemporaries is slowly coming to terms with Darwinism. But feeling and sensation are still utterly Christian. Feeling is unable to draw from the content of natural reality that elevation which it is capable of deriving from the teachings of religion. And

from this conflict of 'modern' minds arises the lack of courage which makes them shrink back from drawing the consequences of their thought-premises. How cowardly seems the talk that science is not far enough to say anything about final questions, compared with the boldness with which Dr. Bautz holds his view of Hell and Purgatory! Where are the modern minds who have courage to think their views to the end? And how are the few who do have it treated! One may think of the hostility Ernst Haeckel has experienced from his professional colleagues, because he not only registered individual facts but erected from his scientific insights an edifice with a modern view of the world.

Characteristic of the way our clever freethinkers behave towards men who have a brave go at highest questions are the views one comes to read about Friedrich Nietzsche. Here was a person who for once burrowed into the deepest problems of knowledge, and did not pause until he had penetrated the foundations of existence. In an incomparably grand way, he confronted faith in the otherworld with a reverence for this world, and developed in the highest sense the cult of this world. But what does all that matter to our 'modern minds'? They have no concern whatever with his views, the thoughts for which he lived and suffered, or from which sprung all his delight in existence. No, they just enjoy Nietzsche the poet. I will certainly deny no one a right to be elevated by the poetic beauties of Nietzsche's presentation. But to hang merely onto the latter seems to me a comfortable way of being able to call this mind great. No, nobody should call him great who cannot value in their full significance the profound thought-processes of *Jenseits von Gut und Böse*. Here is a depth of ideas never yet previously attained in mankind's spiritual history. But to our modern minds this does not matter. If they wanted to go into these fundamental things, they would have to come out for or against these ideas. Their thinking is too incompetent, or lacking in courage. They would rather be exhilarated instead by Zarathustra's *language*. Dullness and slovenliness of thought is often the signature of our 'modern minds'. In this respect they fall behind the devout people who do not want any Darwin Memorial because the tower has collapsed. These devout people have a closed view of the world; but 'moderns' for the most part have just fragments. This thought always arises in me when seeing both conceptions of the world, Christianity and modern naturalism, pitted against each other. My opponents here always please me better than those whose opinion is close to my own. But I like least the conciliatory minds: theologians defending Darwin, and natural scientists coming out for Christianity. By wanting to play such a conciliatory role, one is forced to blur over what is characteristic in each of these views. Health only comes by progressing honestly and openly towards the true consequences of an opinion one has formed. Only its whole personalities have made Christianity great. So too only whole personalities will make the modern way of thinking into a bearer of culture.

The Leaders Among Us

Some three months later, in the issue for 27 November 1897, Rudolf Steiner published in the *Magazin für Litteratur* a further associated article, entitled 'Charles Lyell: on the Centenary of his Birthday':

> Present spiritual life would have a wholly different physiognomy if in this century there had not appeared two books: Darwin's *Origin of Species* and Lyell's *Principles of Geology*. If Darwin and Lyell had not lived, professors in university halls would be speaking differently from how they do about many things. The religious consciousness of educated humanity would be different from what it is. Ibsen would have incorporated into his plays different ideas from those we derive from them. Had we not the named books, dramatic and narrative literature would be living a different life. The content of these books forms an important component of the spiritual air we breathe. Had Darwin and Lyell not injected their thoughts into mankind's spiritual organism, we cannot easily make a mental picture of how we would be thinking. Even someone who has never read a single line of the *Origin of Species* or the *Principles of Geology* is nonetheless standing under the influence of these books. From them not only our thinking but also our feeling-life have received their characteristic stamp. A young man reading these books today will not believe he finds in them anything he does not already know. Many of us grew up with the ideas of Darwin and Lyell before we knew more than the names, or indeed perhaps before we even knew the names, of these great observers of Nature. Many of us must speak to those who have not grown up with these ideas in a quite different language from the one they are used to. We are starting to look on men who do not understand our language as being survivors from a past historical epoch. It is not a question of how many think in this way. The chief thing is that we see in ourselves, who do think in this way, the really true human beings of the present time. We know ourselves to be the young ones, and the others the old ones. We are looking forwards, the others backwards. To a cultural historian of the future, our ideas will be the start of a new epoch of thought. For us, the thought of the future calls forth happiness and delight, because those in the future will look on us as their precursors. Future people will know more, be able to do more than us, but will have feelings related to ours. We stand nearer to them than to any of our contemporary preachers. Lyell and Darwin are the foremost, the greatest, the leaders among us. We are endlessly grateful to them, believing that without them we would

belong to a segment of mankind which was going extinct. Our feeling-life pronounces them sacred. We shudder at the spiritual experience with which we would be living had they not gone before. Since they are for us the most important ones, we have even lost 'proper judgement' about great persons of ancient times. But we do not thereby grieve. We have no wish to take things as objectively as they are; we want to live, and something should still become of our life. It should bear in itself the power of growth. We would sooner look upon what is not yet done than lose ourselves in reflections on what has happened. If we were fairer, we would be less fruitful. Towards minds near to us, we have the partiality of a son who loves his parents more than others distant from him. We love Darwin more than Aristotle, Lyell more than Plato, because Darwin and Lyell are our well-known fathers, Plato and Aristotle ancestral pictures we have hung up in our spiritual mansion. When we read in Lyell and Darwin, it is as if someone were giving us a warm hand; when we study Plato and Aristotle, as if we were walking around an ancestral room. We live with Darwin and Lyell, we learn about Plato and Aristotle.

We do not always agree with Darwin and Lyell. In many things we contradict them, but feel that despite our contradiction of them they still speak our language. We account on our side various people who do battle in the sharpest manner with Darwin and Lyell. But we know that even if our contradiction bears fruit, it could only do so through these two minds. Great minds also bring forth their opponents, and along with their opponents bring mankind forward. Even if a future humanity were to come to essentially different notions than those of Darwin and Lyell, in both men these sons of the future will nonetheless have to revere their fathers.

Lyell gave a new character to thought concerning the formation of the Earth. Before him, this thought was governed by notions which to us now seem childish. We do not perceive why tremendous mountain formations should have emerged through other forces than those still currently dominant. Lyell saw that in the course of observable periods, flowing water dislodges from the mountains the stone masses, and then deposits them in another place. Formations thus disappear from one place, and others reappear at another. This proceeds gradually. But by thinking of such effects continued through immeasurable periods of time, one can imagine that through these forces still dominant today the whole surface of the Earth has taken the shape it currently has. Add to this the alterations which the Earth's surface today receives from floating icebergs, or from wandering glaciers, carrying with them debris and detritus. One may further think of earthquakes and volcanic phenomena raising and lowering the ground, or of wind throwing up dunes, and the slow, gradual erosion of rocks. Everything which has happened up till now in the shaping of the Earth could have happened in such a way that these stated effects were present during long periods of time. We today do not doubt that the matter is so. But human beings before Lyell thought differently. They believed the mighty formations of mountains to have been caused by extraordinary forces acting instantaneously. If a form on the Earth's surface were ripe for decline, the creative power intervened anew, to give our planet a new countenance. So thought our predecessors. We recognize, by investigating the Earth's crust, that a number of earthly epochs existed and then passed away. Those earthly epochs which passed away we find as layers of the Earth's crust piled on top of one another. In each layer we discover fossilized forms of animals and plants. Our predecessors supposed that the power of the Creator ever and again allowed the life of an epoch to pass away, and put another in its place. Lyell showed this not to be the case. Through the gradual working of forces still active today one epoch evolved out of another, and in each succeeding epoch lived those organisms which survived from the previous one and could adapt themselves to new conditions of life. Creatures of more recent earthly periods are successors to those living in older ones.

This thought was endlessly fruitful for Darwin. He recognized that in course of time animal species can change, that they are not created for themselves but are related to one another, have emerged from each other. If this knowledge be taken together with Lyell's thoughts, it then becomes clear that all life on Earth, past and future, forms a great natural unity. The processes we see today with our eyes and understand with our mental powers have always been taking place. There never have been any others. What happens at present occurs without any miracles or superterrestrial influences. Darwin and Lyell have shown that things on Earth have always been going on in this fashion, without miracles. They are thus the creators of an entirely new conception of the world, of an entirely new feeling, of a new way of living.

On our ethical life they have a most far-reaching influence. They have freed us from the feelings we necessarily had towards beings dwelling in wind and weather. A person who sees in a storm an approaching divinity feels differently from someone who believes that storms and earthquakes are just as natural as the effect made by a stone falling on the ground. One who believes in the thoughts of Darwin and Lyell stands differently towards natural forces than does another holding fast to superterrestrial divinities. The gods can no more help him, no more harm him. They cannot reward him, nor punish him. He has become free from fear and hope regarding unresearchable powers. Nature to him is everything, and what is natural can be investigated. It can also be put under compulsion, and into the service of human ideas. One can consciously make oneself lord of the Earth. Deference vanishes, but pride increases. One wants to rule with wisdom, no longer humbly obeying and deferring to inscrutable counsels. In place of a world-conception of humility and subjection, Darwin and Lyell have set a

> world-conception of pride, of the self-conscious human being. What they did for man's freedom cannot be expressed. They taught us not to raise an altar to an 'unknown god', but to present our service to the known spirit of Nature. They taught man not to regard himself as a dwarf, but to work as a hero. They opened a path for acting and willing, because they freed them from the deadweight hung onto them by a will working in the beyond. They have shown knowledge where its domain is, and thus really given it power. Only since Lyell and Darwin can it be felt as a truth that knowledge is power. Defer to what is preordained for you, is what people before Lyell and Darwin were obliged to tell themselves. Do what you perceive is worthwhile, is what they can tell themselves today.
>
> No relapses into an old view of the world will be able to stop the development here described. What Ernst Haeckel said at the foundation of the Ethical Society in Berlin, that modern morality, religiosity and behaviour are based on a modern conception of the world, is an incontrovertible truth...

Haeckel made this statement at the foundation of the Society in 1892, in a speech published at the time in the journal *Die Zukunft*.

Steiner continued:

> ...I cannot speak of Lyell or Darwin without thinking of Haeckel. All three belong together. What Lyell and Darwin began, Haeckel has taken further. He has built it up in full awareness of serving thereby not only scientific necessity, but also man's religious consciousness. He has the most modern mind, because no remnants of old prejudices cling any more onto his conception of the world, as for instance was still the case with Darwin. He is the most modern thinker, because he sees the only domain of thought in what is natural. And he is the most modern feeler, because he wants to have life established in accord with natural measure. We know that he is celebrating Lyell's birthday along with us as a festival, because for him it is necessarily a day which produced one of the founders of the new world-conception. Lyell's festival-day brings us to proper awareness that we belong to the Haeckel congregation. When Haeckel talks with us about processes of Nature, every word has a connotation related to our feeling. He sits at the helm; he steers with power. Although we do not exactly want to pass many places towards which he leads us, he is nonetheless going in the direction we want to take. He received the rudder from the hands of Lyell and Darwin; they could not have given it to anyone better. He will pass it on to others going in his direction. And our congregation goes sailing rapidly forward, leaving behind it the helpless ferrymen of the ancient world-conceptions.
>
> These ideas are stimulated in me by the 14th of November, when Lyell's birthday recurs for the hundredth time.

A Personal Relation

On 8 January 1898 Rudolf Steiner published in the *Magazin für Litteratur* an article on 'Herman Grimm'.

> We feel fortunate to be allowed to live at the same time as certain men. If I were to name such men, among the first would be Herman Grimm, who on the 6th of January celebrates his seventieth birthday. He has shown me directions of spiritual life no one else could have done. Through him I was introduced into a world of conceptions into which no one else could have introduced me. I could only refer to two or three writers of the present of which I can say as of him: with the first sentences of every one of his books I have a *personal* relation to him. He belongs to the writers for whom I have evinced from youth onwards the greatest sympathies. On occasions when I must contradict them, I respect few as I do him. With others a contradiction which we come into with them blunts our love for them. Never with him. I have the feeling that everything he says comes from and must be accepted from lofty regions, even when we believe ourselves obliged to hold another opinion. In regard to Herman Grimm I cannot speak of error.
>
> Everything Herman Grimm writes and speaks has the most personal character of his being. What he researches by industrious scholarly work, what he attains through most careful observation, he expresses as a personal view, as a subjective opinion. He writes no sentence behind which his personality may not be sensed. He expresses personal experiences, whether speaking of Goethe, Homer, Raphael, Michelangelo or Shakespeare: personal experiences of a deep and nobly sensitive mind.
>
> A *distinguished* personality in the noblest sense of the word stands before my mind when I think of Herman Grimm. Everything he touches gains in his hands a particular significance, and can be observed under the idea of distinctiveness. To him belongs the greatness lying in distinction. There are things which remain foreign to him because they do not let themselves be observed from the visual angle of distinction.
>
> Strict researchers holding to so-called objectivity become annoyed with Herman Grimm. Very disparaging judgements could be heard in this regard when his book appeared about Homer...

Homers Ilias was published in two volumes, the first in 1890, the second in 1895.

> ... I have for this book a quite special liking. A purely human interest binds me to the work. Others write about Homer as impersonal 'method' requires. Herman Grimm writes as must be written by someone enjoying with an artistic sensitivity the works of Homer available to us. He thus brings their content much closer to us than can that method of historical philology.
>
> Herman Grimm's works on Michelangelo and Raphael show us these

> artists in a light in which we can only see them through him. His conception will live on in the development of art history.

Leben Michelangelos was published in 1860–3, *Das Leben Raphaels* in 1872.

> Herman Grimm does not consider the breadth of historical evolution. For him great personalities are of the essence. That western culture has produced a Homer, Sophocles, Michelangelo, Raphael, Dante, Shakespeare, Goethe, comprises for him this culture's value. What lies between these spirits is only to be observed for their sake.
>
> Although Herman Grimm opens up to us great historical perspectives, the historical way of observing has never darkened his feeling for the immediate present. He lives in the present, if in his way. We listen with highest interest to his opinion about every more significant question of the present.
>
> The picture of Goethe sketched by Herman Grimm is not in the manner of a Goethean researcher. This is because with every feature, every statement he regards Goethe with personal involvement...

Goethe was published in 1877.

> ...For him the picture of Goethe is a matter he considers quite subjective. Through all his expositions shines the question: what is Goethe *to me*? He considers Goethe as an element actively intervening into his life. He says things about Goethe of which he has the feeling that he has to say them if Goethe is to be of value to him. Things which do not interest Herman Grimm he does not say, even if scholars believe them to be important for understanding Goethe. Herman Grimm's Goethe is not the 'objective' Goethe, but we would not want to miss him as part of our spiritual life.
>
> A few weeks ago Herman Grimm presented us with the third edition of a volume of novels...

Novellen—first published in 1856—came out in 1897 in a third expanded edition.

> ...A deeply heartfelt beauty belongs to all Grimm's novelistic works. Whoever reads them senses through them what culture is in a characteristic case. One has the feeling of confronting a personality leading a stylish life.
>
> *Style in conduct of life* seems to be an outstanding feature in Herman Grimm's personality. Everything particular he does harmonizes with a whole. Nothing falls out from the great impulse coming through him to ourselves.
>
> Our scientific way of regarding things is distant to Herman Grimm. At many points it offends his personal feeling. Human nature as currently lived out before our eyes and as expressed in works of fantasy and reason is his favourite object of observation. How this nature organically developed

from other forms does not by comparison interest him. To him natural feeling seems to give a better explanation than a scientific way of conceiving.

One result of this way of looking at things is Herman Grimm's *style*. Every sentence with him arises from a personal impulse. He does not know how to make one sentence conclude in another one, or to derive judgements from fundamental assumptions. When he progresses from sentence to sentence there are no points of departure and results. Every statement arises from a new experience. If on reading his books we believe we are becoming richer in inner content of life, it may be ascribed to this peculiarity of his style.

He always gives us fresh warm life: therefore we too evince such for him.

Theatre

During this same month of January 1898 the *Magazin für Litteratur* started also to print a theatrical supplement, *Dramaturgische Blätter*. Its issue for 12 February carried an article by Rudolf Steiner on 'Theatre and Criticism'.

> The theme 'theatrical criticism' is not a pleasant one. It is least edifying for theatrical professionals themselves. What is not all found in our newspapers and journals under the heading 'Theatre'? Nowhere perhaps is dilettantism proliferating so lavishly as in this domain.
>
> Criticism of dramatic achievements and of the art of acting stands worst of all. Conditions are better for operatic criticism. In regard to musical achievements, misunderstanding and ignorance are easily evidenced. By reading five lines of a musical critic, one will be in a position to judge whether one is dealing with an expert or with a dilettante. And yet in course of recent decades conditions have substantially worsened in this domain as well. Those belonging to the Wagnerian artistic circle cannot be acquitted from having contributed an immense amount to this deterioration. In the time before critics of the Wagnerian school appeared on the scene, a musical critic was required to speak from an expert standpoint about an achievement's musicality. He had to know what is possible in the art criticized by him, and speak about the architecture of a musical work of art. He had to interpret aural sensations, and musical fantasy demanded its rights. Wagnerian critics began to speak in quite another key. In their expositions scarcely anything further was to be read on music and musical fantasy. All the more was there instead on every conceivable mysterious soul-condition and darkly mystical truth, or even on natural phenomena meant to come to expression in this or that piece of music. Immense mischief was and is caused. The most brilliant refutation of this mischief is Hanslick's fine booklet *Vom Musikalisch-Schönen*. A musical critic who rejects this book

cannot be taken seriously. In his criticisms he will certainly not be speaking about music at all. He will be telling us what is 'expressed' at this or that place in a piece of music; but will omit everything about the architecture of a tonal work, which amounts to what the ear and tonal fantasy perceive.

A setback is already clearly perceivable in this domain. Wagnerian critics are already being rejected by reasonable musicians.

Matters are different with histrionic criticism. Here dilettantism is harder to recognize. Few people know where the border lies between dilettantism and expertise. Expertise can only be attributed to a person who erects his judgement on a work's purely artistic qualities. A play must be built up according to just such strict artistic laws as a symphony.

The subject is however confused by the matter of dramatic art. This matter concerns a critic only in so far as he must decide the question of whether or not some reproach is at all appropriate to a dramatic arrangement. This question does not apply to music. For the latter is wholly form. It has no matter. The injustice of Wagnerian critics consists precisely of wanting forcibly to impose matter onto music.

But in drama the matter comes into account in no other way than that indicated. If further judgement be made about the matter, such judgement is inartistic. Whether matter be in itself important or unimportant, beautiful or ugly, moral or immoral and so on are inartistic questions. These things do not concern a critic. As soon as matter provides what is necessary for dramatic development, a critic must only ask whether the artist has drawn out what lies in the matter, and then how he has treated the matter. He must be indifferent to the 'what' of the play, and be concerned with the 'how'. He should talk about how a poet introduces a conflict, how he draws threads together, how he brings an event to a conclusion.

But unfortunately in our theatrical critiques little of this is discussed. Material interest always stands in the foreground. And material interest is in this respect what is inartistic. One may imagine the spirit of our histrionic criticism transferred onto criticism of painting. We would then be hearing whether a depicted landscape be charming or hideous, beautiful or ugly, attractive or repulsive, whether a person reproduced in the pictures be lovely or dreadful and so on. But we would hear nothing of whether a painter has succeeded in bringing picture and background into a right relation, whether or not he has produced a harmony of colours. We would be hearing about all the things in a picture which do not concern us; but from a critique directed purely at the matter we would be unable to gather anything about the specifically pictorial.

When we require from histrionic art just such expertise as from the judgement of sculptural art, there will be great progress.

However, our theatrical public steps in the way, hindering this progress. Who is aware of the purely artistic qualities of a play? Who demands from the critic a judgement of these qualities? Everything depends on and presses towards the matter! Vainly did Schiller say that in destruction of matter through form lies a master's true artistic secret. Goethe put the same attitude into the words of Faust: 'Consider the "what", but consider more the "how".'

In respect to drama we are stuck in a barbarian taste.

And the art of acting? It is the absolute stepchild of criticism. Wise judges know least how to begin with it. Here not even the most elementary things lie clear.

That two actors must play a role in quite different ways is mostly not considered at all. When acting, an actor unites in himself three persons. The first is his human everyday personality, his figure, his nose, his voice and so forth; the second is the personality the poet gives him to play, Posa, Hamlet, Othello and so on. The third is invisible. It stands above both. It uses the first as an instrument in order to embody the second. And since there are no two men built the same way, just so no two actors can play a role the same way. An actor has to present a compromise between the person the poet depicts and his own natural constitution.

Only a critic who asks himself the question whether an actor has succeeded in presenting that compromise can come into consideration. All else written about the art of acting is empty drivel.

Criticism of drama and of histrionic art is often judged from too low a viewpoint. People basically think anyone can write about these things. And indeed 'anyone' does write about them. Just because judgement of purely material considerations is here so tempting, requirements should be set particularly high. Expertise should be demanded, because expertise is so hard to distinguish from charlatanry.

But the public receives obligingly a couple of trenchant expressions about a play or a histrionic achievement. Claims are here taken at face value whose analogies in another artistic domain would be simply laughed off. A nicely written feature article is worth more than competent artistic judgement. And if the feature-writer is also witty! No one then troubles about his expertise.

It will be hard to bring about better conditions in this domain. But for the benefit of dramatic and histrionic art they *must* be brought about.

A Real Technique of Histrionic Art

In the following week, on 19 February, Rudolf Steiner published in the *Dramaturgische Blätter* a related article on 'Unimportance':

There is hardly any art where unimportance plays such a large role as in the art of acting. The issue is whether an actor for some reason moves this or that facial muscle, or whether he moves his right hand or not. A bad hand-movement from this or that actor can spoil an entire scene.

In the art of drama we are unfortunately not so far as to notice a single bad hand-movement or a false contraction of a facial muscle. Mostly we need a *whole* actor who 'spoils everything' in order to notice how necessary it is for the stage artist to accomodate the poet, so as to bring the latter's intentions to full effect on the stage.

For the theatrical public, an actor is a person who brings the poet's intentions to actual realization.

It therefore seems to me quite superfluous to talk about whether the art of acting is an art of first or second rank. In an ethical respect, differences of rank are very important. In the artistic domain they do not come into question. For in art everything is necessary, even what is seemingly incidental. A work of art must be perfected right into its details, if it is to be according to strict demands adequate to a style perfected in itself. No foreign element should here disturb the harmony of the whole. A great play can be spoiled by an actor playing a role just one degree more banal than it is meant to be.

The question of what rank on the artistic ladder the art of acting takes seems to me irrelevant. What by contrast is for me important is the problem: how can the art of acting do justice to the tasks which poets set upon it?

Everything revolves around this: does the art of acting have an independent significance alongside drama or not?

I believe it certainly does have an independent significance. The work of a stage-artist will only be complete if brought by means of histrionic art onto an actual stage.

Evidence for this can be adduced in a very simple way. In Shakespeare's time, with the means of histrionic art of that time, Hamlet quite certainly had to be acted differently from today.

We do not perhaps act Hamlet better than he was acted in Shakespeare's time, but we do act him differently. If however we acted him today as Shakespeare made him be acted, we would be acting him badly.

When there are different means to realize a thing, and the realization can be one time good and another time bad, the means have an independent significance.

The art of acting is a means, but a means of independent significance.

What matters is *how* X acts Posa, and that he acts him differently from Y.

What the personality of Posa expresses is certainly for all times one and the same thing. How to express it through the art of acting changes from one decade to another.

We should therefore not talk about unimportance in histrionic art. Much rather should we consider what it is in this art which matters. It is laughable to call the art of acting reproductive. Drama is for a true actor what reality,

Nature, is for a playwright. An actor is as productive towards drama as a playwright is productive towards Nature. He raises drama into a new, specially artistic sphere. If drama is a piece of Nature, seen through the temperament of a playwright, the work performed on stage is a drama, seen through the temperament of a producer and actors.

Unless we desire wilfully to lower the rank of histrionic art, we must grant it to be independent, and reflect on its peculiar technical means. It will then present itself as an independent art, of the same kind as other arts.

If we have perceived this, we shall think less about its lower rank. We shall be fairer towards it.

The art of acting needs such fairness. For today it is often seen as a stepchild among the arts.

This prejudice is especially widespread among productive playwrights. It has to be overcome.

And it will be overcome, the moment we are clear about the relation between the art of acting and dramatic poetry.

We lack a real technique of histrionic art. It must first exist. Both poets and actors will then acknowledge it. And both categories of artists will then understand each other.

Such understanding is at present lacking.

Modern Spiritual Life

At the beginning of the next month, on 5 March, the *Magazin für Litteratur* carried an article by Rudolf Steiner entitled 'Untimeliness in School Reform'.

There is much talk now about school reform. On reading the reports concerning negotiations held on this matter, one gains a strange impression. Everything conceivable is talked about, but the main thing very little. There are endless debates over whether or not to set a couple of lessons more or less for Latin and Greek, or whether German essays should be promoted in this or that way. And yet these things are the most irrelevant in the world. The chief deficiency in our *Gymnasium* can be grasped with one's hands. It does absolutely nothing to bring its pupils to a point where they can understand modern spiritual life.

Or is it not correct that a school leaver today stands helpless when facing the actual basis of our view of the world and life, modern *scientific ideas*? What Socrates and Plato taught and what Caesar wrote is no living part of our spiritual life. What Darwin revealed and what modern physiology, physics and biology unveil should become precisely that.

I am not underestimating the formative value of the Greeks and Romans.

But my opinion is that the past only receives the right value in educating our time if seen from a present spiritual angle. Anyone who does not know the educational content of our time can also only come into a lopsided relation to Socrates and Plato.

All teaching in schools must be filled with the spirit of the present. Only human beings permeated by this spirit should be teachers. Let no one say that it is irrelevant whether a teacher of Greek or Latin understands something about modern science or not. In spiritual life everything hangs together. A modern mind will teach a thousand things differently from one rusted into classical philology, knowing nothing except his 'subject'.

The consequences would be unforeseeable for our whole spiritual life if our pupils were brought up in the sense of a scientific view of the world in our time. Our whole public life would take on a different form. We would be spared countless discussions on the relation between religion and science, faith and knowledge, etc. Things would no longer be brought up which have long been dismissed from the standpoint of modern thought.

Let no one object that the views of a scientific world-conception are for the most part still hypotheses which still need first to be proven, and that every doubt about them is justified. I would retort that this applies to every view, old no less than new. But we do not have the task of handing on convictions to our growing generation. We should bring it to use its own power of judgement, its own ability to interpret. It should learn to look into the world with open eyes.

Whether or not we doubt the truth of what we hand on to youth is irrelevant. Our convictions are valid only for ourselves. We bring them to youth, in order to say: 'This is how we see the world. See how it presents itself to you.' We should awaken *capacities*, not transmit *convictions*.

Youth ought not to believe in our 'truths', but in our personality. Those growing up should notice that we are *seekers*. And we should bring them onto the *paths of seekers*. We tell our successors how we come to terms with things, and leave it to them how they manage to do so.

We should not then withhold from pupils the content we have gained for the replacement of religious notions which we have overcome. They should not grow up with feelings contradicting modern thought.

Many will consider what I have said as a monstrous product of fantasy from a man so taken in by ideas of a scientific world-conception that he does not at all notice how much he thereby overlooks the opposite feelings of others. That is not the point. Those others stress their demands. We want to do so with ours. No Catholic bishop will hesitate to reform a school backwards in his direction. We too want to state our opinion regardless, about the path leading to where we want the world to be. Moderation blunts weapons.

Only a Questioner

A fortnight later, on 19 March, Rudolf Steiner published in the *Magazin für Litteratur* an article 'On Ibsen's Seventieth Birthday: 20th of March 1898'.

> When fifty years ago wild storms of revolution were roaring through Europe, Henrik Ibsen was twenty years old. He greeted the movement for freedom with strongest sympathy. The passion of revolutionaries was inwardly related to feelings living in his own soul. Looking back on this time he later says: 'The time was powerfully stirred, the February Revolution, the uprisings in Hungary, the war in Schleswig—all this strongly intervened in my development. To the Magyars I directed thundering poems, urgently admonishing them in the interest of freedom and human rights to hold out in the rightful struggle against tyrants.'
>
> The revolution the twenty-year-old experienced was a herald and symptom for a greater one, the revolutionizing of minds. Political revolution could not bring about what minds promised themselves from it. Transforming movements of the human order are only victorious if expressing newly born views of the world. Christianity was able to found a new order of human relations, because it derived from a revolutionizing of the whole feeling-life. Jesus of Nazareth proclaimed a new relation to the world and to life. He gave human feeling a new direction. Actual conditions had to follow a changed direction of heart. The revolution of the year forty-eight was a purely political one. It was not borne up by any new view of the world.
>
> Only ten years after this revolution, Charles Darwin proclaimed to men the gospel they needed to give content to a new form of life. Goethe already possessed this gospel. The great knowledge had already dawned in him of the purely *natural*, unitary being which produced the dead stone, the still plant, the irrational animal, which also called into existence the human being, and beside which there is in the human being nothing divine. Man to him is the most perfected *natural being*. Nature at its peak has the power to bring forth the rational animal; into this rational animal no divine breath need be breathed.

Reproducing this article in the 1940s, Marie Steiner added at this point a footnote:

> Since today reading is fast and often superficial, we do not regard it superfluous to point out that Dr. R. Steiner is not here reproducing his own views, but those of a time which looked through Darwin's spectacles at things which can also be looked at more deeply.[27] Even if a modern spiritual investigator still looks in the same direction—the gate of scientific knowledge—it is nonetheless one thing to remain standing before the open gate,

and another to step through it and perceive new horizons. There is a need to pass through that gate—but further steps must then be taken.

Rudolf Steiner's text continued:

> But Goethe gained his view of life as a spiritual aristocrat. Only through his individual course of development was it possible so to read the Book of Nature that it made this revelation. Darwin proclaimed the same knowledge in a democratic way. Every person could emulate his mental steps. Not *what* he proclaims makes a man into a prophet, but *how* he proclaims it.
>
> The great secret was unveiled for Goethe by the sight of Greek works of art in Italy. On seeing these works, he called out: 'There is necessity, there is God. I have a supposition that artists when producing these works were acting according to the same laws by which Nature works, and which I am on the track of.'

These combined quotations are from the *Italian Journey*, and were made in Rome respectively on 6 September and 28 January 1787.

> Human work only continues the work of Nature: at that moment Goethe recognized this. What a man creates does not come to him as a gift of grace from Heaven, but rather through developing to a higher level the same forces of Nature active in plant and animal. Goethe's life would have to be emulated if one wanted to come to his knowledge the same way as he did. Darwin taught the same thing. But he indicated common *facts*, expressing such a truth—facts available to every person. He expressed in popular form what Goethe proclaimed for the elect.
>
> It would then be preposterous to ascribe to creative power coming from above what Nature could obviously produce out of herself. Under the influence of a new world-conception all human feeling-life must change. Man sees that he is higher, more perfect than what he evolved out of. Formerly he believed that something standing *above* him transplanted him into existence. His vision now can no longer be directed upwards. He depends on himself and on what is *below* him.
>
> For centuries the human heart was accustomed to ordering itself into this vision directed upwards. Since Darwin's appearance it strives to give up this tendency of feeling.
>
> It is relatively easy for the understanding to adopt new knowledge; it is endlessly difficult for the heart to transform itself accordingly. In the souls of the best people of the last half-century the most difficult struggles were thus played out between the understanding and the heart. Natures unclear in themselves, unharmonious, doubting, searching, are typical for this half-century.
>
> Most of those walking with a more serious attitude among us today still sense these struggles inside them. And even the best people have only a

feeling that satisfaction will come; not that it is already there. From these struggles countless questions arise for us. Only from the future do we hope for answers.

A future historian of our time will have to speak about human beings who were struggling and questioning. And if he wants to depict a single personality in whose soul all the struggles which stirred five decades were mirrored, he will have to depict Henrik Ibsen. All the questionable figures our half-century had to produce meet us in Ibsen's plays. All the questions thrown up by this time we rediscover in these works. Because this time is one of questions which only the future will answer, Ibsen's plays therefore end with questions; and he therefore had to say of himself:

'I mostly question, answering is not my business.'

Ibsen made this statement in 1875 in the course of 'A Rhyming Letter' to Georg Brandes.

One must honour truth and admit that Ibsen was not a man who knew the answer to the time's great questions. He understood how to question with all his might; he was unable to answer. He felt this himself, on saying:

'I for my part will be satisfied by the success of the work in my life's week, if this work can serve to prepare a mood for tomorrow's day. But firstly and above all I will be satisfied if it can help to strengthen minds for that working week following afterwards.'

I like to regard it as fortunate that Ibsen is only a questioner. Being unable to arrive at answers, he is in a position to question deeply and fundamentally. Since we taste with him the utter and profound seriousness of the highest questions, our successors will come to deeper answers. The conflict and dissatisfaction we bear within us today on leaving his plays will change into happiness for those who will loosen what we tie up.

Thus do I understand Ibsen. To me he is a nature who is strong enough to feel the problems of our time as his own grief; but who is not strong enough to fulfil our highest aims.

To me Ibsen is the builder who erects the towers from which we should overlook our world; but who succumbs to dizziness if he himself is to stand on top of these towers.

I imagine that in our time it must be hard to be old. Whoever is young today believes he can keep up in his heart with the culture of understanding in which we are living. To an old man of today, it seems impossible to keep up. Ibsen's own heart has grown too deeply into the very feelings which past centuries have instilled into us for him to live satisfied by the proudly turretted edifice of knowledge he has helped to create.

In his *Baumeister Solness* he has admitted, in the manner of a great man, that he is seized by dizziness in his own work.

I think the old master will rejoice if we tell him today on his birthday that we have understood him. In his fifty years of activity he wanted to lead men into freedom. We want to preserve freedom even towards him. It is not blind admiration but admiring *knowledge* which he should see in us, when we turn to him with greetings on this day.

A Thorough Libertine

On the 31 March 1925, the writer and critic John Schikowski published in the Berlin newspaper *Vorwärts* an obituary notice beginning as follows:

> With Dr. Rudolf Steiner, the anthroposophist, who died yesterday at Dornach near Basel, one of the most remarkable men of our time has departed. Less remarkable by the significance of his person and of his achievement than by the influence this person and achievement exercised on a large part of our contemporaries. Steiner however owed this influence to the spirit of the age, which he did not create but made use of.
>
> I came to know Steiner in the 1890s, and we had much contact with one another at that time. From Weimar, where he . . . had published Goethe's scientific writings, he had moved to Berlin and here become editor of the *Magazin für Litteratur*. In his view of the world he was a Haeckelian, a materialist and atheist. Politically he called himself an anarchist, and we Social Democrats were regarded by him as bourgeois. Which however did not prevent him from giving lectures on literary subjects in the context of Social Democratic training organizations. In his manner of living he was a thorough libertine, full of pleasure in earthly existence and quite unrestrained in his abundant enjoyment of it. I am far from burdening his moral account with the often somewhat questionable adventures whose hero was 'Rudi Steiner'. Many a saint has been on pilgrimage through the dirtiest stations on the earthly path before attaining to purity . . .

A week later, on 7 May 1925, the Frankfurt paper *Die Volksstimme* published over the initials E.B.H. a short 'Recollection of Dr. Rudolf Steiner', written vividly in both present and past tense:

> Otto Erich Hartleben and Rudolf Steiner come deep at night into a Berlin nocturnal café, where a gypsy band were playing their fiddles. Both of them had been bravely carousing and were eagerly discussing a literary subject.
>
> The café was thickly thronged. Only one table has free seats; at it sits a lady called Mathilde. Both of them sit down at Mathilde's table and spin out their subject further. Mathilde, a lady of settled age, listens. Steiner has sat down on the sofa beside her. Otto Erich sits on the side of the table directly opposite.
>
> Steiner then disappears for a while. Hardly has he gone when Mathilde turns to Otto Erich: 'Tell me, has your friend got money too?' Otto Erich

replies with a tone of utter conviction: 'Never!' Mathilde twitches herself together. 'What—and then he still makes poems!' she utters indignantly. Otto Erich smiles behind his dark pince-nez, searches in his breast pocket and pulls out a postcard. On it he writes down Mathilde's statement and sends it to the *Simplizissimus.* A couple of days later, the latter promptly sends him twenty marks royalty. In the evening he goes conscientiously into the café to hand over to Mathilde her first royalty for art and science. But on entering how astonished he was! On the sofa beside Mathilde sat Steiner. And he said that Mathilde was a very decent lady who would not tolerate at her table any unsuitable speeches and replies to these wordlessly by pouring the various drinks standing in front of the relevant person over their skull.

⋆

The two following letters from Hartleben to his friend Ellen Birr, both written on the same day, date from that time. (S = Steiner.)

Berlin, 6th of April 1898
Dorotheestr. 30

You really are an idiotic tiger!

I've just been in your lodging here and Frau T . . . told me you were here last Sunday and expecting me. Unheard-of!

You should've written to the pub where I usually sit at the criminals' table on Saturday evening. This pub is called Restaurant at the Old Artists' Den, run by Georg Stallmann, Dorotheenstr 30. I've come here. No letter for me has arrived. So either you wrote to the wrong restaurant, or the letter was withheld by one of my good friends and fellow criminals, because last Saturday I only arrived at the criminals' table later. But why don't you also write or telegraph to S? Just as you can send him stupid telegrams of homage, you can also tell him seriously when you're arriving here. D'you suppose I wouldn't have had the dull bunch shot with pleasure on Saturday evening to be alone with you? In short, you're an old camel and not worth the thrashing you ought to be given.

I've now had no news of you since a week ago Monday, when you also stood me up. I don't know if my birthday letter arrived. S was in Weimar for a few days, so today I didn't hold out any longer and went to Frau T . . .

When are you coming?

Kisses from

Your Erich

⋆

Berlin, 6th of April 1898.

My dear sweety,

I humbly beg forgiveness! You did everything I accused you of neglecting. Please, please, forgive my rudeness.

Since Saturday I've just seen Dr. S again. He wasn't at home on Saturday afternoon when your telegram arrived at his house. He then came to the criminals' table. I arrived later, and he handed me your letter of last Monday! I was deeply cast down and went home, while the others went on drinking. That doesn't often happen with me.

S had forgotten his key, went with W. . . into the café, on Sunday 'arrived home' drunk, didn't even see your telegram lying there (he 'arrived home' at 3 o'clock on Sunday afternoon). Took his proofs under his arm, went into the café, didn't finish with the proofs (Magazin) so on Sunday night travelled to Weimar, where the magazine is printed on Monday, came back from Weimar at quarter to 10 on Monday and on Tuesday morning finally discovered your telegram of Saturday afternoon! A work of art, isn't it?

For me it's just such a shame that a day of happiness for us had to be lost. All Sunday I sat at home and waited for S—or anyway a letter from him. I couldn't understand at all why I heard nothing from you. Don't be angry with me for having written you today that bitterly angry letter. You're more than ever my blood's unrest and I was so dreadfully sad.

Kisses from

Your Erich

Please don't be angry with me, I want to be well-behaved and shan't do it again.

Your Rudolf S

★

Several decades later, in October 1936, the 77-year-old Rosa Mayreder, who at that earlier time had also been contributing articles to the *Magazin für Litteratur*, made the following entry in her diary:

Steiner's autobiography 'Mein Lebensgang', which I've now read, is in its way a significant work. There he sets out his philosophical development as only a comprehensively educated philosopher can do. And yet this presentation makes a shadowy imprint, because it moves only on a spiritual level. He himself finds that private relationships don't belong to the public: 'They are no concern of theirs.' That isn't true. Certainly what a human being thinks shows the nature of his intellect, but how he behaves characterizes his personality. Only through his private relationships does he come humanly close to us.

I've been thinking over whether I weren't under an obligation to communicate these private relationships of Steiner's, so far as I know them. But they throw such an unfavourable light upon him that I can't bring myself to do so. He's become a spiritual leader to many, who find in him security and comfort. Nonetheless I did tell the Rogers something about him . . .

To recover from Steiner's 'Lebensgang', I again took up Goethe's 'Dichtung und Wahrheit'. What a splendid man speaks there out of every line! In the former the pose of an enlightened wise man. In the latter the first wise man, kind, impartial, recalling with smiling superiority his own youthful follies. Perfect humanity and highest tactfulness in communicating 'private relationships', which in Steiner's opinion don't belong to the public.

A Certain Period of Time

On 25 June 1898 the *Magazin für Litteratur* carried an article by Rudolf Steiner entitled 'Willibald Alexis: for the centenary of his birthday on 29 June 1898'.

There are personalities on observing whom we forget everything happening around them. They seem to draw all the power of their existence from themselves. If we want to grasp the character of their deeds, we enquire into the special nature of their minds. That such men live in a temporal period with quite definite cultural conditions we hardly estimate more highly than that they breathe the air of a certain region of the Earth. These persons appear as closed circles, filled with their own content. I do not mean just those leading spirits in world history whom Emerson calls 'representatives of the human race'. Persons whose life passes by without trace for mankind can also be natures erected on themselves alone.

In contrast to these characters there are others, who in everything they do and pursue remind us of their surroundings, of the age they live in, indeed often of the place where they were born. With such men the relation to the world around interests us more than themselves. And when they belong to the past, all individual interest in them ceases; we observe them just as typical representatives of a certain period of time. This is how I am affected by Willibald Alexis (Wilhelm Heinrich Harding).

His works were produced between the third and seventh decade of our century. The world-conception professed by today's most advanced minds was then just coming into being. Within single especially enlightened heads, the ideas were present in which we are currently brought up. But the majority of the educated grew up in a world of notions foreign to our feeling-life. This world of notions foreign to us was living in the art and artistic view of that time. People wanted then an impersonal, objective art. An artist was to create selflessly, divesting himself of his personality. The more he withdrew behind his work, the higher he was appreciated. There was no wish to discover in his creation his subjective peculiarities, but an objective beauty, subjected to eternal laws raised above every personal or private tendency. It may be recalled what Schopenhauer out of the spirit of this view requires from an artist: he should 'completely disregard his interest, his will, his aims, thus for a time wholly divesting himself of his personality, remaining as *purely cognizing subject*, a clear universal eye'. Philosophers otherwise combating each other with greatest vigour were united in this basic idea. Hegel, the man Schopenhauer hated as perhaps no other person, would scarcely have raised any objection to the above sentence. I have heard a supporter of Herbart, who contradicted Schopenhauer and Hegel with the ease so typical of philosophers, Robert Zimmerman, defending the same artistic view. They were all children of their time, the middle third of our century. And Willibald Alexis was an artist of precisely that time.

Alexis was selfless in a way bordering almost on psychological impossibility. One cannot deny one's being more strongly than he did. Karl Julius Schröer in his *Deutsche Dichtung des neunzehnten Jahrhunderts* recounts a conversation he had with the writer. Alexis particularly emphasized his romantic tendency. Among other things he recounted that as a boy he heard a poem which began: 'Hüll' o Sonne, deine Strahlen . . .' The meaning of this poem was unknown to him. But the sound of the words 'Hüll' o' made him blissfully happy. Nonetheless Alexis became a writer who was above all things concerned with *objectively* reproducing *actual* circumstances. Anyone seeking in his works something to indicate the natural disposition characterized by the above words will seek in vain. He attempts to find the meaning of past times, seeks to be objectively faithful, tries to repress his originally romantic trait. Alexis's relation to Walter Scott bears the mark of a total divestment of self. Admittedly Scott's manner too has often been described as romantic. To me this always appears as if black should be called white because it arises when from the latter light is taken away. Indeed even the Grimm brothers' objective absorption in the German past was given the epithet *romantic* because they were inclined to become absorbed in our people's past like the Romantics, and stand in a certain temporal relation to them. What however matters is not burying oneself in past times, but the *tendency* deriving from this burial. With the Romantics, it is to satisfy an inclination towards the mystical and nebulous, corresponding to past history which disappears into unclarity. With the Grimm brothers, it is trying to grasp historical process in a clear and scientifically transparent way. As clarity relates to mysticism, so does Walter Scott relate to Romanticism. Strongly grasping bygone actuality, strictly realistic—thus is Walter Scott. If the born Romantic Willibald Alexis took Scott as a model, this could only happen through a total surrender of personality.

As if he wanted to prove that to us, Alexis published two novels in 1823 and 1827: *Walladmor*, 'freely after the English of Walter Scott', and *Schloss Avalon*, 'freely after the English of Walter Scott'. He so copied the Englishman's manner that the works could be taken for translations. Such things can only happen with a person who surrenders his own being.

Willibald Alexis was thus as if created to give with historical faithfulness an artistic shape to past times, their battles and conquests, their personalities and conditions. In this way he depicts in *Cabanis* German life at the time of the Seven Years' War, in *Roland von Berlin* the struggles between Berlin's urban representatives and the old nobility, in *Falsch Waldemar* circumstances of life in towns and for knights. The same artistic attitude also predominates in his later novels *Die Hosen des Herrn von Bredow, Ruhe ist die erste Bürgerpflicht* and *Isegrimm.*

As his time thought, so did Willibald Alexis think. Only in formative power was he ahead of his contemporaries. That admittedly is a great deal. And yet such figures must not be mistaken for actually productive spirits, who not only give shape to what everyone feels but also have particular feelings.

Stimulating Matter

Besides such longer articles, Rudolf Steiner would often include in the *Magazin für Litteratur* short editorial notices. Here are some examples from 1898:

> Dr. Kurella has just translated a book *Sozialismus in England,* described by English Socialists, edited by Sidney Webb. Anyone wanting to understand socialism in forms as characteristic as appear in England will derive great benefit from this book. Important questions of the times, like for instance unemployment, are discussed by real authorities. Contributors include the writers William Morris, Robert Blatchford, John Burns and others. A wealth of stimulating matter is considered from fruitful standpoints.
>
> ⋆
>
> On the 30th of June took place the death of Professor Dr. Leo, to whom Shakespearean research is much indebted. He was among the co-founders of the German Shakespeare Society, and for a long time editor of the *Shakespeare-Jahrbuch.* Every year a little collection of German Shakespeare researchers would assemble on the 23rd of April in Weimar, so beloved for such purposes. Leo's characteristic head was always to be seen there. He was among the pillars of this Society.
>
> ⋆
>
> The philosopher Robert Zimmerman died on the 1st of September. For over thirty years he taught philosophy at Vienna University. In his views he was an orthodox pupil of Herbart. From the year 1848 onwards he developed this philosopher's teaching in a good number of works. His

favourite field was aesthetics. He wrote a history of this science and presented in a book his own standpoint in this realm.

★

In London on the 3rd of October Virchow delivered the Huxley lecture opening the winter term of the medical school at Charing Cross Hospital. He characterized Huxley as a bold human thinker who drew the consequences from Darwinian teaching and made its viewpoints fruitful for wide realms of research.

★

A book able to arouse interest in widest circles is Landor's *Auf verbotenen Wegen* (F.A. Brockhaus, Leipzig). The author depicts a thoroughly dangerous, instructive and gripping journey through Tibet, supplying his description with everything for which he as painter is specially endowed.

★

In his love-novel *Eifersucht* (Berlin, Schuster & Löffler) Ernst Brausewetter examines an old problem from a new side. He wants to derive jealousy from suspicious feelings of soul which arise as if by themselves, and do not require outer causes like for instance in Shakespeare's *Othello*.

★

The *Deutsche Rundschau* (Gebrüder Paetel, Berlin) contains in its November issue an article by Ernst Haeckel 'On our Present Knowledge of Man's Origin'. In this lecture, given by Germany's most genial scientist at the fourth International Congress of Zoologists in Cambridge, comprehensive light is shed on most important questions of current natural philosophy.

★

A most remarkable new publication is the book by Mary Wollstonecraft *Eine Verteidigung der Rechte der Frau* (E. Piersons Verlag, Dresden and Leipzig), translated into German by P. Bertold. In a special piece of writing a little while ago the Viennese authoress Helene Richter referred in a splendid way to this first woman in 'whom consciousness awoke with an overwhelming clarity, and who also had courage to speak out that women have rights'. (*Deutsche Worte*, Vienna, 1897.)

★

Karl Henckell brings out a new edition of his *Gedichte*. It comprises all his former poetry collections in essentially shorter form and also a new section at the end. Henckell wanted to make a book containing only those of his lyrical creations which can still stand up today to his own criticism.

To this publication of Henckell's may be added a notice that his commendable undertaking *Sonnenblumen* (repeatedly advertised in this weekly) has recently presented examples of poems and short descriptions by the following poets: Joseph Victor von Scheffel, Franz Evers, Marie Eugenie delle Grazie, Algernon Charles Swinburne . . .

★

Chapter XXVII of Steiner's autobiography ended:

> My continual concern for the *Magazin's* survival cast a shadow over all other events in my life at the time. The weekly's circulation could have been increased if material means had been available to me, despite all difficulties. But a journal which can only pay extremely low royalties, gave me almost no material basis for living, and for which nothing could be done to make it better known, could not flourish upon the small circulation with which I had taken it over.
>
> While I was editor, the *Magazin* was a constant source of anxiety to me.

On occasion it must have been a source of anxiety to others as well. In his previously quoted obituary of Steiner, Max Osborn, who was also contributing articles to the *Magazin*, continued:

> . . . After a brief start Steiner sank into a fantastic editorial laziness. One day we all received a strange circular in which the *Magazin's* great mighty lord told us that unfortunately something fatal had occurred. Yesterday night, when he, Steiner, was wanting to light his pipe, the whole desk had gone up in flames. 'Should you, dear sir, still suspect me to be in possession of unanswered letters or unprocessed manuscripts, I am extremely sorry that . . .' No one ever found out what happened during that dreadful night . . .

Shakespeare's Conception of the World

On 30 July 1898, the *Dramaturgische Blätter* carried an extensive article by Rudolf Steiner entitled 'Another Shakespeare Secret'.

> Over and over again I have to ask myself the question: on what does the wide effect of certain Shakespearean plays depend? *Hamlet, Othello, The Merchant of Venice, Romeo and Juliet* make a equally deep impression on those who are educated and those who are not, on those inclined to the classical and those inclined to the modern, on idealists and on rakes. We people of the present feel that we confront this poet from a relatively long past time as though he were living among us today. One only needs by comparison to think of the effect of poetic creations like for instance Goethe's *Iphigenie* and

Tasso, to have the difference appear in complete clarity before one's eyes. As regards temporal changes in the influence of dramatic works of art, I would draw attention to the decreasing enthusiasm in the course of our century for the creations of Schiller. Only plays by Shakespeare seem to force out the same estimate from every level and type of education, and no less from every time.

Anyone wanting to solve the question here touched on must, I believe, go into the fundamental reasons for the effects made by works of art.

This is not in our time easy. The branch of human thought called today aesthetics is dominated by a host of prejudices which prevent our contemporaries from understanding certain basic artistic questions.

In saying this I am thinking above all of certain critics on whom everything in artistic observation which looks like a view of the world or a philosophy acts like a red rag to a bull. It is supposed to be quite immaterial how a poet *thinks* about things which provide the content of his works. Indeed these critics are even of opinion that an artist is the greater, the lesser he thinks at all. People like to call a poet whom they believe not to think at all 'naive', and become enthusiastic for his creations, praising in all kind of tones his fine 'unconsciousness'. They become mistrustful if they notice that a poet has a view of the world which he expresses in his works.

They believe that he loses thereby the naivety and unconsciousness of creativity. Some observers of art go so far as to say that a poet who does not live like a child in a dream-state which dims and conceals the clarity of thoughts is no true poet at all. I have often heard and read that the greatness of Goethe rests on his having not thought about his artistic achievements, that he was living as though in dreams, and first had to have his dreams explained to him by the more conscious Schiller.

What often amazes me is that for the sake of such a prejudice facts are turned on their head. Just in the case of Goethe it can be proven that the entire manner of his artistic creativity derives from a clear and sharply defined conception of the world. Goethe was a man of cognition. He was unable to see anything around him without fashioning a view which could be clearly formulated in concepts. When Duke Karl August called him to Weimar and had him engage in every possible practical activity, the things he had to deal with in practice became for him sources from which he was continually enriching his knowledge of man and the world. His engagement in the mining works at Ilmenau led him to make a thorough study of geological conditions on the Earth's surface and on this basis gain a comprehensive view of the formation of the Earth. Nor could he surrender himself to the joys of Nature like a mere pleasure-seeker. The duke gave him a garden. He was unable just to enjoy flowers and plants, but was soon searching for the fundamental laws of plant-life, a search leading him to the epoch-making ideas set down in his morphological works. These studies, joined to the observation of works of art in Italy, formed in him a view of the world having sharp conceptual outlines, and out of which necessarily flowed his artistic manner.

This conception of the world must be known. One must have permeated with it one's whole mental life if one wants to receive a proper impression of Goethe's works of art. Goethe is—if we still wish to apply a word badly misused by present-day people—a naturalist. He wanted to know Nature in her purity, and reproduce her in his works. Everything which for explanation of Nature had recourse to things not found in Nature herself was contrary to his way of depicting. He rejected any form of transcendental divine forces from the beyond. He does not connect to a God only working from outside and not moving the innermost part of the world. Every kind of revelation and metaphysics was to him an abomination. The deepest secrets of real natural things must themselves be uncovered by anyone turning their gaze impartially towards them. But he was not like our modern factual fanatics who can see merely the surface of things and 'only of course name what can be seen with eyes, grasped with hands, and measured on the scales.' For him, this superficial reality is just one side, Nature's outer side. He wants to see deeper into the works, seeking in Nature a higher nature. He is not content to observe a wealth of plants and bring it into a system. He wants to discover in them an archetypal form, the primal plant lying at the base of them all; which cannot be seen, but must be grasped as an idea. This he does in every field. It is how he also looks at human beings and their mutual relations. The confused bustle of humanity and its manifold characters he tries to derive from some typical basic forms. In his poetry he seeks to embody these forms, these types—not the manifestations of mundane reality. His Iphigenia, his Tasso present a higher human nature in Nature. The possibility of presenting higher natures was given to him because in tireless cognitional work he had come to a particular view, to a clear world of ideas. Only someone having *his* fundamental view can present human beings and their life together in such a way as he did. And only a person who has made Goethe's conception of the world his own can understand this view. From this fact arises the dependence of Goethe's poetic technique on his conception of the world. A factual fanatic works out his figures in such a way that they appear to us like manifestations of day-to-day life. For this he must also apply technical means which make an impression of lower naturality. Goethe must apply different artistic methods. He must draw lines and colours going beyond the surface of things, super-real and yet working on us with a magic possessed by the necessity of natural existence.

I would like to bring forward other examples which make clear the dependence of artistic technique on a conception of the world. Schiller is a supporter of the so-called moral conception of the world. World history is for him world judgement. A person who meets with evil in the world must have a certain guilt, and deserve his destiny. I do not want to claim that Schiller saw the real world as though every guilt were also followed by a proper punishment. But his view was that this is how it should be, and that any other way of linking things together leaves us morally dissatisfied. He therefore constructs his plays in such a way that they mirror the relationships of the world according to this moral demand. So he makes his heroes end tragically, because they have brought guilt onto themselves. That there exists a dramatic connection between destiny and guilt is the basic requirement of his dramatic technique. Mary Stuart, the Maid of Orleans, Wallenstein must be made guilty so that we can be satisfied by their tragic end.

Compare with this the dramatic technique of Henrik Ibsen in his final period. With him there is no further talk of guilt and expiation. That a human being is destroyed has for him causes quite other than moral. His Oswald in *Ghosts* is innocent like a child and is yet destroyed. A person with a moral conception of the world can only be disgusted by this course of things. But Ibsen has no knowledge of a moral conception of the world. All he knows is an amoral nature-connection; a cold necessity devoid of feeling. As a stone cannot help being shattered when falling on hard ground, so an Ibsenian hero cannot help meeting a bad fate.

We can perceive the same fact in the case of Maeterlinck. He believes in fine, psychic, mysterious connections between all phenomena. If two people are talking with each other, he will not only hear the common content of their speech, but will perceive deeper relations, unspoken circumstances. This mysterious unspoken element he tries to work into the things and human beings whom he presents. Indeed, he regards everything external and visible only as a means for indicating what lies deeper, hidden within the soul. His technique results from this endeavour, and thereby from his conception of the world. No one can understand Maeterlinck without being able to sense the intimated deeper essences of things and people whom he brings onto the stage. Every gesture, every movement, every word on the stage expresses the underlying conception of the world.

Anyone aware of these truths will perceive that Goethe, Schiller, Ibsen and Maeterlinck can only work on a particular circle of people, on those who can live themselves into these poets' world-conceptions, can think and feel like them. This is the reason why the influence of these artists necessarily has boundaries.

Why is this different with Shakespeare? Does Shakespeare for instance have no conception of the world? And is his influence so general because it does not flow out of such a conception and thus is also not limited by it?

No one who observes the conditions more thoroughly can admit this. Shakespeare too has a particular view of the world.

For Goethe the world is an expression of typical basic essences; for

Schiller of moral order; for Ibsen of a purely natural order; for Maeterlinck of a psychic, mysterious relation of things. What is it for Shakespeare?

I believe the most fitting word with which to express Shakespeare's conception of the world is by saying: to him the world is a play. By his nature he observes all things for a certain play-acting effect. Whether they mirror typical basic forms, or are morally connected, or express something mysterious, is to him immaterial. He asks the question: what do they have which, when we look at it, gratifies our satisfaction in pure onlooking, in innocent observing? If he finds in one man that the desire for a spectacle will be most gratified by observing what is typical in him, he turns attention onto this typicality. If he believes that innocent observation has its best money's worth by being offered something mysterious, he places it in the foreground. The desire for a spectacle, however, is the most widespread and general desire. Anyone who meets it will have the largest public. A person who directs his gaze onto one thing can also only reckon on approval from people whose basic sensations are similarly directed onto this one thing. Only the fewest people have a mind directed onto a single thing—even if these fewest are precisely the best, those capable of drawing the most from the world. In order to draw from the depths of the world, one has to think and feel intensively. What this however means is not hanging onto every conceivable thing, but rather enjoying one thing from all sides. Depth, however, is not what Shakespeare had his eye on.

Some resonance of every direction of thought and feeling may be found in everyone. Even the most superficial person can sense what is typical, moral, mysterious, or cruelly natural in the world. But all this will not affect him very intensely. He flits over it and soon wants to pass on to another impression. So everything interests him, but little does so continuously. This is the kind of man who desires a spectacle. He wants to be touched by everything, but not wholly involved in anything. Again it may be stated that everyone has something of this desire for a spectacle, even a person who in general surrenders himself totally—even fanatically—to *one* basic impression. The wide effect of Shakespearean drama is connected to this general disposition of human character. By not being one-sided, it works on every side.

I should not like to see my remarks interpreted in such a way that I were wanting to accuse Shakespeare of a certain superficiality. He penetrates into every one-sidedness with a genial sense of feeling, but in no one-sidedness is he himself engaged. He changes himself from one character into another. His whole being is that of an actor, and thus he is also the most effective playwright.

A person with markedly sharp temperament, for whom everything he touches at once gains a particular colour individual to him, cannot be a good playwright. A person to whom single characters are 'common', who

> changes himself into each one with the same devotion, loving all of them equally and none in particular—that is the born playwright. A certain inconsiderateness must belong to a playwright, a sense for all the world. This is what Shakespeare possesses.

One Small Event

On 5 October 1930 the musician Woldemar Sacks published in the journal *Anthroposophie* an article entitled 'A Memory of Rudolf Steiner'.

> It must have been in about 1897 when I was a regular in Berlin in the Nollendorf café-casino in the Kleitstrasse, the breeding-ground of the 'upper stage' and all subsequent cabarets, and at the same time a gathering-point for all the writers and artists. Ernst von Wolzogen, Peter Hille, Arthur Nikisch, Busoni, Oskar Straus, Richard Strauss, Begas and many others would spend their evenings and nights there in the long-past era of the Kaiser, when police hours did not yet exist. So when one had some important conversation, it would simply be: 'All right—about 2 o'clock in the casino. See you then!' These little rendezvous would not happen in the actual café, but in a club room on its own at the back, where met the 'Bohemians', of whom I was the silently voted 'leader', i.e. I wore a turban, acted simultaneously as host and waiter and named my foundation 'The Musicians' Den'. In the front room, situated on the street, used to sit serious newspaper–readers. My den also gradually became a gathering-place for the 'Coming Generation', as was called the society of writers assembled around the journal *Magazin für Litteratur*, edited by Rudolf Steiner.

In Chapter XXIX of his autobiography Steiner recalled this society in respect to the Jewish poet Ludwig Jacobowski (whom he met in 1898):

> He founded a society, 'The Coming Generation', consisting of writers, artists, scientists and artistically interested persons. Meetings were held once a week. Poets presented their poems. Lectures were given on the most varied domains of knowledge and life. The evening would end with an informal gathering. Ludwig Jacobowski was the centre of this ever-expanding circle. Everyone loved this kindly person full of ideas; in this society he even developed a refined and sensitive humour.

Sacks continued his story:

> So it happened that from time to time Steiner, who read the journals in the front room, also came into the back room. Mostly he would soon again disappear.

Now when I was once more sitting with Wolzogen over our beer, and we were debating violently about the forthcoming 'upper stage', Steiner looked in through the door, greeted me and wanted to escape again. But I did not let go and forced him—who for the most part just looked in earnestly—to take a place in our merry circle. He sat there stiff as a rod, speaking not a word, and when no one was paying attention once again disappeared. A few days later he said to the writer Ludwig Jacobowski, then his chief co-worker: 'A nasty person, that Woldemar Sacks!'

When however a few days later we came to be sitting in the reading-room at the same table, a conversation developed which was so engaging and lasted so long that the young bakers were calling out offers for early buns. From then onwards we were united in a friendship lasting several years, but always coming to expression only in the café. Discourse with Rudolf Steiner was incomparably gripping. He appeared to slide from one theme to another, nibbling now here and now there—but only in appearance! These were in reality the radiations from a universal mind. For he mastered many domains of knowledge! Only his form of conversing was aphoristic. Already then there was a tendency towards mysticism, but he never wholly left the ground of reality. Not much was yet to be perceived of purely theosophical thoughts—for the only mission he felt at the time was as a promoter of literature and editor of a journal.

But more than all conversations it was one small event which to me revealed a truly great man. One evening when we were again debating with each other, Peter Hille, an unforgettable poet and eternal Bohemian, sat down at our table and ordered from the waiter a cup of coffee. Since we all knew that Hille never had any money, we were wondering how he would get out of the matter, for in the café there was no 'credit'. Nonetheless on leaving he called out 'Waiter, I want to pay!' The waiter came up and said: 'The coffee is already paid!' Peter Hille said to us movingly: 'Are there angels flying around here? Which of you was it?' Now it was really not me, and Steiner swore black and blue that he was glad to be able to pay *his* coffee. As no one else was present, Peter Hille went away shaking his head.

When in the early morning hours Steiner and I left the café, he said resignedly (at the time he lived outside Berlin): 'I've got to go home today on foot—I haven't enough money for the tram!' Of course I was too 'burned-out' to be able to help Steiner, but offered to accompany him. When we had been going chatting through the night for about half an hour, he suddenly said: 'You see, Saxy, how good it was that I acted as angel for Hille. Would we otherwise have had this beautiful night walk?'

However small this event may be—it epitomizes the great character of this later spiritual representative of mankind.

Artistic Education

On 6 August 1898 Rudolf Steiner published in the *Magazin für Litteratur* an article on 'Artistic Education'.

> A few days ago I had a dream. I dreamt of a leading article in the *Zukunft*. In a discussion about the justifiability of the Farmers' Union, about Stirner, Nietzsche and monarchist sentiment I read quite clearly a sentence on Kant. I did not believe my eyes, but in this sentence stood literally: 'category of the imperative'. I was—in my dream—deeply amazed, for Maximilian Harden doesn't show such ignorance . . .

Harden was editor of the *Zukunft*.

> . . . He did indeed once write a sentence in a leading article of the *Zukunft* showing that he hasn't any proper concept of Kant's 'categorical imperative'. But that he was even writing 'category of the imperative' instead of 'the categorical imperative' made me—even in dream—astonished. I woke up, rubbed my eyes and said to myself: Oh you dreamer, that too came from such annoyance about writing. You get so dreadfully annoyed about all the rubbish daily meeting your eyes from the 'knights of the pen' that the annoyance follows you into your dream. But my dreams exaggerate. It's not true that 'category of the imperative' was ever to be read in a leading article of the *Zukunft*.
>
> My dreams will probably be right. For Alfred, mein Kerr once told me that I didn't want to go deeply into nonsense and complain to my heart's content. It'll probably be the suppressed fury pursuing me in sleep like a nightmare.

Alfred Kerr (pseudonym for Alfred Kempner) was a writer and critic. The pseudonym is similar to the German word *Kerl*, meaning 'bloke', and Steiner often jokingly referred to him as 'Alfred, mein Kerr'.

> I dressed myself, drank coffee, and then had to get something from a shop in the Potsdamer Strasse. For the first time I saw the two sculptural 'works of art' set up on the Potsdam Bridge. A worthy jovial man sits there, with mild features. I could take him for an honest foreman in a factory producing cable rope and electrical apparatus. It's meant to be Werner Siemens, the greatest electrotechnician. Since I hadn't gone out to study the secrets of sculptural art, I passed by, not particularly dissatisfied by not having found them. The memorial was done by C. Moser.
>
> I reached the other end of the bridge. Another man is sitting there. A schoolmaster, considering how to introduce children to the ABC. And yet no—it's meant to be Hermann Helmholtz. I always thought that along with a person's outer features a sculptural artist should transmit to posterity their

significance. In the case of Helmholtz this doesn't seem to me so terribly difficult. By immersing oneself in his writings one will acquire a sharply defined idea of that man's personality. By comparing this idea with the features of his face one will recognize the harmony of bodily and spiritual physiognomy which in him was so striking. Helmholtz indeed also wrote down reminiscences of his life. In every line anyone who ever saw him will think of the scientist's outer appearance. In no feature does the man sculpted by Max Klein and meant to adorn one end of the Potsdam Bridge recall the writer of those reminiscences.

But there's still more. Hermann Helmholtz is as few other researchers a type within a certain scientific tendency of the present. He isn't a genius like his great teacher Johannes Müller. He didn't give the first impulse to the discoveries and inventions associated with his name. Anyone who doesn't believe what I'm saying here may read about it in the above-mentioned reminiscences. With great perspicacity and untiring work he drew the consequences from his predecessors' achievements. Above many other things I would like to stress the invention of the ophthalmoscope. When Helmholtz embarked on the researches which led him to this invention, the work accomplished by his predecessors was so far advanced that it needed a mere trifle to construct the important instrument, a final step on a precisely demarcated path. And so too in other domains where Helmholtz was at work. He lived at a time which was ripe for quite particular scientific inventions, as preliminary work for them was there in superabundant fullness. That time required exact scientific workers, implementing in detail the scientific ideas of a previous time through astute laboratory work and tireless experimentation. In the first half of the century Johannes Müller, Purkinje and others provided leading ideas. From the viewpoints handed down Helmholtz, Brücke, Ludwig and Du Bois-Reymond arrived at epoch-making individual discoveries. Perspicacity for details of Nature's work, for experimental research and for tireless observation are characteristics of the type of scientist presented by Helmholtz. If one wants to make this type clear through its opposite, one need only recall Ernst Haeckel. He's quite different from those belonging to the named group. He too drew the consequences from a great predecessor. But he not only went in detail further than Charles Darwin. He put up an edifice for which his predecessor supplied the foundation; Helmholtz and the other named persons provided fittings for a completed, but nonetheless internally still vacant building. This typical significance in Helmholtz should be illustrated by the pictorial presentation of his figure.

But in order to do that, the artist allotted such a task would have had to study the scientific peculiarity and significance of Helmholtz from his works. I am so naive as to believe that every artist does this before presenting a man pictorially. However, the Helmholtz Memorial on the Potsdam Bridge in Berlin has convinced me of the contrary.

Books were lying at the scientist's feet, on top a book on whose spine stood—Oh physicist, quickly avert your eyes, before they are too offended—'Die Physiologie der Optik'. The sculptor has thus not even got as far as the title-page—indeed not even as far as the spine of a bound copy—of Helmholtz's *Physiologischer Optik.*

What my dream about a writer only led me to believe has been turned by a sculptor into reality. Saying 'Die Physiologie der Optik' instead of 'Physiologische Optik' is just as if one would say 'category of the imperative' instead of 'categorical imperative'. But that kind of thing isn't even done by the composer of a leading article. We writers are indeed better people.

But 'Die Physiologie der Optik' isn't the only thing characterizing in loud shrieks the 'education' of a sculptural artist. Below this 'Physiologie der Optik' lies yet another book. It's about four centimetres thick. On its spine stands 'Die Erhaltung der Kraft'. Now on this concept dominating modern physics Helmholtz wrote an essay of only a few pages. Herr Max Klein didn't indeed honour with a single glance Helmholtz's existent works, but instead saw in his mind a non-existent one.

Scholars of Berlin newspapers have reprimanded the sin against the spirit of all education; and thus—one of the mistakes has been made good. I don't know if the words read on the Helmholtz Memorial to the annoyance of educated passers-by were changed into their correct reading during sleepy night-time in order to conceal the shame. Today anyway we read the corrected 'Die Physiologische Optik'. By contrast, a well-meaning corrector will still have to make another effort for the second 'inadvertence'. This second book can't be made thinner; but one can ask better newspaper-readers, who'll advise setting on this work 'Tonempfindungen', for better newspaper readers know that Helmholtz wrote a *Lehre von den Tonempfindungen.*

To anyone calling me a petty carper for writing this, I retort that it's basically all the same to me what stands on the memorials of the Potsdam Bridge, but the matter appears to me a distressing symptom. How must it be with the 'education' of scupltural artists to whom such 'inadvertence' occurs? And what picture can an artist transmit to posterity of a man he knows in the way the creator of the Helmholtz Memorial knows his writings?

One may just listen to them, sculptural artists, making fun of omissions about their works made by writers. A writer going over the Potsdam Bridge in Berlin may be comforted that scarcely a 'writer' will write similar nonsense about a 'sculptor' as a 'sculptor' has here sculpted about a 'writer'. Yes, yes, we writers are indeed better human beings, and to none of us can it occur, with whatever fundamental ignorance of Kant's philosophical views, instead of 'categorical imperative' to write 'category of the imperative'. Something like that can only happen to us in a bad, nasty dream.

Empty Phrases

In the following month, on 3 September, the *Magazin für Litteratur* carried an article by Rudolf Steiner 'On the Psychology of Empty Phrases'.

> Anyone wanting to undertake an exhaustive description of the power of catchwords would certainly be setting himself a big task. There must be little in the world working so suggestively as catchwords, and the effects of which are so mysterious. The main thing is that a catchword is on every mouth, that everyone utters it importantly, thinking of nothing thereby, and that everyone also importantly listens to it, again without thereby thinking of the least thing. Both speaker and listener must only be convinced that something significant is meant. At the same time anyone undertaking to ask after a catchword's meaning must be considered stupid. For such a person would destroy the catchword's effect. He has to destroy it. For of course the catchword has a meaning. Simply because every word has a meaning on the lips of whoever uses it first in a certain context. But the effect does not depend on this meaning. It depends on something having nothing to do with the meaning.
>
> A sensible politician uses a word. Within the exposition he gives, it has its proper meaning and is fully justified. It then happens that in the country the politician belongs to we meet this word for a certain time in all political remarks. When used by the first sensible politician, it had a stirring effect, having light shed on it by the meaning of the remaining expositions. But countless others using it do not think of this meaning at all. Bismarck delivers a remarkable speech, a speech which is a political deed. He says in this speech: 'We Germans fear God, but nothing else in the world.' Within his speech these words have a meaning. But they work on as catchwords. In countless speeches they can now be heard. But a prize may well be offered for a reasonable interpretation of the words in these countless speeches. And yet most of these speeches will owe their effect to the circumstance that the speaker used the words.
>
> One may well assert that a word must first lose its meaning if it is to become a catchword. For the multitudes love nothing so much as words; and there is nothing on which they are less keen than on understanding the meaning of words. Man's speech-instruments are ensouled by a tremendous urge for activity, while thought-instruments are the most sluggish organs which an organism possesses. Human beings want to say a very great deal

and to think very little. So there must be as many catchwords and empty phrases as possible, by which one feels a rigid effect without having to think about anything.

Anyone who understands how to observe people's facial expressions will often see the following. Two persons are conversing. They seek to reach understanding in a meaningful way. This goes on for some time. For one of them, understanding suddenly becomes too boring. A catchword occurs to him by which he can end the conversation. Both faces now express the satisfaction they feel from having to speak about the matter no further. The catchword, which has no meaning, brings a long and perhaps not at all meaningless conversation to an end.

The addiction to bring up quotations for statements has a distant similarity to the tendency to work through catchwords. Where quotations are used they mostly lose all meaning, being torn out of their original context.

We meet quotations everywhere. On banners, on memorials, over the entrances to houses, in family albums, in leading articles, on pipe-ends, walking-sticks and so forth. The sight of such a quotation requires us every time to forget the meaning it originally had.

With all this I do not wish to have said anything against catchwords and the use of quotations. For the wittiest turns of phrase in speeches are sometimes achieved by using a quotation in a way which contradicts its original meaning. And yet a collection of observations on how catchwords work would be instructive. By writing this chapter of popular psychology, one could hit two flies with one stroke. For one would also have written a good deal of another chapter of soul-doctrine called 'the thoughtlessness of the multitudes'. How multitudes seek to avoid thinking is best seen precisely in the use of catchwords.

There are journalists who build their whole existence on this characteristic of the multitudes. They write—say every week—an article containing some word suitable for being repeated eight days in succession. For eight days on end readers then have a means for talking about something without activating their thoughts. A whole week long they adduce at every opportunity the latest expression of journalist X. Many journalists can only attain great success because they possess the art of forming words which have beside their meaning also something else by which they work suggestively—by which they work when they discard their meaning. A psychologist of empty phrases will have to investigate what this 'something' is which remains over when meaning is distilled out of a word, and which then has the magic potency of raising the meaningless word to a power ruling over human beings.

This psychology of empty phrases will be an important contribution to herd psychology.

A Theatrical Event of the First Order

In the same issue of the *Magazin für Litteratur* Rudolf Steiner also included this brief notice:

> On the 1st of September the Lessing Theatre brought us a first production by the new director Otto Neumann-Hofer. The performance was of Shakespeare's *King Henry V*. It was a theatrical event of the first order, and I shall return to it in the next issue. At the moment I would just like to say how creditable it was of the new director Otto Neumann-Hofer to produce this interesting work by Shakespeare, which has not been given in Berlin for a long time, and that the presentation was a theatrical achievement of an exemplary kind. A remarkable contribution to solving the question: how should Shakespeare be brought onto the stage today?

The next issue, on 10 September, contained a whole article by Steiner about *King Henry V*:

> In his book *William Shakespeare* Georg Brandes states that *Henry V*, though not among the best, is among the most lovable of Shakespeare's plays. To agree with this judgement one only need observe how Shakespeare portrayed the drama's protagonist. From the second sentence this king speaks he already starts gaining our sympathy, and we feel we shall be following him in both pain and joy. If he develops before us as a great man, we shall take pleasure that an attractive personality is great. If he collapses from his own incapacity, he will gain our pity but not lose our love. While crown prince he was no ascetic. But he takes leave at once from flippant goings-on, and when the crown bedecks his head makes a ruler's strict obligation into his goddess. The poet compels us to love this man, for he loved him himself. He shows us unmistakably what he wanted to say: a real king speaks like this one, is a man like all others, the sky looks to him just as it looks to everyone else, and his senses are subject to general human conditions:
>
>> '. . . his ceremonies laid by, in his nakedness he appears but a man; and though his affections are higher mounted than ours, yet when they stoop they stoop with the like wing.'
>>
>> (Act IV, 1.)
>
> This is how the king appears, when we look into his heart. Nor is he any less significant if we consider his understanding. The Archbishop of Canterbury says of him:
>
>> Hear him but reason in divinity
>> And, all-admiring, with an inward wish

You would desire the King were made a prelate.
Hear him debate of commonwealth affairs
You would say it hath been all in all his study.
List his discourse of war, and you shall hear
A fearful battle rendered you in music.
Turn him to any cause of policy,
The Gordian knot of it he will unloose,
Familiar as his garter, that when he speaks,
The air, a chartered libertine, is still . . .

(Act I, 1.)

I believe Shakespeare wanted to portray in Henry a king of whom he could say: this is what a head of state should be like under whom I am glad to be an English underling.

The play's events are pure history, sweeping along from scene to scene without dramatic tension or inner propelling power. In dialogue form it recounts how Henry sets out to win the throne of France, and after many military adventures achieves his aim and also brings home the French king's daughter. All of this amply interspersed by scenes revealing in the finest way Shakespeare's gift of depicting human beings and presenting the character of whole classes of people. We still enjoy listening when persons like the Welshman Fluellen tell us of things which have nothing to do with the progress of the plot. For a moment we become aware that what we see before us are merely scenes strung together. But if—against all habit—we become so gripped, we abandon all prejudices about the play.

In another sense too Shakespeare shows himself in this play as a lovable poet. The modesty with which he makes his 'chorus' speak about the relation between life, action and poetry is a remarkable feature for the most influential poet there has ever been. The chorus speaks to the audience:

. . . But pardon, gentles all,
The flat unraised spirits that hath dared
On this unworthy scaffold to bring forth
So great an object.

(Prologue.)

and

. . . that mean and gentle all
Behold, as may unworthiness define,
A little touch of Harry in the night.
And so our scene must to the battle fly,
Where—oh for pity!—we shall much disgrace
With four or five most vile and ragged foils
Right ill-disposed in brawl ridiculous

> The name of Agincourt. Yet sit and see
> Minding true things by what their mockeries be.
>
> (Act IV, 1.)

> Great wisdom lies in such sentences. A great art is allocated the right place in comparison to life. Only too often does a meagre art desire to be upraised at the cost of life, and be allocated a place it does not deserve.
>
> *Henry V* is a play from which we come to know Shakespeare the man in his whole lovable greatness. In it he stated what he, as an Englishman, wants to have for a king, and also told us what he thought about the relationship of his art to life.
>
> The play cannot of course be performed today in the Shakespearean manner handed down. On the 1st of September the Lessing Theatre gave a performance which accords to every demand of modern theatrical art. Artistic pedants have naturally a great deal in this presentation to find fault with. One does not even have to be an artistic pedant and may still confess to the opinion that we can already tolerate again more Shakespeare than Dingelstedt allowed . . .

Franz Freiherr von Dingelstedt (who had died in 1881) was a Viennese theatrical manager.

> . . . To the theatrical director I should like to say: 'Via Dingelstedt back to Shakespeare!' And above all things: 'Why such monologues as are held by the insignificant boy serving Nym, Bardolph and Pistol?'
>
> Let critics behave however badly! Some are praising it; others writing that they cannot distinguish Shakespeare's Henry from Wildenbruch's, because on the 1st of September in the Lessing Theatre they held their eyes closed and their hands over their ears. After reading the criticisms by one of these brutes covering his ears, I was just laughing. I have every respect for the gentlemen who brought about the performance on the 1st of September. It is not easy to bungle good Shakespeare to such an extent that one needs to cover one's ears.

Different Opinions

Rudolf Steiner's question in the *Magazin für Litteratur* as to the reason for such monologues as are given in Shakespeare's *Henry V* by the insignificant boy serving Nym, Bardolph and Pistol may have been connected to an article 'About the Monologue in Drama' published by someone under the name or probably pseudonym of Fritz Selten which opened the same week's issue of the *Dramaturgische Blätter*. The same week's issue published 'A Letter to the Editor':

Dear Sir,

Allow me briefly to go into your interesting article 'Another Shakespeare Secret' in No. 30 of the *Magazin für Litteratur*, of which unfortunately I have only recently obtained sight. I am surprised and pleased by the train of thought contained there: that it is nonsense to suppose a poet might without a firm, quite definite conception of real things (view of the world) make a work of art, or even that a work of art be so much better the more 'misty' be the thought-world of the creating person. You even go so far as to say of Goethe: 'These—scientific—studies, joined to the observation of works of art in Italy, formed in him a view of the world having sharp conceptual outlines, and out of which necessarily flowed his artistic manner.' From this one might make an inference you certainly do not intend, as though Goethe's 'artistic manner' had even been secondary—not as it were demanding.

You show very aptly the extent to which definite, in part questionable ideational prejudices or philosophical thought-forms have influenced the writings of Schiller, Ibsen and Maeterlinck. But you then come to a conclusion about Shakespeare which is for me quite inconceivable, namely that Shakespeare's view of the world determined that he always chose for his poetical presentation that subject and that form most suited to bring about 'satisfaction in pure onlooking, in innocent observing.' This however, so you conclude, is a special characteristic of an actor, and so—'His whole being is that of an actor, and thus he is also the most effective playwright.'

One of the most significant readers of Shakespeare, one who drew most nourishment from Shakespeare's 'view of the world', was no less than—Bismarck. If we observe that precisely Shakespeare's 'effect' goes through the centuries without the least diminution, we must in my opinion make clear to ourselves the manner of his effect by such examples as Bismarck. Bismarck did not go much to the theatre, but presumably he sensed the 'dramatic effect' of Shakespeare in its quite 'elementary' manner. What Shakespeare emphasizes seemed also to him worth stressing; as the poet sheds light on things, so also did he see them. The world in its aesthetic effect was for him as for Shakespeare the great lever of zest in life and strength for deeds.

We may now also suppose that Shakespeare did not make an effect on others into the yardstick of his composition; we must then believe the same effect comes in general onto us from a work of art through which the poet in the rapture of his activity wanted to work onto himself.

But was the thing he wanted, which has kept its power down the centuries, the capacity of his plays to call forth 'our satisfaction in pure onlooking, in innocent observing'? I rather believe such 'pure onlooking', such 'innocent observing', which also creates satisfaction, does not exist at all. Pleasure in looking on, the aesthetic enjoyment reposes on the great suggestion which is aroused in us, and unleashes a storm of forces within us through the aroused desire to imitate, even calls forth and creates new powers for activity.

You speak of 'a certain inconsiderateness' in Shakespeare the playwright, to whom his characters are morally 'common', of his 'sense for all the world'—; by comparison I would like to recall such things as his distinctive patriotism, for a kind of squirelike vassal's loyalty, his predilection for human beings of mental and corporeal fullness, for such as have a definite way of thinking, his endeavour always to contrast what is passionately alive with what is dying away and feeling it, his pleasure in lashing out and slaughtering, in a kind of religious subjection under the power of facts. All this in my opinion stands in sharpest contrast to the virtues of the degenerate actor whom you depict; for we may not forget that a modern actor with few exceptions presents his type only in the most degenerate form.

But I shall not go into the psychology of the actor, especially of the actor from Shakespeare's time; I grant you that for an actor nothing so much suggests itself as exploiting the sentimental effect. Nothing by contrast lies, I think, farther from him than the chief ability of a playwright, who as you—not quite to my taste—say, 'changes himself into each character with the same devotion'. I would rather say: 'who is in a position always to put himself at the same time into a number of different characters, in so far as something be found in his own personality uniting and yet individually colouring them all.'—For an actor this would be death. He can certainly on different evenings richly endow different characters according to an inner principle, each time living in a quite different world. Feeling two at the same time is for him completely impossible, except according to the 'Scheme F' applied in rehearsals, with the four temperaments etc., which indeed we know well enough.

I rather believe that Shakespeare's eternally living effect on striving peoples, his privilege of even being loved by such 'heroes' as was Bismarck, his ability to choose with a sure quick hand from the thousand possibilities of dramatic effects containing in themselves that 'enjoyment in onlooking' those which release suggestion into power for deeds—that all this does not indicate as the originator a 'man of semblance', an actor, but rather a man of deeds, an author chained with the most personal interests to all the details of the public and political life of his time.

You would be obliging me by printing these observations in the Mag. f. Lit., and I would be eager to know how you would try to contradict them.

Your devoted

H. Häfker

Rudolf Steiner added a 'Note to the Foregoing':

The editor of a literary journal, I am convinced, is duty bound to allow different opinions on a matter to be recognized. So I have willingly brought into print the foregoing remarks. But I am not of opinion that very much is gained when the author of one opinion contradicts that of another, the latter then again answers him back and so on. The kind of views I have brought forward derive from quite definite premises, from feelings I have gained in course of life by contemplating Shakespeare. Herr Häfker starts out from other feelings. I do not believe we can convince each other. Still less do I believe that a reader can be won over to either view by bringing forward new remarks. A person who looks at things like I do will declare himself for my opinion; a person who starts from Herr Häfker's premises will agree with him. One can just put forward one's own views. Whether agreement be found or not depends on many things which cannot be changed by bringing forward conclusions, deductions, contradictions and so forth. I would therefore like to refrain from adding anything further to my remarks.

Fine Pliers

This gave rise a fortnight later, on 24 September, to another article by the poet Rainer Maria Rilke on 'The Value of the Monologue':

> In these pages the question recently arose: are monologues acceptable in modern drama or not? Monologues acquired a right.
>
> It is perhaps worthwhile to consider for once not so much the monologue as rather the occasion when it necessarily appears.
>
> A monologue occurs at a moment of indecision or helplessness of the person concerned, as it were on the eve of an action, and has the duty of unveiling the man's innermost conflicts, his soul with its doubt and anger, yearning and hope. For in dialogue there is no room for this, and yet it must happen somewhere, as everyone perceives. And what wonderful device can shed light on the most secret depths, where decisions have their root? Remarkably: the word. The very same word which in dialogue proves unusable for grasping finality gains access to all truth as soon as it becomes directed to no further person. One whom we know cannot oversee an outer situation portrays to us at the moment of his conflict the wonderful order of his soul so convincingly that the portrayal, and not some later deed, becomes the main thing in the play; i.e. the epic moment henceforth signifies more than the action. In it lies the decision, the turn, the progress.
>
> And this is perfectly justified, if a monologue is otherwise really capable of disclosing those mysterious twilights in which all decisions are still like clear little springs. But we shall have for once to cease overestimating '*the word*'.

We shall come to perceive that it is only one among many bridges connecting the island of our soul with the great continent of common life—perhaps the widest, but by no means the finest. A feeling will arise that we can never in words be wholly sincere, as they are much too rough pliers, quite unable to touch the tenderest wheels in the great work without immediately crushing them. We will thus give up expecting information about the soul from words, since we do not like going to school with our servant in order to recognize God.

Maybe we shall perceive this sooner in drama than in life. For a play is more concentrated, more surveyable, a kind of experiment where life's elements unite in little tasting-glasses, in similar proportions as they behave outside in their rich immeasurability. Within the limits of the setting presented by a stage, everything appears to have space. No deed is too great for it, no word too significant.

But there are mightier things than deeds and words. In the end the latter are only that by which we share everyday life in common, ladders reaching from our window to the neighbour's house. We would scarcely have needed them had we remained solitary, each person on a star, and indeed have no need of them in moments when we do feel so solitary. Then we are full of a gentler experience, as homecomers into a land with sacred, secret usages, creative in all inactivity and outgrown from words. Certainly our actual life is of such a kind, remaining like a fine accompaniment over our action and repose, and leading and determining us in our final decisions.

To create *for this life* space and rights (and on the stage that means expression) seems to me the predominant task of modern drama—and this latter the monologue with its naive crudity strikes in the very face. It forces what is above things into the things, forgetful that scent only in fact exists because it is freed from the rose and willing to all winds.

If anyone asks what should step into its place, I assert that it leaves no gap in drama at all. The deeper life it is called upon to illuminate must always develop just as containedly and uninterruptedly as the 'outer action' of which it is finally the cause. When this juxtaposing of two actions really comes to effect, no more delays are needed through retrospective epic portrayal of a momentary soul-condition. There is no more need of vistas into the background.

Admittedly, how this should be attained none of the 'moderns' has shown. They all miss the monologue, leave it out instead of making it superfluous; it is then of course lacking, and one knows 'where it should come'. The actor becomes restless, smokes, drums on the window-panes, seems to have a very bad conscience and to beg forgiveness for his taciturnity. That however is no progress.

But one who recognized the power of this gentle experience, more clearly and consciously than those before him, Maeterlinck, stands towards his revelations too much as a priest than as an artist. He seems one-sided in striving to do everything to the glory of the god who fills him and lifts him up.

His figures have lost gravity. They are like stars shrouded in gleaming solitude, meeting each other high in the night. They can only pass each other by, and none can stop the other. They are scents, but the garden they rise from is not seen. This makes the life whose herald Maeterlinck became seem foreign, and his mysticism vanishes more deeply and riddlingly behind the things, which to him are not so bodily and opaque as to us. The genial Belgian's plays seem to me—taking a technical expression from the art of etching—the 'first state' of a new dramatic picture which must still be perfected through other sheets.

So the path goes on beyond Maeterlinck, and will have roughly this purpose: one must learn not to fill out a whole stage with words and gestures, but to leave a little space above them, as if the figures one created ought still to grow. I am convinced that the rest will come by itself: a gentler life will spread over like a warmth, like a radiance, and stay calm and bright above everything, above words and above processes; it must just be given space.

But the question still remains open how this should happen. And yet it can only be answered until someone has come across it—spontaneously.

Until then the monologue has rights. It is like a fine precious curtain (at best) hung in front of wide clear perspectives. One can also take pleasure in a curtain. The poets, actors and public of yesterday find themselves sure in the knowledge of its beauty and of its value.

What lies behind is for those who have already progressed further.

Rudolf Steiner added some editorial 'Remarks':

Viewed from an editor's standpoint, adding observations to particular articles in a journal appears almost like schoolmastering transferred onto another domain. But I cannot help it when after reading the article on 'The Value of the Monologue' something occurs to me which seems worth mentioning. For it seems to me that there was an artist who subscribed to Rilke's words: 'But there are mightier things than deeds and words.' 'To create for this life space and rights seems to me to be the predominant task of modern drama.'—This artist is Richard Wagner. He tried to solve in a quite definite way the problem Rilke poses. He held that what is not in this life expressible in words must be sought by the language of music. The author of the above article, by contrast, leaves the question he raises unanswered. But I also believe he underestimates the word's expressive capacity. Basically a word lets even more be sensed than it brings clearly and plainly to expression. If one holds to this deeper meaning of a word, attainable by sensing, the word can then—in my opinion—indicate even the soul's most hidden depths. Words must not be accused if most people do not take them deeply enough. In themselves they are not actually rough pliers, but fine pliers, mostly employed by rough hands. Rilke seems to me to be one of those critics of the word who attribute to words what actually is lacking to the—ears of listeners.

In a further issue Rilke published a letter to the editor:

Herr Doktor,

Your observations on 'The Value of the Monologue' are striking. They preoccupy me. Allow me a couple of further words on the matter.

It appears indeed as if I had done the 'word' terrible injustice. Do not forget that I was not thinking of that solitary word, in which great past times live wrapped up among us like contemporaries. I was observing the word of intercourse, the little, daily, mobile one, which works in life or seems to work, and therefore even on the stage hinders and promotes the development of events. This is the word I think about when asserting that in it the soul has no space. Indeed it almost seems to me as if words of such kind were like walls in front of men, and a false lost race were slowly wasting away in their heavy shadows. Think of a child which knows itself to be guilty of an offence. Will it be silent? Unquestioned it will place before its little, frightened, freezing soul many, many lofty words, to hide its shame. And the final confession is a stream of tears. Observe two persons, each deep in thought, meeting on a solitary walk. How quickly do they with ready words cover and protect their naked soul, which still for a time hesitates in their eyes. Consider lovers, who in days of discovery press away from one another with words, before recognizing each other in the first silence. Let every person ask himself whether words stand at the high points of his life. Is it not rather with words as with vegetation, which behind the great magnificence in a valley becomes ever more earnest, simple and solemn the higher one climbs, until there remains the timid dwarfwood, not daring to step onto pure splendid ferns?

Every word is a question, and even more so what is felt as the answer. In this regard your observation is correct that words, unable to give revelations, let much be sensed. So it's up to every person to feel a word widely or narrowly, richly or miserably; which is good. 'Du gleichst dem Geist, den du begreifst.'

But on the stage, is something or—let us at once say—what matters, namely the standard effect, thereby attained for a crowd with many aptitudes?—And then with 'sensing' in general: was it not a poor, abandoned world which God *sensed* behind things? Was that not an idle God, a God with hands in lap, who was so modest as to let himself be sensed? Is it not rather finding him, recognizing him, as if surprising him in the workshop creating deeply within himself, in order to possess him?

So I too believe we should not be content with sensing what is behind words. It must sometime be revealed to us. Indeed, who does not recall the moments when quite poor, outworn words met him from beloved lips as if never touched, for the first time, radiant with youth? Someone says: 'light'; and it is as though he were to have said: 'ten thousand suns'. He says: 'day' and you hear 'eternity'. And all at once you know his soul has spoken. Not from him, not through the one little word which tomorrow you will already have forgotten, but through the light, perhaps through the sound, through the landscape. For when a soul speaks, it is in everything. It awakens all things, gives them voices; and what it confesses is always a complete song.

With this I have also betrayed the question and inconclusiveness I left in the previous article. In the broadest sense I desire space for things on stage over and beside the words. For being 'realistic', a stage has for me not one (a fourth) wall too few, but rather three walls too many. I desire space for everything which takes a part in our days, from childhood onwards touching us and determining us. It has just as much share in us as words. As if in a list of characters were to stand a cupboard, a glass, a sound, and much finer and gentler things too. In life all has the same value, and a thing is no worse than a word or a scent or a dream. Little by little this rightfulness must also become law on the stage.

Maybe life for a while carries on in words like a river in a bed. Where it becomes free and strong, it spreads out over everything; and none can perceive its banks.

I leave it to your discretion, Herr Doktor, whether you use something from these remarks for your paper. Anyway I thank you for the stimulus your note imparted to me, and hold myself duty-bound herewith to present you its fruit.

In special esteem,

Your wholly devoted

Rainer Maria Rilke

A Nice Task

In Chapter XXVIII of his autobiography, Rudolf Steiner recalled:

> During this difficult time in my life, the Vorstand of the Workers' Training College approached me with the request that I would teach history and speaking exercises in the College.

In the book *Errinerungen an Rudolf Steiner und seiner Wirksamkeit an der Arbeiter-Bildungsschule in Berlin* (1979), Alwin Alfred Rudolph narrates how he was among the bearers of this request:

On the third floor we found the doorplate: Dr. Rudolf Steiner. We bravely pressed the bell. The door was opened by a young slim lady in a dark dress. A large bright space received us, at the same time living-room and work-room. A wide sofa, padded chairs, not at all in the latest fashion. Books on the walls, many books, some pictures, at the window a desk of enormous extent, laden to excess with papers and books. Dr. Steiner was standing in the middle of the room, highly erect in majestic slenderness, straight and gaunt, dressed in black, with a small black moustache on his upper lip, which was uncut and had grown thin like himself, pince-nez before his eyes, long black hair laid smoothly backwards, around his collar on the breast a long wide bow tie ... His greeting was most friendly. A beneficent atmosphere held sway in the room and we felt at once like good acquaintances, without shyness and without reserve or diffidence. An older lady in the room was introduced to us, but we remained unsure who she was. The one who had opened the door to us was this lady's daughter...

Like a beloved visit, without being asked for our wishes ... we were pressed towards the large table, upon which the coffee-machine soon did its job. The daughter brought in crockery for the coffee. The lady brought a large plate with biscuits. Dr. Steiner took it and offered it to us, we had first to strengthen ourselves...

It was a coffee break just as rare as delightful, for us young lads vastly removed from the usual way of life... We told about ourselves, the family we came from, what we were doing, where we lived, what we had so far read and seen on the stage...

The coffee table was cleared away... Now came our business. The chatting had hitherto left no time for it. The lady assured us that this was no cause for worry, such kind of things were not discussed at table...

We told about the Workers' Training College, its foundation, development, activity, composition, the age and profession of those taking part. We were asked about the intentions and expectations of the audience...

We had to name the previous teachers to Dr. Steiner. He knew them all. If not personally, nonetheless their particular attitude and activity, their hitherto published writings, their significance. Nor did he hold back with recognition or rejection...

And then he held out his hand, completely unexpectedly. We drew back, for we thought we had not achieved anything. But he then said we should return very soon, just as if all was arranged. We should come and tell him what we wanted to hear, and he could imagine he would be taking on a nice task.

Lack of Courage

Chapter XXX of Rudolf Steiner's autobiography includes the following short paragraph:

In the first issue of the *Magazin* for the year 1899 may be found an article by myself with the title 'New Year Reflection by a Heretic'. What is meant here is not heresy against any religious confession, but against the cultural orientation taken by the time.

Steiner went on to quote several passages. The complete article reads as follows:

Recent years have brought us a good number of reflections on the cultural achievements of the expiring century. In the two years of this century we still have to live through, these reflections will in all probability immensely accumulate. Minds who like to emphasize ever anew the self-evident may object that the end of a century is a purely incidental point in the developmental course of mankind, and by another way of reckoning time this point might coincide with a quite different phase of development. Such an objection cannot prevail against the suggestive effect which derives from the century appearing as a numerical totality.

Apart from this general reason, there is at the turn of the present century also a particular reason for glancing at the achievements of our culture and the directions it is currently taking.

On observing these things, what strikes one immediately is the vast wealth of new circumstances for mastering natural forces, and the related progress in practical forms of life. Anyone wishing to invigorate this thought in an all-rounded way would have to pass in review a series of vastly influential inventions, from the railway and steamship to the telephone.

It is no different with the new conditions, created for widening our knowledge of the world. What insights into Nature are provided by spectral analysis, Röntgen's discoveries, studies on the age of the human race, the organic theory of evolution and other matters! Here of course I am not going into them, being only concerned with indicating these things.

But despite all these and various other achievements—for instance in the sphere of art—a person who looks more deeply cannot at present be very happy about the formative content of our time. Our highest spiritual needs yearn for something which the time only sparingly gives.

In Goethe's sense one can say of education that it should lead through the purest culture to the loftiest happiness. Our education does not lead towards this happiness.—It leaves the finest minds in the lurch when trying to satisfy the most intimate needs of their feeling-life. In this respect the end of the century provides a different vista from its beginning. One may recall how a hundred years ago Fichte inflamed people's minds by seeking to bring the totality of education at the time into harmony with the innermost needs of the human spirit. Schelling and Hegel deepened the knowledge of outer things. And how the voices of these spirits were heard!

Around the middle of the century a complete change took place.

Knowledge of external things which were storming without number onto mankind seemed to force totally into the background a capacity to gain insight into the human soul, and to seek for harmony between the outer and inner world.

The change is given really paradoxical expression by the low regard currently enjoyed by philosophy and its bearers. How may one compare such disparagement with Nietzsche's view that the Greek nation stands so high because it places as human ideals not prophets, like other nations do, but its seven *wise men*?

There is no cause for surprise if among these phenomena minds with deeper spiritual needs find the proud thought-edifice of scholasticism more satisfying than the ideational content of our own time. Otto Willmann has written an outstanding book, his *Geschichte des Idealismus* (Braunschweig 1894–97) where he puts himself forward as the eulogist of past centuries. It must be admitted that man's spirit longs for that proud comprehensive illumination of thoughts which human knowledge experienced in the philosophical systems of the scholastics. The spirit will be ever more dissatisfied by confessions like that made a few years ago by the great physicist Hermann Helmholtz in his speech at Weimar about Goethe. He said that in regard to the wealth of our present knowledge it is hardly possible for a comprehensive spirit to appear which would span the totality of this knowledge with a uniform circle of ideas.

The yearning of the human soul to integrate all knowledge into a complete conception able to satisfy the highest spiritual needs faces in our time a *lack of courage* in our thinking, which does not allow such a total conception to be attained.

This lack of courage is a characteristic feature of spiritual life at the turn of the century. It clouds our joy in the achievements of most recent times.

Wherever someone appears who tries to devise a complete picture of our knowledge, there resound innumerable voices witnessing to this lack of courage. They stress how impossible it is to form such a complete picture, and state that our knowledge is still a long way from being ripe for such conclusions. Voices may also be heard defending the impossibility of these conclusions. Precisely through the successes of the sciences, the human mind has seen how incapable it is of knowing anything about those things which were formerly made by philosophers into objects of reflection.

According to the opinion of people who allow such voices to be heard, contentment is to be found in measuring, weighing and comparing things and phenomena, and investigating them with the available apparatus. But never would questions be raised as to the higher *meaning* of things and phenomena.

We have lost our unshakeable faith that thought is called upon to solve the riddles of the world. Only with a few researchers, as for instance Ernst Haeckel, is there a tendency so to penetrate available knowledge that such a *meaning* arises.—It does not matter whether one agrees with the thoughts developed by Haeckel in his *Der Monismus als Band zwischen Religion und Wissenschaft* (Bonn, 1892). The essential thing is that here, with the methods of our mental training, the question is being raised: how can human feeling satisfy its needs through modern knowledge? This is the same question which the religions of all time—as well as scholasticism with its training methods—tried to solve.

But the fact is that thoughts of that kind have little effect today when faced with the common lack of courage, indeed cowardice of human thinking.

It is therefore not at all surprising if in the spiritual domain reaction everywhere raises its head. As long as scientifically formed thinkers are too cowardly to offer a substitute for antiquated religious ideas from the standpoint of their knowledge, persons who need a view of the world will fall back on traditional conceptions; and the few who arrange their lives in the sense of a modern view of the world will remain singers without an audience. I wanted here to explain for what reasons the most advanced minds of the present are so little understood.

In a further instalment of his autobiography written in February 1925 Steiner added:

That is the soul-mood out of which the facts bringing about my anthroposophical activity within the Theosophical Society must be understood. If I immersed myself in the culture of the time in order to have the spiritual background for editing the *Magazin*, there was afterwards a deep need for my mind to 'relax' by reading such works as Willmann's *Geschichte des Idealismus*. Despite the chasm lying between my spiritual conception and Otto Willmann's form of ideas, I nonetheless felt this form of ideas as close to the spirit.

The facts related here show that my aim of communicating the content of the spirit-world had already become a need in my mind *before* giving up the *Magazin*, and is not for instance connected to the impossibility of continuing the *Magazin*.

I entered into an activity whose impulses were in spiritual knowledge, as into my predestined element.

But even today I have a feeling that if the hindrances depicted here had not existed, my attempt to lead to the spirit-world through scientific thinking might have become more promising. What I expressed from 1897 to 1900 I look back on as something which had to be once expressed in regard to the then prevalent way of thinking. On the other hand I look back on it as something in which I underwent my most intense spiritual trial. I learnt to recognize thoroughly where lie the culture-dissolving, culture-destroying forces of the time which strive away from the spirit. Much of this knowledge added to the strength I later needed in order to work out of the spirit.

An Awakener

Alwin Alfred Rudolph described Rudolf Steiner's first lecture on 13 January 1899 in his opening course on 'History from the 16th Century to the Present Time' in the Berlin Workers' Training College:

> The small room was hardly sufficient. Further seating possibilities had to be brought, and not everyone could be placed at tables for writing things down. Ten minutes, five minutes before the scheduled time, most of us became quite nervous. We comforted ourselves that Steiner had perhaps counted on the quarter of an hour allowed between the announced start of an academic lecture and the actual start; this was not customary with us, but I had not told him, as on being questioned I had to admit. I would willingly have fetched him, at least on the first evening, for the maze of streets and the traffic in Berlin could not in the short time have become familiar to him. But this he had decisively declined—replying that he was properly grown-up, half jokingly but more meaningfully. At two minutes to eight he was standing in the doorway, seemingly moved with joy. He probably noticed that most people greeted him with an expression of some relief; so then he said that he had not forgotten. With him were the two ladies, mother and daughter, from his home. He had two admission tickets given to him, and despite our objection that they were not needed for anyone accompanying him, he filled them out.
>
> The two minutes were taken up with these greetings and filling out the tickets, and then Steiner stood on the platform behind a small table and after a quick look at people's faces began to speak. He spoke without any kind of notes in his hand, and went on doing so throughout the evening. This caused some astonishment and aroused in us the opinion that we had to do with a man supplied with comprehensive knowledge and with a memory into which even details were engraved. He only needed to see a face once and hear the name, and would never again forget it.
>
> From this very first lecture we knew that there was something here to be learned. He let his superior knowledge be felt only in order to teach us. There was no arrogance about him. He spoke with inner warmth, filled by the matter and by his words, and so the words entered without trouble into his audience, who pricked their ears and followed him, entranced by his personality. We had announced him as a lecturer, but he did not doceate; he was a caller, an awakener, precisely a teacher who was not seeking after

disciples, not soliciting fellow travellers, not striving after supporters—he served out what he had as knowledge, as cognizance, he awoke a capacity to judge for oneself.

His manner of speaking gradually intensified to the end, hardly needed gestures, never stresses, he never emphatically raised his voice. Sometimes a strand of his black hair drawn smoothly over his head would come loose and fall over his face, and with an energetic shake which was like a command he would send it back to its place. That was as it were like a clock. The stream of speech slowly ebbed away, the insistent warmth of his words withdrew as if turned off, and he finished without any particular formula, almost sprang from the platform and sat down in the room beside the two ladies. When he came, he knew when he had to begin, and could judge exactly when the time assigned for his lecture was over...

Johanna Mücke added:

After the end of the lecture pupils were heard speaking with each other vividly and excitedly. One of them, a particularly active contemporary and a very awake man, came up to me and said with a certain joy: 'Well, that wasn't a materialistic conception of history, but it was interesting!'

General Education

In the following month, on 4 February, Rudolf Steiner published in the *Magazin für Litteratur* an article 'On the Problems of a Journalist and Critic':

A few days ago death took away from us an important personality of the present. Emil Schiff, who died on the 23rd of January, was not a creative artist nor a scholar, not a productive figure. He fructified no domain of spiritual life with new ideas. Everything he wrote was mere reporting; mostly indeed writing purely for the day. He was a journalist. But when stating this about Emil Schiff, one must recall the Goethean saying: 'Think of the *what*, think more of the *how*.' He worked like an embodied protest against the journalism of the present. How would it be with journalism if we had many like him! According to one now generally prevalent view, the concept of journalism is not to be separated from that of superficiality. Who would deny this view a certain justification? What a contrast was Emil Schiff! Every feature-article he wrote smelled of thoroughness. Many a scholar writing on a distant theme, easily mastered on account of its one-sidedness, might take as model this or that newspaper-article by Schiff.

For 25 years Schiff had been Berlin correspondent of the Viennese *Neue Freie Presse*.

A journalist writes for the day. Whoever does that must understand the day. But the day, 'today', results from the whole of man's cultural work. In the smallest phenomenon of the day things can come to light which are only to be judged upon the broadest basis of a quite general education. Imagine a journalist who on the occasion of the death of Helmholtz, Du Bois-Reymond or Treitschke wants to write in a worthy manner! It is certainly easier to write for the most learned magazine about rodents' brains.

People claim that in our time a certain many-sidedness cannot be combined with thoroughness. The abundance of what we have to know today in certain domains, if we want to be 'thorough', cannot be united with a universal mastery of our time's spiritual content. If that were right, so also would be the view that a writer for the day must be superficial. Emil Schiff is the living counterproof of this claim. Through what did he become that counterproof?

One need only assemble a couple of facts to answer this question. From his nineteenth year Emil Schiff studied law. Then he became a journalist. In his twenty-ninth year he began studies of higher mathematics and analytical mechanics, and in his thirty-second of medicine. In his thirty-seventh he was able to write a doctoral dissertation about *Cabanis*, one of the most many-sided persons of the last century. Schiff's friends relate that in the last days of his life he was concerned with English and Roman history, and that Cervantes was to be seen at the dying man's bed. One will therefore hardly make a false judgement in stating that this tireless person included into the wide compass of his knowledge much which cannot be documentarily established.

It would certainly be incorrect if one wished to claim that Schiff only tried to develop his knowledge on every side in such an industrious way in order to become a perfect journalist. To him an all-rounded education was a personal need. Not to know something seemed to disturb his mind, which aimed at universality. But just such persons belong to journalism. Nothing is too good for this calling. Although one would also have to say that a man who so yearned for knowledge should have become the ideal scholar, it is not regrettable that he became a journalist. Since a large part of our educated world absorbs merely the literature of the day, it needs persons like Emil Schiff.

Only through characters of his kind can the world be rid of the journalistic damage which is so often discussed. Human knowledge forms a whole contained in itself. One can if necessary be a specialist, and manage without general education. One must then assemble purely factual matter about Byron's influence on German literature; or report on the propagation of moss, as seen with one's eyes. But it is impossible to report to one's contemporaries a political phenomenon or a scientific discovery without knowing on the basis of a comprehensive education how to incorporate it into the whole cultural activity of the present. Our journalists mostly cannot do that. Unfortunately the lack of such ability is also much too little noticed. Those who understand how to display conceited erudition in a paradoxical way are now much luckier than the Schiffs. A journalist can be as one-sided, indeed as ignorant as possible, if he be only 'amusing'. Yes, amusing! This cannot actually be at all denied. But it only depends for whom he is being amusing. For those who have a serious need to take part in present cultural life, or for those who want to pass the time remaining to them from their vocational business in empty jokes devoid of content. Pamphleteers are accepted today more than knowledgeable and discerning reporters. Article-writers stand in highest regard who have adopted a couple of phrases from the landowners' catechism, and know how to pad them out with a couple of stylistic flourishes from a superficial reading of Nietzsche. Writers of the day are ruled by one-sidedness, superficiality and paradox. The opposite of all this was characteristic of Emil Schiff. He was a proper journalist. He had the reporter's necessary conscience. He could fulfil what his conscience prescribed, for he was ceaselessly at work perfecting his capacity for judgement.

One can hold the view that no one should write about a theatrical piece without knowing at least the basics of Darwinism, and that no one should write about Count Bismarck without understanding the essence of sociology. Emil Schiff fulfilled strict conditions of that kind. He combined the exactness of a scholar with the many-sided interest of a newspaper-writer. Mere empty phrases were quite foreign to him.

Productive natures will probably not find it at all easy to live up to the journalistic calling in such a perfect way as was done by Schiff. They will be too concerned with developing what is their own, to acquire such a large measure of the foreign. Schiff could report about other people and things in such a unique way, because what was his own never bothered him.

All talk about reforms in certain conditions of life and culture is worthless unless it be recognized that such reforms must be erected on a basis of complete human selectivity. We know today that man cannot be developed against his tendencies. Anyone speaking about education who believes that there are general maxims according to which human nature may be formed understands nothing of modern scientific achievements. We can do no more than develop a person's innate tendencies. We must create such conditions that those persons who are specially suited to any sphere of life may also be placed into these. Professional classes will be best provided for if natural conditions are suited for bringing into them those persons who by their nature fit them best.

In order to create such conditions, the persons who have such fitness must however be known and appreciated. The requirements set up in certain callings are ordered according to this knowledge and appreciation. These requirements correspond exactly to what in the domain of national economy is called demand. Supply will always be ordered according to this demand. If our newspaper readers ask for chatterers, Kerrs will be supplied to them; if they require conscientious writers with an all-round education, they will be met with Schiffs. This is an iron law in mankind's spiritual development. Exemplary and unique personalities such as Emil Schiff should therefore not be ignored.

Every circle of readers has the journalists it deserves. Emil Schiff was meant only for a select one. That is not exactly flattering to our time; for basically this man was little regarded. In many circles his articles probably met with scarcely more understanding than those of any sentence-turner with a sparse knowledge of literary history. During his lifetime only few people recognized this man's worth.

From the English

A month later, on 4 March, the *Dramaturgische Blätter* carried an article by Rudolf Steiner on 'The Beginnings of the German Theatre'.

In the series of 'Hochschulvorträge für Jedermann' has appeared a work introducing the original history of the German stage. Prof. Dr. Georg Witkowski deals with the theme *Die Anfänge des deutschen Theaters*. With the brevity necessitated by his task he shows that this important factor in our spiritual life only gained its place late in German culture. In the Middle Ages there was in Germany no actual theatre. The content of the first work to appear in dramatic form was taken from the biblical story, and its performance connected to a church service. At Easter and Christmas festivals, scenes were performed from the Old and New Testament. They did not have the aim which every real dramatic work must have of presenting struggles of soul for their own sake, but wanted to present in living vividness sacred history. Just as little may comic performances promoted by craftsmen and pupils at Shrovetide be really described as dramatic achievements. They mostly dealt with little judgement scenes, marital disputes and coarse fun usually mocking farmers from the standpoint of townsmen ... Performers went from house to house, speaking their parts without any scenic means, and certainly in this way developed very little measure of histrionic art. From where should honest craftsmen and their pupils have acquired it? After the Reformation there were in Germany more promising conditions for drama. Luther favoured pupil performances, believing them to have a good influence on public views. 'For the sake of boys in the school one should not refuse to play comedies, but rather allow and permit them, firstly that they practise the Latin language, and further that in comedies such persons are with fine artistry depicted, portrayed and presented, the people instructed thereby, and every person reminded and warned of his office and position, of what is appropriate to and well befits a servant, lord, young fellow and old, and of what he should do. Indeed, therein are represented and set before the eyes all dignities of station, offices and charges, how everyone should hold himself in his state in outer mode of life, as in a mirror.' In the following period school-drama blossomed. But this could not achieve much, for conceptions of the nature of dramatic technique were of the most primitive kind. They did not go beyond dialogue divided between several persons. The impulse for real dramatic art in Germany came from the English. They developed this art with admirable speed at the end of the sixteenth century. The first theatrical building was erected in London in 1576, and in that town at the end of the century there were more artistic institutes of this kind than today. English drama developed just as quickly, from simple plays with a religious and morally didactic tendency to the masterly creations of Shakespeare.

The art developed there was also carried by wandering troupes of actors into Germany. In the year 1586 such a troupe is found under the leadership of William Kempe at the Dresden court. From that time on, these societies of comedians appear at the most varied places. They perform English plays, partly however in outrageous parody. But plays were also composed by Germans, and such societies then performed them. The leader of such a troupe mostly played the main part, which had to present someone comic. The plays put on had to be brought into a form allowing that leader to appear as the now typical comic figure.—We know about these performances almost solely through council protocols and the towns' tax charts, which show us what charges officials imposed on wandering troupes. At this time there was as yet no theatrical criticism or the like.—Dramatic art in Germany had this character through the last years of the sixteenth and the first third of the seventeenth century. Witkowski tells of a theatrical notice from Nuremberg which lets us see what was on offer: 'Let everyman know that there has arrived here a quite new company of comedians, never before seen here in the land, with a very funny Pickled Herring, who will daily act fine comedies, tragedies, pastorals (sheep-farming) and histories, mixed with lovely and funny interludes, and in fact today they will present a very funny comedy called *Love's Sweetness Changes into Death's Bitterness*. After the comedy will be presented a beautiful ballet, and ludicrous pranks. After the 2nd stroke of noon, lovers of such plays will place themselves at the fencing house, where at precisely the given time a beginning will be made.' Regarding the expression Pickled Herring, that is smoked herring, it must be said that the stated comic figure at the centre of performances was given the name of a favourite food: Hans Sausage, Hans Scarcecheese, Dried Cod and so on.—After 1631 other conditions came about. The English troupes disappear; in their place come 'High German comedians'.

Reference may especially be made to Witkowski's portrayal of the dramatic stage:

'Already long before, the broad space of the court encompassing a large number of people is thickly beset. Those entering found at the door a notice on which is written that a place costs six *Kreuzer* a person. Otherwise the English would often demand more, which this time is not allowed. The public paying out the still high sum (German troupes only received half a *Kreuzer*) sits both in front and around the stage, which has little similarity to the present one. It consisted of a small construction set up on the back wall of the court, taking up only a little part. It was open on three sides, but hung at the back with tapestries, in front of which could be seen a smaller raised construction, led up to by steps. This served a dual purpose. Firstly its platform was always used when there was need of a raised position, like a town wall, a hill or a tower. But its inner space then served to create a second stage on the stage, where in particular scenes played inside the chambers of houses were performed. This second stage was furnished with decorations and closeable by a curtain, so that it could be changed while acting was taking place on the front part; an extremely practical arrangement, coming in very useful for the development of the plays. Later on, the width of the stage was extended over the whole back wall of the building where acting took place, thus establishing the present form of our theatre. This is far distant from the previous simple and yet so sensible usage of the English. But with them we already find the important principle of the front and back stage; here already is the so-to-speak primal cell of the stage of today.'

In Germany itself during the time when theatricality was influenced by the English, there arose only dramatic works of no value for the actual theatre. They copied the Greeks and Romans. Not before Molière and the French art which he developed did fruitful things also come about in Germany. A total collapse of the theatre in the first half of the eighteenth century was followed by an upswing through Gottsched, working in union with the genial stage-artist Neuber. Although even in Germany people freed themselves again from French influence, at that time this influence can only be described as extremely favourable.

12
THE BERLIN CONCLUSIONS

Simplicity and Greatness

Chapter XXXI of Rudolf Steiner's autobiography begins:

> Another collection setting out the nineteenth century's cultural achievements was published at the time by Hans Kraemer. It consisted of lengthy articles on separate branches of cognitional life, technical creation and social development.
>
> I was invited to give an account of literary life. So the evolution of imaginative life in the nineteenth century also passed at the time right through my mind. I did not give descriptions like a philologist working 'out of sources', but portrayed what I had inwardly experienced in the developing life of imagination.
>
> This account, too, was significant for me because I had to speak about phenomena of spiritual life without going into experience of the spirit-world. Actual spiritual impulses from that world, living in the poetic phenomena, remained unmentioned.
>
> Here too there stood before me what soul-life has to say about an existing phenomenon when that life is set at a viewpoint of normal consciousness—without bringing the content of consciousness into such activity that it rises up into experience of the spirit-world.

The work referred to, *Das XIX Jahrhundert in Wort und Bild*, came out in four volumes, the first appearing in or after March 1899. It included a contribution by Steiner on 'Spiritual Life 1795 to 1840'. This began:

> At the end of the eighteenth century *Goethe* had reached the high point of his development. From a spirit looking at details of sensory experience just as impartially as he could investigate the deepest secrets of natural and human life, he had created a view of the world which seemed to fulfil what was yearned after by the best minds of the eighteenth century. The fruitfulness of this view of the world proved for the following time unbounded: an effect like that made by Goethe on the nineteenth century can be compared with scarcely anything else in mankind's spiritual history. Its reason lies in that universality of the Goethean spirit which made Wieland call his great contemporary the 'most human of all men'. This many-sidedness of his mind distinguishes Goethe from those who brought about the great spiritual revolution along with him at the turn of the eighteenth and nineteenth centuries. Voltaire, Rousseau, Lessing, Herder, Kant and

> Schiller accomplished great things by placing their creations into the service of *one* ideal. Goethe by contrast brought to development within himself a multiplicity of human capacities in such a way that they stand in perfect harmony.
>
> Goethe himself expressed in clear words how his natural disposition differed from that of his friend and greatest of contemporaries Schiller: 'He preached the gospel of freedom; I did not want Nature's rights curtailed.'

The quotation, from Goethe's 1820 article 'Influence of Recent Philosophy', had been used in Edmund Reitlinger's 1874 article 'Into the Interior of Nature' reproduced at the end of *Freie Blicke*.

> . . . Schiller started from the ethical demand of freedom, Goethe from observing Nature and the human being. In the piece of writing which Goethe to the end of his life—1832—was working at, *Faust*, he did not present a man wishing to realize an ideal of freedom born from reason, but one who by developing the highest tendencies available in a human being wants to work himself into a free personality. What human nature contains is what should emerge when Faust goes wandering through the 'small and the big world'. Goethe was convinced that Nature is the source of all perfection, and that the best can only be created by following her tracks.
>
> Goethe's youthful works were a protest against the lack of naturalness he could observe in his time. He made Götz von Berlichingen the hero of a play because he wanted to show his contemporaries, who had distanced themselves from Nature through all conceivable artificial ideas, a man whose deeds emanated from the most original and natural feelings. On the other hand, he presented in *Werther* the value of naturalness. The basic idea of this work is that sentimentality contrary to Nature must suffer shipwreck. Goethe's gaze was directed at what a man can experience through his inherent character and the conditions in which destiny has placed him. In his dramatic and narrative works he presented in an incomparable manner life's sorrows and joys played out in variously fashioned human natures, the conflicts life brings and the pleasures it offers. *Clavigo*, *Stella*, *Die Geschwister*, *Egmont*, *Iphigenie* and *Tasso* are soul-pictures created by a mind to whom have been revealed the deepest secrets of human nature.
>
> Goethe's endeavour to proceed in his own creations according to the same laws followed by Nature led him to seek his artistic ideal in the world of antiquity. Greek works of art observed on his Italian journey elicited the statement: 'I have the supposition that the Greeks were proceeding according to laws by which Nature herself proceeds, and which I am on the track of.' Believing himself to have thereby come to know what the purpose of all art must be, he sought to develop further the studies of Nature he had already begun before his Italian journey. He wanted to become acquainted with Nature's creative forces, in order to give expression to them in his

works of art. After his return from Italy, in the year 1788, he was no less active in the domain of science than in that of poetry. That artistic creation was for him a kind of higher stage of natural activity was stated by Goethe in his book about Winckelmann: 'In so far as man is set on Nature's peak, he looks on himself as a whole nature, which must again bring forth a peak within itself. For this purpose he intensifies himself, permeating himself with every perfection and virtue, calling up choice, order, harmony and meaning, and finally raises himself to the production of a work of art.' By disposition Goethe was predestined everywhere to seek in things for what is natural and original; but he believed he had only come to know the actual deeper being of Nature through study of antiquity. His opinion now was that he had indeed been previously faithful to Nature, but that only the ideal beauty of the ancients had raised him onto a higher stage of existence and artistic work. In his youth Goethe had sought to reproduce things and people purely from his own nature. He would now only accept a work of art if natural truth were transfigured to ideal truth, if simple naturalness were subjected to the strict stylistic laws demanded by the sense for beauty of the ancients. Goethe was at this stage of development as the eighteenth century drew to its close. A ripe product of the view of art he then held is the poem composed in 1797, *Hermann und Dorothea*. Life in a small town, genuine and simple folk stand in the narrative like creations of Nature herself, over all of which is poured the simplicity and greatness we admire in works of art by the ancients. A perfect faithfulness to Nature here celebrates its marriage to the highest stylistic art.

Such qualities may be seen in the opening of the part headed 'Erato', which presents a fine simile of a visual after-image. Here it is in the 1838 English translation by William Whewell:

> As when a wandering man, at sunset loitering, once more
> Gazes intent on the orb fast sinking just ere it vanish,
> Then in the thicket's gloom and upon the side of the dark rock
> Sees its similitude float: wherever his vision is turnéd
> Still it dances and glances before him in gorgeöus colours:
> So to Herman's eyes the lovely form of the Maiden
> Softly moved before, along the path of the corn-field...

Romanticism

After examining various other Goethean works from the early nineteenth century, Rudolf Steiner continued:

...Life in a higher ideal reality, to which Goethe had been upraised by long experience and after taking into himself the cultural world of the ancients, seemed to the poets of the following time, who portrayed their direction as Romantic, to be the prerogative of a true artist. These poets are characterized by a yearning for everything which is foreign to normal life and born only out of genius and imagination. In their creations they favoured everything having the appearance of the wonderful, the mysterious, the mystical. Rare feelings entirely foreign to anyone standing amidst real life were specially made by them into the object of poetry.

The account went on to the works of the Schlegel brothers:

... In their own creations the Schlegels only managed to fashion things of no importance. They remained imitators of foreign forms. So much the greater were their achievements as interpreters and transmitters of other people's works. Friedrich Schlegel opened up wide vistas into foreign spiritual trends in his works *Über die Sprache und Weisheit der Inder* and *Geschichte der alten und neuen Literatur*... August Wilhelm Schlegel was a born translator and renderer. Through his Shakespeare translation he created a new epoch in understanding the great British playwright and demonstrated the high extent to which the German folk-spirit is capable of receiving poetry from abroad. Through this transmitting of foreign poetry and immersion in their own people's past the German Romantics profoundly influenced the development of literature ...

Steiner next discussed Tieck's renewal of older German poetry and the collection *Des Knaben Wunderhorn* assembled by von Arnim and Brentano.

After going onto the Grimm brothers, Schelling, Hegel and Schopenhauer, he then returned again to his discussion of poetry, commenting on the works of Wackenroder and Tieck, and continued:

... The deepening soul-life which Romanticism made possible came to expression through the real poets of German feeling: Friedrich von Hardenberg, called Novalis, and Josef von Eichendorff. Novalis wrote his *Hymnen an die Nacht* (1797) out of wonderfully tender and profound sensations. Into these songs, inspired by the highest sweep of fantasy, he poured the deep sufferings caused in him by the death of his bride, and a yearning for his own end. In his novel *Heinrich von Ofterdingen*, set at the time of the Crusades, the feelings of a Romantic spiritual manner gained their most marked expression.

Disregarding the laws of Nature and living in the shapes of a pure fantasy-world often drew the Romantics to the craziest leaps in presenting people and events. At times they fashioned real caricatures of everything natural. What the persons they present accomplish over a period of time does not hang together as with real people, but as with figures appearing to us in dreams. When in *Heinrich von Ofterdingen* both maidens loved by the hero, Mathilde and Cyane, in course of events melt into a single being, this is an

> example of how the Romantics created figures like pictures in a dream. But with Novalis all this was immersed in poesy. Here the Romantic mood spoke out of a true poet...

After examining Eichendorff, Steiner went on to other writers, in the process making general observations about German Romanticism such as its 'leaning towards the unreal and the mystical'.

Like the World's Eternal Music

Rudolf Steiner then continued:

> German literary streams in the second half of the last and first half of this century are marked by a return to original sources of human knowledge. A view of the world was liberated from old mental pictures containing nothing but traditional authority. Art was redeemed from forms—built up in particular under the influence of French classicism—which had gradually turned into pedantic artistic laws and outer mannerisms deadening to any artistic individual.
>
> The high degree to which this latter view of the world and artistic trend had outlived itself is also shown by literary movements at the beginning of the century among the related English people, which took almost exactly the same direction.
>
> Here the three poets of the so-called 'Lake School', William Wordsworth, Robert Southey and Samuel Taylor Coleridge, were the first who tried to emerge from the old-fashioned rigid classicism whose chief representative seemed to them to be Pope. They are combined under the name 'Lake School' because for a time they lived together on the banks of lakes in Westmoreland and Cumberland, and this region's natural beauties provided material for many of their poems. They did not want to peer like their predecessors through the spectacles of mental pictures handed down to them and sing about Nature in traditional artistic forms. Rather they wanted to confront Nature naively and talk in natural language. The most significant of these three poets, Coleridge, has in his being much similarity with the German Romantics. He too sought for the mystical and the rare in the world's phenomena, and lived in a dream-world foreign to reality. Wordsworth was less gifted; his effusion for Nature has something contrivedly naive, and the natural tones struck up in his poems he mostly destroys by a moralizing conclusion. Of Southey's creations, only those produced in youth are interesting through expressing a sense of freedom; in old age the revolutionary developed into a eulogist of reaction.
>
> The poet who exercised the greatest influence at the start of the Romantic Movement in England, the Scotsman Walter Scott, does not in

his creations have anything of the world-encompassing sense of the German Romantics. He did not search for the roots of what is human in the whole world, but only in his own folk. A genuine, natural freshness and real original feeling stream through Scott's 'Lay of the Last Minstrel', coming out in 1805, as through his poem *Lady of the Lake*, published in 1810, but none of the deep longing of German Romanticism. When Scott went over from poetry to prose, his portrayal gave almost a historical reproduction of people and events. He became the creator of the historical novel, depicting natural conditions of a region and historical prerequisites of a particular time. One of the manifold character traits of Romanticism was to discard the overestimation of present cultural conditions, which belonged to the Age of Enlightenment. At that time people only had a sense for such notions of religion, science, custom and so forth as they themselves held to be correct. Romanticism first reawakened a love for human beings and cultures growing out of different conditions than those of the present. Walter Scott developed precisely this character-trait in Romanticism. He allows human beings and facts to grow out of the soil they are born on, and appear in the light of the time they belong to. What historians should regard as an ideal, the portrayal of everything from given conditions, is in Scott's novels fulfilled. That he thereby met a need of his time is shown by the fact that for

Walter Scott

> instance in the year 1822 there were printed 145,000 volumes of Scott's novels. This writer exercised enormous influence on Europe's whole novelistic literature. Everywhere were found imitators of his methods.
>
> Much more genuine Romanticism lived in the Irishman Thomas Moore. He hits on a folk tone, and at the same time revels in the colourful world of the Orient. His *Lalla Rookh* is a poem inspired by luxuriant sensuality and by a fantasy with a wealth of motley pictures. But his most significant achievement is his *Irish Melodies*, begun in 1807, where the humiliation of his Irish people, which endured unexampled suffering under dominion by England, released such great and thrilling tones as have only ever been sung by a singer of freedom.
>
> To this time belong two poets in whom a feeling for Nature springing from the deepest sources of the human soul found exalted lyrical expression: John Keats and Percy Bysshe Shelley. Their spirit seems as though uplifted to the loftiest and most tremendous powers governing the world, and their poems touch the heart like the world's eternal music. Both died young: Keats in 1821 at the age of 26, while Shelley was drowned in the bay of Spezia when not yet 30. Nothing finer can be said about Keats than by repeating the words of Shelley in the lament dedicated to one who was in spirit so closely related to him: 'He is made one with Nature.' For Keats's whole life was a yearning for union with eternal powers. His 'Hyperion', begun in the year 1818, remained unfinished. Byron spoke these words about it: the poem 'is really inspired by the Titans and lofty as Aeschylus'. Allegory was for Keats a favourite form into which he poured his deep feeling for Nature, and in it he attained a great formative power with which hardly anything else can be compared.

Steiner was referring to Keats's habit of introducing allegorical figures into his poems, as for instance in the 'Ode to Autumn', where the season is personified into a living being:

> Season of mists and mellow fruitfulness,
> Close bosom-friend of the maturing Sun,
> Conspiring with him how to load and bless
> With fruit the vines that round the thatch-eaves run;
> To bend with apples the mossed cottage-trees,
> And fill all fruit with ripeness to the core;
> To swell the gourd, and plump the hazel shells
> With a sweet kernel; to set budding more
> And still more, later flowers for the bees,
> Until they think warm days will never cease,
> For summer has o'er brimmed their clammy cells.
>
> Who hath not seen thee oft amid thy store?
> Sometimes whoever seeks abroad may find

Thee sitting careless on a granary floor,
Thy hair soft-lifted by the winnowing wind;
Or on a half-reaped furrow sound asleep,
Drowsed with the fume of poppies, while thy hook
Spares the next swath and all its twinéd flowers;
And sometimes like a gleaner thou dost keep
Steady thy laden head across a brook;
Or by a cider-press, with patient look,
Thou watchest the last oozings hours by hours.

Where are the songs of spring? Aye, where are they?
Think not of them, thou hast thy music too—
While barred clouds bloom the soft-dying day,
And touch the stubble-plains with rosy hue;
Then in a wailful choir the small gnats mourn
Among the river sallows, borne aloft
Or sinking as the light wind lives or dies;
And full-grown lambs loud bleat from hilly bourn;
Hedge-crickets sing; and now with treble soft
The redbreast whistles from a garden-croft;
And gathering swallows twitter in the skies.

Steiner continued:

If one may speak about a philosophy of the heart, it is with this name that the poetry of Shelley must be denoted. His aim was directed to the depths in the secrets of the world. This was not, however, investigative reason at work, but rather a heart desiring to encompass with its love the loftiest things in Nature. In his poems the elements of Nature herself seem to speak in their native language.

This comprehensive sense for Nature was joined in Shelley to a boundless love of freedom. And this love also grew out of his sense for Nature. He was wholly consumed in the life of Nature, which shatters all chains through the power of her forces, so that for him freedom was something without which the world could not be imagined. He therefore confronted *Prometheus Bound* with his 'Unbound', who bears his chains with dignity because he knows the hour is coming when freedom is victorious. Shelley presents this victory of freedom with all the power belonging to a necessary and unconquerable force of Nature.

The absolute urge for freedom derived by Shelley from a feeling for Nature going to the limits of what is human was in George Gordon, Lord Byron, the result of a proud personality confronting with defiance and grandeur anything desiring to limit the development of its innate humanity. In this poet lived a mind which took by storm both heaven and hell. Everything exercising compulsion was from the start his polar opposite.

> Byron is a singer who sings about pride in human nature, and his *Manfred*, begun in 1816, is the song of this pride. Manfred is a great personality, a human being whose soul is not depressed by the consciousness of having drawn onto itself a profound guilt, but wants despite this guilt to do battle with the limits of what is humanly possible. Byron found words to express the loftiest things, but also such words as struck like a sure arrow everything aimed at by his hatred or contempt. He possessed fine expertise in the matter of tracking down pettiness enwrapped in a cloak of greatness. Considered from the viewpoint of tearing away the mask from all hypocrisy, and holding up the lower source to all untruth, his *Don Juan* is a masterpiece. A sense for freedom drove him to devote his energy to the Greek movement, because in the Greeks he saw a people who, abandoned by European powers, wanted to battle out for themselves freedom from Turkish suppressors. Byron placed himself and everything he had at the service of liberating this people. He soon succumbed—though not in battle—to the strains brought about by his desire for deeds.

Byron was educated from 1805 to 1808 at Trinity College Cambridge. Soon after leaving England for good in 1816, he sat in Rome in 1817 for a bust by the Danish sculptor Bertel Thorvaldsen. After Byron's death in

Lord Byron

1824, Thorvaldsen went on in 1829 to sculpt a magnificent statue of Byron, the posture determined by the poet's right club foot. This statue was acquired in 1843 by Trinity College, whose then Master, William Whewell, had it set up in the college library.

In a Similar Way

In May 1899, Rudolf Steiner took up contact again with Ernst Haeckel, sending him the back-number of the *Magazin für Litteratur* containing his article on Charles Lyell.

Three months later, in August, he began to publish in *Die Gesellschaft*—a journal edited by his friend Ludwig Jacobowski—a series of articles on 'Haeckel and his Opponents'. The first began with a lengthy paragraph:

> In his book on Winckelmann, Goethe splendidly expressed the sensation a human being has when observing his place in the world: 'When man's healthy nature works as a whole, when he feels himself in the world as in a great, beautiful, valuable and worthwhile totality, when harmonious contentment grants him pure and free delight: *then the universe, if it could sense itself, would rejoice at having achieved its purpose and marvel at the peak of what it has become and what it is.*' From this feeling arises the most important question man can ask: how is his own development and nature related to that of the whole universe? In a letter to him on the 23rd of August 1794 Schiller aptly depicted the path by which Goethe desired to come to knowledge of human nature: 'From a simple organism you rise step by step to more evolved ones, for the final purpose of building genetically from the material of Nature's whole structure the most evolved of all, man.' This path of Goethe's is also the one which science has for four decades been taking, in order to solve the 'question of all questions for mankind.' Huxley sees this in determining the place which '... Man occupies in Nature and of his relations to the universe of things'...

The quotation is from Huxley's *Evidences as to Man's Place in Nature.*

> ... It is the great credit of Charles Darwin to have created a new scientific basis for reflecting on this question. The facts he communicated in 1859 in his work *On the Origin of Species* and the principles he developed enabled science to show in its way how well founded Goethe's conviction was that Nature 'after a thousandfold animals constructs a being which contains them all: man'...

The slightly altered quotation is from a statement made to Eckermann by the octogenarian Goethe on 20 February 1831. Literally the statement was:

> I may be allowed to revere *Him* who was so great in the wealth of his creations as still to make after a thousandfold plants one in which all others

> are contained and after a thousandfold animals a being which contains them all: man.

Steiner continued.

> ... We look back today on forty years of scientific development under the influence of Darwin's trend of ideas. In his essay *Über unsere gegenwärtige Kenntnis vom Ursprung des Menschen*, reproducing a lecture held on the 26th of August 1898 at the fourth International Congress of Zoologists in Cambridge, Ernst Haeckel could rightly say: 'Forty years of Darwinism! What tremendous progress in our knowledge of Nature! And what a reversal of our most important views, not just in the directly affected realms of the whole of biology, but also in that of anthropology and equally of all so-called spiritual sciences!' From his deep knowledge of Nature Goethe foresaw this turnabout, and recognized its significance for developing man's spiritual culture to its fullest extent. We see this especially clearly from a talk he had with Soret on the 2nd of August 1830. News was then reaching Weimar of the July revolution, which had just begun and was everywhere causing great commotion. On visiting Goethe, Soret was received with the words: 'Now, what do you think about this great event? The volcano has erupted; it's all standing in flames, and there's no longer any hearing behind closed doors!' Soret could of course only believe that Goethe was talking about the July revolution, and rejoined that under the known conditions nothing else was to be expected than that it would end by ousting the royal family. But Goethe meant something quite different. 'I'm not talking about those people at all; it's completely different things which concern me. I'm talking about the conflict between Cuvier and Geoffroy de Sainte-Hilaire which is so highly significant for science and has come to a public outbreak in the Académie!' The conflict was about the question whether each species in which organic Nature abounds has a special design for itself, or whether one is common to them all. Goethe had already decided this question over forty years previously. His assiduous study of the plant and animal world had turned him into an opponent of the Linnaean view that we 'enumerate as many species as different forms have in principle been created'...

The slightly altered quotation is from Linnaeus's *Genera Plantarum*. Literally the text reads:

> There are as many species as different and constant forms have been produced in this globe by the Infinite Being.

Steiner continued:

> ... Whoever holds such an opinion can only trouble to investigate what the organizational designs of living species are. He will above all seek carefully to differentiate these individual forms. Goethe took another path. 'What

Linnaeus sought to keep forcefully apart has to strive, according to the innermost necessity of my being, towards unity.'...

The quotation is from Goethe's *Geschichte meines Botanischen Studiums* of 1817.

... He formed the opinion summarized in 1796 in the 'Lectures on the First Three Chapters of the Draft of a General Introduction into Comparative Anatomy' in the sentence: 'So this we would have achieved: to be allowed to assert unafraid that the more perfected organic natures, under which we see fish, amphibia, birds, mammals and—at the peak of the latter—man, were all formed according to an archetype, which only in its very constant parts is more or less deviating here and there, and still daily evolving and reshaping itself by reproduction.' Already in 1790 in his 'Attempt to Explain the Metamorphosis of Plants' Goethe put forward the primal picture to which all manifold plant-forms may be led back. This way of observing, by which Goethe attempted to recognize the laws of living Nature, is quite similar to the one he requires for the lifeless world in the article he wrote in 1793, 'The Experiment as Mediator of Object and Subject'. 'Nothing occurs in living Nature which does not relate to the whole, and if to us experiences only *appear* isolated, if we can only consider experiments as isolated facts, this is not to say that they *are* isolated. The only issue is: how do we find the relation of these phenomena, these occurences?' Species too *appear* to us just isolated. Goethe searches for their relation. From this it clearly follows that Goethe's endeavour is directed towards *applying the same kind of explanation to observing living beings as leads to the goal in lifeless Nature.* How far with such mental pictures he was ahead of his age becomes evident if one considers that at the same time as Goethe was publishing his writing on metamorphosis, Kant in his *Kritik der Urteilskraft* wanted to prove scientifically the impossibility of explaining living things according to principles valid for lifeless ones. 'For it is quite certain that we do not even sufficiently come to know, much less explain, organisms and their inner possibility according to merely mechanical principles of Nature; and indeed so certain that one can boldly state it to be inconsistent for man even just to conceive such an attempt or to hope that some Newton might once arise who could render understandable even just the creation of a blade of grass according to natural laws which no purpose has ordered. Rather must this insight simply be denied to man.' Haeckel rejects this thought with the words: 'But seventy years later this impossible Newton now really appeared in Darwin and ... and actually solved the task Kant considered utterly insoluble!'...

The quotation is from Haeckel's *Natürliche Schöpfungsgeschichte* of 1868.

... Goethe knew that the reversal in scientific conceptions caused by Darwinism had to come, for it accords with his own kind of mental picturing.

> He recognized his own view in the one defended by Geoffroy de Saint-Hilaire against Cuvier, that all organic forms bear in themselves a 'common plan, just modified here and there'. He could therefore say to Soret: 'Geoffroy de Saint-Hilaire is also now decidedly on our side, and along with him all his significant pupils and followers in France. For me this event is of quite unbelievable importance, and I am right to jubilate over the general victory I have at last experienced of a matter to which I have devoted my life, and which is also quite especially my own.'[28] Now the discoveries of Darwin are of much greater importance for Goethe's view of Nature. The latter relates to Darwinism in a similar way as do the insights of Copernicus and Kepler into the structure and movements of the planetary system to the discovery by Newton of the law of the general attraction of all heavenly bodies. This law shows the scientific reasons why planets move in the way Copernicus and Kepler described. And Darwin found the natural reasons why manifold species reveal the common archetype of all organic beings which Goethe presupposed.

Here is Steiner's fullest adaptation for the organic realm of ideas deriving from Edmund Reitlinger's course at the Viennese Technical College in 1881 on the history of physics, namely the part 'From ancient times to Newton'.

Substantially Diminished

Chapter XXX of Rudolf Steiner's autobiography includes the following passage:

> Before becoming active in the Theosophical Society, in the last period of editing the *Magazin*, I composed my two-volumed book *Welt- und Lebensanschauungen im neunzehnten Jahrhundert.* From the second edition onwards this was expanded by a survey of the developing views of the world from Greek times to the nineteenth century and appeared as *Rätsel der Philosophie.*
>
> The outer cause for the origin of this book may be seen as quite irrelevant. Cronbach, publisher of the *Magazin*, was arranging a series of writings dealing with various domains of knowledge and life in the development of the nineteenth century. In this series he wanted also to present views of the world and of life, and assigned this to me.
>
> The entire substance of the book had occupied me for a long time. My study of views of the world had a personal starting point in that of Goethe. The contrast to Kantianism in which I had to set Goethe's manner of thought, the new philosophic trends at the turn of the eighteenth and nineteenth centuries with Fichte, Schelling, Hegel: all this for me began an

> epoch developing a view of the world. Richard Wahle's ingenious books, presenting the dissolution at the end of the nineteenth century of all philosophical attempts at views of the world, closed this epoch. So the endeavour towards views of the world in the nineteenth century was rounded out to a totality, which existed in my vision and which I willingly took the opportunity to portray.
>
> Looking back at this book, it is precisely in it that the course of my life seems to me to be symptomatically expressed. I did not, as many believe, move forward in contradictions. Were that the case, I would willingly admit it. But that was not the reality in my spiritual development. I moved forward by finding new domains to be added to what was living in my mind . . .

Steiner composed the first volume of this book in the summer and autumn of 1899.

★

During that autumn, from 4 to 15 September, Steiner travelled with Anna Eunicke back to his Austrian homeland and stayed at Mauer near Vienna, visiting friends such as Moritz Zitter and Rosa Mayreder.

In the next month Steiner and Anna Eunicke moved into a Berlin house at 95 Kaiserallee in Friedenau, and on 31 October, after some six years of acquaintance, they were finally married.

★

In early November Steiner once again paid a visit to his home city of Vienna, and on the 7th gave a lecture there to the Austrian Women's Union on 'Goethe and Women'.

Fifteen years previously, this very subject had been discussed in lectures by Karl Julius Schröer, published in 1884 under the title *Goethe und die Liebe*, a book Steiner had reviewed at the time in the Viennese *Deutsche Zeitung*.

Exactly when the last meeting between Steiner and Schröer took place is not recorded, but this occasion in November 1899 would have been the last possibility.

Walter Beck writes:

> It is not known whether and to what extent Schröer in the last three years 1898 to 1900 was still mentally active. There are differing reports about his mental condition. Elisabeth Palme and Edgar von Mojsisovics related—as grandchildren—that during these years their grandfather was physically disadvantaged, but remained mentally bright and lively.
>
> In contrast to the grandchildren's accounts, Payer von Thurn, successor to Schröer in editing the *Chronik*, wrote in an obituary that already from 1894 Schröer's mental and bodily powers had substantially diminished, and

> stated in the annual report of the *Chronik*: 'All of you indeed know that Schröer was we might perhaps say the soul of the Goethe Union, up to the point in time when his mental and bodily powers began to desert him . . .'
>
> In the *Biographischer Jahrbuch* Rudolf von Payer spoke of Schröer's 'infirmity lasting for years'; and Rudolf Steiner, who emphasized to an amazing extent the personality of Schröer, spoke in his lecture of the 23rd of September 1924 about Schröer's senility.

What Steiner said in this lecture was:

> . . . On seeing Schröer, one had the quite distinct perception: this soul is not fully within the body. And then when he grew older one could see how his soul, not being really willing to enter properly into the body of that present time, was little by little withdrawing from that body. Firstly his fingers grew swollen and thick, then the soul withdrew ever further, and indeed Schröer ended in senility.

Only One World

In former years Karl Julius Schröer had published books on German poetry like *Die Deutsche Dichtung im neunzehnten Jahrhundert.* And on 13 January 1900 Steiner published in the *Magazin für Litteratur* an article on this very subject, 'Observations on the Collection *Aus Deutscher Seele*':

> It would doubtless be interesting—now at the turn of two centuries—to investigate how much particular domains of spiritual life have contributed to the mass of foolishness produced by the century which has just passed, following on from that of the Enlightenment. One thing seems certain, that in such statistics on stupidity the thinking on art and poetry would stand high up, by a large percentage. There is no need even to consider the printed rubbish brought forth weekly and daily in this regard by papers and magazines. Merely what books and brochures have achieved in this field would reach an incredibly high figure. On reading aesthetic and critical works of the present, one has in most cases a feeling that the concept of art and poetry had been utterly lost. What remarkable things there meet one's eyes . . . ! Ideas of naive creativity, unconscious production, individuality, intuition and all the rest meet us in a way which shows nothing more than that those who write them down have picked them up in some way and are now throwing them here and there as children do with stones in a kaleidoscope. Learned treatises on art and poetry form absolutely no exception to this general rule. Worthy philologists, professors of the history of literature and of other spiritual sciences regard it as the height of dilettantism if one goes to work 'unscientifically' in proving which idea of

Wieland an idea of Goethe derives from. When they start drivelling in their own way about Goethe's 'naive' way of creating, they prove nothing further than their own—naivety. Just to read five lines of most aesthetic treatises and books makes it clear that their authors have not penetrated to the elements of that knowledge which could explain the essence of human productivity, fantasy, intuition and so on. If 98 per cent were by chance lost of what has been written in the course of the last two decades about Ibsen, Hauptmann and others, posterity would be deprived of nothing, absolutely nothing, possessing any actual value. Although today 'psychology' is being discussed everywhere, knowledge of the human soul currently ranks among the most unknown things in the world. Over hardly anything does such limitless ignorance hold sway as for instance over the essence of *fantasy*.

In such conditions, where can any judgement come from about the artistic or poetical value of new creations? Is it not natural that the concept of art and poetry be in this way actually lost?

In Jacobowski's collection *Aus deutscher Seele* there is—for all those who want to use it—a means to rediscover it. In his 'preface', from which we have given above the most important passages, the editor himself was speaking about the tasks he set himself in his collection. If one might succeed in displacing only a little the 'bazaar wares of popular melody', it would be impossible to say what would thereby be done for people's culture. The day which established that the booklet *Aus deutscher Seele* were noticeably rivalling the Apollo Theatre, the Wintergarten and so on would count among the greatest festival days of the now dawning century. And no less the day when the editor's 'subsidiary intention' could be shown to have come to fulfilment. For there should be no doubt that a poem like 'Die schöne Hannele', given above, contains in itself more poetry than the majority of volumes filled up with so-called 'modern lyricism'.

The editor brings everything to equip him for his task. What matters first is that among poets at present he stands in the front rank. In his *Leuchtende Tage* he showed the source of true poetic creations to be present within him. He is moreover an outstanding expert on the origins of poetry, as he has demonstrated in a series of gripping studies. Where popular fantasy comes from, what relation to life and to other forces of the folk-soul it takes on—this is what his research and observation is directed towards. Articles like the one he has just published in the *Gesellschaft* on the beginnings of the art of storytelling are exemplary. How fantasy develops is what his thought deals with. His manner of research gives quite other perspectives than the petty effects of philological hair-splitters who like to put forward their miniature fantasies as results of exact scientific investigation.

Reading lyrical collections in one go is often not easy. Here it becomes a delight. This is because Jacobowski possesses a compositional ability of the first class for arranging particular spiritual creations. The 'general summary of contents' printed at the front of the collection shows that artistic sense held sway in the arrangement. Nothing follows anything else arbitrarily, everything stands in a necessary connection. The totality of the folk-soul and the sum of human feeling in all conditions of life come into view. And they come into view in such a way that the inner harmony of popular life finds expression. The series opens with songs deriving from the highest and happiest affirmation of life, and ends with sensations about death. The entire content of popular feeling lies between. The individual chapters are: Lucky Love, Avoiding and Parting, Unlucky Love, Marriage, From a Devoted Soul, Verses for Festival Days, Riddles and Comic Rhymes, Ballads, Historical and Cultural Songs, Soldiers' Songs, Class and Lineage Songs, Hunting and Animal Life, Nature, Popular Wisdom, Drunkards' Poetry, Humour, Dying, Death. The beginning and end of this collection cannot be rendered more convincingly than by placing at the front verses wholly upborne by an urge to live:

> Wollt' Gott, ich wär' ein weisser Schwan!
> Ich wollt' mich schwingen über Berg und tiefe Tal,
> Wohl über die wilde See,
> So wüssten all' meine Freunde nicht,
> Wo ich hinkommen wär'!

and by placing at the the end a saying which with deepest wisdom reflects 'eternity' in naive sensation:

> O ewich is so lanck.

What does the artificially constructed concept of 'individuality', behind which the wisdom of our contemporaries trips along like a dandy, look like if observed in the light raying out from such poetry as this book provides? Is for instance individuality less expressed in the poem 'Die schöne Hannele' than in those of many poetic somersaults by our artistic wordwrights? Those who always speak today about 'individuality' should reflect that every person who has immersed himself into the profoundest depths of his individuality has found there something in common with all human beings. For what is it to understand an artist? It is nothing else than finding his individuality in ourselves. How do we understand Shakespeare? Only by us all having in ourselves a secret Shakespeare. To understand Shakespeare is to discover the secret Shakespeare in oneself. Shakespeare's individuality is in our individuality. That a person is single does not stop generality from being revealed to him. Life is like climbing a mountain. Our paths can be different. But we meet on the peak above, and all finally enjoy the same view over the common uniform harmony of the world. One need not become a supporter of those who preach the banal average man. But those who believe each of us to be locked into his own individual snail's house, and that they have to safeguard their own way, simply do not know that for all who look out from their snail's house there is only one world. It is wisely ordained in Nature that one can approach in countless ways the peak on which the glories of the world are revealed to us. But it is just as wise that there is only one such peak.

Common Human Property

In the next issue of the *Magazin für Litteratur* Rudolf Steiner included this notice:

> On the 13th of January the Lessing Theatre presented *Lord Quex*, a comedy in four acts by Arthur W. Pinero. If this presentation had no other importance than of showing us a dramatic work played countless times to great applause in London, one could be gratified. It is good when we have opportunity to become acquainted with what interests another nation. By this alone the performance would already be justified, but it also is in another respect than criticism of the day will admit. The comedy is found to be boring. This however depends completely on an individual. Without in any way overestimating *Lord Quex*: it contains more spirit than does the *Tugendhof* treated with such tender hands by the critics. But Pinero lives in London—that is far away. People there judge more objectively.

⋆

Here is another editorial snippet from this year's *Magazin*:

> We note the highly interesting volumes giving a picture of the 'International Congress of Women 1899':
>
> 1. International Council of Women. Report of Transactions of the Second Quinquennial Meeting held in London, July 1899. With an introduction by the Countess of Aberdeen.
> 2. Women in Education. With an introduction by Miss C.L. Maynard.
>
> 3,4. Women in Professions. With an introduction by Mrs. Bedford Fenwick.
>
> 5. Women in Politics. With an introduction by Miss E.S. Lidgett.
> 6. Women in Industrial Life. With an introduction by Mrs. J.R. Macdonald.
> 7. Women in Social Life. With an introduction by Mrs. Benson
>
> All published in London: Fisher Unwin, Paternoster Square 1900.

⋆

Early in the year Rudolf Steiner collected his articles on 'Haeckel and his Opponents' into a pamphlet, *Haeckel und Seine Gegner*. And when in March the first volume of his *Welt- und Lebensanschauungen im neunzehnten Jahrhundert* finally appeared, it was also to Haeckel that this work was dedicated. In Chapter XXX of his autobiography Steiner explained:

> To me Haeckel was a person who placed himself courageously on a thinker's standpoint in science, while the remaining world of researchers excluded thinking and would only recognize the results of sensory observation. What repeatedly attracted me towards Haeckel was that in exploring reality he set value on *creative* thinking. So I dedicated my book to him, though its content—even in the form it then had—was not composed in his manner at all. But Haeckel did not have a philosophic nature. He stood towards philosophy as a complete layman. The attacks of philosophers hailing down upon him at that very time therefore seemed to me quite uncalled-for. I dedicated the book to Haeckel in opposition to them, just as I had already composed my work *Haeckel und seine Gegner* for the same reason. Haeckel had made thinking into a means of portraying biological reality, in complete naivety towards all philosophy; he was attacked on philosophical grounds which lay on a spiritual domain foreign to him. I believe he never knew what philosophers demanded from him . . .

★

On 5 May Steiner published in another Berlin weekly, *Die Nation*, an article on 'Ludwig Jacobowski'. This began:

> One of the most remarkable depictions of a person's own soul was given by the English poet Richard Jefferies, who died in 1887, in his book *The Story of my Heart*. How may I work through all impressions and experiences so that my soul-forces are in a process of continual growth? How can I transpose inside me all sorrows and joys of existence in such a way that the life of my spirit becomes ever richer? Jefferies spent the greater part of his life under the impress of these questions. Anyone following the poetic career of Ludwig Jacobowski will find that a similar fundamental urge is observable. From his first appearance onwards, with the poetry collection *Aus Bewegten Stunden* (1889) to his most recent works *Loki: Roman eines Gottes* (1898) and *Leuchtende Tage: Neue Gedichte* (1900) there is perceptible in his development a passionate struggle to intensify his soul-forces, to let his inner life grow. Goethe once said to Eckermann: 'The beneficial in poetry is only the truly great and pure, which however stands like a second Nature and either uplifts us towards her or scorns us.' When in the twentieth year of his life Jacobowski published his first poems, he felt now uplifted and now scorned. The subtitle of this collection was *Kontraste*. From the bottom of his soul surge up disharmonies; he anxiously measures his strength against imagined ideals. He is not among persons allowing events of the world to work upon them as mere onlookers, as if they were not themselves involved. His very

> own personal destiny presents to him that of all mankind. The experiences he feels become to him symbols of a great fight which humanity is fighting in order to balance out the contrarieties of life . . .

★

With regard to Goethe, one may recall that Karl Julius Schröer had declared him to be just as much a genius as Newton, and Steiner too in his introductions to the scientific writings had regularly called him a genius.

In the next issue of the *Magazin*, on 12 May, Steiner published a review-article on this very subject entitled 'The Genial Man'. It began:

> What is genius? No less question than this is raised in the book *Der Geniale Mensch* by Hermann Türck. A knowledge of geniality is perhaps connected to that of one of the most important problems in the world. For geniality is spiritual conception. And whoever takes his stand on a modern scientific standpoint can see in spiritual conception, in productivity of soul, nothing else than a higher stage of productivity in the bodily world. How does a new individual arise from the motherly organism? How in course of the spiritual evolution of mankind does there arise a new spiritual object: a musical composition, a poem, a new tool, or shall we say just a new joke? For a modern view of the world these are very much related questions. Genius has to do with creativity, productivity, conceiving. Mentally to work over what was already there and transmit it further does not require any genius. One may carry around all the knowledge in the world—if one has no new thoughts, one has no genius. And one does not need to know very much at all; if something strikes one, be it only a new way of tying one's cravat, there is something genial about one. It should not be denied that in the great geniuses on whom the progress of culture depends there is no particular mystical gift, but only an intensification of those spiritual capacities which appear in every new inventiveness. In this sense genius is common human property. To a certain extent every person has genius. And those who are called in a real sense genial men have only a higher level of this common human property . . .

★

A couple of days later, on 14 May, Steiner wrote a letter to his parents which included the following paragraph:

> Here in Berlin there's a big festival on the 17th of June, the quincentennial memorial festival for the birth of Gutenberg, inventor of the art of printing. I've been chosen to give the festival speech to all Berlin printers (four to five thousand people). I'm curious to know how I manage with my voice. It's a great art speaking to such a large crowd of people. But of course I'm enormously pleased to be able to speak at this festival, which only takes place once every hundred years.

An Artist of Lyric Form

The second volume of *Das XIX Jahrhundert in Wort und Bild* appeared around this time. It included a contribution by Rudolf Steiner on 'Literature and Spiritual Life 1840–1871'.

This was divided into two parts, the first of which covered German and Austrian literature. The second part began by discussing French literature, mentioning *inter alia* the journeys made by Victor Cousin through Germany, and his friendship with Hegel, whose views he transplanted to France.

Steiner then continued:

> The German spirit also worked across to England. The transmitter here was Thomas Carlyle, who immersed himself in the works of Goethe and Schiller with deep understanding. He is an ideally inclined person, with a tendency for bringing out everywhere the highest points in mankind's historical development. This led him to a kind of deification of heroic personalities. Great individuals are for him the bearers of cultural progress. He is less concerned with what ferments among the masses. He wants to understand the minds whom he prefers, and depict their influence on his-

Thomas Carlyle

tory. He worked in the most fruitful way for an understanding in England of the German thought-world and of German art. He portrayed the life of Schiller and translated Goethe's *Wilhelm Meister*. Carlyle's idealism is one basic impulse running at this time through the spiritual development of England. The other is a sober unpoetic view of life, a utilitarian standpoint. Swaying uncertainly back and forth between the two was Edward Lytton-Bulwer, who in his numerous novels shows himself to be a narrator of great ability in characterization and in composing events. However, his gripping method of presentation derives more from a clever, calculating understanding than from a productive figure-creating fantasy. His works nonetheless found a large circle of readers . . .

Bulwer-Lytton, as he came later to be called, was educated in 1822 at Trinity College Cambridge.

. . . But the characteristic qualities of the English spirit were all united in the most effective narrator of this epoch, Charles Dickens, who understood as few did how to create out of the folk-soul. As soon as he made his appearance, this was understood in the widest circles. His *Sketches of London* (1836) and still more the *Pickwick Papers* (1837) made him a writer with a common touch. He knew how to depict in a most delightful manner the cosy proceedings of a family circle, the most mundane events, and the simplest feelings and passions. He observed with finest senses popular customs, thinking and feeling, and presented them with greatest vividness, irresistible kindness, and apt humour. He passed over nothing which stirs a child of the people. Superstition, natural cleverness, a sense of earthiness—all find in his works their justified place. *David Copperfield*, *Little Dorrit*, his Christmas books, especially the thrilling *A Christmas Carol*, are among the widest-read writings of world literature.

The moralizing tendency strongly pronounced in Dickens is also found in William Makepiece Thackeray. He was however lacking in the former's inwardness of mood. Dickens spoke to the heart and thus affected the moral sense, without wanting to preach morals directly. Thackeray's significance lies in the satire with which he chastises customs and relationships. A cutting acuity and humour characterize the physiognomy of his works, translated into many European languages . . .

Thackeray matriculated in 1829 at Trinity College Cambridge, where his tutor was William Whewell. On leaving Cambridge altogether in 1830, he travelled to Weimar and stayed there for six months, meeting the octogenarian Goethe.

. . . Related to him in artistic understanding is the politician Benjamin Disraeli, who however lacks his attractive humour. Dissatisfaction with circumstances of the time also found in England its literary exponents,

Lord Tennyson

namely its lyricist in Thomas Hood and its novelist in Charles Kingsley. Alfred Tennyson, by contrast, is an artist of lyric form, of a light, pleasant-sounding language, which his poems carried into the widest circles. His *Enoch Arden* has become world-famous . . .

Enoch Arden was a narrative poem in blank verse, written in 1861–2. Here is a passage describing the tropical island on which the protagonist suffers shipwreck:

The mountain wooded to the peak, the lawns
And winding glades high up like ways to Heaven,
The slender coco's drooping crown of plumes,
The lightning flash of insect and of bird,
The lustre of the long convolvuluses
That coiled around the stately stems, and ran
Even to the limit of the land, the glows
And glories of the broad belt of the world,
All these he saw; but what he fain had seen
He could not see, the kindly human face,
Nor ever hear a kindly voice, but heard
The myriad shriek of wheeling water-fowl,
The league-long roller thundering on the reef,
The moving whisper of huge trees that branched
And blossomed in the zenith, or the sweep
Of some precipitous rivulet to the wave,
As down the shore he ranged, or all day long
Sat often in the seaward-gazing gorge,
A shipwrecked sailor, waiting for a sail:
No sail from day to day, but every day
The sunrise broken into scarlet shafts
Among the palms and ferns and precipices;

The blaze upon the waters to the east;
The blaze upon his island overhead;
The blaze upon the waters to the west;
Then the great stars that globed themselves in Heaven,
The hollower-bellowing ocean...

Tennyson too was educated, from 1827 to 1831, at Trinity College Cambridge where his tutor was William Whewell, and in due course a statue of him was erected on the north side of the college antechapel alongside the statue of Whewell.

Steiner's account of mid-century English writers ended:

> ...In 1836 a poet rich in thoughts, Robert Browning, entered literature with the play *Paracelsus*. Stimulated by Shelley, he was concerned with the deepest questions of a striving human being. A Faustian impulse runs through all his ideational poems, the plays *Strafford*, *Sordello*, and also through the poetry collections. Subordinate reading-needs were catered for by Frederick Marryat, the material of whose novels is principally taken from sea- and travel-life.

Spiritual Needs

On 16 June 1900 the *Magazin für Litteratur* carried an article by Rudolf Steiner on the play *Das Neue Jahrhundert* by the writer and dramatist Otto Borngräber.

> With his tragedy on Giordano Bruno Otto Borngräber has taken a risk. I fear he will experience many disappointments. I would wish myself to be mistaken. But I doubt that our time will have the impartiality to follow this playwright's intentions. We are living in an epoch of small perspectives. Otto Borngräber has dramatized a man of the greatest possible perspective. Despite the festivities held this February to honour Giordano Bruno, despite the dithyrambic articles written about him, I do not believe the public of this 'superman of another kind', as Ernst Haeckel calls him in his preface to the drama, to be particularly large. I cannot believe in the inner truth of this cult of Giordano Bruno. One experiences symptoms too characteristic of the petty way of thinking in our time. I confess that it is for me really depressing now to observe one of these symptoms in the struggle against Ernst Haeckel's recently published *Die Welträtsel*. How often is there occasion to perceive gladness creeping out from the most hidden corners in the souls of our contemporaries about the attacks observed on a theological side against Haeckel's struggle for a new view of the world. A church historian in Halle, Loofs, no doubt believes that with his brochure *Anti-*

Haeckel, which has now appeared in several editions, he has within the opposition to Haeckel shot the bird down. He found that some chapters in Haeckel's book contravene ideas formed by current ecclesiastical history about the relation of certain facts.

In the relevant chapter Haeckel followed a book by an English agnostic, Stewart Ross, appearing in the German language under the title *Jehovas gesammelte Werke*. In Germany this book is little known. Most of Haeckel's readers will have gained knowledge of its existence from the *Welträtsel*. So too with Loofs. In his *Anti-Haeckel* he has now subjected it to criticism from the standpoint of a present 'enlightened' Protestant church historian. This criticism has turned out devastating. Ross has grievously sinned against 'facts' established by present-day biblical criticism, historical investigation of the Gospels and other sources of ecclesiastical history. Loofs cannot do too much in condemning the book. He describes it as a disgraceful publication, inspired by ignorance of church history and a blasphemous way of thinking. It can now unfortunately be observed that his judgement has made an impression on a large circle of educated people. One can hear it repeated ad nauseam that Haeckel let himself be 'taken in' by the writings of the English ignoramus.

For me all these judgements from the mouths of 'the educated' only prove one thing. Haeckel's view of the world makes them somewhat uncomfortable. Out of indefinite feelings they prefer the old Christian dogmatism to a modern conception of Nature. But this conception is too well founded to be easily fought against. The facts upholding Haeckel speak too clearly. One is allowed too much by openly shutting oneself off from this view of the world. This does not hinder one from feeling inner contentment when a theologian comes along and proves Haeckel's dilettantism in church history. One is here in a position, as if from behind and around, to form a negative judgement about the new world-conception. The Monism of the great natural scientist is not openly confronted. That would need courage. One does not have that. But the judgement can be fitted nicely together that a man like Ernst Haeckel, who is so naively taken in by the ignorance of a Stewart Ross, cannot deeply unsettle us in our ideas. Loofs himself does not hold back from a similar judgement. He virtually strikes Haeckel off the list of serious scientific researchers for basing himself on a supposedly so 'unscientific' book as that of Ross.

But let one just take this book into one's hands. Anyone reading it without bias—I really dare say this—cannot be astonished enough at the deep inner untruthfulness of Loofs's criticism. For according to the latter he must necessarily believe that he has before his eyes the work of a frivolous person not concerned with truth, but rather with mocking convictions sacred to millions of people. Instead of which he has a book by a deeply earnest man, in whose every sentence can be felt a tremendous struggle for truth. He evidently has psychic crises behind him of which people like Loofs in the comfortable cushions of their ecclesiastical history have no conception. A sacred enthusiasm for human welfare and human fortune have here inspired a person to words of wrath against traditional prejudices which he considers human misfortune. One is not dealing with a light-hearted denier, but with an outraged man swinging his scourge because he believes the truth to be distorted by Pharisees.

I need the background of this fact to justify by a remarkable symptom my above-expressed doubts about the public's receptivity to Borngräber's tragedy. I can only state once again: I would like to be thoroughly mistaken and that what Haeckel expresses at the end of his foreword be fulfilled: 'We can only express the heartfelt wish that this great tragedy, standing at the very height of our time, may not only find a wide circle of readers as an ennobling and exciting book, but also through early performance on a larger German stage find the appreciation and influence which it certainly deserves.'

I do not believe the play will find mercy at the judgement-seat of those aesthetes who during the last two decades have fortified themselves in their views. Anyone who considers the dramatic technique of 'moderns' as the only possible one will form no particularly favourable judgement about *Das neue Jahrhundert*. Neither before the naturalistic nor before the symbolically romantic forum of recent years will Borngräber's technique, with its tendency to decorative beauty and stylization, hold its own. A person who goes deeper will admittedly find joy in this stylization, dramatizing a Renaissance hero with unconcealed pleasure in forms appropriate to the Renaissance. I believe that in Borngräber may be recognized a poet who in his tastes has kept himself at a distance from the sympathies and antipathies of the day. For his artistic form he presupposes a public whose joy in formal beauty has not been wholly lost in the leanings of contemporary taste. I do not thus mean to say that I am an unqualified eulogist of the play in an aesthetic respect. I do not find Borngräber to be a master of the style he has chosen. But all this seems to me unimportant beside the great perspective of a world-conception expressed in the work. It will not be a matter of whether to aesthetic judges of this or that direction Borngräber has supplied a faultless tragedy. The matter is whether a tendency exists whereby the great world-conception for which the martyr burned in Rome as its first representative be transmitted by an elite of spiritual fighters onto a larger multitude of people.

Only someone in a position to sense with the global perspective of Bruno can have a feeling for the tragic force expressed in this personality. The tragedy lies in the relation Bruno's personality has to the radical change in world-conception brought about by men like Copernicus or Galilei.

Copernicus and Galilei supplied building-stones for a conception of the world which recent centuries have been working to extend. Bruno is one of those who at that time depicted in broad outlines, with a vision looking far into the future, the effects which must follow from the ideas of Copernicus and Galilei in conceiving the nature of man. He uttered truths of which only the first factual seeds were available. He did it at a time when these seeds did not yet have the capacity to grow, to form themselves out into a conception of the world. Borngräber with fine sense places opposite the figure of Bruno that of Galilei. Galilei is no tragic personality, though undeniably one to whom we owe more than to Bruno, if we consider the building-stones forming our world-conception. I can think Bruno completely away from the process of mental development in recent centuries. Even without him having had the thoughts filling me today, these latter could yet be exactly the same as they are. For Galilei this is not the case. Without Galilei there would be no Newton, without Newton no Lyell and Darwin and without Lyell and Darwin no modern scientific world-conception. All that would still exist without Giordano Bruno. Galilei did not go beyond what his physical foundation necessarily required. Bruno proclaimed things which a person with Galilei's cast of mind can only claim for himself today. Here lies Bruno's deep tragedy.

On reading Borngräber's book I had constantly to think about a lonely fighter of our days, the worthy Eugen Reichel...

Reichel was a regular contributor to the *Magazin*.

...He has placed before our eyes a person of the sixteenth century in whom we find the tragedy for which Giordano Bruno is put to us as a representative by Borngräber realized in yet quite another sense. Reichel is convinced that in 1586 there died a man whom the world of the time looked upon in our present-day spirit, and whose remembrance has hitherto been completely expunged from the memory of mankind.

Reichel believes that, to anyone looking more deeply, Shakespeare's plays and the *Novum Organon* by Bacon of Verulam reveal a tremendous, genial personality equally great as poet and thinker, but who died in oblivion without being understood by the surrounding world. Shakespeare's plays as they lie before us are not the work of their original genial creator, but have arisen by mutilation, dilettante expansion, and revision of the estate. The *Novum Organon* too, in the form handed down to us, is a work where two minds may be perceived: an original one, standing on the height of a Copernican view of Nature and already at the end of the sixteenth century living in the world-conception completed by the three following centuries, and a bungling scholastic. Bacon of Verulam was this bungling scholastic. He acquired the estate of the forgotten genius and 'revised' it in the way indicated, handing over to the surrounding world and

> to posterity the philosophical part under his own name, and the dramatic part under the name of the Stratford actor Shakespeare . . .

All this was set out in Reichel's *Shakespeare-Literatur*, published in 1886.

> . . . Even today I am not in a position to form a judgement about this great question to which Reichel has devoted his powers. Suppose that one could agree with Reichel. In the genius of the sixteenth century which he sees behind the works of Bacon and Shakespeare is then revealed to us a figure of deepest tragedy—of a Bruno tragedy transposed into immensity. A hostile power killed Bruno. It could not destroy his work. He departs from life conscious that his enemies are more afraid of this work than he of their judgement. The lack of judgement among contemporaries destroyed the work by the English genius; it murdered him not just bodily, but spiritually. In his *Meisterkrone* Eugen Reichel gave this tragedy a dramatic form in large strokes. He did not poetically shape a real historical process as Borngräber is doing now, but created the basis for a symbolic act. No doubt the perspective is thus increased for anyone who can feel the tragedy of the personality concerned. But through Borngräber's work the tragic problem at issue is brought closer to a larger public.
>
> Borngräber's play will soon receive a performance in Leipzig arranged by a circle of the work's friends. May others follow it, and may our stages (in Berlin) also soon pluck up courage and open their gates to the Bruno tragedy. They can then fulfil a fine task in the great struggle for the 'new faith'. 'The tremendous struggle between ecclesiastical religion and spiritual religion, between spiritual servitude and spiritual freedom which is just now ringing in "the new century" meets us excitingly in Borngräber's work.' (E. Haeckel in the foreword.) Worthy performances of this play could significantly contribute to an understanding of this struggle. Should the stage give a picture of the world, it must not cut itself off from what is highest for human beings in this world, from spiritual needs.

A Vigorous Co-worker in All Culture

The 'four to five thousand people' expected by Rudolf Steiner as his audience for the speech at the Gutenberg festival on 17 June 1900 turned into an even larger number, for in his autobiography he recalled:

> At the celebration of Gutenberg's jubilee, I was chosen to give the festival speech in a Berlin circus before 7000 setters and printers . . .

The speech was published at the time in the professional journal *Deutscher Buch- und Steindrucker*, under the title 'The Deed of Gutenberg as a Milestone of Cultural Development'.

> One must go back to the founding of Christianity to come across a point of time in mankind's evolutionary history which seems as important as the turn of the fifteenth and sixteenth centuries. With our whole thinking and feeling we stand immeasurably closer to everything which has occurred in the last four centuries than to what took place before. We have a sense that our own cultural life is bound up with the occurrences of this time, and everything previous appears like something detached.
>
> Gutenberg's invention stands there like a great milestone dividing this detached part from the cultural epoch still working on today. If we look more closely, Gutenberg seems to us like a participant in everything which has happened in recent centuries. Our material and spiritual life fully confirms what was expressed soon after Gutenberg by Wimpheling: 'Of no invention or fruit of the mind can we Germans be so proud as of book-printing. What different life stirs up in all classes of people, and who would not gratefully recall the first founder and promoter of this art!'

Jacob Wimpheling was a German humanist of the late fifteenth and early sixteenth centuries.

> But one may also state that no art entered history at the right point of time in such a way as printing. It is as though in the mid-fifteenth century the whole world were waiting for Gutenberg's deed. A turnabout had long been preparing in the communal life of society, in the mental pictures and feelings of men. German mysticism, brought about by the thirteenth, fourteenth and fifteenth centuries, heralds the new epoch. Mystics wanted to free themselves from ideas transmitted to human beings by an old tradition, and which could only be believed on the witness of authorities. People wanted to find the source of all spiritual life inside their own soul. An impulse to liberate the personality and individuality was gaining ground. The individual man wanted to test for himself the thoughts he must follow in carrying out his cultural tasks. From such an impulse grew the need for a new means of gaining human knowledge. Anyone wanting to yield unrestrainedly to authority can do nothing else than go along and have the views of this authority verbally transmitted. Anyone wanting to seek after truth and knowledge for himself, building on his own thinking, needs the book, which makes him independent from authority. Gutenberg pressed the book into men's hands at a time when they most urgently needed it. For Germans, Luther translated the Bible into their mother-tongue. The paths upon which this henceforth comprehensible Bible could wander out into the whole world were smoothed by Gutenberg. The Reformation is unthinkable without the previous invention of printing.
>
> The way by which spiritual treasures made accessible to all men through the art of the printer at first worked shows quite evidently what vast importance this art possesses. Before its invention, knowledge of natural-

scientific laws was a secret for the few. Large multitudes of people, if wanting to have explained to them natural phenomena played out hourly before their eyes, were referred to the worst superstitions. The book made it possible for these multitudes to form ideas about the natural course of what is constantly occurring before their eyes and ears. But the populace, which for centuries had been referred merely to authoritative belief, was little prepared really to form proper notions. In books, ideas were conveyed which had never before been heard about. It was therefore believed that even more must be hiding behind such ideas than the simple plain letters of the new art transmit. This belief smoothed the ground for all conceivable 'secret sciences' and arts, for charlatans who gave themselves out as owners of special higher knowledge and to whom people willingly lent belief, letting themselves be beguiled by them because they could only slowly become used to forming their own independent judgement.

We can observe the incapacity—which had grown through the centuries—of giving simple explanations for natural facts in the profound books of such a select mind as Jacob Böhme (1575–1624). This simple man is really great in presenting everything which can be gained through searching one's own heart and feelings. But he becomes highly adventurous when wanting to explain physical or other natural events.

Such phenomena show what part the deed of Gutenberg plays in expanding the horizon of western humanity. For the greatest part of mankind, insight into Nature was first won through the printer's art.

Through this conquest of natural knowledge the spiritual life of modern times acquired a quite different character. Unworldly and hostile to Nature as is the life of the Middle Ages enclosed in a cloister, just as unworldly is also in effect the whole of education before the fifteenth and sixteenth centuries. What might the object of such education be? Nothing other than what the human being spun out of himself. One was not taught by natural phenomena; one just sharpened the logical weapons of understanding. Scholasticism is a result of such unworldly education. It may well be maintained that scholasticism could only influence spiritual life as long as there were only written books, to most people inaccessible. The educational path which previously had to be trodden by someone who wanted to attain to these books was such that it brought the whole human mind into a direction receptive to scholasticism. The printing of books made it possible to enlist quite new forces for taking part in spiritual culture. People who had not been forced onto a special track were able to collaborate in fostering education. The whole physiognomy of education thus also became different. Human awareness, instead of just being concerned with unworldly scholasticism, was directed onto experience, onto real life. Gutenberg may also be regarded as a quiet participant in all achievements related to the names of Copernicus, Kepler, Galilei and Bacon of Verulam. For both Copernicus's book—so rich in its effects—which pointed out new paths for astronomy, and Kepler's discoveries of the movement of heavenly bodies, could only become properly fruitful for the world when met by a generation which was seeking an education friendly to the world, not foreign therefrom.

Gutenberg made it possible for the great pathfinders of science and art in modern times to address wide circles of people. For a scientific world-conception to flourish depends on as many as possible taking part in education. As long as truth was sought only in the human mind, it sufficed for a few to devote themselves to this search and convey their results to others. But ever since truth has been sought in the immeasurably numerous facts of the outer world, the circle of those interested in enlarging education needs to be as great as possible.

Not only spiritual culture, however, but also social and economic life were waiting just in the fifteenth century for a new means of spreading human thoughts and established facts and experiences. The growth and evolving independence of a merchant class placed higher demands on the personal competence of a single man than had previous conditions. By the totality to which he belonged, and through the social organism into which he was membered, an individual's activity was formerly strictly determined and happened inside quite narrow boundaries. In the fifteenth century all these things underwent enlargement. An individual was liberated from associations which his aims had previously prescribed for him. The whole of life became more complex. Firm companionships had loosened. An individual himself had to make his way through life. No longer the guild was decisive for what had to happen, but the personality. In his writers and procurers a big merchant could henceforth only have regard for personal assiduity. Family considerations and class affiliation, formerly decisive factors as to who should stand in a particular place, now fell right away. The need arose in each single person for a wide view of the world. Man had to orientate himself over what went on in the world. Again it was Gutenberg's invention which made such things possible. In place of primitive means for agreement about world conditions, which alone had been known by the Middle Ages, there appeared printed information. The first 'newspaper' already came out in 1505. It even brought news about Brazil.

Through printed information what is called *public opinion* first became possible. The whole of mankind was so to speak drawn towards the great discussion which guides the course of world events. In leaflets, tractates, pamphlets, a single person spoke to the totality. The seventeenth century developed the newspaper, and with this also the influence of the folk-spirit. Besides cabinets and individual statesmen, people step onto the world stage and join in where great political and cultural questions are involved. An individual statesman sees himself obliged to conform to public opinion if he wants to work successfully. We see statesmen spreading through the press the motives for their actions, so as not to be powerless. In leading personalities we see respect for public opinion increasingly growing. Wallenstein's officers send to the Munich newspapers reports about their deeds of weaponry. The Austrian government complains to the Brandenburgian that Berlin newspapers have an anti-Austrian tendency. It is thanks to the art of printing that the spirit of a people must gradually be reckoned with, as a fully justified element within the bustle of the world.

It is definitely not going too far to see the period of the Enlightenment as substantially conditioned by printing. In Gutenberg's workshop at Mainz a basis was laid for the attitude to which the philosopher Kant gave monumental expression by the words: 'Have the audacity to use your own reason.'...

The quotation is from Kant's *Beantwortung der Frage: Was ist Aufklärung?* (1784).

...For reason must first be gradually educated to such audacity. This it could only be by knowing how to gain continuous information about what is going on in the world. And anyone who wants to gain benefit from using his own reason must also be able to reckon on his say being heard. The eighteenth century was allowed and able to be enlightened, because the seventeenth developed a public opinion and established its value.

What public opinion signifies was learned by the factors in power, but also soon learned by those who wanted to contribute their mite to the progress of spiritual life. We can follow how power and education united with the printer's art, since on this depended a successful result. Printing finds its best foster-places in the proximity of educational institutions, and scholars associate with the new art, indeed themselves become printers, so as to obtain influence in the world for their works. Papal envoys no longer send every week to Rome merely their own reports, but also the newspapers, where the voice of the people has come to expression.

There is a deeply symbolic significance that the printer's art met with a similar mistrust as knowledge and cognition itself. It is characteristic that Gutenberg's companion Fust or Faust was brought into relation with the most interesting cultural and historical saga of modern times. Since man has seized hold of knowledge, of cognition, he has fallen away from God. This is the meaning of the Fall. Man's thirst for knowledge could only be attibuted to intervention by the Devil. The 'black art', a great ally of the thirst for knowledge, was presented as nothing less than a work of hell. It was said of Faust: 'Henceforth he wanted no more to be called a theologian, became a man of the world, called himself a Dr. Medicinae.' That the forming of such a saga became united to knowledge and the printer's art shows their deep inner connection.

The quotation is from the *Historia von D. Johann Fausten* (1587)—the work discussed by Edmund Reitlinger in his article on 'Doctor Faust and Natural Science' published in 1874 in *Freie Blicke*.

> With the spread of the printer's art we see at the same time poetry, all literature, becoming popular. The scholarly touch which spiritual life up till then possessed made place for a new spirit. Merry farce and cheerful prank enter into the art of narrative. It is known that henceforth one can now speak to the populace, and so endeavours are also made to offer them things which relate to their most personal attitude, to their feeling and ideation. And out of the populace itself, which is now taking part in spiritual life, new powers grow. One should not underestimate how much the printer's art has contributed to personalities like for instance Hans Sachs being able to swing up to a significant height of creativity. How much would probably never have appeared before his eyes if printing had not transmitted it to him!
>
> Through Gutenberg a bridge was created between two worlds which are called on to work together and can only bring about a successful process of development for mankind through continual interaction on each other. Fichte in his *Reden an die deutschen Nation* described it as a serious defect of culture if a scholarly class stands over against self-dependent people who do not understand it or gain anew from it fresh driving forces. In the full sense of the word such a judgement may only be made about culture in the Middle Ages. Here the last four centuries have created a complete turnabout through printing. Participation of people in their work has also worked back onto scholars in a most favourable way. The latter had lost all feeling for other classes. This can best be seen by the first scientific books handed out to the people. They were completely interspersed with all possible miracle-stories. It was believed that people were not ready for actual natural truths. Here too one soon learned otherwise, and was—on the contrary—driven to clarify one's own thoughts and give them a better form through wanting to be understood. The need to transmit knowledge thus brought about clarification of knowledge itself. Reflecting began on the art of how to bring education into the widest circles. Comenius's great pedagogical thoughts on the tasks of folk-education presuppose that a people longing for knowledge need to interact vigorously with the carriers of the entire spiritual life.
>
> So we can follow the influence of Gutenberg's deed into the whole of modern life. If other spiritual heroes created the content for this life, it was he who supplied the means for bringing this content to full effect. We are thus so much at home in everything which the last four centuries have brought about; everything is also so foreign to us which we learn historically about times lying before the invention of the art of printing. How man thinks depends more than one is usually inclined to assume on the way he is connected to his fellow human beings, how he interacts with them. Just as

language itself, which first builds a bridge from man to man, is a creator of culture, so is the printed word, that mighty intermediary and potent representative of the spoken word, a co-creator of modern culture. The human being took hold of the printed word in an age when he began to lay the highest value on his individuality, on personal competence. Through this emphasizing of the personality he turned away from the old co-operatives, in which space became too narrow. The art of printing gave him a new means for seeking, in place of the old restrictive union, a new way of coming together, in accord with a widened horizon of life. The more man individualized himself, the more he needed a means freed from his immediate personality, in order once again to attain to the whole. The art of book-printing showed itself to be the uniting bond at a point of time in history when life placed a demanding challenge onto the single man and also onto the single folk: to detach oneself, in order to make oneself capable inside the great struggle for existence.

Ever since the art of printing was invented, it was seen to be a capable ally of human progress. Where the latter attains a certain height, the former comes abettingly to its side. Where progress encounters hindrances, the printer's art also suffers. An eloquent example is the beneficial influence emanating from the union of the 'brothers of the common life'. This was founded by Gerhard Groote (1340–1384) from Deventer and set itself the task of turning education from a scholarly monopoly into a source of popular welfare. This union developed important pedagogical activity. The emergence of a large number of schools may be traced back to its influence. When the printer's art appeared, quite new life entered into the cultural work of the brothers of the common life. They could provide for the widest dissemination of good textbooks. They themselves took in hand to print these books, and thus became promoters of the new art in Holland and the whole of north-west Germany. If this fact demonstrates how progress and book-printing belong together, no less indicative is the backward step taken by the art after the first time of its great flourishing and rapid spread in the sixteenth and seventeenth century. The culture which at the start of the new age had attained a wonderful height is given a series of hard blows by the Peasant Wars, the unhappy religious confusions with their bloody, devastating consequence, and the Thirty Years War. The art of printing now played as much part in the decline of spiritual and material culture as it had previously in their development.

That a lower level of general popular education interacts with the art of printing is unmistakable in the difficulties the latter encountered in Spain. In the fourteenth and fifteenth century, ecclesiastical censorship and dominance over people on the part of the clergy were greater here than in Central Europe. So the printer's art too spread only gradually; and even the little it achieved here may be traced to the influence of single persons with scientific interests. Since in Spain this art had no real basis, in the following time the subjugation of spiritual life by the Jesuits and the Inquisition could find a special home. Turkey shows most glaringly that only a person who is a promoter of Gutenberg's art can play a role in modern cultural life. Right into the eighteenth century the Turks proved themselves utter enemies of this art. In 1483 Sultan Bajazet threatened anyone printing with the death penalty, and his son had the threat renewed. This people had to pay for measures so inimical to printing by losing any importance within the spiritual life of Europe. It is interesting to follow the relation of spiritual life and the printer's art in Hungary. The ruler there in the second half of the fifteenth century was King Matthias Corvinus. He had a deep interest in sciences and arts. Already from 1473 onwards the printer's art was therefore eagerly promoted in the capital of Hungary. A vigorous spiritual life thus held sway in this country, which on account of its geographical position has to struggle with greatest difficulties in regard to cultures.

Man is a being who can only attain to a truly purposeful activity in the future by knowledge of the past. History is his great teacher. One may compare how much more exactly, more intimately we know the last four centuries than previous times when printing was not yet a companion to all culture. For those times we are only too often dependent on mere suppositions and bold hypotheses, since historical tradition leaves us for large stretches in the lurch. The printer's art is thus not only a vigorous co-worker in all culture, it is also the best and most faithful preserver of the treasures of the past, which man so much needs for the future.

In the nineteenth century, the age of scientific knowledge and technology, the printer's art did not in its advances remain behind other cultural factors. With its great technical improvements it can worthily stand beside the other achievements of our present time. And if today we are not living without optimism in the now dawning century and are gladly looking into the future of human evolution, we may thank for no small part of this mood the genius of Johannes Gutenberg.

Into the Widest Circles

Rudolf Steiner's engagement with this same subject is further shown by an associated review-article published six days later, on 23 June, in the *Magazin für Litteratur*. It was entitled 'The Art of Printing: to Celebrate the Quincentenary of its Founder'.

There can be no doubt that the physiognomy of spiritual life in which modern man is standing has been created by the last four centuries. Anyone looking back in history feels at the turn of the fifteenth and sixteenth centuries a shift of culture having few parallels in the evolution of humanity. Whatever school conferences may say to favour study of the ancients, every impartial person feels today how immeasurably closer to him lies everything which spiritual progress since that turn of time has brought forth than everything preceding. He feels the connectedness of this spiritual evolution, and what came before seems like a foreign world closed in on itself. Set against its predecessors, this culture of recent centuries has in it something of victorious confidence, of conquering power, of future certainty. In order to admit this, there is no need to side with habitual condemners of medieval spiritual life. One can keep a free vista for the heights of thinking to which for instance a Thomas Aquinas upraised himself. But did this thinking possess the conquering power inherent in the culture of recent times? It was indeed precisely Thomas Aquinas who had to capitulate before the blindest superstition. The year of his death is also that of the first official burning of witches. For a long time the Church pitted herself against such belief. Her science had no power to overcome it. Before the sixteenth century there really were natural scientists implementing methods and arranging experiments held in the spirit of our own. One only need recall the genial Roger Bacon. What did people take the outcomes of their physical experiments to be? Results of magic arts. Only since the sixteenth century does belief in the naturality of natural processes conduct its campaign of conquest through the world. Only since this time does it feel the power to gain victory.

The centuries preceding the sixteenth prepare us for this belief. The German mysticism of a Tauler, of a Meister Eckhart struggles not to owe truth to a supernatural revelation, but to let it stream out of the human soul in a natural way. And as soon as the belief was established that revelation could be found in man himself, individual need was also increasingly obliged to awaken, to take direct and active part in the development of culture.

Ground was thus gained for a new kind of communication of discovered truths. People had finally to work out for themselves things in relation to which they had formerly sought advice from specially favoured men. The immediate influence of such men lost power. People no longer wanted to accept what they heard. They wanted to think along. A kind of communication was needed free from the direct presence of a person.

The fact cannot be denied away that historiographers of spiritual life have little to say about the centuries of the Middle Ages. What went on there was settled by a few amongst themselves. Spiritual life only gains richness when the number of those who take part in it becomes large.

Johannes Gutenberg called on mankind to take part in it. He transmitted to the world what was formerly the property of a few. In place of an artificial selection of spiritual leaders he set a natural one. It was a matter of chance if among those few who in the Middle Ages took part in spiritual life there was precisely a chosen person. This became different when the art was discovered of carrying education into the widest circles. How differently can a cheap book select from the multitude of human beings those who are called upon to foster culture than did the artificial selection-principle of the Middle Ages!

In the sixteenth century such spreading of culture was among the greatest conceivable historical needs. The scene on which human fortunes were played out became vastly enlarged. Through the discoveries and the related enlargement of all connecting traffic, the world in which man had to develop his activity became more spread-out. An enormous sum of human forces which had till then lain fallow was enlisted to collaborate in the fortunes of the world. This power rested bound up in human beings, in individuals. The individual had to intervene more strongly in the course of evolution. To this end his circle of vision had to be enlarged. The art of printing books liberated countless forces lying bound up in personalities.

Other inventions and discoveries set man greater tasks than he had had to master formerly. The art of printing gave him the possibility of solving these tasks.

It is a deeply indicative symbol that the new art did not emerge from circles of learned education. A man of practice hit upon it, a personality removed from his standing and family. Johannes Gutenberg had grown out of surrounding connections as an individual human being, relying entirely on himself. He did not work inside tradition, like representatives of a scholarly class. He is a type of modern man, wanting to attain what he needs not through possessions handed down by a union he has grown out of, but rather by setting his cause upon himself and his own ability.

No traditional forces grown out of medieval culture could create the new art, but only modern man, the individual placed on his own resources, who is an outcome of changed social connections at the turn of the fifteenth and sixteenth century.

What meaning does the whole quarrel over the home town of the art of printing basically have? Gutenberg's fatherland is the world of modern culture. He had to grow out of all paternity into a genuine modern humanity, in order to create for mankind the international art of printing. Since von der Linde produced his monumental work on the art of book-printing, all quarrelling over other shares in the invention has been settled for good...

The reference is to Antonius von der Linde's three-volumed *Geschichte der Erfindung der Buchdruckerkunst*, published in 1886.

...And it accords with our feeling that an uprooted, typically modern human being of modern times has created its character.

From century to century the Gutenberg festivals became more splendid. Nothing is more natural. Mankind becomes ever more conscious of what it owes to Gutenberg. Every day puts new things into effect which he made possible.

> An extremely creditable work to celebrate the five-hundredth anniversary of Johann Gutenberg is provided by Dr. Heinrich Meisner and Dr. Johannes Luther (*Die Erfindung der Buchdruckerkunst*). Arrangements and images from antiquity and the Middle Ages, which may be considered as in a sense preparing mankind for Gutenberg's art, are depicted in an appealing and transparently clear way. Especially fine is a description of the culture of wood-engraving, the immediate predecessor of typography. One recognizes from this description how the need for the art of printing was born from a desire in the masses for learning and education. That the authors do not overestimate Church influence on the spreading of Gutenberg's art will be welcomed with pleasure by those who recognize the signature of spiritual life in the last four centuries as an anti-ecclesiastical one. For the Church just shrank away from the new education she met in the letter-characters, and was clever enough to reckon with a cultural factor whose effect she could not hold back. It would have lain much more in her spirit to have continued the politics which at the Council of Toulouse found such crass expression in banning the laity from reading and owning the Bible.

In the early thirteenth century, during the struggle in south-west Europe between the Catholic Church and the Cathars, the Councils of Toulouse in 1229 and Béziers in 1233 forbade all reading of the Bible in the vernacular, and in 1234 the Synod of Tarragona went on to prohibit anyone from owning a Bible translation without approval from a bishop.

Steiner ended:

> Gutenberg's personality, his life and deeds are clearly characterized, and the spread of printing during initial decades vividly depicted. The writers have shown a fortunate gift in grouping factual material which is not easy to handle. In view of the quality of the authors, it seems superfluous to remark that their presentation rests wholly on current knowledge of the subject, and therefore anyone may gain instruction from the book in an up-to-date way.
>
> Regarding one point, the fashion of the time to overload books with illustrations is here for once beneficial. To anyone wanting to picture printing's first stages, it is in the highest degree desirable for the first prints to come before his eyes in illustrations.
>
> There will be few cultural deeds in whose history such wide circles have interest as the art of printing. The book takes this circumstance into account in every respect. It thoroughly deserves to become popular.

A Memorial

On Michaelmas Day, 29 September 1900, Rudolf Steiner—by then deeply engaged in his lecturing activity in the Workers' Training College—finally resigned as editor of the *Magazin für Litteratur*, after three years and three months in the post. He was succeeded by two other persons who henceforth edited this journal jointly.

Nonetheless for several further months Steiner still went on contributing articles to the journal, no doubt in order to support his successors. On 6 October he published one entitled 'A Memorial'.

> The life of Austrian Germans at the present time has been described by one politician as a graveyard where a host of hopes lie buried. Only with difficulty will an outsider be able to form a notion of the reasons which in recent decades have decided the destiny of Germans in the country of the Danube and the Alps. But anyone who like myself spent the first thirty years of his life in Austria, and in particular spent the period of his academic study at the beginning of the eighties in Vienna, will find hardly anything in the course of Austrian development inconceivable. For he will have seen numerous single persons playing out individual destinies which are no more than a miniature repetition of this course of development. By taking into account the character and temperament of an Austrian German and—in relation thereto—the peculiarities of spiritual life in his country, everything in these particular cases becomes understandable.
>
> Drawing on the example of a student friend, I would like to show how easily talents which under other circumstances would probably have come to beneficial effect can precisely in Austria collapse. In the eighties I began my studies at the Viennese Technical College. It was a period when a great deal in Austria was decided. Liberalism, which after the defeat at Königgrätz had experienced a brief time of blossom because influential circles were hoping thereby to deliver the state from the total confusion into which bureaucracy had brought it, had sunk in reputation. It had lost the leadership of the Empire, partly from weakness and partly because it had been left too short a time to fulfil its intentions. We young people of that period did not expect from it anything further of relevance. With all the greater enthusiasm did we dedicate ourselves to the up-and-coming German national movement. Its leaders were little concerned with what had previously been called 'Austrian state thoughts'. In this they saw an abstraction foreign to reality. An Austrian state which does not consider the manifoldness of its people's cultures, but on the basis of extremely moderate progress wants to come to terms with a democracy upholding every possible inherited prejudice and right, seemed to younger people preposterous. Younger Germans believed they might look into the future all the happier in their hopes by stressing their own people, immersing themselves in their national culture, and cultivating a relation to the progress of spiritual life in Germany. Academic young people in the eighties lived themselves into such ideals. They did not notice that the development of actual events took a direction in which the

only endeavours with a chance of success were those resting on much grosser presuppositions than theirs. The great activity soon aimed at by Georg von Schönerer who in place of idealistic German tendencies set up the racial standpoint of anti-Semitism could not convert us. In such a case idealists seldom do anything else than break out in laments over the failure to appreciate their justified endeavours. At the time these idealists in Austria had, so to speak, the ground removed from under their feet. Their activity was lamed by a public spirit in whose strivings they did not wish to take part. These words might describe the destiny of a great number of persons who at this given time were engaged in their studies. Only few of them roused themselves to seek satisfaction in callings lying outside the public life of Austria. Many of them sank with unpleasant resignation into a dull philistine existence. But the lives of not a few of them suffered total shipwreck.

In these lines I would like to erect a little memorial to one of them. He is called Rudolf Ronsperger. In the fullest sense of the word he was one of the idealists just described. To those like myself befriended with him during their student years he showed a poetic gift of great promise. The basis on which such talents developed was the idea of German nationality. The shipwreck of this idea experienced by us was accompanied in Ronsperger by something else no less characteristic of Austrian relationships. He had not been educated at a *Gymnasium*, but at an *Oberrealschule*. Austrian *Oberrealschulen* are in a certain respect models of modern training establishments. People there are brought up, without Latin or Greek, to a level of education in all other repects fully equal to that of a *Gymnasium*. But those who have this training miss out precisely on knowledge of Latin and Greek. Admission to a university is therefore denied them. These *Realschulen* bear loud witness to the half-measures familiar in Austria in every domain. Almost everywhere people remain at the point of departure for justifiable aims. Vigour for final consequences is mostly lacking. So it was with the *Realschulen*. They were so arranged that pupils had a modern humanistic education, and the way was then closed off into the only calling which this education gave the more idealistically inclined among them reason to desire. Countless people fall victim to these half-measures in educational arrangements. Ronsperger belonged among them. Through the manner of his gifts, and the direction these gifts had taken in the *Realschule*, he was wholly unsuited to a technical vocation. His energy was insufficient later to make up what would have been opened to him by the gates of the university. He was thus wholly Austrian. He remained in half-measures. The course of his life is an understandable result of his Austrian character and the depicted Austrian conditions. As students, he and I lived through much in common. Later on, life led us apart. In course of our friendly relations he showed me many pleasant poems and some dramatic pieces, among them a play, 'Hannibal', of which Heinrich Laube later expressed his approval. I then only heard that he had become a railway official.—A few months ago his sister, the wife of a respected Berlin writer, handed over to me this student friend's literary estate. At thirty-eight years of age, when all hope had vanished, he put an end to his life.

I do not feel inclined to present anything from the content of this estate of lyric and dramatic pieces, though it includes a comedy in four acts which found praise before judges of a competition in Vienna for its very good dialogue and was only rejected because this person, mistreated by life, had portrayed this life all too unrealistically. It is not these achievements which invite deep sympathy for this unfortunate person, but his life. A document speaking clearly about this life was found in the estate. It is a letter to myself, written several years before Ronsperger's suicide. In this letter he wrote about his dashed hopes and the suffering inflicted on him. He attempts to revive our old friendship, so as to find his way to some extent with my support. He did not send the letter because—he was unable to ask for my address. To me this fact expresses symbolically his whole destiny. He is representative of characters so numerous especially in Austria, who in all their strivings go as far as the point where they are confronted by reality. And if this reality offers hindrances of risible pettiness—as in this instance—they do not confront the reality. I am convinced that countless people of the same age as Rudolf Ronsperger might characterize themselves as he did in this letter. Because I do not consider it a chance single case but something typical, I tell something of it. 'In my outer circumstances of life little has occurred worthy of note. Posted firstly to Leitmeritz, later to Kostomlat, then again to Leitmeritz, and finally since almost two years ago traffic official in Nimburg, I'm now in a post which a subaltern official can't wish to be more pleasant and respected . . . There'd be somewhat more to report about the destinies, or rather transformations which my inner being has in recent years undergone. A lot, maybe everything has changed in my views of the world and man—*one* firm conviction hasn't been lost to me even in the five years of bitter struggles: the conviction of my poetic calling. For me it's stayed alive, though I'm involved in an occupation which otherwise usually takes up the whole man day and night, and mostly robs from him an ability to devote himself to side-thoughts wholly deviating from his official duties and almost incompatible with them. For me it's remained, despite the mocking smiles of all who chanced to gain knowledge of it. And even if in the great world nothing is heard of my scribblings—I believe I may state it boldly: I'm still a poet . . . You'll perhaps call that arrogance. But to anyone like me to whom poetry has become a necessity of life, anyone forced like me to turn all his thinking and feeling into poetry may well be entirely justified in claiming that he's called to be a poet. Even chosen?—That's a question I can't answer with "no", as I'd thereby dash a great deal of my hopes. And a sanguine person of the first order like me doesn't do that. I'm not blind to all the faults I possess, which have contributed to my not so far having achieved what alone could have decisively and indeed conclusively affected the direction of my calling—a success. Of all these faults lack of energy is first and greatest; a deficiency in strength and perseverance, that iron persistence, that tenacity, conscious of its aim and its victory, in pursuing plans once drawn up, which are always the accompanying qualities of talent and help it to break through under the hardest conditions. Without being presumptuous, I can say that I'd have done good things had luck indulged me and a warm ray of sunshine made my capacities blossom, had my desires met no opposition and my attempts been favoured by destiny. I'd have sailed fast with the wind behind me, and perhaps have achieved much which others under similarly favourable circumstances had never attained. I lacked courage and strength to sail against the wind. I make many powerless attempts—and only not having wholly foundered and fallen headlong into the waves still gives me hope that perhaps the wind will turn once more and might drive forward the unskilful boatman, who didn't want to learn how to trim the sail.'

This turn of the wind unfortunately did not come. More energy would have made Rudolf Ronsperger seek his own path, off the tracks marked down by conditions of Austrian culture. Less idealism and feeling would have let him adapt to the work into which these conditions had brought him. He would then have buried the conviction of his poetic calling in the dull sea of everyday life.

Our Complete Trust

Writing this article about Rudolf Ronsperger must have called up in Rudolf Steiner memories of their friendship in Vienna in the early 1880s. In this respect it seems more than just coincidental that on 20 October 1900—only a fortnight after the article about Ronsperger—Steiner published in the *Magazin für Litteratur* a further article entitled 'Thomas Babington Macaulay, born on the 25th of October 1800'.

In course of his letters to Ronsperger of August 1881 Steiner had referred to Macaulay's essay on *Milton*. During the intervening period this essay must have led him onto other works by the same author.

Here is the article:

There are few historical works the reading of which awakens in us such a sure feeling of being led into the spirit of the depicted epoch as Macaulay's *History of England*. Doubtless historians exist who understand how to form their matter more artistically or work out their personalities more vividly, and others who manage to bring forward even greater diligence than Macaulay in the assembling of details. Yet in only quite few historical writers can a harmonious coordination of these three capacities be found in the same way as it is with him. The work's first two volumes came out in 1848. In England their publication was awaited with the very greatest of hopes. Something most exceptional was anticipated from the man who for over twenty years had been regarded with the greatest esteem as an essayist and politician. Macaulay surpassed all expectations. In the shortest conceivable time translations were available in German, French, Dutch, Danish, Swedish, Russian, Italian, Spanish, Polish, Bohemian, Hungarian and Persian. That the book spread so rapidly through the whole educated world is quite understandable if the sure feeling awakened by study of it as mentioned above is taken into account. It belongs among literary achievements which from our first acquaintance with them gain our complete trust. The first two volumes cover the short span of English history from 1685 to 1689; in later volumes Macaulay managed to depict events up to 1704. There were ten years of careful study before publication. Even someone uninstructed about this carefulness from Macaulay's biography will soon learn about it from the work. Every sentence insistently expresses it. The portrayal of facts is so vivid that one almost believes one is listening to a contemporary, and the character-drawing of the personalities depicted often lulls us into the illusion that someone is narrating on the basis of personal acquaintance. This complete maturity of historical judgement results from the course of Macaulay's life and his quite peculiar disposition of character. He was almost always placed into life-situations which offered him the largest conceivable experiential horizon. His father as a sixteen-year-old was sent by a Scottish commercial firm to Jamaica. There he came to know the horrors of slavery. This caused him to devote part of his life to battling against it. After his return to his own country, a society founded for the purpose of freeing slaves gave him the task of colonizing slaves liberated on the coast of Sierra Leone. The character of such a person ripened for cultural tasks of great style must also have contributed to the growth in the son of a great free spirit. In this respect his father deeply influenced the young Macaulay. At his parental home would gather numerous people belonging to widely differing branches of activity. The elder Macaulay did everything to awaken his son's interest in the dealings and work of these men.—When Macaulay was twenty-five years old, his first significant literary work appeared in the *Edinburgh Review* on Milton. At a stroke it turned the author into a famous man. Fame at such a young age upraises a person having preconditions for it to a higher place of activity. It lends the necessary strength to bring his talent into a proper relation to matters and contemporaries. In a country like England the attention of those interested in public life was soon directed onto the young writer. In 1830 he was elected Member of Parliament for Wiltshire. He represented the people during a stirring time. The French Revolution in July kindled everywhere a call to extend liberty. As a parliamentarian Macaulay was allowed in 1831 to take part in the debate on Lord Russell's Reform Bill. The issue was maintenance of English constitutional conditions. Macaulay acted in such a way as added to his fame as a great writer also that of an important politician. Three years later his creative domain was widened again. He was elected a member of the Council of India. He discharged his post in England's colonies on the basis of an ethically uplifted view of life. His activity in India lasted until 1837. It left beneficent traces in the country's material and spiritual culture. From then onwards till the year 1847 Macaulay led a quieter life, almost entirely devoted to extensive studies for his *History of England*. In 1847 he entered Parliament once again. How great his influence was—resting on nothing more than the convincing effect of his words and reasons—can be seen by his having managed in 1853 to bring about by a majority of over a hundred votes a legal proposal, as good as decided by his speech, on expelling from Parliament the Senior Archivist.

That Macaulay could make use of the fortunate positions into which he came in the sense of a comprehensive activity is explained by the extraordinary gifts of his mind. A really wonderful memory was joined to a rare gift of orienting combinations, which as a historian allowed him to shed clear light on one event by another often lying quite far apart. In the domain of practical activity it everywhere allowed him energetically to find means appropriate to the ends he had in view. To characterize this mental ability of his I should like to bring forward one of his brilliant historical analogies. It is found in the essay 'Burleigh and his Times': 'The only event of modern times which can be properly compared with the Reformation is the French Revolution, or, to speak more accurately, that great revolution of political feeling which took place in almost every part of the civilized world during the eighteenth century, and which obtained in France its most terrible and signal triumph. Each of these memorable events may be described as a rising up of the human reason against a caste. One was a struggle of the laity against the clergy for intellectual liberty; the other was a struggle of the people against princes and nobles for political liberty. In both cases, the spirit of innovation was at first encouraged by the class to which it was likely to be most prejudicial. It was under the patronage of Frederic, of Catherine, of Joseph, and of the grandees of France, that the philosophy which afterwards threatened with destruction all the thrones and aristocracies of Europe first became formidable. The ardour with which men betook themselves to liberal studies, at the close of the fifteenth and beginning of the sixteenth century, was zealously encouraged by the heads of that very church to which liberal studies were destined to be fatal. In both cases, when the explosion came, it came with a violence which appalled and disgusted many of those who had previously been distinguished by the freedom of their opinions. The violence of the democratic party in France made Burke a

Tory and Alfieri a courtier. The violence of the chiefs of the German schism made Erasmus a defender of abuses, and turned the author of *Utopia* into a persecutor.'

In reading the character portrayals of historical persons supplied by Macaulay one is often reminded of the monumental manner of Emerson. But while the latter as a rhetorician and moral writer elaborates finely wrought thoughts and gives priority to the excellence of his *aperçus* over naturalistic presentation of reality, with Macaulay the opposite is the case. His immersion in reality is so mature, so established and thoughtful that with him historical fidelity is reshaped by itself into a striking *aperçu*. As when he characterizes Burleigh, Queen Elizabeth's statesman, with the words: 'He never deserted his friends till it was very inconvenient to stand by them, was an excellent Protestant when it was not very advantageous to be a Papist, recommended a tolerant policy to his mistress as strongly as he could recommend it without hazarding her favour, never put to the rack any person from whom it did not seem probable that useful information might be derived, and was so moderate in his desires that he left only three hundred distinct landed estates, though he might, as his honest servant assures us, have left much more, "if he would have taken money out of the Exchequer for his own use, as many Treasurers have done".'

Lord Macaulay

> A model of historical presentation is the chapter in Macaulay's *History of England* about the state of England in 1685. In writing history it is a modern trait to substitute cultural history for the former purely diplomatic and political method. In the mentioned chapter Macaulay becomes an accomplished cultural historian because the inner truth of his subject causes him to be, and because his comprehensive sense makes it impossible for him not to pursue into their furthest corners the relationships linking things together.—This tireless man could not take his historical work beyond the year 1704. Heart disease snatched away his strong life in the year 1858.

It did indeed, but only in the year 1859. Macaulay had been educated from 1818 to 1822 at Trinity College Cambridge, and was then from 1824 to 1831 a Fellow along with William Whewell. In 1868 the college had a statue of him erected in the college antechapel, on the north side where stood also the statue of Whewell.

A New Epoch of Thought

Probably in mid-October 1900 Rudolf Steiner completed the second volume—published in the following year—of his book *Welt- und Lebensanschauungen im 19. Jahrhundert.* One of its chapters was entitled 'Darwinism and World-conception'. It began:

> If the thought of conformity to purpose were to undergo reform in the sense of a naturalistic view of the world, purposeful formations of organic Nature had to be explained in the same way as a physicist or chemist explains lifeless processes. When a magnetic rod attracts to itself iron filings, no physicist thinks that there is a force operative in the rod working towards the aim or purpose of the attraction. When hydrogen and oxygen unite into water, a chemist does not explain this as if something were at work in both materials which has the purpose of water-formation hovering before it. An explanation of living beings governed by that very kind of naturalistic sense would have to tell itself that organisms gain conformity to purpose without something in Nature aiming towards this. Conformity to purpose arises, without being somewhere as such intended. Such an explanation of conformity to purpose was given by Charles Darwin. He placed himself on a standpoint which recognizes that nothing in Nature wants such conformity. For Nature, there is no question if what arises within it is purposeful or not. It thus produces without choosing between what has conformity to purpose and what does not.
>
> What has conformity to purpose at all? Whatever is so arranged that its needs, its conditions of life correspond to outer relationships of existence.

> Where by contrast such is not the case, there is no conformity to purpose. With Nature's complete lack of plan, what will happen between the most purposeful beings and the least purposeful when all grades arise having more or less conformity to purpose? Every being will seek to form its existence according to given conditions. A purposeful being achieves this without further ado, those with more or less conformity to purpose only to a small extent. Another matter must be added: Nature is not a parsimonious housekeeper regarding production of living beings. The number of seeds is enormous. This surplus in production of seeds corresponds to only a limited measure of foodstuffs. The consequence will be that those beings which are more purposefully formed for acquring foodstuffs have easier play for their development. If a purposeful being strives alongside an unpurposeful being for the preservation of its existence, the one with more conformity to purpose will prevail. The latter must go down before the former. The fit, that is to say the purposeful, survives, the unfit, that is to say the unpurposeful, does not. This is the 'struggle for existence'. It means that what has conformity to purpose survives, even if in Nature the unpurposeful arises without any choice beside the purposeful. Through a law which is as objective, as devoid of wisdom, as only a mathematical or mechanical law of Nature can be, the course of natural evolution receives a tendency towards purposefulness, without this tendency being somehow inherent in Nature.
>
> Darwin was led to that thought by a work of the national economist Malthus, *Essay on the Principles of Population*. It is here explained that within human society there takes place a ceaseless competition, because the population grows at a much faster pace than the supply of foodstuffs. This law, set up for the history of mankind, was generalized by Darwin into a comprehensive law for the entire world of life.
>
> Darwin now wanted to show how this struggle for existence becomes the creator of the manifold forms of living beings, how thereby the old Linnaean principle is overturned, that we 'count as many species in the animal and plant kingdoms as different forms have in principle been created'...

The quotation was from the *Genera Plantarum* of 1737.

> ...Doubts concerning this principle were clearly formed in Darwin's mind when finding himself in summer 1835 on a journey to South America and Australia. He relates how these doubts took shape in him...

Steiner now quoted from the introduction to Darwin's *Variation of Animals and Plants Under Domestication*, published in 1868. His translation was based on the 1878 German rendering of Victor Carus, but had some variants.

> 'When I visited during the voyage of H.M.S. Beagle the Galapagos Archipelago, situated in the Pacific Ocean about 500 miles from South

> America, I found myself surrounded by peculiar species of birds, reptiles and plants, existing nowhere else in the world ...'

Instead of 'plants', Steiner's quotation had 'snakes'!

> '... Yet they nearly all of them bore an American stamp. In the song of the mocking-thrush, in the harsh cry of the carrion-hawk, in the great candlestick-like opuntias, I clearly perceived the neighbourhood of America, though the islands were separated by so many miles of ocean from the mainland, and differed much in their geological constitution and climate. Still more surprising was the fact that most of the inhabitants of each separate island in this small archipelago were specifically different, though most closely related to each other ...'

Here Steiner's quotation silently omitted a whole sentence:

> '... The archipelago with its innumerable craters and bare streams of lava appeared to be of recent origin; and thus I fancied myself brought near to the very act of creation ...'

Steiner's quotation continued:

> '... I often asked myself how these many peculiar animals and plants had been produced: the simplest answer seemed to be that the inhabitants of the several islands had descended from each other, undergoing modification in the course of their descent, and that all the inhabitants of the archipelago were descended from those of the nearest land, namely America, whence colonists would naturally have derived. But it long remained to me an inexplicable problem how the necessary degree of modification could have been effected.' The answer to this 'how' lies in the naturalistic conception of the evolution of living organisms. As a physicist brings a substance into different conditions in order to come to know its properties, so Darwin after his return observed the phenomena which result in a living being under different conditions. He made experiments in breeding with pigeons, chickens, dogs, rabbits and cultivated plants. Through these experiments it was shown how living forms continually change in the course of their reproduction. Under certain circumstances certain living beings change so much after a few generations that by comparing the newly appearing forms with their ancestors, one might speak of two quite different species, each of which is directed according to its own organization. Such a variability of forms is used by the breeder in order to bring to development cultivated organisms which accord with certain intentions. He can breed a kind of sheep with especially fine wool, if he allows only those individuals in his herd to reproduce which have the finest wool. In their progeny he again seeks the individuals which are endowed with the finest wool. The fineness of the wool is then enhanced in the course of generations. After some time

> one reaches a species of sheep which is very far removed from its predecessors. The case is the same with other properties of living beings. Two conclusions follow from this fact. Firstly, that in Nature there lies a tendency to change living beings; and secondly, that a property which has started to change in a certain direction increases in that direction when in propagating living beings those individuals are held away which do not yet have this quality. Organic forms thus assume other properties in course of time and keep to the direction of the change they have once begun. They change and transmit changed qualities to their successors.
>
> The natural conclusion from this observation is that change and hereditary transmission are two driving principles in the evolution of living beings. Now if one assumes that beings in the world change in a way conformable to Nature so that the purposeful arises beside the unpurposeful and more or less purposeful, one must also presuppose a struggle between the manifold changed forms. This struggle brings about, without a plan, what the breeder does with a plan. As the latter excludes from reproduction those individuals which would bring into evolution what he does not want, so the struggle for existence removes the unpurposeful. Only what is in conformity to purpose remains for evolution. The tendency towards eternal perfection is laid into this like a mechanical law. After Darwin had recognized this and thus laid a sure foundation for the naturalistic view of the world, he could place at the end of his work *The Origin of Species*, which introduces a new epoch of thought, the enthusiastic words: 'Thus, from the War of Nature, from famine and death, the most exalted object which we are capable of conceiving, namely the production of the higher animals, directly follows. There is grandeur in this view of life, with its several powers having been originally breathed by the Creator into a few forms or into one; and that, whilst this planet has gone cycling on according to the fixed law of gravity, from so simple a beginning endless forms most beautiful and most wonderful have been and are being evolved.'...

This was the very same passage as already quoted in *The Shrewsbury Chronicle* in a letter of 23 January 1894 by Edwin Powell, who originally started the movement for a Darwin Memorial in Shrewsbury, which despite the collapse of the upper part of the spire of St Mary's Church in that town was eventually erected on 10 August 1897 and gave rise to Steiner's article on 'Darwinism and the Present'.

The Development of Thought in England

The next chapter was entitled 'The World as Illusion'. Under this title Rudolf Steiner first discussed various nineteenth-century German thinkers, mostly prominent in scientific fields: Johannes Müller, Hermann Helmholtz, Hippolyte Taine, Jakob Henle, Isidor Rosenthal, Emil DuBois-Reymond, Gustav Kirchhoff and Friedrich Albert Lange.

He then continued:

> By recognizing the scientific way of thought, Friedrich Albert Lange agrees with Monism in so far as he disputes that any other source for knowledge of the real is justified; only he denies this way of thinking any ability to penetrate into the essence of things. In order to move on sure ground, he cuts off the wings of a human way of conceiving. What Lange does in an insistent way corresponds to a tendency of thought deeply rooted in the development of world-conceptions in recent times. This is also shown with full clarity in another domain of the world of ideas in the nineteenth century. Through various phases this world of ideas develops towards viewpoints out of which Herbert Spencer, around the same time in England as Lange in Germany, founds a dualism which on one side strives after full scientific knowledge of the world and on the other side confesses to agnosticism in regard to the nature of existence. When Darwin published his work on the *Origin of Species*, thereby providing Monism with one of its firm supports, he could recognize with praise Spencer's scientific way of thought: 'Mr. Herbert Spencer, in an essay (originally published in the *Leader*, March 1852, and republished in his *Essays* in 1858) has contrasted the theories of the creation and the development of organic beings with remarkable skill and force. He argues from the analogy of domestic productions, from the changes which the embryos of many species undergo, from the difficulty of distinguishing species and varieties, and from the principle of general gradation that species have been modified; and he attributes the modification to the change of circumstances. The author (1855) has also treated psychology on the principle of the necessary acquirement of each mental power and capacity by gradation.' Like the founder of the modern view of life-processes, other scientific thinkers too feel themselves drawn to Spencer, who strives to explain reality, from inorganic fact right up to psychology, in the direction expressed in Darwin's above statement. But Spencer also stands on the side of the agnostics, so that Albert Lange may say: 'Herbert Spencer, kindred to our own standpoint, does homage to a materialism of appearance, whose relative justification in science finds its limits in the thought of an unknowable absolute.'

The quotation is from Lange's *Geschichte des Materialismus*, published in 1866.

> One may imagine that Spencer was led to his standpoint from similar points of departure as Lange. In the development of thought in England he was preceded by minds guided by a double interest. They wanted to determine what man actually possesses in his knowledge. But they also did not want to

> shatter the essence of the world through any doubt and through any reason. In a more or less explicit way they were all governed by the feeling Kant expresses when he says: 'I had to abolish knowledge in order to make place for faith.' (Cf. Vol I. of this history of world-conceptions, p. 146 ff.)

The quotation was from the foreword to the second edition (1781) of the *Kritik der reinen Vernunft*, the relevant passage being quoted more extensively on the page referred to, in the chapter on 'The Age of Kant and Goethe'. Subsequent pages discussed the influence upon Kant of David Hume.

> Before the start of the development of world-conceptions in the nineteenth century there stands in England Thomas Reid (1710–1796). The basic impulse of this man's belief was what Goethe too expresses with the words: 'In the end it is only, as I think, the practical and self-rectifying operations of common sense, which dares to exercise itself in a higher sphere.'...

The quotation was from the final sentence of Goethe's article 'Experience and Science', written in 1798—only a couple of years after Reid's death.

> ... This common sense does not doubt that when observing the facts of the world it has to do with actual real things and processes. Reid considers a world-conception only capable of life if it abides by this basic view of common sense. Even if it were admitted that our observation might be deceiving us and the true essence of things were quite different from what the senses and the understanding are saying, we would not need to trouble ourselves with such a possibility. We only manage in life if we believe our observation; everything else does not concern us. From this viewpoint Reid believes himself to attain really satisfying truths. He does not seek to come to a view about things through complicated arrangements of thought, but by going back to views instinctively supposed by the soul. And the soul possesses what is right instinctively, unconsciously, before it undertakes to shine into its own being with the torch of consciousness. It instinctively knows what it must hold about the qualities and processes in the bodily world; but it also instinctively possesses the direction of its moral behaviour, judgement about good and evil. Through calling upon truths inherent in common sense, Reid leads thinking into soul-observation. From then onwards this tendency to observe the soul remains peculiar to the English development of a world-conception. Prominent personalities within this development are William Hamilton (1788–1856), Henry Mansel (1820–1871), William Whewell (1794 to 1866), John Herschel (1792–1871), James Mill (1773 to 1836), John Stuart Mill (1806–1873), Alexander Bain, Herbert Spencer. They all place psychology at the centre of their view of the world.
>
> For Hamilton too what is true is what the soul originally finds itself obliged to accept as true. With regard to original truths, proving and

conceiving ceases; one can simply register their appearance on the horizon of consciousness. In this sense they are inconceivable. But among original statements of consciousness belongs the statement that each thing in this world is dependent upon something we do not know. We find in the world in which we live only dependent things, nowhere anything definitely independent. And yet there must be such a thing. If dependence is encountered, independence must be presupposed. With our thinking we do not enter independence. Human knowledge is meant for the dependent and wraps itself in contradictions if it applies its thoughts, which are very suitable for dependent things, onto independent ones. Knowledge must therefore withdraw when we approach the entrance to independence. There religious truth is in its place. Man can only be a moral being by confessing that he can know nothing about the essential kernel of the world. He can suppose a God who causes moral order in the world. No logic can steal this faith in an endless God, as soon as it is recognized that all logic is only directed to the dependent, not to the independent.—Mansel is a pupil and continuer of Hamilton. He only clothes the latter's views in even more extreme forms. It is not going too far to say that Mansel is an advocate of faith, who does not judge impartially between religion and knowledge, but enters partially on behalf of religious dogma. He is of the view that the truths of revealed religion necessarily wrap knowledge in contradictions. This however does not derive from a deficiency in revealed truths, but from the limitations of the human mind which can never enter the regions about which revelation makes statements.

The Psychology of Scientific Research

Rudolf Steiner's account continued:

William Whewell believes he can best obtain a view of the significance, origin and value of human knowledge by investigating how pioneering minds in the sciences arrived at their insights. His *History of the Inductive Sciences* (1837) and his *Philosophy of the Inductive Sciences* (1840) set out to examine the psychology of scientific research. From outstanding scientific discoveries he tries to find out how much of our own conceptions belongs to the outer world and how much to man himself. Whewell finds that in every science the mind supplements observation from its own substance. Kepler had the concept of the ellipse before discovering that planets move in ellipses. The sciences accordingly arise not just through mere reception from outside, but through active participation by the human mind, which imprints its laws onto what it receives. Sciences, however, do not extend as far as the ultimate essences of things. They are concerned with the world's details. But just as each particular thing is for instance assumed to have a cause, such a cause must also be presupposed for the whole world. Since in respect to that cause knowledge breaks down, religious dogma must step in as a supplement. Herschel, like Whewell, also tries to gain insight into the genesis of knowledge in the human mind by observing numerous examples. (*A Preliminary Discourse on the Study of Natural Philosophy* appeared in 1831.)

In regard to Whewell, this account briefly summarizes the argument of the second named work, *The Philosophy of the Inductive Sciences*. When writing it Steiner may well have recalled his time at the Viennese Technical College in 1880–2 under Edmund Reitlinger, who was fond of quoting from this particular work. And indeed, since he was later to describe Reitlinger's presentation of Kepler as a masterpiece of scientific lecturing, it is striking that Steiner's summary includes a reference by Whewell to that astronomer. Perhaps the passage concerned had once played some part in Reitlinger's presentation.

The passage is taken from the opening 'book' in the first volume, 'Of Ideas in General'. Its sixth chapter, 'Of Induction', begins with this section:

> When we have become possessed of such ideal conceptions as those just described, cases frequently occur in which we can, by means of such conceptions, connect the facts which we learn from our senses, and thus obtain truths from materials supplied by experience. In such cases, the truth to which we are thus led is said to be collected from the observed facts, *by Induction*.
>
> Thus Hipparchus, tracing the unequal motion of the Sun among the stars in different parts of the year, as learnt from observation, found that this inequality might be fitly represented by the conception of an eccentric—a circle in which the Sun had an equable annual motion, the spectator not being situated in the centre of the circle. And thus he established, by Induction, the truth that the Sun appears to move in such an eccentric. At a later period Kepler, proceeding upon more exact observations, was able to show that, not a circle about an eccentric point, but an ellipse about the focus was the conception which truly agreed with the motion of the Earth and of the other planets about the Sun.[29] And thus the elliptical form of these orbits was established by Induction from many observed facts. Again, to take an example of another kind, the forms of flowers may have applied to them conceptions borrowed from the idea of symmetry of parts; and this symmetry may contain *three* similar portions, as in the lily and its tribe; or *five*, as in the wild rose, and many others. Now it appears by observation of many particular cases that these differences in the kind of symmetry of the flower are conjoined with differences in the seed: the tripartite symmetry prevailing in those seeds which have only one cotyledon, or lobe enveloping the embryo; and the quinquepartite symmetry in those seeds which have two cotyledons. Here then we have a truth concerning the laws of vegetable form, established by Induction. (*Hist. Inductive Sciences*, iii. 338.)

> In these, and in all cases of Induction, the ideal conception which the mind itself supplies is *superinduced* upon the facts as they are originally presented to observation. Before the inductive truth is detected, the facts are there, but they are many and unconnected. The conception which the discoverer applies to them gives them connexion and unity. Before Hipparchus it was known that the motion of the Sun was not equable, but it appeared to be irregular and lawless; all parts of the motion became regular and orderly by the introduction of the conception of the eccentric. In the case of Hipparchus we can only conjecture the nature of the efforts by which the conception was discovered and applied to the facts. But in Kepler's case we know from his own narrative how hard he struggled and laboured to find the right conception; how many conceptions he tried and rejected; what corrections and adjustments of his first guesses he afterwards introduced. In his case we see in the most conspicuous manner the philosopher impressing his own ideal conception upon the facts; the facts being exactly fitted to this conception, although no one before had detected such a fitness. And in like manner, in all other cases, the discovery of a truth by induction consists in finding a conception or combination of conceptions which agrees with, connects, and arranges the facts.

It is evident that Steiner—and maybe Reitlinger before him—was using the original edition of 1840. For in the second edition of 1847 Whewell remodelled the entire 'book' 'Of Ideas in General', and although this example of Kepler and the ellipse was with some changes retained, the further paragraph about conceptions supplied by the mind being superinduced upon the facts was replaced by different material.

The remainder of Steiner's description may best be illustrated by the final paragraphs of the work. They bring to a close a chapter on 'Induction of Causes' concluding the 'book' on 'Methods Employed in the Formation of Science' at the end of the second volume. In this chapter a section headed 'Induction of Ulterior Causes' has a subsection 'Of the Supreme Cause'—which in 1845 Whewell went on to include as the final set piece in his anthology *Indications of the Creator*. This subsection ended as follows:

> We have already passed beyond the boundary of those speculations which we proposed to ourselves as the basis of our conclusions. Yet we may be allowed to add one other reflection. If we find in ourselves ideas of good and evil, manifestly bestowed upon us to be the guides of our conduct, which guides we find it impossible consistently to obey; if we find ourselves directed, even by our natural light, to aim at a perfection of our moral nature from which we are constantly deviating through weakness and perverseness; if, when we thus lapse and err, we can find, in the region of human philosophy, no power which can efface our aberrations, or reconcile

our actual with our ideal being, or give us any steady hope and trust with regard to our actions, after we have thus discovered their incongruity with their genuine standard; if we discern that this is our condition, how can we fail to see that it is in the highest degree consistent with all the indications supplied by such a philosophy as that of which we have been attempting to lay the foundations, that the Supreme Cause, through whom man exists as a moral being of vast capacities and infinite hopes, should have Himself provided a teaching for our ignorance, a propitiation for our sin, a support for our weakness, a purification and sanctification of our nature?

And thus, in concluding our long survey of the grounds and structure of science, and of the lessons which the study of it teaches us, we find ourselves brought to a point of view in which we can cordially sympathize, and more than sympathize, with all the loftiest expressions of admiration and reverence and hope and trust, which have been uttered by those who in former times have spoken of the elevated thoughts to which the contemplation of the nature and progress of human knowledge gives rise. We can not only hold with Galen and Harvey and all the great physiologists that the organs of animals give evidence of a purpose; not only assert with Cuvier that this conviction of a purpose can alone enable us to understand every part of every living thing; not only say with Newton that 'every true step made in philosophy brings us nearer to the First Cause, and is on that account highly to be valued'; and that 'the business of natural philosophy is to deduce causes from effects, till we come to the very First Cause, which certainly is not mechanical'; but we can go much further, and declare, still with Newton, that 'this beautiful system could have its origin no other way than by the purpose and command of an intelligent and powerful Being, who governs all things, not as the soul of the world, but as the Lord of the Universe; who is not only God, but Lord and Governor'.

When we have advanced so far, there yet remains one step. We may recollect the prayer of one, the master in this school of the philosophy of science: 'This also we humbly and earnestly beg: that human things may not prejudice such as are divine; neither that from the unlocking of the gates of sense, and the kindling of a greater natural light, anything may arise of incredulity or intellectual night towards divine mysteries; but rather that by our minds thoroughly purged and cleansed from fancy and vanity, and yet subject and perfectly given up to the divine oracles, there may be given unto faith the things that are faith's.' When we are thus prepared for a higher teaching, we may be ready to listen to a greater than Bacon, when he says to those who have sought their God in the material universe: 'Whom ye ignorantly worship, Him declare I unto you.' And when we recollect how utterly inadequate all human language has been shown to be, to express the nature of that Supreme Cause of the natural, and rational, and moral, and spiritual world to which our philosophy points with trembling finger and shaded eyes, we may receive, with the less wonder but with the more reverence, the declaration which has been vouchsafed to us:

ΕΝ ΑΡΧΗ ΗΝ 'Ο ΛΟΓΟΣ, ΚΑΙ 'Ο ΛΟΓΟΣ ΗΝ ΠΡΟΣ ΤΟΝ ΘΕΟΝ, ΚΑΙ ΘΕΟΣ ΗΝ 'Ο ΛΟΓΟΣ.

One-sidedness

On 24 November 1900 Rudolf Steiner published in the *Magazin für Litteratur* an article about the Anglicized German scholar Max Müller, formerly Professor of Comparative Philology in the University of Oxford:

> On the 28th of October 1900 died one of the most popular scholars of our time. The way people spoke about Max Müller when news arrived of his death recalled the high esteem to be heard a few years ago on the demise of Hermann Helmholtz. Anyone laying claim today to a certain general education will associate with the names of both scholars similar mental pictures. And yet what goes on inside the heads of our contemporaries is not the same if they cite one name like the other. Hermann Helmholtz people know to be among the greatest physicists. He belonged to those who, in an old saying, are more famed than read. Many will probably recall that we had to experience the sight of the great physicist's statue on the Potsdam Bridge in Berlin adorned with the incorrect title of one of his books. With Max Müller the matter is different. He is actually read. Countless notions about the development of language or about religions set down in his delightfully written works have become a component in the learning of our time. He placed the spiritual development of eastern peoples into the general education of the West. He knew how to do this in such a way that even those not placed in any scholarly profession concern themselves with his works. He was among the most significant spiritual stimulators of the present. Colleagues in his subject, researchers into language and religion, do not esteem his works as highly as others. As a Sanskrit researcher and mythologist he was for them not even a scholar nameable in the very first rank. They say that hardly a single one of his basic conceptions can be maintained in the present state of knowledge. No one should presume to pass any judgement on this matter who is not a specialist in the domain of linguistic research.
>
> But a non-specialist can state one thing about Max Müller. What he achieved for our western cultural life, purely in the extent of his work, is as significant as the creations of only quite few writers. He published the oldest monument of Indian spiritual life (*Rigveda*) in six large volumes (London 1849–1874); he arranged the publication of one of the most monumental works of our time, the entire *Sacred Books of the East*, at which scholars from

nearly all cultured nations are working, and to which he himself made important contributions. And while attempting so tirelessly to bring before the eyes of Europeans the educational treasures of the East, he tried to present the laws of mankind's spiritual development in lectures on *The Science of Language* (appearing in German in 1875), in his *Essays* and in a large number of other works and treatises.

The way Max Müller did all this corresponded in large measure to needs and tendencies in the second half of the century. A *historical* way of observing was sympathetic to this time, which is thus in essence differentiated from the preceding age. The latter believed it could come to conclusions about human nature, about laws of language, of morality and of religion by observing the nature of *present* man—as a completed single being. In proportion as the century progressed, this became different. People wanted to explain man of the present from man of the past. They no longer believed that observing a fully evolved human being could for instance provide information about how religious needs arise, or from where moral conceptions derive.

People wanted to come to know the first beginnings of such conceptions, and by grasping the more undeveloped cultures slowly rise to grasping present ones. They also wanted to find out how different cultural folks become educated, so as to fathom by comparison the laws of mankind's development. More and more they gave up observing man as an individual; they learnt to look on him as a member of the whole of humanity. The thoughts of Max Müller lie completely inside such a conceptional trend. He opened up the East, in order to show the agreements and differences of manifold cultures, and thus attain knowledge of the great laws holding sway in everything.

Only towards the end of the century did people begin to perceive that this way of observation also harbours one-sidedness. A most stimulating writing by Friedrich Nietzsche is the *Unzeitgemässe Betrachtung: Vom Nutzen und Nachteil der Historie für das Leben*. He sought to show how man spoils life at present by always looking into historical development. It is Nietzsche's opinion that life stands higher than knowledge of life. If I ask myself how each of my mental pictures has come about, I lame my freedom to get on with life. With each step I believe I must first consider whether it also lies in accord with previous regular development. We have so often had to hear that when in recent decades a new impulse wanted to arise, confessors of the historical way of observation immediately came and said it was unhistorical. Through the historical way of observation the philosophical one has slowly been lost. We have been obliged to experience this worst of all with philosophy itself. Our time has become poor in new philosophical thoughts. Indeed, people look down with contempt on those who still want to produce such thoughts. They have even denied to our time the capacity to give new laws before the process of emergence of legal development has been fully penetrated.

In the spreading of such a mood lie the shadow sides of a work such as that of Max Müller. Here we have arrived at a point where this important writer leaves those of our contemporaries who are striving forwards dissatisfied. How far he is being overtaken by the linguistic science and religious research of the present we can calmly leave to specialists to decide. That his philosophical aptitudes were not very significant is what must disturb those who search in present literary achievements for elements to be considered within the great questions for views of the world. Max Müller could not grasp why Ernest Renan regretted that he became a historian and not a scientist. This is related to Max Müller's characterized philosophical aptitudes. He always remained quite distant from science. He could not decide to cross the 'Rubicon of the spirit' which leads from the human being into the rest of Nature. He followed historically the evolution of language as far as *history*, the science of man, can do. Whoever wants to know how language emerges from capacities of a lower kind must leave the historical method of observation and pass over to a scientific one. Müller enumerates 121 linguistic roots underlying the language of the Aryans. They are meant to express as many original concepts. Thus far does a historian attain. A scientist reaches further. He seeks in animal capacities for the origin of everything appearing in a human being. Anyone rejecting everything inaccessible to history never reaches such origins. A scientist investigates natural laws of the present. From out of the present he illuminates the past. The historical method of observation will slowly have to widen to a scientific one, if it wants to fructify our view of the world. We can never understand the present merely from how it has become; rather must we grasp becoming, development, from out of the present. A geologist investigates the causes which are today still altering the surface of the Earth. From there his perspective opens out into the past. Observation of man must also learn how to change into this direction. But in the writings of Max Müller there is little such knowledge to be found. This separated him from the way of thinking of scientists. It will increasingly be recognized as a defect of his work.

Perfection of Form

The third volume of *Das XIX Jahrhundert in Wort und Bild* was published around this time. It included a contribution by Rudolf Steiner on 'Literature and Spiritual Life 1871 to 1899'. Again, this was in two halves, of which the first covered German and Austrian literature. The second half began by examining French, Dutch and Belgian literature, and then continued as follows:

> English poetry of this time receives its characteristic stamp from the creations of Algernon Charles Swinburne. By nature romantically inclined, he is a fiery depicter of sensuality and a portrayer of great passions, but also of tender movements in the soul and of atmospheric Nature pictures. His favourite realm is the sea with its manifold beauties. His cradle-songs are characteristic of his practical mood. In the dramatic realm (*Atalanta in Calydon*) he strove for a Greek perfection of form . . .

Atalanta in Calydon is an early work by Swinburne, begun in 1863 on the Isle of Wight and completed in 1864 at Tintagel in Cornwall. The play's subject comes from Greek legend, and among its formal characteristics are a wide variety of metres. Here for instance is a section from the final scene:

Meleager:

Let your hands meet
  Round the weight of my head;
Lift ye my feet
  As the feet of the dead;
For the flesh of my body is molten, the limbs of it molten as lead.

Chorus:

O thy luminous face,
  Thine imperious eyes!
O the grief, O the grace,
  As of day when it dies!
Who is this bending over thee, lord, with tears and suppression of sighs?

Meleager:

Is a bride so fair?
  Is a maid so meek?
With unchapleted hair,
  With unfilleted cheek,
Atalanta, the pure among women, whose name is as blessing to speak.

Atalanta:

I would that with feet
  Unsandalled, unshod,
Overbold, overfleet,
  I had swum not, nor trod
From Arcadia to Calydon northward, a blast of the envy of God.

Meleager:

Unto each man his fate;
Unto each as he saith
In whose fingers the weight
Of the world is as breath.
Yet I would that in clamour of battle mine hands had laid hold upon death.

Chorus:

Not with cleaving of shields
And their clash in thine ear,
When the lord of fought fields
Breaketh spearshaft from spear,
Thou art broken, our lord, thou art broken with travail and labour and fear.

Meleager:

Would God he had found me
Beneath the fresh boughs!
Would God he had bound me
Unawares in mine house,
With light in mine eyes, and songs on my lips and a crown on my brows!

After his discussion of Swinburne, Steiner continued:

> ... Beside him also come into consideration Matthew Arnold and Dante Gabriel Rossetti. In his view of the world and manner of expression the former recalls Byron, while the latter seeks to attain a simple style through old-fashioned artistic means. William Morris is an original character with a powerful gift of portrayal. Rudyard Kipling depicts Anglo-Indian life with penetrating observation in gripping novels, stories and folkloric-sounding poems.

Steiner could compare these latter with the poems of his own friend Ludwig Jacobowski, who however died on 2 December 1900.

Concluding Event

In the final chapter of his biography of Karl Julius Schröer, Walter Beck describes events during that month in Vienna:

> On the 15th of December 1900, after a preparation of twenty-two years, the Goethe Memorial according to Hellmer's design was unveiled before

Goethe Memorial in Vienna

illustrious society. Franz Joseph himself graciously performed the festive act. Orders and diplomas are handed out. Schröer is accorded 'all-highest recognition', whereby however 'all-highest' refers not to any height of recognition, but rather to the highness of His Apostolic Majesty.

Schröer was not present. He had indeed received an official invitation, but it was known that he would not appear. A *Festschrift* was drawn up and Hellmer named honorary member of the Goethe Union.

The unveiling of the Memorial—taking place in Schröer's absence—can despite inconsistency and all differences be looked upon as the so to speak symbolical concluding event of his life's work. On the following day, the 16th of December 1900, Schröer died.

Beck then summarized the matter:

The plan pursued by Schröer for years on end of the Goethe Memorial showing a picture of a productive Goethe pointing into the future was not fulfilled. Schröer's intention was not understood, though admittedly it is also impossible to understand it without insight into Schröer's spiritual experiences.

Schröer's endeavours to present an inner picture of Goethe had begun with his early poems, and continued with his writings on Goethe's poetry and the latter's *Faust*. In all pictures of Goethe's outer appearance he sought to make visible that picture of Goethe in the background which ever since his youth had stood before his eyes. To show this figure in a Memorial was Schröer's intention in his strivings down the long years for the Goethe Memorial. Every connection which might help to demonstrate the agreement between tradition and personal vision was to him of great importance.

In order to confront the world around him with central questions of Goethe's thought he had given the stimulus to found the Goethe Union, written his articles in the *Chronik* about 'The Double Kingdom' (in Goethe's fairy tale and in the Helen scene), the 'eternal feminine' and reincarnation (in Goethe's statement to Frau von Stein: 'Oh, in past times you were my sister or my wife.')

Schröer started out from a real overview, from a designated idea, and not from details. Thus the Schröerian chronicle stands out as one of the clearest documents of Goetheanism in the second half of the previous century.

In pursuing these endeavours, Schröer believed he had discovered in Tilgner's design for the Goethe Memorial *the* Goethe whose presentation he considered absolutely necessary. Only if this connection is grasped in its reality will insight arise into Schröer's struggle for the Goethe Memorial.[30]

He wanted to set *that* Goethe as an example before the world around, to give human beings of the present a support for finding new possibilities of perception and opening a way into the future—those 'high tracks' which he had already expressed as a young man in the fifties in his 'Poem of the Time', so as 'to conquer that world', namely gain insight into a world of spirit.

Already at an early age Schröer recognized that he could indeed indicate such a path, but—after initial successful attempts—could not go along it himself and would therefore have to leave this step to another.

★

On 13 January 1901—just four weeks after the unveiling of the Goethe Memorial—Rudolf Steiner published in a Viennese medical weekly, the *Wiener klinische Rundschau*, an article on 'Goethe and Medicine'. It began as follows:

> That the great poet to whom the capital of Austria has now also erected a memorial had a relation to natural sciences which is of profound interest to the scientist is evidenced by a wealth of available literature on this subject. A number of most significant scientists have endeavoured to portray Goethe's importance for their science. One only need recall the relevant writings of Virchow (*Goethe als Naturforscher und in besonderer Beziehung auf Schiller*, 1861), of Helmholtz (*Über Goethes naturwissenschaftliche Arbeiten* and *Goethes Vorahnungen kommender naturwissenschaftlicher Ideen*, 1892), of Haeckel (*Goethe, Lamarck und Darwin*, 1882), of Cohn (*Goethe als Botaniker*, 1881) to

> have a vivid notion of the high value competent experts attach to the poet's scientific works. The author of this article has himself tried to present the significance of Goethe's scientific ideas and their place within the scientific development of the nineteenth century through a series of works (introductions to *Goethes Naturwissenschaftliche Schriften* in Kürschner's Goethe edition, 1883 to 1897, and *Goethes Weltanschauung*, 1897). Whatever people may think about this significance, according to the works mentioned one thing seems beyond doubt. In looking back on his scientific endeavours Goethe was right to say: 'Not through exceptional mental gifts, not through a *momentary inspiration*, unexpected and unique, but rather through *consequential endeavours* have I finally arrived at such a gratifying result'...

This quoted sentence forms the penultimate paragraph of the *Geschichte meines botanischen Studiums*—among the very works which in 1883 Steiner had included in the first volume of the Kürschner series edited under guidance from Schröer.

Steiner went on:

> ... In Goethe's ideas on natural science we have before us not merely the lightning flashes of a genial personality, but the results of strictly methodical work. If we follow historically Goethe's endeavours, what leaps above all to the eye is how close his type of work stands to the spirit of modern scientific methods ...

Both Goethe's ideas on natural science and the spirit of modern scientific methods were the very subjects to which Schröer had formed no proper relation.

Very Interesting

Two days after the appearance of Rudolf Steiner's article, on 15 January, a writer denoting him or herself by the initials 'A.A.L.' published in Britain in *The Theosophical Review* an article entitled 'Reasons for Believing Francis Bacon a Rosicrucian'. It began:

> On looking back into rather a dim past we find unquestionably the existence of a certain mysterious body, the Order of the Rosy Cross, claiming as its founder Ormus, a 'convert of S. Mark', in A.D. 46. A confraternity bound by solemn oath and obligation to conceal its tenets, and offer help and succour to its members. We find these veiling themselves at times in impenetrable secrecy, at other times adopting pseudonyms under which their opinions became known, while they still practised silence with regard to themselves and their doings, which included unremitting and noiseless labour in the interests of humanity, notably by the practice of medicine and

> of the healing art generally, having for their goal the extension and preservation of human life.
>
> 'Custodians of human learning', these wise and beneficent philosophers, as the centuries rolled by, added sheaf to sheaf, increasing greatly the rich stores of human knowledge, and supplying to the world, as occasion warranted, wheat-ears from their threshing-floors and hidden granaries. This Order, scattered over the globe, separated by lands and seas, corresponded by means of a concealed language, whose alphabets were many.
>
> Swift and secret messengers flew north, south, east and west at the bidding of its masters . . .

After further such elaborations the article went on to describe in this style the Templar Order and then the Masons, in a way which implied that both of these orders were really much the same as the Rosicrucians.

The article then continued:

> The term Fra. or Frater (Brother) is used by the Rosicrucians of one another. They study in solitude the works of the Great Architect of the Universe, themselves builders in His Courts, fellow-labourers with the Lord of Two Worlds, Master-builders in a Temple not made by hands, emulating the flight of the golden bird of Zeus, that gazes unblinded on the Sun. Great scientific discoveries are the product of these masters of physical science, who possess the key of treasuries not more safe than Pandora's box to unlock. Gradually, as occasion warrants, or rule permits, they, like the bees, furnish honey from their cells, or, like true pioneers, gold and rare jewels dug from some deep, dark mine of truth and science.
>
> Some of these natural philosophers have been known to the world as the honoured councillors of kings, as wise orators, and jurists in courts of law. 'Occult, jealous of intrusion' is Gabriel Rossetti's description of them, and he speaks as one having authority, alluding to one great author of old in England as 'the wisest of all wise men', or words to that effect. To whom did he refer?
>
> We know that Paracelsus (whose real name was Hohenheim) was the bright particular star of Germany in 1493; that Robert Fludd, M.D., was called 'the most prominent Rosicrucian of the British Isles' in 1600; that Elias Ashmole, the occult philosopher, founder of the Ashmolean Museum at Oxford in 1682, was another; that in Italy, Battista Porta, in 1605, was a chief of the Rosy-cross band, who under cover of his comedies instructed initiates in things human and divine.
>
> Wickliffe, W. Lollard, Chaucer, Dante, Petrarch, Boccaccio, Voltaire, Goethe, Lessing, Swedenborg, Mesmer and Jacob Böhme are today openly accepted as brethren of the craft, men who taught by symbols and parables, the keys of which were held only by comparatively few. Reliable Masonic

works state in so many words that many other well-known names might be quoted in their list of Knights of the Red Cross, without giving any reason for these omissions. The mystery of secrecy which 'doth hedge' these men throws difficulties in the way of those who seek for their names either at home or abroad, in the history of occultism. The names of William Shakespeare and Francis Bacon are both missing. And yet we hold that though his identity has been closely veiled by the impenetrable secrecy which his Order assumes at will, the man called Francis Bacon was the founder of modern speculative Masonry, and the earthly cornerstone of the Knights of the White and Black Eagle; also that he was the greatest, or one of the greatest, Rosicrucian philosophers of the seventeenth century, the possessor of a key—the Open Sesame of the cave of the liberal sciences, the seven mystic sciences of which he was the Thrice Puissant Master—a key which helped to make him the great and powerful influence we believe him to have been in the world of literature and art, science and natural philosophy—our British Fra. St. Albone, who was 'not for an age, but for all time'.

To find reasons for our beliefs we have but to look very closely into what is recorded of the life of Bacon. First, we find him almost always referred to by his contemporaries as Lord St. Alban, not as Lord Bacon, after he once received his title of the Earl of Verulam, Viscount St. Albans.

His own signature, in almost all the private and public documents which I have seen, is Fra. S. Alban (never Albans). Heading a list of renowned Englishmen acknowledged by the craft as members of their body, we find St. Alban, G.M. in Britain, 287 A.D. Alter the date to 1599 and it *may* reveal under what pseudonym Francis Bacon figures in Masonry. His intimate friend and ally, W.H., Earl of Pembroke, stands as an initiate in 1618; their attendant architect, Inigo Jones, as well as King James I, is entered as joining in 1603. It is significant to find so eminent a philosopher as Lord Verulam, so good an operative architect, so learned a master of literature, science and art, so versed in the wisdom of the Ancients from the depths of which modern speculative Masonry was unquestionably developed, so deep a scholar of languages, living and dead, excluded from mention. This is one of the links in our chain.

The conspiracy of silence with repect to Bacon's private life which faces us at every turn is explained by the fact that he was a prominent, if not the most prominent, member of one of the highest and most secret Orders known.

The foundation on which modern Masonry rests, given or suggested in the great *Masonic Cyclopaedia*, is the body of learned Rosicrucians of the seventeenth century. In another dependable work published by the Craft it is clearly stated that 'Speculative Masonry had fixed firmly on in England by the end of the sixteenth century'. If so, who 'fixed' it? Without hesitation I answer—Francis Bacon.

Let us turn for confirmation of this statement to Aubrey's description of Verulam House, 'the most ingeniously contrived little pile that ever I saw'. Whose mind imagined and fashioned it within and without? 'No question but His Lordship was the chiefest architect.' It had a 'delicate staircase of carved wood'. A spiral stair being a specially mystic feature sacred to Masonry, it is not unnatural to ask: was this one?...

Here are some extracts from further paragraphs:

If we descend by the 'delicate staircase' and step out to the Verulam House fishponds, which Aubrey tells us were 'curiously perfected' by His Lordship, we find 'in the middle of the middlemost pond, in the island', a 'curious banqueting house of Roman architecture, paved with black and white marble, covered with Cornish slate and neatly wainscoted'...

The alternate squares in black and white of the tessellated pavement in memory of the mosaic pavement of King Solomon's Temple, and the fountains for lustration, signifying the 'Fountain of Life', are both necessary adjuncts or furniture in a Lodge-room of the high degrees...

Lustration is a foremost rite in Baconry—I mean, forgive me, Masonry—and represents the New Birth, a term often used by Francis Bacon. 'Outward bark for all', his works, like those of all Rosicrucians, contain 'internal pith, food for the few'. Petrarch says: 'It is folly to believe that poets concealed nothing under their outward words.'

There is yet another link in our strong chain of evidence, and then I have done. Sir Thomas Meautys, one of Lord St. Albans's many secretaries, raised a monument to him after his 'supposed' death in 1626. It stands in a niche in the wall of the little church of St Michael's, Gorhambury. The life-size figure of 'Fra. S. Alban' is seated, and the attitude is significant. Raised on three steps (three is a sacred number among Rosicrucians), he gazes up, unblinded, into the open face of heaven. One foot is in advance of the other, and he *leans his head upon his left hand*. To those instructed in the secret signs of the Degree of the Knights of the Black and White Eagle, this will say much. To them as well as to the uninitiated I put this question: if Francis Bacon were not a Rosicrucian, why did he fashion his works, 'inventions', life, death and burial in such close accordance with Rosicrucian rules and tenets?

⋆

In Germany, almost three months later, Rudolf Steiner sent his first letter to Marie von Sivers:

Friedenau-Berlin, 13th of April 1901

Highly honoured gracious lady,

Many thanks for the 'Theosophical Review'. I am returning it to you

> under separate cover. The article about Bacon is very interesting. It gives me food for thought in the most various directions. But I have the most decided feeling that the author takes the matter somewhat lightly. In particular I cannot share his view that the Baconian philosophical writings conceal an esoteric meaning. This is surely necessary if one wants to treat him as a Rosicrucian. I beg you many times to forgive me for the delay.
>
> With best recommendations,
>
> your wholly devoted
>
> Dr. Rudolf Steiner

Goethe's Manner of Conception

A few months later, on 3 July, Rudolf Steiner published his last article in the *Magazin für Litteratur.* It was entitled 'Herman Grimm. Deceased on the 16th June 1901'.

> Herman Grimm died on the 16th of June. On hearing of his passing, anyone who valued his cast of mind was overcome by the feeling that with him a person has left us to whom those following an educational path in the last third of the past century are inexpressibly grateful. For us he was a living link to the age of Goethe. Those who follow us will have no contemporaries able to speak about Goethe like Herman Grimm. Even though at Goethe's death he was only four years old, Herman Grimm may yet be spoken of as one of Goethe's contemporaries. He was the son-in-law of Bettina, who entered completely into Goethe's world of ideas and from whom we have the fine book *Goethes Briefwechsel mit einem Kinde* . . .

Bettina von Arnim published this book in 1835, just three years after Goethe's death.

> . . . Herman Grimm himself was quite at home in an ideational world drawing its nourishment from a directly personal relation to Goethe. Out of this kind of ideation he judged everything, not just Goethe himself. Only a man who stood to Goethe like Herman Grimm could write his books about Michelangelo, about Raphael, in the way he did. People can also assess these geniuses in other ways, and different judgements must be made from other artistic perspectives and needs of the time. But scarcely any age will be able to come closer to them in manner of conception than Goethe's. That they are written in the mentality of the Goethean age will always give Herman Grimm's works an incomparable value.
>
> Anyone who personally knew Herman Grimm had to the highest degree a feeling as if Goethe himself were speaking through this man directly to him.—One whose personal contact with Herman Grimm lasted such a short time as that of the writer of this article also had this impression. I often

think of the beautiful hours I was able to spend with him in Weimar. Especially vivid is a conversation I had with him on my own, when he once invited me to share lunch with him in a Weimar hotel. He spoke of his history of German fantasy as of a work summarizing for him what he had thought about the course of evolution of the German people. How he could indicate characteristic places where a people's cultural substance was gathered as in a focus! One wanted to think about something more or less differently from him, but with each of his explanations the feeling came over one with lightning speed that his viewpoint was in some way justified, and in the highest measure significant and fruiftful. In my opinion, through nothing could the actual manner of German culture in the second third of the nineteenth century so be seen before one's eyes as by hearing persons like Herman Grimm speaking. I also made the acquaintance of another man who had a similar effect, my highly revered teacher Karl Julius Schröer. He died a few months ago in Vienna. I have a heartfelt necessity soon to draw the picture, just as it lives in my mind, of this so unrecognized person. In a rather different way from Herman Grimm, he too was living completely in Goethe's manner of conception. It lies in the nature of our age that those who are only eight or ten years younger than my contemporaries will have to form a quite different picture of such persons than we do.

Now Steiner's later pupil Walter Johannes Stein was not just 'eight or ten years' but some 30 years younger than Steiner's contemporaries, and although for that reason he had 'a quite different picture' of such persons than Steiner, he was nonetheless through intimacy with the latter also able to explain in what way Schröer's involvement 'in Goethe's manner of conception' was 'rather different' from that of Herman Grimm:

> The path taken by Herman Grimm of praising Goethe's *Doctrine of Colours* as a stylistic masterpiece, while disregarding the content, Schröer could not follow . . .

Steiner ended:

> In a certain sense Herman Grimm stood quite distant to the basic needs of *our* time. Social troubles in our days were removed from his understanding, and he was probably always gripped by a frosty feeling towards the views of Haeckel and Darwin. But for that very reason—however paradoxical it may at first glance appear, when one says this—his book on Goethe is a historical document of which not many exist. No one can any longer write about Goethe in that way. Neither our present culture nor any subsequent one will be able to. Goethe's generation was followed by one which still had so much of Goethe that it could retain his picture undisturbed by everything following. Herman Grimm belonged to that generation. Whatever may still be said about Goethe, Grimm's *Goethe* cannot be surpassed. No one will any

longer be able to feel about Goethe as he did; but only in these feelings about Goethe was the Goethean age fully alive.

Those calling themselves scholars in the 'real sense' did not wish to number Herman Grimm among them. They deny him any 'strict method'. He could smile about it. He neither wanted to be compared with these 'scholars' nor to be numbered among them. He knew too well how it is with 'method'. It is mostly a crutch for all those who from lack of personal strength are unable to go on their own feet, and of themselves come to nothing. He knew that only a person can deny him 'method' who 'himself has nothing but method'. He was convinced that 'the single personality within its limited circle will always remain what is valuable'.

This final quotation was from Grimm's *Beiträge zur deutschen Kulturgeschichte* of 1897.

Steiner's article was altogether a fine appreciation of Herman Grimm.[31] It is however striking that although he evidently intended soon also 'to draw the picture' living within him of Karl Julius Schröer, in the event he did *not* at the time carry out this intention. His 'heartfelt necessity' to do so could not yet find suitable expression precisely because the Schröerian mission was still insufficiently fulfilled.

Rudolf Steiner in the Workers' Training College

A Tremendous Effect

Over the winter of 1901–2 Rudolf Steiner gave lectures in the Theosophical Society on 'Christianity as Mystical Fact'.

A few months later, in mid-April 1902, he began another course in the Workers' Training College, entitled 'The History of Literature from Luther to the Present'. The mention of Luther sufficiently indicates that the literature in question was mainly German. It is therefore peculiarly ironic that the only lecture in this course of which any transcript has survived is that given on 6 May about 'William Shakespeare'.

According to a statement by the famous writer Georg Brandes, Shakespeare must also be accounted among the German classics. Considering that Shakespeare, after becoming known again in Germany particularly through Lessing in the mid-eighteenth century, exercised an extraordinary influence on Goethe, Schiller, and the whole development of German literature—especially through the excellent translations of his works by Schlegel and Tieck—one would have to agree with this statement.

Around Shakespeare has arisen a complete legend. Whole libraries have been written about each one of his works. Scholars have both placed into and read out of his works everything conceivable. A number of writers held that this actor who had no learned education was incapable of conceiving all the thoughts they found in Shakespeare's works. They finally came up with the hypothesis that William Shakespeare, the actor at the Globe Theatre, did not write the works bearing his name; some important and highly educated man, such as Lord Francis Bacon of Verulam, was the poet who concealed himself under the actor's name at a time when literary activity was not much appreciated. These suppositions are based on the fact of manuscripts in Shakespeare's hand not having been found; then on a notebook discovered in a London library where people wanted to find particular passages corresponding to passages in Shakespeare's works, and so on.

Testimony for Shakespeare's authorship is however supplied by the works themselves. His plays speak of having been written by a man who knew the theatre most intimately, and had the finest understanding for histrionic effects.

If Shakespeare himself arranged no edition of his works, this was just a general custom of the time. Not a single one of his plays was printed in his lifetime. The plays were closely guarded from becoming known through print. People were meant to come into the theatre and there see the plays, not read them at home. All that could arise at the time were pirated editions, copied out during performances with help from the then incipient stenography; so they did not contain the authentic text, but numerous mutilations and mistakes.

These partial gaps and mistakes have led certain researchers to claim that Shakespeare's works as they stand are not particular works of art at all, but were originally assembled quite differently. One representative of this view is Eugen Reichel, who believes he can see in the poet of Shakespearean drama the representative of a particular view of the world. By contrast the fact remains that these plays, just as they are, make such an extraordinary impression. We see this thrilling effect with works which are known to be garbled, as for instance *Macbeth*. Evidence was given by a performance of *Henry V* produced by Neumann-Hofer at the opening of the Lessing Theatre. Despite a ridiculously bad translation and no good production, it made a tremendous impression.

Shakespeare's plays are in the first place character plays. The tremendous interest of these works does not lie chiefly in the action, but in the magnificent development of individual characters. The poet places before us a human character, lets him live in front of us and portrays him in all his thinking and feeling. He presents an individual person.

This artistic evolution culminating in Shakespeare was only possible through the preceding cultural development of the Renaissance period. Only through the higher appreciation of the single person provided by this Renaissance culture were Shakespeare's character plays made possible. In the early Middle Ages we see even in Dante, despite all his strong personality, basically the expression of Christian ideas as then set out. Into the foreground stepped the Christian type of his time, in contrast to the single person. This was just a common conception. The Christian principle had no interest in the single person. Only slowly did interest in the single person develop under a new manner of conceiving.

The circumstance that Shakespeare's fame spread around so soon is proof that he found an audience possessing great interest in the theatre. They therefore brought a large measure of sense for and understanding of the presentation of personality as offered by Shakespeare. What mattered to Shakespeare was to present characters; he was far from developing for his audience ethical or moral ideas. The idea of tragic guilt, for instance, which Schiller believed he had to burden his hero with in order to justify his downfall, was completely foreign to Shakespeare. He lets events develop consequentially, one deriving from another, but uninfluenced by the thought of guilt and atonement. It would be hard to demonstrate a concept of guilt in this sense in any of the Shakespearean plays.

Shakespeare was also not concerned to present an idea, neither jealousy in *Othello* nor ambition in *Macbeth*. No, he wanted to present the particular character of Othello, of Hamlet, of Macbeth. He was able to create such great characters precisely by not encumbering his figures with any theory. He had a basic knowledge of the stage and knew how to present a process effectively. Just as a practitioner he could develop a process in such a way as to carry a listener along with him.—In the whole of world literature there are no plays so much thought out from a histrionic standpoint. This secures the actor Shakespeare the fame of having composed these plays.

Shakespeare was born in Stratford in the year 1564. His father was a prosperous townsman, and he attended the Latin school in his home town. Legends have often been formed about his youth: it is stated that he was a poacher and led an adventurous life; all this has been brought up against Shakespeare's authorship. Yet it was all precisely of benefit to his compositions. The very circumstance that although provided with good schooling he nonetheless remained spared from actually studying enabled him to stand towards things much more freely and impartially, viewing them without being laden by a pile of learning. It is just the poet's adventurous nature which explains some of the greatest merits of his works. Daring flights of fantasy, sudden changes of events, passions and boldness—all this speaks for a man who had also been much thrown about, and must himself have led a stirring life.

Under his father's worsening financial circumstances, Shakespeare came to London in the year 1585. His theatrical career began in the most subordinate activity conceivable. He held the horses of visitors to the theatre while they were attending performances. Later he rose to supervisor of a number of such grooms, until finally he found employment on the stage itself and could play his first great role in the year 1592.

His fame as actor and theatrical poet now soon spread. With it grew his prosperity, so that already in the year 1597 he could buy a house in Stratford. Especially after becoming joint owner of the Globe Theatre, he turned into a very prosperous man.

The plays of Shakespeare's first period, *Love's Labour's Lost*, *As You Like It*, or some of the kings' plays are not yet so essentially different from other plays of the same time created by Marlowe and others. Their expressive power, purity and naturalness was also impaired by a certain artificiality of speech corresponding to the fashion of the time. Only gradually did the great character-plays then follow: *Othello*, *Hamlet*, *Macbeth*, *King Lear*, *Julius Caesar*, *Coriolanus*, which were to establish Shakespeare's fame for all time. From a number of his last works some of his biographers and portrayers wish to deduce bleak events and experiences then befalling the poet and leading him to a bitter view of life. But precisely with Shakespeare such a deduction is very hard to prove, for he withdraws behind his figures like no other poet. He does not bring to expression through the mouth of his figures what he thinks about a matter. Rather, he lets each one think and act according to their character.

It therefore seems futile to ask what standpoint Shakespeare himself took towards various questions . . . Hamlet broods over being or not being; he is scared by the ghost of his father, as Macbeth by the witches on the heath. Whether Shakespeare believed in witches or ghosts, whether he was a believer or a freethinker is of no matter at all. The question he asked himself was how to present on stage a ghost or a witch in order to produce the effect he intended on a listener. That the effect of Shakespearean figures has remained equally great up until today just shows how he answered this question.

It should also not be forgotten that the circumstances of our present-day stage are actually not particularly favourable to the effect of Shakespearean plays. The value placed today on fittings, all kinds of subsidiary props, frequent changes of scenery—all this reduces the effect of character portrayal which remains the principal matter. In Shakespeare's time, when a change of scene was indicated simply by hanging up a sign, and a chair and table sufficed for a royal palace, the effect must in this regard have been significantly greater.

With a present writer such an endless amount in a performance depends on all the fittings. Most writers prescribe quite exactly the fittings of the rooms and so on right into every detail, so that in a bad performance the effect is completely lost. Shakespeare's plays have a tremendous effect even in the most inadequate of performances.

If a time comes when we again look more at what is essential than is the case today, the effect of Shakespeare's art will become ever more tremendous through its power of character portrayal, in which it has remained alive and unequalled through the centuries.

Unprecedented Tension

In 1941 the Austrian-born writer Stefan Zweig published his autobiography *Die Welt von Gestern*, which *inter alia* described his arrival in Berlin in 1902:

> I had received from Viennese friends a whole series of recommendations. But not a single one of them did I take up. For the actual aim of my escapade was to get away from that secure and bourgeois atmosphere and lead instead a liberated life, completely dependent on myself. I wished to meet exclusively people to whom I had found the way through my own literary efforts—and if possible interesting people. After all, one had not read the *Bohème* in vain, and as a twenty-year-old it was a matter of course to wish to lead such a life.
>
> There was no need to search long for a wild circle thrown indiscriminately together. From Vienna I had for some time been contributing to the leading journal of the Berlin 'moderns' named almost ironically *Die Gesellschaft* and edited by Ludwig Jacobowski. Shortly before his death, this young poet had founded a club with what was for youthful people a seductive name, 'The Coming Generation', meeting once a week on the first floor of a café on the Nollendorfplatz. In this vast company modelled on the Parisian 'Closerie des Lilas' the most heterogeneous people thronged together, poets and architects, snobs and journalists, girls draped up as craftswomen or sculptresses, Russian students and snow-white Scandinavians wanting to perfect themselves in the German tongue. Germany itself had representatives from all its provinces, strong-boned Westphalians, worthy Bavarians, Silesian Jews, all crowded together in wild discussions and complete informality. From time to time poems or plays were read out, but the main thing for everyone was getting to know each other. Among

these young folk consciously behaving as Bohemians, there sat like Father Christmas an old grey-bearded man, respected and loved by all because he was a real poet and a real Bohemian: Peter Hille. This septuagenarian with his blue doggy eyes would look with good-natured innocence into this peculiar swarm of children, always wrapped up in his grey mackintosh which concealed a totally frayed suit and very dirty washing. On our insistence, he willingly let himself be tempted to bring out from his jacket pockets wholly crumpled manuscripts and read out his poems. They were poems of dissimilar kind, actually improvisations by a lyrical genius, just formed too loosely, too accidentally. He would write them with a pencil in the tram or the café, then forget them and have trouble finding the words again on the blurred and stained papers. He never had money, but did not bother about money, sleeping as a guest now with this person now with that, and his forgetfulness of the world, his absolute lack of ambition had something captivatingly genuine. One did not actually understand when and how this good woodman had landed up in the city of Berlin and what he wanted here. But he did not want anything at all, not to be famous, not celebrated, and thanks to his poetic dreaminess was more careless and free than I have ever later seen in another man. Around him the ambitious disputants would yell and shout; he would listen mildly, disputing with none, sometimes lifting his glass towards one with a friendly greeting, but hardly ever becoming involved in conversation. One felt as if even during the wildest tumult verses and words were seeking each other in his shaggy and rather tired head, without entirely touching or finding each other.

The genuineness and childlikeness emanating from this naive poet—who even in Germany is today almost forgotten—perhaps drew my attention and feelings away from the elected chairperson of the 'Coming Generation'; and yet this was a man whose ideas and words were later decisive in shaping the lives of countless persons. Here in Rudolf Steiner, for whom as founder of Anthoposophy the most splendid schools and academies were later built by adherents to carry out his teaching, I met again for the first time after Theodor Herzl a man to whom destiny was to give the mission of becoming a guide to millions of people . . . In his dark eyes there lived a hypnotic power, and I listened to him better and more critically when looking away from him, for his ascetically gaunt face marked by spiritual passion was certainly calculated to make a convincing effect not only on the ladies. At that time Rudolf Steiner had not yet reached a teaching of his own, but was still a seeker and learner himself. Sometimes he would lecture to us on Goethe's doctrine of colour, the picture of which as presented by him became more Faustian and Paracelsan. He was stimulating to listen to, for his learning was stupendous and wonderfully many-sided compared to ours, which was limited just to literature. From his lectures and many good private talks I always returned home simultaneously enthused and rather

> depressed. Nonetheless when asking myself today whether at the time I would have prophesied for this young man such a philosophical and ethical effect on the masses, I must to my shame deny it . . . However, to meet a man of such magnetic power just at that early stage where he was still friendly and undogmatic in communicating himself to younger persons was for me an invaluable gain. From his fantastic and at the same time profound knowledge I recognized that a true universality, which we overestimators of our *Gymnasium* education imagined ourselves to have already mastered, cannot be attained by cursory reading and discussion, but only through burning endeavour continued over years.

★

In regard to discussion, Hermann Friedmann in his autobiography *Sinnvolle Odyssee* (1950) described Steiner in the same circle:

> My great conception of his personality was not acquired from particular qualities, but from the *relations* which certain of his qualities bore to one another. When for instance I said that in discussion he especially 'stood out', that should not be taken to mean that when discussing he spoke a lot and made a considerable impression. Others could also have done this, without for that reason having ascribed to them the quality of greatness. On subjects which he had not himself brought forward, Steiner on the contrary expressed himself for the most part with taciturnity or not at all; but at the same time he was listening with every organ, and no one could have said that his 'involvement' in the discussion had not been exceptional. I believe he heard, saw, felt and understood the person who was speaking. This alone would in itself be worthy of admiration. But what was great in my eyes was rather the relation of this nearly mystical silence—i.e. of a mystic's receptive silence (σιγη) in contrast to the silence of indifference—the *relation* of this wordless listening to the forcefulness of his own speech on his own subject, when he would strain, tear, gasp and shout. From these relations—one would like to say disparities—there sprang up a tremendous dynamic, and a discharge of unprecedented tension. So in my opinion just hearing him speak did not yet render one capable to encompass entirely the phenomenon of the effect of his speech. His silence and capacity to listen must also be borne in mind. Admittedly, when engaged himself in speaking he would harangue another as overwhelmingly as he would disengage himself when listening to another. Each of these actions could therefore make in itself an immeasurably strong impression. At times he would just state in a short sentence: 'You stand exactly where I do, only you don't know it.' One could believe him, because it was no manner of speech or feint, but preceded by the evidential power of his most devoted attention to the opposing speech. On the other hand, the drilling ferocity and forcefulness of his self-assurance could of course annihilate any contradiction. But what I wish to

bring out here is not his power to convince, but the testimony of his greatness; and such in my eyes is that tension and dynamic I described as a 'relation'...

The Divine Tragedy of Hamlet

By June 1902, Rudolf Steiner was finalizing a written text of the lectures he had given over the previous winter on 'Christianity as Mystical Fact'. (In the present selection, all words, phrases or sentences added or substituted in the later edition of 1910 are enclosed in square brackets.)

The first chapter was entitled 'Points of View':

> Scientific thinking has profoundly influenced the conceptual life of modern times. It is becoming ever more impossible to speak about spiritual needs or 'soul-life' without engaging oneself with the methods of thought and the conclusions of science. Admittedly, there are still many human beings who are satisfied by these needs without letting their circle be troubled by the scientific stream in spiritual life. Those who listen to the pulse-beat of the time cannot belong among them. Minds are captivated with increasing speed by conceptions drawn from knowledge of Nature; and hearts follow too, if much less willingly, if often without courage and apprehensively. It is not only a matter of the *number* of those who are captivated, but that inherent in scientific thinking is a power which convinces the observant that the future will belong to this thinking [that this thinking contains something which a present view of the world cannot pass by without receiving significant impressions]. Easygoing denial, indeed mockery of 'raw materialistic science' is no longer in place ... [Many outgrowths of this thinking *necessitate* a justified denial of its ideas. But one cannot stop there] ... in an age when wide strata of the population [circles] turn towards this way of thinking and are drawn by it as though by a magic power. Nor is this altered by the fact that single persons in refined spiritual exclusiveness declare that 'people' have long got ... [perceive how real science by itself has 'long' gone] ... past the 'shallow wisdom of force and matter' in materialism. Much rather, it seems, should attention be payed to those who boldly declare that a new religion must also be erected upon scientific ideas. Even if such people also appear shallow and superficial to one who knows mankind's deeper spiritual interests, he must yet listen to them, for the attention of the present turns towards them; and reasons exist for believing that they will gain ever more attention in the immediate future. Others also come into account who with the interests of their hearts have remained behind those of their heads. They are those whose understanding cannot escape from scientific ideas. The burden of proof oppresses them. But the religious needs of their feeling cannot be satisfied by these ideas. The latter provide

> too comfortless a perspective for such satisfaction. Should the human soul be enthused for heights of beauty, truth and goodness in order to be in every single case swept away into nothingness like a bubble raised by the material brain? This is a feeling which oppresses many people like a nightmare. But scientific ideas also oppress them [because they are imposed with tremendously authoritative power]. As long as they can, such people remain blind to this discord in their souls. Indeed they comfort themselves by saying that in these things the human soul is not given complete clarity. They think scientifically, as far as the experience of the senses and the logic of understanding demand it; but they keep to the religious sentiments in which they have been brought up and prefer to remain in darkness about these matters, a darkness which clouds their understanding. They have not the courage to struggle through to clarity.
>
> So there can be no doubt that the scientific way of thinking is the most powerful force in the spiritual life of modern times. And anyone who speaks about the spiritual interests of mankind may not heedlessly pass it by. But there is also no doubt that the way it at first satisfies spiritual needs is superficial and shallow. The outlook would be comfortless if this way were the right one. Or would it not be depressing to have to agree as soon as a person said: 'Thought is a form of force. We walk with the same force with which we think. Man is an organism that changes several forms of force into thought-force. Man is a machine into which we put what we call food, and produce what we call thought. Think of that wonderful chemistry by which bread was changed into the divine tragedy of *Hamlet*.' This is written in a brochure by Robert G. Ingersoll, bearing the title *Moderne Götterdammerung* . . .

Ingersoll was an American political speaker and writer, who had died three years previously in 1899. The work referred to was a German translation of a lecture he had held at Fairbury, Illinois on 29 January 1872, under the title *The Gods*. The German title was more elaborate.

Steiner continued:

> . . . Even if such thoughts find outwardly little agreement when one or other person expresses them, that is all the same. The main thing is that countless people believe [see] themselves virtually forced to such confessions by the scientific way of thinking [forced by the scientific way of thinking to align themselves to the processes of the world in the sense of the above sentences, even if they believe they are not doing so].

A note added to the 1910 edition read:

> Ingersoll's words are not brought forward at this point in the book merely with reference to those people who express them as their conviction in exactly the same formulations. Many people will not do this and yet have

> such ideas about natural phenomena and man that if they were really consequent, they would have to come to these statements. It does not matter what someone expresses as his conviction theoretically, but whether this conviction really follows from his whole way of thinking. Someone may for his own person even abhor the above words or find them laughable; if he forms an explanation of them which takes into account mere externality without rising to the spiritual foundations underlying natural phenomena, another will make out of it as a logical consequence a materialistic philosophy.

The main text went on:

> Certainly these things would be comfortless, if science itself forced us to the creed proclaimed by many of its recent prophets. Most comfortless for anyone who from the content of this science has become convinced that its way of thinking is valid, its methods unshakeable in its domain of Nature. For such a person must say to himself: however much people may still argue over particular questions, though volumes after volumes be written, observations upon observations collected about the 'struggle for existence' and its meaninglessness, about the 'omnipotence' or 'powerlessness' of 'natural selection', science itself is moving in a direction which [within certain limits] *must* find agreement to an ever higher degree.

A note added to the 1910 edition stated:

> For anyone who can rightly perceive, the 'Spirit of Nature' speaks with tremendous power in the facts currently dealt with by the catchphrases 'struggle for existence', 'omnipotence of natural selection', etc. Not in the *opinions* science forms about them today. The first circumstance contains the reason why science will be heard in ever wider circles. But it follows from the second circumstance that the opinions of science should not be accepted as if they necessarily belonged to knowledge of the facts. However, the possibility of being tempted so to accept them is immeasurably great at the present time.

The main text continued:

> But are the demands of science really those spoken about by some of its representatives? That they are not is shown precisely by the behaviour of these representatives themselves. Their behaviour in its own field is not such as many describe it, and demand for other fields. Or would Darwin and Ernst Haeckel ever have made the great discoveries in the domain of evolutionary biology if instead of observing life and the structure of living beings they had gone into the laboratory in order to set up *chemical* experiments about a piece of tissue cut out of an organism? Would Lyell have been able to present the development of the Earth's crust not by

> investigating its strata and their content but instead by testing countless stones for their chemical qualities? Let anyone *really* tread in the footsteps of these explorers who appear like monumental figures within the development of modern science! He will then be acting in higher domains of spiritual life as they acted in the field of observation of Nature. He will not then believe he has grasped the essence of the 'divine' tragedy of *Hamlet* by saying that a wonderful chemical process transformed a quantum of food[32] into that tragedy . . .

The Idea of Hamlet

After this preliminary chapter, there followed further chapters on 'Mysteries and Mystery Wisdom', 'Greek Sages before Plato in the Light of Mystery Wisdom', 'Plato as a Mystic' and 'Mystery Wisdom and Myth'.

A chapter on 'Egyptian Mystery Wisdom' then gradually also led into a discussion of Buddha and Jesus. It was followed by a chapter on 'The Gospels', presenting 'the standpoint of a "mystical" origin of the Gospels', and applying this standpoint to such phenomena as 'miracles'.

★

The next chapter was entitled 'The Miracle of Lazarus'. It began as follows:

> Among the 'miracles' attributed to Jesus, quite particular significance must be ascribed to the raising of Lazarus in Bethany. Everything unites to assign a prominent position in the 'New Testament' to what the evangelist here relates. One must consider that the account stands only in the Gospel of John, of that evangelist who demands through the significant introductory words of his Gospel a quite particular interpretation of what he relates. John begins with the sentences: 'In the [primal] beginning was the Word, and the Word was with God, and [a] God was the Word. And the Word became flesh, and dwelt amongst us, and we saw his glory, a glory of the only-begotten Son of the Father, full of grace [dedication] and truth.' Anyone placing such words at the beginning of his expositions is indicating as it were with fingers that he wants to be interpreted in an especially profound sense. Whoever wishes to come up here with merely intellectual explanations or other things remaining on the surface is like a person who opines that Othello had 'really' murdered Desdemona on the stage . . .

★

Throughout the remainder of this chapter Steiner then presented his own interpretation of the raising of Lazarus. It included the following passage:

> ... There dawns a certainty which no logical interpretation, no attempt at rational explanation can give. A mystery in the true sense of the word stands before us. Into Lazarus the 'eternal word' has entered. Speaking in the sense of the Mysteries, he has become an initiate. (Cf. p. 81 ff.) ...

The bracketed reference was to passages in the chapter on 'Egyptian Mystery Wisdom'. In 1910 Steiner changed the reference to give a more general indication of an even earlier chapter:

> (Cf. 'Mysteries and Mystery Wisdom'.)

The text went on:

> ... And the event recounted to us must be a process of initiation.
>
> Let us once place the whole event before us as an initiation. Lazarus is loved by Jesus. (John 11:36). No affection in the usual sense can here be meant. That would contradict the spirit of John's Gospel, in which Jesus is the 'Word'. Jesus loved Lazarus because he considered him ready for the awakening of the 'Word' within him. There existed relationships between Jesus and the family in Bethany. That only means that Jesus prepared everything in that family which was to lead to the great final act of the drama: to the raising of Lazarus. The latter is a pupil of Jesus. He is a pupil of such a kind that Jesus can with certainty expect the awakening to be one day accomplished within him. The final act of a drama of awakening consisted in a symbolical action [a pictorial action revealing the spirit]. The human being had not only to grasp the 'Die and become'; he had to accomplish it himself in a symbolically [spiritually] real action. The earthliness of which the higher human being in the sense of the Mysteries must be ashamed was to be laid aside. The earthly human being had to die a symbolically [pictorially] real death. That his body was then put for three days into a somnambulistic sleep can indeed only be described, in regard to the great transformation of life taking place, as a symbolically real action [as an outer event to which an incomparably more important spiritual one corresponds]. But this action was indeed also an experience dividing the life of the mystic into two parts. Anyone who does not know the higher content of such actions in living fullness is unable to understand them. One can only bring them close to him by a comparison.—The whole content of Shakespeare's *Hamlet* can be summarized in a couple of words. Anyone who has command of these words can in a certain sense say that he knows the content of *Hamlet*. And logically he does know it too. But a person who lets himself be affected by the whole wealth of the Shakespearean play knows it differently. A living content has passed through his soul which is not replaceable by any mere description. The idea of *Hamlet* has for him become artistic, personal experience ...

Important

There followed further chapters on 'The Apocalypse of John', 'Jesus and his Historical Background' and 'The Essence of Christianity'.

The penultimate chapter was headed 'Christianity and Pagan Wisdom'. Its concluding paragraphs stated that

> ... The more intimate sense by which alone the Word could become flesh was given by the whole development of ancient world-conceptions. Plato indeed recounts the macrocosmic tale: God has stretched the soul of the world onto the body of the world *in the form of a cross* ...

In his earlier chapter on 'Plato as a Mystic', Rudolf Steiner had referred to a passage from the *Timaeus*[33] as follows:

> ... The Father made the world from the cosmic body and the cosmic soul. He harmoniously mixed the elements which arose [came into being] when he gave [offered] up a separate existence of his own by pouring himself out. From this arose the body of the world. And onto this body of the world the soul of the world is outstretched *in the form of a cross*. It is the divine in the world. It met death on the cross, so that the world might exist ...

The passage in the *Timaeus* actually reads:

> Such then was the sum of the reasoning of the ever-existing God concerning the God who was one day to be existent, whereby He made Him smooth and even and equal on all sides from the centre, a whole and perfect body compounded of perfect bodies. And in the midst thereof He set the soul, which He stretched throughout the whole of Him, and therewith enveloped also the exterior of His body ...
>
> Next He split all this which was put together into two parts lengthwise; and then laid the two one against the other, the middle of one to the middle of the other, like a 'chi' (οἷον χι) ...

This image was elaborated by Vincenz Knauer in his work *Die Hauptprobleme der Philosophie* (1892). The relevant sentence, heavily marked in Steiner's copy, reads:

> About which, the myth reports in the *Timaeus* that God laid this soul of the world through the universe in the form of a cross and stretched out over it the body of the world.

In his chapter on 'Christianity and Pagan Wisdom', Steiner continued:

> ... This soul of the world is the Logos. If the Logos is to become flesh, it must then repeat in fleshly existence the cosmic process of the world. It must be hammered onto the cross and rise again. This most important thought of

> Christianity was long foreshadowed as a spiritual idea in ancient world-conceptions. The mystic underwent it as a personal experience during 'initiation'. The Logos become man had to undergo it as a fact, valid for the whole of mankind. Something which was thus a Mystery event in the development of ancient wisdom is indicated through Christianity as [becomes through Christianity] a historical fact. Christianity thereby became the fulfilment not only of what Jewish prophets had foretold, but also of what had previously been formed by the Mysteries.—The cross on Golgotha is the Mystery cult of antiquity condensed into a fact. We encounter this cross first in the ancient world-conceptions; at the starting point of Christianity we meet it as [within] a unique event, meant to be valid for the whole of mankind. The mystical element in Christianity can be grasped from this point of view. Christianity as mystical fact is a stage of development of Mystery Wisdom.

In 1910 this ending was changed and expanded, thus:

> . . . Christianity as mystical fact is a stage of development in the evolution of mankind; the events in the Mysteries and the effects occasioned by them are the preparation for this mystical fact.

★

The preface to the 1910 edition began:

> *Das Christentum als mystische Tatsache* was the title given to this work by its author when summarizing in it eight years ago the content of lectures he had held in the year 1902. That title was meant to indicate the particular character of the book, which did not just attempt to present historically the mystical content of Christianity, but was meant to describe how Christianity arose out of *mystical conception*. Underlying it was the thought that in this process *spiritual facts* were at work, which can only be seen through such conception . . .

Fifteen years later, in an instalment of his autobiography first published in February 1925 and now standing as part of Chapter XXX, Steiner once again referred to the title of his book:

> . . . It was then that I held the course of lectures which I summarized in the book *Das Christentum als mystische Tatsache*.
>
> I let it be known from the start that the choice of title 'as mystical fact' is important. For I did not want simply to present the mystical content of Christianity. My aim was to present evolution from the ancient Mysteries to the Mystery of Golgotha in such a way that not just earthly historical forces are working in this evolution, but spiritual extraterrestrial impulses. I wanted to show that in the ancient Mysteries cultic pictures were given of cosmic

> processes, which in the Mystery of Golgotha were then accomplished on the plane of history as a *fact* transferred from the cosmos onto the earth ...

The German word *Tatsache*, 'fact', is a combination of two other words: *Tat*, 'deed', and *Sache*, 'thing'. The combination is first recorded in 1756 as a translational borrowing of the English phrase 'matter of fact'. And early users of the English phrase, attested since 1581, included Francis Bacon.[34]

Now that Rudolf Steiner in June 1902 had given such prominence to this Baconian term in the very title of his forthcoming book *Das Christentum als mystische Tatsache*, his own visits to Britain could begin.

NOTES

1. My work *Rudolf Steiner in Britain* was reprinted in 2009 (with corrections to the text, and rescanned photographs) and may be ordered by interested readers from Temple Lodge Publishing, or directly from the distributor at orders@booksource.net. Owners of the original 2004 edition may also request from the publisher copies of the rescanned plates free of charge.
2. It is curious that Rudolf Steiner's autobiography, the instalments of which he brought out under the title *Mein Lebensgang* (in English *The Course of My Life*), has never been published in Britain. Both existing English versions appeared in America, that by Olin Wannamaker in 1926 (revised in 1951), and that by Rita Stebbing in 1977.

   As with all of Steiner's works, this autobiography presents great difficulties to a translator. Indeed at times it seems unsurpassed in translational intractability by any other of Steiner's prose writings. The Wannamaker version keeps fairly closely to the original syntax, at the cost of some stylistic awkwardness. The Stebbing version is more freely conceived and has an admirable fluency, but at a proportionate cost in accuracy. In the present work I have made use of both translations in making my own versions, which try to steer a middle course between these two extremes.
3. Maria von Nagy in memoirs published under the title *Rudolf Steiner über seine Letzte Ansprache, über Ungarn und über die Schweiz* (1974) records that in conversations with Steiner at Easter 1924 he spoke with her about the need for Hungarian translations of his writings: 'He wanted to see these himself and correct them. He said he still knew the necessary Hungarian...'
4. Francis Bacon plays a prominent role in Rudolf Steiner's 1924 karma lectures, where his previous life as Harun-al-Rashid is frequently discussed, often in conjunction with an unnamed 'wise counsellor' who for his part reincarnated as Amos Comenius. Why Steiner did not name the counsellor is hard to say. It seems reasonable to suppose that he was referring to Yahya ben Barmak.
5. On Hochstetter's part in the development of Steiner's geological ideas, cf. now the great work by Dankmar Bosse: *Die gemeinsame Evolution von Erde und Mensch* (2002), p. 56.
6. Faraday's invention of the electric motor in 1821 was followed exactly ten years later, in 1831, by his epoch-making discovery of electromagnetic induction. James Hamilton states at another point in his biography: 'The discoveries that Faraday made in science in the 1830s had electricity as their vibrant centre. In this decade Faraday transformed the public's perception of electricity, such as it was, from a novelty with uses limited to attempting to heal the sick or making toys revolve, to a power which would one day light cities or drive ships...'
7. On 18 January 1825, the 75-year-old Goethe remarked to Eckermann:

'*Hermann and Dorothea* is almost the only one of my longer poems which I still enjoy. I can never read it without being interested and moved.'

Whewell's first reference to this poem was in a letter written a couple of years later, in 1827—still during Goethe's lifetime: 'The great beauty of the book is the truth of the characters and the admirable manner in which the story is brought out . . .'

8. Darwin's only journey to the European Continent was as an 18-year-old in 1827, when he accompanied his uncle, the famous potter Josiah Wedgwood, on a journey to Paris. Nothing is known of what he saw there. In the first volume, *Journeying* (1995), of her Darwin biography, Janet Browne moots the interesting possibility that the Parisian sights which he visited could have included the Muséum d'Histoire Naturelle made famous at the time by Georges Cuvier.
9. In course of his Munich lecture on 26 August 1912 Rudolf Steiner stated: '. . . I could give examples of what I have just told you about the sometimes disconcerting reappearance of initiates in such a way that one might believe them to have come down from their height, and you would probably be astonished to the highest degree if I told you in what manner for instance Dante was incarnated again in the nineteenth century. But I have not here the task of discussing further what was for myself the result of research, and for me is certain . . .'

In no subsequent lecture did Steiner ever return to this example. But in his biography *Carl Gustav Carus* (1999), Ekkehard Meffert records that Steiner did subsequently inform Ita Wegman, Albert Steffen and Mathilde Scholl that the Italian poet reincarnated as King John of Saxony.

John of Saxony, born in 1801, grew up as an ardent admirer of Dantean poetry. As Saxon prince, between 1821 and 1849 he translated the *Divine Comedy* into German under the pseudonym 'Philalethes', and during this period gathered around him in Dresden a circle of other Dantists which included Carus and Tieck. In 1854 he finally succeeded to the Saxon throne, and on the foundation in 1865 of the German Dante Society became its patron. He died in 1873.

In his biography Meffert also intimates (as his own idea) the undeniably interesting and attractive possibility that Carus—who made extensive journeys to Italy in 1821, 1828 and 1841—might well be considered as the reborn Brunetto Latini, a figure repeatedly discussed in Steiner's karma lectures of 1924.

It may be added that Steffen's interest in Dante and his period is especially highlighted in a passage from Rudolf Steiner's letter to Marie Steiner of 27 February 1925: 'One must understand Steffen by looking back on him as Giotto. The whole change from Cimabue to G. is that from a lucid spiritualism, from spirituality in colour, conception and form to naturalism; and only in Raphael and the great artists does something still remain of what came to an end and is somewhat preserved only in Cimabue. That is all expressed in Steffen's psyche. He works with the forces thrusting against him from the change of that time, goes for reality, in almost the only way possible in the twentieth century. G. had beauty before him, which he grew out of. That idealizes his naturalism. Steffen was surrounded everywhere by non-art; that materializes the spiritualism slumbering inside him to begin with . . .' On all this see now Erdmuth Grosse's *Das Rätsel des Urvorstandes* (2008).

10. In 1844, on learning that Whewell had translated into English *Hermann und Dorothea*, Carus commented on 'the difficulty of attempting English hexameters'. When five years later, in 1849, Whewell went on to publish *English Hexameter Translations*, a recipient of the book sent him the following verses:

    Thanks, many thanks, Master, for your most acceptable present,
    Just come from Murray's shop, but sent by the editor also,
    Brimful of hexameters, translated all from the German,
    Except some very few from Greek original authors—
    Almost impossible, in our own inharmonious English
    Harsh words to modulate, and arrange in rhythmical order,
    Such as might please the ear of a staunch admirer of Homer.
    Quantity, which regulates all the flow of classical verses,
    With well-known fixt laws, in our tongue is an element unknown,
    While accent ill supplies its place in versification.
    That which I complain of, in our English hexameters,
    Is a want of spondees, and the too great number of dactyls,
    But still more I object to the want of a natural pause or
    Suspension of the verse, *caesura* we commonly call it.
    But time forbids me to extend my remarks any further,
    So no more just now from your most obedient servant.

11. In the present context it may be added that the financial profits from the Great Exhibition were used to purchase a piece of land in South Kensington on which were later built the Science Museum, the Geological Museum and—at the insistence of Richard Owen, whose statue now commands the sweeping double staircase in the entrance hall—the Natural History Museum. Rudolf Steiner, describing in his autobiography his first visit to London in 1902, when he was staying in Bayswater, must have been partly referring to the collections housed in these buildings when stating: 'I tried to use the intervals I had left from attending the Conference meetings to make careful visits of the scientific and artistic collections in London. I may say that from these scientific and historical collections many ideas arose in me concerning the evolution of Nature and mankind.'
12. It was peculiarly appropriate that in 1852 Whewell (who at the time was translating elegies about Rome) should have met the author of *Die römischen Päpste*, the eminent German historian Leopold von Ranke. For in the karma lecture given at Dornach on 12 April 1924 Rudolf Steiner described Ranke as 'a pre-earthly pupil of Lord Bacon', and indeed as 'Bacon's most significant posthumous pupil'.
13. In contrast to the ever-increasing literature relating to Charles Darwin, there

were no further works published concerning William Whewell. But at the very end of the nineteenth century, Leslie Stephen composed an extensive and carefully researched entry on Whewell for Vol. XX, appearing in 1899, of that monumental literary compendium of the late Victorian age, the *Dictionary of National Biography*. He gave a full bibliography of Whewell's writings and referred to the works edited by Isaac Todhunter and Janet Stairs Douglas as well as to various other obituaries and reminiscences. From this account any interested person could obtain a reasonably good idea of Whewell's life and destiny. The portrayal by the present writer was mainly constructed by following the various tracks opened out through the indications in Stephen's entry.

In the further developing scientific climate of the early twentieth century Whewell's works were regarded as superseded, and he was largely forgotten. By the time in 1924 when he received mention in Steiner's *Lebensgang* few readers would probably even have heard of him. Only later in the century, with the slowly burgeoning growth of interest in the Victorian age, did Whewell begin to re-enter historical consciousness. During the 1960s and 70s various of his scientific works were reprinted. Finally in 1991 there appeared two separate books about him: Menachem Fisch published *William Whewell: Philosopher of Science*, over 200 pages in length, and along with Simon Schaffer also edited a collection of over 400 pages entitled *William Whewell: A Composite Portrait*, to which various scholars contributed. But although both works discussed in enormous detail Whewell's scientific writings within the historical context of early- and mid-nineteenth-century philosophy, neither of them showed any interest in or desire at all to present Whewell's actual *life*!

It may be added that the account of Whewell in the present book has been taken entirely from published sources, and that much further documentary material about him still lies unpublished in the archives of Trinity College Cambridge. These archives have however been used by Laura J. Snyder in her fine work *The Philosophical Breakfast Club* (2011), which only appeared while the present book was already at press. It examines the intertwining scientific impulses and friendship between William Whewell, John Herschel, Richard Jones and Charles Babbage.

14. What Rudolf Steiner said was: 'I was happy in this friendship. The girlfriend was like sunshine in my life. Yet later this life led us apart. Happy hours spent together still lingered on in the form of a brief correspondence, and then only remained as a wistful memory of the beautiful period of life we had spent, a memory which ever since has risen again and again from the depths of my soul.'

Only one letter from Rudolf Steiner to Radegunde Fehr has survived, from the Viennese period itself (15 July 1888). The letter, though quite friendly, also gives expression to Steiner's reserve, being written in a formal style ('Sehr geehrtes Fräulein . . .'). It largely concerns details of the *Deutsche Wochenschrift* he was then editing, and includes the memorable statement: 'When writing something, I set my whole thinking and feeling so much into the matter that I am not then indifferent to the way it is received. That is: I am generally little concerned with approval from the multitude, but all the more so with approval from those to whose spirit and heart I am devoted . . .'

Gundi Fehr died in Vienna in 1903, aged only 35.

15. Thomas Reid is appreciatively discussed in the book by Ernst Lehrs: *Man or Matter* (1951, revised in 1958 and again in 1985), especially in Chapter VII, 'Except We Become . . .' In a note to this chapter Lehrs states: 'The present writer's interest in Reid was first aroused by a remark of Rudolf Steiner, in his book *A Theory of Knowledge*.'

    In connection to Aberdeen, where he taught, Reid is also mentioned by Karl König in his autobiographical fragment now published in the collection *Karl König: My Task* (2008).

16. During various karma lectures in 1924 Rudolf Steiner identified a previous incarnation of Byron as an Eastern European adventurer of the early Middle Ages, 'about one or two centuries before the Crusades', who travelled to Constantinople in an unsuccessful attempt to carry off the legendary—and carefully guarded—Palladium and bring it to Russia. Since the Crusades began towards the end of the eleventh century, Steiner's chronological indication suggests roughly the tenth century.

    Of interest in this connection is a passage in Benita Eisler's biography *Byron: Child of Passion, Fool of Fame* (1999), describing an episode during the poet's visit to Constantinople in 1810:

    'For Byron, the most evocative experience was riding on horseback inland along the ramparts of the fifth-century Theodosian land-walls. "Imagine, four miles of immense triple battlements covered with ivy," he wrote to his mother, "surmounted with 218 towers, and on the other side of the road Turkish burying grounds (the loveliest spots on earth) full of enormous cypresses. I have seen the ruins of Athens, of Ephesus, and Delphi, I have traversed great parts of Turkey, and many other parts of Europe and some of Asia, but I never beheld a work of Nature or Art which yielded an impression like the prospect on each side, from the Seven Towers to the end of the Golden Horn." '

17. In Chapter XIV of his autobiography, Steiner stated: 'Suphan's previous post had been that of teacher in a Berlin *Gymnasium*. At the same time he had begun to edit the works of Herder. Thus he seemed well qualified also to take on the management of the Goethe edition.'

    Suphan's edition of Herder was published continuously from 1877 onwards for the rest of his life, in what eventually became 33 volumes.

    After another couple of paragraphs, Steiner continued: 'Suphan was faithfully attached to Herman Grimm. Previously, in Berlin, he had been looked on as a member of Grimm's household, had breathed in the spiritual atmosphere of that house. But inside him lay something which did not allow him to come to terms with life. It was indeed possible to speak with him about the highest spiritual matters; but something sour, emanating from his feeling, easily entered the conversation. This sourness held sway above all in his own mind; he then sought relief from this feeling through a dry humour. So one could not become warm with him. In the same breath he could express understanding for greatness, and without any transition, fall into pettiness and triviality. He was constantly well-meaning towards me. But he did not share at all in the spiritual interests living in my soul...'

Kurt Franz David in an article reprinted in Peter Selg's work *Rudolf Steiners Innere Situation zur Zeit der 'Philosophie der Freiheit'* (2007) states: 'Steiner's letters to his Viennese friends and the description in *Mein Lebensgang* give sufficient insight as to how little of the necessary understanding for his viewpoints he managed to find in Suphan. Their relationship with each other was subjected to ever greater burdens...'

One very striking statement was made by Steiner in a letter to Pauline Specht on 20 May 1891: '... Here in Weimar I stand towards everything as strange and cool as possible, most of all towards the Judas of humaneness, the false Herder-apostle Suphan.'

This characterization proved uncannily prescient. For when 20 years later in 1911 Suphan finally committed suicide, it was by hanging himself—just as Judas had done centuries previously. The manner was symbolical. Climbing onto the piled-up volumes of his Herder edition, he tied to a window-cross a rope knotted around his neck, and then kicked his Herder edition away.

In the above-mentioned book Selg adds: 'Rudolf Steiner's call to Weimar took place in a complex network of human connections and circumstances. But without Karl Julius Schröer and Bernhard Suphan neither Steiner's entry into the Goethe and Schiller Archive nor his work there would have been possible. Only to a very limited extent did both these persons, Schröer and Suphan, recognize Steiner and the working motif which was living within him; yet they stood by him and were part of his path of destiny...'

18. On 10 April 1829 Eckermann recorded:

'"While we are waiting for the soup, I shall give you some refreshment for your eyes." With these obliging words Goethe put before me a volume of landscapes by Claude Lorrain.

'"Here for once," he said, "you may see a complete man, who thought and felt beautifully and in whose mind there was a world the like of which you will not easily find anywhere in external reality. These pictures are supremely true, but not in the least realistic. Claude Lorrain knew the real world by heart down to its minutest details, and he used it as a means to express the world of his own exquisite sensibility. And that indeed is true ideality: so to use realistic means that the higher truth thus manifesting itself produces the semblance of being real."

'"I call that a good saying," I remarked, "and one which would apply just as well to literature as to the visual arts." "Precisely so," said Goethe.'

19. The previous incarnation of Haeckel indicated by Rudolf Steiner was as Pope Gregory VII, who reigned 1073–85. Among Gregory's close connections was that to Countess Beatrice of Tuscany and her daughter Matilde, on which cf. note 30 below.
20. Quite unconnected to the ongoing correspondence on Darwin in *The*

Shrewsbury Chronicle was an arresting little article appearing in the issue of March 1894 under the title: 'Is It The Strongest Or The Fittest That Survive?':

'The survival of the fittest, it must be remembered, does not always, or perhaps ever, mean the survival of the merely strongest, or the merely self-ishest. The very powerful or the excessively selfish man or animal often becomes acutely obnoxious to other men and animals; and his powerful selfishness may be the very cause of his destruction rather than of his survival. The wisest, not the cunningest, but the wisest animal, the creature who has the finest appreciation of the principle of "live and let live", would appear to be the one most adapted for survival in a world where struggles and battles and alliances and the seeking of help from all possible quarters is the order of the day. In such a world those creatures which on the one hand make the least demands upon others and on the other hand show the greatest capacity and willingness to render services to others are surely the most fitted for survival; and as a matter of fact it seems undoubted that such are the creatures which survive. In our judgement the doctrine of the "survival of the fittest" is sound in philosophy; and the principle in fact and practice is not only discoverable but is of the highest service to the world.'

Cf. here Rudolf Steiner's lecture on 23 November 1905 in Berlin, entitled 'Brotherhood and the Struggle for Existence'.

21. The historical lack of interest in Britain for researches into colour of a kind which contest Newtonian doctrine was made strikingly clear to the present writer in 2010 when consulting in the Bodleian Library in Oxford University its copy of Dr Joseph Reade's book quoted by Goethe in this passage, *Experimental Outlines for a new theory of colours, light and vision, with critical remarks on Sir Isaac Newton's opinions* (1816). Its pages were still uncut!
22. *Arden of Faversham* was an anonymous play published in 1592, sometimes attributed to Shakespeare. The attribution is uncertain.
23. Sterne was one of Goethe's favourite English-language authors. He read both *Tristram Shandy* and *A Sentimental Journey* in Strassburg in 1770/1, soon after their first appearance. From then onwards he was praising Sterne's novels to his friends, reading from them in gatherings, and alluding to characters and episodes from them in his letters. Down the years the number of passing references to Sterne in Goethe's writings goes into three figures. In 1817 he reread both Sterne's works, and in 1826 acknowledged the extent of his personal indebtedness to him in a brief essay entitled 'Lorenz Sterne'. In 1828 he again reread *A Sentimental Jouney*, and went on to reproduce a series of laudatory reflections on Sterne in the aphoristic collection 'Aus Makariens Archiv' included in the expanded 1829 edition of his last novel *Wilhelm Meisters Wanderjahre*. Finally in 1830 he again reread *Tristram Shandy*.
24. *The Koran* was not actually by Sterne as Goethe (and later Nietzsche) mis-takenly supposed. Its author was in fact Richard Griffith, a talented Sternean imitator.
25. In October 1897, Rudolf Steiner revisited Weimar to attend the Annual General Meeting of the Goethe Society. His account of the occasion ended:

'... On the 9th the theatre presented visitors with Shakespeare's *A Winter's Tale*, directed by Karl Weiser and performed in the chief roles by Fräulein Richard (Hermione), and Karl Weiser (Leontes).'

26. Cf. Richard Ramsbotham: *Who Wrote Bacon?* (2004). The content of this book is excellent and can scarcely be too highly commended. In the opinion of the present writer, however, its catchy title is restrictive and misleading, and does not do proper justice to the content. This opinion is clearly shared by others, for the book has now been translated into German under the more appropriate title *Jakob I: Inspirator von Shakespeare und Bacon* (2007).

Of further relevance to Ramsbotham's book, though nowhere referred to by him, is the memorable, one might almost say archetypal experience undergone by Karl König at Christmas 1938:

'I was sitting in a tiny room, in one of the hundreds of back streets in London. Alone, a drop in the vast human sea of a city, a stranger, a foreigner. I knew that together with me, tens of thousands of people shared the same fate. Men and women, old and young, children and adults, we were all in the same boat. It was the boat of loneliness; a ship without a destination, a life uprooted from the native soil and barely saved, like a plant which is given a handful of earth in a little plot of clay. How shall we survive?

'The small candle in front of me lit the few green branches on the mantelpiece, and the gas fire hummed a low song. My thoughts went out into the future. Will it be possible to turn this lonely life into order and shape again? Will the fragments of my existence be put together so that they may build a new frame? I was one of the many who were just too young to be a soldier in the First World War. Then came a time of breathtaking recovery and all seemed to be well, when gradually a second war appeared on the horizon. And here I was, thrown out of my work; I felt like one who after a shipwreck was cast onto a lonely, unknown island.

'The flame of the candle jerked and quivered, throwing strange shadows onto the wall. I had left Europe behind me. Here it was no more the land of Europe; it was a country of the western world. The language was foreign to me; the people were strangers. Their way of living was not my way, their past was almost unknown to me. I had a different background, different modes of existence, different thoughts. Some of these strangers had turned to me with a friendly gesture; others, on whom I had previously counted, showed no more interest than just the limits of good behaviour would permit.

'I was alone! Will I again have the strength to begin anew? In a few days my wife and children were to arrive, and in several countries on the continent a number of young friends were waiting to join me. Join me in what? Will I be permitted to work? And if so, what kind of work was I to do? A house had been found in the north of Scotland where we could start to live together. But what kind of life will we live? It will become only an enclave in this land; we will be strangers in a big community. And what is our task?

'The light of the candle now was quiet and bright, and my eyes turned to a small book which a kind person had given me as a Christmas present. It was an

English Bible; never before had I held one in my hands. I was astonished to realize that the present translation was sponsored by James I, a man and monarch for whom, for many years, I had had the highest esteem. I had learnt to admire this "wisest fool in Christendom", and I now read the following words in the dedication: "... to go forward with the confidence and resolution of a man in maintaining the truth of Christ, and propagating it far and near..."

'I asked myself: "Is this not common ground on which I may stand?"

'It was common ground. And now I saw and knew some more about the future task which lay before me. I saw Austria overrun and conquered by men who had betrayed the very essence of the destiny of Europe. They had turned it into a camp of nationalists, searching for might and power. Europe was overcome by their vainglory and was preparing to become a battlefield. Could we not take a morsel of the true European destiny and make it into a seed, so that some of its real task may be preserved? A piece of its humanity, of its inner freedom, of its longing for peace, of its dignity?

'If this were possible, would it not be worthwhile to live and work again? Let us try to become a morsel of this Europe which, at the moment, had to disappear. Let us not do it in words, but in deeds. To serve and not to rule; to help and not to force; to love and not to harm, will be our task. Thus I was thinking.

'I understood my thoughts. They had emerged after weeks of trial and need and now stood before me, helping me to clarify the problem of my existence. On this Christmas Eve, neither Camphill nor the Movement existed. The future was shrouded, but a will started to find its way.'

The decisive part played here by the King James Bible in stimulating König's thoughts in such a way as also to activate his will can certainly be related to his ongoing absorption at the time in the historical destiny of Wallenstein and associated figures from the seventeenth century, as noted in diary entries referred to by Hans Müller-Wiedemann when quoting parts of this passage in his great biography *Karl König* (1992).

27. On the subject of Darwinism Steiner was naturally also able to make suitable distinctions. In an article on 'The Social Question' published in the *Magazin für Litteratur* on 16 July 1898 he stated:

'... In this domain I have noticed that the kind of thinking our researchers have under the influence of Darwinism made their own is *at the moment* not yet working at all beneficially. Let me not be misunderstood. I perceive that with the Darwinist way of thinking one of the greatest advances has been achieved which mankind could make. I believe that Darwinism must work beneficially in all domains of human thought if applied properly, i.e. according to its spirit. In my *Philosophie der Freiheit* I have myself provided a book written in my opinion completely in the spirit of Darwinism. What happened to me on conceiving this book was very strange. I reflected about the most intimate questions of human spiritual life. I did not thereby concern myself with Darwinism at all. And when my thought-edifice was complete, the idea came to me: "You have actually made a contribution to Darwinism."

'Now I find that sociologists do not do this. They first ask the Darwinistically thinking scientists: how do you do it? And then they transpose the method of the latter onto their own domain. They thus make a big mistake. They simply transpose natural laws holding sway in the realm of organic nature onto the domain of human spiritual life: exactly the same should apply for human development as may be observed in animal evolution. Doubtless in this view there lies a healthy kernel. In the whole world a similar conformity to law is certainly to be found. But it is not necessary at all for the *same* laws to be therefore valid for all domains. Laws discovered by Darwinists act in the animal and plant realm. In the human realm we must look for laws thought out in the spirit of the Darwinian ones—but which are just as specifically particular to this realm as the organic laws of evolution to the given realms of Nature. We must search for particular laws of human development, though these will also be thought in the spirit of Darwinism. A simple transposal of the laws of Darwinism onto human development will not lead to satisfactory conceptions.'

28. Regarding Goethe's upholding of the views of Saint-Hilaire, it may be mentioned that in the 'Historical Sketch' prefacing *The Origin of Species* (added in 1860 to both the American edition and to Heinrich Bronn's German translation, and from 1861 onwards reproduced in all subsequent editions), Charles Darwin included the following footnote:

'I have taken the date of the first publication of Lamarck from Isid. Geoffroy Saint-Hilaire's (*Hist. Nat. Générale*, tom. ii. p. 405, 1859) excellent history of opinion on this subject. In this work a full account is given of Buffon's conclusions on the same subject. It is curious how largely my grandfather, Dr. Erasmus Darwin, anticipated the views and erroneous grounds of opinion of Lamarck in his *Zoonomia* (vol. i pp. 500–510), published in 1794. According to Isid. Geoffroy there is no doubt that Goethe was an extreme partisan of similar views, as shown in the introduction to a work written in 1794 and 1795, but not published till long afterwards: he has pointedly remarked (*Goethe als Naturforscher*, von Dr. Karl Meding, s. 34) that the future question for naturalists will be how, for instance, cattle got their horns, and not for what they are used. It is rather a singular instance of the manner in which similar views arise at about the same time that Goethe in Germany, Dr. Darwin in England, and Geoffroy Saint-Hilaire (as we shall immediately see) in France, came to the same conclusion on the origin of species in the years 1794–5.'

29. In 1849 Whewell further re-examined the example of Kepler and the ellipse in his work *Of Induction*, which in 1860 was republished as an appendix to the third volume, *On the Philosophy of Discovery*, of the redesigned *Philosophy of the Inductive Sciences*.

30. During a lecture given in Berlin on 6 February 1913 as the last in the course *Die Mysterien des Morgenlandes und des Christentums* (attended *inter alia* by Herbert and Mabel Heywood-Smith), Rudolf Steiner mentioned previous incarnations of Goethe as an Egyptian initiate and later as an ancient Greek

sculptor. Eleven years later, he expanded on the latter incarnation in karma lectures given at Breslau on 9 June and at Dornach on 23 September 1924. In this last lecture he also revealed Schröer's incarnation in a former life as Plato, whose eye fell onto this Greek sculptor, then a young man, and who harboured love towards him. Reincarnated into the nineteenth century, Schröer then developed his fervent admiration for Goethe, which according to Steiner found expression in Schröer's writings and in his intended Goethe biography.

But this admiration was also and much more strikingly expressed by Schröer's engagement in the Goethe Memorial, which Steiner in his lecture did not mention at all. It seems quite legitimate to perceive in this lengthy engagement—might one almost say obsession?—that the nature of Goethe's Greek incarnation had become profoundy fixed into Schröer's mind on a quite unconscious level: Goethe for him *had* to appear not merely in various kinds of written form designed for inner consumption by the literate, but also outwardly projected into three dimensions on the material plane: in *sculptural* form, in *marble*, and looking *young*. The incarnational background to this psychic necessity makes it quite understandable that when eventually the last two specifications were found by others unacceptable, Schröer—whose admiration for Goethe had in Steiner's words 'something extremely personal'—could feel no further connection to the project.

31. Herman Grimm features in Steiner's karma lecture of 23 April 1924, where his previous lives—in Roman antiquity as Pliny, and in the Middle Ages as Beatrice of Tuscany—are examined in relation to previous lives of Emerson. (This relation is further explored in the useful article 'Studies in Successive Earth-lives' published by William Mann, Joan and Siegfried Rudel and Brien Masters in the 1977 issue of *The Golden Blade*.) But however instructive such *historical* relations may be, perhaps even more revealing is a private communication about Grimm's *posthumous* activity made by Steiner ten years earlier, in Paris in May 1914, to Herman Joachim, as recorded in the latter's notebook. It reads:

   'The following spirits now belong to a closed community with a high mission: Gladstone, Tennyson, Emerson, J. Joachim [Joachim's father], Herman Grimm, Bettina v. Arnim, Hallam. The special task of Herman Grimm consists in bringing sceptics who are truly striving towards higher things onto the right path.'

32. The phrase 'a quantum of food' was an embellishment by the German translator, Wolfgang Schaumburg, for the simple noun 'bread' as found in the quotation from Ingersoll's lecture. Steiner of course never read this lecture in the original English, but only in German translation.

33. In a footnote to the latest (1989) edition of *Das Christentum als mystische Tatsache* (GA 8), David Hoffman writes:

   'Neither Plato's *Timaeus*, to which Rudolf Steiner in the text refers, nor Vincent Knauer's *Hauptprobleme der Philosophie*, where he strongly marked the corresponding passage, seem however to be *sources* for the picture here presented. Steiner rather found in these philosophers a (somewhat modified) *trace* of the image discovered independently by himself, which would also explain the divergences from the presentations by Plato and Knauer. In his autobiography *Mein Lebensgang* he describes this method of picturing and verifying his spiritual knowledge through historical traditions (Chap. XXVI):

'"My relationship to Christianity makes it fully clear that in spiritual science I neither sought nor found anything at all along pathways ascribed to me by many people. They intimate that I put together spiritual knowledge from ancient traditions. I am supposed to have elaborated Gnostic and other teachings. The spiritual insight gained in *Christianity as Mystical Fact* is brought directly out of the world of spirit itself. Only in order to show to the audience at these lectures and to readers of the book the harmony between what is perceived in the spirit and historical traditions did I examine the latter and incorporate them into the content. But I placed nothing which stands in these documents into the content without *first* having it before me in the spirit."'

34. Further details on the origin of the German word *Tatsache* are found in my work *Rudolf Steiner in Britain*, pp. 661–2, note 3.

SELECT BIBLIOGRAPHY

Beck, Walter, *Rudolf Steiner—Das Jahr der Entscheidung*, Dornach 1984
—*Karl Julius Schröer*, Dornach 1993
Boyd, James, *Goethe's Knowledge of English Literature*, Oxford 1932
Browne, Janet, *Charles Darwin: Voyaging. Volume I of a Biography*, London 1995
—*Charles Darwin: The Power of Place: Volume II of a Biography,* London 2002
Eisler, Benita, *Byron: Child of Passion, Fool of Fame*, London 1999
Goethe, J.W., *Conversations and Encounters*, edited by David Luke and Robert Pick, London 1966
—*Naturwissenschaftliche Schriften*, edited by Rudolf Steiner, Dornach reprint, 1975
Hamilton, James, *Faraday: the Life*, London 2002
Hecker, Jutta, *Rudolf Steiner in Weimar*, Dornach 1988
Hoffman, David, Kugler, Walter and Trapp, Ulla (eds), *Rudolf Steiners Dissertation*, Dornach 1991
Jardine, Lisa, *The Curious Life of Robert Hooke*, London 2003
Jardine, Lisa and Stewart, Alan, *Hostage to Fortune: the Troubled Life of Francis Bacon*, London 1998
Kannenberg, Manfred, *Rudolf Steiner in Berlin*, Dornach 2011
Lehrs, Ernst, *Man or Matter*, London, third edition, 1985
Lindenberg, Christoph, *Rudolf Steiner: eine Chronik*, Dornach 1988
—*Rudolf Steiner: eine Biographie*, Dornach 1997
Mandelbrote, Scott, *Footprints of the Lion: Isaac Newton at Work*, Cambridge 2001
Meffert, Ekkehard: *Carl Gustav Carus*, Basel 1999
Meyer, Thomas (ed.), *Der Briefwechsel Ralph Waldo Emerson/Herman Grimm*, Basel 2007
—*Rudolf Steiners 'eigenste Mission'*, Basel 2009
Selg, Peter: *Rudolf Steiners innere Situation zur Zeit der 'Philosophie der Freiheit'*, Dornach 2007
—*Rudolf Steiner und Felix Koguzki*, Arlesheim 2009
Steiner, Rudolf, *Einleitungen zu Goethes Naturwissenschaftlichen Schriften* (GA 1)
—*Grundlinien einer Erkenntnistheorie* (GA 2)
—*Wahrheit und Wissenschaft* (GA 3)
—*Die Philosophie der Freiheit* (GA 4)
—*Dokumente zur 'Philosophie der Freiheit'* (GA 4a)
—*Goethes Weltanschauung* (GA 6)
—*Das Christentum als mystische Tatsache* (GA 8)
—*Die Rätsel der Philosophie* (GA 18)
—*Mein Lebensgang* (GA 28)
—*Gesammelte Aufsätze zur Dramaturgie 1889–1900* (GA 29)
—*Methodische Grundlagen der Anthroposophie 1884–1901* (GA 30)
—*Gesammelte Aufsätze zur Literatur 1884–1902* (GA 32)

—*Biographien und biographische Skizzen* (GA 33)
—*Briefe* (GA 38–9)
Snyder, Laura, J., *The Philosophical Breakfast Club*, New York 2011
Sterne, Laurence, *Tristram Shandy*, York and London 1759–67
—*A Sentimental Journey*, London 1768
Vögele, Wolfgang G. (ed.), *Der Andere Rudolf Steiner*, Dornach 2005
Westfall, Richard S., *Never at Rest: A Biography of Isaac Newton*, Cambridge 1980

THE SAME AUTHOR:

Rudolf Steiner in Britain
A Documentation of his Ten Visits
Volume I, 1902–1921 / Volume II, 1922–1925

Crispian Villeneuve

Rudolf Steiner, the founder of Anthroposophy, spent some five months of his life in Britain, visiting it ten times between the years 1902 and 1924. With the exception of German-speaking countries, the longest time Steiner spent abroad was in Britain, a place he clearly considered as central to his work.

In this extraordinarily thorough study of over 1,200 pages and dozens of illustrations, Crispian Villeneuve documents these important visits, reproducing letters, articles, records and other archival material—much of it published for the first time. He also studies the interconnected theme of the life and work of D.N. Dunlop, Rudolf Steiner's closest British colleague.

Rudolf Steiner in Britain has special significance for English-speaking peoples around the world, as well as for those seeking to understand how and why Steiner disseminated his spiritual world-view. Villeneuve's two-volume opus, the fruit of a decade of research, is finally available in a paperback edition.

'*The author makes no claims to great historical writing, comprehensive judgements or assessments. He wants to stimulate further research and to hold himself completely back. And yet he repeatedly attains, often through the mere arrangement of material, surprising insights into the whole development of Anthroposophy as it was coming into existence . . .*'—Johannes Kiersch in *Das Goetheanum*

2 volumes, 1280pp + 48pp illust; 23.5 x 15.5 cm; paperback;
ISBN 9781906999032